PROFILES
OF AFRICAN-AMERICAN MISSIONARIES

Profiles of African-Americans Missionaries is a book that should be in every library. It is an indispensable and invaluable tool. It will increase God's servants' prospective of His plan of reconciliation through His church and the ministry of missions. It is incredible to read about the commitment of many faithful African-American missionaries that have served under many life-threatening circumstances. Certainly the challenge is before us, especially in this era.

Supt. Vincent E. Mathews Sr., *All Nations Church of God in Christ, Port Huron, Michigan*

I am delighted to encourage anyone who desires to be informed about the history of African Americans in missions to devour this very informative and inspiring work that details the challenges and God-given victories by African Americans seeking to obey Christ by going into the entire world, with the good news for all men.

Bishop Emery Lindsay, *Senior Bishop, Church of Christ Holiness, USA*

In 1994, as senior pastor of Calvary Evangelical Baptist Church, I had the opportunity to visit Liberia, West Africa to assist in organizing a major reconciliation conference where I served as one of the speakers. I saw firsthand the result of the war. Since that time my church and I have been increasingly engaged in world missions. Global missions has allowed us to open new doors for reconciliation between African-American Christians and White American Christians by developing strategic partnerships. I am pleased to endorse this book as a tool in the hands of our Mighty God regarding missions.

Allen R. McFarland, *Senior Pastor, Calvary Evangelical Baptist Church*

Profiles of African-American Missionaries is an extraordinary book which is a must read for anyone interested and concerned about missions, particularly within the context of the African-American faith community. It really should, on the one hand, help us celebrate those who in many ways are unknown heroes and heroines in the field of missions. Yet it should also challenge and inspire us, particularly within the African-American church family, to become far more engaged in connecting with our global family, and moving well beyond our comfort zone of daily existence. Brian Johnson, one of my mentors in the ministry of missions, is an incredible "doer of the word" when it comes to exhorting people to live and share their faith in a most compelling way to advance the Kingdom of God. If you have a desire to influence the world for Christ, *Profiles of African-American Missionaries* will let you examine how others were pacesetters in that regard. This book will hopefully propel you to step it up in your life's work and leave a legacy of winning more souls for the Lord Jesus Christ and of fostering greater human understanding.

Rev. Jonathan L. Weaver, *Pastor, Greater Mt. Nebo African Methodist Episcopal Church* and *President, Pan African Collective*

PROFILES
OF AFRICAN-AMERICAN MISSIONARIES

EDITED BY
ROBERT J. STEVENS
BRIAN JOHNSON

Profiles of African-American Missionaries
Copyright © 2012 by The Cooperative Missions Network of the African Dispersion (COMINAD)
All rights reserved.

No part of this book may be reproduced, stored in a retrieval system, or transmitted in any form or by any means—electronic, mechanical, photocopy, recording, or otherwise—without prior written permission of the publisher, except brief quoatations used in connection with reviews in magazines or newspapers.

Scripture quotations marked (NIV) are taken from the Holy Bible, New International Version®, NIV®. Copyright © 1973, 1978, 1984, 2011 by Biblica, Inc.™ Used by permission of Zondervan. All rights reserved worldwide. www.zondervan.com The "NIV" and "New International Version" are trademarks registered in the United States Patent and Trademark Office by Biblica, Inc.™

Scripture quotations marked (RSV) are from Revised Standard Version of the Bible, copyright © 1946, 1952, and 1971 National Council of the Churches of Christ in the United States of America. Used by permission. All rights reserved.

Scripture quotations marked (NKJV) are taken from the New King James Version. Copyright © 1982 by Thomas Nelson, Inc. Used by permission. All rights reserved.

Published by William Carey Library
1605 E. Elizabeth Street
Pasadena, CA 91104 | www.missionbooks.org

Ms. Jean Voss, copyeditor
Francesca Gacho, editor
Josie Leung, graphic design
Rose Lee-Norman, indexer

A ministry of the U.S. Center for World Mission
Pasadena, CA | www.uscwm.org

16 15 14 13 12 5 4 3 2 1 BP1000
Printed in the United States of America
Front cover photos courtesy of Brian Johnson: From top left—Arnold and Gerri Polk; Missionary surgeon Michael Johnson; Missionary nurse, Julia King; Myra Smith.

Library of Congress Cataloging-in-Publication Data

   Stevens, Robert J., 1955-
  Profiles of African-American missionaries / by Robert Stevens and Brian Johnson.
      p. cm.
   ISBN 978-0-87808-008-3
  1. African American missionaries--History. I. Johnson, Brian. II. Title.
  BV2417.A47S74 2011
  266.0092'396073--dc23
                          2011026651

Contents

Foreword
  Brian Johnson ix
Foreword
  Robert J. Stevens xi
Preface xiii

1600s Era: Christianity and the Slave
Chapter 1 Christanity and the Slave [1600s]
  Robert J. Stevens 3

1700–1780 Era
Chapter 2 African American Outreach Begins: 1700s–1780s
  Robert J. Stevens 7
Chapter 3 George Liele: Missions Pioneer
  Mark Sidwell 9
Chapter 4 The Origins of the Pentecostal Movement
  Vinson Synan, Ph.D. 13

1781–1819 Era: Independent and Black Evangelists
Chapter 5 Independent and Black Evangelists
  Robert J. Stevens 19
Chapter 6 AME and AMEZ History
  Bishop William Jacob Walls 22
Chapter 7 Lutherans and Mission History
  Richard C. Dickinson 32
Chapter 8 Lott Carey
  Mark Sidwell 47
Chapter 9 John Stewart: The Missionary Pioneer
  Joseph Mitchell 52

1820–1860 Era: Second Great Awakening and Missionary Rise
Chapter 10 The Second Great Awakening and Missionary Rise: African-American Missionary Movement
  Robert J. Stevens 59
Chapter 11 Betsey Stockton: Stranger in a Strange Land
  Eileen Moffett and Dr. John Andrew III 62
Chapter 12 Alexander Crummell (1819–1898)
  William Edward Burghardt DuBois, edited by Robert J. Stevens 74

1861–1894 Era: Civil War and Holiness Movement
Chapter 13 The Civil War (1861–1865) and Holiness Movement
  Robert J. Stevens 81
Chapter 14 Coloured American ME History
  Bishop Charles Henry Phillips 84

Chapter 15 Thomas Lewis Johnson: Africa For Christ—28 Years a Slave
  Thomas Lewis Johnson 91
Chapter 16 The Story of the Lord's Dealings with Mrs. Amanda Smith
  Amanda Smith 102
Chapter 17 William Sheppard: Congo's African American Livingstone
  William Phipps 107

1895–1919 Era: Reconstruction
Chapter 18 Reconstruction (1895–1919)
  Robert J. Stevens 125
Chapter 19 Lott Carey Convention
  Leroy Fitts and Mark Sidwell 127
Chapter 20 Rev. John Chilembwe: African Missionary Extraordinaire
  Pastor Esker Jerome Harris 134
Chapter 21 Far From Home: A Biography of Emma B. Delaney, Missionary to Africa 1902–1922
  Willie Mae Hardy Ashley 140
Chapter 22 The Life and Work of Rev. Landon N. Cheek: Excerpts from *The Bones of My Ancestors*
  Margaret J. Durham 158

1920–1954 Era: Hindrances [Time of Garvey]
Chapter 23 1920–1954 Era: Hindrances [Time of Garvey] 171
Chapter 24 Montrose Waite: A Man Who Could Not Wait
  Eugene Seals and John McNeal, Jr. 173
Chapter 25 Efrain Alphonse: Translator
  Jim Wilson, Wycliffe Bible Translators 183
Chapter 26 Gladys East: A Missionary Daughter With Vision
  Dr. Benjamin W. Johnson, Sr. 185

1955–1974 Era: Redefinition [Time of Civil Rights]
Chapter 27 Redefinition [Time of Civil Rights]
  Robert J. Stevens 191
Chapter 28 Andrew Foster
  Rhoda Rynearson and Berta Foster 193
Chapter 29 Take A Giant Step: The Life Story of Elgin and Dorothy Taylor
  Elgin Taylor 199
Chapter 30 Bob Harrison: When God Was Black
  Bob Harrison 206
Chapter 31 The Life and Work of Daisie Whaley
  Nene Bi Tra Albert 218
Chapter 32 The Mable McCombs Story
  Dorris E. Ngaujah 222

1975–Present Era: African American Rise in Mission
Chapter 33 AFA Rise in Mission: 1976–Present
  Robert J. Stevens 229
Chapter 34 Reconciliation in Mission—Brian Johnson's Story
  Miss Jean and Dorris Ngaujah 231
Chapter 35 Jacqueline Huggins
  Dorris E. Ngaujah 249
Chapter 36 David Cornelius: My Missionary Experience
  David Cornelius 260

Chapter 37 Michael Johnson: What Does it Cost to do Missions?
Michael Johnson *266*

Chapter 38 Hakim Scott Stands Tall as a Missionary to China
Thomas M. Watkins *277*

Chapter 39 Virgil Amos: Seeing Ourselves as Agents of God
Virgil Lee Amos *280*

Chapter 40 The Cal Neighbor Story
Dorris E. Ngaujah *283*

Resources *290*
Timeline *294*
Bibliography *311*
Index *316*

Foreword

by Brian Johnson

The church in the African-American community is and has been a great blessing to the African-American people as a whole. The church, more than any other institution, has been the change agent that informed and supplied an ethical foundation to our politics, social action, health care, entrepreneurial innovation, education and family. The African-American church has always seen God's mission in the United States as holistic, and it was no different when African-American missionaries began to leave the shores of the United States, to make Christ known to people who were living without the loving Savior. Missionaries immediately immersed themselves in issues of justice, health care, education, entrepreneurial training, etc., while teaching the word of God in formal and nonformal settings.

This book features the life and ministry of some of those faithful African-American missionary servants, who were and are unique within the African-American church. It can be said of some of them, "Of whom the world was not worthy" (Heb 11:38). Just as Jesus willingly undertook the mission of the Father—"As My Father has sent me, so send I you" (John 20:21)—these missionaries willingly accepted the same mission under the authority and blessing of Christ. Prior to the publishing of this book some of these faithful servants have already passed on to be with Christ, so it is a blessing to share their lives through this book. It has been a privilege for us to see how God cared for these special people over the years. It is God's faithfulness that has been an encouragement to other African-American Christians who desire to step out in faith in order to serve people who are not of their own ethnic group.

Each individual featured in this book worked on two fronts: serving the indigenous people in the countries where God sent them, and mobilizing other African Americans in the United States to reach out in greater ways to God's global mission of reaching all human beings with the love of Christ. This dual passion is true of every African-American missionary that I have ever met.

We are so thankful to Bob Stevens and the Southeast Office of the U.S. Center for World Mission, and William Carey Library for their contribution to making this book possible. May God bless and continue to keep you all.

Brian Johnson
COMINAD

Foreword

by Robert J. Stevens

I had the privilege of helping edit, *African-American Experience in World Mission: A Call Beyond Community*. A publisher told us to use the many biographical sketches we had discovered for a second volume. Stories of real people who accomplished much at great personal sacrifice always stimulate the reader to reach higher. This collection is no exception in the long story of telling of the mighty works of God as the Kingdom of God continues it destined advance to bless each and every people group on Earth.

There are so many remarkable stories, encouragements and praises that can be gained by going through each story in this collection. I found myself many times giving thanks to God for his marvelous workers, who against remarkable odds, advanced the Kingdom of God and left a wonderful legacy.

Emma Delaney demonstrated a "purpose and fortitude from above." The Liberians wrote of her, "Truly she suffered [from malaria] enough to have caused any ordinary woman to throw up the sponge, but not so with our subject." In spite of the surrounding spiritual darkness and loneliness, she persevered to bring a major blessing to the Seuhn Industrial Mission. She was a bright light of hope, of salvation, and the practical help of training and schooling to so many.

Don't miss the story of Bob Harrison, who served five years with the Billy Graham Crusade team. God opened his eyes to the world of missions and he was on fire, helping blacks to see the vision. He was realistic about the roadblocks from the white community but then, in the fullness of His time, God opened a door, and Bob kept going through those open doors.

Montrose Waite persevered over many years to finally go with the Christian & Missionary Alliance to Africa (C&MA). Even when the C&MA dropped his support after two years and in the middle of the Great Depression, God continued to provide for him so that he could raise his family on the mission field and do God's work.

If you like adventures, the life of William Sheppard is better than a movie. He recorded 22 bouts with malaria during his first two years in the Congo. He publicized the terror and extortion used by the rubber companies against the native population. He was treated as a hero in America and shared the stage with the likes of Booker T. Washington and W. E. B. DuBois. Sheppard was a mover and a shaker on three continents. He was received in the White House by two presidents. No one did more to stir up forces of liberation in the Congo, Europe, and the USA!

Read them all!

Bob Stevens
afabooks2@gmail.com

Preface

It is with great appreciation and wonder that we applaud the research efforts taken by each contributor to the historical writings of these pioneer African-American missionaries. Against all odds, they prevailed in their calling and obeyed God in proclaiming the gospel of Jesus Christ and His love cross-culturally to those who were lost. We've chosen only a few, but tried to choose the "first," the "frontier" workers, the "mission to an unreached people group," and the famous or those little known, but all faithful. We also sought some contemporary workers who began mission ministries of their own, began the first African-American work within another mission organization, or began the first African-American foreign work within an evangelical denomination. We've included a few COMINAD members who continue to commence to gathering and mobilizing, with assistance of pastors and African Americans for responding to the call to mission, and who, in their own lives, live out that call. May God grant His blessings on this work to His honor and His glory until He comes again!

1600s Era: Christianity and the Slave

Chapter 1
Christanity and the Slave [1600s]

by Robert J. Stevens

What a history African Americans have in World Mission! Each mission story has a definite divine intervention for calling, going, and multiplication as well as divine power to overcome the surmounting obstacles along the way.

The first Africans who came to America were indentured servants and it is widely believed by historians that they were not Christians.[1] There are no records available of what the "Negro" actually did or thought religiously prior to 1619. We have every reason to believe that he did give thought to the spiritual things in life. His religious background emphasized his beliefs in spirits and the practice of "Black Art." Every "Negro" slave entering the colonies in this and succeeding years was indoctrinated in the native interpretations of good versus evil spirits. No death, in so far as the slave or "Negro" was concerned, was due to natural causes. If a man died by drowning, the water spirit triumphed; if he succumbed to disease, those individual spirits conquered. In other words, no "Negro" had personal control of his own destinies.[2] American slavery was one of the only slave systems in world history that was based on racial status. Therefore, the American and the European theologians used several biblical texts and social theories to justify their inhuman practices of slavery and the slave trade.[3] With prevailing opinions pertaining to slavery by all Europe and the Church of England spilling over to the colonial churches, it is no wonder the churches in America did little for the conversion of the early slave. However, paradoxical situations existed in the minds of so many Christians. It was firmly believed that Christians could not enslave other Christians. Therefore, should any slave who accepted Christ as LORD, be manumitted? Can a slave be baptized? Eventually, royal decrees and special statutes were issued. These documents "guaranteed" that if the slave converted to Christianity that he/she would still be a slave and would not be manumitted. This ruling fulfilled the desire of the slaveholder, the current legislators, and the church.[4]

---

1 John Hope Franklin, *From Slavery to Freedom* (New York: Knopf, 1974), 57.
2 David Henry Bradley, Sr., *History of the African Methodist Episcopal Zion Church: Book Three: Mother Methodism, at Home and Abroad* (Nashville, TN: The Parthenon Press, 1956).
3 Marilyn Lewis, "Independent Study Assignment: The African-American in Christian Mission," Th.M. Candidate, Dallas Theological Seminary, #788, 1993, 10.
4 Peter Marshall and David Manual, *The Light and the Glory* (Grand Rapids: Revel, 1977), 226.

Contrary to belief, even before the battle concerning the "Negro's" capabilities was joined—his salvation was not wholly neglected. When on February 16, 1623, the names, "Anthony, Negro; Isabell, Negro; William, their child, baptized" were recorded in the document, "List of name of those living in VA, Elizabeth City Co." the authority relating the account exclaimed that this was a Red Letter Day for the "Negro" for it was the beginning of his stewardship in spiritual things.[5] The first successful worker among the slaves and freed men was a Reverend Samuel Thomas, who labored in the Goose Creek Parish of SC. He began his work around 1695, and ten years later had at least 20 Africans, as they were commonly called, in his congregation. By 1705, it is said that he had around 1,000 slaves under his instruction. One writer states that in "some of the congregations, Negroes constituted one half of the communicants."[6]

---

5 David Henry Bradley, Sr., *History of the African Methodist Episcopal Zion Church: Book Three: Mother Methodism, at Home and Abroad* (Nashville, TN: The Parthenon Press, 1956).
6 Ibid.

1700–1780 Era

Chapter 2

African American Outreach Begins: 1700s–1780s

by Robert J. Stevens

Overall, little was done for evangelization and full acceptance of African-American Christians until the Holy Spirit in 1702 prompted Reverend Dr. Thomas Bray to obtain a charter from King William III which founded the Society for the Propagation of the Gospel in Foreign Parts among the Negroes in the Colonies. He had been sent by the Bishop of London in 1701 to America where he visited MD. There he found the Church of England in the American Colonies disorganized and with very little spiritual vitality.[1] The London organizers felt that missionaries as the evangelists of the Society should be utilized as a "direct means to convert the heathen of all races whether Europeans, Indians or Negroes."[2] To gain success, the Society added some new teachings. The Society challenged the slaveholders to evangelize the slaves stating that a Christian slave was a better servant. Using biblical passages it emphasized that the slave should serve the slave holder as he/she was "found"; that the slave should serve the slave holder as serving God; and, that the hope of the slave is not in manumission but it is in the future kingdom. The Society also felt that the slaves could then be added to the Protestant lines of the faith and not be forced to succumb to the "errors of the Roman Catholic church."[3]

Of course many slaves felt that if they were converted they would be ostracized by others and considered to have discarded their African culture. Many evangelists in the colonies expressed the opinion that the "wicked life of the slave holders were a major obstacle" to the conversion of the slaves. In the northern regions the Society encountered much success. Many slaves were regarded as a "member of the family" and were included in family prayers, Bible reading, and religious instruction.[4] Work in NC began in 1712, when Reverend Ranford Chowan baptized three Negroes and boasted of the fact that in one year he had baptized 20 slaves and freed men. In 1714 work among Negroes in Albany, NY, had begun and later in New Rochelle, NY, in 1737.[5]

---

1 www.uspg.org.uk/history.html.
2 C. E. Pierre, "The Work of the Society for the Propagation of the Gospel in Foreign Parts Among Negroes of the Colonies," *Journal of Negro History* 1 (1916): 349.
3 Albert J. Rabotearu, *Slave Religion: The Invisible Institution in the Antebellum South* (New York: Oxford University Press, 1978), 102.
4 Carter G. Woodson, *History of the Negro Church* (Washington, D.C.: Associated Publishers, 1985), 7.
5 David Henry Bradley, Sr., *History of the African Methodist Episcopal Zion Church: Book Three: Mother Methodism, at Home and Abroad* (Nashville, TN: The Parthenon Press, 1956).

The Society felt that to complete their job effectively, all black Christians had to be taught to read and write. In 1743, the Society founded a special school for training African Americans to participate in this evangelistic work in Charleston, SC.[6] The evangelists desired to convert whites, blacks, and Indians (all of the souls that did not know Christ). In 1741, the Bishop of Canterbury expressed his gratitude at the large number of African Americans who were brought into the church.[7] Even though the Society had the predominate white churches begin to "think about" entering the arena for the evangelization of the African American, a new spiritual fire was needed. That fire came in the form of spiritual awakenings.[8]

The Spiritual Awakenings

What is known as the Great Awakening (1730–1760), a phenomena of the colonial era, swept throughout America. African Americans both enslaved and free were among those who were "lifted to new heights of religious excitement" by these teaching Revivalists.[9] African Americans flocked to hear the preachings and teachings of Jonathan Edwards and George Whitfield in the north who started a movement for popular education, political democracy, and social revolution which was greatly felt in the African-American communities. Revivalist went to the South and to the West and continued to spread their teachings in their new manner: camp tent meeting revivals. The Revivalists visualized and personalized the state of sin, the need for salvation, the existence of hell, and the eternal state of the elect.[10] The Baptists and Methodists Revivalists taught that Christianity was the "experience of conviction, repentance, and regeneration."[11] The evangelistic enterprise was fostered chiefly by three denominations, the Methodists, the Baptist, and the Scotch Irish Presbyterians.[12] African Americans seem to be attracted to their teaching and the denominations of the Baptists and the Methodists were reaping a harvest of black members throughout many of the regions of the U.S.[13] In contrast, were the Anglican Revivalists, who were more educational in their presentations. They taught the Ten Commandments, the Apostles Creed, and the Lord's Prayer. ... They grew as well acquiring mostly freed blacks and almost no slaves.[14]

---

6 Carter G. Woodson, *History of the Negro Church* (Washington, D.C.: Associated Publishers, 1985), 7.
7 C. E. Pierre, "The Work of the Society for the Propagation of the Gospel in Foreign Parts Among Negroes of the Colonies," *Journal of Negro History* 1 (1916): 349.
8 Marilyn Lewis, "Independent Study Assignment: The African-American in Christian Mission," Th.M. Candidate, Dallas Theological Seminary, #788, 1993, 17.
9 Justo Gonzalez, *The Story of Christianity*, vol. 2 (New York: Harper and Row,1984), 229.
10 Albert J. Raboteau, *Slave Religion: The Invisible Institution in the Antebellum South* (New York: Oxford University Press, 1978), 128.
11 Ibid., 133.
12 David Henry Bradley, Sr., *History of the African Methodist Episcopal Zion Church: Book Three: Mother Methodism, at Home and Abroad* (Nashville, TN: The Parthenon Press, 1956).
13 Ibid., 133.
14 Franklin Frazier and C. Eric Lincoln, *The Negro Church in America* (New York: Schocken Books, 1974), 24.

Chapter 3
George Liele: Missions Pioneer

by Mark Sidwell

A pioneer is someone who launches into the unknown. He might be a settler clearing a wilderness, or he might be a scientist seeking a cure for a deadly disease through a new line of research. In Christian history, a pioneer is one who carries the gospel to an area where the name of Jesus Christ is little known or to a people who are being ignored by the rest of the Christian world. George Liele was a true Christian pioneer. Relatively early in his Christian life, he helped found one of the first black churches in America. Then, forced by necessity to leave his home, he went to Jamaica as a missionary more than ten years before Englishman William Carey launched the modern foreign missions movement.

Early Years and Conversion

George Liele was born a slave around 1750 in VA. Like many slaves, he was separated from his parents when he was young. All he knew about his father from secondhand stories was that the elder Liele had been a deeply religious man.

As a young man, George knew almost nothing of salvation through Christ. "I always had a natural fear of God from my youth," he later wrote, "and was often checked in conscience with thoughts of death, which barred me from many sins and bad company. I knew no other way at that time to hope for salvation but only in the performance of my good works." Henry Sharpe, Liele's owner, was a Baptist deacon, a God-fearing man, and a kind master. When Sharpe moved his family to Burke County, GA, around 1770, Liele began attending the white Baptist church with his master. On hearing the gospel preached plainly there, Liele realized that there was no salvation in his "best behaviour and good works." He explained, "I was convinced that I was not in the way to heaven, but in the way to hell." Burdened for five or six months by a sense of conviction of sin, Liele was finally converted in 1773. He testified, "I saw my condemnation in my own heart, and I found no way wherein I could escape the damnation of hell, only through the merits of my dying Lord and Saviour Jesus Christ, which caused me to make intercession with Christ, for the salvation of my poor immortal soul." Then he added, "I requested of my Lord and Master to give me a work. I did not care how mean it was, only to try and see how good I would do it."

First Ministry

The first work that God had for George Liele to do others might have indeed thought "mean," or contemptible—explaining the Scripture to other slaves. His success in that ministry caught the

---

Mark Sidwell has a B.A. in history and M.A. and Ph.D. in church history from Bob Jones University (BJU) where he teaches history and serves as director of a resource center in J. S. Mack Library. He is the author of *The Dividing Line* as well as coauthor of *United States History for Christian Schools*, second edition. Dr. Sidwell also edits and writes for *Biblical Viewpoints*, the journal of the BJU School of Religion. Article, "Free Indeed: Heroes of Black Christian History" by Mark Sidwell. Greenville, SC: Bob Jones University Press, 1995.

Used by permission.

attention of the pastor of his master's church. At the urging of the minister, the church licensed Liele to preach. (Some historians believe that George Liele was the first ordained African-American Baptist pastor in America.) His master, Henry Sharpe, gave Liele his freedom to allow him to preach without hindrance.

Because historical records are so incomplete and sketchy, there is much debate about when and where the first black Church in America was founded. George Liele helped establish in the 1770s what was at least one of the first: the Silver Bluff Baptist Church in SC, across the Savannah River from Augusta, GA. This was a "plantation church," one operated on a plantation with the permission of a sympathetic slave owner. Liele also preached even more extensively and with great Success in Savannah, GA, and the surrounding area. Many future African-American Christian leaders were coworkers with Liele or converts under his preaching. Helping to found the Silver Bluff work was David George, who later became a minister in Nova Scotia and the British colony of Sierra Leone in Africa. Among the converts was Andrew Bryan, founder of the First African Baptist Church in Savannah, the first major black church in the South.

During the American Revolutionary War, the British occupied Savannah. This situation offered little hardship to Liele; his former master was a Loyalist who served as an officer with the British forces. Liele therefore was able to continue his work with little interference. Henry Sharpe was killed in battle, however, and Sharpe's heirs tried to reenslave Liele. The black preacher was jailed, but he quickly won his freedom by producing the papers that showed he was a free man. Nonetheless, the incident made Liele fearful about his future in GA. When the British evacuated Savannah at the end of the war, he thought it safer to leave with them. Liele "indentured" himself as servant to a British officer named Colonel Kirkland. This meant that in return for passage for him and his family (as well as some debt that Liele owed Kirkland), Liele would work for the colonel until the amount was repaid. As a result, George Liele left America with his family for Jamaica.

Preacher in Jamaica

Jamaica, the island to which George Liele came, was at that time a British colony. Christopher Columbus had landed on the island in 1494, and it remained a Spanish colony until 1655, when the British took over. The native islanders died out, and then the Spanish—and later the British—brought in slaves to work on the island's extensive sugar plantations. As a result, most of the population were of African descent—and most of them were slaves with little knowledge of salvation through Christ.

Liele and his family arrived in Kingston, Jamaica's main city, in 1783. He served the colonel and paid for his indenture. Once his debt was paid, Liele began preaching among the slaves and free blacks, and he formed a church in a private home in September, 1784.

Soon the former slave was gathering a large number of listeners to hear the gospel. Liele certainly did not try to entice them with brief services that could be squeezed into the corners of a busy schedule. His church held two services on Sunday, one from 10:00 to 12:00 in the morning and the other from 4:00 to 6:00 in the afternoon. He held hour-long services on Tuesday and Thursday evenings, and the church also organized meetings for smaller groups on Monday evenings. Baptismal ser,vices were regular and very public. Every three months, Liele and his church members made a procession through the town to an outdoor site, either in the ocean or in a river, where they publicly baptized professing converts. Because of this practice, converts openly declared their identification with the cause of Christ.

Liele said of himself and his flock, "We hold to live as nigh the scriptures as we possibly can." His congregation certainly reflected the truth of the Scriptures' claim that "not many wise men after the flesh, not many mighty, not many noble, are called" (1 Cor 1:26 KJV). The pastor said of his congregation that "the chiefest part of our society are poor illiterate slaves, some living on sugar estates, some on mountains, pens, and other settlements, that have no learning, no not so much as to know a letter in the book."

The poverty of the people became evident when they began constructing a church building in Kingston in 1789. Progress was slow. "The chief part of our congregation are slaves," Liele explained in a letter, "and their owners allow them ... but three or four bits [around 50 cents] per week for allowance to feed themselves; and out of so small a sum we cannot expect anything that can be of service from them; ... and the free people in our society are but poor, but they are willing, both free and slaves, to do what they can." The building was finally finished in 1793 with financial help from English Baptists.

The poverty of his congregation also forced Liele to find a means besides the ministry to support himself financially. He farmed, but the income from farming was too irregular and insufficient to take care of his family. Therefore, he also kept a wagon and team of horses so that he and his sons could earn money by hauling goods. Liele lamented that financial pressures often forced him to be "too much entangled with the affairs of the world." He considered this need for supporting himself "a hindrance to the Gospel in one way" but in another way it at least allowed him "to set a good example" by proving that he was not trying to wring an easy living for himself from the poor.

However lacking the church was materially, God prospered the work spiritually. By 1793, Liele had baptized some 500 converts. He was able to establish congregations in other towns and to recruit other preachers to spread the work. He also established a free school for the children of slaves and free blacks. In April of 1793, a deacon in Liele's church and teacher in his school wrote:

> We have great reason in this island to praise and glorify the Lord, for his goodness and loving kindness in sending his blessed Gospel amongst us by our well-beloved minister, Brother Liele. We were living in slavery to sin and Satan, and the Lord hath redeemed our souls to a state of happiness to praise his glorious and ever blessed name; and we hope to enjoy everlasting peace by the promise of our Lord and Master Jesus Christ. The blessed Gospel is spreading wonderfully in this island: believers are daily coming into the church.

Opposition and Persecution

Liele tried to keep from offending the whites in Jamaica by allowing in his congregation only slaves who had their masters' permission to attend. His church covenant explicitly said, "We permit no slaves to join the church without first having a few lines from their owners of their good behavior." In fact, some modern black writers criticize him, or at least question his wisdom, because of these attempts to accommodate slavery. He should have opposed that institution, they argue, as part of his proclamation of the gospel. Liele apparently did not think so, but despite his caution many whites opposed him. Some white masters thought that blacks were like animals, having no souls, and that therefore preaching to them was useless. Others feared that their slaves might become more troublesome if they became religious or that they might use church meetings to plot rebellions. In 1791, Liele reported, "The people at first persecuted us, both at meetings and baptisms, but God be praised, they seldom interrupt us now." Little did he know what was yet to come.

Beginning in the late 1790s, persecution came in waves. Sometimes the opposition was simply petty harassment. On one occasion, as Liele's congregation was about to partake of the Lord's Supper, a white man rode his horse directly into the church. "Come, old Liele," he said, "give my horse the Sacrament!" Staring the intruder down, Liele replied, "No, Sir, you are not fit yourself to receive it." The pastor in his pulpit faced the mounted rider as several uneasy moments passed until the arrogant trespasser finally turned his horse and left.

Then Liele was jailed in 1797, falsely charged with encouraging rebellion through his preaching. The courts acquitted him, but he was immediately jailed again for almost three and a half years for a debt owed to the builder of his church. (Liele had paid much of the cost of the building himself and was legally responsible for its debts.) He remained in prison until the debt was paid, although we do not know how he, or his friends, raised the money. While in jail, Liele continued to minister to others. He preached to the other prisoners and gave the Lord's Supper to other Christians in prison. His church continued to function in his absence under the leadership of his son and the deacons of the church. But it also suffered through a lawsuit initiated by one of the deacons—a suit that ended in a split in the church.

After Liele's imprisonment, the persecution became fiercer and more widespread. There was a harsh crackdown on preaching to slaves. Anyone who preached to slaves without legal approval was subject to imprisonment. Slaves found guilty of preaching illegally were subject to whipping. One man reportedly was hanged for the "crimes" of preaching to slaves and baptizing them. Outside the law, vicious gangs attempted to break up black services.

One of the worst atrocities occurred not directly under Liele's ministry but under the ministry of one of his converts and fellow preachers, Moses Hall. Determined to put an end to slave meetings, some slave owners broke up a prayer meeting being led by a slave named David, one of Moses Hall's assistants. They seized David, murdered him, cut off his head, and placed it on a pole in the center of the village as a warning to the other slaves. They dragged Moses Hall up to the grisly object.

"Now, Moses Hall, whose head is that?" the leader of the murderers asked.

"David's," Moses replied.

"Do you know why he is up here?"

"For praying, Sir," said Moses.

"No more of your prayer meetings," he said. "If we catch you at it, we shall serve you as we have served David."

As the crowd watched, Moses knelt beside the pole and said, "Let us pray." The other blacks gathered around and knelt with him as he prayed for the salvation of the murderers. Astounded, the slave owners departed, leaving Moses and his followers unharmed.

Final Years

We have little record of Liele's later ministry. We know that between 1801, the end of his imprisonment, and 1810 he conducted work in the interior of Jamaica, establishing churches there. That would seem to be the pattern of his final years: ministering to the works he had established and establishing new works wherever he could. Liele died in 1828. His pioneer work in Jamaica was fruitful. Baptists were a small and struggling sect in Jamaica when he came. By 1814, they numbered 8,000, and within five years of his death they totaled over 20,000. Obviously, George Liele was not responsible for all of this growth by himself. For one thing, other faithful preachers—many of whom Liele had pointed to Christ—shared in the work. Above all, it was the blessing of God's Spirit upon George Liele and the others that brought thousands to salvation. The God who calls "not many wise men after the flesh, not many mighty, not many noble" is the One Who "hath chosen the foolish things of the world to confound the wise; and …the weak things of the world to confound the things which are mighty" (1 Cor 1:27 KJV).

Questions for Thought

1. In what ways could we say that George Liele was a "pioneer" for Christ?
2. Henry Sharpe, Liele's master, was a Christian who even gave Liele his freedom in order to preach the gospel. Yet Sharpe saw no moral problem with slavery. How can you explain this apparent contradiction?
3. How would public baptisms such as those Liele practiced in Jamaica be a testimony to the unsaved? What challenges might the practice present to the participants?
4. How did Liele feel about having to work other jobs to support his ministry? In what other ways could a situation such as this work to the advantage and/or disadvantage of a missionary?
5. Was George Liele right to try to cooperate with slave owners in his ministry to Jamaica? Why or why not?
6. Read 1 Corinthians 4:1-4, 9-16 and 1 Thessalonians 2:9. How was Liele's situation similar to that of the Apostle Paul?

Chapter 4

The Origins of the Pentecostal Movement

by Vinson Synan, Ph.D.

The Pentecostal movement is by far the largest and most important religious movement to originate in the U.S. Although the Pentecostal movement had its beginnings in the U.S., it owed much of its basic theology to earlier British perfectionist and charismatic movements. At least three of these, the Methodist/Holiness movement, the Catholic Apostolic movement of Edward Irving, and the British Keswick "Higher Life" movement prepared the way for what appeared to be a spontaneous outpouring of the Holy Spirit in America.

From John Wesley, the Pentecostals inherited the idea of a subsequent crisis experience variously called "entire sanctification," "perfect love," "Christian perfection," or "heart purity." It was John Wesley who posited such a possibility in his influential tract, "A Plain Account of Christian Perfection" (1766). It was from Wesley that the Holiness Movement developed the theology of a "second blessing." It was Wesley's colleague, John Fletcher, however, who first called this second blessing a "baptism in the Holy Spirit," an experience which brought spiritual power to the recipient as well as inner cleansing. This was explained in his major work, "Checks to Antinominianism" (1771). During the 19th century, thousands of Methodists claimed to receive this experience although no one at the time saw any connection with this spiritually in tongues or any of the other charisms.

In the following century, Edward Irving and his friends in London suggested the possibility of a restoration of the charisms in the modern church. A popular Presbyterian pastor in London, Irving led the first attempt at "charismatic renewal" in his Regents Square Presbyterian Church in 1831. Although tongues and prophecies were experienced in his church, Irving was not successful in his quest for a restoration of New Testament Christianity. In the end, the Catholic Apostolic Church which was founded by his followers, attempted to restore the "five-fold ministries" (of apostles, prophets, evangelists, pastors, and teachers) in addition to the charisms. While his movement failed in England, Irving did succeed in pointing to glossolalia [tongue] as the "standing sign" of the baptism in the Holy Spirit, a major facet in the future theology of the Pentecostals.

Another predecessor to Pentecostalism was the Keswick "Higher Life" movement which flourished in England after 1875. Led at first by American holiness teachers such as Hannah Whitall Smith and William E. Boardman, the Keswick teachers soon changed the goal and content of the "second blessing" from the Wesleyan emphasis on "heart purity" to that of an "endue-

Dr. Vinson Synan received his B.A. from the University of Richmond, his M.A. and Ph.D. from the University of Georgia. He is currently Dean of the School of Divinity at Regent University, Virginia Beach, VA. He is the author of *The Old-Time Power: History of the Pentecostal Holiness Church*, Advocate Press; *Charismatic Bridges*, Word of Life; *Aspects of Pentecostal/Charismatic Origins*, Logos; *Azusa Street*, Bridge Publ; *In the Latter Days*, Servant; *The Twentieth-Century Pentecostal Explosion*, Creation House; *Launching the Decade of Evangelization*, N Amer Renewal Srv Comm; *Under His Banner: A History of the FGBMFI*, Gift Publ; *The Spirit Said Grow*, MARC, World Vision.

Article used by permission.

ment of spiritual power for service." Thus, by the time of the Pentecostal outbreak in America in 1901, there had been at least a century of movements emphasizing a second blessing called the "baptism of the Holy Spirit" with various interpretations concerning the content and results of the experience. In America, such Keswik teachers as A. B. Simpson and A. J. Gordon also added to the movement at large an emphasis on divine healing "as in the atonement" and the premillenial rapture of the church.

Indeed, for the first decade practically all Pentecostals, both in America and around the world, had been active in holiness churches or camp meetings. Most of them were either Methodists, former Methodists, or people from kindred movements that had adopted the Methodist view of the second blessing. They were overwhelmingly [Jacob] Arminian in their basic theology and were strongly perfectionistic in their spirituality and lifestyle.

In the years immediately preceding 1900, American Methodism experienced a major holiness revival in a crusade that originated in NY, NJ and PA, following the Civil War. ... Leaders in this movement were Methodists such as Phoebe Palmer, (also a leading advocate of women's right to minister); John Inskip, a pastor from New York City, and Alfred Cookman, a pastor from NJ.

The first Pentecostal churches in the world were produced by the holiness movement prior to 1901 and, after becoming Pentecostal, retained most of their perfectionistic teachings. These included the predominantly African-American Church of God in Christ (1897), the Pentecostal Holiness Church (1898), the Church of God with headquarters in Cleveland, TN (1906), and other similar groups. These churches, which had been formed as "second blessing" holiness denominations, simply added the baptism of the Holy Spirit with glossolalia as "initial evidence" of a "third blessing."

Pentecostal pioneers who had been Methodists included Charles Fox Parham, the formulator of the "initial evidence" theology; William J. Seymour, the pastor of the Azusa Street Mission in Los Angeles who spread the movement to the nations of the world; J. H. King of the Pentecostal Holiness Church, who led his denomination into the Pentecostal movement in 1907-1908; and Thomas Ball Barratt, the father of European Pentecostalism. All of these men retained most of the Wesleyan teaching on entire sanctification as a part of their theological systems. In essence, their position was that a sanctified "clean heart" was a necessary prerequisite to the baptism in the Holy Spirit as evidenced by speaking in tongues.

The first "Pentecostals" in the modern sense appeared on the scene in 1901 in the city of Topeka, KS, in a Bible school conducted by Charles Fox Parham, a holiness teacher and former Methodist pastor. ... The first person to be baptized in the Holy Spirit accompanied by speaking in tongues was Agnes Ozman, one of Parham's Bible School students. ... According to J. Roswell Flower, the founding Secretary of the Assemblies of God, Ozman's experience was the "touch felt round the world," an event which "made the Pentecostal Movement of the Twentieth Century."

As a result of this Topeka Pentecost, Parham formulated the doctrine that tongues was the "Biblical evidence" of the baptism in the Holy Spirit. He also taught that tongues was a supernatural impartation of human language (xenoglossolalia) for the purpose of world evangelization. Henceforth, he taught, missionaries need not study foreign languages since they would be able to preach in miraculous tongues all over the world. Armed with this new theology, Parham founded a church movement which he called the "Apostolic Faith" and began a whirlwind revival tour of the American middle west to promote this exciting new experience.

It was not until 1906, however, that Pentecostalism achieved world-wide attention through the Azusa Street revival in Los Angeles led by the African-American preacher William Joseph Seymour. He learned about the tongues-attested baptism in a Bible school that Parham conducted in Houston, TX, in 1905. Invited to pastor a black holiness church in Los Angeles in 1906, Seymour opened the historic meeting in April 1906, in a former African Methodist Episcopal (AME) church building at 312 Azusa Street in downtown Los Angeles.

What happened at Azusa Street has fascinated church historians for decades and has yet to be fully understood and explained. For over three years, the Azusa Street, "Apostolic Faith Mission" conducted three services a day, seven days a week, where thousands of seekers received the tongues of baptism. ... From Azusa Street Pentecostalism spread rapidly around the world and began its force towards becoming a major force in Christendom.

The expressive worship and praise at Azusa Street, which included shouting and dancing, had been common among Appalachian whites as well as Southern blacks. The admixture of tongues and other charisms with black music and worship styles created a new and indigenous form of Pentecostalism that was to prove extremely attractive to disinherited and deprived people, both in America and other nations of the world.

As early as 1972 Sidney Ahlstrom, the noted church historian from Yale University, said that Seymour was "the most influential black leader in American religious history." Seymour, along with Charles Parham, could well be called the "co-founders" of world Pentecostalism.

1781–1819 Era: Independent and Black Evangelists

Chapter 5

Independent and Black Evangelists

by Robert J. Stevens

After the American Revolutionary War, and the formation of the Protestant Episcopal Church in America, that church began forming Black congregations and ordaining Black priests to serve them. Two early African-American figures in the Episcopal church were Absalom Jones and Richard Allen. Jones was born a slave in DE in 1746. He taught himself to read using the New Testament. In 1784, he was able to buy his freedom. Allen, too, was born a slave in Philadelphia and was able to purchase his freedom. In 1787 Jones and Allen founded the free African Religious Society. Later Absalom Jones became the first Black minister of any denomination in the U.S. Allen, committed to the principles of Methodism joined others in forming the African Methodist Episcopal Church.[1] Evident of a needed evangelical outreach to African Americans as well as others, the Baptist did not limit the pastoral education and calling and appeared to readily accept the southern slave and the southern white. By 1790, it is estimated that the African-American Baptists made up at least one-fourth to one-third of the total church membership.[2]

A large number of African Americans joined the Methodist in the North. ... It appears that the Methodists had no barrier for membership, and welcomed those who felt a desire for righteousness. Also, many of the African Americans liked the hymns, the ritual, and the services of the Methodists.[3] The Methodists did not license individuals who felt a desire to preach. Calling them "exhorters," these black preachers were the first "black evangelists."[4]

In the aftermath of the Great Awakening (and later the Great Western Revival), true Christianity crossed the color line, and became more accessible to the average American.[5] Throughout the next two decades, 1790–1810, black evangelists traveled the countryside in the manner of Revivalist preachers, informing all who would listen to the gospel, of the impending judgment if one did not accept Christ.[6]

---

1 "The Black Experience within the Episcopal Church," Kathleen A. McAdams, M.Div. Candidate, Church Divinity School of the Pacific, September 1988.
2 Franklin Frazier, *The Negro Church in America* (New York: Schocken Books, 1974), 24.
3 William McClain, *Black People in the Methodist Church: Whither Thou Goest?* (Cambridge: Schenkman, 1984), 21.
4 Marilyn Lewis, "Independent Study Assignment: The African-American in Christian Mission," Th.M. Candidate, Dallas Theological Seminary, #788, 1993, 20.
5 William Pope Harrison, *The Gospel Among the Slaves* (TN: Publishing House, Methodist Episcopal Church, 1893), 138.
6 Marilyn Lewis, "Independent Study Assignment: The African-American in Christian Mission," Th.M. Candidate, Dallas Theological Seminary, #788, 1993, 21.

1791 Toussaint L' Ouverture—Haiti

In 1791, the revolt of Haitian slaves influenced the slaves in the states. Haiti had 40,000 whites, 28,000 freedmen, and 500,000 slaves. In April 1794, Toussaint L'Ouverture, a man of rare courage and remarkable leadership, who had attained high rank in the Spanish Army as the head of 4,000 troops, deserted the Spanish and his defection led to the surrender of the Spanish garrison in Santo Domingo. L'Ouverture, Dessalines, and Christophe led the slave revolt in Haiti against French rule. Toussaint L'Ouverture issued a constitution which abolished slavery. They had established a negro controlled nation in which all inhabitants were free. It is said that some 13,000 black Americans migrated to free Haiti after this revolution, where they found refuge.[7]

One such leader, and a strong abolitionist, Episcopal bishop, James Theodore Holly, took advantage of this open freedom in Haiti.[8] Holly was born, baptized and raised a Catholic but converted to the Episcopal Church in 1852. Holly had founded the earliest known national organization among African-American Episcopalians in 1856: Protestant Episcopal Society for Promoting the Extension of the Church Among Colored People. The Society, like all African Americans, was divided over the issues of emigration to Africa or Canada for immediate freedom, or remaining in the U.S. for eventual freedom.[9] Supported by James Redpath, in 1861, Holly (then a rector) along with 100 of St. Luke's, New Haven, CT, fellow church members, moved to Haiti and began an Episcopal mission. As an experienced Masonic leader and scholar, he visited the Masonic temples in Haiti to win friends among their elitist members. He offered to perform their funerals. In 1874, he became an Episcopal Bishop.[10]

African Americans began to consider other options when confronted with racism in the white churches. One opinion was the development of independent black denominations. This event was something more significant than the independent black church on a plantation. For the first time, the African American had a right to manage his or her own churches, train and select leaders, worship in their own style, ordain their own ministers, establish their own bylaws, and design their own church creeds. The independent African-American church, but more importantly the separate denominations, provided the necessary basis for the molding and shaping of black Christian leadership and the impetus for the "competition" in the Christian Mission Movement.[11]

Richard Allen, Absalom Jones, and William White were the three men instrumental in the establishment of the first separated denomination. ... It all took place in the Philadelphia region where Allen was well known and had a following which kept increasing. The white congregation continued to segregate the black delegation. This segregation and hostility were so evident that in the midst of the black delegation praying, the white deacons felt compelled to interrupt and request that they leave. The African Americans arose from the altar, and withdrew from the church. This withdrawal resulted in the establishment of the African Bethel church which later developed into the African Methodist Episcopal denomination (1794, AME).[12]

The Great Western Revival 1800, Gabriel Prosser

In the summer of 1800, inspired by the success of Toussaint L'Ouverture, Gabriel Prosser, of Henrico County, VA, organized about 1,000 slaves, armed them with the clubs, knives, and guns and marched on Richmond. ... On the day appointed, there occurred one of the heaviest rain storms in the history of the area, washing out roads and bridges. Slave revolts were numerous in those days, and agitation from antislavery groups was mounting.[13]

Although the slaves could not read, they were not unlearned, because they were quick to master the teachings of the Scriptures. They also

---

7 Bishop Jacob Walls, *African-Methodist Episcopal Zion Church* (Charlotte, NC: A.M.E. Zion Publishing, 1974).

8 Richard C. Dickinson, *Roses and Thorns* (St. Louis, MO: Concordia Publishing House, 1997).

9 "Precursors to the Union of Black Episcopalians," www.ube.org/precurso.htm.

10 David Dean, *Defender of the Race: James Theodore Holly, Black Nationalist Bishop* (Boston: Lambeth Press, 1979).

11 Marilyn Lewis, "Independent Study Assignment: The African-American in Christian Mission," Th.M. Candidate, Dallas Theological Seminary, #788, 1993, 30.

12 Carol George, *Segregated Sabbaths: Richard Allen and the Emergence of Independent Black Churches, 1760-1840* (New York: Oxford University Press,1973), 52.

13 Richard C. Dickinson, *Roses and Thorns* (St. Louis, MO: Concordia Publishing House, 1997).

showed an uncanny quality for applying these sacred teachings to their position and condition. The masters monitored the religious teachings to which the slaves were exposed, because the clandestine, unauthorized black preacher could easily foment rebellion right out of the pages of God's Holy Word. A common practice, in many churches, especially in the churches of the northern states, was to mark a certain section of pews with the letters "B.M." meaning black members. In some instances, separate churches were built for slaves where white pastors, or approved colored preachers, were in charge.[14]

The first breakthrough came in 1807 with the passage of a bill prohibiting the slave trade. Ownership of slaves, however, was still permitted. There was something in the peculiar attitude of Methodists too, which seemed to bear out the contention that these people who emphasized "heart strangely warmed" process, created more unrest among slaves. Time after time in listing runaway slaves the owner declared that he was a Methodist who did a little preaching. ... Some of these preachers from various denominations either remained on in slavery or obtained their freedom legally and were well known for their work.[15]

Black Preachers Continued

The Baptists and Methodists continued to send out black evangelists to work with the slaves until the state legislators and ecclesiastical bodies forbade the practice. Many continued and the "slave preachers who traveled generally did so unofficially on the strength of their own charisma and their reputation among whites and blacks."[16] The importance of these black evangelists "official" and "unofficial" before, during and between the Awakenings needs to be appreciated for nurturing the birth of Christianity in the African-American communities.

Some of the great black religious leaders who were gifted in the pulpit were: Josiah Bishop, VA; John Stewart, OH; "Simon" of the Roanoke Association; Joseph Willis, MS and LA; John Chavis, NC; John Jasper, VA; Uncle Jack, VA; Henry Evins, NC; Harry Hosier, NY, who traveled with Francis Asbury, Thomas Coke and Richard Whatcoat; Thomas Paul, MA, NYC and on to West Indies.[17]

---

14 Ibid.
15 David Henry Bradley, Sr., *History of the African Methodist Episcopal Zion Church: Book Three: Mother Methodism, at Home and Abroad* (Nashville, TN: The Parthenon Press, 1956).
16 Katherine Dvorak, *An African-American Exodus: The Segregation of the Southern Churches* (New York: Carlson Publishing Inc., 1992), 47.
17 Marilyn Lewis, "Independent Study Assignment: The African-American in Christian Mission," Th.M. Candidate, Dallas Theological Seminary, #788, 1993, 21–24.

Chapter 6
AME and AMEZ History

by Bishop William Jacob Walls

Bishop William Jacob Walls (1885–1975), was the 42nd Bishop of the African Methodist Episcopal Zion Church. In 1899 he entered Livingstone College where he received his license to preach and in the first year became the noted "Boy Evangelist" or "Boy Preacher," and graduated with highest honors in 1908. He continued his studies at Columbia University, NY, in 1922, and the University of Chicago, 1941 where he received an A.M. Degree in Christian Education. Honorary degrees of D.D. and LL.D. were conferred on him by Livingstone College. He received a B.D. Degree from Hood Theological Seminary in 1913. In NC and OH he successfully pastored, built, and planted churches.

He was elected editor of *The Star of Zion*, 1920; consecrated Bishop in the A.M.E. Zion Church, 1924; secretary of Board of Bishops, 1941–1965; and chairman of the Board of Christian Education (1924–1968). Also was chairman of the Board of Trustees of Livingstone College (1941–1973).

Bishop Wall authored a number of published works. He was one of the co-founders of Roosevelt University, IL, 1945; Founder of Camp Dorothy Walls, NC; and organized the Harriet Tubman Home Foundation Board, NY, 1953. He departed April 2, 1975.

First appeared as "Book Five" from *African Methodist Episcopal Zion Church—Reality of the Black Church* by Bishop William Jacob Walls, A.M.E. Zion Publishing, Charlotte, NC, ©1974. Used by permission.

Methodist Beginnings

John Wesley's Thoughts on Slavery, in an attempt to awaken his fellow-citizens regarding parts of Africa "whence the Negroes were brought," Guinea, states:

> You know how populous, how fruitful, how pleasant it was, a few years ago. You know, the people were not stupid, not wanting in sense, considering the few means of improvement they enjoyed. Neither did you find them savage, fierce, cruel, treacherous, or unkind to strangers. On the contrary, they were, in most parts, a sensible and ingenious people. They were kind and friendly, courteous and obliging, and remarkably fair and just in their dealings. Such are the men whom you hire their own countrymen to tear away from this lovely country; part by stealth; part by force, part made captives in those wars which you raise or foment on purpose. You have seen them torn away—children from their parents, parents from their children; husbands from their wives, wives from their beloved husbands, brethren and sisters from each other. You have dragged them who had never done you any wrong, perhaps in chains, from their native shore. You have forced them into your ships like a herd of swine;—them who had souls immortal as your own; only some of them leaped into the sea, and resolutely stayed under water, till they could suffer no more from you. You have stowed them together as close as ever they could lie, without any regard either to decency or convenience. And when many of them have been poisoned by foul air, or had sunk under various hardships, you have seen their remains delivered to the deep, till the sea should give up his dead. You have carried the survivors into the vilest slavery, never to end but with life.

Therefore, the story of the Negro minister and Christianity among Negroes took place largely in America, where the slave trade became paramount. The European used his slave trade in his colonies in America. Incidentally and persistently, the major colonizers of the Western world who brought their brawn and endurance to the colonies were black men. By a narrow margin, the vote came near putting abolition of slavery into the Constitution. At that time there was no Negro church general organization. There was only here and there a congregation sparsely organized. As we read the history of these turbulent and struggling days, we see that all the black churches were born in white congregations, East, West, North and South. Organized Christianity is the major thing the black race got out of slavery, second to which was the English language.

Besides the fact that Methodism was a friend of the black race long before it was introduced on the American continent, it had the evangelistical appeal to this suffering and despised race, and the system of the class meetings, to not only instruct the members for the good of their souls, but "to watch over one another in love…and help each other to work our their own salvation." These, along with Wesley's strong opposition to human bondage, made the strongest kind of impact upon the Negro population in the U.S. and West Indies during the late 18th and early 19th centuries. John Wesley baptized his first converted Negro into a Protestant Church on November 29, 1758,…. The conflict within the family of Methodists on the slave question grew exceedingly until the climactic division which created the Methodist Episcopal Church and the Methodist Episcopal Church, South, in 1844, which lasted for nearly a century.

By the first half of the 18th century, New York had the largest slave population north of the plantation states, both in numbers and as a percentage of the population. Negroes in New York were generally kept under close watch, and could not have any meetings of any nature among themselves.

In 1766, when Irishman Philip Embury, who had been licensed by John Wesley, held the first Methodist meeting on American soil in his home in Augusta Street (then Barrack Street), exhorting to an audience of five, one black person was present. She was Betty, the slave of Barbara Heck, who had requested the meeting of her fellow countryman out of necessity to save their people from "hell." As they grew, their slaves and other blacks were privileged to join the movement. As they outgrew the house, they soon obtained a more commodious facility for meeting, and a little later, moved into the Rigging or Sail Loft at 120 William Street.

We observe, from journals and reports of early missionaries sent to America by Wesley, that the black membership of John Street Church, in the beginning, was principally slave.

While meeting in the Riggin Loft, when the subscriptions for Wesley Chapel (the first John Street Church) were circulated, two dedicated young slave girls contributed;… But the itinerantcy of the traveling preachers at John Street Church (the "New York Circuit") during its first 30 years of existence was part of the problem that caused the establishment of the African Methodist Episcopal [AME] Zion Church.

Many more black men were interested in the Methodist religion, and were holding private meetings among themselves in their homes. In the interest of the race, they refused to be a party to segregated services. Thus, several of the earliest leaders in the Zion Church movement were not members of the John Street Church or New York Circuit.

In 1791, the revolt of Haitian slaves … brought about a new assertiveness among the blacks in America. In New York City, the members of the "New York Circuit" numbered 575 whites and 135 blacks. The leading black members were beginning to lay concrete plans for the new movement of Methodism which could create a new emphasis in freedom and self-expression. They planned hard and well and reached the crest of their fondest dream in 1796. After prodding their way through numerous obstructions, they made their move to a humble house on Cross Street. Few in numbers, poor and despised, they prayerfully and zealously fought their way to victory by 1821.

James Varick manifested his hatred to slavery by leading his few noble followers out of the Methodist Episcopal Church in 1796, and thus became a pioneer Negro anti-slavery leader. Bishop Hood stated in his history that:

In the days of slavery the Zion ministers were generally leaders of the anti-slavery movement and their pulpits were always open to anti-slavery lectures. If no other house could be obtained for an anti-slavery meeting it was known that the Zion Church could be had. The doors of this church were never closed against one who wanted to plead for the oppressed.

Emancipation heroes and heroines were: James Varick (Bishop); William Hamilton; Christopher Rush (Bishop); Reverends Beman and James; Frederick Douglas; Sojourner Truth; Bishop Jermain Wesley Lognen; Harriet Tubman; John Jamison Moore; Joseph Pascal Thompson; Eliza Ann Gardner; and Catherine Harris.

From the beginning, this independent movement of the AME Zion Church was largely influenced and structured by James Varick. [Other leaders—Father Abraham Thompson, June Scott and William Miller—did not stay.] Varick was the most prominent name from the beginning and played the diplomat between Zion and other churches, both the Methodist Episcopal Church and Bethel movement, but maintained the constancy and unity of AME Zion movement.

The original pioneers when the separate meetings commenced were: James Varick; Abraham Thompson; June Scott; William Miller; Francis Jacobs; William Brown; Peter Williams; William Hamilton; Thomas Miller; and Samuel Pointer. For the most part, the church leaders were free, although quite a number of the members were still slaves. They themselves fitted up the house with seats, pulpit, and gallery. There were three licensed preachers in NY: James Varick; Abraham Thompson; and June Scott, the first three Africans of this state to be ordained in the Methodist Church. In the beginning of the Christian movement, they were known as Apostles. The AME Zion Church was firmly established in 1820, when the leaders voted themselves out of the Methodist Episcopal Church and published their first Discipline.

[March 23, 1810] … a movement led by William Hamilton, the New York African Society for Mutual Relief, was begun and received a state charter…with Hamilton its first president. Its object was "to raise a fund to be appropriated toward the relief of the widows and orphans of the deceased members." Its members were composed chiefly of businessmen, many of them members of the AME Zion Church, and several preachers (practically all the black preachers of the city of that day). James Varick was elected its first chaplain and functioned in the various services, especially anniversary celebrations, annually held in Zion Church. This organization was still in existence in 1969, when a historic marker was placed on the site.

The first Lodge of Freemasonry was established in New York State in 1812, when Peter Lew, Grand Master of Prince Hall Grand Lodge, Boston, granted a warrant to nine Master Masons to open and work a Lodge of Master Masons in New York City under the title of Boyer Lodge No. 1 F. & A.M. It was named in honor of General Jean Boyer, the Haitian general. Sandy Lattion, Worshipful Master, had created deep concern among the white lodges when he announced his meetings in the city newspaper. So far as is definitely known, he was the first Master. Sandy Lattion was a member of the AME Zion Church, both Zion and Asbury, where he was an original trustee.

On January 17, 1817, the New York African Bible Society was established in William Miller's schoolroom in his home at 36 Mulberry Street, where he also operated his cabinet-maker's shop. The group met and drew up its constitution and chose the following gentlemen as managers: William Miller, president; James Varick, Jacob Matthews, and Thomas Miller, vice-presidents; George Collins, secretary; Lewis Carter, treasurer; George DeGrass, Sandy Lattion, Robert F. Williams, Andrew Smith, and William Lambert. The Society continued to grow, along with a sister group, "The New York Female Bible Society of People of Colour," which raised large sums for the distribution of the Bibles and reported to the American Bible Society.

Varick once again came to the front in behalf of his race when a group of black ministers and businessmen met in New York City, and appointed Thomas Sipkins secretary of the committee to petition the NY State Constitutional Convention regarding their right to vote. Varick figured prominently, also, in the black man's effort to start a newspaper for his race.

The influence of the abolition movements, and the aftermath of the Nat Turner Insurrection of 1831, increased repugnance among pro-slavery groups, both North and South. From 1834 on, "Negro preachers were gradually outlawed in many Southern states and slaves were required to attend the church of their masters." As described above, a noted pioneer in this struggle was the second bishop of the AME Zion Church, Christopher Rush, Varick's successor. He attended and participated in the National Conventions from the first one in 1830. He was "one of the Giants of the reform movement of the 1830's—one of the group of courageous militant leaders who built the Negro Convention movement, together with Bishop Richard Allen, Nathanial Paul, Peter Williams, Jr., Samuel Cornish, and others."

Outside of expanding the AME Zion Church from Philadelphia to Washington, D.C. and Pittsburgh, Rush was best known as a prime organizer and president of the Phoenix Society of New York City, for many years after it was organized in 1833. "The Society was composed of Negro and white members, men and women, old and young, rich and poor; it was perhaps the most progressive and democratic organization in the country. Its aim was to prepare and educate the people for a new day of freedom, unity, equality and peace. Its immediate aim was 'to promote the improvement of the coloured people in morals, literature, and the mechanics arts.'

The General Conference sessions were still being held in conjunction with the NY Annual Conference. On Sunday, May 24, 1840, the Sixth Session of the General Conference convened at Asbury Church, New York City, in joint session with the 20th Annual Session of the NY Conference. About 40 ministerial delegates "from the East, West, and North," were present, with Bishop Christopher Rush presiding, assisted by Rev. William Miller. The making of an assistant superintendent without having defined the office in the Discipline, "was the rock upon which the church split" in 1853. The genesis of the trouble appears to have stemmed from the strong Wesleyan group, whose attitude of independence and self-assertion, and different views regarding church government, had been felt ever since the beginning of the connection in 1820. William Miller was at this time pastoring Wesley Church in Philadelphia.

The Church Spreads Abroad

Before the Foreign Missions Department and the Women's Home and Foreign Missionary Society were formed, churches were established in several areas outside the U.S. Much of it did not survive for various reasons, mainly for the lack of preachers and financial support. However, some of our early churches in foreign territories, such as Demerara and British Guianea (Guyana), were set on a firm foundation before Emancipation and continue modestly in the course of Zion history.

Efforts to establish the AME Zion Church on foreign soil began with Bishop Rush two days after the close of the NY Annual Conference session, on May 28, 1829, when Rev. Hamilton Johnson arrived from Prescott, Upper Canada, hoping to be in time to join the conference and represented a Zion Society there. From this time forward, AME Zion Church had work intermittently in Canada.

One thing that hindered our work abroad was the lack of men. We did not have enough preachers after the Civil War to develop the South, to hold Canada and the distant North, and to send missionaries to new territories. The church began to concentrate on spreading the borders to the West Indies and Africa, the first decade after its abundant growth in the South.

The Christianization of Africa was the dream of the African-American Church. The Christian churches had gone ahead and were developing missions in Africa. We felt it our responsibility as a race church to drive into the vast continent and develop our Fatherland for Christ Jesus. Bishop Alexander Walters states the following on our commencement of our work in Africa:

While Scotland can boast of her David Livingstone ... And while the Methodist Episcopal Church can boast of her Melville Cox, ... our Zion can boast of her rugged old hero. Andrew Cartwright, and Dudley, [Frank] Arthur and Wright; nor can we forget their services, who are the connecting links between our Church and Africa.

All honor to Bishop Small ... who felt the burden of African redemption ... It is known to a good many of us that out of his own private purse he aided Frank Arthur and other African students, who matriculated at Livingstone College. Several of them he kept in his home, providing liberally for their physical needs.

After organizing and building 12 churches in 10 years, Rev. Andrew Cartwright left Plymouth, NC, and sailed for Africa on January 7, 1876. He organized the first AME Zion Church on the continent in Brewerville, Liberia, on February 7, 1878, and one in Clay Ashland, November 1878. By 1880, he reported another church organized at Atherton, for a total of three. A formal report was sent to the General Conference assembled in Montgomery, AL, May 1880, from Liberia, signed by Josephus Samuel Baker and others, stating the splendid beginnings of Brother Cartwright and requesting the General Conference to give Cartwright power to call a conference, and enable him to gather in more preachers for the work. This is the historic General Conference which made concrete plans for our work in Africa by forming the Woman's Home and Foreign Missionary Society.

In 1886 he organized another church with 40 members and 50 Sunday school scholars at Cape Palmas, but due to shortage of funds, the flock scattered and soon joined another denomination. The General Conference Committee on Districts recommended that the African Mission be left in the hands of the Board of Bishops to be supplied, and "that some one of them visit the work yearly."

This same year, after passing through some difficulty in securing a woman teacher to help him start a school for Zion in this territory, he employed his wife, Carrie E. S. Cartwright, sanctioned by the Board of Bishops, for $300 per year. She made a report of her labors on the organization and operation of the AME Zion Mission School at Brewerville, Liberia, to the 1892 General Conference, and the delegates were stimulated to move forward in the interest of Africa. In October, 1892, Bishop Walters requested Cartwright to accept the presiding eldership in Africa over his own work. He willingly did so, yet he felt that he should have been acknowledged as superintendent of African missions, with responsibilities equivalent to a bishop of the church, on the African continent. He served in this capacity until the 1896 General Conference and reported his labors there. A special committee on the status of Reverend Andrew Cartwright resolved that the was a "missionary to Africa acting in the capacity of Presiding Elder by the appointment of Bishop Alexander Walters of the Seventh Episcopal District." The Committee on Episcopal Address acquiesced with the bishops of the church and recommended to the General Conference that a member of the Board of Bishops visit the work in Africa at least annually, feeling that there was not a need for the election of a missionary bishop.

Carwright had opened the door for Zion in Africa, and blessings were in store for the church on this vast continent. The General Conference elected John Bryan Small a bishop and assigned him to MS ... Small's father was a strong member of the Church of England of Barbados, 'and so educated his son for the ministry of that church; but while in Honduras he professed hope in Christ and joined the Wesleyan Methodist Church.' In 1871, on his way to England, he came to the U.S., and through the influence of Reverend R. H. G. Dyson and Bishop J. J. Clinton, he joined the AME Zion Church two weeks after his arrival.

"He [Bishop Small] is the first Bishop of our Zion who feels or has felt divinely called to go to Africa. ... Africa, the land that afforded the child Jesus refuge when wicked Herod sought His life; whose teeming millions are as yet hardly touched by the Christian Church, notwithstanding the fact that there are now 40 missionary societies represented there by earnest, heroic missionary toilers, and the Bible has been translated in whole or in part into 66 of its dialects, is waiting and ready to receive from the dark sons of Ham, like Bishop Small, the glorious light of the gospel."

Bishop Small had made a number of friends and contacts on this, his first trip to the Fatherland, and had attempted to bring other students over with him to study at Livingstone College, and return home equipped to extend the borders of Zion. While on the Gold Coast, he had offered James E. Kwegyir Aggrey and his closest friend, Kobina Osam Pinanko (Frank Arthur), the opportunity to come to America to study, but they refused. The offer was renewed. A close associate of Aggrey's, Mr. Aanman, urged Aggrey to accept it; other friends pressed money upon him; and on July 10, 1898, he sailed ... thence to America. Frank Arthur evidently arrived only a few months after Aggrey, as Aggrey and Hockman were one term ahead of him at Livingstone College by 1900.

There was also an attempt to organize a Zion Society at Cape Coast by Reverend F. Egyir Asaam after Small's trip. "That society would have succeeded and grown like a bay tree," but our inadequate foreign missions program, which was in its infancy, and Rev. Asaam's ill health soon caused this work to expire. Zion was more successful however, in Kwitta (now known as Keta). Reverend Thomas B. Freeman, our missionary to Kwitta, established a flourishing mission there, and had made strenuous efforts to establish similar work at Accra, Lagos, and other places. Reverend Dr. Owen L. W. Smith of Wilson, NC, who had been appointed by President McKinley as Minister Resident and Consul General to Liberia in 1898, was also an asset to Zion in Africa. While serving the government, Bishop Small made him a presiding elder of the Liberian work. During this time, he also sent $50 to Reverend Freeman to help him firmly establish this and other mission work on the Gold Coast (now Ghana).

Much of the credit is due to churches in Mobile, AL, for mothering foreign missions, just as Zion history records the noble deeds of the New England Conference in sponsoring its first missionaries to the South after the Civil War. If it had not been for the churches in Mobile, Bishop

Small could not have taken either of his trips to Africa or the West Indies. Accompanied by William Hockman, one of the African young men whom he brought to this country, educated at Livingstone College for the foreign work, Bishop Small sailed on June 21, and arrived in Cape Coast, West Africa, on Thursday morning, July 24. "While in Cape Coast, at his request, Mrs. Christine M. Selby, an educated African lady, who spends the greater part of her time in Europe, presented to him, in conjunction with her brother, Mr. Charles A. Albert Barnes, a large plot of ground, 50 feet wide and 200 feet long, in the town of Cape Coast on which to erect a church and church appliances for the AME Zion Church." Although the people were anxious for him to start a church in Cape Coast while he was there, he would not do so. Bishop Small, the brilliant penman, accomplished poet, conqueror of several African languages, established The (Zion) Missionary Star, in 1901 to stimulate the work in foreign territory.

After his return home, on the first day of August 1903, he sent Reverend Frank Arthur (Pinanko), who had just completed his studies at Livingstone College, to Cape Coast, and the work in this area, both churches and schools grew abundantly under the leadership of this unusually sober, scholarly, and upright Christian gentleman, and a trustworthy servant in that field."

On his African trip in 1902, Bishop Small visited Accra, Gold Coast, and felt it was very easy to establish an excellent church there. He then went to Kwitta, where Zion had a flourishing church organization with zealous workers and a school connected with the church. His leading missionary, Rev. Joseph D. Taylor, was engaged in a noble work assisted by William Hockman, S. F. Abban, and C. L. Acolatse.

From Kwitta the Bishop journeyed to Brewerville, Liberia, and at the request of the members of our mother church in Africa, he ordained to the order of deacon Brother Lewis B. Dudley, and placed him in charge of the church at Brewerville. Reverend Andrew Cartwright was appointed presiding elder … This faithful pioneer in Africa, Cartwright, died at his post on January 14, 1903. He was succeeded by Reverend H. T. Wright whom Bishop Small sent from Philadelphia to Liberia with wife and child, on February 27, 1900, to take charge of the Brewerville Church. Reverend Wright was succeeded by Rev. J. Drybauld Taylor, a native of Africa. The work in this section of Liberia became greatly stimulated when Bishop Walters appointed Rev. J. J. Pearce, during the organization of the Liberian Conference. Eight mission points had been established, and another four or five opened up by letter, and in all these places Americans and Liberians were working together in the best interest of Zion.

While holding the West Alabama Conference in November 1904, he [Bishop Small] has a severe attack. His death occurred Sunday, January 5, 1905.

Bishop Alexander Walters, assigned the foreign work at the General Conference of 1908, made his trip to West Africa in 1910. Walters, who was one of the prime organizers of the Pan-African Conference in London, July 1900, was intensely interested in enhancing the cause of African peoples throughout the world.

He left New York on January 26, 1910, and arrived in Liverpool on February 1, accompanied by Bishop I. B. Scott, resident bishop of Monrovia of the Methodist Episcopal Church. They sailed for Monrovia on the 9th, stopping first at Freetown, Sierra Leone, and making a safe arrival in Monrovia around February 26. After a brief stay in the capital city, Walters journeyed to Brewerville and organized the Liberia Annual Conference, March 3, 1910. He was greatly assisted in this conference by Reverends J. D. Taylor and J. J. Pearce. Missions were established in Monrovia, Po River, Roysville, Pleasant Hill, Suahn, and River Cess. Bishop Walters ordained several missionaries in each area that he visited to carry on the work. He left Monrovia for Cape Coast, where he arrived several days ahead of his planned schedule. Reverend Pinanko, by authorization of Bishop Walters, had organized the West Gold Coast Annual Conference the previous year, and on March 17, 1910, Bishop Walters presided over the second session at Cape Coast. Walters was warmly and enthusiastically received by the people, and the work was greatly blessed. Several mission churches and training schools had been opened for the people in the towns and villages, and nearly 1,200 additional souls had been brought to Christ during this quadrennium.

Bishop Walters left Cape Coast on March 28 for Kwittah, his last stop on the West Coast of

Africa, accompanied by Rev. Pinanko, presiding elder, and Rev. Harold N. Kwaun, a delegate from Kwitta to the conference held at Cape Coast. He organized and held the first session of the East Gold Coast Conference at Kwitta, March 31, 1910, with five ministers and nine lay delegates present. He ordained Brothers Harold N. Kwaun and G. A. Tay deacons, and three other young men of our teaching force were admitted to this conference. He found over 300 members in Kwitta, and a day school of 270 scholars. He was greatly assisted in this part of Africa by our staunch missionary, Rev. W. E. Shaw, who was a trained physician, "and eminently prepared by literary training and experience" to give ample service in the redemption of Africa. The bishops praised the work and the fine coterie of consecrated workers who were serving in Africa, and stated they were proud to send both Mrs. Henrietta Peters and Miss Lillian Tshabalala to Kwitta, and Mr. T. D. Davis to the Mt. Coffee farm in Liberia, all of whom were fine accessions to our foreign work.

Bishop George C. Clement succeeded Bishop Walters as presiding bishop of the African work in 1917. Reverend Pearce had returned from Liberia in 1915, and the work was without supervision until August 1919, when Reverend Thomas E. Davis was employed by the Board of Foreign Missions and appointed by Bishop Clement to take charge of the work in Liberia, while Rev. Pinanko was still carrying on the work in the West Gold Coast Conference. The East Gold Coast Conference was being directed by Reverend R. E. Peters, who had been on the field for six years. It was felt by the natives, however, that the African work needed close-up episcopal supervision, and their sentiment was expressed by the Corresponding Secretary of the Foreign Missions, Reverend W. W. Matthews, at the 1924 General Conference. He recommended that we send an American resident bishop—"one who is willing to enter heartily into their lives and problems, willing to live among them, to sympathize with them, to supervise and direct affairs and Zion's destinies in the Fatherland. After operating nearly a half-century in the Fatherland, this historic General Conference answered the plea and elected the largest class of bishops in the history of the denomination, at that time, making two additional ones, and assigned to Africa a resident bishop, Cameron Chesterfield Alleyne.

Bishop Alleyne and his wife, Annie L. Washington Alleyne, made their departure within the year for their new work. In Liberia, the bishop found Reverend and Mrs. Daniel Carleton Pope, stationed at Brewerville and Mount Coffee Farm, already at work for Zion. In the West Gold Coast Conference he found the churches divided and the flock scattered. With efficacy he united the people and saved them all to Zion. He was abounding in gratitude to Professor James E. K. Aggrey, who had passed away during the quadrennium and had aided materially and helped to save Zion in the Gold Coast. He found Rev. Pinanko, the pioneering, painstaking, and progressive servant for 25 years, still reliable, loyal and true. His wife, Victoria Osam-Pinanko, was working in the schools as sewing teacher to great benefit. He found Rev. Isaac Sackey to be one of our most constructive pastors and leading church builders on the coast. The missionary workers from America had also been zealous and courageous, with unquenchable enthusiasm for the African work. Reverence W. D. Francis, who had lived and preached Christ among an appreciative people, remained at his post when his devoted wife, Martha B. Francis, who was an asset to the work, broke down in health and was confined at home, Reverend and Mrs. D. G. Garland served at Mt. Coffee Mission from 1922–1923.

Mrs. Harriet Mae Green, the trained registered nurse who went to the field with Bishop and Mrs. Alleyne, was resplendent in her duties. While in Africa, Bishop Alleyne and our competent preaching and teaching ministry the Rev. and Mrs. R. F. Pile, Revs. P. D. Ofosuhene, D. K. Brown, Isaac Cole, G. B. Eninful, Moses D. Frans, P. O. Okyir, Alfred Eshun, Coffie, Qyason, G. B. Ado, Mr. Walter K. Dolly (later minister), and others made vast improvements to the work and left in course of erection more than a half-dozen churches in Cape Coast.

Bishop Alleyne's successor, Bishop W. W. Matthews, associated by the zealous missionaries from the home field, his wife, Alice J. Matthews, and daughter, Juanita Matthews, Oliver L. Sims, and Rev. Miss Almena Smith, made substantial enhancements of the total work in Africa. Working in close association with them were African leaders, including Reverends. Henry Bassa, Henry Anaman, K. M. Medu-Kyirpua, J. H. Phillips, and the eager and enthusiastic layman, Ben Brew.

The Nigerian Conference was organized and received into the fellowship of Zion at the time of the joint sessions of the East and West Gold Coast (Ghana) Conferences, February 24-29, 1932, with 28 churches, 11 native preachers, and 2,345 members. By 1932, 18,000 members were reported in the conferences of West Africa. Later, Miss Arwilda G. Robinson of Philadelphia, "a young woman of fine spirit, good preparation and fully devoted to the cause," was sent to Liberia, as well as Rev. and Mrs. A. W. Ricks, who took up the work at the school and farm at Mt. Coffee, Liberia. Reverend A. A. Adjahoe was sent to Keta, and served as preacher, superintendent, and school master with phenomenal success, assisted by Rev. F. K. Fiawoo, who had been trained in the U.S., and returned to Keta to serve his native land.

After supervising the African work for eight years, Bishop Matthews was succeeded by Bishop James W. Brown. The small society in Monrovia organized during Bishop Walters' day had long since been lost, and Bishop Brown organized a church for the second time in this capital city, with 50 members, and erected a church building. Reverend S. Dorme Lartey became its first pastor. The Bishop's wife, Andrades Lindsay Brown, Rev. G. A. Tay of Nigeria, and Rev. and Mrs. S. W. Peacock rendered valuable services with the others on the field. Bishop J. W. Brown was reassigned to the African Conferences by the General Conference of 1940. He met with a fatal accident in New York City, when an automobile struck him down on February 27, 1941.

The Board of Bishops assigned the work to the experienced Bishop Alleyne. He was prevented from visiting the field because of the emerging conditions of World War II, but through ponderous correspondence and proxies on the field, the work met with surprising success throughout the dismal war years.

Bishop Edgar B. Watson was elected in 1944 and assigned the African Conference along with two Home Mission Conferences. He and his wife, Mary J. Watson, spent considerable time in Africa, and he was given help from the Sesqui-Centennial Fund with which he did some development of the work. In 1948, the newly elected Bishop Hampton T. Medford, who served as corresponding secretary of the Foreign Missions Department, was assigned to the African work. He appointed Mrs. Cordella Medford Fauntleroy, his daughter, missionary supervisor. She accompanied him on his first trip to Africa, because of the illness of his wife, Mrs. Mary Elizabeth Medford, who could not serve and soon passed away. His daughter, Mrs. Fauntleroy, also died five weeks after returning from their first mission, reportedly from some illness she contracted in Africa.

The work had been enhanced through the significant contributions of Dr. and Mrs. J. A. Babington-Johnson of Nigeria, who later transferred to America where Dr. Babington-Johnson pastored until his death in 1971; Dr. and Mrs. S. Dorme Lartey of Liberia, and Dr. A. W. Appiah, Revs. Isaac Cole and K. O. Okyir from the Gold Coast. The notable servant, Rev. Frank Arthur Osam-Pinanko, passed away on March 15, 1946, after 43 years of dedicated services.

The International Christian Endeavor Conventions

In the early part of the 20th century, though there was an International Christian Endeavor Society movement, there was also the World Christian Endeavor movement, which graduated into the International Society of Christian Endeavor. It is well known that Reverend Daniel A. Poling became the world renowned leader in helping to spread this united movement around the world. The AME Zion Church was represented in these separate conventions by its General Secretary of Christian Endeavor, Mr. James W. Eichelberger, and the faithful Secretary of Christian Endeavor, Mr. Aaron Brown, Sr.. Mr. Brown served as a member of the International Christian Endeavor faculty in 1929. After the demise of Bishop Alexander Walters, another methodical denominational spokesman, Bishop Lynwood W. Kyles, took up the cudgels attending meetings in Europe and North America, and became a voice of significance in the International Christian Endeavor Society. He sustained a place of distinction by his masterly contributions to the program.

Mr. Eichelberger became a noted spokesman in this organization. He served on executive committees and as a trustee and became a potent voice for Christian action in serving the needs of youth throughout the world. Succeeding him in faithfully attending these conventions and executing the work of Christian Endeavor is the present General Secretary of Christian Education, Dr. George Lincoln Blackwell, II, who is presently a trustee of this Society along with Bishops W. J. Walls and H. B. Shaw.

The youth representation has always been far-reaching from the AME Zion Church. In 1947, Reverend William H. Coleman, Jr., attended the International Christian Endeavor Convention at San Francisco and was the official youth representative of the AME Zion Church.

AME Zion Colleges—Livingstone College

The urgent necessity for a theological and collegiate institution had been increasingly felt throughout the connection for several years. This need found a voice in the NC conference which met in Salisbury in November, 1877. In the meantime, Zion was developing Reverend C. R. Harris, an apostle of lore; serving also as principal of the High School in Charlotte, and when the school was eventually started in Concord, he became the first principal. Zion Wesley Institute subsequently held it first session in December 1879, in the frame house across the road from Scotia Seminary, with three students in attendance and four teachers, on the first day. After a brief recess, classes resumed the first Monday in January 1880. At this school session over 20 pupils were enrolled, some of them preachers in the traveling connection. In the meantime, the delegates of the AME Zion Church to the Ecumenical Conference held in London, England, September, 1881, Bishops J. W. Hood, J. P. Thompson, Reverends J. McFarley, and J. C. Price, "presented the opportunity of bringing the needs of our education work before the people of Great Britain—a people who have ever listened with sympathetic ear to the appeals of the American Negro for the amelioration of his unfortunate condition." Price's extraordinary talents were necessary to the church and race at that time. While the subject of foreign missions was being discussed, Price digressed to say, "the work that presents itself to the American Negro to go there (to Africa) to save the immortal souls of his people," and continued that this can be better assured, "by preparing those in America." He further stated:

"Six or seven million Negroes in America are the instruments to elevate their brethren in Africa, and since they have not the training schools in Africa, my idea is that we encourage the schools that we have in America and send the people…intelligent, moral, and well prepared men, to preach the gospel of Christ in Africa."

The immortal J. C. Price planted the school on a firm foundation, toiling the remaining 11 years of his life to build a creditable race institution. At Dr. Price's suggestion, the board voted to change the name of the institution to Livingstone College in 1885, in memory of the great explorer and missionary to Africa, David Livingstone, and a charter was procured. "In a little more than a brief decade he was known in Great Britain and the U.S., both on the Pacific and Atlantic, as a peerless orator … His fame rests not alone upon his popularity within his own church or his own race, for the evidence is conclusive that though unmistakably identified with the Negro, Democratic whites and whole communities recognized his worth, highly esteemed him, honored him in life and esteemed him in death."

Mrs. Meriah Gion Harris, pioneer teacher in 1879, and became first matron of Livingston College. First Secretary of the Women's Home and Foreign Missionary Society, 1880–1892. Mrs. Victoria Richardson, niece of Bishop Harris, also a pioneer teacher, with her brother Professor A. S. Richardson, in 1879. Miss Richardson also organized the Young Women's Department of the Women's Home and Foreign Missionary Society in 1912. One of the most distinguished graduates of the school and the most noted African of the first half-century was James Emman Kwegyir Aggrey of the Gold Coast (Ghana); co-founder of Achimota College in Ghana. The spirit of Livingstone College is the spirit of Joseph Charles Price. Dr. William Harvey Goler, Theologian and Philosopher, companion with the great Price in building Livingstone College and became its second president.

AME Zion Colleges—Hood Theological Seminary

Though the primary object of establishing Livingstone College was religious training, it had also soon developed courses in the classical arts and trades. There were efforts of having a religious department in the school. Dr. George Lincoln Blackwell, a graduate of Livingstone College and Boston University School of Theology, became the first to head the theological department of Livingstone College, and was recognized as the dean of the theological department. The need of a regular theological department at

Livingstone College and other schools had been voiced strongly throughout the denomination.

After much urgency on the part of the bishops and others, a regular organized theological school, for which theological teachers were selected, was begun the fall of 1903 by President W. H. Goler, ... The Board of Trustees voted to name the newly established department in honor and appreciation of the services of Senior Bishop J. W. Hood, first chairman of the Board of Trustees of Livingstone College, and plans got immediately on the way for a new building. The denomination rallied to the cause, and the first Hood Theological Seminary building was completed and opened for operation in October 1910. After the General Conference of 1912, they voted to make Hood Theological Seminary the sponsorship of Livingstone College.

The list of colleges is as follows:
- Zion Wesley Institute, Concord, NC, 1879, later changed to Livingstone College in 1885
- Hood Theological Seminary opened in 1910
- Clinton Junior College opened in 1894, SC
- Clinton Institute, Rock Hill, SC, opened in 1940
- Lomax-Hannon Junior College, Greenville, AL, opened in 1893
- Zion Institute or Josephine Allen Institute, Mobile, AL, opened in 1900
- Greenville High School, Greenville, TN, 1887, later changed to Greenville College
- Madisonville High School, KY, opened in 1889, later changed to Atkinson College in 1896
- Eastern NC Academy, New Bern, NC, opened in 1904
- Ashley County High School, 1892, AK, later moved to Warren, AK, and changed to Walters Institute in 1906, later became Walters-Southland Institute in 1936 located in Wilmot, AK, and later moved to Lexa, AK, in 1948
- Tuskegee Institute, AL, opened in 1881
- Dinwiddie Agricultural and Industrial School of AME Zion Church (Dinwiddie Institute) opened in 1910 in Dinwiddie, VA
- Jonson Rural High School, Batesville, MS, opened in 1920, later became Johnson Memorial Institute
- Institute of Black Ministries, Philadelphia, PA, opened in 1972

Chapter 7
Lutherans and Mission History

by Richard C. Dickinson

Richard C. Dickinson, from AL, is a lifelong Lutheran. He attended Lutheran and Presbyterian schools. He received his B.S. degree from Barber Scotia College, Concord, NC. He received his M.Div. from Immanuel Lutheran Seminary in Greensboro, NC; his M.A. degree from Concordia University, River Forest, IL; and his D.Min. from Chicago Theological Seminary, IL. He also was awarded the degree of Doctor of Divinity by Concordia Seminary, St. Louis, MO.

Dr. Dickinson spent 25 years as a parish pastor, 5 years as a District Executive, and 14 years as the Executive Director of the Commission on Black Ministry for the LC-MS. Besides the ministry work in the LC-MS, he makes frequent trips to Africa visiting mission sites, doing teaching, preaching, encouraging, and counseling.

Excerpts are taken from Richard C. Dickinson, *Roses and Thorns* (St. Louis, MO: Concordia Publishing House, 1997) and from Dr. Rosa J. Young, *This I Remember*, 1995. All other quotes are noted.

Collection of articles/information from LC-MS archives submitted by Dr. Richard C. Dickinson, Sr., Dept. of World Mission, 1333 S. Kirkwood Road, St. Louis, MO 63122-7295, 1999.

All references used by permission.

To understand the history of black American Lutherans in missions, the history of blacks in America must wind in and out of the black mission endeavors of church denominations.

The institutional patterns of American slavery were established in the islands of the West Indies, where the Africans were subjected to "the Break-in System." Whites tried to strip blacks of their African heritage and culture, including language and religion. It was in the West Indies that the organized churches began a systematic effort to bring the Christian faith to the African slaves.

The first organized effort to give religious instruction to the slaves in the American Colonies was made in 1702, in SC, by the London Society for the Propagation of the Gospel. The Moravians began their work among the Negroes in SC in 1738. Later the Methodist and the Baptists became involved in this work. The Lutheran Salzburgers, who settled in GA as early as 1734, were opposed to human slavery, and were open to ministry to their servants. Most Lutheran slaveholders lived in the states of NC, SC, GA and TN. Under Toussaint L'Ouverture and his successor, Dessallines, slaves in Haiti had led a successful revolution against their masters and the governments that had supported them. They had established a Negro-controlled nation in which all inhabitants were free.

In the summer of 1800, inspired by the success of Toussaint L'Ouverture, Gabriel Prosser, slave revolts were numerous in those days, and agitation from antislavery groups was mounting.

After the Civil War there was a mass exodus of Negroes out of the churches of their former masters. The black Lutherans were no exception to this rule. One Southern Lutheran writer said, "One reason was the disorganized condition of the Southern Lutheran Church after the war. Another was the paucity of her ministers and the poverty of her members. A third, he states, was the urgent need for looking after and caring for her white members, who were relatively in the majority and were widely dispersed. These groups of scattered sheep demanded her pastoral care and they were wanting the men and means to raise up suddenly a colored ministry for the colored people."

Four Lutheran synods have been singled out for their activity on behalf of the slaves and freedmen in their areas:

Probably the first black person to be licensed to preach by the NC Synod, organized in 1803, was the Reverend Michael Coble. In many ways, the NC Field can be considered the oldest field of Lutheran endeavor among black people in the U.S. The first established organized black Lutheran congregation of record is Trinity Lutheran Church, Elon College, NC. In fact, it goes far back into slavery, predating even the organization of the Lutheran Church-Missouri Synod (LC-MS) as a corporate body. ... This predates the resolution of 1877 by at least one year. Many families can trace their lineage back to plantations whose masters were Lutheran. Since many of the slaves took on the surnames of their masters after they were freed, an interesting pastime is to isolate all the German and Scandinavian names among the black Lutherans from the area and try to link them up with the corresponding plantation names.

The Synod of SC could boast of producing the first educated black Lutheran pastor in the U.S. A young boy by the name of Daniel Payne was confirmed by the Rev. Dr. John Bachman, Pastor of St. John's Church, Charleston, SC. Dr. Bachman sent him to the Lutheran Seminary at Gettysburg, PA. He would have been the first Lutheran pastor to be fully educated in one of our Lutheran seminaries and to serve in the Lutheran Church, but because of his race, there was no place for him in the ministry of the Lutheran Church. He turned his talents and abilities to the Methodist Church ... Libraries, universities, seminaries, schools, and other projects in the Methodist church are named in his honor. The TN Synod is distinguished because it probably produced the first licensed black Lutheran preacher in the country. Thomas Frye was not privileged to preach longer than three months before the Lord called him to his eternal reward.

The Synod of GA reported black accessions to their membership as late as 1870.

The LC-MS was established in 1847, and during the early years, the synod was too weak to support a foreign mission program. The Evangelical Synod of Missouri, OH, and other states began its missions program by contributing to two outstanding missionary societies in Germany through which it had done its foreign mission work. They were the Leipzig Society and the Hermannsburg Society. These societies were involved in foreign mission in places like China, India and South Africa.

In 1869, C. F. W. Walther, the great leader of the Missouri Synod, and one of the greatest theologians of his time, wrote a letter to Reverend F. Sievers in which he said, among other things, "It will be difficult to begin mission work among the colored people so long as we have not more men who are conversant with the English language."

After the Franco-German war of 1870, the Second Reich was born. The LC-MS could no longer declare how and where they wanted their money used. They discontinued contributing to these societies and looked around for a mission project that they could fully support and control. After preliminary meetings in January and November of 1871, the Synodical Conference was officially organized on the 10th of July, 1872. It originally consisted of the synods of OH, MO, WI, IL, MN, and the Norwegian Synod.

In this age of the pioneer and explorer, and the afterglow of the David Livingstone reports, Dr. C. F. W. Walther, and Ferdinand Sievers were preparing The LC-MS, then known as The Evangelical Lutheran Synod of MO, OH, and Other States, to become more active and more directly engaged in the field of mission outreach to the "heathen."

Eighteen seventy-seven was the year of the Hayes-Tilden compromise. In 1877, Ferdinand Sievers raised his voice on behalf of a broader missionary spirit. In 1877, the Synodical Conference voted to embark upon a foreign mission project upon American soil. The four million Negroes, recently freed and almost all living in the deep South at that time, were singled out as the object of this new mission endeavor. The segregation laws and the discrimination practices had made them virtually a nation within a nation. Black ministry in America was considered as a "foreign mission field," and the professional church workers in this field were called missionaries.

The issue of foreign missionary work in Africa was one of the rationales for establishing the historically black Lutheran college and seminary in the U.S. From Letter from Rev. Nils Jules Bakke, pioneer missionary to NC and first pastor of Grace Church:[1]

> Dear Pioneer, —I offer to donate three or four acres of land in the eastern part of Concord, known as the Litaker property, as a building site for a Colored Lutheran College and Seminary. This is the summary of a docu-

---
1 *The Lutheran Pioneer*, June 17, 1892, 26 (St. Louis, MO: Concordia Publishing House).

ment which Honorable Warren C. Coleman, an enterprising merchant of Concord and our representative colored man of the "North State," handed to your Missionary the other evening. A Lutheran College and Seminary, a colored Concordia, if you please, for the classical and theological education of colored young men for the ministry in our church is a long-felt want. Without it we can not, for obvious reasons, carry on successfully the mission work we have undertaken. What the colored people of the South need and must have are thoroughly educated Christian men of their own race, men that will not work for their own selfish ends, but by faithful instruction in church and at school lift their fellowmen out of their ignorance and degradation. The day may not be distant when the Evangelical-Lutheran Synodical Conference need missionaries for the dark tribes of the dark continent. Who would be better fitted to undertake the cause of Christ among those Africans than the Southern negro boys, who with the mother milk, as it were, have drank in the great glorious doctrines of our church ... — Missionary.

Immanuel Lutheran College and Seminary was started in Concord, NC, in 1903, and it was moved to Greensboro, NC, in 1905 and was located on East Market Street adjacent to A&T University.

The AL Field of mission endeavor was the last to be started by the Evangelical Lutheran Synodical Conference of North America. The Synodical Conference had almost 40 years of experience to draw on when this mission field was started. In 1916, Nils Jules Bakke went there and had a strong congregation going in less than 8 months and 25 growing congregations in about ten years. It was in AL that he assisted Rosa Young in her ministry endeavors.

African-American Rosa Young's Lutheran Mission

The Lutheran Church missions among the black people in AL had its beginning in a private school.
[The following quotes are taken from *Light in the Dark Belt, The Story of Rosa Young as Told by Herself*.[2]]

---

[2] *Light in the Dark Belt, The Story of Rosa Young as Told by Herself* (St. Louis, MO: Concordia Publishing House, 1950). Used by permission.

I was born at Rosebud, in Wilcox County, AL, May 14, 1890, in a church that stood on a plot of land about one mile from the present site of our oldest Lutheran mission. My parents were Grant and Nancy Young, devout Christians and very dutiful in church attendance. My father was an African Methodist pastor for about 20 years, my mother a woman of high morals. Much credit is given to her by all who know her for the manner in which she raised her family of ten children.

As long as I can remember, I would tell all who asked me that I was going to be a teacher. The morning after my graduation [from Payne University], June 2, 1909, I left for my old home in the country at Rosebud.

There were no mirrors ... no timepieces ... no factory-made brooms ... no cooking stoves ... no sheets ... no washbowls. The women usually wore one-piece dresses tied around the waist with a string. They combed their hair with a table fork and tied their braids with string. Men wore their trousers rolled up halfway to the knees and held them up with one homemade suspender. All went barefoot. They did not bother to wash their feet before retiring at night, even at the end of a rainy day.

Far below everything else was their religious training. The little colored children did not know any prayers. They did not know that God had made them. They did not know that God made the world. They did not know what was meant by a Bible verse. They did not know how to sing. They did not know what was right and what was wrong. They had no knowledge of the Bible.

At that time there were in this part of the country some very peculiar local laws pertaining to the public schools in certain districts. One was that if the colored people failed to have a public school for any one scholastic year, the public school money would be returned to the county and be given to the support of the white schools. Most of the so-called public school teachers were not able to pass the state examination and secure a state certificate.

I resolved to render some service to my race by teaching them for each year in as many of these vacant schools as I could and thus help them retain the small public fund that had been set aside for colored youth. The children advanced in their studies and made good progress along secular lines. I taught them the Lord's Prayer and some Bible verses. I did not have the least idea of what was to be done, but the Lord instilled in me the thought of building a school, gave me the strength to begin this work, and sustained me. I decided that it was necessary to secure the good will and approval of all the white people in the community before presenting my proposition to the colored people.

The next thing I decided to do was draw up a course of study and to devise plans to raise money for buying the land, erecting the school building, and supporting the school, as there were no funds appropriated for such a school. A school meeting was called in the Methodist Church. After much discussion by both men and women, the resolution was accepted. Thus, on July 8, 1912, was organized the Rosebud Literary and Industrial School. Rosa J. Young opened the Rosebud School on the first Monday in October, 1912, with seven children. The enrollment reached 215.

In the fall of 1914, when the time came to open our school, things looked very dark. Business was dull, and World War I had broken out. I called together our board of trustees. At this meeting we all agreed to offer the school to the African Methodist Episcopal Church. The Presiding Elders' Council met at Prattville that August. The men began to fight each other. When Bishop Jones saw that nothing could be done, he disbanded the first committee and appointed a new committee of three men. Miss Rosa, … you went out since your graduation, built a school, and gave us the first offer, but we are unable to take it.

I took the appeal to the Aunt Jean's Fund. This appeal was denied. I applied to the agent of the Rosewald Fund and was denied. I appealed to the authorities of the Slater Fund, but with no success. I cried in vain to the Reformed Presbyterian Church, the United Presbyterian Church, and the American Presbyterian Church. I wrote to the mission board of the Congregational Church. Then I decided that I would write one more letter. If no relief came then, I would close the school. Now, that letter was to go to Dr. Booker T. Washington, our great leader.

At last, one day a letter came from Tuskegee Institute signed by Booker T. Washington himself. In this letter he told me he was unable to help me in the least; but he would advise me to write to the Board of Colored Mission for the Lutheran Church. He said they were doing more for the colored race than any other denomination he knew of.

A short time passed, and one day a letter came from the sainted Rev. Nils J. Bakke. In his letter Rev. Bakke stated that although he doubted nothing that I had stated in my letters, he would rather come and investigate the matter for himself. When the train stopped, Papa was standing on the platform. Pastor Bakke came limping down from the coach on the train with a crutch under his arm and a walking stick in his hand. When he returned to St. Louis, God moved him to make a favorable report. The Board instructed Rev. Bakke to return to AL and stay there until the work was well organized.

Missions came into possession of the property in 1916. By the help of the Lord I succeeded in purchasing 45 long benches from the Methodist church body, five heaters, one large school bell, a sewing machine, and in paying a reasonable amount on a nice piano. I received a gift of 150 Bibles and New Testaments for our Bible Training Department from the American Bible Society at Philadelphia and a nice collection of useful books to begin a school library from Knox Academy, belonging to the Reformed Presbyterian church and school at Selma.

In the face of combined forces, adverse circumstances and threats and false reports, Rev. Bakke continued to preach Christ crucified, the Son of God and the Savior of the world. On Palm Sunday, April 16, 1916, 70 were confirmed and 12 were baptized. On Easter Sunday following, 49 were baptized. Reverend

Bakke then organized the first Lutheran Church in AL for blacks and called it Christ Evangelical Lutheran Church. Using the Christian day school as the chief model for mission outreach, the growth of the work was phenomenal.

The very day on which I severed my relations with the African Methodist Church and joined the Evangelical Lutheran Church, willing to work for Jesus, was the day on which the devil turned the people against me....
The leaders in the sectarian churches pledged themselves to overthrow the Lutheran Church. Preachers stood up and proclaimed from their pulpits, "Rosa Young hath a devil." "Rosa Young is a Jezebel, an antichrist, a false prophet." "Rosa Young is a Democrat; she is working for the white people."

Booker T. Washington is quoted as saying during this time that the religion of the Negro is Baptist. Many Negroes are Methodist. When he found a Negro who was a member of any other denomination, such as Presbyterian or Lutheran, Washington knew that some white person had been messing with that man's religion.

Rosa Young is tearing up churches; that she was leading the people to hell for money; that she ought to be Ku-kluxed, skinned alive, burned at the stake. At another time I was at a place where my Church was accused of being a German church. It was during the World War.

June 30, 1931, was a memorable day for me, for it was on that day I started on my first trip North. I arrived late on the 3rd of July at the great Union Station in St. Louis. Pastor Schultze had arranged that on my return (mission speaking trip to northern states) I should lecture in the Emmaus Church hall in St. Louis. A large audience was assembled. A large offering was given at that time for starting the work in Africa, which had not yet begun.

African-American Lutheran Mission to Africa

Missions work was begun in Africa in 1877. Rev. Joseph G. Lavalais was the first black person to be elected to the Plenary Board of the Lutheran Synodical Conference. This was the board that set the policies and controlled the work among black people both in America and also in Africa from 1877 to 1965. Dr. Lavalais was the first black person to be called for service as a foreign missionary to Nigeria. He had to decline due to health complications from diabetes. The other "first" black missionary during this time was Betty Dickens, a nurse, sent by Transfiguration Lutheran Church in St. Louis, MO, to the Lutheran hospital in Eket, Nigeria, West Africa.

The General Conference was an official conference of black Lutheran congregations. This General Conference reported a meeting in Concord to *The Lutheran Pioneer*.

"Grace Lutheran Church, Concord, N.C., Entertains the General Conference.

The General Conference of Colored Missions convened Thursday morning, August 12-16, at Grace Lutheran Church, Concord, NC. In the Thursday morning session a hearty welcome in behalf of the city of Concord was made by Mr. C. F. Ritchie, a prominent business man, who urged upon the members of the convention that they be consecrated and zealous in mission-work.

The Rev. J. P. Smith, superintendent of the southeastern field, gave a brief historical sketch, showing that the work in NC had its inception in Grace Church and that the beginning of Immanuel Lutheran College and Theological Seminary likewise was made in Grace School. Friday's sessions were devoted to the hearing of a doctrinal paper on "The Image of God," by Dr. H. Nau, president of Immanuel Lutheran College—I. J. A.[3]

In Verhandlungen der zweiunddreiss-tigsten Versammlungder Ev-Luth Synodalkonferenz von Nordamerica, 1930, pg. 64, Mission in Africa, (Report, p. 57, No. 10). Translated it reads: Proceedings of the 32nd meeting of the Evangelical Lutheran Synodical Conference of North America, (28-36th). These were Board copies of the minutes of the sessions of Synodical Conference. [The minutes of the Evagelical Lutheran Synodical of North America were all written in German from its beginnings in 1872 until 1934 when the move to English prevailed.]

---

[3] It will interest our readers to know that the General Conference, after long and earnest discussion, passed strong resolutions on the great desirability of beginning mission work in Africa in the near future and thus to bring the Gospel blessings also to our African brethren, as an expression of our gratitude to God for His favors to us.

"WHEREAS, The synods constituting the Synodical Conference have encouraged the Synodical Conference to make an exploration of mission possibilities in Africa; and

WHEREAS, Approximately $6,000 for this purpose has been collected, chiefly by our colored brethren; therefore be it

Resolved, That the Missionary Board be instructed to select a committee of capable men to do all preliminary work preparatory to an exploration in Africa; and be it further

Resolved, That said committee submit its findings to the Missionary Board and report to the Synodical Conference at its next meeting; and be it further

Resolved, That said committee carry out this exploration in Africa pending the approval and decision of the Synodical Conference.

Adopted."

It was natural for black people in America, who were effectively isolated from the main stream of American culture by legal segregation and ruthless exploitation, to establish their society and culture, and to look for other black people in the world to expand their relationships. The same could be said of the poor black Lutherans, who were also effectively isolated from the mainstream of their church. They had no fellowship with the Lutheran synods that created them, but these black Lutherans had established their own church conferences every year, and the General Conference met every other year. Each field had its own special mission project, but until 1925 the common mission field project of the General Conference was the China Mission Drive. In 1925 the change was made, and from that time until black ministry became a part of the LC-MS, African Mission was the primary project of black Lutheran congregations in the Synodical Conference.

Those resolutions at the General Conference meeting in 1925, started a sustained drive which established that mission work in Nigeria, West Africa in 1936. The reason for the delay can be found in the Proceedings of the Thirty-Third Convention.[4]

"Resolved, That the Missionary Board be instructed to select a committee of capable men to do all preliminary work preparatory to an exploration in Africa."

The organization of this committee was effected May 21, 1931. The committee was fully persuaded of the extraordinary importance of this petition, and it elected a special committee of three—Pastors E. L. Wilson; O. C. A. Boecler; and G. A. Schmidt—to make further investigation and to obtain the necessary information from the properly constituted governmental authorities and missionary societies.

The replies were unfavorable. The International Missionary Council London declared:

The Qua Iboe District of Nigeria is an area already over crowded. The Church of Scotland, Qua Iboe, and the Primitive Methodist Missionary Society have been treading on each other's toes for a long time, and even now, though they have reached a friendly agreement regarding spheres of influence, difficulties still arise. It seems a pity that a new society should plunge into the tangle when there are so many areas where there are no missions at all.

The Qua Iboe Mission, with headquarters in Belfast, which has worked in Southern Nigeria for upwards of 40 years, communicated the same adding: "We feel strongly about this matter, especially in view of the fact that there are large countries in West Africa altogether untouched."

The committee's response was:

As yet neither your Committee nor the Missionary Board is able to present definite recommendation. On the other hand, this missionary society has pointed to us fields, quite accessible, where thousands upon thousands may be reached who have never heard the Gospel. In the mean while a young Nigerian native belonging to the Ibesikpo United Church, Mr. Jonathan Udo Ekong, is pursuing his studies at our institution in Greensboro in order that he may in due time return to his native country, and, if God wills, preach the Gospel to his people. But it is his prayer that work may be begun in Africa before that time.

Even after going through Britain, the colonial power in Nigeria at that time, advised that the

---

[4] Evangelical Lutheran Synodical Conference of North America, "Mission in Africa" report, 1932, 32–33.

work not start there. The LC-MS did indeed start it.

Jonathan Udo Ekong's "Footprints of the Lord"

The following are excerpts from The Missionary Lutheran, 1934, when Jonathan Udo Ekong, Afaha, Nigeria, Africa, shared his life story in a three-part series.

The southern part of Nigeria, between the Niger on the West and the Cross River on the East, bordering in the South, the Gulf of Guinea and defined in the North by an imaginary line drawn from a point 150 miles north from the mouth of the Niger River in an easterly direction to the great bend of the Cross River, is the land of the Ibibios, a strong tribe, numbering millions of Efik people. Owing to their trade relations with coastal towns and century-old contact with Europeans they have also acquired many European customs and vices.

My grandfather, Ndem Ekpin, was the head chief of the Ibibio tribe. He, being a heathen, married many wives and had many children. After his death some of his sons succeeded him in the chieftainship, among whom was also my father. He was chief of the town of Afaha in Ibesikpo. He married fifteen wives and over 60 children were born to my father.

The custom of voluntary mutilation for the sake of beauty is now rapidly disappearing. Thus the upper and lower front teeth were filed into sharp points. I still carry on both temples the mark of my tribe cut with a razor. Many middle aged men and women can be seen whose body is dotted with numerous beauty scars on arms, chest, and abdomen.

The houses are mostly sun-dried mud. Father owned a large tract of land, woodland, palm groves, farmland, and real estate in town. His wives and children were a blessing to him. When I was born, my father named me Oyop Idem, that is, sacred palm. My mother called me Akai, that is, grave.

The staple foods of our people are cassava, yams, bananas, plantains, and beans. Yams, after they have been cooked, are eaten like Irish potatoes together with palm oil or a chili sauce, and fish or any other kind of meat, preferably goat.... Fruits of all kinds are found in great abundance.

The belief in a supreme being is universal. The heathen Ibibios call it 'abasi', and they conceive that Abasi as being the creator, preservor and protector, from whom no evil comes. Of Abasi no image is made, but sacrifices are rendered. The blood, which is considered the life of the animal, is given as the most precious gift.

The next important, or even more important, element in the heathen religion of our people is spirits. The most prominent of the spirits are accorded to the souls of departed men. These need food and care. Accidents, failure of crops, sickness, etc., are ascribed to the work of evil spirits of dead men, which, therefore, must be placated by sacrifice, while the witch doctor tries to undo by charms or enchantments. A main part of the heathen religion is, furthermore, the fetish. A fetish is a rag, string, root grown on a grave, a tooth, hair, nail, leaves, etc., into which magic power has been coaxed by the witch doctor. Intimately connected with the fetishism is the very common ancestor worship. Father and mother were heathens during my entire youth. They worshipped idols made of clay and wood and representing sun, moon, and stars, ancestors, certain trees, snakes and other animals. Especially were they given to conjuring, incantations, witchcraft, and ancestor worship.

Heathen farmers began to clear the bush only after a sacrifice has been made by the fetish priest, and they will also not eat of the new crop before a similar sacrifice is made to Idio, the god of the workers. Many of our people are engaged in the palm oil and palm kernel business. From some of these trees we get palm wine, from others coconuts and coconut oil. Occasionally epidemics of smallpox, typhoid fever, dysentery and cholera sweep over the country and kill many people. Malaria is always with us.

Father was very disappointed that I refused to accompany him to the heathen worship. Every heathen family in my country has what they call Ibok ukpon, that is a medicine for the purpose of protecting the soul of the children in the family. While this nasty stuff is boiling the witchdoctor calls upon the names of the gods and his deceased predecessors in witchcraft to give protecting power to the concoction in the pot. This over, he smears the evil smelling stuff into the face of everybody in the house. If they caught me, there was no way to escape and I had to stand the torture, but as soon as they turned their back I would run to the next water pool and wash off the horrid stuff.

There were schools and Christian churches in other parts of Nigeria, in Calabar, Iboe, and Lagos. When I was a little boy the Qua Iboa Mission, a mission society from Belfast, Ireland, began to evangelize the Ibibio country. … Some years after hearing the first rumors about the foreign missionaries I asked my half brother, and a son of a friend of my father, to go with me to see [the missionary]. … After two weeks we went back to church. This time we were seven boys. Next time we were fifteen. Father and mother gave me a frightful thrashing after the people of the town had bitterly complained that I was the ring-leader and the ruin of their children. My half-brother suggested that I be sent to a friend of his in Calabar to attend school there. He made me his chore boy.

Being a heathen he frequently made sacrifices to his gods and most of the time compelled me to eat before his idol. … In six months my half brother came down again on a business trip and inquired about me. I told him I was not going to stay. …

Soon after my return I found my old playmates and friends and we discussed how we could arrange matters so that we could receive a fair school education. … As a number of boys who desired education increased we asked the white missionary, in charge of the Qua Iboe mission in Aka, to establish a school in our town. … At last he announced his coming to our parents. They were very angry. … He held a meeting with them and the chiefs of the town, and all present promised to help establish a school and a church. They even promised to give a small piece of land for the building of a school house. Hardly had the missionary left town when they all very promptly changed their mind.

Since, however, the chiefs of the town were not willing to part with even a small plot of ground for the erection of a school and church, I asked my mother for permission to donate the piece of land she had bought for me. … Poor father, he had to pay a high price for his silent consent. In a meeting of the secret and half-secret societies of which he was a member, Ekpo, Ekon and Ekpe poison was administered to him in food in consequence of which he died. Seeing I had given a small lot for the church, my half brother, Udo Mbon, came forward and did the same, also a few other friends of the mission. After the church, building of mud walls and palm leaf roof, had been erected Mr. Esien Oka of the United Free Church ministered to us till 1918, when he died of influenza in his own village. … The Christian congregation in 1918, numbered about 200. The congregation, from its very beginning, contributed to the support of its catechist-teacher.

After the death of the catechist-teacher, Esien Oka, the United Free Church transferred us, without our consent, to the Qua Iboe Mission. … Till 1926 we struggled in the Qua Iboe Mission. … I addressed the chiefs with much humility and respect, showed them the present condition, spiritual and political, in Ibesikpo, and pointed out the needs and ways to meet these needs. The chiefs were very much pleased, promised to grant the land for the central school and a supply of materials for school and dormitories, and went home in high spirits. After three weeks they made good their promise and in the beginning of 1927 we began to clear the bush in order to build the school.

As the work of God progressed in Ibesikpo, Christians began to talk about having a trained minister of their own in their midst. They cast about for a proper person whom they might send to the United Free Church Seminary in Calabar. When the vote was taken, I was chosen. Since we were under the Qua Iboe Mission we went to Rev. Westgarth and he promised to lay the matter before the Field Conference. This Conference decided against my going to Calabar to the Free Church seminary and also turned down a request of my people to send me to England for training.

When we came back from Conference we called a meeting in which Mr. Okom Edem, a native of Calabar and a teacher in a native school, was present. He injected the idea of sending me to America. Okom knew something of Howard University and promised to get in touch with that university if my people would raise enough money to send me to America. In about three months I received a letter from Howard University which Okom read for us and in three more months my people sent $250 to Howard University for my support and education.

Now began a battle royal for a passport and endorsement of the passport, lasting about a year and a half. May 19, 1928, I sailed to America with the good wishes of my people and the request to interest an American Church in the work in the Ibesikpo country. Mr. Brown, of the school of religion of Howard University, took a special interest in me. Dr. Brown tried to acquaint me with the churches of different denominations in Washington. Thus the first church I attended in America was Lutheran.

I never enrolled in Howard University as a student, because I had not received an education which actually prepared me for entrance into the university.

In the fall of 1930 I read in the "Afro-American," a colored newspaper, that the Lutheran Synodical Conference which conducts Negro Missions in this country was thinking of opening up mission work somewhere in Africa. ... Pastor Vorice gave me the address of the late Rev. C. F. Drewes, Executive Secretary to the Missionary Board of the Synodical Conference, to whom I now appealed on behalf of my people. The Missionary Board seriously considered by request and I left Salisbury to become a student in Immanuel College, Greensboro, NC. When my people, hard hit by the depression in the palm oil trade, failed to send my support, the Missionary Board graciously supported me, and has always listened to my frequent appeals for my people.

A paragraph from the Golden Julbilee Edition reads:

The Church grew at Afaha and so did the sphere of influence of Qua Iboe Mission. By 1925, there were 60 Churches in Missionary Westgarth's district, at least 14 of them in Ibesikpo villages.

In America, Jonathan Ekong was trying out schools and churches. One Sunday morning he visited St. John's Lutheran Church in Salisbury. I am sure that pastor Felton Vorice had made no special preparation that morning, but Mr. Ekong was so impressed with that sermon and his subsequent interview ... that be considered his search at an end. The pastor took Mr. Ekong in his car ... and introduced him to Dr. Henry Nau, the President of Immanuel Lutheran College and Seminary. Mr. Ekong was given some financial aid and work study so that he could enroll in the college at Immanuel. Even sweeter to Mr. Ekong's ear was the story about the project of the General Conference. Their churches and Sunday schools were continuously and consistently raising funds to send missionaries from our church to Africa to spread the Gospel.

A report on Africa was printed in the "Proceedings of the Thirty-Fourth Convention of the Evangelical Synodical Convention of North America,"[5]

Your Board for Colored Missions was instructed at the regular meeting of the Synodical Conference at Mankato to carry on its investigations regarding Africa and to gather more definite information regarding the possibility of mission—work in that country.

The Dark Continent Calls for Light

A group of people known as the Ibesikpo United Church, living in the Protectorate of Nigeria, on the West Coast of Africa, has petitioned the Lutheran Synodical Conference of North America to undertake aggressive mission—work in the Ibesikpo country. Then, as God may prosper our

---

5 Evangelical Lutheran Synodical Conference of North America, 1934, 96–105.

work, to extend it into unoccupied fields in Nigeria or in parts of Africa adjacent to Nigeria.

In a mysterious manner the welcome news penetrated to the interior of Africa that a large church-body in the U.S., known as the Lutheran Church, is conducting successful missionary activities among the Negroes of our country. The interested natives did not know whom to direct their appeals, but by a combination of fortunate circumstances their letter ultimately reached our Missionary Board in St. Louis.

Shortly, thereafter, Jonathan Udo Ekong, a young Nigerian native, came into contact with our coloured mission in Salisbury, NC, and after receiving Christian instruction, was received into membership with our Church. This young man had been sent to America by the Ibesikpo people for the purpose of preparing him to become a Christian missionary to his brethren in the homeland.

The fervor and earnestness of their appeal is manifested by the following excerpt from a letter under date of January 22, 1934:

> We have informed the government officials in Nigeria about your coming into Ibesikpo as a missionary to the Gospel of Christ. They have given their approval, and no objection is offered by them. We hope that, when the Lutheran Synodical Conference will hold its convention in 1934, they will give deep consideration about Ibesikpo appeal and be ready to bring the Good News into our land. Do not despise our tears. We have waited so many years to have you.

A carefully selected number of doctrinal and devotional books, catechisms, Bible histories, pamphlets, tracts, etc., was promptly forwarded to Africa by our Board. In acknowledgment, we received the following reply under date of March 6, 1934:

> We hope you will be very pleased to hear that the tracts and literature you sent us have thrown a great light upon our people. We have distributed these pamphlets and tracts to friends afar, and they are anxious to get more. We have already informed you that we have established Lutheran churches in Ibesikpo from the time we have received the literature, books, and catechisms from you. The impression we are getting from these books moves us to form a reading room in the center for all our teachers to meet once each [word omitted] for the study of the Gospel.

> We are now conducting services in our churches according to the Lutheran order of service. We are now asking that the order of services should be sent to us in a pamphlet, so that we may be able to follow step by step.

> Pending the anxiously awaiting coming of the Lutheran Church, the Ibesikpo people are carrying on heroically. Not only 20 towns in the Ibesikpo country are ready to accept the services of our Lutheran Church, but we are informed that 'many more towns are standing by watching hopefully whether the appeal of the 20 towns will be granted.

In September, 1938, a report was printed in *The Missionary Lutheran*, excerpts from a letter by Nigerian missionary Koeper, p. 66.

[*The Missionary Lutheran* replaced *The Lutheran Pioneer*. It was published monthly from about 1930 until about 1963. Its purpose was to inform the church about the mission fields both among black people in America and in Africa. It was edited by workers on the field and published by Concordia Publishing House in St. Louis, MO. In 1963 the Synodical Conference dissolved. At that time there had been four synods in the Conference: The LC-MS, The Wisconsin Synod, The Slovak Synod, and The Norwegian Synod.]

Although missionary Koeper was not black, his article described well what missionaries actually encountered.

> There is so much to do that one hardly has the time to think of the hardships and inconveniences of the country. The heat, the dampness, the insects, the fever, the poor food—but the large number of natives, their ignorance and sin, their desire to learn about God and their Savior, the help we can give in cases of sickness, and the hundreds of children in the schools—these all far outweigh the other difficulties. The work really is enjoyable, and it brings a satisfaction which nothing else has ever brought.

When we started work, these churches were not proper congregations, but just groups of people eager to hear the Word of God. They had a little knowledge of Christianity but it was surprisingly shallow. Their Christian life was hardly different from that of the heathen. They practiced polygamy, killed twins, took part in heathen dances, burials, and sacrifices, and even practiced heathen forms of witchcraft.

Since the beginning of the work we have been following the principle that we can do nothing until we have people with Christian knowledge, conviction, and life in these churches. Aside from being able to teach the children to read and to write and to present a few simple stories without application, the native teachers are practically useless because they have but an eighth grade secular education with no religious training.

We have insisted that each person who wishes to be baptized or attend communion must pass an examination before the missionary and the entire congregation. Now we have a nucleus of good Christians in almost every church, and we can begin to grow. Of course many of the people who were in the churches at first have left us. They couldn't do without their two or three wives or for some reason they couldn't follow our instructions.

We have seen much sickness. Twice this past week Mrs. Koeper has gone into the bush to find mothers who had given birth to twins. We have watched people die of pneumonia, and seen them all cut to pieces by machetes. We try to do what we can to help them, especially by taking them to the hospital, but in most cases they wait until it is too late before they call for help. Even the teachers are ignorant in these things. One of them had a compound fracture of the leg. I carefully explained that gangrene would enter the open wound and he would lose his leg if not his life and, therefore, should go to the hospital. He insisted that he would first try a native doctor for two weeks. Exactly two weeks later I carried him back to his native village in a motor car, and he died on the way.

On the same page was this announcement:

Under the auspices of the Missionary Board of the Lutheran Synodical Conference of North America a service was held Sunday evening, July 3, 1938, at St. Luke's Evangelical Lutheran Church, Chicago, IL, at which Candidate of Theology Jonathan Udo Ekong was ordained and commissioned as a missionary among the people of the Anang country in Nigeria.

[The LC-MS currently has the Jonathan Ekong Memorial Lutheran Seminary in Obot Idim, Uyo, Akwa Ibom State. In June, 2005, it graduated seven pastors and eleven evangelists, all sent out to the harvest fields.]

Although the Christian church was active in Africa since 1836 and much work was being done by American Lutherans in Nigeria since 1936, the first black American-born missionaries, James and Billie Tyler, were not sent to Nigeria until November 27, 1981.

The Reporter had a series of articles on the Tylers. The first article was, "Tylers Find Nigeria Another Door to Work Among Cultural Groups."[6]

For Rev. James Tyler and his wife Billie, their new assignment in Nigeria is the culmination of two decades of hopes for mission work in Africa. The diversity of languages (estimates range from a minimum of 395 to a maximum of 850) also reflects the diversity of groups which come together in the city. "When they do come to the city, it is basically English that they speak," Tyler said. "Being a black missionary," Tyler said, may be "almost a hindrance. We look like them and yet we're not" ... "I thought before it would be a help, but when I think of the cultural differences, I realize the mistakes I would make will be more glaring; they will look at me and say, 'you're one of us and yet you're not doing it like one of us.'"

Four years later, in January 1985 *The Reporter* reads:

Missionary James Tyler and his wife, Billie, who began work in Nigeria three years prior for the Missouri Synod Board for Mission

---

6 December 7, 1981, vol. 7, no. 48, 1–2 (St. Louis, MO: LC-MS Department of Communication).

Services, say their black American heritage has helped them in Africa. The couple agreed that as black English-speaking foreigners, they are more readily accepted by Nigerians than if they had been born in that country. "We're neutral strangers," explained James Tyler. "We don't belong to any particular African village so we are accepted by everyone. The fact that we are black did not help us to adjust—it helped us to be accepted." Tyler says that he would like to see more black workers in African missions in the years to come.

Some of God's rewards were shown in the article, "God's Power is Strong in Nigeria," written by the Tylers:

> Quite a few of our group were going to visit a family of church members, whose only son in a family of eight girls had died five days before. We read Scripture, sang and prayed to console the grieving father. As we were leaving, he blurted out: "I am beyond consolation, my youngest female child is even now dying. We have tried giving her glucose by mouth; she does not take it. She is now with the mother, in a house of a woman who has knowledge. She has not taken food in three days. She is dying."
>
> We saw them outside the door—relatives, friends and neighbors—looking at us with hate and disagreement. We sensed the oppressive presence of Satan. It was frightening. Our parting words, "Your child will not die. The God you trust, whose love you know through Jesus Christ, will show His loving power to you." Even so, as the others were leaving, the father fell on Jim's shoulder and sobbed. "Pastor, she will die. Please know that I will not run from my God, even if I have sorrow to my grave." ... But they are all out there—my enemies, my neighbors, my relatives—they are laughing at me. They mock my children. They warn me that my child should be allowed to die or there will be no peace in this family. (We understood that according to tradition, this child's death would be a type of passive sacrifice for the sudden death of the only male child. This was the demand of one of their traditional gods.)
>
> Jim gave the father some money and asked him to bring the baby and mother to our house the next day. Jim promised that if we could not find a hospital with proper medication on hand we would try oral rehydration and prayer. They did not come, so we went to their house. Emson, the father, was returning home as we left his house. He seemed embarrassed. Then by some strange impulse he said, "Pastor, would you like to see where the baby is?"
>
> We came to the place—a very small dark room with about seven people sitting around. We sat on one of the beds with the mother. The child, appearing lifeless, was lying across the lap of one woman. The child's feet were cold, but her body was hot. "Did she take any fluids today?" "No, she won't take." "Let's take her to the hospital. She must have treatment tonight." The mother looked to her friends, who indicated, "No." We felt heavily burdened and had a strange fear. The heavy darkness we felt was something more than the night. These people could blame us if the cursed lived, and the parents could be troubled in their faith if she died.
>
> The hospital at first refused us because the doctor was gone for the evening. We begged the nurses to do something to try to save the child's life. The next day, the baby was better. On the second day she was active and eating. We were jubilant! Alas, on the third day, little Seiyefer was taken out of the hospital by her mother and taken back to the house of the lady with 'special knowledge.' We felt angry and were despondent. We visited the parent's house—the baby was not there.
>
> One male relative, just back from America, talked with us. "Be patient," he begged, "you must be patient with our traditional beliefs." All right, we said to ourselves, that's it. We have worked, taught and prayed with this family. "Oh, Lord, do you want these non-Christians to continue to mock this man? It is all in your hands, Lord," we prayed.
>
> God's answer: the little girl lived. Two weeks later, the entire family came to church and asked for time to speak, to give thanks and praise to God that His power is stronger than that of Satan, and His love is wonderful.

In a later article, "Nigerian Mission Not Easy, But Satisfying," Rev. Jim Tyler writes:

> It took us almost three years to get to know the Nigerian people and their ways. To be effective, we had to learn how the church could expand its urban ministry. From 1861 to 1946, as an English protectorate, Nigeria suffered segregation that divided the people. Groups were used against each other to keep the country from uniting. These divisions persist, even though Nigeria became an independent nation in 1960. Some people are still ready to fight over tribal or religious differences. But the expansion of the Lutheran Church of Nigeria depends on people being one in Christ.
>
> The church operated under the same family system. We started Bible study groups in homes, and these grew into worship centers. With God's help we established four churches from such groups. When we left, two groups had bought land and were building facilities. The third rented a school for services; the fourth is negotiating to buy land for a church.

The results of the mission work in Nigeria was written in a "PRAY FOR US" article for Missions, 1986:

The most populous of the African nations with 101 million people, Nigeria is located on the southern coast of West Africa. Religious preference is divided with an almost equal number of people committed to either Islam or Christianity. Many people still adhere to their traditional animistic tribal religions. The church has been in Nigeria for 150 years, and a strong Lutheran effort began 50 years ago.

One of the key ingredients to evangelizing Nigeria is the training and equipping of pastors and lay preachers who carry on the evangelization and nurture of their people. Hand in hand with this ministry is the task of putting God's Word into the language of the people. The complete Bokyi Bible was dedicated in 1985. The New Testament has been translated into both Yala and Kukele. Translation work is also a vital ingredient in the total mission picture. In addition to hospitals in Eket and Yahe, rural health programs are conducted among three different tribal groups.

Local congregations are organizing vernacular literacy training programs to aid the people to read their own language— and the Bible—in their own tongue. Theological Education by Extension (TEE) is used to continue the training process of both laity and clergymen.

Rev. James and Billie Tyler have served as urban missionaries in Port Harcourt since 1981. They helped the Lutheran Church of Nigeria to integrate its urban membership, which is comprised of various ethnic and tribal backgrounds. There are 750,000 people living in this city where the news is broadcast in English and five local languages. Along with their regular work of training workers, setting up Bible centers and establishing preaching centers, the Tylers help to produce local radio and TV programs in English.

John Nau says of his father, Dr. Henry Nau,

> His work in Africa was always pointed to the establishment of an indigenous church. He urged the congregations in the U.S., through its national mission organization, to permit the Africans to support their own native congregations and to build their own native churches and schools, and to staff them with their own native people. The church at home should supply the necessary know-how through dedicated, consecrated, and fearless missionaries who would act as advisers and not policy makers.

Dr. Henry Nau was very unhappy with and often complained about the way that the missionary board changed its earliest policy and assumed "dictatorial" powers (back in the U.S.). Not only were the white missionaries watched very closely and often warned about the dual social system of the South, but also the black Lutheran workers were not immune to similar treatment and/or persecution in those days. Anyone who seemed to threaten the system took his life in his hands.

It could have been that difficulties in working with the dual social system of the South and realities of the white and black caste relationship, influenced the board to establish strong central control in St. Louis.

Students of black history may look with dismay at the fact that at the beginning of World War II there was not a single black nation in Africa that was not controlled in some way by a white nation. Ethiopia and Liberia can be considered possible exceptions, but Ethiopia was, in many ways, controlled by Italy, and Liberia was in many ways controlled by the U.S.

Integrating black ministry as an intregal part of the LC-MS from 1930–1963. Black Lutherans, such as myself, were the product of the cooperative efforts of the many constituent synods of the Evangelical Lutheran Synodical Conference of North America, but we were products which none of these Synods would accept into their fellowship at that time. They turned inward upon themselves and organized their own conferences. They then sought cooperation and coalition with each other ... 1967 was a time of unrest among blacks in the U.S. riots and burnings were very prevalent all over the nation. The Black Clergy Caucus emerged to address problems in black ministry. The interchange between the conferences and cooperative efforts in the field of mission endeavor, such as China and Africa and the many other projects which they pursued in common, gave the sense of worth to their efforts and the feeling of achievement which nurtures and bolsters personal and corporate pride.

When the Commission on Black Ministry was created in the Synod (1977), ... this was the first time in over 100 years that black people were asked to give serious input into the policies and practices of black ministries. After I had become the Executive Director of the newly established Commission on Black Ministry of the LC-MS, my opportunity [to go to Africa] came. One day, early 1980, President Preus came by my office on that day and asked me how I would like to go to Nigeria. In Nigeria, President Unwene took me to the home of Dr. Jonathan Udo Ekong. Dr. Ekong was blind, and his health quite fragile, but his enthusiasm and joy at meeting me truly warmed my heart. He was full of questions. I could hardly finish one answer before he was asking another question; but then he got very serious and said, 'I thought that they would send one of my classmates home with me to help me with this work. You are the first pastor of my race to come to this field. Why did it take so long? I thought that I would not live to see the day, but THANKS BE TO GOD! You are here.' I was resolved that I would not be the last one, but simply a forerunner of many more blacks coming over from America to work.

In the Fall of 1980, the Executive Director of the Board for Mission Services went to Nigeria. Shortly after he returned, some positive action was taken to break the racial barrier in African missions. One morning I received a telephone call from Dr. Paul Heerboth, Director of Personnel of the Board of Mission Services. He wanted to know if I knew of a black pastor who wanted to serve as a missionary to Nigeria. The one who was the most enthusiastic was Rev. James Tyler.

1990, The Charlotte Convocation re-established our connection with Africa and invited Dr. Nelson Unwene to be the Keynote Speaker for the 1991 Convocation in Selma, AL.

In conclusion, Rosa Young and Rev. Nils J. Bakke were the two most influential people in beginning Lutheran churches and Lutheran Schools among the blacks as well as helping to encourage the LC-MS for doing missions work in Africa. The five black African Missionaries sent by the LC-MS were Betty Dickson, James and Billie Tyler, and Wendell and Jean Edwards. The Lutherans had called Rev. Joseph G. Lavalais to go to Africa but he could not go. The first African native to be trained in America and sent back was Jonathan Udo Ekong, but there have been many others such as: Paul Fynn of Ghana; and from Nigeria—Nelson Unwene; O.U. Idiong; Imo John Ikpe; Immanuel David Akpan; Ebong Ukpong; and Samuel Udofio. Prior to Betty Dickens and the Tylers, there were no other "non-ordained" or "ordained" black Lutheran Americans sent as missionaries, teachers or Christian workers. [In June 2003, 27 pastors graduated at the Jonathan Ekong Memorial Seminary in Nigeria, the largest class ever.]

The LC-MS did not send a missionary to replace the Tylers in Port Harcourt, Nigeria. It was no longer considered a "mission field." Congregations had been organized there. They had become members of the Lutheran Church of Nigeria (the LCN) and native pastors of the LCN have served these congregations and continued to expand the work. Originally the LCN was started in the rural areas of southern Nigeria. After about 40 years the mass migration to the cities could no longer be ignored. The LCN was trying to emerge from what it had become, an ethnic church body, tied to the Efik language and Ibibio culture. It wanted to discover how to be a church for all of the 394 languages and cultures of Nigeria. They wanted another black person to help them get started in urban ministry in a northern city. So the request for Wendell and Jean Edwards for their specific assignment to Jos, Nigeria. The LC-MS did not send another missionary to replace Wendell and Jean. That congregation is now served by a native pastor, Christian Ekong, a close relative of Dr. Jonathan Udo Ekong, the founder of the LCN.

Although I deplore much about what the [Lutheran] church has done and is doing today in black ministries, I am as proud of the message today as I ever was. Older Lutherans boast about the Word of God in its truth and purity, and I feel that any person who can read today can also have the Word of God in its truth and purity. I will boast of God's plan of salvation in all its clarity, unadulterated by synergism and other work-righteous schemes. "Therefore, we conclude that a man is justified by faith and without the deeds of the Law" (Rom 3:28–30 or Gal 2:16). "If the Son therefore shall make you free, you shall be free indeed" (John 8:36 KJV).

I want to be a part of this ministry of reconciliation. May God speed the day when race and nationality are meaningless and faith in our Savior Jesus Christ is all in all!

Chapter 8
Lott Carey
by Mark Sidwell

Englishman William Carey, who went as a missionary to India in 1794, has gone down in history as the Father of Modern Missions. Yet there is another man of the same last name who was part of that great expansion of missions in the early 19th century. This "other Carey" in the history of foreign missions is less renowned than William Carey and other famous missionary heroes. Yet, Lott Carey, a former slave in America went as a pioneer missionary to Africa to help free that continent from enslavement to sin. His work on the western coast of Africa inspired a major African-American effort in foreign missions and foreshadowed the spread of the gospel across that continent.

Early Years

Lott Carey was born around 1780 on a plantation in Charles City County, VA. As is the case with many slaves, little is known of his parents. Carey did maintain a fond memory of a godly grandmother. When he was a child, his grandmother told him of Africa and how people there did not know God. He asked, "And do all of them think that the great God lives far away from them and does not love them?" She replied that they needed to be told, but that she was too old ever to tell them. "Son, you will grow strong," she told him. "You will lead many, and perhaps it may be you who will travel over the big seas to carry the great secret to my people."

There were many steps between that grandmother's wish and its fulfillment. The first step was taken in 1804 when Carey's master hired him out to work in the Richmond Tobacco Warehouse. At first, the change seemed to be for the worse. Although still enslaved, Carey found ample opportunity to get drunk, and he had enough "freedom of speech" to become well practiced in profanity. In that city, however, he heard the gospel at Richmond's First Baptist Church and was converted in 1807. The change in his life showed plainly as he became an excellent worker in the warehouse and was promoted to foreman.

After his conversion came a desire for learning. Like most slaves, Carey had never been taught to read and write. Listening to his pastor tell the story of Christ and Nicodemus from John 3, Carey felt a yearning to read that passage for himself—and the rest of the Bible as well. Painstakingly, he memorized passages of Scripture, then compared them with the printed words to figure out what they said. After learning to read, he spent all his spare moments at the warehouse reading. Carey also began attending a night school for blacks taught by a deacon at First Baptist Church.

Mark Sidwell has a B.A. in history and M.A. and Ph.D. in church history from Bob Jones University (BJU) where he teaches history and serves as director of a resource center in J. S. Mack Library. He is the author of *The Dividing Line* as well as coauthor of *United States History for Christian Schools,* second edition.

Dr. Sidwell also edits and writes for *Biblical Viewpoints,* the journal of the BJU School of Religion. Article, "Free Indeed: Heroes of Black Christian History" by Mark Sidwell. Published by Bob Jones University Press, 1995.

Used by permission.

Having found spiritual freedom in Christ, Carey was next able to secure freedom from physical enslavement. In 1813 he purchased his freedom and that of his two children for $850. Nothing is known of his first wife, but in 1815 he married for the second time. With the support of his new bride, Carey became an "exhorter" (lay preacher) among blacks. His skill and success impressed the white leaders of First Baptist Church, and they licensed him to preach.

Another black preacher told a white minister, "I tell you I don't hear any of your white ministers that can preach like Lott Carey." Through God's blessing on his powerful, earnest sermons, Carey gathered a congregation of 800.

A Burden for Africa

This ministry among Richmond's blacks led to Carey's involvement in foreign missions. While attending night school, Carey heard the report of a missionary tour of Africa. Much impressed, he said, "I have been determined for a long time to go to Africa and at least to see the country for myself." In 1815 he became secretary of the Richmond African Missionary Society, an organization designed to raise funds for work in Africa. The formation of this society, Carey said, made him wonder, "Am I satisfying God's requirement of me as a preacher of the Gospel? … Was my grandmother… right when she suggested, … 'perhaps it may be you who will travel over the big seas to carry the great secret to my people'?" Lott Carey believed that God would have him go to Africa to preach the "great secret" of the gospel.

Carey's interest in Africa arose during the time of America's first great surge of missionary effort. The country was in the midst of the Second Great Awakening, a great revival that brought spiritual renewal to the young nation. In churches, on college campuses, and on the frontier, thousands were finding new life in Christ.

The awakening also sparked a great push toward missions. During one of the college revivals, a group of students at Williams College in MA began to meet for prayer. During one outdoor prayer session in 1806, a thunderstorm drove the little group to the shelter of a haystack. As they waited out the storm, the students began to discuss the need for the gospel not just in America but around the world. Someone needed to take the gospel to other lands, they thought.

Then one of them, Samuel J. Mills said, "Why should we not be the ones? We can do it if we will!" Mills himself was never able to go to the field, but he founded a mission board and made trips abroad to scout out lands for foreign missions. (Mills wrote the report on Africa that caused Carey to express an interest in going to that continent.) Other missionary pioneers joined the cause, notably. Adoniram Judson, the Baptist missionary to Burma, who probably did more than any other man to confront the American church with the call of the mission field. And in the forefront of this wave of American Christians taking the gospel to foreign lands was Lott Carey.

Carey willingly explained his motives for wanting to go. Despite his work among the blacks of Richmond, Carey believed he could do more overseas. He saw mission work as an opportunity to serve God without running into the obstacle of racism that he had found in the U.S. "I am an African, and in this country, however meritorious my conduct and respectable my character, I cannot receive the credit due to either," he said. "I wish to go to a country where I shall be estimated by my merits, not by my complexion, and I feel bound to labor for my suffering race." In his farewell sermon before leaving for Africa, he said,

> *I am about to leave you, probably to see your faces no more. I am going to Africa, a land of heathenish darkness and degradation, to spread the light of salvation there. Jesus Christ commands me to go, and I must obey Him. I know not what may befall me, nor am I anxious about it. I may find a grave in the ocean, or among the savage men or beasts in the wilds of Africa. I long to preach the Gospel there to those who have never heard it. And I fear there may be thousands in this country who preach the Gospel, or profess obedience to Jesus Christ, who are not half awake to the magnitude of his requirements.*

Carey challenged his hearers to share the burden that he felt. He described the final judgment and imagined Christ saying, "I commanded you to go into all the world, and preach the Gospel to every creature—have you obeyed me? Where have you been? Have you fulfilled the task I gave you, or have you sought your own ease and satisfaction regardless of my commands?"

On May 1, 1819, the Baptist Board of Foreign Missions accepted Lott Carey as a candidate for the field. The tobacco warehouse immediately offered him a hefty raise to stay with the warehouse and not go to Africa. Carey refused. As he said shortly before leaving, "This step is not taken to promote my own fortune, nor am I influenced by any sudden impulse. I have counted the cost and have sacrificed all my worldly possessions to this undertaking. I am prepared to meet imprisonment or even death in carrying out the purpose of my heart. It may be that I shall behold you no more on this side of the grave, but I feel bound to labor for my brothers, perishing as they are in the far distant land of Africa. For their sake and for Christ's sake I am happy in leaving all and venturing all."

There remained much preparation before going to Africa. Carey organized a congregation among the prospective settlers before he left, planning to transplant the church to Africa. Unfortunately, the Baptist mission board asked Carey to work with the American Colonization Society. Carey was not entirely pleased with this situation. The society sought to settle the problem of slavery in America by acquiring territory in Africa in which to resettle American blacks. The scheme was impractical to begin with, and many whites were much more interested in getting free blacks out of America than actually finding a way to end slavery. Carey feared—justifiably, as it turned out—that a secular organization so dedicated to solving the slavery problem would prove a poor vehicle for promoting the spread of the gospel. He wrote to the Baptist mission board, "If you intend on doing anything for Africa you must not wait for the Colonization Society, nor for government, for neither of these are in search of missionary grounds, but of colonizing grounds; if it should not suit missionary needs, you cannot expect to gather in a missionary crop." His concerns, however, were not heeded.

Africa at Last

Finally, everything was ready. Carey and his small band of settlers sailed on January 23, 1821, for Sierra Leone, a British colony established on the western coast of Africa as a haven for freed blacks and rescued slaves. Just before his departure, Carey wrote to the General Convention of the Baptists that, "we shall hoist our sails for Africa ... with our bibles and our utensils, and our hopes in God our Savior."

The party landed in Freetown, Sierra Leone, in March. If Carey had any rosy dreams about the work he was undertaking, they were quickly shattered. The American Colonization Society had failed to purchase land in Africa for their colony. The missionary arrived, therefore, without official standing and without any means of support. Carey and the others worked for a time as farm laborers as they waited for their promised aid from America. Then a second, more serious trial occurred: Carey's wife became sick and died shortly after arrival. He was left now to raise his family alone.

Finally, in December 1821, the American Colonization Society "purchased" territory from the natives to form the colony of Liberia. (As part of the "negotiations" for the purchase, an American naval officer held a pistol to the head of an African chief to encourage him to sign the purchase agreement.) Carey moved there in 1822, hoping to begin his mission work in earnest. The limited number of settlers, however, and the daunting task they faced forced all the colonists to fill several roles. Carey was made "Health Officer and Government Inspector" and often functioned as a physician when disease afflicted the little colony. The governor, in fact, reported that Carey was forced to spend up to half of his time ministering to the sick.

The work was hard and often unrewarding. During the rough early days, Carey confronted one group of discouraged settlers and talked them out of returning to Sierra Leone. Some of the native tribes resented the establishing of the colony near their lands, and they harried it with raids. Carey compared the battles in building Liberia to those of Nehemiah and the children of Israel in rebuilding the walls of Jerusalem, even to the point of holding weapons close at hand as they worked. Yet he said, "There never has been an hour, or a minute, no, not even when the [bullets] were flying around my head, when I could wish myself again in America."

Ministering on the Dark Continent

Most of Carey's mission work centered on the church he pastored in Monrovia, the capital of Liberia. His congregation was an interesting mixture. Carey ministered to immigrants from America, slaves rescued by the British from slave traders, and a handful of natives. It was among the Africans rescued by the British that Carey saw most of his few converts from the African tribal religions. The greater part of his increase came from black American immigrants. There were some scattered successes among the nearby natives, however, one native had heard a little of the gospel in Sierra Leone. Seeking a fuller understanding of Christ and the way of salvation, he traveled 80 miles to speak with Carey. The seeker was converted, and Carey baptized him and gave him his first communion. In halting English, the new convert gave his testimony:

> All the time my heart trouble me—all day—all night me can't sleep—by and by my heart grow too big—me fall down this time—now me can pray—me say Lord—have mercy. Then light come in my heart—make me glad—make me light—make me love the Son of God—make me love everybody."

By 1825, Carey had 60 members in his church, and he wrote, "The Lord has in mercy visited the settlement, and I have had the happiness to baptize nine converts."

Carey also strove to promote education in Monrovia among both the colonists and the natives, but the lack of funds often hampered his work. He urged his brethren back home to send help: "O American Christians! Look this way! come this way! and help, if you cannot come! Send help for the Lord's sake! help Africa's sons out of the devil's bush into the kingdom of God: the harvest is already white." Eager to set an example, he even set up the Monrovia Mission Society among the Liberian Christians to raise money for missions.

Some American blacks opposed the Liberian work because it was associated with the American Colonization Society. They saw the work as mere camouflage for efforts to move free blacks from the U.S.. Carey took pains to distinguish his work from that of the society. He urged black Christians back home to support his work for the sake of the souls on the continent. "Africa suffers for gospel truth," he wrote, "and she will suffer, until missionaries can be sent, and settled in different parts of her continent." Just as William Carey, saw his work in India as an opening to reach that whole subcontinent for Christ, Lott Carey saw Liberia as the starting point to carry the gospel to all of Africa.

Still, the burdens of government continued to interfere with Carey's work. He became the spokesman for a group of colonists who were dissatisfied with the way the governor of the colony, Jehudi Ashmun, was handling property disputes. The American Colonization Society ruled against Carey's faction, and the black missionary was forbidden even to preach for a time. He became reconciled to Ashmun, however, and in 1826, Carey was made assistant to the governor. When Ashmun left Liberia in March, 1828, and died later that year, Carey became acting governor.

Carey did not long enjoy this honor. Trouble broke out again with one of the native tribes and with a slave trader. Carey began organizing the defense of the colony. He and several other colonists were preparing cartridges on November 8, 1828, when someone knocked a candle over into the gunpowder. The ensuing explosion fatally injured eight people. Among them was Carey, who died two days later.

Heritage

Lott Carey died after only a little more than eight years on the field. The results he had seen were, humanly speaking, small. But as is often the case with Christian work, Carey's heritage was far more extensive than he could have dreamed. In 1847, the colony of Liberia became an independent republic. It thus became the first republic in Africa and the only nation of that continent never to fall under colonial rule. Then in 1897, a group of black Christians in America founded the Lott Carey Foreign Mission Convention, a major missions agency of African-American Baptists.

As important as Lott Carey was as a "founding father" of an African republic and as an inspiration to African-American Christians, even more notable was his example to Christians of all races. Carey became the forerunner to Christian work across the continent of Africa. Just before Carey left the U.S., he received a letter from a representative of the American Baptist Board of Foreign Missions. Quoting Psalm 68:31, the man wrote to the departing missionary, "Let nothing discourage you. Ethiopia shall stretch forth her hands unto God. You are engaged in the service of Him who can make the crooked straight, and the rough places plain." Neither that writer nor Carey himself fully realized the prophetic nature of those words. Africa indeed soon stretched out her hands unto God. Carey's dream "to spread the light of salvation" on that continent was not fulfilled in his brief lifetime, but the decades that followed saw thousands of missionaries and African preachers bringing, as Carey's grandmother called it, "the great secret" of salvation in Christ to the people of Africa.

Questions for Thought

1. When he went to the mission field, Lott Carey left a large ministry among the blacks of Richmond, VA, and he had much less numerical success in Africa. How would you answer someone who said that Carey made a poor choice in changing his ministry?
2. Carey compared the trials he faced in Liberia to those of Nehemiah in rebuilding the walls of Jerusalem. Read Nehemiah 4. In what ways was Carey's situation similar to that of Nehemiah? In what ways was it different?
3. Carey often had to perform many duties that kept him from direct missionary work, such as doctoring the sick. Do you think such work was a help or a hindrance to his mission work? Why?
4. Lott Carey was not eager to work with the American Colonization Society. Was he justified in his hesitation? (Support your answer by citing evidence from the chapter.) Do you think Carey should have worked with the society at all? Why or why not?
5. Lott Carey said, "I wish to go to a country where I shall be estimated by my merits, not by my complexion." Compare this with Martin Luther King's famous statement. "I have a dream that my four little children will one day live in a nation where they will not be judged by the color of their skin but by the content of their character." In what ways were the sentiments of Carey and King similar? In what ways were they different?

Chapter 9

John Stewart: The Missionary Pioneer

by Joseph Mitchell

Anyone who has ever rejoiced in the fact that "the Gospel of Christ…is the power of God unto salvation to every one that believeth; to the Jew first, and also to the Greek" (Rom 1:16 KJV)—and anyone who has ever marveled at how "There is neither Jew nor Greek, there is neither bond nor free, there is neither male nor female: for ye are all one in Christ Jesus" (Gal 3:28 KJV)—should find the story of the life and labors of John Stewart to be spiritually encouraging and challenging. The Missionary Pioneer chronicles the unique circumstances which this black Christian missionary faced while fearlessly taking the Gospel of Jesus Christ to the Wyandott Indian tribe in the early 19th century American wilderness. His story is one of phenomenal courage, commitment to Christ, and triumph in the midst of numerous obstacles, dangers and personal opposition.

From "Foreword" by G. Wm. Foster, Jr., Connelly Memorial Baptist Church, Roanoke, VA, March, 1998.

Missionary Pioneer

John Stewart was born in Powhatan County, VA, to parents who were free (colored), and members of the Baptist Church. John by age 21 was a careless sinner. In this situation he was robbed of all his property while on his way from VA to Marietta, OH, at age 25. This circumstance brought him to reflect seriously on the state of his soul; but grief and vexation prevailed over hope and patience. He commenced a course of excessive drinking at a public house, which continued until his nerves became affected. He remained in this condition for some time determined to destroy his life. His landlord discovered his intention and withheld spirituous liquors from him. He more deliberately reflected on his miserable condition and cried out, "Oh! wretched man that I am, who shall deliver me" (Rom 7:24 KJV). He resolved to cast himself on the mercy of God, for support and salvation and took to reading, meditation, prayer, and seeking the Lord in private. Soon, he returned to shameful acts and not until his lady companion suddenly died and he thought of suicide, did he seek the Lord "carefully with tears."

There being no Baptist church near, he did not join himself to any religious Society. In his youth he had imbibed strong prejudices against other denominations, particularly the Methodist. He soon neglected his repentance. One evening he heard the sound of a Methodist meeting and he resolved to enter and make known his case. Here he was encouraged to seek with all his heart

Originally published in 1827 as: *The Missionary Pioneer, or a Brief Memoir of the Life, Labours, and Death of John Stewart, (man of colour,) Founder, under God, of the Mission among the Wyandotts at Upper Sandusky, Ohio.* Published by Joseph Mitchell. Reprinted in *The African Preachers*, Harrisonburg, VA: Sprinkle Publications, P.O. Box 1094, Harrisburg, VA 22803, 1988.

Used by permission.

the last blessing. Soon after, at a Camp-Meeting, he united himself to the people whom he had formerly held in contempt.

One evening at private devotion, suddenly he heard a sound which much alarmed him: and a voice (as he thought) said to him—"Thou shalt declare My counsel faithfully"; at the same time a view appeared to open to him in a Northwest direction, and a strong impression was made on his mind, that he must go out that course into the world to declare the counsel of God. Judging himself entirely unqualified for such a work, he determined to avoid it if possible, and accordingly made ready to follow his friends to the state of TN. A severe illness prevented him [from going]. He resolved, that if it should please the Lord to spare his life, he would go and see where he should be conducted, although he feared he should be killed by the first Indians he should meet with. He was restored to health and set out without credentials, directions of the way, money or bread.

As he proceeded he was met by sundry persons who, having learned something of the nature of his undertaking, strove in vain to dissuade him from the pursuit. On his way he met with some Indians who appeared friendly. They conducted him and introduced him to the tribe of Delawares at Pipe-Town, on the Sandusky river. Here he endeavored to enter into conversation, but found they understood little of his language.

As they contemplated having a dance that day, their actions produced some fears in him that they were about to kill him. They soon desisted from their exercise and he took out his hymn book and sung a hymn, during which there was a profound silence. When he had ceased singing, one spoke in English and said, "Sing more," he then sang again, and asked for an interpreter; in a short time one was produced (an old Delaware, named Lyons,) the Indians placed themselves in a position to hear, and he delivered to them a speech. On this occasion the Indians appeared attentive, and at the close, a kind of entertainment was provided and he reposed, fully believing that he had now accomplished the design of his little and singular mission, intending the next day to return towards Marietta, from thence to the state of TN. But to his great surprise, on the next morning he still felt strong impressions to pursue his journey to the Northwest.

Having found amongst these people so much friendship and hospitality, "he thanked God and took courage." He proceeded towards Upper Sandusky and upon arrival called at the house of Mr. Walker, sub-agent amongst the Indians. Mr. Walker, being fully satisfied that he was not a runaway slave, directed him to Jonathan Pointer, a black man, who in his youth had been taken prisoner by the Wyandotts, and had learned to speak the tongue of the nation fluently. Jonathan was not pleased with his company, or conversation, and gave evasive and unsatisfactory answers. Stewart asked him whether it would be convenient to have the Indians collected together for the purpose of preaching to them. Jonathan replied that it would be of no use because many great and learned men of different denominations had attempted in vain. Stewart was not to be discouraged and asked to join Jonathan in going to a feast held in the neighborhood that day.

At the feast there were a large number of Indians dancing. At the close of the ceremonies he asked permission to make a speech, which was granted. He spoke through Jonathan. At the end he asked if they entertained friendship towards him that they would give them their hands. An old Chief, named Two Logs arose and addressing the assembly said it would be perfectly correct to show him friendship, especially as he was a stranger, but it would be in conformity to their established rules of hospitality. They all then gave the proposed mark of friendship; and after making an appointment to preach at Jonathan's house, they dispersed. A goodly number met and Stewart addressed them on the subject of striving "to flee from the wrath to come." This was November 1816.

The doctrine of repentance was not well received by Jonathan, and he would state the substance of Stewart's discourse, and say, "so he says, I do not know whether it is so or not, nor do I care; all I care about is to interpret faithfully what he says, to you; you must not think that I care whether you believe it or not." The word was not without its good effects for many were soon convinced of their lost and undone condition, and began earnestly to inquire the way of salvation, calling upon God for mercy. Jonathan changed as well from Stewart's message.

A few white traders advised the Indians to drive him out the country stating that he was not a licensed preacher; but a runaway slave, a villain, etc., and that he had only come among them for protection. This was readily believed by many. Stewart appeared before Mr. Walker and informed him that the Chiefs would, under their advice, drive him out of their country. Mr. Walker advised him to pay no attention, but to go on preaching, and to refer to him any who manifest dissatisfaction. During this time of trial Jonathan remained faithful to his friend. Many of those people, having been members of the Roman Catholic Church, were partially instructed in those doctrines. Stewart had many difficulties to encounter. Finding that Stewart taught doctrines so different from those which they had learned from the Romish Priest, they concluded that he did not teach from a genuine Bible, or at least there must be a discrepancy between his Bible and that used by the priests, and that, consequently, it must be wrong for them to hear or encourage him as the doctrines taught by him was heresy.

Some of the principle men went to Mr. Walker. He had Stewart present himself with his books for the purpose of examining them in the presence of the Chiefs. He informed them that he had carefully examined Stewart's Bible, and that it was most certainly the same kind used by the priests, and was, as he believed, the word of God—the same kind, only theirs was in Latin and Stewart's was in English. New spirits appeared to enliven their hearts. The next objection—he had no written permission to preach. Mr. Walker asked if he had performed the rite of matrimony or baptism; they answered that he did not. No valid objection could be brought against him for endeavoring to persuade sinners to serve God and save their souls. Stewart continued to teach the way of eternal life. However, he had left untouched their absurd notions respecting the powers of magicians, witches, feasts, dances, and many other ridiculous ceremonies. Many found it hard to renounce them, although they were seriously told, that if they wished to become the followers of the Lord Jesus Christ, they must abandon them all.

Mr. Stewart made pointed remarks against their old system of heathenism. At the close of his discourse he offered any to speak if they had objections to his doctrines. John Hicks, one of the chiefs, spoke. "I, for one, feel myself called upon to rise in defense of the religion of my fathers;—a system of religion the Great Spirit has given his red children, as their guide and the rule of their faith. Your declaiming so violently against our modes of worshipping the Great Spirit, is, in my opinion, not calculated to benefit us as a nation; we are willing to receive good advice from you, but we are not willing to have the customs and institutions which have been kept sacred by our Fathers, thus assailed and abused."

Manoncue, another chief, arose and said, "I do not doubt but what you state faithfully what your book says; but let me correct an error in which you appear to have run, and that is, your belief that the Great Spirit designed that his red children should be instructed out of it ... Let me call your attention to another important fact. Where did the Son of God first make His appearance? According to your book He first made His appearance away in the East, among the white people and we never heard of His name until white people themselves told us. If it had been the will of the Great Spirit that we should be instructed out of this book, He would have provided some way for us to understand the art of making and reading the books that contain His word. Ours is a religion that suits the red people, and we intend to keep and preserve it sacred among us, believing that the Great Spirit gave it to our grandfathers in ancient days."

Stewart replied that it was stated in this book, that the Son of God, before He ascended into Heaven, commanded His disciples to "go ye into all the world, and preach the Gospel unto every creature (Mark 16:15 KJV);" saying at the same time, that "He that believeth and is baptized shall be saved; but he that believeth not, shall be damned" (Mark 16:16 KJV). And in another place it is said, "And this Gospel of the kingdom shall be preached in all the world for a witness unto all nations; and then shall the end come" (Matt 24:14 KJV). Addressing himself particularly to the Wyandotts, he said, "you certainly consider yourselves a nation composed of human beings; if so, then you may rest assured that this Gospel will be preached not only to you, but to all nations of Indians and not only Indians, but to all nations under the Heavens, before the end of the world shall come." Rest assured the curse will fall upon you, especially upon you chiefs, who have so great an influence over your people; lead them not to destruction, I entreat you!"

Manoncue came to Hicks privately and said, "my friend, I begin to feel somewhat inclined to abandon a good many of our Indian customs, but I cannot agree to give up painting my face; this

I think would be wrong, inasmuch as ceasing to paint will be jeopardizing my health." At almost every meeting there was less or more disputing between Stewart and some of the principle men of the nation ... One thing is that not a single instance occurred during the time Stewart labored among them of their treating his person with any indignity or violence.

There did not appear to be any who evidenced a genuine conversion, though many appeared to be really hopeful penitents, and mourning for "errors past." There being no preacher among them, who was authorized to form them into a Society ... it will not be surprising that many grew weary in well doing and relapsed.

At a meeting in February 1817, he preached a sermon on the day of Judgment. Alarm appeared evident in every countenance. Another meeting was appointed at early candlelight. A few assembled. Stewart began to sing and the people assembled and in a few minutes the house was pretty well filled; he then rose up and began to exhort them to seek the Lord Jesus as the Saviour of sinners, and escape the impending wrath of an offended God. A few came forward, principally women—it was not long before some of the idle spectators were struck to the ground, to all appearance dead, and in a few minutes there were many slain, some crying for mercy, while others appeared to have no life in them. Some cried to Jonathan to desist from singing. Thereupon, an old woman sprang up having found "the pearl of great price," began to clap her hands and rejoice with great joy, and went through all the crowd, proclaiming that God, for Jesus' sake, had forgiven all her sins.

Stewart advised the people "they are not dying, or insane as you suppose; though some of them, I trust, are dying to sin and struggling into a life of righteousness, peace and the joy in the Holy Ghost". None, however, were converted at this meeting, except the old woman. John Hicks and Manoncue sat as silent spectators. There was a dance held afterwards to show the preacher how they worshipped the Great Spirit. Manocue had earlier forsaken all his Indian customs except for face painting but now could not refrain from joining in the dances. Stewart gave a farewell sermon on Acts 20:32 when he planned to return to Marietta. He began again to enforce the necessity of total abandonment of their heathenish customs and notions. "Wherefore I take you to record this day, that I am pure from your blood; I feel now that I have discharged my duty to you. God sent me here to warn you to flee the wrath to come, and I have done so; but, Lord, who hath believed the report?"

During the sermon a dead silence reigned. And as he sung, he proceeded around among the people, taking each by the hand—even his most violent opposers were constrained to drop a tear, on his bidding them adieu. He promised to return. Situated as they were, it was difficult to determine who were Christian and who were not, for the righteous and the unrighteous were all mixed together. Deprived as they were of the ordinances of God's house, such as baptism, the Lord's supper, marriage, etc., and not having the advantages of class-meetings, discipline, etc., were causes of the work not appearing so flattering as it otherwise might.

While away from them, some wicked and designing white men informed some of them that Stewart's master had come out from the state of VA to OH in pursuit of him, had found him and taken him, and carried him back to VA in irons. It created considerable uneasiness among his friends. John Stewart wrote them a letter sent through Mr. Walker, telling them "to faint not" in their faith. He did return later and found that some remained faithful.

He now found many Wyandotts whom he had not seen when he was first among them (they had been out hunting). There arose a violent opposition among some of the principal leaders of the nation, Manocue and Two Logs, to prevent the success of Stewart's ministry. Two Logs said, "I do not believe the Great Spirit will punish His red children for dancing, feasting, etc." "The Great Spirit," said he, "never created Negroes, they were created by the Evil Spirit." Many were the visions, revelations, prophecies, etc., which were sounded about the whole neighborhood: all appearing to aim at the destruction of Stewart's preaching. Nothing remarkable transpired during this summer; Stewart continued preaching.—Those who professed to believe in the Christian religion still appeared to manifest good desires, but took no active part either way.

In August 1817, a treaty was called by the Commissioners on part of the general Government, to be held a Fort Meigs with the Wyandotts and other nations of Indians, for the purpose of purchasing their lands. Stewart deemed it advisable to return to Marietta. He came back the later part of 1818 and encountered new opposition. Certain Missionaries in traveling to the North called with the Wyandotts, among whom Stewart was laboring, and spent a short time preaching to them. On ascertaining how remarkably useful Stewart's labors had been in bringing the Indians to the knowledge of the truth, and how highly he was esteemed by most of them, they proposed to receive him as a member of their church, and to employ him as one of their Missionaries on that station, at a very comfortable salary; but as from a difference in religious opinions from them, he could not accept their offer.

They demanded the authority by which he was acting as a gospel minister and as a Methodist Missionary. He confessed he had none. This news was employed by the white traders and opposing Indians as certain evidence that he was an impostor. He told of this situation to the Quarterly-Meeting Conference of Mad River district. He was advised by letter to continue his labors until a license could be procured. Until now it was unknown in the white settlement that any religious excitement existed among the Indians, or that Stewart was among them, or even that such a man existed. The Quarterly Conference sent Moses M. Henkle to visit the Indians to aid the good work. He had just entered the ministry and volunteered for this work. In February, 1818, he came and spent some time laboring among the Wyandotts. Many professed to have found "the pearl of great price," and many others were inquiring the way to Zion, deeply mourning the sins of their past. During his stay he had good opportunity to witness Stewart's piety and usefulness.

He brought Stewart a certificate of membership which he had obtained at Marietta, a certificate of his having been there recommended by his class for license to exhort, and also certificates of his character and usefulness, from the time of his first appearing in Sandusky. Stewart attended the Quarterly Conference at Urbana in March 1819, where he was regularly licensed to preach the Gospel. Stewart continued with his labors.

The difficulties which he had to encounter, while striving to build up the walls of Zion in this once howling wilderness, required much Christian fortitude and patience. Sometime after the Treaty at Fort Meigs, a number of the Wyandott people made application to the chiefs, for liberty to settle Stewart permanently on the section of land, in the center of their reservation, which was by the provisions of the treaty, set apart for the support of a Missionary. They said he should stay until the Missionary, provided for, had come.

Although the principle charge and care of this flock was now given to Mr. Henkle, after he began to labor in concert with Mr. Stewart, Between-the-Logs, Peacock, John Hicks and Manocue, that once violent enemy and opposer of religion, united themselves with those who were striving to serve the Lord and save their souls. In 1821, James Finley, missionary, was appointed to build a school. All that was now wanting was the doors of the invisible church to be thrown open, and the invitation given; a large number was ready and willing to come in—Some sound converts ready to come and shout glory to God in the highest, and some true penitents ready to come in and fall at the altar and cry, "God be merciful to me a sinner." From this time, the work went on in a most prosperous manner.

In 1823, Stewart experienced ill health but continued to labor for the salvation of others. He died in December with these last words to his wife, "wife, be faithful." It should be noted that near death Two-Logs resolved that if the Lord would spare his life, he would turn and seek salvation. He was restored and died a devoted Christian in peace.

1820–1860 Era: Second Great Awakening and Missionary Rise

Chapter 10
The Second Great Awakening and Missionary Rise
African-American Missionary Movement

by Robert J. Stevens

Daniel Coker organized the first branch of the AME church in Liberia 1820. In 1820, at the instigation of the Church Missionary Society, the Domestic and Foreign Missionary Society of the Protestant Episcopal Church in the U.S. began operation. However, it was not until ten years later that missionaries of the church were sent out. Lott Carey and Colin Teague sailed for Liberia in 1821.[1] The expansion of the AME was so rapid that it was soon necessary to establish a western conference. Wishing to further extend its operations, the AME church ordained its first foreign missionary, Baltimore Minister Scripio Beans in 1827, to do evangelism work on the island of Haiti.[2] Others followed: American Baptist Church in USA (1814); American Baptist Foreign Missionary Union (1815). The Methodist Episcopal Church followed the early mission interest of the Congregationalists and Baptists with the formation of the Foreign Mission Board of the MEC in 1819 for the work of evangelization at home and abroad. Its original work was among native Americans.[3]

The Missionary Movement gained momentum after 1830, and by the end of the nineteenth century, mission sentiment existed in most of the churches in the Western world. Methodist Protestant Church (established in 1830). Many para church organizations were established for the sole purpose of evangelization. Missions had a sense of world destiny. The African American felt an involvement in the mission movement. They believed God desired them to enter the mission arena.[4] Finally, of the larger Protestant churches in Africa, the Presbyterian Church in the U.S.A. organized the Foreign Mission Board of the Presbyterian Church in 1837, after separation from the American Board. The Presbyterian Church in the U.S.A. began work among Coptic Christians and Muslims of Egypt in 1854 (the first American church to begin

---

1 Sylvia Jacobs, "Black Americans and The Missionary Movement in Africa," *Contributions in Afro-American and African Studies*, no. 66 (Westport, CT: Greenwood Press, 1982).
2 Carter G. Woodson, *History of the Negro Church* (Washington, D.C.: Associated Publishers, 1985), 87.
3 Sylvia Jacobs, *Black Americans and The Missionary Movement in Africa, Contributions in Afro-American and African Studies*, no. 66 (Westport, CT: Greenwood Press, 1982).
4 Marilyn Lewis, "Independent Study Assignment: The African-American in Christian Mission," Th.M. Candidate, Dallas Theological Seminary, #788, 1993, 33.

work in this area.) By 1868, 12 of the 13 Presbyterian U.S. staff members in Liberia were African American.[5]

Reasons why one desires to be a missionary sent to Africa should best be answered by the missionaries themselves. Many were attracted to Africa because of the culture and racial ties, geographical stories, commitment to the race, and the desire to propagate the gospel.[6] Alexander Crummell's father stated that he came from Sierra Leone and had relatives and friends who had immigrated to Liberia. Whatever the reasons, one of the most interesting insights was that the African-American missionary's first preference for activity was the home continent of Africa.[7]

"Who has motivated the black individual to return to Africa? Who, but the Spirit of God is moving these Christian remnants of black society, this seed of civilization from the West Indies and America to the coast of Africa. Who, but God Himself, alas called and elected this germ of Christianity to a great work of duty in the land of their fathers? And what use then ... to seize upon this movement to plant their own phrase of Christianity in villages and towns along the course and the interior of Africa?"[8]

The Second Awakening

God sent another spiritual fire. The Second Great Awakening (1840–1860) was not marked by great emotional outbursts, but rather by sudden earnestness in religious devotion and godly living. Attendance at worship increased noticeably and many spoke of having an experience of conversion.[9] The Awakening resulted in the rise of abolitionist movement and led to an increase in nineteenth century mission sentiment.[10] This Awakening opened the "eyes" of the African-American Christians to the belief that he/she was "competent" to lead their own churches without being relegated to separated sections.[11] The first African-American involvement in mission really started near the Revolutionary War era. However, during and after the Second Great Awakening, another missionary drive started. This second drive sent the first African American to the West Indies but it sent the majority of the African Americans to Africa.

Five major Protestant denominations in the U.S. began to send missionaries to Africa in the nineteenth century: The Congregationalists, the Baptists, the Methodists, the Episcopalians, and Presbyterians. By 1840, all of these religious sects had organized foreign mission societies and had established mission stations in Africa.[12]

Methodist Episcopal Church South (established 1843). Wesleyan Church (established 1843). Southern Baptist Convention (established 1845). By 1846, a year after the founding of its Foreign Mission Board, the new convention had appointed two African Americans as missionaries (John Day and A. L. Jones). Over the next 40 years, the board either appointed or gave support to at least 62 black missionaries. The vast majority of these served in Africa.[13]

Lutheran Church-Missouri Synod (established 1847). In 1877 it called its first missionary to Africa, Joseph G. Lavalis, but he declined due to health issues.[14] Coloured Black Baptist Convention (established 1853). Free Methodist (established 1860). The competition for the "souls of the Africans" was being played in the black churches as well as the white churches. It was believed that all churches needed a "foreign mission field." The European explorers were describing the "rich mission field" of the African pagan, the churches were praying for the Lord to send people to Africa, the press was telling more

---

5 Sylvia Jacobs, *Black Americans and The Missionary Movement in Africa, Contributions in Afro-American and African Studies*, no. 66 (Westport, CT: Greenwood Press, 1982).

6 Marilyn Lewis, "Independent Study Assignment: The African-American in Christian Mission," Th.M. Candidate, Dallas Theological Seminary, #788, 1993, 34.

7 Ibid., 36.

8 Milton C. Semen, *Afro-American Religious History: A Documentary Witness* (Durham, NC: Duke University Press, 1985), 258.

9 Richard M. Riis, *A Survey of 20th Century Revival Movements in North America* (Peabody: MA: Hendrickson Press, 1988), 13–14.

10 Ibid., 18.

11 Marilyn Lewis, "Independent Study Assignment: The African-American in Christian Mission," Th.M. Candidate, Dallas Theological Seminary, #788, 1993, 25.

12 Sylvia Jacobs, *Black Americans and The Missionary Movement in Africa, Contributions in Afro-American and African Studies*, no. 66 (Westport, CT: Greenwood Press, 1982), 7.

13 David Cornelius, "A Brief Historical Survey of African-American Involvement in International Missions", in *African-American Experience in World Mission: A Call Beyond Community*, edited by Vaughn J. Walston and Robert Stevens (Pasadena, CA: William Carey Library, 2002) with Cooperative Mission Network of the African Dispersion (COMINAD).

14 Richard C. Dickenson, *Roses and Thorns* (St. Louis, MO: Concordia Publishing House, 1997).

stories (true or false) about African missions and the desire and call of missions increased. Yet, just like the first missionary movement thrust of the African Americans slowed down because of another war—the battle for emancipation.[15]

---

[15] Marilyn Lewis, "Independent Study Assignment: The African-American in Christian Mission," Th.M. Candidate, Dallas Theological Seminary, #788, 1993, 39–40.

Chapter 11
Betsey Stockton: Stranger in a Strange Land

by Eileen Moffett and Dr. John Andrew III

Eileen Moffett, a graduate of Princeton Theological Seminary and missionary in Korea (Presbyterian Church, USA) 1956-81, taught courses in English and Christian Education at the Presbyterian Theological College in Seoul, served as director of the Korean Bible Club Movement 1976-81, and is the author of an illustrated book for children, *Korean Ways*. She lives with her husband, Samuel H. Moffett, in Princeton, NJ. From *International Bulletin of Missionary Research*, April 1995.

Used by permission.

Dr. John A. Andrew III, is an assistant professor in the Department of History at Franklin and Marshall College. From *Journal of Presbyterian History*, Summer 1974. Published by the Presbyterian Historical Society, Philadelphia, PA.

Used by permission.

On November 19, 1822, the brig Thames pulled away from its New Haven, CT, pier and set sail for the Sandwich Islands. Both the pious and the curious crowded the waterfront to attend the festivities, and the religious press throughout New England lauded the embarkation of a reinforcement to the Sandwich Islands Mission. Enraptured by visions of an ever-expanding Christianity, supporters of foreign missions hoped that the Gospel would find a permanent station in the Pacific. From these islands Bibles and missionaries could accompany the sandalwood to the pagodas of China. Owyhee (Hawaii), the Boston Recorder predicted, would become a "radiating point of religion."[1]

On board the Thames were 14 men and women to reinforce the Sandwich Islands Mission, and among them was a black woman—Betsey Stockton. The missionaries would provide instruction in agricultural techniques, improve the lot of Sandwich Island natives, and make Hawaii an international showplace; an example of what missionary labors could accomplish. The islands would, of course, be unique—but only for a short while. Soon this system would spread to all heathen lands. Promoters of foreign missions took great care, therefore, to conduct their enterprise so as to avoid controversy and not inflame prejudices.[2]

The appointment of Betsey Stockton to the first reinforcement of Sandwich Island missionaries seems unusual in light of this concern. The country had just passed through the agitation of the slavery issue in the MO crisis. Many contributions to the American Board, moreover, came from slaveholders and Southerners. Concerned with all sectors of the country and society, yet confronted by economic instability and uncertainty at home, the American Board hoped to build up greater support throughout the South and West. It could ill-afford to alienate contributors, and preferred to gently nudge people toward Christian benevolence rather than stridently exclude anyone.[3]

Who was Betsey Stockton? Her name fails to appear in the standard history of the Hawaiian Islands. Neither does she re-

---

1 *Boston Recorder*, 7 (30 November 1822), 190.
2 John A. Andrew III, "Betsey Stockton: Stranger in a Strange Land," *Journal of Presbyterian History*, Summer 1974, (Presbyterian Historical Society, Philadelphia, PA), 157.
3 For a larger view of the activities of the American Board see my dissertation, "Rebuilding the Christian Commonwealth: New England Congregationalists and Foreign Missions, 1800–1830," (University of Texas, 1973).

ceive notice in Kenneth Porter's article on blacks in early Hawaii.[4] What position did she occupy in the mission, and how was she received in Hawaii? The answers to these questions provide some surprising commentary on the objectives and ideals of the early promoters of foreign missions. They also compel us to revise present interpretations of the benevolent crusade and its directors. These men were not elitist reactionaries attempting to prevent change and preserve status, but sensitive Christians anxious about the future of the American republic.[5] Seeking to promote Christian principles, directors of the American Board of Commissioners for Foreign Missions sent a black to labor with whites among the Sandwich Island natives. They did so because she fulfilled the qualifications of a Christian missionary, not because she was black. But her appointment reflected visions of a Christian society far beyond those held by most Americans. Instead of being too conservative for their times, they were, indeed, almost too radical.[6]

Born to a slave mother about 1798, Betsey Stockton passed her childhood as the property of Robert Stockton of Princeton, NJ. Her mother was owned by Robert Stockton, one of Princeton's distinguished citizens whose home was "Constitution Hill." Robert was a cousin of Richard Stockton, one of the signers of the Declaration of Independence, and both of them were grandsons of one of the original pioneer settlers of the town. There is no record of Betsey's father at all, and it seems likely that she never knew who he was, though either her father or grandfather was probably a white man, since in her will she describes herself as a mulatto.[7]

Major Stockton gave the young little servant girl to his oldest daughter, Elizabeth, married to Ashbel Green, a Presbyterian minister in Philadelphia.[8] The Greens had three sons, Robert, Jacob, and James. James, the youngest, was six years old when, back in Princeton on his grandfather Stockton's farm, the little slave girl, Betsey Stockton, was born.[9] Betsey served the Green family as a domestic servant for several years.[10]

Much later, Dr. Green, in a letter of recommendation for Betsey, supporting her application as a missionary candidate, wrote: "By me and my wife she was never intended to be held as a slave." Dr. Green was a strong antislavery advocate of his day, as was his Presbyterian minister father before him. Green's letter continued:

> We deliberated seriously on the subject of dedicating her to God in baptism. But on the whole concluded not to do it. Betsey gave no evidence of piety, or of any permanent seriousness till she was near 20 years old. One the contrary, she was, at least till the age of 13 or 14, wile and thoughtless, if not vicious. She always, however, manifested a great degree of natural sensibility, and of attachment to me and to her first mistress; and a great aptitude for mental improvement.[11]

---

4 "The standard history of Hawaii remains," Ralph S. Kuykendall, *The Hawaiian Kingdom*, 3 vols (Honolulu, HI). Volume I narrates the early history. Kenneth Porter mentions several blacks in early Hawaii, including a few who resided there as late as the 1860s. See "Notes on Negroes in Early Hawaii," *Journal of Negro History*, 19 (April 1934): 193–197.

5 Representative of the status-reactionary school is Clifford Griffin, *Their Brothers' Keepers: Moral Stewardship in the United States, 1800–1865*, (New Brunswick, N.J., 1960). See also John R. Bodo, *The Protestant Clergy and Public Issues, 1812–1848*, (Princeton, 1954), Raymond Mohl, *Poverty in New York, 1783–1825*, (New York, 1971); Charles C. Cole, *The Social Ideas of the Northern Evangelists, 1820–1860*, (New York, 1954); and Charles I. Foster, *An Errand Of Mercy: The Evangelical United Front, 1790–1837*, (Chapel Hill, 1960). A recent corrective is Lois Banner, "Religious Benevolence as Social Control: A Critique of an Interpretation," *Journal of American History*, 60 (June 1973): 23–41. The counterweight to the "social control" theme of the "republic in peril."

6 John A. Andrew III, "Betsey Stockton: Stranger in a Strange Land," *Journal of Presbyterian History*, Summer 1974 (Presbyterian Historical Society, Philadelphia, PA), 158.

7 Thomas French, *The Missionary Whaleship*, (New York, 1961), 113-4; Hawaiian Mission Children's Society (HMCS), *Missionary Album*, (Honolulu, 1937), 177; *The Freeman's Journal* (Cooperstown, N.Y.), Nov. 3, 1865: 2. Ashbel Green was later president of the College of New Jersey (Princeton). Betsey apparently took her name from Elizabeth Stockton, although Green had a sister named Betsy. See "Calvin Green's 'Diary': The Life of Calvin Green," *New Jersey Historical Society*, Proceedings, 69 (April, 1951), 116n.

8 John A. Andrew III, "Betsey Stockton: Stranger in a Strange Land," *Journal of Presbyterian History*, Summer 1974 (Presbyterian Historical Society, Philadelphia, PA), 158.

9 Eileen F. Moffett, "Betsey Stockton: Pioneer American Missionary," *International Bulletin of Missionary Research*, April 1995 (New Haven, CT: Overseas Ministries Study Center), 71.

10 John A. Andrew III, "Betsey Stockton: Stranger in a Strange Land," *Journal of Presbyterian History*, Summer 1974 (Presbyterian Historical Society, Philadelphia, PA), 158.

11 Ashbel Green to the American Board of Commissioners for Foreign Missions, Princeton, NJ, September 3, 1821, ABCFM archives, vol. 4, no. 210.

So we know that Elizabeth and Ashbel Green had discussed the question of her baptism. There was, however, some ambiguity in Presbyterian Church law as to whether believing masters and mistresses who had slave children under their care should see it as their duty and responsibility to baptize them and oversee their Christian nurture—or whether such children might be presented only by believing parents.[12] For whatever the reason, the Greens decided not to sponsor her baptism, even though they took seriously their responsibility to instruct and nurture her and their other domestics in Christian faith and life.[13]

Of Betsey's growing-up years we have only snatches of information. We know that she was precocious and, by Dr. Green's account, became alarmingly wild and willful, but very bright. She remained with the Greens in Philadelphia. During these years Ashbel Green took an interest in his precocious servant and became concerned for her future welfare. She was systematically tutored in the academic and spiritual disciplines given their own children. Elizabeth Stockton Green died in 1807, when Betsey was about nine years old. Betsey stayed on with the family for all but three or four of her childhood and early teenage years. She was included in family prayers and "home-schooled" by Dr. Green, who often heard her catechism lessons, and by his son, James, who took a particular interest in her education. She developed a sisterly affection for James and his older brother, Jacob, and later in Hawaii took pains to collect and send home to Jacob from the island of Maui a number of interesting and unusual specimens of seashells and insects for his scientific research.[14]

To save Betsey from the evils of the urban Philadelphia atmosphere, he sent her to live in the country with his niece and her husband, Reverend Nathaniel Todd. ... Four or five years later, when Todd moved away and the Greens moved to Princeton in 1812, Betsey returned to live with the Princeton pastor.[15] Ashbel Green took up duties as the eighth president of the College of New Jersey (now Princeton University). He married a second time in 1809 and was the father of another baby son, Ashbel, Jr..[16] In her 20th year he freed her, but she chose to remain in his family as a hired woman. During her years in the Green household Betsey took advantage of her freedom and surroundings to educate herself. Ashbel Green's library and intellect assisted her in this pursuit.[17]

During the winter term of 1814-15 at the college in Princeton, a remarkable and spontaneous "revival of religion" took place under Dr. Green's tenure. As well as reinstating the study of Latin and Greek into the curriculum, Green had organized a College Bible Society and offered regular instruction in the sacred Scriptures, examining the students himself on their knowledge of the Bible. Each Sabbath day the young men of the college and of the theological seminary next door gathered together at Nasaue Hall for worship. When the revival broke out in early 1815, the atmosphere of community life among the students was greatly affected for good, and this eventually spilled over into Betsey's life. She attributes her conversion, though, to the ministry of a seminary student, Eliphat Wheeler Gilbert, over a year later, in the summer of 1816, while sitting in the gallery of Princeton's First Presbyterian (now Nassau) Church.[18]

The session minutes of that congregation record that on September 20, 1816, "Betsey Stockton, a coloured woman living in the family of the Rev.

---

12 *Boston Recorder*, Friday, May 6, 1836, article on the baptism of slave children (taken from the Journal and Luminary).

13 Joseph H. Jones, D.D., ed., *The Life of Ashbel Green, V.D.M.*, begun to be written by himself in his eighty-second year and continued to his eighty-fourth (New York: Robert Carter and Brothers, 1849), in an appended memoir, appearing as chapter 29, written by Green's Philadelphia colleague Rev. Dr. J. Janeway, 572.

14 Eileen F. Moffett, "Betsey Stockton: Pioneer American Missionary," *International Bulletin of Missionary Research*, April 1995 (New Haven, CT: Overseas Ministries Study Center), 71–72.

15 John A. Andrew, III, "Betsey Stockton: Stranger in a Strange Land," *Journal of Presbyterian History*, Summer 1974, (Presbyterian Historical Society, Philadelphia, PA).

16 Eileen F. Moffett, "Betsey Stockton: Pioneer American Missionary," *International Bulletin of Missionary Research*, April 1995 (New Haven, CT: Overseas Ministries Study Center), 72.

17 See letter to (unnamed person) from Ashbel Green, 3 Sept. 1821, ABC 6, vol. 4, no. 210, American Board of Commissioners for Foreign Missions Archives, Houghton Library, Harvard University. She was one of thirty-one blacks to join the Presbyterian Church in Princeton during the pastorate of the Reverend William Schenck. See John F. Hageman, *History of Princeton and its Institutions, Philadelphia, 1879*, 11, 116; Ashbel Green, *The Life of Ashbel Green* (New York, 1849), 619. Betsey apparently had some regular correspondence with the Reverend (1774–1858), a Presbyterian minister and colleague of Green, but no letters appear to have survived.

18 Eileen F. Moffett, "Betsey Stockton: Pioneer American Missionary," *International Bulletin of Missionary Research*, April 1995 (New Haven, CT: Overseas Ministries Study Center), 72.

Dr. Green, applied for admission to the Lord's table." The session was satisfied as to the evidence of what they called her "experimental acquaintance with religion" and her good conduct and agreed to receive her into full communicant membership.[19] She was publicly baptized at that time and admitted to the Lord's Table. It was sometime later that year or within the next two years that she was legally manumitted by Dr. Green.[20]

Betsey's Growing Interest in Mission

Betsey's maturing Christian faith gradually gave form in her mind to a sense of the duty that Christians bear toward the "lost" of the world. This was a clear reflection of the American evangelical faith of her times represented by Dr. Green, by the seminary students who were her Bible teachers, and by her own pastor in the First Presbyterian Church in Princeton. All of them shared this Christian worldview, which was grounded on the premise of the love of God in Jesus Christ for the whole world—and the conviction that salvation is found only in Christ. Betsey believed with all her heart that it is the sacred duty of Christians to offer themselves in humble obedience to God's call to carry out His plan of salvation through Jesus Christ for the world.[21] This persuasion soon blossomed into a desire to go to Africa as a missionary. Some of her friends opposed her plan, but she continued to read and study, hoping for such an opportunity.

During this time she started a little class of instruction for several black children of the Princeton community. And for about a year and a half she was a member of a Sabbath school class taught by a seminary student, Michael Osborn, who was impressed by her serious scholarship. When eventually called upon for a letter of recommendation, he wrote: "She has a larger acquaintance with sacred history and the Mosaic Institutions than almost any ordinary person, old or young, I have ever known," (He explained that by "ordinary" he meant one not a member of the clergy or a candidate for the ministry.) Osborn went on to say: "I recollect a multitude of instances where, for my own information, I have questioned her about some fact in Biblical history, or some minute point in Jewish antiquities, and have immediately received a correct answer."[22]

Dr. Green was not among those who tried to discourage Betsey's missionary ambitions, although he must have wondered what opportunity she might every have for such a commission, particularly as a single woman.[23]

American Protestants were not yet ready to send single women overseas without a protector. There were all kinds of problems to overcome in even considering such a radical step. For one thing, there was the danger that a single woman, who would be expected to live in a married missionary's home, might be imposed upon to act as little more than a domestic servant or built-in babysitter. And there was also the risk that the people among whom they worked would assume that the male missionary kept two wives.[24]

Betsey Stockton and a Princeton Seminary student, Charles Stewart, had been acquainted for several years, since he had been in and out of the Greens' home often from his earliest days as a college student. Stewart had been one of those converted during the period of spiritual awakening among the students in 1815, and he attributed to Dr. Green's preaching and counsel the first effectual turning of his heart to the Lord and to a missionary purpose.

When Betsey learned this young friend and his bride-to-be were going out as missionaries to the Sandwich Islands, her heart must have skipped a beat in wondering whether it might be possible for her to accompany them. She was well trained in domestic concerns, had skills as a nurse through useful life experience, and was also well

---

19 Session Minutes, First Presbyterian Church, September 20, 1816, Archives of Princeton Theological Seminary.

20 Eileen F. Moffett, "Betsey Stockton: Pioneer American Missionary," *International Bulletin of Missionary Research*, April 1995 (New Haven, CT: Overseas Ministries Study Center), 72.

21 Donald Philip Corr, "The Field Is the World—Proclaiming, Translating, and Serving by the American Board of Commissioners for Foreign Missions, 1810–1840" (Ph.D. diss., Fuller Theological Seminary, 1993), 27. In a general discussion of the principal motivating factors of ABCFM board administrators, missionaries, and supporters between 1810 and 1840.

22 Michael Osborn to Jeremiah Evarts, Corresponding Secretary of the American Board of Commissioners for Foreign Missions, Princeton, October 27, 1821, archives of the ABCFM, vol. 4, no. 209.

23 Eileen F. Moffett, "Betsey Stockton: Pioneer American Missionary," *International Bulletin of Missionary Research*, April 1995 (New Haven, CT: Overseas Ministries Study Center), 72.

24 See discussion of this problem in Beaver, *American Protestant Women in World Mission*, 62.

prepared as a teacher, though without a day of public instruction in her life, apart from that received as home and church. But the possibility of her accompanying the Stewarts as a missionary must have seemed at first preposterous.[25]

Nevertheless, on September 3, 1821, Dr. Ashbel Green wrote a letter to the secretary of the American Board of Commissioners for Foreign Missions recommending Charles Stewart as a missionary candidate and, as he noted in his diary, another "one for my Betty."[26] "She had saved her wages," he said, "by which, with some small assistance from myself, she was able to prepare her outfit for the mission."[27]

We can only guess at the negotiations that had been taking place in designing the innovative plan that resulted in her trailblazing appointment. While the "mission family" concept was not guaranteed to forestall a possible misunderstanding about a missionary keeping two wives, it did at least provide protection and security for a single woman. The arrangement agreed upon was that Betsey would become part of Charles and Harriet Stewart's family.

Stewart had graduated from Princeton Seminary in 1821 and was married in June of 1822. Five months later, on November 19, the Stewarts and Betsey, bound as a family in this unique, but happy, association, joined the little band of eleven other missionaries and four native islanders leaving American shores to go as the first reinforcements to the Sandwich Islands mission establishment by its pioneers three years earlier. These islands, which we now call Hawaii, were discovered by Captain James Cook in 1778, and named for the Earl of Sandwich, who had invented one of the most enduring fast foods of the Western world. The mission was under the direction of the American Board of Commissioners for Foreign Missions, with its headquarters in Boston. This board, known as the ABCFM, was the joint missionary agency of the Presbyterian and Congregational churches in America at that time.[28]

A testimonial letter to Jeremiah Evarts, Corresponding Secretary of the ABCFM, outlined her qualifications for missionary work:

> *I would say in general, as the result of an intimate acquaintance with her, that I think her pious, intelligent, industrious, skillful in the management of domestic affairs, apt to teach, and endued [sic] with a large portion of the active, persevering, self-sacrificing, spirit of a missionary. From my first acquaintance with her she has expressed a decided wish to go to the heathen.*[29]

The correspondent went on to note that she had attended Sunday School and knew the Scriptures. Betsey also loved to teach children, and had "appropriated a part of every week to the instruction of a number of coloured children." Her other accomplishments included a "respectable" knowledge of geography, legible writing, and some effort at "cyphering in compound multiplication."[30]

In short, Betsey Stockton was a well-educated, pious Christian who sought to evangelize the heathen. No one mentioned her color. The American Board's silence was no oversight, and revealed the Prudential Committee's primary concern for Christian principles.

Yet all persons interested in her welfare realized that her color might become a point of contention. In October 1822, soon after her assignment to the mission, Ashbel Green and Charles Stewart sat down with Betsey and formulated her precise role in the mission company. Jeremiah Evarts ratified this agreement for the ABCFM the day before her departure. The contract was unusual but then so was her appointment. Besides specifying her duties, the document illuminated the unspoken fears and anxieties of Betsey's supporters. In so doing it

---

25 Eileen F. Moffett, "Betsey Stockton: Pioneer American Missionary," *International Bulletin of Missionary Research*, April 1995 (New Haven, CT: Overseas Ministries Study Center), 72

26 Notes from the diary of Ashbel Green, Sepetember 3, 1821, Princeton University Rare Books and Archives.

27 Jones, *The Life of Ashbel Green*, 326.

28 Eileen F. Moffett, "Betsey Stockton: Pioneer American Missionary," *International Bulletin of Missionary Research*, April 1995 (New Haven, CT: Overseas Ministries Study Center), 72–73.

29 Michael Osborn to Jeremiah Evarts, 5 Sept. 1821, ABC 6, vol. 4, no. 209, A.B.C.F.M. Archives. Quoted by permission.

30 Ibid.

also laid bare certain assumptions about the drift of American society.[31]

It was still true then, and for quite a while longer, that only the ordained men had a vote in the mission and were officially the appointed "missionaries." Wives and single women were "assistant missionaries," without vote. But it is only fair to say that the same was true for a time, of unordained men such as physicians and printers. And one of the reasons for that was undoubtedly the fact that American evangelical Christians between 1810 and 1840 considered the proclamation (i.e., preaching) of the Gospel to be he highest priority in missions. Wives, teachers, physicians, and other workers were important partners to the preachers, but in a secondary role.[32] It was the preachers who most unequivocally bore the name "missionary." So, it was as a member of a "mission family" that Betsey's dream of becoming a missionary, even an "assistant missionary," was worked out.[33]

The position of Betsey Stockton in the Sandwich Islands Mission was a unique one. She was entirely under the control of the American Board, yet not a full-fledged missionary. The Stewarts were her "particular friends and patrons," not her masters. "In this family," the agreement noted, "she is to be regarded and treated neither as an equal nor as a servant-but as a humble Christian friend."[34] Miss Stockton was neither servant nor slave nor an equal among fellow Christian missionaries. She was to serve the Stewarts and the mission under the Board's paternal umbrella.

The Prudential Committee's dilemma in resolving the position Betsey Stockton reflected a common predicament of all white Americans. If slaves were freed, what should be their role in American society? Convinced that black people did not deserve slavery, perplexed Christians were not sure that they merited equality either. Caught between racial prejudice and Christian humanism, they paused—unwilling to make the ultimate moral choice. So too with Betsey Stockton. She received her freedom, but it was a qualified freedom.[35]

Her contract with the Board, however, became more radical with each section. Although section one placed her explicitly under the control of the ABCFM, section seven, the final, allowed her to break the agreement at any time. With the agreement severed, she would "remain under the care and superintendence of the Board, like any other missionary."[36] The contract was obviously designed to protect her from exploitation by the other missionaries. That such protection was deemed necessary is itself intriguing. This promised equality, but did so in such a manner so as to forestall domestic criticism of the Board for promoting the abolition of slavery. The likelihood that such a separation might occur before the reinforcement reached Hawaii seemed remote, so Betsey left the country as a servant. That she might become a free woman in the far-off Pacific did not frighten the Prudential Committee, nor was it likely to affect the flow of contributions to the Board's treasury from supporters of slavery. Distance relieved anxiety.[37]

Yet despite mental doubts and physical adversity the adventure beckoned, and she insisted that "I am as happy as I ever was in my life."[38]

Fired by an ambition to evangelize the heathen, in the winter of 1822-23, Betsey Stockton found herself treated as an equal while shipping with a detachment of white missionaries to the Sandwich Islands. That this equality received open acknowledgment only after the Thames left port merely heightened the symbolic nature of the missionary venture. These men and women believed themselves to be the heralds of the future, the advance agents of a millennial age in which Christianity would suffuse the globe and unite mankind.[39]

---

31 John A. Andrew III, "Betsey Stockton: Stranger in a Strange Land," *Journal of Presbyterian History*, Summer 1974 (Presbyterian Historical Society, Philadelphia, PA), 159.

32 Corr, "The Field Is the World," 31.

33 Eileen F. Moffett, "Betsey Stockton: Pioneer American Missionary," *International Bulletin of Missionary Research*, April 1995 (New Haven, CT: Overseas Ministries Study Center), 73.

34 Her contract is in the archives of the Hawaiian Mission Children's Society (HMCS) in Honolulu, Hawaii. Permission to quote is gratefully acknowledged.

35 John A. Andrew III, "Betsey Stockton: Stranger in a Strange Land," *Journal of Presbyterian History*, Summer 1974 (Presbyterian Historical Society, Philadelphia, PA), 159–160.

36 Her contract is in the archives of the Hawaiian Mission Children's Society (HMCS) in Honolulu, Hawaii. Permission to quote is gratefully acknowledged.

37 John A. Andrew III, "Betsey Stockton: Stranger in a Strange Land," *Journal of Presbyterian History*, Summer 1974, (Presbyterian Historical Society, Philadelphia, PA), 160.

38 Letter to Ashbel Green, December 19, 1822 in ibid., 425.

39 John A. Andrew III, "Betsey Stockton: Stranger in a Strange Land," *Journal of Presbyterian History*, Summer 1974 (Presbyterian Historical Society, Philadelphia, PA), 160.

In the first letter that Betsey wrote home to Dr. Green during the long five-month voyage, she confessed to "the most deathlike sickness I ever felt in my life, occasioned by the motion of the ship. Every person in the mission, except Mr. Stuart and Kermoola [one of the islanders], was sick at the same time. The weather became very boisterous. I am happy to tell you that since I left home, in all the storms and dangers I have been called to witness, I have never lost my self-possession. This I consider as a fulfillment of the promise that 'as my day is, so my strength shall be.'"[40] Sea sickness, the terror of ocean storms, and a fear that her religious commitment might decline haunted Betsey as well as the other missionaries. Only a few days out of New Haven she wrote Green:

> But we have not yet come to the most trying part of the voyage. We are now near the coast of Africa, and I fear I shall not act the Christian in the thunder storms which are to be expected there. But I am glad to have it in my power to say, that notwithstanding all our difficulties, I have never looked toward home with a longing eye. I cannot say indeed, sir, that I have not longed to see your family. You are all as dear to me as life itself; and nothing but the consoling thought that we are destined to meet where parting will be no more, could support me.[41]

She continued:

> I wish it was in my power to give the ladies of your family some account of our manner of living, sometimes in imagination, I visit them in the night, and get a piece of bread; for there is nothing I have wanted so much since I left home, of the provision kind, as bread. Ours is pilot-bread and crackers, and by using them in our seasickness I took a dislike to them. But we have pudding, boiled rice, and mush once a week, and beans, potatoes, boiled onions, fruit, etc.. The cook, however, is a dirty man, and we are obliged to eat without asking questions. While I was sick, they gave me a mug of chicken soup—the grease, the pepper, and the feathers, floated together on the surface." She went on to describe their sleeping arrangements and how her hammock pitched and rolled, "Whenever my head went to leeward and my feet to windward, which was the case every five minutes, it made me very sick. The second night the ship rolled without pitching, and I was thrown back and forth as fast as I could go, until about 12 o'clock at night, when ... I was thrown up, first against the ceiling and then on the dining table. The water running on the deck, and the trunks falling in the cabin, allowed me to think very little of myself."[42] Later on a calmer day she wrote in her journal, "If it were in my power I would like to describe the phosphorescence of the sea. But to do this would require the pen of a Milton; and he, I think, would fail, were he to attempt it."[43]

Native warriors in their canoes greeted the missionaries on their arrival at the Sandwich Islands. The sight appalled the little band, and Betsey recorded her own reaction:

> When they first came on board, the sight chilled our very hearts. They were mostly naked except for a narrow strip of tapa around their loins. The ladies retired to the cabin, and burst into tears; some of the gentlemen turned pale: ... my own soul sickened within me, and every nerve trembled. Are these, thought I, the beings with whom I must spend the remainder of my life? They are men and have souls—was the reply which conscience made. We informed them that we were missionaries, come to live with them, and do them good. At which an old man exclaimed, in his native dialect. That is very good. By and by know God.[44]

No prior training could have provided adequate preparation for these conditions. But

---

40 *The Christian Advocate*, 1 (Sept. 1823), 424. Ashbel Green printed some of her letters and excerpts from her journal in *The Christian Advocate* from 1823 to 1825, noting that she was "a young woman of African descent, who was never sent to school a day in her life ... " From Betsey Stockton's journal, in Ibid., 3 (January 1825), 39.

41 The quotes in this paragraph are all from the letter of Betsey Stockton to Dr. Ashbel Green, written on board the ship Thames bound for the Sandwhich Islands, December 19, 1822, excerpts of which were published in *The Christian Advocate*, 1 (September 1823): 423-426.

42 Ibid.

43 Journal of Betsey Stockton, December 31, 1822, written on board the ship *Thames* at sea, published by Ashbel Green in *The Christian Advocate* 2 (May 1824): 233-234.

44 *The Christian Advocate*, 1 (September 1823): 423-426.

personal experience as a slave gave Betsey a sense of empathy; Christian conviction and duty instilled motivation. God had commanded that the world be evangelized, and God did not demand the impossible.[45]

Betsey went on to say:

> In a short time our unpleasant feelings were much dissipated. One morning a few days after they had landed, the queen spoke to a messenger asking solicitously, "Have they hog still?" "Yes," he answered. "Any dog?" "No eat dog." "Any potatoes?" "No." "Any melons?" "No." An order was immediately given, and two men were dispatched with potatoes and melons for the missionaries. "In fact," they wrote, "no Christian congregation in American could, in this respect, have received a clergyman, coming to administer the word of life to them, with greater hospitality, or stronger expressions of love and good will.[46]

Work began almost immediately. After about a month at the mission base in Honolulu, Betsey Stockton and her family, Charles and Harriet Stewart, together with Mr. and Mrs. Richards, were sent to open a new mission station on the island of Maui at a place called Lahaina. Betsey established a school and began instruction in English to six Hawaiians and four English youth. Harriet Stewart gave birth to a son, Charles Stewart, in April 1823, while on board ship. His care and training also fell to Betsey. Together these chores occupied almost every waking hour, leaving little opportunity for loneliness to creep in. Alone at first, the new missionary had now found both friends and commitment. "When you think of me as a stranger in a strange land," she wrote, "think of me still as one who has kind friends, to guide and protect her."[47]

Betsey performed a variety of duties throughout her missionary activities. She looked after the Stewarts and their household (which was also her own), taught school, and served as unofficial doctor and nurse to a variety of persons and injuries. All the time she maintained her religious zeal amid dirt and deprivation.[48] Among her most poignant experiences was a meeting with another black American, Anthony Allen, who had "resided on the island 20 years and had never before seen a coloured female." Betsey noted that, "Mr. Allen was very kind to me, and seemed happy to see one of his own country people. His wife is a native woman, but very pleasant, and to all appearances innocent. They are in good circumstances, and friendly to the mission. I regretted leaving them very much."[49] A few days later she sailed with the Stewarts to Lahaina. It was at Lahaina, isolated from Allen and most of the mission company, that the shadows of solitude deepened her loneliness.[50]

In 1824, the mission at Lahaina opened a school for the education and training of the chiefs' domestics and dependents. The first teacher was Betsey Stockton.[51] The mulatto woman now had reached a plateau equivalent to that of many white women in New England; she had become a schoolteacher.[52] It is significant that she helped to organize and was put in charge of the first school on the islands open to commoners—predominantly farmers. She wrote to Ashbel Green in 1824: "I have now a fine school of the... lower class of people, the first, I believe, that has ever been established."[53] Charles Stewart wrote that these common folk had made application for books and slates and a teacher. So, beginning with about 30 individuals, this school was formed in the chapel, meeting every afternoon

---

45 John A. Andrew III, "Betsey Stockton: Stranger in a Strange Land," *Journal of Presbyterian History*, Summer 1974 (Presbyterian Historical Society, Philadelphia, PA), 161.

46 *Missionary Herald* (ABCFM, Boston) 21 (February 1825): 41, from the journal of Messrs. Richards and Stewart.

47 From Betsey Stockton's journal, in ibid., 3 (January 1825), 36f. (my italics). Her early activities at Maui are noted in ibid., 41, a letter from Charles Stewart to (unnamed person), 24 May 1823 in ibid., (May 1824), 233.

48 Details of her activities are in ibid., 2 (May 1824), 232, 236; and Charles Stewart *Private Journal of a Voyage to the Pacific Ocean, and a Residence at the Sandwich Islands, in the Years, 1822-1825*, (New York, 1828), 202. Hereafter cited as *Residence*.

49 *The Christian Advocate*, 3 (January 1825), 40. Allen was a prosperous farmer.

50 John A. Andrew III, "Betsey Stockton: Stranger in a Strange Land," *Journal of Presbyterian History*, Summer,1974 (Presbyterian Historical Society, Philadelphia, PA), 161.

51 Stewart, *Residence*, 258. See also *The Christian Advocate*, 1825), 374; *Missionary Herald*, 22 (February 1826), 38.

52 John A. Andrew III, "Betsey Stockton: Stranger in a Strange Land," *Journal of Presbyterian History*, Summer 1974 (Presbyterian Historical Society, Philadelphia, PA), 161.

53 Betsey Stockton to Ashbel Green, September 16, 1824, published in *The Christian Advocate* 3 (April 1825): 1854. Eileen F. Moffett, "Betsey Stockton: Pioneer American Missionary," *International Bulletin of Missionary Research*, April 1995 (New Haven, CT: Overseas Ministries Study Center), 73.

under the superintendence of Betsey, who, he said, "is quite familiar with the native tongue," Other missionaries had established the first schools in the islands, usually attended by the upper classes. Betsey, the former slave, was the first to organize a school for the disadvantaged.

During the early 19th century teaching school remained one of the very few respectable occupations for young American women who sought employment outside the home. In an age when the mere instruction of blacks occasioned excitement and hostility even in New England, the appearance of a black schoolteacher working alongside her white counterparts was unusual. Although the distance between Hawaii and New England and the character of her pupils dimmed its impact, the American Board, nonetheless, gave little publicity to this new development. Even in religious circles few learned of Miss Stockton's achievement, and still fewer knew of her color. Abolitionist excitement would not advance the Board's objectives.[54]

Formation of a school for local farmers and their families marked a major accomplishment for the mission company at Lahaina. Education must precede religious training, for knowledge of the English language remained a precondition for study of the Bible. Books and slates, Charles Stewart wrote, were the "most effectual means of withdrawing them from their idle and vicious habits; and of bringing them more readily under the influence of our teachings in morality and religion."[55] The missionaries' objectives encompassed not only the introduction of Christianity, but all the attributes of New England society and civilization.[56]

Though she labored diligently both for the American Board and for the Stewarts, missionary correspondence reveals only occasional glimpses into Betsey Stockton's activities. The evidence indicates that the other members of the mission regarded her as an attachment to the Stewart family, and hints at some uneasiness in her relation to the mission. This unique position and isolation from others of her color compounded any difficulties and enhanced the loneliness. Several times during her three years at the Sandwich Islands Betsey admitted to a "want of spiritual food and Christian converse."[57]

Her reaction to Lahaina reflected a slight homesickness, as she took particular notice of the green vegetation—the first trees "that looked green and beautiful since we left home...." Betsey also experienced some respiratory problems, with chest pains and "a little spitting of blood." The prevailing remedy for nearly all ills—bleeding—was applied. She recovered quickly.[58]

After a year at Lahaina, however, Betsey appeared to tire of foreign mission work. Novelty had turned to regularity, and she complained to Ashbel Green of sinking spirits:

> In your last letter you tell me "to keep up my spirits." I wish it was in my power to say that I have always done so; but here I fear I must plead guilty. My spirits often sink low; and that this is criminal I do not pretend to deny. I knew that the work in which I was to be engaged was great and glorious, and that it demanded all my faculties of body and mind in its performance.[59]

Secular duties and the problems of subsistence consumed most of her time, leaving little for religious activities. With other women of the mission—Mrs. Bingham, Mrs. Stewart and Mrs. Loomis—Miss Stockton conducted the annual examination of scholars at the school.[60] But her unusual position in the mission aggravated her difficulties, and her many duties to the Stewart family (now enlarged with Mrs. Stewart's illness) filled whatever free time she might have enjoyed. She was all too frequently left on the fringes of missionary life. Betsey's letters to Green reveal a touch of sadness, and perhaps resignation: "When in my native land, my Christian privileges constituted much of my happiness; and now, the privilege of mourn-

---

[54] John A. Andrew III, "Betsey Stockton: Stranger in a Strange Land," *Journal of Presbyterian History*, Summer 1974 (Presbyterian Historical Society, Philadelphia, PA), 161–162.

[55] Joseph Tracy, et. al., *History of American Missions to the Heathen, from their Commencement to the Present Time*, (Worcester: Spooner & Howland, 1840), 153.

[56] John A. Andrew III, "Betsey Stockton: Stranger in a Strange Land," *Journal of Presbyterian History*, Summer 1974 (Presbyterian Historical Society, Philadelphia, PA), 162.

[57] Letter in *The Christian Advocate*, 3 (April 1825), 188.

[58] Ibid., 3 (Jan. 1825), 40.

[59] Ibid., 3 (April 1825), 188.

[60] Hiram Bingham, *A Residence of Twenty-one Years in the Sandwich Islands* (New York: 1855), 249. This is Bingham's only mention of Betsey Stockton in his history of the mission.

ing their loss will surely not be denied me. But though sorrowful, yet I rejoice. The missionary's sorrows and the missionary's joys are mine. The missionary's grave, and perhaps the missionary's heaven, will also be mine."[61]

By 1825, the rapid deterioration of Mrs. Stewart's health forced her husband to make preparations to return to the U.S. Betsey undoubtedly welcomed a chance to return to her native country with the Stewart family, including a new little daughter born to the Stewarts during that time. On October 17, 1825, the Stewart family left the Sandwich Islands. Elisha Loomis recorded that "Betsey Stockton, the colored woman attached to their family, of course, returns with them."[62] They were offered a gratuitous passage to England by Captain Dale of the English whaleship Fawn. After a six-month voyage, from October 15, 1825, until April 1826, they arrived at the English port of Gravesend. Following a layover of several months in London, they continued the return journey to America, arriving at New York in August.[63]

Loomis reflected what appears to have been the prevailing attitude toward the missionary teacher. Although granted her independence by contract, and allowed to exercise it in her missionary activities, Betsey could not completely overcome that sense of difference that prevailed among her fellow workers. They included her in all their activities, but as an adjunct of the Stewart family. The American Board of Commissioners made no effort to publicize her presence at the mission station. Only persistent readers of The Christian Advocate or the Missionary Herald, the Board's official publication, ever became aware that a black woman had labored as a missionary at the Sandwich Islands.[64]

By 1826, Betsey Stockton was back in Cooperstown, NY, with the Stewarts. Little information remains about her activities after her return to the U.S.. Her commitment to missionary and benevolent work, however, did not wane once she was reunited with old friends in familiar surroundings. Apparently she established an infant school for Negro children in Philadelphia.[65] But because of Harriet Stewart's continuing frail health, she stood ready and went on a number of occasions to help care for Harriet and the children. Charles Stewart had been forced to resign his missionary commission because of his wife's health and had joined the navy chaplaincy. Betsey was with Harriet and the children in Cooperstown, NY, during the winter of 1826 and probably through most of 1827.[66] For four months during the summer of 1827, their "Aunt Betsey" and the children were in Albany, NY, while Mrs. Stewart was away travelling with her husband.[67]

Sometime in the summer or autumn of 1829, a Methodist missionary, Mr. William Case, travelled to Philadelphia, where Betsey was living again, with the purpose of trying to persuade the young woman to answer another missionary call and go with him to organize schools and instruct native Indian children at Grape Island across the border in Canada, near upstate New York.[68] She went for a few months and on her return brought a birchbark canoe about three or four feet long to little Charles Stewart, then about six years old. The family was in New Haven, CT, that year, staying with Harriet's "adopted" father while Charles Stewart was away with his ship.[69]

When Harriet Stewart died in 1830, just four years after they had returned from Hawaii, "Aunt

---

61 The Christian Advocate, 3 (April 1825), 188. She did spend some time collecting shells for Green, however. See ibid., 189.

62 William D. Westervelt (Comp.), "Copy of the Journal Hawaii, 1824–1826, of Loomis," typescript, University of Hawaii, 1937, 49.

63 Joseph Tracy, et. al., History of American Missions to the Heathen, from their Commencement to the Present Time, (Worcester: Spooner & Howland, 1840), 153.

64 John A. Andrew III, "Betsey Stockton: Stranger in a Strange Land," Journal of Presbyterian History, Summer 1974 (Presbyterian Historical Society, Philadelphia, PA), 163.

65 Letter from one of the Stewart's children to Martha Chamberlain, October 27, 1899 in HMCS Manuscript Collection. French, in The Missionary Whaleship, 116f does not mention this Canadian episode. He notes that she remained in Cooperstown for ten years, leaving in 1836–1837 to go to Philadelphia. Another reference to Canada is in HMCS, Missionary Album, 177.

66 Harriet Bradford Tiffany Stewart to Miss Olivia Murray, Barclay St., New York, March 21, 1827 (among the Chas. Stewart Papers in the James Fennimore Cooper Library in Cooperstown, NY).

67 Rev. Charles S. Stewart to Levi Chamberlain, Island of Oahu, Sandwhich Islands, October 29, 1827. Hawaiian Mission Children's Society Library, Honolulu, Hawaii.

68 The information that Betsey Stockton served on Grape Island comes from an article written by Constance K. Escher, "She Calls Herself Betsey Stockton," Princeton History, no. 10 (1991):87.

69 Gen. Charles Seaforth Stewart to Miss Martha A. Chamberlain, Corresponding Secretary of the Hawaiian Mission Children's Society, Honolulu, Hawaii, October 27, 1899, written from Cooperstown, New York.

Betsey" answered a call again and went to Cooperstown, NY, to care for the three motherless children. Their father soon had to leave again, as he so often did for long stretches of time when his ship was away at sea.[70]

In 1833, Betsey decided to move the children and herself back to Princeton, even though Dr. Green and his household had been living again in Philadelphia for the past eleven years. James Green, her childhood family tutor, had married and established a notable law practice in Princeton. So Betsey undoubtedly had his family to help her relocate to the town she thought of as home, though under very changed circumstances. She enrolled young Charles, then about eleven years old, in the Edgehill School on Hibben Road.[71] Once again her desire to help the poor and downtrodden united with Christian duty. Considerable confusion exists as to the nature of this school in Princeton. Her obituary in the Freeman's Journal indicated that it was a state school.[72] Public schools did not exist in Princeton, however, until 1857. Anthony Simmons, a Negro storekeeper and caterer, formed a school the Session House of the First Presbyterian Church. Betsey, member of this church since 1816, probably taught here.[73]

Charles Stewart, the children's father, remarried in 1835 and they went back with him to New York. But Betsey stayed on in Princeton. She was truly alone for the first time in her life and had some depressing bouts of illness. It was a very distressing time for her. Should she go back into domestic services to earn her living? Where was her family? And who was her family? After a while she moved beyond the time of gloomy loneliness and anxiety over her future and succeeded in opening a public, or "common," school for black children, which she served with great distinction for many years as a principal. During the time of her early years back in Princeton, there was some racial tension at the First Presbyterian Church, Betsey's home church. In the mid-1830's an opportunity arose for the black members of the church to separate and form their own congregation a few blocks away.[74]

Active in Princeton's First Presbyterian Church, in 1845, she joined a petition campaign among black church members to separate and form their own church. Sparked by the increasing interest in antislavery activity, black members of the First Church met December 21, 1845, and unanimously agreed to request a dismission from the Presbytery of New Brunswick. A formal petition followed on March 10, 1846, and the Presbytery granted them a dismission. Ninety-two persons formed the First Presbyterian Church of Colour of Princeton—renamed the Witherspoon Street Church in 1848. Betsey Stockton's name headed the list of petitioners.[75]

Throughout the remainder of her life Betsey retained a lively interest in the welfare of Princeton's black community.[76] The former missionary labored here until her death in 1865.[77]

Betsey's Stockton's name heads the list of the founding members of the Witherspoon Street Presbyterian Church of Princeton. She helped found a Sabbath school for children and young people in connection with the church and was its most faithful teacher for 25 or 30 years. Providentially, the records of this school for about a ten-year period have been preserved and are now lodged in the Rare Books and Archives section of Princeton University's Firestone Library. Among the early superintendents, most of whom were drawn from among students at the theological seminary, was John L. Nevius, later of China missionary fame, known widely for his Nevius Method of missionary strategy, so successfully used in Korea and often referred to as the Three-Self Movement.[78]

---

70 Eileen F. Moffett, "Betsey Stockton: Pioneer American Missionary," *International Bulletin of Missionary Research*, April 1995 (New Haven, CT: Overseas Ministries Study Center), 74.

71 Ibid, 74.

72 *Freeman's Journal* (Cooperstown, New York), 3 Nov. 1865, 2.

73 I am grateful to Miss Genevieve Cobb of the Historical Society of Princeton, New Jersey for information on this point. Her prodigious research proved valuable in snaring elusive segments of Betsey's life.

74 Eileen F. Moffett, "Betsey Stockton: Pioneer American Missionary," *International Bulletin of Missionary Research*, April 1995 (New Haven, CT: Overseas Ministries Study Center), 74.

75 The request and notice of the meeting are in the Presbyterian Historical Society, MS, P9375. See also Hageman, *History of Princeton*, 11, 209f, Anna Smith, *Reminiscences of Colored People of Princeton, N.J., 1800–1900*, 7; Andrew Murray, *Presbyterians and the Negro-A History*, (Philadelphia, PA), 37f.

76 John A. Andrew III, "Betsey Stockton: Stranger in a Strange Land," *Journal of Presbyterian History*, Summer 1974 (Presbyterian Historical Society, Philadelphia, PA), 164.

77 Ibid, 164.

78 Eileen F. Moffett, "Betsey Stockton: Pioneer American Missionary," *International Bulletin of Missionary Research*, April 1995 (New Haven, CT: Overseas Ministries Study Center), 74.

Mr. Nevius, in a letter to his future wife, wrote from Princeton in 1852, "Mr. Williams [a fellow seminary student], of whom I have spoken to you, intends going with his wife to the islands of Corisco, Africa, and thinks of taking with him a negress named Aunt Betsy, and all my ... Sunday School class!"[79] It was probably wishful thinking but indicated the high regard in which he held them.[80]

She also persuaded a student at the seminary in Princeton, the Rev. Lewis W. Mudge, to open a night school for young black men and women who were employed during the day. According to Constance Escher, a Princeton teacher and writer, "[Betsey] Stockton used to read Caeser's Commentaries on the Gallic Wars in Latin with Mudge."[81]

"Aunt Betsey" grew to be one of Princeton's most admired and beloved figures, though unassuming and gentle in spirit. She had a quiet, steady Christian influence, particularly on young people, with whom she was always surrounded in weekday school and in Sunday school. Escher mentions that "one of the first women teachers at the [Witherspoon Street] Sabbath School, Cecilia Van Tyne, went to Rio de Janeiro in 1848 as a missionary." It is not hard to trace the influence of Betsey Stockton in the life of this young woman.

The three Stewart children were very close to her heart. Young Charles, who was nurtured and trained by "Aunt Betsey" from the moment of his birth until the time of her death, and was as close as she ever got to having a son of her own, graduated with highest honors at the head of his class in the military academy at West Point and went on to a distinguished career as a brigadier general. The children, for their part, loved her dearly. And when she died in 1865, a few months after President Abraham Lincoln was assassinated, her funeral was conducted by the president of Princeton college, Dr. John Maclean, who preached the sermon; by Professor Duffield, of Nassau Hall; and by Dr. Charles Hodge, senior professor of the theological seminary at Princeton. She was lovingly laid to rest in beautiful Lakewood Cemetery in Cooperstown, NY, overlooking Lake Otsego, beside the rest of her Stewart family, some of whom died before she did, and some after.[82]

Betsey Stockton was a remarkable 19th century woman missionary pioneer. She must have faced what many today would call daunting identity problems. She was obviously marginalized and often lonely, perhaps feeling that she did not completely belong to anyone or any place. She might well have carried a burden of resentment. But that would have been a costly burden to bear, too costly for Betsey. Instead, like a much earlier missionary pioneer, she discovered a secret that became her victory over loneliness and despair. Paul described it as being "in Christ." Betsey learned that secret, too, through a lifetime of walking with her Lord. She learned the happy secret that "in Christ," one does not live altogether "under the circumstances," whatever they may be.[83]

Betsey Stockton was but one of many men and women who sought to improve American society in the early decades of the 19th century. Sparked by the Second Great Awakening and an evangelical Christianity, many Americans expressed a new concern for Christian principles and a benevolent humanitarianism.[84] One reinforced the other, as proponents of benevolent reform struggled to realize a Christian commonwealth at home and abroad. Not purposively conservative or radical, these reformers sought ways to unify Americans in the face of social change, and to carry their message to the world. But economic speculation and political partisanship pulled men in other directions, and the reformers' successes were slim. The hopes of Betsey Stockton exemplified the aims of this reform, and her failures, its failures.[85]

---

79 Helen S. Coan Nevius, *The Life of John Livingston Nevius* (New York: Fleming H. Revell, 1895), 95.

80 Eileen F. Moffett, "Betsey Stockton: Pioneer American Missionary," *International Bulletin of Missionary Research*, April 1995 (New Haven, CT: Overseas Ministries Study Center), 74.

81 Escher, "She Calls Herself Betsey Stockton," 93.

82 Eileen F. Moffett, "Betsey Stockton: Pioneer American Missionary," *International Bulletin of Missionary Research*, April 1995 (New Haven, CT: Overseas Ministries Study Center), 75–76.

83 Ibid., 76.

84 Andrew, "Rebuilding the Christian Commonwealth," Chapters 4–5.

85 John A. Andrew III, "Betsey Stockton: Stranger in a Strange Land," *Journal of Presbyterian History*, Summer 1974 (Presbyterian Historical Society, Philadelphia, PA), 164.

Chapter 12
Alexander Crummell (1819–1898)

William Edward Burghardt DuBois, edited by Robert J. Stevens

Having known Alexander Crummell, William E. B. DuBois wrote a number of comments in his book, *The Souls Of Black Folk*, which is now in the public domain in the U.S. and can be quoted freely.

W. E. B. DuBois began a writing career as early as 15 as a local correspondent for the *New York Globe*. He attended Fisk College (now University) 1885-88. He attended Harvard and later received a scholarship to study at the University of Berlin, Germany. He returned to Harvard for his doctorate. He taught at Wilberforce in OH, then received a fellowship at the University of PA. His scientific approach to studying social phenomena had him acknowledged as the father of Social Science. He then taught at Atlanta University where he wrote *The Souls of Black Folk* (1903).

He went to Africa, returned to Atlanta, and returned to Africa where he died in Accra, Ghana, in 1963. He was a pioneering Pan-Africanist who wrote and studied Negro morality, ubanization, Negroes in business, college-bred Negroes, the Negro church, and Negro crime. He wrote his views on both the African's and the African American's quest for freedom.

"This is the story of a human heart, the tale of a black boy who many long years ago began to struggle with life that he might know the world and know himself. Three temptations he met on those dark dunes that lay gray and dismal before the wonder-eyes of the child; the temptation of Hate, that stood out against the red dawn; the temptation of Despair, that darkened noonday; and the temptation of Doubt, that ever steals along with twilight. Above all, you must hear of the vales he crossed—the Valley of Humiliation and the Valley of the Shadow of Death."[1]

In 1819, Alexander, was born in lower Manhattan, in New York City, to the son of a West African prince (Temme tribe) and a free mother, Charity. (Lewis) His father, Boston Crummell, announced to his master that he would serve him no longer and left for freedom.

"He was born with the Missouri Compromise and lay a-dying amid the echoes of Manila and ElCaney; stirring times for living, times dark to look back upon, darker to look forward to. ... The slave-ship still groaned across the Atlantic, faint cries burdened the Southern breeze, and the great black father whispered mad tales of cruelty into those young ears. From the low doorway the mother silently watched her boy at play, and at nightfall sought him eagerly lest the shadows bear him away to the land of slaves.

So his young mind worked and winced and shaped curiously a vision of Life; and in the midst of that vision ever stood one figure alone—ever with the hard, thick countenance of that bitter father, and a form that fell in vast and shapeless folds. Thus the temptation of Hate grew and shadowed the growing child—gliding stealthily into his laughter, fading into his play, and seizing his dreams by day and by night with rough, rude turbulence."[2]

In New York his family lived among the most freedom conscious blacks of the time. Alexander attended an interracial abolitionist school at Canaan, NH; one he "had traveled cold and hungry four hundred miles" to attend.[3] His home was the founding place of the first African-American newspaper, *Freedoms Journal*.

---

1 W.E.B. DuBois, *The Souls of Black Folk* (Chicago: A. C. McChig & Co., 1903), 152.
2 Ibid., 153.
3 Marilyn Lewis, "Independent Study Assignment: The African-American In Christian Mission: From Slave to Evangelist to Missionary," M.Th. Degree, January 1993.

But the godly farmers hitched ninety yoke of oxen to the abolition schoolhouse and dragged it into the middle of the swamp. The black boy trudged away.

So in that little Oneida school there came to those schoolboys a revelation of thought and longing beneath one black skin, of which they had not dreamed before. And to the lonely boy came a new dawn of sympathy and inspiration. The shadowy, formless thing—the temptation of Hate, that hovered between him and the world—grew fainter and less sinister. ... A vision of life came to the growing boy—mystic, wonderful. He raised his head, stretched himself, breathed deep of the fresh new air. Yonder, behind the forests, he heard strange sounds; then glinting through the trees he saw, far, far away, the bronzed hosts of a nation calling—calling faintly, calling loudly. He heard the hateful clank of their chains; he felt them cringe and grovel, and there rose within him a protest and a prophesy. And he girded himself to walk down to the world.[4]

Later he attended an institute in Whitesboro, NY, which was run by abolitionists and combined manual labor and the classical curriculum.(Lewis) His father assured his academic success by hiring private tutors. In his early years, Crummell was an outspoken advocate for the abolition of slavery and the removal of legal restrictions on black Americans. He fought for the right to vote and recommended the establishment of Negro schools.[5]

Denied admission to the General Theological Seminary of the Episcopal church in 1839 because of his race, Crummell studied theology privately. He was ordained as an Episcopal clergyman in the Diocese of Massachusetts in 1844, when he was 25 years old, but was excluded from a meeting of priests of the diocese, and moved to England.[6]

A voice and a vision called him to be a priest—a seer to lead the uncalled out of the house of bondage. He saw the headless host turn toward him like the whirling of mad waters—he stretched forth his hands eagerly, and then, even as he stretched them, suddenly there swept across the vision the temptation of Despair.

They were not wicked men,—the problem of life is not the problem of the wicked—they were calm, good men, Bishops of the Apostolic Church of God, and strove toward righteousness. They said slowly, "It is all very natural—it is even commendable; but the General Theological Seminary of the Episcopal Church cannot admit a Negro." And when that thin, half-grotesque figure still haunted their doors, they put their hands kindly, half sorrowfully, on his shoulders, and said, "Now—of course—we know how YOU feel about it; but you see it is impossible—that is—well—it is premature. Sometime, we trust—sincerely trust—all such distinctions will fade away; but now the world is as it is."

This was the temptation of Despair; and the young man fought it doggedly. ... And yet the fire through which Alexander Crummell went did not burn in vain. Slowly and more soberly he took up again his plan of life. More critically he studied the situation. Deep down below the slavery and servitude of the Negro people he saw their fatal weaknesses, which long years of mistreatment had emphasized. The dearth of moral character, of unbending righteousness, he felt, was their great shortcoming, and here he would begin. He would gather the best of his people into some Episcopal chapel and there lead, teach, and inspire them, till the leaven spread, till the children grew, till the world hearkened—till and then across his dream gleamed some faint after-glow of that first fair vision of youth—only an after-glow, for there had passed a glory from the earth.[7]

He journeyed to England about 1848 to raise funds for a church for poor blacks, and soon

---

4 DuBois, *The Souls of Black Folk*, 154–155.
5 Marilyn Lewis, "Independent Study Assignment: The African-American In Christian Mission: From Slave to Evangelist to Missionary," M.Th. Degree, January 1993.
6 James Keifer, The Episcopal Calendar, 1994 edition, Alexander Crummell, Priest, Missionary, Educator (September 10, 1898).

7 DuBois, *The Souls of Black Folk*, 155.

began a course of study at Queen's College, Cambridge.[8]

> He found a chapel in New York—the church of his father; he labored for it in poverty and starvation, scorned by his fellow priest. Half in despair, he wandered across the sea, a beggar with outstretched hands. Englishmen clasped them—Wilberforce and Stanley, Thirwell and Ingles, and even Froude and Macaulay; Sir Benjamin Brodie bade him rest awhile at Queen's College in Cambridge, and there he lingered, struggling for health of body and mind.[9]

He graduated from the Queen's College of Cambridge University in 1853. In the same year he was sent by the British Anglical Church as a missionary to Liberia. This was a white denomination which supported African missionary efforts.(Lewis) Crummell hoped to see established in Liberia a black Christian republic, combining the best of European and African culture, and led by a Western-educated black bishop. He visited the U.S. and urged blacks to join him in Liberia and swell the ranks of the church there.[10]

During his stay in Liberia he worked as a missionary for the Episcopal church and professor at Liberia College. Alexander became one of the leading intellectuals in Liberia and his speeches and writings were internationally known. He became a citizen of the new republic and a strong proponent of Liberian nationalism. Crummell found the racism of the mulattos in Liberia to be intolerable. Even though Alexander Crummell had many health problems and personality conflicts in Liberia, he stayed there for 20 years. Alexander felt that the only hope for the African was the Gospel, not industrial education. Alexander felt that Africa could only be civilized by the black missionaries from the U.S. He felt this because he believed that the African Americans had a special adaptation to the climate, that they had a special relationship to the Africans, and that the theory of Divine Providence was true.[11]

His work in Liberia ran into opposition and indifference, and he returned to America in 1873. He returned to Washington, D.C., were he was appointed "missionary at large of the coloured people."[12] He undertook the founding and strengthening of urban black congregations that would provide worship, education, and social services for their communities.[13]

> Out of the temptation of Hate, and burned by the fire of Despair, triumphant over Doubt, and steeled by Sacrifice against Humiliation, he turned at last home across the waters, humble and strong, gentle and determined. He bent to all the gibes and prejudices, to all hatred and discrimination, with that rare courtesy which is the armor of pure souls. He fought among his own, the low, the grasping, and the wicked, with that unbending righteousness which is the sword of the just. He never faltered, he seldom complained; he simply worked, inspiring young, rebuking the old, helping the weak, guiding the strong.[14]

Throughout his life he would continue to urge the Christianization and civilization of Africa by skilled, educated blacks from all over the world. His book was entitled African and American and it was published in 1891.

Late in his career, he wrote and lectured widely against the increasingly entrenched racism of post-Reconstruction America, appealing to the educated blacks to provide leadership. He was a founder of the American Negro Academy (ANA) on March 5, 1897. One of the first to promote black intellectual and artistic ideas in response to the prevailing philosophy of Booker T. Washington.[15] Like many of the men gathered before him, Crummell defined culture in terms of a group's highest achievements in the arts, literature, and

---

8 Marilyn Lewis, "Independent Study Assignment: The African-American In Christian Mission: From Slave to Evangelist to Missionary," M. Th. Degree, January 1993.
9 DuBois, *The Souls of Black Folk*, 158.
10 James Keifer, The Episcopal Calendar, 1994 edition, Alexander Crummell, Priest, Missionary, Educator (September 10, 1898).
11 Marilyn Lewis, "Independent Study Assignment: The African-American In Christian Mission: From Slave to Evangelist to Missionary," M.Th. Degree, January 1993.
12 Ibid.
13 James Keifer, The Episcopal Calendar, 1994 edition, Alexander Crummell, Priest, Missionary, Educator (September 10, 1898).
14 DuBois, *The Souls of Black Folk*, 159.
15 Marilyn Lewis, "Independent Study Assignment: The African-American In Christian Mission: From Slave to Evangelist to Missionary," M.Th. Degree, January 1993.

scholarship.[16] After ANA's inception, five major objectives were instituted:

1. Defense of the Negro against vicious assaults.
2. Publication of scholarly works.
3. Fostering higher education among Negroes.
4. Formulation of intellectual taste.
5. Promotion of literature, science, and art.

Crummell emphasized African-American self-help and the need for education that was solid and practical.[17] It should be noted that ANA was the first and only body in America, at that time, to bring together Negro artists and scholars from all over the world. Eleven years after the founding of ANA, Alexander Crummell died (September 12, 1908) and Dr. W. E. B. DeBois was elected president.

DuBois wrote:

> I saw Alexander Crummell first at a Wilberforce commencement season, amid its bustle and crush. Tall, frail, and black he stood, with simple dignity and an unmistakable air of good breeding. I talked with him apart, where the storming of the lusty young orators could not harm us. I spoke to him politely, then curiously, then eagerly, as I began to feel the fineness of his character—his calm, courtesy, the sweetness of his strength, and his fair blending of the hope and truth of life. Instinctively I bowed before this man, as one bows before the prophets of the world. Some seer he seemed, that came not from the crimson Past or the gray To-come, but from the pulsing Now—that wandered in this same world of mine, within the Veil.[18]

---

16 Sandy Adell, "Foreword." *The Dictionary of Twentieth Century Culture: African American Culture*. Gale Group, University of Wisconsin, Madison, Afro-American Studies Homepage, http://polyglost.lss.wisc.edu/aas/adell.html.

17 Marilyn Lewis, "Independent Study Assignment: The African-American In Christian Mission: From Slave to Evangelist to Missionary," Master of Theology Degree, January 1993.

18 DuBois, *The Souls of Black Folk*, 152.

Bibliography

"African-American Historical Figures," http://www.brightmoments.com/black history/ncrummel.stm.

Adell, Sandy. "Foreword." *The Dictionary of Twentieth Century Culture: African American Culture*. Gale Group, University of Wisconsin, Madison, Afro-American Studies Homepage http://polyglost.lss.wisc.edu/aas/adell.html.

Crummell, Alexander. http://search.eb.com/blackhistory/micro/727/79.html.

Kiefer, James. The Episcopal Calendar, 1994 edition, Alexander Crummell, Priest, Missionary, Educator (September 10, 1898).

Lewis, Marilyn. "Independent Study Assignment: The African-American In Christian Mission: From Slave to Evangelist to Missionary," Master of Theology Degree, January 1993.

The Black Academy of Arts and Letters, Inc., 26th Anniversary, History. [BAAL, 1997 name changed in the state of Texas.] http://www.tbaal.org/history.htm.

William E. B. DuBois, *The Souls of Black Folk: Essays and Sketches*, Chapter 12, "Of Alexander Crummell," Chicago: A. C. McChig & Co.; [Cambridge]; University Press, Johnson & Son, Cambridge, U.S.A., 1903. Republished by Bantam Books, a division of Bantam Doubleday Dell Publishing Group, Inc. 1989.

1861–1894 Era: Civil War and Holiness Movement

Chapter 13
The Civil War (1861–1865) and Holiness Movement

by Robert J. Stevens

The Civil War was a "tense" moment in African-American history. Black evangelists went underground. During the Civil War, there were no recorded African-American missionaries travelling from the country.[1] During this time the first African-American Catholic priest, Augustus Tolton, was to be sent as a missionary to Africa but they kept him in the U.S. (about 1863).[2]

Missionary Boards Open Up Again

General missionary activity increased after the Civil War as the number of free blacks increased from 68,000 to over 665,000 and schools were open to pro-missionary advocates. The gains made in education and politics and civil rights began to manifest themselves on the mission field until 1877. By 1868, 12 of the 13 Presbyterian U.S.A. staff members in Liberia were blacks. Blacks serving under the Protestant Episcopal Church outnumbered whites by 21 to 5 in 1876.[3]

When the Civil War was over some of the churches, denominations and mission sending boards were active but much was changing with the African Americans. There was a new desire to establish an African-American national entity to allow them to carry out mission work. Lack of funds was a major hindrance. Some decided to join white mission-sending societies and others were refused help or decided to begin their own in order to carry out their work.

Integrated mission work was stressful on African Americans. The missionaries sent from all boards complained that when they were hired by the white missionary boards or churches, they were expected to work at a considerably lower salary than their white brethren (on the same mission field and many times doing the same work!).[4]

In a society dominated by patriarchal values, the Black Church became especially important for black men who were denied the normative masculine role in every area of social life. From the period of slavery until the civil rights era [1867], adult males were usually called "boy" by white southerners and only the black

---

1 Justo Gonzales, *The Story of Christianity*, vol. 1 (New York: Harpers and Row, 1984), 253.
2 Cyprian Davis, O. S. B., *History of Black Catholics in the United States* (New York: Crossroads, 1990).
3 http://wycliffe.org/history/blackmissions.htm.
4 Walter L. Williams, "Black American Attitudes Toward Africa, 1877–1900," *Pan African Journal* 4, Spring 1971.

minister was given a title such as "preacher" or "Reverend." Men and women of talent were called to be preachers and only the most politically astute could reach the levels of power as bishops and presidents of the black denominations and as the pastors of large congregations.[5]

Women's Role in Mission Changed

After the Civil War, so many men died that women were either widowed or unlikely to marry. This forced women into an unusual range of responsibilities. Since missionary boards still refused to send women directly to the work, women simply organized their own boards. First was the Women's Union Missionary Society. In the years to follow, many others were created. Their funds were raised above and beyond the regular denominational mission giving. Besides rousing women to go overseas, more than 100,000 women's missionary societies became active in local churches, an unmatched base for prayer and funding.[6] These women assisted a number of African-American missionaries to the field.

Education—A Key to Mission Advancement

No other area of black life received a higher priority from black churches than education. Sunday schools were often the first places where black people made contact with the educational process, first hearing, then memorizing, and finally learning to read Bible stories. With the aid of the Freedman's Bureau, some white philanthropists, and missionaries from the American Mission Society, individual black churches began to establish schools. A few of these schools, which were often housed in the basement of black churches, later became famous black colleges. Morehouse College in Atlanta, for example, traced its history to a school founded after 1866 in the basement of Springfield Baptist Church in Augusta. Started as a school in the basement of Friendship Baptist Church in Atlanta, Spelman College is also a vivid contemporary example of the role of the Black Church in education.[7]

One of the most important missionary and philanthropic endeavors on the African coast were the activities of Booker T. Washington and Emmett J. Scott from Tuskegee Institute. Tuskegee Institute opened in AL in 1881. Washington and Scott introduced a variety of agricultural programs in Togo and Liberia, supported by the British colonial government. Under President Robert R. Morton's administration, "Tuskegee emerged as a model for educational systems throughout British colonial Africa. Hundreds of missionaries, political administrators, and educators studied Tuskegee Institute's programs, visited the campus, and applauded its president."[8]

Holiness Movement

Christian Unions began with a mountain revival, 1886. Many of the African Americans became part of this "pentecostal" movement and as missionaries were self supported, or, if felt the call of God, went forward in faith to teach and preach. (Later this was called the Holiness Movement, then Holiness Church, and later established as Church of God in 1907.)

A confusion as to the distinction between Holiness and Pentecostal groups persists to the present time, and is exacerbated by the fact that in actual practice the lines distinguishing the two groups have been substantially blurred. Accurate statistics for either Holiness or Pentecostal groups are problematical, although the Pentecostals are widely acknowledged to be the fastest-growing segment of the black religious family.[9] The Church of God in Christ today is by far the largest of the Black Pentecostal groups.

Golden Age of Mission

The years of 1880 through 1910 are seen as the "Golden Age." Some 200 African-American missionaries were serving throughout the world—mostly throughout Africa—but also the

---

5 C. Eric Lincoln and Lawrence H. Mamiya, *The Black Church in the African-American Experience* (Durham, NC: Duke University Press, 1990), 206.

6 Marguerite Kraft and Meg Crossman, "Women in Mission," in *Perspectives on the World Christian Movement, A Reader*, 3rd edition, eds. by Ralph D. Winter and Steven C. Hawthorne (Pasadena, CA: William Carey Library, 2002), 271.

7 C. Eric Lincoln and Lawrence H. Mamiya, *The Black Church in the African-American Experience* (Durham, NC: Duke University Press, 1990), 251.

8 Sylvia Jacobs, "Black Americans and the Missionary Movement in Africa," *Contributions in Afro-American and African Studies*, no. 66 (Westport, CT: Greenwood Press, 1982).

9 C. Eric Lincoln and Lawrence H. Mamiya, *The Black Church in the African-American Experience* (Durham, NC: Duke University Press, 1990), 77.

West Indies. At this time the two large supporting blocks were the African-American church and white missionary organizations.[10]

Between 1863 and 1895, African Americans continued seeking to "flesh-out" their God-given mandate of sending missionaries to evangelize Africa. A number of outstanding African-American missionaries moved these efforts forward.[11]

---

10 Marilyn Lewis, "Overcoming Obstacles: The Broad Sweep of the African-American and Missions," *Mission Frontiers*, April 2000, 23.

11 David Cornelius, "African-Americans in Missions," in *Perspectives on the World Christian Movement, A Reader,* 3rd edition, eds. Ralph D. Winter and Steven C. Hawthorne (Pasadena, CA: William Carey Library, 1999), 289.

Chapter 14
Coloured American ME History

by Bishop Charles Henry Phillips

In Lovely Lane Chapel, in Baltimore, MD, where the first General Conference was held when American Methodism was put into organized form, centenary exercises were held. The various branches of Methodism sent representatives. Other noted gatherings of the year were the General Conferences of the Methodist Episcopal Church, at Philadelphia; the African Methodist Episcopal Church, at Baltimore; and the African Methodist Episcopal Zion Church, at New York.

"The General Conference of the Methodist Episcopal Church South—Important Question Asked and Answered—Religious Oversight of the Slave before the War—Some White Preachers who Labored for their Spiritual Good—M.E. Church, South, Takes Initiatory Steps Looking toward the Organization of Its Colored Contingent into a Separate Church."

When the General Conference of the Methodist Episcopal Church, South, met in April, 1866, in the city of New Orleans, this important question was asked by that body: "What shall be done to promote the religious interest of the colored people?" It was indispensably necessary that such a query should be raised. The war had just ended, and amid the changes of fortune and the vicissitudes of time the relation of slave to master had undergone a radical change.

When the war came on, the Methodist Episcopal Church, South, had 207,000 colored communicants. Their spiritual wants were administered to by faithful and earnest ministers of the Southern Methodist Church. GA and SC alone had as many as 60 ministers who served as missionaries to slaves.

Bishop James Osgood Andrew, ninth bishop of the Methodist Episcopal Church and secondary bishop of the Methodist Episcopal Church, South, having become connected with slavery by reason of a colored girl in his possession bequeathed to him by a lady, also by reason of a boy belonging to his daughter, and other legal slaves of his whom he secured to his second wife, actually became unacceptable to many Northern Conferences, and precipitated the occasion, if not the cause, of the great split in Methodism in 1844.

It was not unnatural that the Southern Methodist Church should, after the war, have shown a disposition to do what was best for her colored contingent. Gradually this contingent was either going into the African Methodist Episcopal Zion Church and African Methodist Episcopal Church. Such were the persecutions, misrepresentation, ridicule, and stratagems brought to bear against the Church, South, and especially its colored communicants, that many were tolled away; for, out of the 207,000 on the roll before the

From *Book Four: History of Colored Methodist Episcopal Church in America*, by Bishop Charles Henry Phillips, A.M., M.D., D.D., L.L.D., Publishing House C.M.E. Church, Jackson, TN, ©1925.

Used by permission.

Civil War, only 78,000 were found at its close. To save this remnant was the supreme though of the leaders of the Church, South. To organize them into an ecclesiastical body occurred to them as the only feasible thing to be done.

It was found at the General Conference of the Church, South, which met in Memphis in 1870, that five Annual Conferences had been organized, whereupon the bishops, in their message, inserted these words: "It is our purpose, unless you otherwise order, to call a General Conference to be holden next winter for the purpose of organizing them into an entirely separate Church, thus enabling them to become their own guides and governors."

The men that composed this General Conference and formed these committees were the pioneers of our Methodism. The work they accomplished has stood the test of more than 25 years. Truth, and an unselfish love for the general welfare of the Church, illuminated their thoughts and seemed to direct their way to wise conclusions.

There was absolutely no difficulty in giving a name to the new Church institution. The eight members of that committee, representing eight Annual Conferences, were of one mind, soul, and spirit. Their knowledge of early Methodism enabled them to select a name that would be closely related to the one by which the followers of John Wesley were first known in this country.

> Whereas we are a part of that same Church, never having seceded or separated from the Church; but in the division of the Church by the General Conference in 1844, we naturally belonged to the South, and have been in that division ever since; and now, as we belong to the colored race, we simply prefix the word "colored" to the name, and for ourselves adopt the name, as we are in fact a part of the original Church, as old as any in America; therefore be it Resolved, 1. That our name be the "Colored Methodist Episcopal Church in America."

In these days there arose an estranged relation between the African Methodist Episcopal Church and the Colored Methodist Episcopal Church, by reason of the former Church occupying property belonging to the latter, to which, by the action of the Methodist Episcopal Church, South, it was justly entitled.

In the antebellum days the colored Methodists of the South held their membership in the Methodist Episcopal Church, South; nor was said membership held by choice, but by necessity; they could not do otherwise. They were not allowed to form organizations among themselves, as they had done in the North. Hence when the African Methodist Episcopal Church made the attempt to gather them together, that Church was driving out as an Ishmael; but when the war had knocked off the shackles from the slaves, "Bethel" again came upon the scene and gathered many under her banner. This was not all; churches that belonged to the Colored Methodist Episcopal Connection, which had been turned over to it by the Church, South, the African Methodist Episcopal Church held for its own use, and many were never recovered.

This article by R. T. White, a prominent preacher in the GA Conference, appeared in the Christian Index, May 11, 1895:

> The Colored Methodist Episcopal Church in America was ushered into the world under the most unfavorable circumstances, and at a period that most critical ever known in the annals of Church history. The political struggle of the country had just terminated, leaving colored men what has been called a free man. Over this blessed bone the colored people went with enthusiasm. In the midst of universal rejoicing and gladness, though was given the Church as to how best to arrange for our people. Among the leaders of the race some cried one thing and some another. Propositions coming in from the North and also from the South, the leaders of the Colored Methodist Episcopal Church accepted the offer made them by the Methodist Episcopal Church, South, which resulted in what is known as the independent Colored Methodist Episcopal Church, a Church the very type and image of the one organized and set up by Christ himself; not noted for wealth or culture, but a Church noted for piety, integrity, and truth. The object of her organization was never more or less than the education of the race and the salvation of precious souls. Her mission, like his, is among the poor, the sick, and the needy.

The third General Conference was held in Louisville, KY, in August, 1874. The bishops' message was looked forward to with interest. The section on Missions was as follows:

> The missionary operations of the Church are important items, and come up for your review and inspection. We need money and other means to extend the kingdom of the Redeemer and to expose the desolate places throughout the country to the benign influences of the gospel of Christ. Something has been done in this direction, and something more may be and must be done in this particular before we can expect much from this part of our labour in the vineyard of our Lord. The great command is to "go into all the world, and preach the gospel to every creature." Nothing is more distinctive of a living, vital, and active Christianity than a healthy and successful missionary plan. The death of the missionary spirit in the Church is the prediction of the early death of the Church itself. It is intimately and inseparably connected with the interest of the Church at large, and is so inherent in and congenial to the gospel and Church of Christ that the destruction of the former would be the fatal, inevitable extinction of the latter. These are the appointed means and instruments employed by the great Head of the Church to make know his will to man. Whatever, therefore, impedes the one obstructs the other; and as a natural consequence the cause suffers, languishes, and dies. Hence the importance of the missionary work and the duty of the Church are apparent to all thinking minds.

In 1892, there were many important gatherings. The General Conference of the Methodist Episcopal Church met in Omaha, NE; the General Conference of the African Methodist Episcopal Church assembled in Philadelphia, PA; and the General Conference of the African Methodist Episcopal Zion Church convened in Pittsburgh, VA. In the two latter bodies the question of organic union was discussed at great length, and committees from both Conferences were appointed to meet and make arrangements for uniting. Upon the adjournment of these bodies it appeared from the surface that union was just in the distance; that plans necessary to lead up to such a desire realization had been consummated; and that a confederation of these two largest denominations of negro Methodists was no longer to be a forlorn hope. Suddenly, some complications arose; organic union was declared impracticable, if not impossible …

In October, 1896, the African Methodist Episcopal Zion Church, celebrated, in New York City, its 100th anniversary. The writer, who was an invited speaker, with no delegated authority, attended, and, at the request of the Programme Committee, made an address on "The Relation of the Colored Methodist Episcopal to the African Methodist Episcopal Zion Church." The celebration was a great success.

Senior Bishop J. A. Beebe called the Board to meet in Nashville, at Caper's Chapel, July 6, 1898. The Missionary Society was launched and I. S. Person, on the first ballot, was elected its Secretary. One of the liveliest discussions of the meeting was had over the adoption of a society for the young people of the Church. Some favored the Christian Endeavor organization, others the Epworth League. The Epworth League advocates finally won out and R. A. Carter, on the second ballot, was elected its first Secretary.

In the fall of 1898, Bishop Holsey continued his visits to the Annual Conferences of the Church, South, in the interest of Paine College. The Epworth League and Missionary Secretaries were moving over the Church with rapidity, getting acquainted with the Conference and the men, and explaining and giving information concerning their departments and their operations.

A gathering of particular interest was the Tripartite Conference of the bishops of the Colored Methodist Episcopal Church, the African Methodist Episcopal Church, and the African Methodist Episcopal Zion Church, which met in Washington, D.C., February 12, 1908. It was the first meeting of the kind ever held among Methodist bishops. It was remarkable in the spectacle which it presented, the brother fellowship by which it was characterized, and the harmonious action which marked the deliberations.

September 14, 1911, J. W. Gilbert sailed from New York to London, where he was to join Bishop W. R. Lambuth, of the Methodist Episcopal Church, South, and together they would journey to the heart of Southwest Africa, where they had hoped to establish a mission in the name of the Colored Methodist Episcopal Church. In the Christian Index this was printed:

> Occasionally you hear one speaking of offering himself for a candidate as bishop for

mission work in Africa. Sometimes such a person knows very little of the necessary qualifications for that service. No person should even think of going to Africa as a missionary who has not the mental qualifications. Zeal, earnestness, an abundance of religion are all desired, but without mental preparation, person possessing those fitnesses might be of some service in Christian work in America, but not in Africa. Dr. Gilbert and Bishop Lambuth informs us that he and Bishop Lambuth studied the native language of the Congo and Kassai Districts, known as the Baluba-Lulua, and made pretty good progress in that language.

At Teneriffe, the metropolis of the Canary Islands, they tarried some five or six hours. In his letter to the Christian Index of November 8, 1911, Dr. Gilbert wrote as follows:

> It is here at Tenneriffe that we donned our helmets, khaki suits, mosquito boots, and leather leggings. The amount of special outfits for the Congo is appalling—tents, filters, walking shoes, canvas low-cut shoes, helmets, leggings, mosquito nets, doubled covered white umbrella covers for helmets, medicine of 50 different kinds, Austrian blankets. Indian merino gauze for underwear, spine pads, pots, pans, plates, and a myriad of other things. Ours will be a pure camp life under our tent by night and on our feet by day. While at present we think well of the territory near the conference of the Kassai and Lulua Rivers, yet Bishop Lambuth seems anxious to go on clear across the continent to Lake Tanganyika, and thence perhaps to the Red Sea, or to the Indian Ocean at the mouth of the Zambezi. I shall stick to him until the last. Bishop Lambuth is so kind, considerate, brotherly, and consecrated to his African work that I love him with all my heart. One can't help it.

It is generally known that the religious services on the Belgian ships are Catholic. One Sabbath, in the Congo, these two travelers desired a service of their own, so they were joined by a Mr. Powell, a white Baptist missionary, and held a service in their own stateroom. Of this service Dr. Gilbert wrote the following interesting excerpt:

> The 15th chapter of St. John was read. Each one in turn commented on the reading, and each one in turn took the lead in prayer. There were four in that cabin, for the Holy Spirit joined us with such might and power that tears of joy and exclamations of praise to God made us forget the angry waves that lashed our vessel and the hungry deep that yawned for our bodies.

Bishop Lambuth and Dr. Gilbert desired to locate among the Batetel Tribe, some 450 miles from Luebo, after first traveling about 300 miles into the interior of Africa, making a total of 700 miles from Luebo. En route they encamped in 22 different villages, passed through 53 other villages, addressed more than 5,000 natives in thatch-covered arbors. In their break for the land of the Batetela they were accompanied by 80 natives. Dr. Gilbert, by studying the various mission posts, their methods, policy, and success, discovered that there were 39 Protestant and 53 Catholic mission stations in the Congo. Probably there has been an increase of missions since he wrote, late in 1911. Still, these mission posts are too few to do the work among the teeming millions of that dark region. Dr. Gilbert says, in the Index of March 14, 1912, writing from Lusambo, Congo Belge, Africa:

> As for me, I intend to do all in my power during the rest of my life for the evangelization of Africa. At home many preachers preach to the few. Here, a few preachers preach to the many, and they, too, being the most needy as well as the most neglected of the earth's heathen races. It certainly does seem that this field, the only mission field open to Negro Christianity, ought not to be neglected by our race. I am glad that the large Colored denominations at home have entered it in several places. The African Methodist Episcopals, the African Methodist Episcopal Zions, the Colored as well as the white brethren of the Methodist Episcopal Church, the Colored as well as the White Northern Presbyterians, the Colored and White Southern Presbyterians, Colored Baptists, white Baptists, are all here working side by side with no distinction as to color. Negro Catholics are here too in large numbers, having been trained for the work by various branches of the Catholic Church. Yes, and God helping me to be upheld in this effort by the Colored Methodist Episcopal Church, as well as by the Methodist Episcopal Church, South, I never expect to rest till my great Church

is at work here too. I am willing to risk wild beasts, wild men, and a treacherous climate in order to do so. I have learned that there are many such men in the ministry of my Church.

I have heard from my family in America but twice since last September. I don't know whether death or any calamity has befallen my family since the 23rd of last October, the date of the last letter from home. But I leave all those possibilities in the hands of my God, whose humble but willing servant I am. I hope my brethren will sing: "I am a stranger here, Within a foreign land," etc., and think of and pray for me when singing this song so expressive of my heart yearnings for the salvation of these poor, heathen, naked brethren of mine. Don't think of me as being unhappy here in the heart of the Dark Continent. Jesus is with me as never before. Hence I am the child of the King with him as my Saviour.

Bishop Lambuth and Dr. Gilbert, after crossing rivers and streams and being daily bitten by the dreaded Tsetse fly, the bite of which causes sleeping sickness, arrived safely at the village of the great chief, Wembo-Niama, on Thursday, February 1, 1912. They regarded this a splendid location. So, here, in the village of Chief Wembo-Niama and the surrounding country, "at an altitude of 2,500 feet above sea-level and on a slope admitting of excellent drainage four degrees south of the Equator," Bishop Lambuth located a mission for his Church. Of this location the Bishop says:

The climate is healthful, with cool nights. One can sleep under a blanket the year round. The food is abundant, including maize, millet, hill rice, yams, beans, mandioca or cassava, plantains, sugar cane, and pineapples. The soil is fertile and is capable of producing a variety of cereals and vegetables. One finds chickens, eggs, sheep, goats, antelope, buffalo meat, and fish in the streams. If the missionary desires it, a variety can be secured by adding snails, ants, caterpillars, and palm worms. The ants are half an inch long and are dried. With a little salt they are not bad, and resemble old bacon in taste. The caterpillars are broiled, dipped in palm oil, and swallowed head foremost. This station, the village of Wembo-Niama, is accessible, being only nine days' march from Bena Debele, on the Sankuru River, which empties into the Kassai, a southern tributary of the Congo, 80 miles above Stanely Pool. An even shorter road or trail can be cut through the forests. To reach it one would land at Matadi, at the head of navigation on the Lower Congo, travel two days by rail to Stanley Pool, take the Lapsley or a river boat, 14 days journey up the Congo, the Kassai, and the Sankuru to Bene Debele, on the east bank, and then on foot or by hammock, nine days, through forests and open veldt. The Batetela, half a million strong, are a vigorous tribe of warriors who migrated westward from the Laulaba River, which was explored by David Livingstone in the 70's. The bulk of the tribe are now found between the Lubefu and the Lomani Rivers. They are independent and self-respecting, never having been in slavery. They are open-eyed, alert, expert hunters and builders, and women are good agriculturists. I saw no native house on the Upper Congo comparable to those erected from the hard wood and the Borassus palm by the Batetela. The main streets of their village are over 100 feet wide and have from one to two rows of shade trees.

Bishop Lambuth found an open door on all sides. In the Congo Belge and surrounding country he thought there were twenty million men and women who had not heard of Christ. A few had a faint glimmer of light and had heard of men who would bring them the Mukanda (the book), but they were long in coming, said some of them to Bishop Lambuth, and "when it did come, we could not read it," said those anxious people seeking and longing for light, longing to be taught how to read the Mukanda. In these words Bishop Lambuth made a challenge to his Church and mine:

Professor Gilbert and I have pioneered the way by 5,000 miles of travel, 1,000 of which was on foot. We sought the place of deepest need, and under God found it the place of greatest encouragement. We visited many tribes, not a few of them cannibals, conferred with 50 chiefs, passed through 200 villages, ministered to over 400 sick, and found an open door on every side. We have led the way. Who will follow?

The Methodist Episcopal Church, South, accepted the challenge and opened a mission in the

Betetela tribe. The Congo Mission includes all the work of that Church in the Congo Belge, Africa.

The Colored Methodist Episcopal Church made a mistake, doubtless, in not taking steps, during the lifetime of Dr. Gilbert, in not accepting his and Bishop Lambuth's challenge to help assume the responsibility of African evangelization.

Our Church will be recreant to the great command of our Lord "to go into all the world and preach the gospel to every creature," till she kindles the camp fires of Christianity in the very bosom of Africa. When this is done, then will John Wesley Gilbert, the skillful linguist, the great Greek scholar, be remembered and most tenderly regarded as the pioneer, the pathfinder who blazed the way for the establishment of the Colored Methodist Episcopal Church in the Congo Belge, Africa.

The Twelfth Quadrennial General Conference met in St. Louis, Missouri, May 6, 1914, and closed on the 20th of the month. The message of the bishops, written and read by Bishop Williams, was delivered on the second day of the Conference. The message dealt with such subjects as "The Church," "Our Institutions of Learning," "The Epworth League," "Sunday School Department," "New Movements in the Church," "The General Departments," "Moving the Time-limit," "Raising the General Funds," "Our African Mission," "Cooperation with the Methodist Episcopal Church, South," and "The Election of More Bishops." Respecting cooperation with the Church, South, the message observed that our Church had already cooperated with that Church in educational work and that now it appeared Providence had intervened to make it possible for us to cooperate with our Mother Church to establish a mission work in Africa, Bishop Lambuth, of that Church, and John W. Gilbert, of ours, having founded a mission in the heard of the Dark Continent. In another chapter I pointed out the fact that nothing had been done by the Church up to this time to do mission work to any appreciable degree in Africa.

From May, 1918, to May, 1922, was a quadrennium full of vital interest and many varied and important happenings in the world, our own denomination as well as throughout Methodism generally. It has already been observed that the World War ended in 1918, and that the Armistice was signed on November 11 of this year. The industrial unrest, which had been considerably intensified during the war; the government control of big industries which had raised the question of making government and municipal ownership permanent; how to lay the foundation for the rehabilitation of the industrial, economic, educational businesses which had been greatly disturbed by the war were among the many problems that confronted the nation.

The General Conference of the Methodist Episcopal Church, South, meeting in May, in Atlanta, GA, elected to the College of Bishops Drs. John M. Moore, William F. McMurray, Urlan V. W. Darlington, Horace M. DuBose, William N. Ainsworth, and James Cannon, Jr.. The General Conference continued the Commission on Unification and voted to raise several millions of dollars during the quadrennial for education, Church extension, missionary work, and for retired ministers. It voted also, in connection with the Methodist Episcopal Church, which pledged itself to raise $80 million to celebrate the centenary of the beginning of Methodist missions, and for that purpose asked the Commission for $35 million.

In a word, the Centenary Movement was to advance the cause of home missions; to awaken the Church to a full appreciation of its relation to the industrial problems of the present day; to emphasize the possibility of fundamental changes in the social order so that the Church might begin a process of adaptation if it would hold its place as the most effective force in the world for good, and to push forward foreign-mission work along evangelistical, educational, and medical lines and "give 30,000,000 pagan black people the Gospel and thus protect them from the evils of advancing European civilization."

The Colored Methodist Episcopal Church sought to raise $1,000,000 as a centenary offering for education and missions. While this amount was not raised in its completeness, it is safe to say that more money was raised for all purposes for the Church during this quadrennium than any four years in history.

The celebration furnished an occasion for a revival in religion, education, in home and foreign missions, and in all the principles, doctrines, and spirit of Methodism generally.

In a former chapter we saw that the General Conference of 1918 decided, by a vote 304 to 48, in favor of organic union with the African Methodist Episcopal and African Methodist Episcopal Zion Churches. The question of unification was supposed, then, to be submitted to the Annual Conferences and various mission, circuits, and stations of the Connection. But it is rather remarkable that Bishop Smith should have failed to chronicle the action of the General Conference (and the Birmingham plan).

Bishop Smith in his "History of the African Methodist Episcopal Church" says that an effort was made to unite these two Churches in 1864. There was a stipulation in the plan that all the articles of agreement were to be submitted to the Annual and Quarterly Conferences of the two Churches.

The Zion Church carried out their agreement but the African Methodist Episcopal Church failed to do so. When, therefore, in 1868, the African Methodist Episcopal Church proposed a new plan for union the African Methodist Episcopal Zion Church rejected the plan because of the failure of that Church in 1864 to live up to its agreement of that year.

In 1886, the Commissions of the two Churches met in Philadelphia and adjourned to meet in 1887, in Atlantic City, NJ. Bishop S. T. Jones, of the African Methodist Episcopal Zion Church, being the only bishop of his denomination present, nothing was accomplished.

Accordingly, another effort at organic union was attempted when the African Methodist Episcopal General Conference met in Philadelphia, PA, in May, 1892, and the General Conference of the African Methodist Episcopal Zion Church met in May in Pittsburgh, PA.

The most difficult problem of this year in the way of unification seemed to have been the adoption of a name for the united Church.

The General Conference of the African Methodist Episcopal Zion Church proposed "African Zion Methodist Episcopal Church" as the title for the Church. It appears that the Commission of the African Methodist Episcopal Church, being in attendance upon the African Methodist Episcopal Zion General Conference at Pittsburgh, was in constant touch with its General Conference at Philadelphia. Finally, Bishop C. R. Harris, of the African Methodist Episcopal Zion Church, telegraphed to Philadelphia that "We prefer the title adopted by Commission, but, in spirit of accommodation, will accept African and Zion Methodist Episcopal Church."

But all the proposed names were rejected and organic union of the two Churches failed. The unification of these Churches was not attempted again till the Colored Methodist Episcopal Church joined the tripartite movement in 1918 and 1920. If they could not affect union when the Colored Methodist Episcopal Church was not involved, on what hypothesis could the Colored Methodist Episcopal Church be made a scapegoat because it would not accomplish for these two denominations what they could not achieve for themselves?

It is commendable to say that the failure of organic union left no bitterness in the ranks of the Colored Methodist Episcopal Church nor in any respect estranged its relation with the other two Churches.

Organic union is one of the most difficult problems that confronts Methodism. It is a subject quite easily talked about but very difficult to accomplish.

During the sessions of the African Methodist Episcopal General Conference at Philadelphia in 1892, where the unification of that Church with the African Methodist Episcopal Zion Church was defeated, Bishop D. A. Payne wrote and lad, according to Smith's history, this remarkable statement recorded:

The blessed Saviour, just before his betrayal by Judah to be crucified, knelt down in and prayed that all his people might be a universal unity. In accordance with the spirit of that prayer, I, as an individual, am willing to give up every name for the Church's sake. And I want to say now, that he who gets between the fulfillment of that prayer and God's Church will surely be crushed. God will sweep him from the face of the earth as a woman sweeps away dust with a broom. I am surprised that any brother should quibble over so small a thing as a name when it conflicts with the interest of God's Church.

The name African is not Scriptural but Zion is. Africa represents only a continent but Zion represents the Church—the whole Church. I hope that you will adopt the words of the telegram.

Bishop Payne's statement, dramatic and florid as it was, did not save the day for union.

A name for the new Church became the rock on which the contemplated organic-union ship of the African Methodist Episcopal and African Methodist Episcopal Churches was wrecked, just as the Birmingham plan became the quicksand in which the unification of the three Churches was drowned.

Chapter 15
Thomas Lewis Johnson: Africa For Christ–28 Years a Slave

by Thomas Lewis Johnson

GOD has indeed been gracious to me, in permitting me to awaken a deeper interest in African mission-work among my own people, chiefly in the Western States of America; so that I feel today I am doing more good for Africa than if I had been permitted to continue my labours there. ... Earnestly requesting the prayers of God's people on behalf of this great work, that Africa may soon be won to Christ, I am, yours truly for Africa."

Reverend Thos. L. Johnson, Preface to the Sixth Edition, "Shalom" House, 134, Upper Parliament Street, Liverpool, January 5th, 1892.

According to information I received from my mother, I was born August 7th, a1836, at a place called Rock-Rayman, in the State of VA; but I do not know the place, as I was removed when a child. ... My father was an octoroon (one-eighth negro blood) and a free man. When I was nearly three years old, Mr. Brent, who owned me, removed to Alexandria, VA. My father wanted to purchase my mother and myself, but the master would not sell. A free man was permitted to marry a slave woman, but her children would be slaves. My father died when I was nine years old. My mother said he left money for me to purchase myself when I became a man; but the white people got it, and I never received it.[1]

I can well remember how happy I used to be, playing in the yard with other children like myself, not knowing we were slaves. Sometimes we saw mother and others of slaves crying, and whispering to each other, but did not know what it meant. ... I remember one day seeing John, who was much older than the rest, with a small bundle in his hand, saying good-bye to his mother, while a white man stood waiting in the hall for him. ... Soon we heard that the man who took John was the "Georgia Trader." ... What seemed worse than all was the discovery that our mothers, whom we looked upon as our only protectors, could not help us. Often we were reminded that, if we were not good the white people would sell us to GA, which place we dreaded above all others on earth.[2]

Mr. Brent held some office in the Government, and he removed to WA when I was about seven or eight year old. If a slave was known to teach another he would be liable to be sent to the whipping post or to be sold; the law was very strict in regard to slaves being taught how to read and write. My mother's heartfelt desire

---

Thomas Lewis Johnson, b. 1836 first edition 2001, ca. 250K, Academic Affairs Library, UNC-CH, University of North Carolina at Chapel Hill.

Africa for Christ: Twenty-Eight Years A Slave by Rev. Thomas L. Johnson, a returned missionary from Africa, 112p., ill., London: ALEXANDER AND SHEPHEARD, 21 AND 22, FURNIVAL STREET, E.C., [1892]. Call number E185.97.J62A3 1892 (University of Virginia Libraries).

The electronic edition is a part of the UNC-CH digitization project. Documenting the American South. Used by permission.

---

1 Thomas L. Johnson, *African for Christ: Twenty-Eight Years A Slave* (London: Alexander and Shepheard, 1892) 9–10.
2 Ibid., 10–11.

seems to have been that I should be taught these things; and no opportunity was lost in trying to inspire me to look forward to freedom and an education. She told me what she knew about heaven, where there would be no slaves—all would be free. Then she would talk of Africa—how that we were all free there, but white people stole us from our country and made slaves of us. This seems to have been all she knew. To her, as to thousands of poor slaves, the Bible was almost a sealed book.[3]

Mr. Brent was sent on Government business to Buenos Aires. At this time I was sent on the farm. After his return, he settled down on a farm near Alexandria, VA, where in two years he died. It was my lot to fall into the hands of the son who used to cuff me so much about his slippers (not knowing left from right). His name was Arthur Lee Brent, and he was a doctor. The family were related to General R. E. Lee, of the Confederate Army. When only 12 years of age, I often thought of freedom, and, as time passed, I made inquiries about Canada. Accustomed to nothing but cruelty at the hands of the white people, we had never imagined that a great ruler, so kind to coloured people, could be otherwise than black; so the impression was that Queen Victoria must be black.[4]

I would often think of my mother's parting blessing. "Good-bye, my son; God bless you; be a good boy, say your prayers, and try to 'seek religion.'" At last I resolved to try to seek "religion." I was nearly 18 years of age. My master was a member of the church, and would teach me to say prayers, the Apostle's Creed, and read to me about Abraham's servants, and Isaac's servants, and Jacob's servants, and "servants obey your masters." He would read these nice things over to me so carefully, have prayers, and then when he felt like it (which he often did), give me a lashing. Yet with all this, my lot was much better than that of many around me. But whenever I commenced to think seriously on this matter, there was one obstacle which presented itself, I was superstitious, and believed in witchcraft and ghosts, as did all on the plantation. It was natural, we should. Superstition is characteristic of the race in Africa, having been brought to America, not permitted to be taught to read the Bible, and having every avenue to education closed against us. One day, I was out gathering black-berries, and commenced to pray the Lord's Prayer. I knew not what else to say. As I prayed, a rabbit jumped up from under the bush. I felt sure this was the devil. … I was never more frightened in my life.[5]

In the year 1835 Mr. Brent took to himself a wife, when I was to his brother, who lived in Richmond, VA. Here I met again my dear mother. This brother, Mr. William Brent, had always been kind to his slaves, and every member of his family followed his example. From this time I received better treatment. During all these years I had not lost sight of the lessons my dear mother had taught me. While away from her I worked hard to be able to make the letters of the alphabet, and had learned to spell a large number of words, which much delighted her.

I commenced after a while to pocket the nice-looking letters I saw, and, when my work was over, I would go to my room and try to make letters like them. But after I had copied them, I could not understand them. I did not know what to call them. The youngest son of Mr. Brent had a copy-book. I made up my mind to have one like it. I got on nicely, but another difficulty presented itself—I could not spell. I purchased a spelling book, kept it in my pocket, and every opportunity I would look into it. But there were so many words I could not understand. In the course of time young Mr. Brent became very kind and free with me, and would often read to me portions of his lessons. If I liked it and wanted to hear it again, I would say, "Lor's o'er me, Mos Carrol, read that again," which he often did. There was a large map of the U.S. hanging on the wall in the dining-room. In the course of time, I learned to spell nearly all the cities along the R. W. route from Richmond to Boston. … During this time I was thinking more or less about seeking religion. But how to get religion was what perplexed me; yet I felt it was essential to my happiness both here and hereafter.[6]

In the year 1857 there was a great revival in America. Many coloured people said the Judgment-day was coming. I often listened to the converts telling their experience, and I heard some say that, when they set out, the devil set out with them; that, while seeking, they would "fast and pray"; that the devil would do all he could to

---

3 Ibid., 11–12.
4 Ibid., 13–14.

5 Ibid., 15–16.
6 Ibid., 16–19.

turn them back. After about two weeks, having fasted all I could some days, on others taking a hearty meal, and having lost so much rest night after night, I got at last into a state I cannot describe. I can only say it was a living death.

After three weeks, I met a coloured man on the street, named Stepheny Brown. He was a Christian, and quite an intelligent man. He explained to me the simple Gospel, and how he had found peace. He told me to go to God, and say: "Lord, have mercy on me, a hell-deserving sinner, for Jesus' sake; set me out Thy way, and not mine, for Jesus' sake." "But," said he, "when you ask, you must believe that He will hear you and answer your prayer. I again resolved, if I lived a thousand years, I would never stop praying for "Jesus' sake." I went into the dining-room, fell down on my knees, and said, "O Lord have mercy upon me, a hell-deserving sinner, for Jesus' sake."

Everything appeared to be different to me. I did not see any great sights, but there was an inward rejoicing. The Lord Jesus was not one whom I had merely heard about but was now MY blessed Jesus—Jesus, the sinner's personal friend. But now, I thought if the master would only come to Jesus, he could be saved. I commenced to pray for the white people.[7]

I was anxious to unite with the Baptist Church. This I could not do, unless I had a "pass" from my master. He at once said, "No, you shall not unite with the Baptist Church." I think it was near three months before I again ventured to ask him. This time I received it at once in answer to prayer. When the Sabbath appointed for baptizing again arrived, my mother and I "went down into the water," hand-in-hand, and were baptized. Soon after my conversion, I felt a deep desire to preach the Gospel; but two difficulties presented themselves. First, I was a slave. Then, secondly, I could not read the Bible understandingly. … I often met with slaves in some secret place for prayer, though we knew, if we were found out, we would be locked up for the night, and the next morning receive from five to thirty-nine lashes, for unlawfully assembling together. Oh, we used to have such a nice time at these meetings, all the time watching for the policeman.[8]

I was in Richmond at the commencement of the war. I had to go into the army with young Mr. Brent, to cook. During the second year of the war Mr. Brent died. After his death, I had to be at home most of the time.

In 1863 I was married. My wife was maid to Mrs. Cooper, the wife of General S. S. Cooper, of the Confederacy. Mrs. Cooper was a sister of General R. E. Lee. By this time I could read fairly, as well as write, and could understand much in the papers. Many of the coloured people believed that the 11th chapter of Daniel referred directly to the war; we often met and read (in our own way) this chapter. Whenever we met, all our talk would be about what we had heard, and about freedom.

On Sunday, April 2nd, 1865, there was great excitement in Richmond; General Grant had taken Petersburg, and was closing in around Richmond. In the afternoon, many of the families commenced to leave the city. Late in the evening Mr. Jefferson Davis left … also General Cooper. About 4 o'clock on Monday morning, April 3rd, 1865, the magazine was blown up—the report was heard for miles. About 8 o'clock the U.S. troupes came in and took possession of the city. Many of the old men and women had prayed for the day they then beheld, and could hardly realise it. No doubt the sublimest State paper ever issued in America was the Emancipation Proclamation, which was sent forth on the 1st of January, 1863, by President Lincoln, who fell a martyr to American freedom.[9]

Just at this time many of our friends were perplexed to know what to do with us. Thousands were homeless, and, having been deprived of intellectual light and spiritual instruction, they were ignorant. But in the Northern States there were thousands of true-hearted Christians. Every branch of the Christian Church commenced to help the poor freedmen. The government established the Freedman's Bureau, General O. O. Howard was appointed superintendent. Through the kindness of Lieut. George Browning, U.S., I sailed with the soldiers for New York early in August. I soon got a situation in an hotel. In seven weeks I had enough money to send for my wife. Then I commenced again to study. After a year, I sent my wife back to the South to see if she could

---

7 Ibid., 19–22.
8 Ibid., 22–24.

9 Ibid., 24–26.

find her people—there were seventeen children in all. When she returned on this occasion she found her mother and father were dead. Eleven of the sisters were living. Mrs. Richardson, wife of Rev. C. H. Richardson, who went with me to Africa, was the youngest.[10]

Having heard much of the great West, I left New York in September, 1866, for Chicago, IL. Here I made up my mind to study hard, and try to consecrate myself more to the Master's work. I united with Olivet Baptist Church (coloured), composed of nearly all freedmen and commenced to do what I could. I went to work for Mr. H. M. Kinsley, a first-class caterer, in Chicago, who became a friend to me, and I thank God is one among those FRIENDS whom God has raised up for me, who continues to be a friend. ... All this time I was studying all I could. My principal studies were in my Bible.[11]

[The *Chicago Tribune* — at Kinsley's Thomas was made head-waiter. Mr. Kinsley could tell you if he pleased, of the great crush in the restaurant the night Grant was first nominated, and how, Thomas, the head waiter, buckled to work ... and took twenty orders at once at one table, and brought back the twenty complete dinners exactly as ordered. He had an extraordinary memory.][12]

In the spring of 1869, I was sent out to Denver City, Colorado Territory, to take care of a little church of freedmen, and to do mission work. They were not able to give me more than L57 a year. Hence my wife and I would work to make up a balance of our support. Many of my friends became deeply interested about Africa, from hearing me speak so much of the country and its people—for Africa was in my talk, in my prayers, and in my addresses. After spending three years in Denver, I left to go to Africa.

When I returned to Chicago, my friends persuaded me not to go, but to remain in the State. In 1873, I was called to Providence Baptist Church, Chicago, IL. Some of my hearers knew more than I did. What I wanted to know was the Bible. Dr. Blackall, of the Bible and Publication Society, had given me—"The Preacher's Prayer." It was an address given by Mr. Spurgeon before his students. It told me if I wished to "reap in the pulpit, I must plough in the closet ... " Oh! how often since have I felt the presence of my blessed Jesus with me when I have gone from my knees to the pulpit. I had charge of the church three years and six months, during which time we enlarged it and paid the debt.[13]

At last, I made up my mind that, as soon as I could save money enough, I would go to Africa on one of the American Colonisation Society's vessels. The American Baptist Missionary Society were not then sending out missionaries to Africa. I earnestly prayed over the matter, and begged the Lord, if it was His will that I should go to Africa, to open the way for me. On February 1st, 1876, I gave the church notice that in six months I expected to leave them and go to Africa. "I have no money, but I have faith." It was about this time that Dr. Murdock, of the American Baptist Missionary Society, called to see me, and promised to pay our passage to Liberia. We expected, after we got there, to trust the Lord for support. A few weeks after this I received two letters from England ... of the Young Men's Christian Association, Manchester, saying that if I could pay my way to England they would see that an opportunity should be afforded me of taking a course of studies before going to Africa. I wrote at once to say that I would come, and wrote to Mr. Murdock thanking him for his kind offer.[14]

On the 1st of September 1876 we arrived in Manchester. It was quite strange to me at first to see no coloured folks, but everywhere I was very kindly received. The way was opened for me to enter Mr. Spurgeon's College, where I commenced my first regular course of studies at forty years of age! When a slave in VA before the War, I heard of my owners talk of Mr. Spurgeon. I had often thought how much I would like to hear Mr. Spurgeon preach. Well, my blessed Jesus knew this, and granted me more than my desire, but it was a hard struggle. A short time in College proved that I did not actually know how backward I really was. I could not succeed until I asked help from my blessed Jesus.[15]

In August 1877, the Rev. C. H. Richardson and his wife came to England, to go with us to Africa. We went under the auspices of the Baptist Missionary Society of Great Britain. On the afternoon of November 9th we sailed from Liver-

---

10 Ibid., 26–28.
11 Ibid., 28.
12 Ibid., 84.

13 Ibid., 28–30.
14 Ibid., 30–33.
15 Ibid., 33–35.

pool on the ss. Kinsembo, and in the evening of November 22nd we came in sight of Cape Verde, on the West Coast of Africa.

"Delight thyself also in the Lord; and He shall give thee the desires of thine heart. Commit thy way unto the Lord; trust also in Him; and He shall bring it to pass." So delighted was I to be near the coast of the land for which I had prayed, and of which I had dreamed, that I could sleep but little. It was not long before we found ourselves anchored at the beautiful little town of Bathurst, on the Gambia River. The Gambia River is a magnificent stream, and is said to be navigable to a distance of nearly 400 miles. What is better still, here the messengers of "Life" have met great success in proclaiming the everlasting Gospel.[16]

On the morning of November 27th we entered the harbour of Free Town. The most pleasing feature in Free Town, and, from what I hear in the colony also, is the great progress made by the messengers of peace. Nothing has or can civilise and elevate like the Word of God. Christian schools have long since been established, and for years have made most wonderful progress. Our next stop was Grand Bassa, Republic of Liberia. It is formed entirely by coloured men from America and their descendants. The first article in her Code of Laws is that Christianity is the foundation of all law; the next is that education is a necessity admitting of no neglect. There are 30,000 of freed slaves from America and their descendants, with 2,000,000 natives, subject to their control.[17]

November 30th, at six o'clock in the morning, we arrived at Nifou, on the coast of Liberia. At twenty-five minutes to ten we stopped at Grand Cess, Liberia. Here, fifteen canoes came out, with from three to twenty men in each. These belonged to the Kroo tribe, the aborigines of a part of Liberia. All the steamers reaching Sierra Leone and the coast of Liberia take on board a gang of "Kroomen" to do the work of the ship in the hot climate. We thank God that to-day hundreds of boys and girls and young men and women from Africa are in schools and colleges of Europe and America, being prepared to return as teachers and missionaries.[18]

"Native African Boys being educated in Central Tennessee College, Nashville, U.S. Momolu Massaqui (Albert Thompson)… a member of the Vey tribe, dwelling on the West Coast of Africa. He was educated in the Episcopalian School in Sierra Leone. Benjamin Payne is fifteen years old, and is a member of the Bassa tribe. He had received some training in Miss Sharp's school, at Monrovia. Frank and Harold are of the Kroo tribe. Frank has attended a feast of the cannibals of his tribe, and tasted the flesh, which he says was good. Frank has a strong body and will, and exhibits some of the traits of an undisciplined boy. Gilbert Haven is of the Dey tribe. He is willing to get his lessons, and behaves in school with much more decorum than some boys who have had their birth in a Christian land. They all seem to understand that they are here to be educated for teachers of their people in Africa." —Chicago Appeal.[19]

The more important towns on the West Coast include Elmina … Accra … Lagos. Bonny, one of our stopping places, was in past years a favourite rendezvous for slave ships. Only about 12 or 15 years since they were all cannibals. … Archdeacon Crowther, a native, who has charge of the mission work, invited me to dine with him. Not only has the preaching of the Gospel done great good in Bonny, but far in the interior they are giving up their idols, and bowing to the "one true God."[20]

After stopping a short time at the Island of Fernando Po, where we were entertained by the wife of the British Consul, we arrived at Victoria, Cameroons, on the afternoon of Saturday, December 14th, 1878. This was our destination. … Here I had the opportunity, for the first time in my life, to speak for my blessed Jesus in Africa, the land of my fathers. I took for my text "Believe on the Lord Jesus Christ, and thou shalt be saved" (Acts 16:31).

For years Victoria has been a city of refuge. … Here no one is allowed to hold slaves or sell his daughters for wives, and no one is allowed to be punished for witchcraft, etc.. Today there are over 400 of these refugees in Victoria, where they are brought under the influence of the Gospel, and their children taught in the day-school. Many of them have become Christians.[21]

---

16 Ibid., 36–38.
17 Ibid., 38–40.
18 Ibid., 42–43.

19 Ibid., 43–45.
20 Ibid., 45–46.
21 Ibid., 49–51.

Dear friend, you who now read these pages—you who were born in this Christian land, where you have the Gospel. My prayer is that, if you cannot go to Africa and preach the Gospel or teach the people, you will at once resolve to do all you can to send others to teach and preach. While we are in this Christian land enjoying Gospel privileges, millions are slaves to superstition and witchcraft in Africa, perishing for want of the Word of Life.[22]

We had not been in Victoria three days before I was taken with the fever. On January 20th, Rev. C. H. Richardson and Rev. Q. W. Thomson left for the interior, to select a new station; I, being ill, could not go. On the 4th of February Mr. Thomson returned. Mr. Richardson having suffered with fever, had been left at Bakundu, 80 miles in the interior, with two native Christians. Bakundu had been selected as the new mission station. Although we knew that the traders along the river objected to interior mission work, we concluded we would go by water on account of the ladies. The Rev. G. Grenfell volunteered to go with us.[23]

These people can talk to each other on their drums almost as well as we can send a message in this country by telegraph.

On this occasion, this man said on his drum, "White man come to take our country." Saturday morning ... several canoes passed us with from 15 to 20 men in each. Seeing they were well armed with guns and cutlasses, I began to feel suspicious. Soon we were off. About 10 o'clock we came up to them. They had all stopped on the beach, put on their war caps, and stood in a line along the river. We were ordered to come ashore. We told them we would not; if they had anything to say, they must come out in their canoes. ... I do not know of any time in my life when I realised the promise of my blessed Jesus more than in this hour, "Lo, I am with you alway." I said to my wife and her sister, Mrs. Richardson, "We lean upon the Lord." ... We soon found it was impossible to proceed; hence we had to return as prisoners to Mungo. We were within six hours of Bakundu beach.[24]

There were many of the traders at Mungo who could talk broken English, and who knew how the English protected the missionaries. Mr. Grenfell, who had been several years in Africa and knew something of the people, threatened them with English authority. After the king...held a consultation, he said to me, "You must pay for passing through my country." To this we agreed. I gave him a large overcoat, a bag of rice, a box of sugar, a blanket, and a barrel of crackers.[25]

I have already mentioned that the best roads in this part of Africa are mere footpaths through the forest ... on which the natives walk single file ...each man with his load on his head and his cutlass in his hand ... to defend himself against any beast or serpent that may be in the path. ... There are some eight or ten towns between Victoria and Bankundu. ... We had a company of 30 men with us when we arrived. ... The first thing I was struck with was the joy of the king. For years he had desired to have a missionary in his town. ... On Sunday we held a meeting in an old unoccupied house. We found the people slaves to superstition and witchcraft.[26]

The custom of giving cass-wood juice prevailed here. The first case we heard of was a young man in the town who was accused of witching his sister's child. He was made very ill from the effects of the juice, but finally recovered. As soon as we heard of it, Mr. Richardson ... went at once to the king and told him how wrong it was to allow such a practice. The king promised to put a stop to it. He kept his word.[27]

When we first arrived at Bakundu we could hardly sleep at night for the yells of the people and their dance and the beating of their drums. They knew nothing of the Sabbath. ... Mr. Richardson went to the king to have a law passed that no work or drum-beating or dancing should be done on the Sabbath. The old man consented. ... They had great faith in what the Bible said. On one occasion, while Mr. Richardson was away with men at Victoria, the women came to me to get me to ask the Bible if their husbands were safe.[28]

Soon after our arrival in Bakundu we all commenced to pray that God would convert the king. ... One day he sent for me, and I found him very ill. ... He said: "Witch make me sick, tell me not to take white man's medicine, and I take this medicine, get my stomach full, old witch come in my mouth, go in my stomach, he get blind and come

---

22 Ibid., 52.
23 Ibid., 52–53.
24 Ibid., 53–54.

25 Ibid., 54.
26 Ibid., 55–56.
27 Ibid., 56.
28 Ibid., 57.

out." I tried to persuade him to believe that all power was in the hands of God; that by believing and trusting Him all these fears would leave him. … One Sabbath afternoon my wife and I both lay ill in bed. …We were sent for. I was hardly able to get out of bed, but we were soon in his presence. … The old man was very weak, and it seemed he would soon pass from time into eternity. … His youngest son, "Ngatee," about ten years old, was called to his side. … "I give this boy to you. Take him and bring him up as you own child; dress him like white man; teach him to talk English and to read and write. His brothers will get a wife for him." … "Don't fear; I'm going now. … Take care of him; be a father to him and the people." … Mr. Richardson then told again the story of God's great love, and that if he would believe and trust in the Word of God we would meet him in heaven. I then said, "Ta Ta Nambulee" (for that is what he was called), "you say you are going now; are you prepared to meet God?" "Ah!" said the old man, "I have been ill these ten days, and He has taken care of me; I can still trust Him." … After we had gone, he said to his son who was to succeed him, "Etau, whatever these men tell you, believe it; I have found them to be true men." … We arrived in Bakundu, February 22nd, 1879. The king died in the latter part of June. Oh! what gratitude we ought to feel that we have been favoured with the Gospel.[29]

The attention the people gave to the preached word Sabbath after Sabbath was very encouraging. The young king passed a law that "if any man or woman worked on the Sabbath that they should pay a cow. If they had no cow, their house should be pulled down over their heads." The Bakundu, as in all the towns along the route, the children are all naked. … As soon as they became more acquainted with us they wanted us to give them clothing. … They are very kind-hearted, and in every way differ much from the surrounding and coast tribes. Many of the West African tribes are continually at war. You hear of their drinking the blood and eating the hearts of their enemies; of walls covered with human skulls; of a pavement made of human skulls, to walk on. Truly, "the dark places of the earth are full of the habitations of cruelty."[30]

These people have queer superstitions, and one must be among them to realise what slaves they are to them. … These people have their Ju Ju houses, or Fetish temples, like the rest of the tribes; there are three in Bankundu. Here they have their sacred meetings. What they do, and how, I could never find out; but this I know, that the preaching of the Gospel and the untiring zeal of Mr. Richardson, fighting against error, have been the means of many of the young men losing faith in Ju Ju. … They believe that there is a Great Being who has great power, but make no connection between Him and themselves. They do not expect anything from Him; neither do they attribute to Him any qualities good or bad. Their gods are many. … I was greatly impressed with the intense desire of the people to be taught. … One Sabbath evening after service some 15 or 20 came to our house to be more fully informed about the plan of salvation, and this too, without having been invited to come. … But it will take many years to get them out of their superstitions.[31]

About the 1st of March, 1879, my dear, faithful, good, loving, Christian wife (after nursing me until I got better) was taken down with a fever. … From that time until her death she was never well. … Day after day, from morning till night, and from week to week, she would find no greater comfort than reading her Bible. On Sunday morning, June 29th, I lay in bed ill. … On Friday, July 4th, she was taken down with the fever. The following Monday she slept nearly all day. At night she said, "All of this day has been lost; I have not read my Bible any." I read for her. Her favorite text was "I shall be satisfied when I awake with thy likeness" (Ps 17:15 KJV). Though she could speak but a few words of the language, she was indeed dearly beloved by the men, women, and children of Bakundu. They all called her, "mamma." I do not think a more devoted wife ever lived.[32]

From the time of my arrival at Bakundu … to November, I do not think I spent two weeks in succession of good health. … After suffering from month to month, unable to do my duty, … Rev. Q. W. Thomson, … sent the Rev. Mr. Wilson, … up from the coast to accompany me to Victoria. I was so ill I had to be carried 80 miles in a hammock by the natives. I returned to England, hoping soon to recover, and after five or six months to be able to return to Africa, and again

---

29 Ibid., 57–59.
30 Ibid., 60–61.
31 Ibid., 61–64.
32 Ibid., 64–66.

enter upon my work But after medical examination, I was advised not to return to Africa. ... I do not remember having a more trying time than this, unless it was when I first set out "to seek religion." ... All I could do was to take the matter to my blessed Jesus in prayer. ...and I am indeed thankful to say my prayer was answered.[33]

The Committee furnished me with means to return home. Mrs. Spurgeon made me a present of some nice books, and Mr. Spurgeon of L10. I shall never forget the words he said to me as I took leave of him: "If you don't get on, let us know. We will not forget you."[34]

Starting from Liverpool, August 4th, 1880, I arrived the 1st of September I met the Wood River Baptist Association, composed entirely of coloured people. I presented the claim of Africa and urged upon them the necessity for their united effort to commence at once mission work in Africa. [T]he following is a synopsis of their report which was received and adopted—"From the shores of Africa, teeming with millions in grossest darkness of heathenism, we see more clearly than ever the prophetic picture of Ethiopia 'stretching out her hand unto God,' and praying for teachers of His Word to be sent to teach them the way of the true and living God. ... We advise that the Board immediately appoint Rev. Thomas L. Johnson, returned missionary from Africa, as its missionary and agent in both its domestic and foreign work."[35]

I then visited two Associations in the State of MO. ... In November of the same year, I met ... two other Associations, representing in all a membership of over 60,000 freed men. So anxious were the people for information about Africa and what I had seen, that I published a little pamphlet of 64 pages, telling of my visit to Africa and setting forth her claims. ... At meeting after meeting I would see strong men and women weeping, as I would tell the story of what I saw in Africa. ... I can now see more than ever the hand of God in my return to America. Among other returned missionaries to America, God was pleased to use me in the Western States and Territories. My health continued bad, yet I thank God, I was able to work on most of the time. ... The one thought and desire of my soul was, AFRICA FOR CHRIST. Our object was to secure the cooperation of the coloured Baptist of the North-west for the purpose of raising funds, and appointing and sustaining missionaries of our own race among the long-benighted people in Africa. Thank God! This has been accomplished.[36]

At the Seventh Annual Meeting of the Baptist General Association of the Western States and Territories, the following resolutions were unanimously adopted:

1. To send qualified missionaries to Africa.
2. To establish mission-stations on the Congo, and wherever in the dark neglected land of Africa the Lord may direct.
3. The enlistment of the interest of the Coloured Churches of the U.S. in the African mission work.
4. That five thousand dollars be raised, and one or more missionaries be immediately employed, and as soon as practicable commence mission work in Africa.
5. That the Executive Board of this body take such steps as in their judgment may be best for the prosecution of this work, and suggest quarterly missionary meetings in every church, and at all annual meetings of the District Associations in each State. That all churches and Sabbath-schools connected with the District Associations form mission circles to raise funds for this purpose.

In the month of July, 1881 ... I was married to my second wife and returned to England. ... I was informed ... that it was the intention of the brethren to request me to become the Financial Agent of the mission. I wrote to say I would serve, etc. ... I discovered I had a grand opportunity to do good for two countries at the same time. Raise up friends for Africa by winning souls for Jesus in England. ... I attended all kinds of missions and meetings in England, Ireland, Scotland, and several towns in Wales. I visited ragged schools; mission halls; mother's meetings; working men's meetings; Bible-classes; Band of Hope meetings; blue ribbon meetings; Gospel Temperance meetings; meetings for railway men; meetings for postmen; noon meetings in shops; warehouse meetings; noon meetings in machine shops and foundries; the theatrical mission in London; Y.M.C.A. meetings; Y.W.C.A. meetings; tea meet-

---

33 Ibid., 66–67.
34 Ibid., 67.
35 Ibid., 67–68.

36 Ibid. 68–70.

ings, and Christian policemen meetings, and, thank God, it was my privilege to attend many Bible readings and Consecration meetings.[37]

Extract from the Annual Report for 1884 of the Executive Board to the General Association of the Western States and Territories:

Twelve years ago the General Association of the Western States and Territories was organised by the coloured Baptist at Mexico, Adrian County, MO. At the time of its organisation the coloured people of the U.S. had been only ten years out of bondage. ... In 1880 a special meeting was called. ... The Rev. Thomas L. Johnson, having returned from Africa, ... was present at this meeting.[38]

Accordingly the General Association adjourned to meet in Chicago, IL, in 1881. At this meeting it was resolved to go immediately to work to raise a fund for establishing, at the earliest practical time, a mission in Africa. To facilitate this work, by furnishing information, and to aid in organising in the churches, auxiliaries, and mission bands, it was resolved to publish a religious weekly paper as soon as funds could be obtained to commence its issue. A plan was adopted to that effect for the work proposed. But the poverty of the people, who had so recently been slaves, and the constant strain to provide for the support of religion amongst themselves, had been the hindering cause, retarding the laid out by the brethren at this meeting.[39]

The attention that is now being given to African missions in the Western States and Territories is in a large degree the result of the labours of Rev. Thomas L. Johnson since his return from Africa. ... The encouragement he has received from Christians of all denominations in Great Britain, who have with their characteristic Christian liberality responded with generous donations upon his presentations of his work for Africa, has caused his brethren on this side of the ocean to take courage and go forward.[40]

By divine Providence, "a great door and effectual is open to us all," to plant evangelical Christian missions into the interior of the continent of Africa. This is most encouraging to us, since the establishment of a Free State in Central Africa, under the protectorate of the powerful Christian nations of Europe and America, in which absolute religious freedom and protection is guaranteed to missionaries to the natives.[41]

Then comes the transfer of the Livingstone Inland Mission on the Congo, to the American Baptist Missionary Union, by the Christian men and women in Great Britain who established and equipped it. And from this society comes the invitation to the coloured brethren in America, descendants of the African race, to co-operate with them in this mission."[42]

The *Chicago Herald*:

> A brilliant assemblage in Kinsley's Banquet Hall yesterday afternoon pays tribute to the worth of a most deserving coloured man. The negro is Thomas L. Johnson. ...born a slave, entered the employ of Kinsley as a dish-washer, was promoted to the post of head waiter at 100 dols. a month, felt himself called upon to engage in missionary work, was successful. ... He returns to Chicago as the accredited agent of the African Missionary Society; he enters a hall into which, until yesterday, no coloured man had gone except as a servitor; he is the honoured guest of his former employer. ... Johnson is six feet in height, with pronounced African lips and nose. He has the forehead of a Caucasian, an honest eye, and a face on which energy and kindness are written."[43]

> I hardly know what I am: I am not an octoroon, a quadroon, nor a mulatto, but I believe that my grandfather looked like that" (pointing to a large picture of the typical negro of the Guinea coast of Africa). "Wooly head, thick lips, flat nose, black negro. I am not black, you see, as was my grandfather, and in Africa I was always spoken of as a white man." ... To hear the story of Johnson' African experience was a rare treat. ... In the Congo Free State there are 5,000 miles of fine waterway, and over fifty millions of people. In Africa to-day 250,000,000 are stretching out their hands and straining their eyes, praying for the light. Of missionaries there are three to every million inhabitants. The horrors of cannibalism and slavery were pictured. ... Africa for centuries

---

37 Ibid., 70–72.
38 Ibid., 80–81.
39 Ibid., 81.
40 Ibid., 82.

41 Ibid., 82.
42 Ibid., 82.
43 Ibid., 86–87.

has been a manhunting land, and nearly every other nation had had a hand in making slaves of negroes. ... The Hottentot, the Nubian, and the aborigines of Australia all came in for mention, the conclusion reached being that the white man cannot Christianise Africa owing to the climate. ... Calling his coloured friends to his side, Johnson sang a solo, and all united in the chorus. It is no exaggeration to say that sweeter music has rarely been heard in Chicago than the notes which had been fitted to these words.

> O, Africa, thou long hast been
>
> Of sin and ignorance the scene,
>
> For ages trodden in the dust,
>
> The slaves of selfish men of lust;
>
> How long has densest darkness reigned,
>
> And cruelty her way obtained,
>
> O'er thy poor sons whom God designed
>
> To worship Him with heart and mind.[44]

Johnson brings from Africa a rare collection of curiosites, which he exhibited to *The Herald* reporter at the conclusion of his lecture. A large necklace is braided of sea shells, which are the coin of certain tribes. He has a cutlass once used by an Arab slave trader, and the iron neck-yoke and twenty-pound shackles now worn by slaves while being driven in droves to the coast. He has the full costume of an African chief, with spear made from ironwood. ... Of the numerous specimens of African handiwork which Mr. Johnson exhibits, there is one napkin made of grass which will rival anything of European manufacture in delicacy of texture. [O]ne day engaged in explaining the Darwinian theory to a very intelligent chief. ...the chief assured him that Darwin had "completely reversed the real facts of the case." "Many suns and moons ago," explained the Mungo sage, "some of our fathers and brothers who were hunting became separated from the tribe and wandered off into the forests. Such became their destitution that they were obliged to feed on the food of animals. By-and-by they became like brutes, and the monkeys and apes which are found in our forests are the descendants of those who, many, many suns and moons ago, were the ancestors of our great-grandfathers." ... The Hottentots are the treacherous and ferocious, but six of their languages are now printed, and the missionaries are lifting them up out of the degradation which slavery has imposed. On the Mungo the people can talk to each other on their drums by a system of sound resembling the Morse telegraphic alphabet.[45]

Johnson is labouring to evangelise Africa with the same faithful, conscientious effort which characterised him when he was a waiter in this city. His salary is 75 dols. a month. ... "My only object in alluding to my former condition of bondage is this: I want to encourage the young coloured men of this country to persevere in the right direction. No matter what their present discouragements are, they must learn to labour and to wait."[46]

Chicago Conservator February 23, 1889. Evansville, IN, February 18, 1889. —

> The coloured people of Indiana, as in other sections of this country, are deeply interested in the changes which will take place when the new administration shall take the reins of government. ... For this reason, ...the undersigned, ...ask the use of your columns to suggest the appointment of Rev. Thos. L. Johnson, of Chicago, as Minister to Liberia. ... The subject of this sketch is a man of marked ability, fine culture, and national reputation. He is known and highly endorsed by the best men of the Old and New Worlds. That a man of his calibre is needed to fill posts of so high a degree of honour, goes without saying. ... The Conservator cordially endorses the letter which presents his name, and will add that IL has no coloured citizen more acceptable as a representative than the distinguished traveller, Rev. Thomas L. Johnson.[47]

---

44 Ibid., 88–89.
45 Ibid., 89–90.
46 Ibid., 90.
47 Ibid., 92–93.

Herald, July 1889: —

The motto of my soul has been —"Africa for Christ." For years this one prayer has gone up from my heart to God. Oh, God, give me Africa for Jesus. And this was not only the prayer of daily devotion, but often in the silent hours of the night, when after awakening from sleep. Africa, Africa, poor long neglected Africa, land of my fathers, would come before me, and as I would contemplate the scheme of my life, the conditions of Africa's millions, of how little was being done, of how much there was to be done, from the depth of my soul would come—"Oh, God, give me Africa for Jesus." ... From month to month I have struggled on, often suffering severe pains, sometimes so weak that I could hardly hold out. But "Africa for Christ" would inspire me. ... Now the time has come that I must stop travelling in the interest of Africa. This seems to be God's will. Bless the Lord, He never made a mistake. Thank God the work will not stop. ... Brethren, pray for me that if it is God's will I may yet do a great work for Africa."[48]

After long years of slow progress and preparation, the time has now come for Liberia to enter upon her great mission of sending the Gospel to the millions in the interior. ... Today the Liberians are more than ever awake to their privileges. ... I believe Africans must be sent as missionaries to Africa. ... We are tied to that people by ties of consanguinity, of suffering and wrong. ... The history of the returning exiled sons and daughters of Africa to the Republic of Liberia, and their success, is a standing proof that the freemen of America can stand the climate and hence are better suited as missionaries.[49]

There are two missionaries now in England who will go with me to Africa ... Rev. R. L. Stewart, and Miss Virginia Jones. ... There are hundreds of young (coloured) men and women in America, with good common education, whose souls yearn for Africa; all they need is Bible and Mission training for six months or a year. I shall be thankful to any friend who read this little book who will assist me in my mission by selling copies.[50]

---

48 Ibid., 93–95.

49 Ibid., 96–98.
50 Ibid., 102.

Chapter 16

The Story of the Lord's Dealings with Mrs. Amanda Smith

by Amanda Smith

Amanda Smith: "God's Image Carved in Ebony"

On the plantation of Darby Insor, Long Green, MD, Amanda Smith was born, January 23, 1837, a slave child. Her mother, Miriam Matthew's, was a slave of Dr. Shadrach Green. Her father, Samuel Berry "Smith," was quite an enterprising entrepreneur. He made and sold brooms and husk mats which helped him to buy freedom for himself and his five children. Amanda was the oldest girl.

Her parents had 13 children in all, and both Amanda's mother and grandmother were dedicated Christians. "My father and mother both could read. ... Always on Sunday morning after breakfast he would call us children around and read the Bible to us. I never knew him to sit down to a meal, no matter how scant, but what he would ask God's blessing before eating."[1] "I never remember a time when I went to bed without saying the Lord's Prayer as it was taught me by my mother."[2] Amanda was mainly self-educated ... "and had only 3 1/2 months of actual schooling, but she was a young lady with determination. " ... [M]y brother and I walked five and a half miles each day, in going and returning, and the attention we received while there was only such as the teacher could give after the requirements of the more favored pupils had been met."[3] At 13 she began working for a widow with five children in Strausburg, PA. There she attended a revival in the Methodist Episcopal Church which she later joined. "I went home and resolved I would be the Lord's and live for him."[4] Bishop William Taylor was her friend.

Amanda's only experience with slavery was with her father's assistance with the underground railroad. "One night during camp meeting. ... A man came and knocked at the door. ... He had come away from LA. ... someone shouted, ... 'We want that nigger you are harbouring, he is a runaway nigger.' The man jumped and ran up stairs. ...they were beating father and trampling all over us children on the floor. We were screaming. ... The poor man jumped out of the window upstairs and ran about two

---

All inserted quotes from *An Autobiography. The Story of the Lord's Dealings with Mrs. Amanda Smith the Coloured Evangelist; Containing an Account of Her Life Work of Faith, and Her Travels in America, England, Ireland, Scotland, India, and Africa, as an Independent Missionary*: Electronic Edition. (Rare Book Collection, UNC at Chapel Hill.) Documenting the American South (http://docsouth.unc.edu), The University of North Carolina at Chapel Hill.

Used by permission.

---

1 Amanda Smith, *An Autobiography. The Story of the Lord's Dealings with Mrs. Amanda Smith the Coloured Evangelist; Containing an Account of Her Life Work of Faith, and Her Travels in America, England, Ireland, Scotland, India, and Africa, as an Independent Missionary*, Electronic edition, 25–26.
2 Ibid., 26.
3 Ibid., iv.
4 Ibid., 28.

hundred yards, when Ben Crout's blood-hound caught him and held him till they came. ... That was the first and last darkey they ever got out of Sam Berry's clutches."[5]

Spiritually, she believed as the Methodist and sought the second blessing of sanctification.

> "One day as I was busy about my room I seemed to feel the conscious presence of Jesus. I saw nothing with my eyes, but I seemed to be conscious of the presence of a Holy Being by me and around me, and I talked with Him, and I was saying, 'Now, if anyone should ask me to tell the difference between justification and sanctification, how could I tell them? There is a difference; I know it; I feel it; but I don't know how to tell it.' And the dear Lord Jesus seemed to answer my question by asking another. He said, 'What is the difference between sunlight and moonlight?' In a moment I saw it. I knew the beauty of the lovely moonlight. I had read by its brightness, and had often sewed at night, and it was beautiful. That was my justified state. How many times, I did not understand clearly, as in the sunlight; but the deeper experience was in power like sunlight in the natural world. It penetrates the dark corners. If there is even a small nail-hole in a door, or crack anywhere, the sun finds it out and looks through; then it heats up everything all about it. There can be no frost where the sunlight is; but it is tropical all the time. There were deep recesses in my heart that the moonlight did not reveal, but when the great sunlight of sanctification came, how it seemed almost to eclipse the moonlight state of justification, save the abiding consciousness of the time when God wrought that first work in my soul. ...
>
> That means two distinct states as real as the moonlight and sunlight. I knew it was true, but, O, why should there be a December in my heart when I may have the beaming sun? When the Holy Ghost came to my soul in sanctifying power it was the inaugural of a perpetual May-day that shall go on increasing in faith, and light, and strength, and power, and thanksgiving, and praise, and rest, and peace, and triumph forever and ever and ever. Amen. Amen."[6]

She married Clavin M. Devine, September 1854. Amanda married young believing all the promises made when Calvin wooed her. "He could talk on the subject of religion very sensibly at times; but when strong drink would get the better of him, which I am sorry to say was quite often, then he was profane and unreasonable. We had two children. The first died; the other, my daughter Maze."[7] Life was hard and her finances were few. Amanda had a reputation for her MD biscuits and her fried chicken. She ironed and washed clothes for a living. Her sister, Frances, was forced back into slavery because her papers were destroyed. With her money from cooking she repurchased Frances. Clavin was gone. When the Civil War broke out he became a soldier in the Federal Army and never came home.

In 1855, Amanda was very ill, close to death:

> One day my father said to me, "Amanda, my child, you know the doctors say you must die; they can do no more for you, and now my child you must pray." O, I did not want to pray, I was so tired I wanted to sleep. ... I fell asleep ... I seemed to go into a kind of trance or vision, and I saw on the foot of my bed a most beautiful angel. ... it said "Go back," three times. Then it seemed, I went to a Camp Meeting..., and I was to preach ... a large Bible opened and I was preaching from these words—"And if I be lifted up will draw all men unto me."[8]

In 1856, Amanda went forward in a Baptist church in Columbia, PA. Seeking peace afterwards, she fasted and prayed about her decision. "'O, Lord, if Thou wilt help me I will believe Thee,' and in the act of telling God I would, I did. ...This witness of God' spirit to my conversion has been what has held me amid all the storms of temptation and trial that I have passed through."[9]

Her second husband was James Smith, an ordained deacon in the A.M.E. church. He later died in 1869. Amanda always thanked God of His manifold blessings. One of which was her sanctification that came to her through a sermon by Brother John Inskip at the Green Street Church, "There are a great many persons who are troubled

---

5 Ibid., 32–33.
6 Ibid., 104–105.
7 Ibid., 42.
8 Ibid., 42–43.
9 Ibid., 47, 49.

about the blessing of sanctification; how they can keep it if they get it. ... You don't need to fix any way for God to live in you; get God in you in all His fullness and he will live Himself."[10] After this Amanda wrote, "how many mother's hearts I have cheered when I told them that the blessing of sanctification did not mean isolation from all the natural and legitimate duties of life, as some seem to think. Not at all. It means God in you, supplying all your needs according to His riches in glory by Christ Jesus; our need of grace and patience and long suffering and forbearance, for we have to learn how not only to bear, but also to forbear with infirmities or ourselves and others as well."[11]

Amanda had three outstanding careers. One was a traveling evangelist, the other a missionary, and the third was one of a singer.

As a traveling evangelist, she encountered segregation and racism. She was refused lodging in many places. She wore a plain poke bonnet and a Quaker wrapper usually brown or black and carried in her hand a carpetbag with her few belongings.

> It is often said to me, "How nicely you get on, Mrs. Smith; everybody seems to treat you so kindly, and you always seem to get on so well." ... I said, "But I have much more to contend with than you may think." ... "But if you would want to know and understand properly what Amanda Smith has to contend with, just turn black and go about as I do, and you will come to a different conclusion." And I think some people would understand the quintessence of sanctifying grace if they could be black about twenty-four hours.[12]

Not all occasions had negative outcomes. Many opportunities when Amanda Smith was asked to speak led to conversions and at times great revivals. Her first national Holiness Camp Meeting was at Oakington, MD, July, 1870, when she went to work for Mrs. Margaret Clark. Mrs. Clark encouraged her to trust the Lord for provisions to attend the meeting and receive its benefits. The Lord did provided and she attended as a guest.

> In the afternoon I went into the tent where Brother Purdy was leading a meeting; he was probing and testing those who were seeking full salvation He probes deep, praise the Lord. ... I stepped up and said, "Brother Brady, would you like to try your probe on me?" ... "Can you stand it, Amanda?" ... "Yes, sir;" .... The power of the Lord came down upon us, and O, what a meeting; sinners were converted, believers sanctified. ...[13]

Another occasion was at the General Conference of the A.M.E. Church held in Nashville, TN. "This was the first time in all these years that this religious body of black men, with a black church from beginning to end, was to be assembled south of the Mason and Dixon's line."[14] Again, after much prayer, the Lord opened the way for her to attend. Again, she was a visitor and chose a seat in the back. Professor White saw Amanda.

> Holding me by the hand, he escorted me to the platform and introduced me to the large audience, who, in the midst of overwhelming amazement, applauded. ... Then he said, "I'm going to ask Mrs. Smith to sing that same song she sang in Boston, and the Jubilee Singers will join in the chorus. If ever the Lord did help me, he helped me that day. And the Spirit of the Lord seemed to fall on all the people. ... They wept and shouted 'Amen!' 'Praise the Lord!'"[15]

In 1876, friends who saw that her spiritual life was deepening and that she was able to give others a deeper understanding and greater experience of God, and what He could do, paid for her travel to England. The passage on the steamer was first class!

During the voyage she understood more fully the book of Philippians and had the honor of conducting religious services. This dynamic woman of God not only did evangelistic work in London, but also in Scotland, Liverpool, Leeds, Manchester, Cambridge, and Plymouth.

Amanda had her daughter, Maze, with her as well. God did show her He wanted her to go. She received enough money to cover her fare, buy new clothes, and had a small amount of cash left.

---

10 Ibid., 76.
11 Ibid., 103.
12 Ibid., 166–167.
13 Ibid., 167–168.
14 Ibid., 199.
15 Ibid., 203–204.

She also received enough to provide winter clothing, and three months board for her daughter.

Her ministry is a prime example of faith missions:

> "Amanda, it is wonderful how the Lord is putting it into the hearts of the people to help you financially. Several have come to me and put in my hands money for you." ... Then I saw it was in direct answer to prayer, as I had asked the Lord on my way.[16]

From London she visited Egypt.

If this was not enough excitement in her life, the Lord "marvelously" opened the way for her travel to India in 1879. This came about near the end of her England tour. A friend, Mrs. Drake, asked her to come to India with her. At first Amanda refused having no previous interest in India, but she prayed to God that, if He wanted her to go to India, He should make it very clear and plain to her. And, if He did that, she would obey Him and leave everything and go. They visited various places where the M. E. churches had been established. When they reached Bombay, Mrs. Drake stayed and Amanda then had Miss Jennie Frow, a missionary, as a companion, who went with her to Calcutta. Enroute she spoke at camp meetings on the subject of temperance. She also took a trip to Burma to do mission work there. She spoke by invitation at numerous Methodist, Baptist, and Lutheran mission stations. After one meeting at a mission station a great rain came bringing on a great flood. A landslide took place and she witnessed the death of many people and in the midst of the shock, horror and sorrow, she had to literally be dragged to a safer location. She went on to preach to sailors, orphans, the sick, the poor in many more mission station areas.

J. M. Thoburn, Calcutta, October 22, 1891 wrote:

> During the summer of 1876, while attending a camp meeting in Epworth Heights, near Cincinnati, my attention was drawn to a coloured lady dressed in very plain garb. ... She suddenly broke out with a triumphant song, and while I was startled by the change in the order of the meeting, I was once absorbed with interest in the song and the singer. ... From that time onward I regarded her as a gifted worker in the Lord's vineyard, but I had still to learn that the enduement of the Spirit had given her more than one gift of spiritual power. ... During the 17 years that I have lived in Calcutta, ... I have never known anyone who could draw and hold so large an audience as Mrs. Smith.[17]

> I have already spoken of her clearness of perception and power of stating the undimmed truth of the Gospel of Christ. ... She sometimes was touched by the pictures of misery which she saw around her, but never hopeless. She was of cheerful temperament, it is true, but aside from personal feeling, she always possessed a buoyant hope and an overcoming faith, which made it easy for her to believe, that the Saviour, whom she loved and served, really intended to save and transform India. ... As she left the country she could look back upon a hundred homes which were brighter and better because of her coming.[18]

Ten years prior to her trip to India, in 1872, Amanda had gone to a Methodist Camp Meeting. Here she heard some talk about missionaries from Asia and South America. That meeting fascinated and inspired her. She asked about Africa and whether all the people there had been converted and was told the story of Melville B. Cox, the first M.E. missionary to Africa and the history of the needs there. While in England a friend told her of a current missionary to Africa and she later said that it made a deep impression on her mind and heart. She returned from India in 1881 to England for the Ecumenical Conference sponsored by the Methodists. In January 1882, she went to Liberia after only being in England for two months.

Monrovia, Cape Palmas, Clay-Ashland, Virginia and Tubman Town, Upper and Lower Buchanan in Bassa, Edina, Harford, Greenville, Lexington, Louisiana, Bluntville, Farmersville, Old Calabar, Cape Mount, were the places she preached and taught. She organized woman's band meetings, young men's praying bands, Gospel Temperance societies, and children's

---
16 Ibid., 262.

17 Ibid., v, vii.
18 Ibid., viii, ix–x.

meetings for the promotion of holiness. She was asked to preach and speak at gatherings of Methodists, Presbyterians, Baptists, Episcopals, Congregationalists, and others. She adopted an African boy, Bob, whose parents brought to her to teach the ways of God. Bishop Taylor and Sister Betty Tubman were witnesses as the parent signed him over. And she was given a girl, Frances, whose parents had died. She brought Bob to England and God supplied the means for him to go to school. Frances was always sick and could not adjust to the travel so was left behind. God provided enough for Amanda to cover all expenses for Frances. (It is believed that the young man was educated and returned home to Africa.)

I calmly looked over all my mind, and my work in Africa. I felt that while there was so much to be done, and I had only done a little, yet that I had God's approval that I had done all I could. I went to Africa at His bidding, and did not leave till I was sure I had His sanction.[19]

Amanda returned from Africa to Liverpool in 1980, experiencing a terrible bout with "la grippe" so much so that she only thought she had "three weeks to live,"[20] and so went home to America. She conducted the Amanda Smith's Orphan Home for Colored Children in Harvey, IL. She died on February 24, 1915. A minister who knew her well referred to her as "God's Image Carved in Ebony."

---

19 Ibid., 487.
20 Ibid., 486.

Chapter 17

William Sheppard: Congo's African American Livingstone

by William Phipps

William Sheppard (1890–1910) and Other African Americans at the Presbyterian Mission Stations in the Congo

William Henry Sheppard Jr. was born March 8, 1865, a month before slavery was eradicated in the U.S. by the confederate surrender at Appomatox. ... His mother's maiden name was Sarah Frances Martin ... She was registered there as a "dark mulatto" who was born free in 1837. According to the 1705 Virginia Code, "All children shall be bond or free according to the condition of their mother." Thus, William was not born into slavery even though Jefferson Davis was his president.[1]

His family first lived in Waynesboro, VA. His father, William Sheppard Sr., was a barber and although illiterate had a fantastic memory which aided him in his work. He was chosen to serve as a Sexton. His "mother never turned any one away from her door who came begging, whether white or coloured."[2] They were devoted Presbyterians.

William helped the family by doing odd jobs and errands for added income. Then at age 12 he became a stable boy for a dentist, and the family grew to love him.

He became a McCurdy House waiter in towns west of Staunton, advancing to become the headwaiter at Covington. In 1880 he took the money he had saved and enrolled in Hampton Normal and Industrial Institute on the VA coast. ... General Samuel Armstrong had founded Hampton as a place where blacks could receive mental, manual, and religious training.[3] Part of the school's outreach, William taught Sunday School in VA.

Prior to going to AL in 1881 to establish Tuskegee Institute, Booker T. Washington taught at Hampton, where he graduated in 1875. He had organized a night school during his last year at Hampton, and Sheppard was among his few students. The routine was rigorous; excepting Sunday, ten hours of manual work preceded two hours of evening instruction.[4]

William Phipps is an ordained minister in the Presbyterian Church (USA) and the author of *The Wisdom and Wit of Rabbi Jesus* (Westminster: John Knox Press). He was Professor of Bible at Peace College in Raleigh, NC before becoming Professor of Religion and Philosophy and Chair of the Philosophy Department at Davis and Elkins College in Elkins, WV.

William Sheppard, *Congo's African American Livingstone*, ©2002, by William Phipps (Louisville, KY: Geneva Press).

Used by permission.

Marilyn Lewis received her masters degree at Dallas Theological Seminary. She was laying the groundwork at U.S. Center for World Mission in Pasadena, CA, for the long-desired African-American Mobilization Division. While manning this project, teaching high school, and taking courses for her doctorate at Fuller Theological Seminary School of World Mission, the Lord called her home on February 20, 2000. Her short paragraphs written about Sheppard prompted the search for more of his story.

We wish to honor Marilyn with this entry.

---

1 William E. Phipps, *William Sheppard, Congo's African-American Livingstone* (Louisville, KY: Geneva Press, 2002), Preparation, 1. Further noted as "Phipps." Quote taken from *June Guild, Black Laws of Virginia* (Richmond:Whittet, 1936), 50.

2 Marilyn Lewis, January, 1993, "The African-American in Christian Missions, " Masters of Theology paper, Dallas Theological Seminary. Further noted as "Lewis." Quote taken from William Sheppard, *Presbyterian Pioneers in the Congo* (Richmond, VA: Presbyterian Committee of Publication, 1917). Further noted as PPC.

3 Phipps, Preparation, 5.

4 Ibid, 6.

Pastor McCutcheon recommended Sheppard to Dr. Charles Stillman, the president of the Tuscaloosa Theological Institute in AL, which would be named Stillman College after his death in 1895.[5]

During his three years at Tuscaloosa, Sheppard continued the pattern of home mission work begun in Hampton by visiting and praying with the sick in AL communities. During that time one concern was much on his mind: "A question asked me in my examination by both the Presbytery in Waynesboro, VA, and by the faculty of Tuscaloosa Institute was: 'If you are called upon to go to Africa as a missionary, would you be willing to go?' I promptly answered, 'I would go, and with pleasure.'"[6]

As a pastor of Presbyterian churches in Montgomery and Atlanta, Sheppard did not adapt well to the black congregations. Inwardly he felt a call for mission service in Africa. He petitioned over and over again for missionary service in the 1880's even traveling miles to present his request personally. However, the Presbyterian hierarchy had refused to send an African-American male as their sole leader of the foreign mission stations.[7]

Funding was recognized as the main obstacle to establishing a mission in Africa by African Americans, and an attempt to get the Northern Presbyterians to cooperate in a joint Congo operation was not successful.[8] Sheppard had declined appointment by the Baptist to their Congo Bolobo Mission, and the Northern Presbyterians to their work elsewhere in Africa, because he preferred to represent his own denomination.[9]

When the mission board later began its mission to the Congo finally in 1889, Samuel Norvell Lapsley became interested in missionary work. He was the only applicant other than Sheppard and the first white man in over ten years to dedicate himself to missions. "Sheppard and Lapsley met with the Foreign Mission Committee and received their approval. The two "brethren" were told that they were to work as "coequals."[10] Now at last, Sheppard would join Lapsley and together they ventured to a country for which little was known.

Before embarking, Lapsley and Sheppard began to establish a support network by visiting churches and cities in several states. Senator John Morgan, a former partner of Judge Lapsley in a leading AL law firm, assisted them in Washington by making political connections that could help their mission. An appointment was made for the judge and his son to visit President Benjamin Harrison in the White House. Harrison expressed his sympathy for the undertaking and attempted to offer comfort.[11]

Lapsley and Sheppard left NY and headed for London. In March, Lapsley was invited to Brussels by Henry Sanford to visit with Belgians who had Congo interests. Sanford made these arrangements after receiving a letter from Senator Morgan on behalf of the American missionaries. ... Lapsley described him in this way: "He is a zealous Congo man, not a visionary, for he has large interests there. He treats me as if I were on his business; directs all my movements, takes me to see everybody of importance to me."[12] ... After his brief trip to Brussels, Lapsley returned to London. Sheppard reported to Lapsley's mother, "We spent a month in England, being together always."[13]

Passage had been booked on the Afrikaan, a small Dutch vessel, because the Belgians had no merchant marine. For much of the three-week trip from England to the Congo, nausea was the principal concern.[14] Lapsley and Sheppard took the arduous journey and arrived in the Congo and selected the Luebo Station in the Kasai Valley of the Southern portion of the country for their ministry.[15]

The missionaries stopped over at a trading post named Banana, near Shark's Point. Sheppard noted that those place names were appropriate because thousands of banana trees were growing

---

5 Ibid., 9

6 Ibid., 10. Quote taken from Ernest T. Thompson, *Presbyterian Missions in the Southern United States* (Richmond, VA: Presbyterian Committee of Publication, 1934), 18, 210, 212.

7 Lewis, D-40.

8 Phipps, Preparation, 11. Quote taken from Minutes of the Executive Committee of Foreign Missions, PCUS (Montreat archives), October 15, 1889, #168.

9 Phipps, Preparation, 11.

10 Phipps, Preparation, 13. Quote taken from *Winefred and Lachlan Vass, The Lapsley Saga*, (Franklin, TN: Providence House, 1997), 7.

11 Phipps, Preparation, 14. Taken from James Lapsley, ed., *Life and Letters of Samuel Norvill Lapsley* (Richmond, VA: Whittet & Shepperson, 1893), 21. Further noted as "Lapsley, *Life*".

12 Phipps, Preparation, 17. Quote taken from Lapsley, *Life*, 23, 45.

13 Phipps, Preparation, 18. Quote taken from PPC, 15.

14 Phipps, Preparation, 19.

15 Lewis, D-40.

in the delta area, and "the river swarmed with man-eating sharks."[16]

Sheppard was elated and felt that this was the work that God had called for him and he was warmly received by the Africans.[17] Lapsley reported,

"Sheppard preached to the Sierra Leone men, ... after which they spoke to him freely of their condition. One of them said, 'No good here for Sierra Leone man; plenty sick, too much flog.'"[18] The mortality rate at that time was much higher in Africa than for any other area of missionary activity. ... At Tunduwa both Lapsley and Sheppard experienced what they called "blackwater fever," meaning that their urine became like black ink. It was accompanied by intense chills and temperatures as high as 105 degrees. ... Sheppard recorded 22 bouts with malaria during his first two years in Congo.[19]

When Sheppard learned that there was a famine in one area, he bravely took his gun and killed a hippopotamus to feed them. He had the ability to learn and speak the native languages quickly. He began to spend his days hunting and was quite good at it, once jumping into the waters to fetch a dead hippo only to confront hungry alligators. Quickly he got out of the water and learned from the Africans, "they will come to shore, just wait," and they did.[20]

When Lapsley returned to the American Baptist station in Kinshasa, he wrote his home headquarters:

Brother Sheppard has, in every way; justified the predictions of his friends. He has won the esteem of all the missionaries as a true man and a gentleman, while with the natives he is, according to Dr. Sims, the most popular man that ever came to this station. He has the constitution needed, and the gift of getting along in Africa. While I was away he devoted much time to hunting on the river, and has actually brought home twelve "hippos," to the great delight of the blacks and admiration of Europeans.[21]

Lapsley wrote, "It seems as if the words and lives of the missionaries were having no effect on these poor people. To earn the trust of the Africans, you had to be a black white man."[22] The Bateka think there is nobody like "Mundele Ndom," ... Mundele means "man with clothes" but it the usual word for white men, as none but white men wear clothes. So, "black Man with Clothes" was the literal meaning of one of Sheppard's Congo names.[23]

Sheppard was not only concerned with the evangelization but he could not avoid being concerned with the living conditions of his African brethren. In 1890, the Belgian government commanded that it desired all of the Congolese men to work to "help pay for the colonial government." Therefore, in 1891, the government imposed a heavy tax upon the Kasai people. These people were forced to work for the Europeans to secure monies for the tax. The tax was quite beneficial for the Europeans. The European companies received cheap labor and provided no benefits and almost no salaries for the African laborer. To make sure that the African male was working and available for work, the government hired the feared cannibalistic Zappo-Zap soldiers to collect the tax. The people were scared and acquiesced to the government's demands. However, the Zap soldiers also used the tax collections as future information for slave raids and cannibalism.[24]

When Lapsley and Sheppard were in Kinshasa, another African-American Protestant clergyman, and eminent historian, was also visiting there. George Williams wrote an open letter at that time to Leopold about his six-month tour of upper Congo, boldly informing the king that the "King of Kings" was not pleased with what was happening in the Congo. ... A year later Williams died, which left the publicizing of human rights abuses in the Congo mainly to Sheppard and Lapsley.[25]

But trying to separate themselves from political issues, Lapsley and Sheppard continued their mission work. Sheppard and Lapsley were relieved to find a promising place to establish the American Presbyterian Congo Mission [APCM]

---

16 Phipps, *Beginnings in Africa*, 29. Quote taken from PPC, 21, 22.
17 Lewis, D-40.
18 Lewis, quote taken from Lapsley, *Life*, 58.
19 Phipps, Beginnings, 31, 32. Last sentence quote taken from *Southern Workman*, 12/1893, 182.
20 Lewis, D-40.
21 Phipps, *Beginnings*, 40. Quote taken from *The Missionary*, 1/1891, 34.
22 Lewis. Reference to Lapsley, *Life*.
23 Phipps, *Beginnings*, 39.
24 Lewis, D-41.
25 Phipps, *Beginnings*, 38–39.

mission soon after arriving in the Lulua area of the Kasai. ... Lapsley clearly recognized the pivotal importance of the Luebo site: "It is the centre of influence from which the lines of trade radiate."[26] The missionaries realized that several major tribes could be contacted at Leubo. The Kubas were continually passing through because they ruled over the tribes surrounding Luebo.

Both men preached, taught, provided medical assistance, ransomed slaves, and established relationships with the African Kete.[27] Describing the way he and Lapsley went about accommodating their eating habits to the environment, Sheppard wrote: "With the help of the natives we began to clear the forest, take up the stumps, and clean up generally. A chicken, parrot and monkey house was soon built, for they were all good for food."[28] There were also other foods that the missionaries learned to like: crickets, manioc or cassava root, and live white ants.

Sheppard preceded Lapsley in moving from tent to cottage, but found that did not immediately prove advantageous. The day after he moved in, ferocious black ants attacked. Lapsley made this diary entry:

> *Midnight—a great commotion. Sheppard was moving about very rapidly, and even dancing, and addressing the people [several camp attendants] in impassioned tones. On inquiry, I learned that a column of driver ants had entered his house and taken possession. They even came under his blankets and covered him; hence his animation. They happened to be marching by and smelt the palm oil inside. We made various reconnaissance's with torches and candles, found many columns pouring across the open space. ... One line had reached my tent door just as I got up. A fire stopped them. I looked around and met another body of them making for the back of the tent, where there was a greasy spot, black with them.*[29]

Sheppard's explanation of his predicament contained none of Lapsley's detachment:

> *I was alarmed by a band of big, broad-headed, determined driver ants. ... There were millions. They were in my head, my eyes, my nose, and pulling at my toes. when I found it was not a dream, I didn't tarry long. ... In an incredible short space of time they can kill any goat, chicken, duck, hog or dog on the place. In a few hours there is not a rat, mouse, snake, centipede, spider or scorpion in your house, as they are chased, killed and carried away. ... We were told by the natives that when there are triplets born in a family it is considered very bad luck, so one of the babies is taken by the witch doctor and put into a deep hole where these ants live and the child is soon scented by them and eaten. We scraped the acquaintance of these soldier ants by being severely bitten and stung. They are near the size of a wasp and use both ends with splendid effect.*[30]

While trying to adjust to their new environment, the missionaries relied on body language and pantomime for communicating. ... To improve on their rudimentary vocabulary, each day they took notebooks into the adjacent Teke village to record the oral languages of the upper Kasai. ... Sheppard commented on this laborious process: "After several months we had thus collected subjects, prepositions, pronouns, verbs, etc."[31]

Most of the students were redeemed Luba slaves who had been purchased back by the missionaries for several dozen bandannas each.[32] ... Sheppard told how he and Lapsley sat beneath a palm tree daily to teach gospel stories to any who might be interested. One story about Jesus stimulated a girl to ask, "What is his Father's name?" Lapsley answered, "Here you call him Nzambi, the Great Spirit." Further questions, such as "Where is his native village?" produced more explanation.[33] That girl could have been N'Tumba. Decades later Sheppard published a children's story about how an ex-slave girl became an evangelist.[34]

---

26 Phipps, *Beginnings*, 51. Quote from Lapsley, *Life*, 103.
27 Lewis, D-40.
28 Phipps, *Beginnings*, 55. Quote from PPC, 67.
29 Phipps, *Beginnings*, 56. Quote from Lapsley, *Life*, 165–166, 170–171.
30 Phipps, *Beginnings*, 56. Quote from PPC, 68.
31 Phipps, *Beginnings*, 58. Quote from *Missionary Review*, October 1905, 742.
32 Ibid., 58.
33 Phipps, *Beginnings*, 59. Quote from PPC, 64.
34 Ibid., 59.

Finding many people suffering from various diseases, they were distressed to find reliance on some ineffective remedies. ... Presuming that even without special training he could improve on some of the witch doctors' prescriptions, Lapsley administered medicines he had for common sicknesses. The people quickly learned that his therapy was often more effective than traditional medicine.[35]

Settling into their surrounding, Lapsley and Sheppard began constructing a settlement resembling a plantation from U.S. Sheppard also took natives hunting and even performed dentistry and began to wear daily his now famous outfit: A pith helmet, white pants and shirt and heavy boots. Even though they did all they could to reach the Kete, it was difficult. "Honestly," Sheppard wrote, "those people would swallow pills just as long as you would deal them out, but they would not swallow the story of Jesus."[36]

Sheppard, being quite tall and robust, evidently had physical strength. He had the ability to learn and to speak the native languages, and displayed skill as a hunter. Eventually, Sheppard would be the primary contact from the mission station to the Africans. He was responsible for directing the practical needs of the mission. Lapsley on the other hand, managed the finances and dealt with the white colonial officials. The team of Lapsley and Sheppard worked well together.[37]

Lapsley started to look for another tribe to evangelize—the Zappo-Zap. They "have been cannibals of lately, without a doubt. The [Kete] say they eat dogs and people," he wrote. "But the Zappo-Zap are the finest people about—magnificent men and handsome women, and carry themselves quite aristocracy."[38] "In Arab-dominated parts of Africa, they spoke Swahili and wore robes. Among Europeans, they learned French or English, ate on China plates, and wore pants."[39]

Sheppard and Lapsley could not agree on reaching this people group. They settled for the Kuba and the unknown kingdom of its leader. Sheppard set out into Kuba country to make contact. While he was gone, the lifestyle of the Kete tormented Lapsley and he wrote, "the isolation from Christian influences, even all books except my Bible and English hymn book, and the constant contact of godless influences, has certainly lowered by level of Christian life, chilled me, and kept me always in a series of inward apologetics."[40]

Sheppard made contact not far from Luebo and as soon as Lapsley had learned of his find, he set out rejoicing and ready to hire workmen. Along the way he caught another fever. The men he found for hire were not working men but refugees, running from burned villages or repeated beatings. He returned to Sheppard with 22 sick and poor people and these were only the beginning as others heard of the place of refuge that these two Presbyterian missionaries offered.

Luebo mission was growing but they still wished to reach the Kuba. The Presbyterian Church was turned down for land acquisition nearby. Lapsley decided to go by ship to meet with the governor-general. Weak and struggling with sickness, he was still able to get a deed at Matadi, but he died of black water fever in March 1892. [The Lapsley file at the Presbyterian Historical Society contains the original document in French certifying the APCM ownership of twenty-five acres on the right bank of the Lulua River.][41]

Sheppard was now the sole leader of the mission station and the first African American in a position of authority. While awaiting Lapsley's replacement he concentrated on evangelization of the Bakuba. Converts were needed to keep the Congo mission funded. He took great care to understand habits, customs, and cultural differences of the Africans. It was evident in his correspondence that he recognized and respected the differences among the African societies and that they worked well together.

Plans had been made for an expedition to the Kuba capital after Lapsely returned from the lower Congo. He and Sheppard had recognized the advantages of planting Christianity in the center of a kingdom with a population of about 200,000, that was culturally advanced, politically powerful, and economically prosperous. ... The Kuba king had prohibited all people from other lands coming into his kingdom. ... While Lapsley was away, Sheppard concentrated on learning

---

35 Phipps, *Beginnings*, 61.
36 Lewis. Taken from Sheppard, PPC.
37 Lewis, D-40.
38 Lewis, Taken from Lapsley, *Life*.
39 Pagan Kennedy, *Black Livingston—A True Tale of Adventure in the Nineteenth-century Congo* (Viking Press, 2002). Further noted as "Kennedy, *Livingston*."

40 Lewis. Taken from Lapsley, *Life*.
41 Phipps, *Beginnings*, 65.

the Kuba language. ... When the Kubas came to dinner they not only enriched his vocabulary but informed him of the names of villages, along with their chiefs, between Luebo and Mushenge (capital). ... Lapsley's death gave Sheppard a stronger determination to fulfill plans they had made jointly.[42]

No outsider had ever entered the capital or seen their king and lived. Sheppard ventured close to the Kuba capital and, by a series of events only God could have orchestrated, he was confronted by a representative of the king. Sheppard later told about the way his exploration incensed the Kuba king, whose title was Nyimi in Bushonga, the Kuba language, or Lukengu (or Lukenga) in Tshiluba:

The king called for his sons; called for his forty fighting men, who use bows six feet high and can send an arrow through a buffalo; gave his spear and knife to his son Toen-zaida and said, "Go down to Bishibing and bring back the chief, the foreigners, the villagers—all—and I will behead them." The next morning, as I was reading a copy of the *Daily News*—a copy two years old—I heard a great noise out in the village. A herald of Lukenga had come storming in and was proclaiming, "Hear the king's message. The king commands you all to come before him; ... because you have entertained a foreigner you are all to be beheaded." The whole village was in intense excitement.... It was too late to run away. I could not rescue my people by force, but I sent for the king's son. ... I said, "These people are not to blame. I have had no guide; no one showed me the way. Last night the chief begged me to go away; but I did not go. I am the only one that is guilty."[43]

The prince was flabbergasted to hear Bushonga spoken so fluently by one who was dressed in the clothes of a distant culture. Also, he could not figure how anyone could come so far into his hidden kingdom without a Kuba guide, or why he was willing to sacrifice his life for a Kuba chief. ... They concluded that the large, mysterious person was a previous Kuba king whose spirit had become reincarnated in a foreign man. Toen-zaida and other princes returned to Bishibing to tell its father's wise men, who declared, "He is no stranger, but Bope Mekabe of your own family; who has returned to earth."[44]

The Kuba had pagan witch hunts. If the way you looked with your eyes was not accepted, you were a witch and must die—drinking poison. He concluded, "Seeing these awful customs practiced by these people for ages makes you indignant and depressed and also fills you with pity. Only by preaching God's word, having faith, patience and love will we eradicate the deep-rooted evil.[45] Of course, they had ancestral worship so Sheppard was accepted as a lost ancestor and placed in a high position under the king. Sheppard took copious notes and collected items from this capital city. "Their knowledge of weaving, embroidering, wood carving, and smelting was the highest in the equatorial Africa," he wrote.[46]

Lukengu gave Sheppard permission to tell everywhere "about the Great Spirit, a great King."[47] ... Sheppard learned from the king about Kuba religious beliefs. They had a vague belief in an invisible God who was responsible for the creation and control of nature. According to their mythology, Sheppard reported, the "first people, man and woman, were let down from the skies by a rope, from which they untied themselves and the rope was drawn up."[48] Weather calamities and agricultural failures were interpreted as signs of the anger of this God, called Chembe, a name corresponding to Nzambi of the lower Congo. This Supreme Being was feared but not worshipped.[49]

Not forgetting why he was there, Sheppard asked the king for nine acres of land in the capital to build a mission. Sheppard could not wait to get back to tell of this advanced culture, the acquired land for a new mission, and begged the king to let him go. Finally, though reluctantly, the king agreed as long as he returned in one year. He truly trusted Sheppard.

George and Margaret Adamson, members of the Free Church of Scotland, took charge of the

---

42 Phipps, *The Kuba People*, 68, 69.
43 Phipps, *The Kuba People*, 70. Quote from PPC,121.
44 Phipps, *The Kuba People*, 70, 71. Quote taken from *Southern Workman*, December 1893, 185.
45 Phipps, *The Kuba People*, 92. Quote from PPC, 131.
46 Lewis. Taken from PPC, 137.
47 Phipps, *The Kuba People*, 75. Quote from PPC, 111; *Southern Workman*, December 1893, 185.
48 Phipps, *The Kuba People*, 78. Quoted in Adam Hoshschild, *King Leopold's Ghost*, (New York: Houghton Mifflin, 1998), 157.
49 Phipps, *The Kuba People*, 78. Quote taken from *Southern Workman*, December 1893, 185, 187.

APCM during his furlough. ... While awaiting his ship at Matadi, Sheppard met four additional APCM appointees, the Rev. Arthur Rowbotham from England and his wife Margaret, as well as DeWitt Snyder, a druggist from America, and his wife May.[50] The Congo was especially unkind to white women. The first one to enter the Kasi basin, Margaret Adamson, became the first to be buried in the missionary cemetery in Luebo. Then Margaret Rowbotham's chronic illness caused the Rowbothams to decide to leave the Congo mission with her infant son four months after arriving in Luebo.

The Snyders continued on until 1896, when May died of malaria.[51]

Sheppard left Kuba and went to London in 1893, he was made a Fellow in the Royal Geographic Society. He gave a speech in London's Exeter Hall of the missionary exploits of Lapsley, and he showed Kuba works of art telling of their advanced culture. He went on to the U.S. and met with President Grover Cleveland, presenting him also with Kuba art and telling of its advanced society.

Upon Sheppard's return to America, he used his furlough as an effort to stir up interest in missions in the African-American community. His fame on arriving in America was increased by his having been made a Fellow.[52] In his home state, Sheppard's address at Hampton Institute entitled, "Into the Heart of Africa" was published in 1893, providing the first written record of the Kuba culture. He received an enthusiastic hearing at a meeting of the PCUS Synod of VA. Because of his speeches and his eloquent mannerisms, African Americans made monetary contributions to this ministry.

Sheppard was engaged to Lucy Gantt, an Alabaman two years younger than himself. She was born in Tuscaloosa to a former slave, Eliza Gantt, who had been abandoned by her impregnator prior to the baby's birth. ... When this only child of Eliza was old enough to go to school, the mother joined her in order to learn to read the Bible. ... At 11 she was admitted to a school for blacks in Talladega, AL, which had been started along with Hampton and Fisk by the Missionary Association of the Congregational Church. Here she studied for nine years and was placed under the supervision of Maria Fearing.[53] When enrolled at Talladega, Lucy engaged in her first missionary work. Her summers were spent in spartan conditions while teaching basic literacy to blacks.[54] When the teenaged Tuscaloosan returned to her hometown for the holidays, she and Sheppard met and fell in love.[55]

Lucy Gantt traveled with the Lousdin Jubilee Singers, which was formerly called the Fisk Jubilee Singers. After college she became a teacher. She taught in a one room schoolhouse in Grayton, AL, and then in Birmingham City Schools for over seven years. She had been corresponding with William since he had been a student at Stillman and through his writings had a glimpse of what was ahead for them all.[56] Both Lucy and William were college educated, Christians, they had a sincere desire for the mission field, both were considered middle class, and both were articulate about issues and events.[57] In 1893 she was delighted to receive a London cable from "Sheppard, F.R.G.S.," announcing that he would see her in a few weeks.[58]

Realizing that the APCM might close unless the Luebo staff were increased, Sheppard was eager to recruit new personnel for the mission. The Sheppards persuaded Henry P. Hawkins and two fellow Talladega alumni, Maria Fearing and Lillian Thomas, to join them back to Luebo in May, 1894.[59] Together they ran the first all black mission station for the Presbyterian Church. In 1896 William wrote to his supporters at home promising to prove that he merited the trust they have placed in him. By 1898, these African-American missionaries had fully established a new branch mission station on the Bakuba frontier. Two years later the mission station had a total of 350 converts.[60]

It was not easy to go to Africa as a black missionary. Henry P. Hawkins, whose wife was refused by the Presbyterian Mission Board to

---

50 Phipps, *Mission Development*, 95.
51 Phipps, *Mission Development*, 96.
52 Lewis, D-41.
53 Lewis, D-24. Talladega College was the first in AL to be opened to blacks and it offered degrees regardless of race. It continues to be affiliated with the United Church of Christ.
54 Lewis. Quote taken from Juia Kellersberger, *Lucy Gantt Sheppard* (Atlanta: PCUS, Committee on Women's Work, n.d.), 5–8. Further noted as "Kellersberger, *Sheppard.*"
55 Phipps, *Mission Development*, 96, 97.
56 Lewis, D-24.
57 Lewis, D-24.
58 Phipps, *Mission Development*, 97. Quote taken from Kellersberger, *Sheppard*, 8–10.
59 Lewis, 50.
60 Lewis, D-41.

join him, was a newly ordained minister from Stillman Seminary. He reported in 1899 that his most difficult task was to make the Africans feel the quietness of Christianity. He wrote about the forced labor of the Africans by the imperialistic government of the Belgians.[61]

Lillian Thomas DeYamert arrived in 1902. She was born September 14, 1872, in Mobile, AL, to James and Lydia Randolph Thomas. She was a member of the Congregational Church and attended Emerson Institute and later entered Talledega College. Lillian was sponsored by the Presbyterian Church in the U.S.. She became superintendent of the Pantops Home for Girls. In the early days when printing was introduced into the Congo, she helped to teach the Congolese how to set type. She also helped start the Luebo Day School.[62]

Lillian, as well as Maria Fearing, were colleagues of Lucy Gantt. Maria was born a slave in Gainesville, AL, 1838, to Mary and Jesse Fearing. She was brought up by the Presbyterians and freed at the age of 27. A minister, noticing her determination to become educated, enabled her to enter Talledega College. After completing the ninth grade at Talledega College, AL, she taught in a rural school in Anniston, AL.[63]

Inspired by William Sheppard's speech, she offered her services. She was 56 and the Committee refused to support her because of age and lack of education. Maria begged Judge J. W. Lapsley to buy her house, with the sale, other savings, and pledged support by the Congregational Church in Talledega, she was granted permission by the Executive Committee of the Presbyterian Church to go with Sheppard. She was the first self-supporting PCUS missionary.[64]

Lillian DeYamert learned the language of the Baluba Lulua people and started teaching in the mission station. During the week she traveled to nearby villages and taught religious lessons to small groups of Africans. She was highly respected by the Africans because of her age, wisdom, and her domestic skills. She worked well with older women, mothers and children. She worked with almost 100 young ladies. She assisted in the construction of small dormitory dwellings. Once the Mission Board saw its benefit, they supported the home financially. Along with domestic chores she taught Bible verses and Christian prayers. In her spare time she continued evangelization in the surrounding communities.[65]

Althea Maria Brown arrived in 1902. Born Christmas 1874 in Rosseville, AL, to Robert and Molly Suggs Brown, her parents were happy because she was "born free." Educated at home, Althea later entered Fisk and graduated with high honor in 1901 and was the only woman to speak at the Commencement Program. Her message was "What Missions Have Done For the World." After graduation she studied at the Chicago Training School for city and foreign missions. In Africa, she studied languages under William N. Morrison.[66]

As Sheppard's wife, Lucy had much to contend with. Sheppard became delirious with malaria en route to Africa, their steamer was attacked by hostile villagers retaliating because State officers on the previous boat attacked them. While on the steamer there was a food shortage and Sheppard, who had acquired the name Ngele, meaning "hunter" shot a hippo for food. On returning to Luebo, Sheppard found that the station that had been left under George Anderson's oversight was now nearly in shambles.[67] Following the death of his wife, Adamson had resigned from the mission. The Snyders were the only missionaries left in Luebo, and there were no professing Christians among the natives.[68]

The Sheppard's first residence was a hut made of sticks and mud with a leaky thatched roof and rotting mats on a dirt floor. ... When a python crawled over the bed in which he and Lucy were sleeping, Sheppard ... slithered out of bed and killed it. In that hut Lucy gave birth to their first child, Miriam Sheppard. There was little joy because the mother "came very near death."[69] Although Miriam was six weeks premature, she appeared to be in good health until her sudden

---

61 Lewis, D-29.
62 Lewis, D-50.
63 Lewis, D-63.
64 Lewis, D-21.
65 Lewis, D-21, D-22.
66 Lewis, D-5, D-6.
67 Phipps, *Mission Development*, 102. Last sentence from Robert Benedetto, *Presbyterian Reformers in Central Africa* (Leiden:Brill, 1996), 56–57. Further noted as "Benedetto, *Reformers*."
68 Phipps, *Mission Development*, 102.
69 Phipps, *Mission Development*, 102. Quote taken from *The Missionary*, 6/1895, 265.

death a few weeks later.[70] Poignantly, the baby was buried in a bamboo coffin lined and covered with her mother's wedding dress.[71] Sheppard built a new five-room house for Lucy and himself that was comparatively more comfortable.

Sheppard's pet monkey again proved to be an asset to the evangelist. At the end of a day's march he brought forth Tippo Tib to amuse the villagers while tents were being set up. Following this, Sheppard said,

We quietly moved Tippo on the inside, and we had a full congregation for a Gospel service. They give excellent attention while you are speaking and singing; but when you say, "let us pray," and have concluded your petitions, and open your eyes, you will be surprised, and also amused, to find the greater part of your congregation away up the street." At those services Lucy started off with the hymn "E Jisus kusa"—"Yes, Jesus Loves Me."[72]

Lucy conducted evangelistic tours, taught school, and instructed at the girl's home. She gave training in domestic chores in her home and she worked as a nurse. She formed the First Women's Society of the Congo which met once a week for prayer, worship and fellowship. Lucy had few instructional materials until 1910 when funds were provided. She acquired a small printing press, elementary grade readers, biblical parables and song sheets. Lucy never regretted giving herself to the missionary work in the Congo and the mission station was considered one of the most productive stations in Africa.[73]

Lucy reported on the first APCM baptismal service, explaining the requirements for becoming a church member: "In April 1895, five young men wanted to profess faith. ... These were carefully instructed and trained, and after some months when we had seen evidence of their changed lives, we received them into the church. At once these five started out as missionaries of Jesus." One of those youths, Kachunga, was unusually intelligent and was selected to go to America to assist in translation work.[74]

Because of her former training and experience, Lucy had oversight of the APCM educational work. She first had to learn Tshiluba, of course, and for that there were no manuals. As her husband had done several years earlier, she mingled daily with villagers in the market place, straining to pick up every nuance of inflection. Her ear was so sensitive that the vocabulary she compiled was published in the first Tshiluba dictionary.[75]

The Presbyterian mission quickly replaced Lapsley and sent Samuel Phillips Verner as business manager. On his first night in Luebo, Sheppard and Lucy had him for dinner. The next morning Lucy gave birth to Lucille Sheppard. A sickly child, in 1897 she also died. Verner, who had not adjusted to Africa well, was on the verge of a nervous breakdown and left that same year.

A budding young lawyer, William Morrison, who felt called to missions, arrived as his replacement in the spring of 1897. Sheppard continued his desire to plant a church for the Presbyterians among the Kuba people. However, the old king had died and a new clan had taken control. He went into the jungle to those who had not seen a Western man and set up a new mission station among Kuba.

Previously, Sheppard's reincarnation of Bope Mekabe, presumed by the earlier Lukengu, saved his life, but now his honorary membership in the Kuba royal family made him suspect in the eyes of Kot aMbeweeky's successors. Sheppard and Morrison waited at Ibanche (also spelled Ibaanc, Ibanj, Ibanshe, and Ibonge!) on the border of the central Kuba area, about 40 miles from Mushenge and 40 miles north of Luebo. … However, Mishaape had no interest in showing favors toward Sheppard. He was especially peeved because Maxamalinge, who was under suspicion as the son of the preceding Lukengu, was being sheltered by Sheppard at Ibanche.[76]

Sheppard told of the tense confrontation:

---

70 Phipps, *Mission Development*, 103, from Letter in Snyder paper, Montreat archives, December 27, 1894.

71 Phipps, *Mission Development*, 103. Quote taken from Kellersbergr, *Sheppard*, 15–16.

72 Phipps, *Mission Development*, 105. Quote taken from *Christian Observer*, March 25, 1896, 10.

73 Lewis, D-24, D-25.

74 Phipps, *Mission Developments*, 107. Taken from *Lucy Sheppard, From Talladega College to Africa*, (New York: American Missionary Association, n.d.), 5; Robert Bedinger, *Triumphs of the Gospel in the Belgian Congo* (Richmond: Presbyterian Committee of Publication, 1905), 127. Further noted as "Bedinger, *Triumphs*."

75 Phipps, *Mission Development*, 107. Taken from Kellersberger, *Sheppard*, 20, 24.

76 Phipps, *Mission Development*, 111.

> We sat down, turned face to face, folded our legs, and began talking. ... "Do you not know," he said, "that it is the custom when the crown passes from one family to another to murder all the sons of the old king?" ... Then he added, can we settle this thing now?" I said, "I hope so," and all I could see was murder in his eyes. Then he took some strong medicine out of the leopard skin and put it into the banana leaf. After sitting a while he had it tied up and gave it to a servant, telling him to throw it into the Lingadi River. The king said, "I cannot call it back and it will not come back. Just so everything is gone that was between us which I had in my heart against you. He said, "Now, what are you going to do?" I said, "If you will allow me I will kneel here on the mat with you and pray." After prayers we went to our houses, I stayed with him a week and then went back to Ibanj.[77]

The APCM reluctantly decided that Ibanche was as near to the Kuba heartland as a station could safely be established.

In 1898, the Sheppards had a third daughter, Wilhelmina. Native soldiers armed with modern rifles had revolted against the State officials and had vowed to kill every foreigner in the district. This threatening situation, along with Lucy's exhaustion from illness, caused her to take the advice that she should return to America with her child.[78] Lucy took Wilhelmina back to the U.S. to visit her mother and to leave her daughter with William's sister to raise.

In October, 1898, Lucy spoke to the Women's Society's at First Presbyterian Church. Her presentation was typical of those given to supporting congregations:

> Mrs. Sheppard gave interesting sketches of different phases in African life, showing us both the encouraging and the discouraging features. She seemed thoroughly happy in her work, and can even speak cheerfully of leaving her little baby here in the home land when she returns to her post in Africa ... everyone enjoyed her signing ...[79]

During her stay in VA, Lucy took time to compile a book that she could carry copies of back to Luebo. After she translated 46 hymns in 1898 for APCM use, they were published by Curtiss Press in Richmond. The hymnal, entitled Musambu ws Nzambi (Songs of God) became the first printed material ever made in the Tshiluba language.[80]

In, 1899, the fierce Belgian take over of Kasai country for costly rubber came close to Sheppard's new station. The Belgians had hired the Zappo-Zap tribe to destroy the entire Kuba district. The Africans thought Sheppard should help them, after all, he had a gun and knew how to use it. He refused. Morrison requested that he stop the raid. "These were orders," Sheppard wrote, "I had to go; there was nothing else I could do."[81] He went from dwelling to dwelling to convince his African friends to join him. Finally he did. Off they went straight towards the Zappo-Zap. "At a curve in the forest we met face-to-face with the Zappo-Zap, who, with lightening speed, cocked their guns, and took aim," Sheppard wrote, "I jumped forward, threw up my hands and cried in a loud voice, 'Don't shoot, 'I am Sheppard!'"[82] Chebambu considered Sheppard a friend and when Sheppard asked to be taken into the Zappo-Zap stockade, he agreed. Their leader was the feared Malumba.

Sheppard took advantage of their confidence. He listened to their conquests and asked specific questions like, "How did you do that?" Proudly they gave graphic answers with tales of cutting off baskets full of hands, and hanging bodies around a village to show their exploits. He heard of their meals and saw the flesh that was taken for them. He saw women chained and placed in tight pens. He even offered to buy the freedom of some. He took photos and again copious notes while smelling the dead flesh and seeing the gathering of their spoils of human parts and hearing of their cannibalism. After two days he left and rushed his report by runners to the mis-

---

77 Phipps, *Mission Development*, 112. Taken from *Southern Workman*, April 1898, 172–173.
78 Phipps, *Mission Development*, 112.
79 Phipps, *Mission Development*, 114. Taken from "Minutes of the Foreign Missions Committee of the Society for Women's Work, First Presbyterian Church, Stauton," October 13, 1898, unpublished.
80 Phipps, *Mission Development*, 114.
81 Lewis, from William Sheppard, PPC.
82 Lewis, from William Sheppard, PPC.

sionaries in Luebo and to Morrison. He then fell apart. Morrison took the report further to State headquarters.

At this time Lucy was returning to Africa not knowing of what had taken place in her absence. In NY, she met with Dr. Snyder, who had a new wife since his first wife had died, ready to return to the rebuilt mission station.

Lucy was also ready for the modern conveniences now at the mission station.

It was not to be. When she arrived she had to treck into the jungle to Ibanche which was another mess to be cleaned up and to a husband who was in spiritual depths of despair. It was a time of healing for them, a strengthening of their marriage, and continuation of the work of missions together. Neither William or Lucy spoke of this time and not a lot was mentioned until much later when both were home on furlough, and a glaring report about Sheppard accompanied them.

By 1902 the APCM was convinced that neither the State agents in the Congo nor the Belgian king would effect substantive changes in African labor practices without strong international pressure. On his return home from Africa in spring of 1903, Morrison was invited to speak to the Aborigines Protection Society in London. ... After Morrison addressed the Aborigines Protection Society, a motion was passed urging the British government to use its considerable international power to secure humane treatment for the Congolese.[83] Liberal party member Herbert Samuel then alerted fellow House of Commons legislators to the forced-labor tyranny in the Congo and to Sheppard's riveting account of "80 human hands being slowly dried over a fire."[84]

Soon after Morrison returned to America, he spoke to the PCUS General Assembly. He told of the abominations that Sheppard had reported years earlier and he pleaded for the "emancipation of the Congolese." The alarmed Assembly expressed its approval for what Morrison and Sheppard were doing in making Belgian atrocities known to the world.[85]

On the basis of Sheppard's findings of the atrocities the Belgians brought upon the Congolese, the Presbyterian Mission called for a state inquiry into the situation. The story was made public and caused the Mission Board to appeal to the United States Department of State to protest directly to King Leopold. Sheppard was fully supported by other missionaries both black and white.[86] Morrison went again in 1903 to London with further reports.

Alonzo Leaucort Edminston, a Stillman graduate, arrived in 1904. He met Althea Brown and they married the next year. Henry P. Hawkins and Lillian Thomas were the "best man" and "bridesmaid." They had two children, Sherman Lucas and Alonzo Leaucourt both had to come to America because of poor health. Alonzo was considered a preacher and a teacher of the Bible.[87] Together they achieved 72 years of service with the APCM. Alonzo pioneered in providing agricultural training for youth. Althea was an outstanding linguist, and her 600-page Grammar and Dictionary of the Bushonga or Bukua Language was eventually published in 1932 at Luebo.[88]

A year after Brown arrived, the Sheppards went on a long furlough--his first in a decade. Shortly after they left in 1904, hostilities between the State and the Kubas resulted in the destruction of Ibanche and several other villages. ... Unfortunately, Sheppard was not on hand to use his persuasive powers to moderate the insurrection. ... After the Kuba calmed down, Ibanche was gradually rebuilt and the mission work resumed.[89]

The Shepherds spent much of their furlough in Staunton with their daughter and his parents. ... After their family reunion, Lucy and her husband traveled widely to tell of APCM developments. Newspaper reports told of the response given to Sheppard. ... The report told of "spellbound" listeners and concluded, "His experiences have been even more thrilling than any recorded by

---

83 Phipps, Atrocities Protest, 151. Taken from Benedetto, *Reformers*, 165.
84 Phipps, Atrocities Protest, 151. Taken from Bedinger, *Triumphs*, 202.
85 Phipps, Atrocities Protest, 152. Taken from Minutes of the General Assembly (Richmond:Presbyterian Committee on Publication, 1903) 43, 483, 504.

86 Lewis, D-41.
87 Lewis, D-20.
88 Phipps, *Mission Development*, 122. Taken from Sylvia Jacobs, ed., Black Americans and the Misionary Movement in Africa (Westport, CT: Greenwood, 1982), 167.
89 Phipps, *Mission Development*, 123-124. Taken from *The Missionary*, 5/1905, 213.

the great African explorer, Henry M. Stanley."[90] Sheppard noted that he was giving "on an average of six or seven lectures a week."[91]

In 1906 the Sheppards tore themselves away from their daughter, whom they left with relatives in Staunton, and returned to the Congo by the usual circuitous route. In London they joined William and Bertha Morrison, who had recently married in MS. Also traveling with them were two black missionary recruits: Anne Taylor, a Tuscaloosa native of high ability, and Adolphus Rochester, who became her husband.[92]

Shortly after the Sheppards returned to Ibanche, Kot aPe visited the Mission with a large retinue. He apologized for his soldiers burning down the station during the period of their absence by not distinguishing more carefully between different types of foreigners. Lukengu recognized that he needed to ally himself with the APCM, and with Sheppard in particular, in his effort to defend his people. ... The Sheppards requested that the king supply some girls for the Maria Carey Home, which was being developed along the lines of the Pantops Home in Luebo. The king had become convinced of the advantages of literacy and health training, so he commanded his villages to send to Ibanche one girl each. When forty girls arrived a day later, Sheppard asked him to send fifty boys to the station for instruction. Again, this was immediately accomplished, and among them was a nephew of the king who became a Christian.

Even though Sheppard and other missionaries expressed paternalism at the beginning, their long-term goal of an indigenous church came to fruition. ... By 1907 a number of church officers could be found on the Presbyterian mission stations, marking "the beginning of a turnover to the native Christians the management of the internal affairs of the native church."[93]

With help both Morrison and Sheppard continued the campaign to reveal the inhumane treatment of the European company. In 1907, Sheppard publicized the use of terror and extortion by rubber companies in the Belgian Congo. One year later, Sheppard refused to retract his charges that the European Kasai Company caused the decline of the African Bukuba Society. The Kasai company sued him for libel. After a trial, that was supported by two American men who showed up unexpectedly, Sheppard was found not guilty.[94]

Sheppard was so successful that the Government had to desist its activities. Following the trial he returned to America a heroic celebrity and launched an extended lecture tour, headlining newspaper articles even when he shared the stage with such luminaries as W. E. B. DuBois and Booker T. Washington.

In 1909 Edminston furloughed back in the U.S. to raise money. His wife was helping to translate the Bakuba language and reduce it into a grammar, dictionary, song book and other learning aids.

After more than four decades as a cunning and ruthless despot, Leopold at last received some retribution. Many in the international community detested him because of his African policies. He had finally become such an embarrassment to his own people that they took his Congo possession away from him a year before he died. ... Sheppard's two decades in the Congo were a period of rapid transformation. When he arrived, Leopold's rubber realm was just beginning to develop. His years there coincided with the era of the worst atrocities in central African history. The depopulation of the Congo during the 25 years of Leopold's rule by approximately 50 percent was similar to what had happened earlier when slavers were kidnapping along the African coast. More people were killed by the village raids of state agents than there were slaves sold in the New World.[95]

As an advocate for missions, Sheppard was also instrumental in helping to establish fair social practices and in respecting the African. Sheppard regarded the African as equal with the European as well as the African American. The only problem with the African focused upon his lack of education and lack of knowledge of the true God. Therefore, Sheppard's mannerism with the Africans were quite different than that of the European missionaries.[96]

---

90 Phipps, *Mission Development*, 125. Taken from letter to Miss Davis, written in Louisville, November 8, 1904, Montreat Archives.
91 Phipps, *Mission Development*, 125–126.
92 Phipps, *Mission Development*, 127. Taken from William Sheppard manuscript in the Hampton archives.
93 Phipps, *Mission Developments*, 126–127. Taken from *Kasai Herald*, January 1908.

94 Lewis, D-41.
95 Phipps, *Atrocities Protest*, 173–175.
96 Lewis, D-41, D-42.

He served in the mission station for approximately 20 years. After the trial, in the spring of 1910, Sheppard returned to the U.S. and met with the Foreign Missions Department. It was here that the reports had come that while Lucy was absent in U.S., Sheppard had taken an African woman and had a son the local Africans called "Sheppete." Lucy had learned about this upon her return to Africa and had forgiven him.

The two APCM stations, Luebo and Ibanche, had a total of 7,705 members and over 20,000 adherents by 1910. Most of the 5,700 in the weekday schools and the 8,000 in the Sunday schools would eventually become full members. This increase was not due to the requirements for membership being lowered, for candidates for baptism were required to complete instruction that took almost a year.[97]

Maria Fearing had gone earlier on furlough in 1906 and spoke to religious groups about her work. She returned to Africa later that year. Her second leave of absence came in 1915 along with Lucius DeYampert. At this time she did not return to Africa because of unforeseen circumstances. She remained in America and lived with the Missionaries DeYamperts in Selma, AL.[98] She served on the mission field for over 21 years. Fearing was instrumental in working with hundreds of African young women teaching them skills she learned as a slave.[99] Many of the women who had become Christians were trying very hard to live better lives. She referred to her young women as "our Little Home Missionaries."

Alonzo and Althea Maria (nee Brown) Edminston returned in 1911 to the Congo without their two children who had to stay in America because of their poor health. Althea helped translate the Bakuba language and reduced it into a grammar, dictionary, song book and other learning aids.[100] Along with her translation work she taught in the day school and became the head. She taught Sunday School and was supervisor of the Marie Carey Home for Girls. She was a leader in the missionary assignments in the villages.[101] He and Althea were located at Bulape near the Bakuba capital as resident missionaries. Their service was a attended by as many as two thousand people. However after one year it was decided that the Edminstons should be withdrawn from the region. In 1920, the Edminstons took another furlough and stayed in America for one year.[102]

It was the end of an era. By 1920 the Foreign Mission Board had changed its policies, and now discouraged African Americans from applying for jobs in Africa. This was partly because, with the advent of Marcus Garvey, Americans of color could no longer travel to the Congo whenever they wished. The Edminstons did return in 1921 and were transferred to the Mutoto station. Both he and his wife provided services for the Africans and had good relationships with them. After four years of work, he fell ill and became a victim of the sleeping sickness disease. They both returned to Brussels, New York City and to Nashville for treatments. The Edminstons returned to the Congo and stayed until 1937.[103]

Lillian Thomas wrote many articles in the *Kasai Herald*, a journal of the American Presbyterian Congo Mission. She believed that education was the most important task before the people, practically as well as spiritually. She had high blood pressure which finally caused a heart attack on May 29, 1930.[104]

A dozen African Americans, equally divided in gender, served the APCM, and nearly all of them were recruited by the Sheppards. They were: Henry Hawkins, 1894–1910; Maria Fearing, 1984–1917; Lillian Thomas (DeYampert), 1894-1918; Joseph Phipps, 1895–1908; Althea Brown (Edminston), 1902–1937; Lucius DeYampert, 1902-1918; Alonzo Edminston, 1903–1941; Adolphus Rochester, 1906-1939; Annie Taylor (Rochester), 1906–1914; and Edna Atkinson (Rochester), 1923–1939.[105]

A year after William and Lucy Sheppard's return to the U.S. he was given a pastorate at Grace Presbyterian Church, Louisville, KY. During 1912, Sheppard's first year as pastor of Grace Church ... sixty new members were added—a 50

---

97 Phipps, *Mission Development*, 129. Taken from *The Missionary*, 5/1910, 249; Mavumi-s Kiantndu, "A Study of the Contribution of American Presbyterians to the Formation of the Church in Zaire" (dissertation, Union Theological Seminary in VA, 1978), 175–177.
98 Lewis, D-22.
99 Lewis, 52.
100 Ibid.
101 Lewis, D-6.
102 Lewis, D-20.
103 Ibid.
104 Lewis, D-50.
105 Phipps, *Mission Development*, 122–123.

percent increase in the congregation's size. In 1913 he worked with a group of boys to renew his church building at Hancock and Roselane.[106]

Sheppard traveled as a preacher and speaker. He helped run an inner-city mission with Lucy and they were instrumental in building a recreational center and a park, later called William Sheppard Park.

Lucy helped organize cooking, sewing, and choral clubs. Her husband gave oversight to the carpentry and shoe repairing schools and to the recreational facilities.[107]

The Sheppards often crossed the Ohio River at Louisville to visit the Indiana Reformatory. ... To guide African-American boys so that they would not become inmates in the penal system, Sheppard was active for years in the Louisville Council of the Boy Scouts of America and provided entertainment at the summer scout camp.[108] Lucy taught in the Sunday School, trained the Choir, organized the Junior Choir, and lectured about her mission work.

That Foreign Missions officials had obviously forgiven him of his adulterous behavior many years earlier. In support of his use of superlatives, Chester stated:

> He is the only minister on our roll holding a fellowship in the Royal Geographic Society of London. On behalf of the Executive Committee of Foreign Missions, I wish to say that there is no missionary on our roll more beloved or more highly esteemed by the Committee under which he serves. During the time of his missionary service he has been called to represent us on many important occasions. He has stood before kings, both white kings and black kings, as our representative. He has never represented us anywhere that we have not had reason to be proud of the manner in which he has done it. He is now both recognized in London and Brussels as one of the greatest of African missionaries. That for which the Committee of Foreign Missions esteems him most is not the fact that he has achieved this prominence and recognition, but that, having achieved it, he has come back to us the same simple-hearted, humble, earnest Christian man that he was when we first sent him out.[109]

William Sheppard died, November 1927, a year after a stroke paralyzed him at age 61. Lucy continued ministry until she was 70 years old. "She served on the board of the Colored Red Cross Hospital, became a sought-after speaker, and was the first black woman ever voted into the Presbyterian Kentucky Synod."[110] The date of her death is unknown, but believed to be in 1940.

William Sheppard was a team with Samuel Norvell Lapsley. When death separated them, Sheppard continued the mission outreach. A team member again with the African Americans who returned with him to Luebo, they built a strong Presbyterian mission in the Congo. He joined in the cry for justice for the Congolese and won. He came out to tell the world of Congo's actual beauty and its real life horrors. Without him the Presbyterian mission would not have remained strong nor would it have grown. But, he could not do it alone. He needed the help of the Lord, dedicated African-American co-workers, and many, many others who supported the mission work and believed it should continue in spite of the seemingly insurmountable obstacles.

While African Americans were generally marginalized in the U.S., Sheppard could proudly claim to have been a mover and shaker of people on three continents. What other black American who lived most of his years in the nineteenth century can claim to have been received in the White House by two presidents and to have been discussed at a cabinet meeting by a third president? No other African American during that period did more to stir up forces of liberation in the Congo, in Europe, and in the U.S.[111]

---

109 Phipps, *After Leaving the Congo*, 186. Taken from PPC, 14.
110 Kennedy, *Livingston*.
111 Phipps, *After Leaving the Congo*, 181.

---

106 Phipps, *After Leaving the Congo*, 184. Taken from Minutes of the Presbytery of Louisville, April 9, 1914, 27–28.
107 Phipps, *After Leaving the Congo*, 184.
108 Phipps, *After Leaving the Congo*, 185.

Bibliography

Benedetto, Robert. *Presbyterian Reformers in Central Africa*. Leiden: Brill, 1996.

Hampton University Archives. Hampton, VA.

Harr, Wilbur. "The Negro as an American Protestant Missionary in Africa." Doctoral dissertation, University of Chicago Divinity School, 1945.

Hoshschild, Adam. *King Leopold's Ghost*. New York: Houghton Mifflin, 1998.

Jacobs, Sylvia, ed. *Black Americans and the Misionary Movement in Africa*. Westport, CT: Greenwood, 1982.

Kellerrsburger, Julia Luke. *Lucy Gantt Sheppard: Shepherdess of His Sheep on Two Continents*. Atlanta: PCUA Committee on Women's Work, n.d.

Kennedy, Pagan. *Black Livingston—A True Tale of Adventure in the Nineteenth-century Congo*. New York: Viking Press, 2002.

Lapsley, James, ed. *Life and Letters of Samuel Norvill Lapsley*. Richmond: Whittet & Shepperson, 1893.

Lewis, Marlyn. "The African American In Christian Missions." Masters paper, Dallas Theological Seminary, 1993.

Myers, John Brown. *The Congo for Christ: The Story of the Congo Mission*. New York: Fleming R. Revell Co., 1985.

Phipps, William E. *William Sheppard: Congo's African American Livingstone*. Louisville, KY: Geneva Press, 2002.

Presbyterian Historical Society. Montreat, NC.

Roth, Daniel. "Grace Not Race: Southern Negro Church Leaders, Black Identity and Mission to West Africa, 1865–1919." Dissertation, University of Texas at Austin, 1975.

Sheppard, William. "Into the Heart of Africa." *Southern Workman* 22 (1893).

Sheppard, William. "Light in Darkest Africa." *Southern Workman*. Southern Presbyterian Church, April 1905.

Sheppard, William. "Pioneers Missionary to the Congo." Nashville: Executive Committee of Foreign Missions, PCUS, 1942.

Sheppard, William. "Presbyterian Pioneers." Richmond, VA: Presbyterian Committee of Publications, 1916.

Slade, Ruth. "English Speaking Missions in The Congo Independent State, 1878–1908." Brussels: Academie Royale des Sciences D'Outre Mer, 1959.

Thompson, Ernest T. *Presbyterian Missions in the Southern United States*. Richmond: Presbyterian Committee of Publication, 1934.

Vass, Winefred K. and Lachlan C. Vass III. *The Lapsley Saga*. Franklin, TN: Providence House, 1997.

"William Sheppard: Christian Fighter for African Rights," *Southern Workman* 39 (Jan. 1910).

Williams, Walter. *Black Americans and the Evangelization of Africa 1877–1900*. Madison, WI: The University of Wisconsin Press, 1982.

1895–1919 Era: Reconstruction

Chapter 18
Reconstruction (1895–1919)

by Robert J. Stevens

The African-American missionaries encouraged the African to come to America, acquire an education and return home to assist "your people." During this time, most of the African-American missionaries had trained a local pastorate to minister to the needs of the African Christian community. In contrast, the white missionaries trained Africans too, but these Africans always remained in positions subordinate to the whites, whereas the African Americans provided the Africans with positions of authority, decision making, and responsibility.[1]

In one newspaper, the *Christian Express*, the articles warned that the Africans educated in African-American schools returned "indoctrinated" with the poison of race hatred. Also it was believed that the notions of democracy, liberty, education, equality, and self government could not possibly help the African to submit to his place in the pre-Apartheid government.[2]

In his article, "Black Man's Burden," Robert Gordon lists seven factors for what he called the decline of African-American involvement in missions in the 20th century.[3] Two areas not already addressed by Jacobs were recruiting and economics.

One area of major missions recruiting has always been among university students. The Student Volunteer Movement was the most influential means of recruiting missionaries, [starting] in the late 19th century (1888–1920). "Recruitment was aimed at university campuses—precisely where blacks were least likely to be found." While thousands of university students were making commitments to give their lives to foreign missions, the African-American community was fighting for its very survival in the U.S.[4]

By the 1900's, the European colonists started developing an open policy of prohibiting the African-American missionary

---

1 Sylvia Jacobs, "Black Americans and the Missionary Movement in Africa," *Contributions in Afro-American and African Studies*, no. 66 (Westport, CT: Greenwood Press,1982), 209.
2 Marilyn Lewis, "Independent Study Assignment: The African-American in Christian Mission," Th.M. Candidate, Dallas Theological Seminary, #788, 1993, 56.
3 Robert Gordon, "Black Man's Burden," *Evangelical Missions Quarterly* (Fall 1973).
4 Vaughn Walston, "Moblizing the African-American Church for Global Evangelization," in *African-American Experience in World Mission: A Call Beyond Community* (Pasadena, CA: William Carey Library Publishers, 2002) by Cooperative Mission Network of the African Dispersion (COMINAD).

from serving in Africa. The restriction of visas was the most mentioned problem. In addition to visa regulations, "it was necessary for each missionary or teacher to secure the permission of the governor of a colony before entering for mission service."[5]

---

5 Sylvia Jacobs, "Black Americans and the Missionary Movement in Africa," *Contributions in Afro-American and African Studies*, no. 66 (Westport, CT: Greenwood Press, 1982), 204.

Chapter 19
Lott Carey Convention

by Leroy Fitts and Mark Sidwell

Leroy Fitts—Shaw University, B.A. 1967; Southeastern Baptist Theological Seminary, M.Div., 1970; VA Seminary, D.Div., 1975; D.H.L., 1990; Princeton University (HEH Inst.), 1984; Baltimore Hebrew University, M.A., 1985. Editor, Lott Carey Baptist Convention, 1975–1990; Board of Managers, VA Seminary and College, 1980; member NAACP, Association for the Study of Negro History, 1978–present; Board of Managers, St. Mary's Seminary and University.

Author, *Lott Carey First Black Missionary to Africa*, 1978; *A History of Black Baptists* (Nashville, TN: Broadman Press, 1985).

Used by permission.

Mark Sidwell has a B.A. in history and M.A. and Ph.D. in church history from Bob Jones University (BJU) where he teaches history and serves as director of a resource center in J. S. Mack Library. He is the author of *The Dividing Line* as well as coauthor of *United States History for Christian Schools*, second edition. Dr. Sidwell also edits and writes for *Biblical Viewpoints*, the journal of the BJU School of Religion.

Author, *Free Indeed: Heroes of Black Christian History* (Greenville, SC: Bob Jones University Press, 1995).

Used by permission.

Lott Carey's Mission Spirit

Black preacher, and former slave, Lott Carey, was missionary pioneer in West Africa and inspired a major African-American effort in foreign missions. Carey was born on a plantation in Charles City, about 30 miles south of Richmond, VA, around 1790. As the case with many slaves, little is known of his parents. When he was a child his godly grandmother told him, "Son, you will grow strong. You will lead many, perhaps it may be you who will travel over the big seas to carry the great secret to my people." In 1800, he moved to Richmond where his master hired him out to work at the Shockoe tobacco warehouse.

It is said that shortly after moving to Richmond, he fell victim to the vices of the city for about three years. Despite this fact, however, Carey eventually was converted in 1807 by the preaching of the Reverend John Courtney, pastor of the First Baptist Church. Upon his baptism, Carey became a member of that church. By carefully saving his earnings and with contributions from whites who enjoyed his preaching, Carey was able to buy his freedom and that of his two children for the price of $850.

Lott Carey learned to read and write by attending a night school during 1815–1817. This project was conducted by William Crane and other white persons who held the class in the white church building.

In 1814, this building had been sold to the Black members and the new congregation became known as the First African Baptist Church of Richmond. In 1815, Carey became a powerful preacher, not only to blacks, but to whites as well.

Lott Carey organized the African Baptist Foreign Missionary Society in 1815. This was the first organization for foreign missions founded by blacks in this country. He was secretary of that society from the time of its organization until he sailed for Africa in 1821.

During this period, there was a growing concern among some whites over the ultimate disposition of the free blacks whose new status caused many whites to fear that these people posed a threat to such peace and tranquillity as was found among the slaves. One of the proposed solutions was that the free blacks be transported to Africa. The organization advocating this view was the American Colonization Society, founded in 1816. Most of the free blacks and some whites were opposed to this idea. Some conceived of the Colonization as "a sort of unholy alliance" between its organizers and southern slaveholders, and as a scheme to get rid of free blacks and to make slavery more secure. The leading blacks inveighed against it in no uncertain terms. ...Yet the Colonization Society moved ahead with its plans and sent representatives to West Africa to explore the area for a suitable site for the settlement of the expatriated blacks.

In 1816, the African Colonization Society was organized in Washington, D.C., as a scheme for the re-settlement of captured enslaved and freed African Americans on the coast of Africa committed to the care of the U.S. government. However, large numbers of African Americans did not participate in the scheme of the American Colonization Society due to strong opposition from the African-American leadership in the U.S. The center of opposition was in Philadelphia, PA. The majority opinion was that African Americans should remain in the U.S. and assimilate into the mainstream of American culture. However, they were aware of the fact that such assimilation was going to be a long-term struggle. Moreover, the objection was not to missionary activity, but to the fundamental motive of colonization.

Whatever may have been the attitudes with respect to American blacks settling in Africa, Lott Carey worked persistently toward his objective of taking the message of the Gospel to the land of his forefathers. He was assisted in his efforts by Colin Teague, also a free black preacher, who shared Carey's ambition to convert the Africans to Christianity. When it was ascertained by his employers at the tobacco warehouse that he was contemplating a missionary ministry in Africa, they offered to raise his salary to $1,000 if he would remain in this country. This had no influence in changing his views of duty to God and to his black brethren in Africa.

Unfortunately, the Baptist mission board asked Carey to work with the American Colonization Society. Carey objected. William Crane was quite pleased when he learned of Carey's intention to go to Africa. He subsequently made various contacts with philanthropic-minded people in VA and missionary organizations. In addition, the Richmond Baptist Missionary Society petitioned the largest organization of Baptists in the country, the General Baptist Convention, which met every three years, to support Carey and Teague as missionaries to Africa. Using money from his own savings, the sale of his farm for $1,500, a contribution of $700 from the African Baptist Missionary Society which he organized in Richmond, and contributions from some whites including $200 in cash and $100 in books from the Triennial Convention of the General Baptist, plus the support of the American Colonization Society, Carey and Teague sailed on the "Nautilus" to Liberia, January 1821.

The small group of African-American Baptists, taking advantage of the opportunity offered by the Society, arrived and found that the report sent to the U.S. urging government sponsorship of a free-slave colony on Sherbo Island, the request having been granted with the protection of the U.S. Navy and the preliminary employment of native (tribal) labor for clearing land and building shelters for the prospective colonists, had not taken place. Lott Carey and other American settlers had to spend their first month as refugees in the British refugee colony of Sierra Leone, West Africa. A small farm was rented and they had to cultivate it for their support and for the support of the Africans; and pay as much of the rent as they could. This option would last until the lands were purchased by the Colonization Society.

However, these shattering political experiences as a refugee in Freetown, Sierra Leone, did not prevent Lott Carey from keeping the missionary cause paramount in his mind. Each political obstacle tended to remind Carey of his grandmother's counsel and the stirring. Lott Carey recognized that the cause of Christ was not always best advanced through an alliance with political agencies. To be sure, the judgment of the Foreign Mission Board of the Triennial Convention to link its African mission with the American Colonization Society was, as Carey suggested, "a detriment to the missionary cause in Africa."

In Carey's letter to Reverend Mr. Straughton, Foreign Mission Board, March 13, 1821, he wrote:

I have not been able to write an information relative to the state of the country, which can be of much use to the board. I intend taking a small excursion in the country, but cannot promise when that will be, as the rains will set in soon, my wife is sick, and we are desirous to get a small crop on the way, as early as possible. ...I, however, have the promise of some friends to take me down as far as the Bagroo, as soon as I am ready to go. I believe that just over on the Bullom side is a beautiful field for missionary labors, among the Mandingoes.

The test of Carey's missionary spirit was again manifested through the sickness of his second wife. Her health had been in a declining state even before she left America. During the last critical hours, Lott Carey was careful to meet his wife's every need. Much of his time then had to be spent in maintaining a family of three children. However, Carey did not allow this new situation to deter him from the missionary cause in West Africa. He not only preached as often as opportunity permitted him, but he also established a mission among the Mandingoes.

After some negotiations with the leading chief around the Cape, King Peter, for a portion of land between Sierra Leone and the Gold Coast. Initially King Peter proved slow in his negotiation procedures. Thereupon, the U.S. government agent cut short the prolonged negotiations in a summary way by pointing a pistol at King Peter's head. Naturally, this surprise of power convinced King Peter to put his mark to a treaty by which he ceded in perpetuity an ill-defined tract of land which was the nucleus of what later became the Republic of Liberia.

The colonizers found their new home offered a great challenge to the founding of a new colony because of its uncultivated state and the hostility of the native tribes. The rains were approaching and provisions were running short. Carey's determination and persistence to remain was able to save the colony because he prevailed upon others to stay. They organized and were put into a state of readiness for an enemy attack. The tribal warriors were already grouping as an attack force with their war drums sounding day and night. During the war Lott Carey proved to be one of the bravest men and lent his well-directed and vigorous support to the measures Jehudi Ashmun who had taken over the management of the colony. In one of his letters, Lott Carey compared the little exposed colony on Cape Montserado at that time to the Jews who, in rebuilding their city, "grasped a weapon in one hand, while they labored with the other," but added emphatically, "there never has been an hour or minute, no, not even when the balls were flying round my head, when I could wish myself again in America."

During the first few years the colonists experienced severe economic, political, and health problems. The missionary career of Reverend Lott Carey went beyond the ministry of preaching and teaching. He also served the colony as a medical missionary. Having been appointed to the position of health officer of the colony early August 1822. Lott Carey advanced his expertise in the area of medical science.

Notwithstanding the unsettled state of the colony and the active part he was compelled to take in its general interests, Lott Carey never forgot his divine calling to be a gospel preacher and African missionary. Carey preached several times each week and, in addition, gave religious instruction to many of the native children.

On April 2, 1825, the board of the American Colonization Society passes a motion to organize a permanent government for the colony. The colony became known as "Liberia," derived from the Latin meaning "Place of Freedom." The capital, Monrovia, was named in honor of President Monroe of the U.S. under whose administration the final arrangements were concluded.

Carey later proposed a specific plan for an emigrant's program to Liberia. This was the first of such programs to be proposed on the basis of medical science. In a letter to the free coloured people of the U.S. he wrote: "The true character of the African climate is not well understood in other countries. Its inhabitants are as robust, as healthy, as long lived, to say the least, as those of any other country. Nothing like an epidemic has ever appeared in this colony; nor can we learn from the natives, that the calamity of a sweeping sickness ever yet visited this part of the continent. But the change from a temperate to a tropical country is a great one; too great, not to affect the health more or less—in the cases of old people and very young children, it often causes death." Carey proposed that the emigrants plan to leave only during the months from April to November. He concluded that, if emigrants would observe this program, then they could expect a long and prosperous life in Liberia.

Lott Carey, the versatile black preacher, participated with Governor Ashmun in the development of a stable colony. Hence, Ashmun and Carey with the input of the advisory council launched a vigorous construction project of schools and churches. The principal teaching responsibilities in the schools were carried on by

Lott Carey. He made many urgent appeals to the Christian and philanthropic spirit of Americans that the Africans in the colonial region were very eager for education.

Upon finally settling in Liberia, Lott Carey began the process of establishing himself as a bulwark of Christian inspiration there, especially among the Vai people of Grand Cape Mount County. Carey established the Providence Baptist Church in Monrovia. In 1826, he led the congregation in establishing a missionary society to raise money for missions. Carey did not attempt to do everything in the church himself; he shared responsibilities and developed leaders. Still, the burdens of government continued to interfere with Carey's work. He became the spokesman for a group of colonists who were dissatisfied with the way the governor of the colony, Jehudi Ashmun, was handling property disputes. Jehudi Ashmun published the announcement that there were in the colony more than a dozen healthy persons who would not receive any more provisions out of the public store until they earned them in useful labor. The colonists demanded that the agent rescind his order.

Carey acknowledged his influence on others and told the agent that it was his wish hereafter to receive no more supplies from the Colonization Society, and to live less intimately with secular connections. Carey became reconciled to Ashmun when he professed, "his willingness to be useful in the way the Agent thought fit to propose." Ashmun expressed no desire to project Carey as an enemy of the colonial government. He knew and trusted Carey's sincerity.

In 1826, the citizens of Liberia encouraged Lott Carey to extend his missionary career in still another field of service. He was elected to the Vice Agency of the colony and was now Ashmun's assistant. In March 1828, Governor Ashmun fell ill and returned to America leaving the entire government of the colony in the hands of Lott Carey. Upon his death, Ashmun urged that Lott Carey be made permanent agent of Liberia. Lott Carey was appointed governor of Liberia. He followed Ashmun's requests in completing work on the Government House, put the jail in complete order, had guns and armaments in a proper state, and got the new settlers located on their lands. He proposed a scheme to facilitate improved communication by the purchase, or aid in the purchase of a vessel to run constantly from this, to America, to bring out our own supplies." He proposed the construction of a new road from Boatswain's to Millsburg. More significantly, Carey negotiated the purchase of the Millsburg lands from the regional kings. He also took measures to strengthen the military security of the colony.

At the same time he became a leading figure in defending his settlement against hostile tribes. In 1829, Bassa parties began raiding outlying colonial settlements. Carey dispatched three trusted emissaries to intercede with chief King Bristol. Bristol responded by seizing the emissaries and making them prisoners. Lott Carey organized a volunteer relief force to rescue his lieutenants. In a strange turn of circumstances, while he was engaged in preparations of making cartridges for defense against an attack by hostile tribes, Carey was killed by an accidental explosion of loose gunpowder by a candle which appears to have been accidentally upset. Eight persons died. Six persons survived until the 9th, and Mr. Carey and one other until the 10th of November 1829.

In brief, Lott Carey laid the foundations for Christian missions in West Africa. He was the "founding father" of an African republic. They settled in what became the Colony of Liberia and organized a missionary program among the native Africans and the settlers. Part of the resolution read and adopted at the annual meeting of the Richmond African Baptist Missionary Society in 1829 is, as follows: "His discriminating judgment, his honesty of heart, and decision of character, qualified him eminently, for this service."

Carey made a clear distinction between a search for "missionary grounds" and in colonizing grounds." He explained, "Africa suffers for gospel truth, and she will suffer, until missionaries can be sent, and settled in different parts of her continent."

Objectively, he always affirmed that the success of the African mission was the result of the hands of Divine Providence. Carey believed that Christian faith must be linked dynamically with a positive view of man in which the concepts of equality and dignity stand out. He clearly believed that through Jesus Christ a person became a it new creature." Carey believed that Christian missions must be adjusted to the particular needs of the mission field. Christian missions, in the thinking of Lott Carey, must be about the business of alleviating human suffering in any form and the removal of tangible and intangible blocks to the ultimate goal of freedom and dignity of all. Carey believed that God works effectively for oppressed people in such a way as to transcend any artificial separation of the religious and secular. This is why Lott Carey could take on diversified roles on the missionary field. He could be at once a preacher and teacher, a pastor and governor of the colony, and a soldier of the cross and soldier in defense of his people. His impact on the Christian missionary enterprise is enduring.

History of the Lott Carey Convention

While in Africa, Lott Carey maintained communication with many African-American church leaders back in the U.S. He sought to show how missionary-minded men and women could overshadow the colonization motif with a distinctive missionary one.

While the colony was being established, the nation back in America became increasingly divided over the slavery issue, while some of the slaves themselves from time to time rose up in violent revolt against their condition. The historian of slave revolts, Herbert Apthenker, reports finding it records of approximately 250 slave revolts and conspiracies in the history of American Negro slavery." The most notable of these were one led by Denmark Vesey, a free black who had purchased his freedom in Charleston, SC in 1822, and Nat Turner's rebellion in 1831, in Southhampton, VA. Turner was an influential religious leader, able to read and write, who felt that his insurrection was ordained of God. He gathered an inspired following, and in the uprising he led, more than 57 whites were killed before Turner was captured and he and his followers executed.

It was not until the early national period that the spirit of Lott Carey took hold within the African-American Christian community. By this time, African-American Baptists had developed many of their own independent boards to advance African missions. In 1840, the Black Baptist of America organized their first convention with a national purpose: The American Baptist Missionary Convention. The ABMU came into being as a result of many calls and requests from Africa to send missionaries and resources to continue the enterprise of the late Reverend Lott Carey.

In 1897, the National Baptist Convention, USA met in Boston, MA, with debate centered around key issues: (1) the advisability of the removal of the FMB from Richmond to Louisville; (2) the use of American Baptist literature and cooperation with the white Baptists in general; and (3) the primacy of foreign missions as a greater emphasis for the convention.

Several clergymen from VA and NC held firmly to their contention of the primacy of the foreign mission emphasis and cooperation with white Baptists. These 28 distinguished clergymen organized the Lott Carey Convention in a way that would reflect the spirit of Rev. Lott Carey.

Lott Carey Foreign Mission Convention

In 1898, a controversy was brewing. Up until that time in history, the black Baptist churches had been using Sunday school and other religious educational materials published by the Northern Baptist Convention. Some of the agents for marketing this literature were clergy of the National Baptist Convention. There were, however, some of the brethren who felt strongly that the National Baptist Convention was capable of and morally obligated to prepare its own religious educational materials. It was a matter of racial pride that prompted this point of view. At the convention of 1897, Rev. Harvey Johnson, the leading Baptist minister in Baltimore, MD, urged the black Baptist to establish their own institutions in "order to better achieve the kind of experience and enjoy the positions that would result in the development of leaders."

In 1898, the Reverend E. K. Love of GA recommended to the Convention that it create its own publishing house and produce its own literature. The recommendation threatened the financial benefits which those brethren who were agents of the American Baptist Publications Society of the Northern Baptist Convention were receiving. The National Baptist Convention, however, voted overwhelmingly to adopt Dr. Love's recommendation. Following this, the men whose finances were adversely affected by the move were instrumental in forming the Lott Carey Baptist Foreign Mission Convention which has continued since that time to carry on an active missionary enterprise.

The founding fathers of the Lott Carey Convention established a two-fold policy of cooperation "with any and all existing Baptist organizations in doing missionary work" and primacy of foreign missions. With the spirit of women's missionary labor at an all-time high, President C. S. Brown led several women of high esteem to formulate a nominating committee to recommend women of great leadership abilities to develop a viable women's auxiliary to the convention. Since its organization the Women's Auxiliary has worked diligently alongside of the parent body. The women of the convention were especially instrumental in the enlistment of youth to work for the cause of missions.

The Lott Carey Convention opened its first Mission in Brewerville, Liberia, under the leadership of Rev. J. O. Hayes. A native of NC, he affiliated himself with the convention immediately after its founding in 1897. Prior to his affiliation he had labored in Liberia under the BFMC since 1881. The Lott Carey Convention opened its first Mission in Brewerville, Liberia. Rev. Hayes reported to the LCC in 1902 that the church was experiencing slow growth due to the "heathen influence with which the Christians have to contend."

The mission work extended beyond the establishment of a church. In 1902, Rev. J. O. Hayes operated an industrial school for the training of boys who came into the villages from the interior of the country.

In 1909, LCC sent Rev. and Mrs. W. H. Thomas to Brewerville, Liberia. Mrs. Thomas worked faithfully with her husband until she died. Mr. Thomas extended the mission of LCC with journalism. He operated the only printing press among the Negro Baptists in Liberia. The intelligence of Liberia was greatly enhanced by the Watchman, a monthly paper which was organized in 1909 in his mission station.

In 1917, he reported to the LCC that the Alexander Chapel was completed and used as a church, Sunday school, and day school. He also stated that work was in progress on the "Salle Mile Building" home house for the missionaries.

Consistent with its basic philosophy, the LCC established a program of cooperation with other bodies doing mission work. In 1916, it established organic cooperation with Liberian Baptist Convention in the operation of Ricks Institute. Not only did the LCC support programs of evangelism, and vocational education, but it also made early strides in medical missions.

From the outset of its organization, the LCC expressed interest in Haiti. In 1916, the LCC began its work in Haiti in cooperation with Baptist pastors and private school teachers who were supplementing their small salaries by doing mission work on the island. The pioneers were Rev. Lucius Hippolite, Rev. Jeannes Jacques, Rev. Delfort Eustache, Rev. De Lattree, Miss Alice Pierealexis, Rev. Dumay Pierealexis, and Rev. L. Ton Evans. The Haitian mission represented another example of the LCC commitment to cooperation with other bodies in foreign missions.

We have a peculiar interest in Haiti, because it is the only Negro republic in the Western World, and because the people are inclined to be Baptist. By mutual agreement, the American Baptist Home Mission Society has consented to assist in the evangelization of Haiti.

South Africa attracted the missionary arm of the LCC. The Convention's pioneer missionary in South Africa was Rev. John Tule, in 1899. By 1915, the state law of South Africa provided that "colored people including missionaries shall not emigrate" into the country. Consequently, the LCC, for the first time, was required, of necessity, to cooperate with the South African Baptist Union. Native churches would not be recognized by the Government of South Africa unless they were commissioned by the SABU. In fact, the SABU took charge of the LCC stations in South Africa. In 1926, Rev. B. F. Mdodona, gained approval of the British Baptist Union of South Africa to serve freely under LCC. He caused the name of LCC to be exalted in South Africa.

The LCC's initial contact in the Congo was in 1901. Rev. and Mrs. C. C. Boone, pioneer preacher and physician, established a mission house, a chapel for preaching, and industrial school rooms—compliments of the Missionary Union of Boston with which LCC cooperated.

The LCC opened its missionary work in India in 1926. Manmatha Nath Biswas and Mrs. Sukoda Bannerjee began a work in Calcutta. In the late 1940's, the LCC established a school in the slums of Delhi.

The LCC began its missionary work in Nigeria in 1961 under the leadership of Rev. Charles Ebong. By 1963, the LCC had been organized into the Wendell Baptist Convention of Africa. In 1964 the WBCA began construction of an educational facility.

In 1964, Dr. A. Carlyle Miller petitioned the LCC to accept the educational and missionary program he had initiated and carried on for 18 years in Guyana. Dr. Miller was from Guyana, received his degree in the U.S. and practiced near the Covenant Avenue Baptist Church in New York City. He then studied at Virginia Theological Seminary and College in Lynchburg, VA. Upon his return to Guyana he set up his work and the Covenant Avenue Baptist Church help to develop his dream of a Christian mission.

Chapter 20

Rev. John Chilembwe: African Missionary Extraordinaire

by Pastor Esker Jerome Harris

Pastor Harris was in Malawi, March 1977–July 2001, as an appointed missionary by his National Baptist Church. He taught in a new Bible school and was active in church development.

Born in Memphis, TN, Pastor Harris grew up third in a family of seven. Upon graduation from high school he was awarded a football scholarship to UCLA. He graduated from UCLA, after military service, with a B.A. in Physical Science and Mathematics. In 1964, he joined IBM as a Systems Engineer. He enjoyed a 30 year career with almost 15 years in the Corporate Headquarters as staff to the VP of Marketing and served three years in Paris, France.

In Paris, Esker was converted and made a new creature in Christ through the witness of God's transforming his sister's life. A year later, the Lord made him aware of his sins and a need for a Savior and at the same time gave him to know his sins were forgiven in Christ. With a God-given mentor he was able to grow rapidly in the Lord. Upon return to the U.S. he enrolled in the New York School of the Bible. Pastor Harris then studied nights at Alliance Theological Seminary while at IBM. After retirement, he received his M.Div, in 1996, at Chandler School of Theology and was ordained in a National Baptist Church. He served as an associate pastor until his appointment as a missionary to Malawi. He received his doctorate from Fuller Theological Seminary, Pasadena, CA, 2011.

Missionary Movements in Africa

The West has a long-standing practice of sending missionaries to Africa. The first "modern-day" attempt to introduce Christianity into Africa was made by Roman Catholics in 1481, when the King of Portugal sent ten ships with soldiers, laborers, and priests as missionaries to work in Elmina.[1] The Moravians followed by introducing Protestant missionaries in Africa beginning in 1736 and continuing until 1770, but with only marginal success. The Wesleyans came next with mission stations in 1792. The Church Missionary Society began sending missionaries in 1804. However, it was not until the early 1820's that the first African Mission was established.[2] Thereafter, throughout the nineteenth century many missionary societies established mission stations in Africa through the work of African-American as well as Anglo American missionaries. However, at the dawn of the 20th century the Foreign Mission Board of the National Baptist Convention, USA, Inc., took a bold step forward in its decision to send an African, Rev. John Chilembwe, back to his home country as a pioneer missionary. In the providence of God, John Chilembwe took a circuitous route to the point of being educated in America, ordained as a Baptist minister, appointed to break a new ground in taking the gospel to his people, and ultimately in giving his life for the cause of his people.

Missionary or Mercenary

Rev. John Chilembwe is probably best known today as a social activist or freedom fighter because most of the volumes that have been written about him concentrate on his role in 1915 in leading a rebellion—which has been referred to in the literature as a "Rising"—against the injustices of colonial domination in British Central Africa. Yes, John Chilembwe was a social activist, but that is not all that he was, nor is it the most important role he played. According to D. D. Phiri, writing in *Let Us Die For Africa*, "Chilembwe was also an educator, spiritual leader

---

1 Edward W. Blyden, *Christianity, Islam and the Negro Race* (1967), 48. "The Romish mission thus founded, lingered on for a period of 241 years,… and then disappeared altogether from West Africa. They made no impression except upon their immediate dependents; and what little impression they made on them was soon totally obliterated."

2 Ibid, 48, 49.

and even a pan-Africanist of sorts."[3] He was, from the start of his mission, concerned with "helping Africans of various tribes to modernize themselves."[4] Rev. John Chilembwe's calling as a minister of God has been relegated to the background. The objective of this biography is to bring it to the forefront.

John Chilembwe was born June 1871 near a hill called Sangano in the village of Chiradzulu in the colony of Nyasaland[5], which was in British Central Africa. His father moved the family as he deemed necessary in pursuit of better living conditions and educational opportunities for his children. Chilembwe, the gifted young African with distinct leadership capabilities, passed the "Standard Three" exam in 1891. This was equivalent to approximately seven years of education under the Scottish-based school system, which was considered to be excellent. He did not continue with senior primary education at that time, possibly due to shortages in family finances. Yet, even at that point, his potential had begun to bud for he had acquired a level of proficiency in English to converse with a prospective employer and to write a brief application in intelligible English.[6] This enabled him to make a key contact which set in motion a sequence of events that marked the life and death of an African legend.

Chilembwe and Booth

In autumn of 1892, Chilembwe applied for a job as a "cook-boy" for a British missionary named Joseph Booth. Landing this position proved to be the key to his conversion to Christianity and later development into an effective leader of his people. Booth lost his wife from pneumonia in October, 1891, while living in Australia. Yet, three weeks after his wife's death, and against sage council to the contrary, he set sail for England, as the fist leg of his missionary journey to Africa, with a motherless teen-aged son and a nine year old daughter.[7] His son died of malaria in 1894, but the young daughter, Emily, came to know and respect John Chilembwe, who cooked, cleaned, and cared for her during her father's long absences due to his work as a missionary. Years later Emily wrote of the character of Chilembwe by stating that:

The coming of John was to mean to us much more than merely having found, at last, a dependable cook-boy. In that capacity he did all that could be expected of a native boy who had acquired only a little something of the ways of the white people. He had a great desire to learn to write, and to gain the truths of Christianity. Being a cook-boy was only a means to an end. While neither his cooking nor his English were astounding in their perfection, they served both our needs and his. It was in greater qualities than these that our John excelled... He was so kind and true—so thoughtful and unselfish. Without his faithfulness and dependability I doubt very much if I could have survived, or if Father could have completed the seeking-out, and buying of new land for a mission station.[8]

As a missionary, Joseph Booth earned a notorious reputation for being difficult to cooperate with because of his many broken relationships with various mission agencies operating in Nyasaland. However, to his credit, Booth also had a reputation of taking sides with Africans in opposition to their suffering the blatant injustices of colonial rule. This, in no small measure, contributed to the acrimony between him and the white settlers there. Chilembwe came to work for Booth primarily because of his reputation for fairness, and the working relationship proved to be mutually beneficial. Since Chilembwe spoke the two different native languages of his mother and his father (i.e., Yao and Nyanja), he frequently served as interpreter, and, as though it were by reciprocity, he improved his verbal writing skills in English through his association with Joseph Booth. However, the most significant result of their relationship was Chilembwe's conversion.

John Chilembwe chose his own Christian name as an adjunct to his tribal names; for this

---

[3] D. D. Phiri, *Let Us Die For Africa* (1999), ix. Phiri, a Malawian, provides "an African perspective on the life and death of John Chilembwe of Nyasaland."

[4] Ibid. 16.

[5] Nyasaland, which is in Central Africa, gained its independence in 1964 and is currently named Malawi. It is the region of Africa where David Livingstone did a great deal of his missionary work. The largest city and business center of the country is named Blantyre, which is the name of Livingstone's birthplace in Scotland.

[6] D. D. Phiri. *Let Us Die For Africa* (1999), 2.

[7] Shepperdson and Price, *Independent African* (2000), 27.

[8] Ibid., 37, 38.

was a common practice of many Africans who interacted with the new world of Europeans.[9] He selected the name "John" because of John, the disciple whom Jesus loved, and not John the Baptist, although Chilembwe later described himself as being responsible for "taking the light" to his people.[10] Nevertheless, there was no clear evidence that Chilembwe was a Christian when he met Booth in 1892.[11] Joseph Booth noted in his records that he baptized John Chilembwe as his first convert in Nyasaland on July 17, 1893.[12] In the years that followed, Chilembwe matured as a Christian and learned a great deal about developing and running a mission as he saw Booth build a new mission station from the ground-up. This knowledge would serve him well in later years.

By the end of 1895, after severing relationships with several mission stations in Nyasaland, Booth made his first trip to the U.S. to gain new sources of support for his outreach from "American Negroes, who enjoyed nostalgia for the motherland and who were contemplating returning 'home' to assist in the Christianization and development of the so-called 'Dark Continent'."[13] In 1897, Booth promoted a scheme in Nyasaland called the African Christian Union. John Chilembwe was a prominent signatory along with Alexander Dickie, an English missionary, and Morrison Malinki, a Seventh Day Adventist missionary. The essence of this Union was "an appeal to Africans to unite and work for their own redemption—religious, political, economic and spiritual—instead of relying on Europeans. Its slogan was 'Africa for the African'."[14] It became clear that this slogan referred to "Africans" of the diaspora. Booth sought financial and spiritual backing for the African Christian Union from blacks in America and sympathetic whites. He decided to take an African along to convince potential contributors that this scheme "had the welfare of the African at heart and that the indigenous African was inviting his American brothers to 'come home'."[15]

Booth choose Chilembwe to accompany him on his fundraising jaunt to America primarily because of Chilembwe's loyalty and his zeal for God and knowledge. This decision was providential; it opened opportunities for Chilembwe's further growth and development.

Separation from Booth

Chilembwe's separation from Booth in America came at the insistence of Negro preachers who were pragmatic in light of racial innuendo in America three decades after the Civil War. At a large gathering of Negro ministers in Philadelphia, Chilembwe said openly, "Mr. Booth we must part. God has brought me to good friends. I am now a man and can walk alone."[16] Chilembwe further maintained that he new friends would care for him and send him back when ready. They knew well the ways of the whites towards blacks better than Booth did.[17] It is a gross understatement to quote Shepperson and Price in stating that "race relations in the U.S. at the end of the 19th century were not good."[18] African Americans were not only disappointed that the hopes of the Civil War and emancipation from slavery had not been realized, but the disenfranchisement of blacks had been institutionalized such that government agencies cooperated in enforcing the exclusion of blacks from political, social and economic influence. Chilembwe was exposed to all the evils of America' socio-economic "apartheid." This did not escape Chilembwe, but he remained focused on his primary objective of attaining an education and qualifications for ministry.

Education in America

The National Baptist Convention, USA, assumed responsibility for the welfare of Chilembwe after this break with Booth. "The most important man in the chain of friends and helpers Chilembwe developed in America was Dr. Lewis Garnet Jordan, the Secretary of the Foreign Mission Board of the National Baptist Convention. ... Jordan took Chilembwe to Roanoke, VA, where he handed him over to Pastor William W. Brown ... This man of God agreed to pay for Chilembwe's

---

9 There is no record available that indicates when this choice was made, but presumably this was a decision made as a youth before Chilembwe met Joseph Booth.
10 Shepperson and Price, *Independent African* (2000), 39.
11 Ibid., 47.
12 Ibid., 48.
13 D. D. Phiri, *Let Us Die for Africa* (1999), 6.
14 Ibid., 6.
15 Ibid., 9.

16 Shepperson and Price, *Independent African* (2000), 93.
17 Ibid., 93.
18 Shepperson and Price, *Independent African* (2000), 94.

schooling."[19] Chilembwe was enrolled in the Virginia Theological Seminary and College in Lynchburg, where he studied for almost three years and achieved the Bachelor of Arts and Bachelor of Divinity degrees (B.A., B.D.). According to Phiri, some people cavil at the actual nature and value of such degrees, but the real question perhaps should be: what is the nature of the light that Chilembwe acquired in America—which he was not taking home to his people?"[20] At the Lynchburg campus Chilembwe was a proud African, confident of his commitment to Christ and commitment to excel in his studies in order to be prepared to minister to his people at home. While studying in America, Chilembwe was exposed to the best of the teachings of W. E. B. DuBois and Booker T. Washington. Whereas the two "adversaries" would have viewed themselves as being on opposite sides of the table, Chilembwe integrated into his own philosophy the assertiveness of DuBois and the industriousness of Washington.

Chilembwe Goes Home

Prior to returning to Nyasaland, Chilembwe became acutely ill with asthma. He was ordered by his physician to return to Nyasaland immediately. The account of his response to this severe setback was given by Rev. Jordan, who told of Chilembwe's near-death experience:

> We can never forget, at a farewell meeting at Newport News, VA, about 2 o'clock in the morning, with the rain coming down in torrents, the thunder fairly shaking the house wherein we dwelled, and the lightening playing about on the electric wires on the front of the building, we supposed this young African dying. We had propped up his head with a chair to see him die. As we stood, after looking into his face with pity, we remember having said to him; Bro.Chilembwe, if anything should happen to you, what must I write to your people? He was then to us breathing his last. Rolling his eyes toward us, unable to speak scarcely, he said, "Brudder Jordan, I no going to die. God bring me to this land to get light to take back to me people. He is not going to kill me here." Deep in our hearts we admired his faith, but would not have given a ten cents for his life. But the next morning he was yet living.[21]

In the providence of God, Chilembwe lived to return to Nyasaland as the first African who had been prepared through training in America to be a fully qualified and ordained as a Baptist minister. "He was the first African from this part of the world who had been to America, and returned. He had come back from overseas not as a slave or soldier or servant but as an independent minister, with the backing of one of the greatest forces of organized Negroes in the world."[22] He knew his charge, his "raison d' etre," and set about to address it.

When Chilembwe returned to Chiradzulu, Nyasaland in 1900, his first challenge was to acquire land for building a mission station. Through financial support from the Foreign Mission Board of the National Baptist Convention in America, and by the grace of God, Chilembwe was finally able to purchase 93 acres of prime farm land near his birthplace despite deliberate delay tactics by Commissioner Alfred Sharpe.[23] Chilembwe initially named the site "Ajawa Providence Industrial Mission," but later dropped the "Ajawa" designation, which referred to his tribal chauvinism. The Providence Industrial Mission (P.I.M.) was the auspicious start of a "light house" for Africans in that region who were lost without Christ. Chilembwe laid the foundation for P.I.M. for just over a year, and in 1901 Rev. Landon N. Cheek arrived to assist him. About a year after Cheek arrived, Miss Emma B. Delaney came in 1902 to offer further assistance, especially in working with women.[24] Delaney returned to America in 1905 and Cheek in 1906.

Innovative Changes

John Chilembwe wrote a letter to the Central African Times on December 8, 1900 which showed the influence of American Negroes like Booker T. Washington, William E. DuBois, and Marcus Garvey which expressed his sense of an independent spirit in applying their approaches to Africa:

---

19 D. D. Phiri. *Let Us Die For Africa* (1999), 10.
20 Ibid., 12.

21 Shepperson and Price, *Independent African* (2000), 122.
22 Ibid., 128.
23 Ibid., 131.
24 Harvey, *Bridges Of Faith Across The Seas* (1989), 44.

[B]y giving the children of Africa good training they will be able to possess indomitable spirits and firm dependence upon God's helping and sustaining hand. And make observations which will be of greatest use to different tribes of African Sons, who only need the quickening and enlightening influence of the Gospel of Christ to lift them from this state of degradation, and make them suitable members of the Great human family.[25]

Rev. Chilembwe had a "magnetic personality," and he was a charismatic leader. He established schools at P.I.M. with curriculum that included English, arithmetic, Bible, some history and a little geography. By 1905, there were 71 students and 11 new converts awaiting baptism. By 1910, he had established 5 churches with a total of 800 members, 7 assistants and 625 students. In 1912, there were 906 students—200 of which were physically at P.I.M. while the rest were spread among other village schools. There were 6 satellite schools along with the main school at P.I.M., and the colonial government instructed him "not to open any more than that."[26] When the government stopped his expansion of schools, Chilembwe turned his energies toward improvements at the P.I.M. headquarters. "About 1911, he started work on a scheme which was to prove a monument to his aspirations, a crystallization of his assertions that Negro people were capable of doing great things without white supervision."[27] The church membership was 492 and with visitors in attendance, the capacity of the church built earlier was now exceeded. Chilembwe took on the task of raising funds to build a new church. Whereas Booker T. Washington often appealed to wealthy, kind-hearted whites for needed development funds, Chilembwe rejected this approach. He opted first to attempt to raise money among his own people. If that was unsuccessful, he would appeal to his American Negro friends. The church members had virtually no funds, so they volunteered their services in kneading mud, baking bricks, cutting poles, etc. By 1913, the church was completed and it was a marvel to behold. Photographs were made, and many found it difficult to believe that the Chilembwe crew of volunteers had done the job all alone with unturtored labor.[28]

Women's Rights

"From the start of P.I.M., Chilembwe saw to it that a girls' boarding home was setup side by side with that of the boys. He was devoted to women's progress."[29] He was especially concerned with the training and development of African women. His desire was "to pull the African women of Nyasaland out of the tribal state, and to model them on the contemporary European woman, as a progressive ideal. His concept had all the shades of European female respectability of the time."[30] A quotation from a letter Chilembwe wrote in 1912 to the Secretary of the Foreign Mission Board of the National Baptist Convention illustrates his ideal for African women:

I feel safe in saying that I am doing good to my countrymen, as it is time everywhere that men are developing faster than the women. But there can be not healthy progress if such is the case. We believe there is an urgent need for special work to be done among the wives of the people, whom you are privileged by God's grace to bring out of darkness into light. The world will not go forward as it should till women have been taught and have learned to take the place God has ordained for them as man's helpmeet—his equal, not his slave.[31]

Chilembwe had an enlightened perspective on the role of women in ministry in 1912. In some Christian circles today his perspective still eludes their grasp.

Chilembwe's Christian Ministry

As the founder of P.I.M., Rev. Chilembwe was driven primarily by his desire to fulfill the Great Commission found in Matthew 28:19–20 (NIV), "Therefore go and make disciples of all nations, baptizing them in the name of the Father and of the Son and of the Holy Spirit, and teaching them to obey everything I have commanded you. And surely I am with you always, to the very end of the age."

---

25 Shepperson and Price, *Independent African* (2000), 127.
26 D. D. Phiri, *Let Us Die For Africa* (1999), 20, 21.
27 Ibid., 21.
28 Ibid., 22.
29 D. D. Phiri, *Let Us Die For Africa* (1999), 19.
30 Ibid., 175.
31 Ibid.

The *Weekend Nation*, a local newspaper, published an article in August 2000, in celebration of the Centennial for P.I.M. The article, "Chilembwe: Pioneer and Patriot," states:

> If we remember Chilembwe only as a man who led the 1915 Rising, we do not do him full honor. We should remember Chilembwe for believing and preaching that Africans could do great things independent of the white man's supervision.

The evidence of his commitment to the call and his dedication to the work of the ministry may be seen in his hand-written correspondence. In one letter he wrote to a brother about a recent trip to Mozambique, where he frequently went elephant hunting to supplement the income for P.I.M., saying:

> Yes, I have just returned from my hunting trip nothing successful to please men, but I have done a great work in preaching the words of God to our poor people until the Portuguese thought to lay hand on me, but they failed ... I know this is the work I was born for.

In a second letter he wrote:

> I only heard the call of God for the salvation of the poor African brothers and [to] lay foundation for future welfare in the right hand of God ... Pray for me that I may not fail for the money in my heart. I value nothing for I have weighed the world and its riches and find nothing comparing [to] the love I got for my people and our God.

In a third citation, regarding his getting needed financial assistance, he said:

> I am only laboured [sic] not for my own, but in the name of God for my countrymen. I am sure, it was by revelation of Christ I find you in the time of my struggling to be my constant helper as I had faith in you in all its totality.

Ignored Yet Recognized

The local government of Nyasaland did not recognize P.I.M.'s existence in the Government Census of 1911 although it included the other, smaller white sectarian missions. Nevertheless, Rev. Chilembwe's name and that of P.I.M. appeared in the report of the Commission of the first World Missionary Conference at Edinburgh in 1910. His name appeared as Rev. John Chilembwe (National Baptist Convention), Blantyre. So he was recognized and accepted in the world community of missions although he was ignored at home.

Conclusions[32]

John Chilembwe exemplifies a missionaire who gave his life to his people in his work of ministry and gave his life for his people in leading "The Rising" against the abuses of colonial rule. The revolt was quelled and he was killed in 1915 while attempting to escape into Mozambique. However, his legacy lives on in the embodiment of P.I.M. today, which has extended its mission outreach to include the establishment of churches throughout Malawi (i.e. the modern name for Nyasaland), in Mozambique, Zambia, Zimbabwe, and South Africa.

---

[32] Note from the author: My doctoral studies are aimed at motivating African-American churches for cross-cultural missions work. I will return to the mission field in Malawi upon graduation from Fuller in order to re-start the Bible school and develop people to continue its operation. My long-term aspirations are to become a catalyst to motivate African Americans for missions.

Bibliography

Blyden, Edward W. 1967 *Christianity, Islam and the Negro Race* (Edinburgh: At the University Press, 1967). First edition: Edinburgh University Press, 1887.

Harvey, William J., III. *Bridges of Faith Across the Seas* (Philadelphia, PA: Foreign Mission Board, National Baptist Convention, U.S.A., Inc., 1989).

Phiri, D. D. *Let Us Die For Africa* (Blantyre, Malawi: Central African Limited, 1999).

Shepperson, George and Thomas Price. *Independent African* (Blantyre, Malawi: Christian Literature Association in Malawi (CLAIM), 1958). This 2000 edition was made from the 1987 paperback edition.

Chapter 21

Far From Home: A Biography of Emma B. Delaney, Missionary to Africa 1902–1922

by Willie Mae Hardy Ashley

Willie Mae Ashley, a native of Fernandina Beach, FL, graduated from Peck High School and is a member of the First Missionary Baptist Church, the home of Missionary Emma B. Delaney. She received her B.S. Degree from Bethune Cookman College, Daytona Beach, FL, did further study at the University of Michigan, Ann Arbor, MI, and was awarded a master of education degree from Florida A&M University, Tallahassee, FL.

During her 35 years of service in Nassau County, FL, she served as a classroom teacher, an elementary school coordinator, and a guidance counselor. She retired in 1977.

The author is very active in religious, civic, and professional organizations and has been the recipient of several citations and awards. She has traveled widely throughout the U.S., Europe, and West and South Africa (including Johannesburg and Soweto). Her trip to Africa in 1978 included a visit to the Suehn Industrial Mission in Liberia, West Africa.

She was contacted for Fernandina Beach's African-American heritage for the historic facts on Emma B. Delaney for her representation in the Great Floridians 2000 program, which the Florida's Legislature established in 1997. This contact brought a resolution nominating Emma B. Delaney to be included. A plaque, paid for by the city, was placed at First Missionary Baptist (for Delaney), located at 22 S. Ninth Street.

On March 6, 2004, the City of Fernandina Beach, FL, held an event at which they named their Peck Center Auditorium in her honor.

From the Foreword

The history of Christendom will never be complete until the contribution of the Black American Baptist is included.

As early as 1880, Black Baptist were concerned to the point of organizing a foreign mission convention for the sole purpose of sending missionaries to Africa. In 1882 this convention sent six missionaries to Liberia, West Africa. Three of them were women who accompanied their husbands to the mission field. In 1900, the pioneer women missionary was Emma B. Delaney, who served with Rev. L. N. Cheek in opening the Providence Industrial Mission in Nyasaland under the guiding hand of Rev. John Chilembwe, a native African. In an age when women were relegated to household duties or to being mothers or maiden ladies with no recognizable administrative responsibilities, Emma Delaney defied tradition and, with determination and zeal, launched out into the depths of missionary service. In 1912, she single-handedly opened and supervised the Suehn Industrial Mission in Liberia, West Africa, thereby defying the local African custom of relegating women to the position of second-class citizens.

Though the role of Black women serving as missionaries in Africa has been mentioned, no work has specified the role of women as Willie Mae Ashley's has, especially about this pioneer missionary of the National Baptist Convention, Inc., U.S.A., Mrs. Ashley is to be commended for this definite work on Emma B. Delaney—a work of loving concern that her name and work will not be forgotten. Fortunately, most of the information she received was oral from the few people now living who knew Emma Delaney personally.

Dr. William J. Harvey, III
Executive Secretary
Foreign Mission Board National Baptist Convention, Inc., U.S.A.
Philadelphia, PA

From the Preface

Far From Home, the biography of Emma Beard Delaney, has been compiled and written from "firsthand" information, from published and unpublished records, and from oral history obtained through intensive interviews. A very few minor discrepancies and repetitions may be noted apparently due to the varied sources of information. No attempt, however, was made to edit materials quoted from other sources even though facts may vary slightly based on my research.

From Chapter I: Carrying "The Light" — The First Journey

Jan. 1902—Sailed to British Central Africa. Aided in establishing the Providence Industrial Mission in Malawi.

It was a very cold Wednesday, January 15, 1902, when Emma B. Delaney boarded a ship bound for British Central Africa (now Malawi), a distance of more than 14,000 miles from her native home of Fernandina Beach, FL, U.S.. The journey ahead was very, very long and the hazardous travel over thousands of miles on water brought physical stress she had never experienced in her lifetime of preparation for this journey.

Some of the time on board the ship was shared with fellow travelers M. W. Gilbert, J. T. Brown, and others. ...

There was never, NEVER a minute of doubt in her mind about accepting "the call" to go on this missionary journey. That "call" had come to her long, long ago as a child. Her mind was filled, however, with the miraculous chain of events which led to the resolution of April 1899. This resolution, sending her to Africa, was introduced by the General Florida State Convention (endorsed by the Women's Missionary and Education Convention and approved by the National Baptist Foreign Mission, Inc., U.S.A.). The fact that this resolution was introduced and passed at a convention held at her "home church" in Fernandina Beach, FL, her birthplace, seemed to increase the faith that God's mission plan had been entrusted to her.

It was God's plan. It was His mission. Her direct physical link, however, started with John Chilembwe, an African.

John Chilembwe[1] was a native of British Central Africa Nyasaland, now Malawi. In 1893 he became a convert of Joseph Booth, A Seventh Day Adventist missionary. Chilembwe became Booth's apprentice, helping him as an interpreter and family friend. They spent about five years in Africa together before coming to the U.S.

This trip to America provided many new experiences and acquaintances for Chilembwe, who was about 20. Gregory W. Hayes, an American Negro minister who was president of Virginia Theological Seminary in Lynchburg, VA, met him and helped him obtain an education. ...

At an end of formal education, Chilembwe went to Philadelphia, PA, although he was in poor health. Finally, he returned to his native home in Africa with the backing of the National Baptist Convention. He began work on his school and the first independent African church of Baptist beliefs. He named it the Providence Industrial Mission.

Chilembwe returned home to his family and friends, who had been a bit displeased about his coming to the U.S. ... Some of them were skeptical about his clothing style and his expressing what they considered "the white man's religion." These problems and his general poor health made his work suffer. He needed help! He needed strong, immediate help if the mission was to take roots and grow.

His help came in part through the National Baptist Convention in the U.S. in the form of Emma Beard Delaney. So "Emma," the little girl who promised at the age of eight to go to Africa, found herself linked to Chilembwe's struggles. ...

Missionary Delaney's superior preparation through high school in Fernandina, FL, and her distinct college training at Spelman in Atlanta, GA, gave her great influence, especially in the women's movement. Her expertise was a valuable source of excellent training, given through sewing and general education classes intermixed with learning regular forms of social life. The celebration of Christmas became a recognized feature of mission life also. Her direct personal influence and teaching, especially among the women, led to a special pride and Christian spirit resulting in many opportunities.

By 1904, Missionary Delaney's influence on the Christian spirit, deep pride, and physical condition of the mission had become evident as seen in the following letter written to the women of the National Baptist Convention.[2]

> If I may compare the place to-day with the place two years ago, I would say that we have already reached a degree of civilization. In

---

[1] George Shepperson and Thomas Price, *Independent African—John Chilembwe and The Origin, Setting and Significance of the Nyasaland Native Uprising of 1915* (Edinburgh, Scotland: The University Press, 1958).

[2] Ibid., 209.

front of the house where one year ago only stumps, thorns and crooked trees were growing you will find to-day scarlet geraniums, a few blooming roses and other flowers, while the red leaf hedge forms the walk and divides the yard into squares. ... To the right of the house a few hundred yards were dilapidated huts and another field of grass, trees, etc.; to-day you will find a brick church, certainly not a very handsome building, for architects here are self-taught, and native labor very crude, but nevertheless God's Temple reared to his glory.

Another letter written in 1905 shows an interesting contrast:[3]

If you could have been here today, you could have gone to a witch dance. They were dancing to find out who are the witches, that are eating the lives out of the people in a village; for here, no one dies unless he or she is bewitched. While they are dancing, the witch doctor by method chooses the witches, and they are forced to drink Mari; this is a poison. If he or she is able to vomit, he or she is not the witch. If the person dies, he is guilty, and his body is thrown aside, for the birds and beasts to devour. No one would be found guilty of burning the body of a witch. If it is proved that the accused is not a witch, his accusers are made to pay dearly for their false accusation to the chief of the district, in money, clothing, or slaves.

These people have many curious customs and superstitious ideas. There is a man who comes here for medical treatment whose body is thickly covered with hair and he has a tail like a monkey. He is indeed a peculiar looking man. He must be the missing link.

Mrs. Blanch of Cholo is here and has tried to take his picture. Don't know yet if they will be good. The natives believe when you look at them through a camera, that you can see through them and when you take their picture, you steal their shadow; without their shadow they will die. So it is hard to get the picture of many of them.

[3] Ibid.

The work is moving on slowly, 25 have been baptized already this year and many others are interested. We are hoping that much good will be accomplished for the Master.

The fever attacks one in many ways. In my last attack something appeared on my limbs like a boil, and the suffering was intense. I opened it. Imagine to my surprise on seeing a live worm an eighth of an inch long. I have been told by one of the missionaries, that they are frequently found in the flesh of the arms and legs, and the often attain the length of an inch. They very often cause blood poison, if allowed to remain in the limb a long time.

Yours for the redemption of Africa.

Delaney's work with Chilembwe through the National Baptist Convention, Inc., U.S.A., shares a very important role in the history of an independent Africa.

One of Chilembwe's four children was named Emma as a loving tribute to this dynamic missionary.

After struggling for a few years, Chilembwe led an uprising against the British Colonialist, the Nyasaland Native Uprising of 1915. He was killed in this uprising along with several other natives. His life's work, Providence Industrial Mission, was demolished with dynamite after an attempt to destroy it by fire had failed. Although Chilembwe's life work ended in chaos, he has been hailed by many contemporary black Africans as the father of the independent Africa idea. He was the first to promote this dream in such a tangible work.

From Chapter II—Commissioned for Her Mission

For days and days Emma had been thinking, wondering, and planning. The right plan suddenly came to her during the night: "As soon as I am old enough I will go to Africa myself and help the poor jungle girls and boys who cannot read or write and do not know about Jesus!"

Emma was eight years old then and several weeks earlier she had gone to church with her mother and sister Anna to hear missionaries tell about their work in Africa. ... Then weeks later she did not talk to anyone about her idea until the final decision was made. ... And so, the very next day after that decision had been made Emma calmly announced to her mother at the breakfast table, "I am going to Africa when I grow up to teach the jungle children about Jesus."

So the commission for her mission to Africa as a missionary came at an early age. Only time was needed for fulfillment. Her family circle made it possible for Emma to mature in the direction of her dreams.

She was born in Fernandina, FL, on Tuesday, January 17, 1871. ... Emma's parents, Daniel Sharpe Delaney and Anna Delaney, were members of a highly respected pioneer family which had deep roots in the community, state, and nation. Her father was a pilot for 30 years on the Revenue Cutter Boutwell, the only "colored" pilot in that kind of service making trips between Cumberland Island and Fernandina. Her mother was a strong, beautiful God-fearing woman who reared Emma and her sister Anna with the best that "colored people" of that day and area enjoyed. ... Many family members distinguished themselves in occupations such as college president, lawyers, teachers, doctors, ministers, politicians, and nurses, while others were just outstanding citizens of the U.S.. She is first cousin to the famous Delaney sisters of Having Our Say. Their father, the late Bishop Henry Beard Delaney, is Emma Beard Delaney's godfather in addition to uncle.

Emma completed high school at the Catholic Convent in 1889 and then went to Spelman Seminary in Atlanta, GA. ... The following account of her is taken from *The Story of Spelman College* as one of its outstanding graduates.[4]

> Emma DeLaney, the fifth Spelmanite to go to Africa, entered Spelman from FL in 1888. ... She graduated from Spelman Seminary in 1894, and from Missionary Training Course in 1896. She had already completed Spelman's Nurse Training Course, and she was determined to work for the people of Africa. She had to wait a few years before she received an appointment from the National Baptist Convention (Negro), but her purpose did not faker [sic]. She sailed on Jan. 15, 1902, on assignment to an entirely new field in British East Africa, Chiradzula, Blantyre, Nyasaland. The nearest mission was 12 miles away manned by Mr. and Mrs. Dreyer and supported by Baptists in Scotland. The Seventh Day Adventist later in 1902 "brought out a mission" and sent Mr. Branch and his family from the western U.S. They lived at a station 60 miles away. ... Mr. Dreyer had a heart attack. Their departure left Miss DeLaney very much isolated, in a strange country, with a strange language, and in a community not yet civilized. She lived in a two-room mud house. She put bricks together to use as a stove. When hard showers came, rain poured through the grass roof. The weather was very cold. The smoke came down the chimney and heat went up. She was plagued by lice. She had a nasty attack of fever. In fact, she suffered from frequent attacks of "fever"—from malaria and other causes. But she could enjoy a view of snow-topped Chirandzule mountain by standing in her doorway. Besides, she was learning the native language and had much work to do.
>
> The people were peaceful. There were three distinct tribes—the Angona, the original settlers; the Yao, who conquered the Angonies; and the Angulus—recent comers and the lowest in the scale of intelligence. Their belief in witches led to unnecessary suffering and even death.
>
> Before she could speak the language, Miss DeLaney began to teach the people to make a garden, and to make and burn bricks. She made some progress in teaching the girls to sew and boys to cook. One new boy who came as a helper was told to make a fire in the stove, and put water in the pot and the pot on the stove. Instead he put the water on the bricks which were the stove, and made the fire in the pot! Fortunately the error was discovered in time to save her only pot from destruction. Her best helper was an earnest youth named Daniel Malekebu. The native food was hard to take. Leopards made visits close to her center, and occasionally a lion. Three persons were killed by lions between the mission and the place Daniel had to go to get the mail.
>
> The superstitions that existed are hard to believe. For example, when a person was accused of stealing, a pot of water was put on the fire.

---

4 Florence Matilda Read, *The Story of Spelman College* (Princeton University Press, 1961), 349.

When it came to a boil, the accused was made to drop two rocks into the boiling water and take them out with his hands. Sometimes, just enough meal was put in the water to stick to the skin. If the skin peeled off, the person was guilty, if not, he was innocent.

With all the difficulties and hardships, Miss DeLaney wrote in 1902: "These things will never discourage a Spelmanite when I remember what the Founders of that grand institute had to pass through in order for it to stand as it does today. I take fresh courage ... today if its pioneer workers had grown discouraged from hardships."

A brick house for Miss DeLaney was completed early in the 1900's with windows inside, and a verandah outside, whose pillars held up the thatched roof. This was not only a great comfort to her but it inspired the people to keep their own houses in better order. They began to want chairs and a table and even a bed and flowers growing. A few coffee trees, a few hills of corn, several acres of cotton also made the outlook more hopeful. The medicines Miss DeLaney received after long delay enabled her to heal many serious wounds. The people came long distances to have them tended. Some came on their hands and knees, some had to be carried on the backs of husbands or fathers. Many of the wounds were from jiggers; some from bites either from each other or from insects; but the majority were from burns. They slept around a fire in the middle of the hut; many got horrible burns, and some were burned to death. With all the wounds that came to Miss DeLaney's care, not one person had lost a limb or a joint.

Perhaps the most important thing Miss DeLaney accomplished—because it left something to build on after the World War and its aftermath—was to organize a school to train native leaders. This was in operation when in 1905, with health impaired, she left to return home. After 4 years in Nyasaland, she further had the satisfaction of seeing considerable improvement in the homes of the people around the mission; of having 64 students regularly attend her school (a ratio of about two boys to one girl); of leaving at the station 25 grownup women who were trying to be Christians.

Two African children who became friends of Miss DeLaney were Daniel Malekabu and his sister Ruth. Their parents were opposed to "the foreign woman." When Miss DeLaney got ready to leave for America, she grieved that she did not have the money to take her two little girls—Ruth Malekebu and one other. The boy, Daniel, begged to go with her, but it was impossible for her to become responsible for him. His parents also refused to approve and appointed guards to watch him until his teacher had been gone for three days. Then he ran away. He started on foot to follow Miss DeLaney to the coast but never was able to overtake her. It was a journey of over 200 miles. He climbed trees at night to escape from the lions and leopards. But he reached Beira, East Africa, before the steamer sailed for England, and persuaded the captain to allow him to work for his passage to England. He earned his way to America in the same way. He attended Selma University in AL, and then Meharry Medical College. He and Miss DeLaney were guests of Miss Clara Howard at Spelman for several days. There he met Flora Zeto. After he completed his medical course, they were married in the chapel at Spelman on March 22, 1919.

Chapter III—"Lead, Kindly Light"—The Mission

The hymn, "Lead, Kindly Light" had a special meaning to Emma Beard Delaney. Mrs. Celestine Davis Kegler, a Fernandian, related the following account:

I recall going to one of Miss Delaney's lectures after she had been to Africa. ... She told us how hard, how lonesome, how frightening it was to be so far from home. One evening when she was sad, so lonesome not knowing what the next day would bring she thought of this song, "Lead, Kindly Light" and began to sing it. ... It seemed that some inner peace or brave feeling would come through the words and melody. …She sang it always as her favorite hymn."⁵

"Lead, kindly Light! amid th'encircling gloom, Lead Thou me on;

The night is dark, and I am far from home, Lead Thou me on;

Keep Thou my feet; I do not ask to see The distant scene; one step enough for me. I was not ever thus, nor prayed that Thou Shouldst lead me on;

I loved to choose and see my path, but now, Lead Thou me on;

I loved the garnish day, and spite of fears, Pride ruled Thy will; remember not past years. So long Thy pow'r has blessed me, sure it still Will lead me on;

O'er moor and fen, o'er crag and torrent, till the night is gone; And with the morn those angel faces smile Which I have loved long since, and lost awhile! Amen."

The following account is given of her mission and the founding of Suehn Industrial Mission "in a heathen land":⁶

To The National Baptist Foreign Mission Board Philadelphia, PA Greetings from Liberia, Africa: We, the recipients of your hospitality and brotherly kindness in Christ Jesus, as well as our native brothers, take this method to show our appreciation and gratitude for having sent to us such an efficient women as Miss E. B. Delaney.

We shall also try to give to you a brief sketch of adventures and success since she has been in our country.

According to her record, she left U.S. on June 8, 1912, and after a weary journey and intermediate stops, she arrived in our country July 12. She made her appearance in Arthington, July 16, where she remained one and a half years, detained by sickness and waiting for grant of land from the government and a suitable building in which to move. While in Arthington, mind you, do not glean the idea that she sat with folded hands waiting for something to turn up. We are persuaded to believe that she set about turning up too many things, and that her constant activity possibly brought on some of her illness. The malaria went quite hard with her. Truly she suffered enough to have caused any ordinary women to throw up the sponge, but not so with our subject. She came with a purpose and with that fortitude born from above, she said, "I will." We Americo-Liberians insisted that she stop and establish a school permanently among us, but she answered, "Not here, but in the midst of the heathen will I plant the work." "What! A lone woman, and among raw heathen?" "Yes, I came especially to settle among the heathen, and to heathen I am going."

While in Arthington she maintained an industrial school, helped the poor, and kept busy along these lines. After one [and] half years in Arthington, under the most adverse circumstances, she succeeded in getting deeds to a grant of twenty-five acres of land from the government. On December 3, she made her appearance at Seutown, which is at least eight miles from the settlement of Arthington. In this town one of the most memorial battles was fought in 1900. The natives made an advance on this town about 2:30 a.m. on the 7th of November, and were it not for the braveness of the ex-President, W. D. Coleman, of Liberia, who was in the town when the natives attacked the town, perhaps hundreds of lives would have been lost. The memory of this battle is upon the annals of Liberian history. Miss Delaneys' arrival at Seuhn with a number of children, at a site possibly about three-quarters of a mile north of Saw Town, brought into existence an institution that will possibly be forever known as the Seuhn Industrial Mission. Being settled did not end hardships and adversities; here, new obstacles confronted her; yea, new ones on every side, but faith in God and pluck called up the offenses known as success. And now

---

5 "Lead, Kindly Light," over 50 years old. Open to public for reproduction.
6 Unpublished Minutes of the Baptist Convention in Liberia, West Africa (June 1915).

she enjoys or rather she labors in a mission whose surroundings look beautiful and inviting. Under the roof of S. I. Mission, 60 boys and girls, Americo-Liberians and aborigines, find shelter, food and education; yea, and best of all a number have found the Christ of God. Many from the settlement of Arthington have visited S. I. Mission and the effects of the principal, Miss E. B. Delaney, have their hearty approbation. On December 21, 1914, the old veteran and sage of Arthington, in the person of Mr. Solomon Hill. Sr., made a visit to the S. I. Mission in company with Pastor R. B. Wicker, of the St. Paul Baptist Church, of Arthington. The old veteran was so pleased that God had answered his prayers in sending such a competent woman, filled with the push and go, from the civilized world. I say that he was so pleased that he has shown how grateful he was for the mission, and has cheerfully donated two hundred (200) acres of land to the mission ... so most or all its bread stuffs can be raised by the students. The object is to make it as near self-supporting as possible. Verily, her ideas are worthy of commendation. The mission is raising some of her bread stuffs already. The work is too much for one person, yet with bulldog tenacity she is forging ahead. Verily, we are grateful for such a character in our midst and we most earnestly pray that the Foreign Mission Board will give the most of interest in Liberia for the training of our children and native brethren in the Seuhn Industrial Mission, because it's the only school in Montserrado County, Liberia, that is planted among heathen.

Our native brethren take delight in sending their children to school, which gives us courage to believe that heathenism is about to take its flight, and in the place which was a seat of war 15 years ago, a candlestick has been placed, and the light of civilization is now bursting forth. We cannot but give praise for his living kindness. Freely we can say the Lord has answered our prayers, that our brethren in America have sent such an efficient women of our kith and kind to assist in fostering civilization among our heathen brethren in this benighted land."

Signed by some of the leading elders and members in the Baptist Convention in Liberia, this 30th day of June, A.D. 1915.

Rev. T. H. Tyler, B.D.; Deacon G. W. Ashie, Sr.; Rev. A. C. Harris, D.D.; Deacon Elic Ponder; Dr.Rev. W. L. Shaw; Deacon Moses Fuket, Sr.; Rev. Owen Lavall; Deacon M. F. Smallwood; Deacon A. C. Harris, Jr.; Deacon E. S. Moore, Sr.; Rev. R. F. Walker; Deacon James H. Rolhac; Rev. E. L. Parker; M. K. Wilkens; Rev. F. W. Madison; J. C. Taylor, Jr.; Rev. Charles M. Bryant; Francis W. Hill; Deacon J. O. Cassell; Solomon Askik; Deacon Solomon Hill, Sr.; A. M. D. Crusoe; Deacon F. C. Taylor, Sr.; Mrs. Mary E. Andrews; Deacon C. R. Branch; Mrs. H. M. Walker.

1912—Returned to Africa (Liberia) and founded the Suehn Industrial Mission. This mission continues today as an outstanding mission near Monrovia (Liberia), Africa. The recent civil wars in Liberia have greatly affected the status of the Suehn Industrial Mission (other missions also). The challenge we face today is restoration of the mission.

Although Dr. Daniel Malekebu did not work with his beloved "Mother Delaney" he was in touch with her and gave the following narration when asked about her mission in West Africa.[7]

When Mother Delaney came back to the States from East Africa, she spent these years preparing for 1912, the trip to Liberia. Now when she went to Liberia this is her first time she didn't want to live in a city or too close to the city so she went to Suehn. She had heard about Suehn and that is about 50 miles from Monrovia. There was a man who was the president of Liberia at that time. His name was Howard, President Howard. So President Howard told mother Delaney don't go that far because even our people here are afraid. The officer, etc., are afraid to go back that far into the interior because the Africans were not so nice, should I say?

---

7 Taped interview with Dr. Daniel S. Malekebu and Mrs. Flora Zeto Malekebu (Atlanta, GA, July 9, 1974).

So being a woman, don't go there, we'd be afraid for you. But she said, "No, I'm going I must go. I must go."

So, at that time there were no good roads and so she fixed herself and she went on 50 miles from Monrovia and tried to establish a church. Suehn is a little town, a little native town. Right across from there from this town she established Suehn Industrial Mission. It was HARD in those days "ruff" so r-u-f-f-, so far as the Africans were concerned. But she was bold, she was a bold and brave woman, too. In Liberia they call her one woman and four men.

So, she established there with the money she was raising here in this country. She raised enough money to have some company to make or to build a frame house or ...a prefabricated house. Yes, she took the already made house with her to Liberia. ... So from that time she went alone and made a deep impression, a deep impression with the Africans in Africa.

She stayed there straight until time to come back home and the reason what she wanted was knowing I was here being educated she wanted me to go to the Suehn and take charge of the school by the time she was leaving.

1922—Returned to the U.S. and died on Saturday, October 7, of Black Tropical Fever contacted in Africa. Buried at Bosquo Bello, Fernandina Beach, FL.

The Story of Spellman College also included this account about one of its illustrious alumni and her work in Africa:[8]

One of Emma DeLaney's African friends said of her that she was two women in one. It surely seems that she accomplished the work for two or more women. After she returned home on furlough in 1906, and found that permission would not then be given for a return to Nyasaland, she set herself that task of raising money for establishing a mission in Liberia. In 1912, she went to Monrovia under the National Baptist Convention (Negro).

She selected a spot in the jungle not far from Monrovia, cleared the land, built houses, set out trees, and established the Suehn Industrial Mission.

In one of her letters (October, 1919) she wrote: "Liberia is ...the only open door for Negroes in Africa. President George Sale told me this." It was Miss DeLaney's plan to make the center at Suehn a model station from which to start a chain of industrial settlements, all to be under general supervision of a staff who would travel up and down the river on a mission steamer.

There was great difficulty to keep going during the First World War, even to keep alive. The food shortage was extreme. For three months, with the rice harvest not due for three months longer, she was not able to buy a single quart of rice in a radius of three day's walk; not a quart was to be had in Monrovia. Nor could she buy potatoes or cassava. There was also the danger from the war. Communication with the outside world was shut off. Miss DeLaney was nine months without receiving a letter; then 50 came all at once on August 12, 1918. Miss DeLaney remained at the Suehn Industrial Mission for eight years. Then, although in wretched health, she returned to the U.S. mainly for the purpose of raising funds for further work. She was at Spellman in June 1922, full of plans and hope for the Mission. A few months later, in October, she died of blackwater fever at her mother's home in Fernandina, FL.

From Chapter IV—Missionary Delaney's "House Boy" Grows Under the Ntundu Tree

1905, 1906—Returned to the U.S. followed by one of her pupils, Daniel S. Malekebu. Dr. Malekebu was educated in the U.S., was active as supervisor of missions in East, Central, and South Africa, established many churches and was president of the National Baptist Assembly of Africa. Dr. Malekebu died in 1978 in the village of his birth, although he had lived in the U.S. for years.

Daniel was one of Delaney's first pupils in the area. His village was about 50 miles from Blantyre. He was about 13 years old when he came to

---

8 *Spelman Messenger*, Vol. 18, no. 5 (Atlanta, GA, Spelman Seminary Press, February 1902).

the mission, although his exact birth date had not been established following the native custom of the time. ...

One morning, according to his story,[9] he got a message saying that the "missionary" wanted to see him. He related the following interesting story:

> Well, the missionary has just come here and there are so many boys here, what does she know about me?
>
> So, I say all right, I don't know what but the Missionary wanted me to be her boy, her house boy. Well now I was glad. ... She showed me how to cook; she showed me how to wash plates, dishes and wait on the table, and from that time on I was her "house boy." Then she was teaching me English and I was teaching her the native language. So we were exchanging learning.
>
> Yes, yes, that was really beautiful. When Mother Delaney arrived at the mission she moved into the mud house where John Chilembwe had lived.
>
> I was converted and baptized by Mother Delaney in March 1902. She changed my name to Daniel Sharpe which was her father's name. ... Now, she left to come to the States. Now, I was anxious to come with her to the States to go to school. I think you could call it a vision. I wanted to come to the U.S., get my schooling and go back home and teach people. Now, when my people heard this they said, "No. Oh, no, no our son go to the States? It was bad enough for him to leave the village and go to the mission and learn the white people's customs. Now you talk about going to America. No, they'll eat him up and we will never see our son." That's what they said, that's what they believed.
>
> ... And when she left the country she did not know that I'd follow her. ...And I left the country and walked until—It is a railroad built now from in East Africa to the coast to Malawi—walked through this area to the coast and one day I saw something floating on the water and they told me that it was a steamer. Well, it was going to England. So I made my way to the captain and told him—and there was no need to mention money because there was no money here at all. ... So I worked my way from Malawi to England and from England I took another ship with a man named Allen, a white man named Allen who had transported stuff for Mother Delaney.
>
> ... You see, I'd received communication between him and Mother Delaney so it was easy for me to get to him. ... A beautiful sight as our ship went on by the Liberty, the Statue of Liberty. ...They sent us to Ellis Island to stay until somebody come to take us way from there. ...Then the officer said now.... Don't you have some friends in America who can come and get you? And I said, yes, I have my teacher in Africa, Mother Delaney. Well he said, give us her name and we will send a telegram. ... But Mother Delaney was not there. So they sent the telegram but the office of the Foreign Mission Board was in Louisville, KY, at that time. Then, Mr. Jordan, sent a telegram to Newark, NJ, to a man named Mr. Brown and told him to go pick up a boy named Daniel from Ellis Island for Miss Delaney. So, he came. ...
>
> It was Friday evening at Mt. Zion Baptist Church. They were having a meeting. They took me and introduced me and said here is a boy who just now I went to get him from Ellis Island and 12:00 o'clock at night the train was going to Columbus, OH, so they got me a ticket and put me on there and told the conductor—now this boy is going to OH. You see, Mother Delaney was not in Fernandina at that time but in OH attending a convention. She told them when she got the news, "That must be Daniel send him to me!" So now that night some men came to the train station and I went a long, long time to her. Some men got me and took me to this big, great big building hall and sat me up on the stage. Mother Delaney had not come there yet that night. They were telling the people about the boy who came, who came all the way from the African jungle to see his teacher. I heard them talking like away far off because I was thinking, looking, waiting to see her. And then I looked—I looked and SAW

---

9 Taped interview with Dr. Daniel S. Malekebu (Fernandina Beach, FL, November 16, 1974).

Mother Delaney come through the door and I jumped off the stage like wild—just jumped off that high place and ran to her. That was great, great joyous time! That long time run away trip was over! I was in America! I was with my Mother Delaney. I was no more afraid!

Well, she took me then. We stayed there a few days and then we came back home to Fernandina. Well now, so much begin to happen. There were new people, new places with Mother Delaney. I didn't know a physical birthdate... They said, well some one said look like he is about 16, 16 years old from what we can see. So I put it that in 1905 I was 16 so I go back there and I took baptism date and spiritual and natural birth date and add. Yes, so that's the way it was.

Now you see since we've been here in the States we learned and we started our people to put down the date of birth—put down the date of marriage—put down the day somebody dies and on and on. So they are doing that kind of thing now.

So here now I am here in America in Fernandina with Mother Delaney and she said, "You must go to school, you must go to school." Somehow, she and other friends got together and I went to school, too.

My first school in America was Selma University, Selma, AL. National Training School. This gave me a chance to go to the first YMCA conference for Negroes in the U.S. I was a delegate. The meeting was held in NC.

I finished my medical training at Meharry Medical College in 1917. ... Then after that I came to Philadelphia to take special courses in tropical medicine at the University of Pennsylvania and received an honorary certificate of membership to the Anthropological Society of the University. I took my internship at Mudgett Hospital in Philadelphia. At the same time a professor heard about me, in fact he saw me. So, he invited me to help in the Department of Anthropology—You see giving lectures on Africa and so on. Later he wanted me to be his assistant but I couldn't do that because I had to do my own work. So, that's it.

History records that Daniel Sharpe Malekebu, "the house boy" now grown up, did much more than just finish medical training at Meharry. According to the record presented in *The Compass*,[10]

> Among the hundreds of graduates none are more outstanding in their achievements and results of whom Meharry is more proud than Daniel Malekebu. For the nine years following his graduation, he received practical experience in the Mudgett hospital in Philadelphia and returned to Nyasaland, his native home, as a medical missionary helped by the Foreign Mission Board of the National Baptist Convention.
>
> In 1967, Dr. Melekebu, then Superintendent of the total work in Central and East Africa, was called to U.S. to received the highest award of his Alma Mater: The President Award (a gold plaque presented for 50 years of service to humanity). In conjunction with this special award he received the Red Carpet Club Award; Special Letter of Commendation from the White House, Lyndon B. Johnson, President; The Mayor's Award; and The Keys to the City of Nashville, TN.
>
> Baptist were cognizant of the great recognition accorded by Meharry and provided many courtesies which offered the experience of speaking at conferences and programs of recognition in OH and PA. In Philadelphia, he had a special conference with Reverend William Harvey III, Corresponding secretary of the Foreign Mission Board, National Baptist Convention, Inc., U.S.A.
>
> In Washington, D.C., he attended a reception honoring the President of Malawi, Dr. Hastings K. Banda who is also a graduate of Meharry. Dr. Malekubu also made an impromptu address at the Sunday School and Baptist Training Union Congress in Milwaukee, WI.

---

10 Prepared by W. W. Douglas, Washington D.C., *The Compass—A Guide For Trail Explorers Unit One* (Nashville, TN, Department of Christian Education and the Sunday School Publishing Board, n.d.).

His response to all of this attention was: "It was good, so very good to see and visit after 50 years. I was pleased to know that somebody liked what I did—yes, so, so, pleased."

His complete record shows that he established many churches and schools in Malawi, Northern and Southern Rhodesia (Malawi), Portuguese East Africa, and the Union of South Africa. He constructed two hospitals at Providence Industrial Mission; organized the Malawi Farmers Association; the Chiradzula District Association; and the National Baptist Assembly of Africa, Inc., the most powerful Christian body in Africa with over 200,000 members; baptized over 20,000 converts and ordained about 30 ministers; and served as supervisor of the mission in East, Central, and Southern Africa.

After years in Africa, Dr. Malekebu and his wife returned to the States and resettled in Atlanta, GA. They retired after giving 45 years of missionary service to God's work. Thousands of people owe their salvation either directly or indirectly to these two Christians. …

Dr. Malekebu returned to his native land in 1977 after the death of his wife, who had ably and capably assisted him in all of his accomplishments. He died there in St. Elizabeth's Hospital, Blantrye, Malawi, on October 8, 1978. … He was buried in the village of Ntupanyama, his birthplace.

Great was the work of this unusual servant of God whose life came under the direct influence of his beloved "Mother Delaney." His astounding results were made possible to a major degree though the dynamic qualities of his wife, Flora, also a native of Africa. A very brief story of her life gives us an awareness of the great destiny accorded this unique personality.

Flora Zeto Melekebu[11] was born in the Belgian Congo at a time of tribal wars, slavery and cannibalism. A white missionary from England rescued a baby from a tribe, named her Flora and kept her as his own child. Her natural family was killed in this tribal war. The missionary kept her until his wife died, then he gave her to another missionary Clara Howard, a graduate of Spelman and friend of Emma B. Delaney. Miss Howard brought Flora back to the Spelman campus when she returned to the U.S.

This child, Flora, became known as "The Spelman Baby" and acquired the name Zeto when she started school. Zeto was a big city in the Congo where she was born. The name meant that she would be a great woman. As a campus child, she was cared for, shared and nurtured by students, other missionaries, as well as her adopted mother. In school she learned quickly, showing exceptional skills in music. She graduated with high honors and later worked for the U.S. Government as a Red Cross Reserve. In spite of her work she was always longing to go back to Africa to help "her people." She did a great work, too, although her deep longing to return to her native land, The Belgian Congo, was never fulfilled.

She was a gifted musician, a teacher, a lecturer, and organizer and friend to many. She assisted her husband in every endeavor and singularly organized and directed women's mission groups in the areas of his work. She was president of the Women's Auxiliary of the National Baptist Assembly of Africa, an organization consisting of thousands of members. In later years she was confined to a wheelchair but continued her role whenever possible. She died in September 1976, and was buried in Atlanta, GA.

From Chapter V—The Pioneer—The Worker

A brief biography of Mrs. Emma B. Delaney, founder of the Suehn Industrial Mission and the Bethel Delaney Baptist Church-Suehn Mission.[12]

Miss Emma B. Delaney according to reliable sources came to Liberia in the year 1912 as a pioneer Afro Missionary. Upon her arrival in Liberia which is one of the oldest west African republics, Miss Emma B. Delaney first went to one of the settlements along the Saint Paul River called Arthington and stopped in the home of one Mr. Solomon Hill where she

---

[11] A ten-year summary of the Foreign Mission Board (1930–1940), Mission Herald, August 1940, 20.

[12] A letter from Solomon J. Scott containing a biographical report on Missionary Delaney (Monrovia, Liberia, West Africa, January 27, 1979).

spent some time while trying to find a place to establish a Mission School. It was during her stay in Mr. Solomon Hill's home that she asked him to show her a place to establish her mission in Liberia. Mr. Hill then recommended a town called Suehn to her that was the only possible place she would find a spot. This was a clan in the Lofu Gola Chiefdom in the Western provinces of Liberia known at the time as the Suehn Bopolu District, Western Province, Republic of Liberia (now the Township of Suehn, Bommi Territory, Republic of Liberia since March 15, 1958). She then told Mr. Hill that she has since heard about Suehn and there where God has directed her to go and establish her Mission School.

During those days there were no motor roads in this part of the interior of Liberia (1912) and so she rode a four boys hammock going up and down hills, mountains, and through dense forests, swamps, creeks and wild animal trails until she reached a town known as Suehn Town after which the Suehn Industrial Mission is named. Upon arriving in Suehn Town she met with the paramount Chief in person of Jeremiah Johnson and the clan chief in person of Jallah Baikpoh who were residing in Suehn Town.

Miss Emma B. Delaney then requested the two tribal chiefs to kindly give her a spot to open a mission. The chiefs and their elders in response to Miss Emma B. Delaney's request told her to choose any spot near the town. After walking through the bush by a native guide of the tribal people, she chose the spot where the Suehn Industrial Mission stands today (1912 to 1979). Having chosen this spot and making her report to the chiefs and their people, she was later informed that this identical spot she has chosen was the traditional society bush of the tribal people (the Golas) and also the battle ground where the tribal people fought many wars and there where many of the victims of the war killed from the fighting were buried. Even though she was informed of the danger of the selected spot, she insisted that this was the spot that God has shown her to choose for the establishment of the Mission School.

At this junction the chiefs permitted her to have the spot. Fortunately, as God would have it, laborers were provided for her by the chiefs to clear the bush from the spot. At the completion of the cleaning of the spot she erected an imported house that she has brought with her from America which was called Delaney Hall. The carpenters who erected the house were also provided her by the chiefs who showed much kindness to her. During the clearing of bush and the erection of her imported house, she resided in Suehn Town with the chiefs and their people with whom she held church services to tell them about Christ. After the completion of the house (Delaney Hall) she moved on the campus with about three or four girls from the tribal areas. Later on she built a large country thatched shade where she held church services with the tribal people of the neighboring villages of Suehn. But she was frequently molested with the tribal drum beating and war dances at night by the natives whose intention was not to harm her and few girls on campus, but only to frighten them. For fear of any future danger or harm, she appealed to the President of Liberia at that time for protection. In reply to her request the Liberian Government dispatched a squad of soldiers to keep guard over the mission for sometime until all threats of war drum beating and dancing were ceased.

When she had lived on campus for some indefinite period of time with the few girls that she had gotten from the tribal homes she began to get few male students after putting up a few more buildings.

Miss Delaney's Report[13]
Another Year's Work Recorded

Relying upon God for strength and guidance, I took up my abode at the mission eight months ago. I had been to the mission before, but could not remain for lack of shelter. Every effort was put forth to get things on the station in working order. However, this was impossible when I was 15 miles away, so as soon as a floor was laid, regardless to green plank, I moved in.

… When I reached the place to turn from the main road to go up to the house, I expected

---
[13] *Mission Herald*, October 1914, 2–3.

to find a road cleared of bushes, for I had paid a man to cut one, but the bushes were over my head, and stumps of old trees that had stood for years were everywhere to be seen, even in the out-kitchen, or the frame for a kitchen, there were stumps three feet in diameter waiting to be removed. Myself, the girl that was with me, and a few laborers, lost no time in clearing around the place.

I saw the difficulties and the responsibilities of this work before it was started, yet I made up my mind that in God's strength I could assume the one, and surmount the other. When discouraging, as well as encouraging features had to be dealt with, I simply took hold as a proof of the fact that God is with me.

The Religious Work for the Year

It was my privilege to lend all the assistance possible in the revival meeting conducted in the Baptist Church in the settlement where I was stopping while waiting for the mission house. Sixty souls were saved and among this number quite a few were heathens. We have no place at the mission station in which to conduct services. I mean by this, a place large enough for the villagers. Certainly, we have services daily for the students on the station. For this reason the native worker and I have been going to different villages each Sunday during the dry season. I have oftimes wondered if this was not a mistake instead of calling them to the mission I have gotten them accustomed to sitting around in their villages and waiting for us to come to them. If it was a mistake, it grew out of the fact that it was the best we could do at the time. And now, that the six months' rains are on, there is no hope of getting a place until they are over. We have had some very excellent meetings: many have heard God's word even if they did not care to, as in the case of a man who was converted in the village a few months ago. He refused to come out to the meeting when asked, but remained in his hut stretched on his mat. On Monday, he came to me, and with the assistance of an interpreter, he said: "Mamma, I would not come out to that "God Palaver" you were talking, but I heard it all, and I tried to forget it, but it just laid down in my heart, and turned over and over everywhere I went, and something told me to come to you yesterday, but I would not. Last night I could not sleep (his wife and the woman in the next hut were witnesses to the fact that he prayed all night), and this morning my heart came up (their way of saying they are happy) and a man told me to come to you and tell you all about it, and also to tell you to take me to the stream and wash my face (baptise him)." I don't know where he got this washing from, for he has never seen a person baptized, and I am positively sure I have said nothing about since I have been out here.

He is a Mandingo, and, like many others, took refuge here during the cruel war in Bopora. The government has ordered them all back before the end of the year. He, with others, has gone to clear up and get their rice farms planted. I pray he will keep the assurance; his light is so small, and there is so much darkness, and with no knowledge of what it means to be a Christian, I tremble for him.

Bopora is about four hard days' walk from here. Whenever this convert sees a messenger coming down this way he sends me word, 'he is still on God's side.' I am told there are a number of Mohammedans above us, and I fear he will unite with them, for his tribe takes to that creed.

Yet, I must say that the Mandingoes, though Mohammedans, have been very attentive and respectful at all meetings. They are more easily impressed than the raw heathen, and they are very prompt in attending the meetings in their villages. Sometime ago we had quite a stormy Sunday morning, and I did not go to the village. … There are customs here which make everything so uncertain, especially with women and children. Only last week a man that I have always thought was above the average, told me that he would bring his little girl to school the next day. … I learned to my disgust that the man had bought an ox of his uncle a year ago, and had never paid for it. The uncle being in need of money, came to his nephew and demanded that the debt be paid at once. The nephew had no money so the little girl, who was to have been put into school, was given to the uncle for the debt. The probabilities are that the girl will never be redeemed; hence, she will be the property of this uncle all her life. And so it goes. … A women and her children may be with the husband and father today in this village, and tomorrow they will be owned by some other man in a village miles away. One can readily understand how they sold their children into slavery centuries ago. I trust that Christianity will destroy these customs in years to come. …

I say like the child to you, this year's work on paper seems a mere trifle, but my Father in heaven knows I have done my best. I take comfort in this fact; He cannot read wrong. And while—
"The world crowns success. God crowns faithfulness ... With this thought to cheer, I press on in His service."

From Chapter VI—The Legacy Lives

Her body rests in Bosquo Bello (Quiet Woods) Cemetery in her hometown where she was born and reared. Her burial place is an old Spanish city cemetery located at the top of a hill. It has been in use since 1798.

1928 Name "Bethel Baptist Church" given in honor of Miss Delaney's work in Africa by Mrs. Sarah Williamson Coleman of Washington, D.C., the missionary to Suehn from 1924-1929, for the newly erected church.

I went to Liberia, November, 1924, and found at Suehn the grant of land given to Emma B. Delaney by Chief Jallah. "Delaney Hall," I called it, was a corrugated iron house brought from America to Liberia by her. It was brought in sections and assembled by workers on the spot. It was in my plans to keep it forever. It served as the only house to live in for five years and I used it for every need. The natives helped me to prop it up until I could have workmen come up from Monrovia and repair it. I made a road to the door from the main road. Remember there were only bush paths and wild cats on the entire hill!

The government wanted to take away the grant of land when Emma Delaney passed because it was on that hill where the last battle was fought between the American Liberians and the natives. Emma B. Delaney name named the mission Suehn because from that last battle blood ran down the hill. Suehn means "running blood."

I named the church that God bless me to help lay the foundation in 1928 "Bethel Delaney Baptist Church." I was anxious although only in my early twenties to keep sacred the memory of Emma B. Delaney the founder of Suehn Mission.

The African government wanted the land back so that they could make a historical spot. But the Foreign Mission Board "held on." Thousands have followed this light in the jungle and accepted Jesus as their Savior.[14]

The work of this true and faithful servant never ceased after her physical death, but continues in her spirit through the hearts and works of others. Years later, the women of the National Baptist Convention saw the need to memorialize this sainted missionary as shown by the following resolution:

Resolution Passed and Recorded[15]

That a monument to the memory of Miss Emma B. Delaney (who twice crossed the ocean and founded the Suehn Mission School in West Africa which stands to the credit and pride of American Baptist) be ordered and made. ...

1932—The fund treasurer reported $375 at the General State Convention. The committee was increased and given authority to solicit funds through Spelman College also.

1935—Emma B. Delaney's monument was unveiled at Bosquo Bello by the General State Convention.

At the church and cemetery a beautiful and impressive memorial[16] was held. Those who spoke on her life of usefulness were Mrs. G. P. McKinney with whom she worked pleasantly and successfully for several years. Mrs. J. C. Mapp of Chicago, first vise president of the Women's National Convention, who had worked with Miss Delaney in the interest of Foreign Mission after her second return from Africa, Dr. W. C. Brown, once a student of Miss Delaney at the Florida Institute and Mrs. A. E. Duhart a school mate of Miss Delaney at Spelman Seminary in Atlanta, GA.

1973—A Resolution was passed by the Women's Auxiliary to the General Baptist Convention of FL proclaiming Emma B. Delaney's Day the third Sunday of May.

---

14 Written report by Mrs. Sarah Williamson Coleman, Missionary at Suehn Liberia, West Africa 1924–1929 (Washington, D.C., Dec. 1978).

15 *Historical Facts of the Women's Missionary and Educational State Convention Auxiliary of Florida* 1980–1941, 34, 49 (n.d.).

16 A memorial for the Reverand Henry Beard Delaney is at St. Augustine College Chapel, Raleigh, NC. He was the father of the famous Delaney sisters, Dr. Bessie and Miss Sadie wrote their autobiography *Having Our Say* at ages 101 and 103.

1974—Emma B. Delaney Hour was held at First Baptist Church, Rev. Robert Flagler, Pastor at Fernandina Beach, FL; sponsored by the Foreign Mission Committee of the Baptist General State Convention of FL, Inc.. Dr. Susie C. Holley, President; Mrs. W. L. Smith, Chairman; Mrs. A. Atchison, Co-Chairman.

1979—The pastor, officers and congregation of the First Missionary Baptist Church, honored her memory by erecting a building named E. B. Delaney Fellowship Hall.

The Dedicatorial Service was held on Sunday, August 26, 1979, with the pastor Rev. Dr. Robert Flager presiding. The dedicatorial message was given by Rev. Allen Weaver, Pastor of Bethel Baptist Church, Daytona Beach, FL. The Florida Women's auxiliary was represented through a message by the president, Dr. Susie C. Holley, Sister Willie Lee Smith and Alleen C. Bradley. The church congregation was represented as follows: Dea. Clarence Harvey, Chairman of the Deacons; Bro. John Baker, Chairman Building Committee; Sis. Carie Coakley, Beautification; Sis. Mamie Delaney, Missionary Society President and Venita Edwards, Pulpit Aid Board President; and Hospitality Building Committee members. The Dedicatory Planning Committee Chairman was Sis. Alleen D. Gilyard with Sis. Willie Mae Ashley, Co-Chairman.

From Chapter VII—Remembering E. B. Delaney—Echoes From Home

1949—A portrait was unveiled at a special tribute at First Baptist Church in Fernandina Beach, FL.

Dr. D. S. Malekebu, Atlanta, GA, July 1974:

Yes, the picture hanging in our church can tell you how she looked but the other part—I don't know if I can actually describe her. ...Yes, —and she didn't like to take—to take what word shall I use?—to take foolishness perhaps that would fit in. ... Mother Delaney was a passionate, kind lady with pride and determination like nothing you could see now. She stood erect, carrying herself with a strong, strong sense of self. Her penetrating eyes, though kind, left an indelible impression on me. She was really outspoken but she had a way, a diplomatic way they call it, of handling you. ...

She was stylish too in the up to date styles of the day and immaculate. I especially remember her "hair do" or whatever you'd say. She wore long skirts with pretty blouses and stylish buckled up shoes. ...

Mother Delaney was a great teacher, too.... You know, in those day in my country girls couldn't go to school like boys. ... [S]he taught my sister Ruth. Ruth became the first native female in my country to pass the English proficiency test. She became the first English teacher.

Nancy Verdier McDonald, Fernandina Beach, FL, February 1973:

Another remembrance was the funeral— You know, in those days there were not many cars among our people. But I remember that large number of cars seen in the streets with our people—"colored people" as we were called then—driving them. ... The funeral procession from the church to Bosque Bello stretched for a long long ways.

Johnnie Benton Delaney, Fernandina Beach, FL, May 1974:

She said one day after she had had a nap she woke up, looked up in the ceiling of the hut tent-like house and there was this huge snake stretched out on one of the open rafters. It looked like it was ready to jump. She was so afraid but quick movement and yelling brought her house boy. He and the other boys struggled until that snake was knocked down, cornered and killed.

Carrie Marshall Randolph, Fernandina Beach, FL, March 24, 1974:

... One evening a bit after dark she returned to her hut carrying a light as usual. As soon as she walked in, a glance at an old mirror on her "make shift dresser" revealed a native crouched in the corner with a knife or something in his hand just like he was going to attack her. ... although her back was turned toward him she began praying—asking God to help her brother describing him just as he was looking at that minute. ... Not realizing that she was seeing him in the looking glass; he was puzzled— After a few minutes in utter amazement the scared young man came forth, hands out-

stretched, dropped the crude instrument and ran from the hut. God spared her life.

Irene Brown Smith, Jacksonville, FL/Richmond, VA, April 1973:

In those days, you know, we didn't have fountain pens like you all have now. We had to use the pen and dip it in the ink well. I remember her as being very good, neat writer and she demanded without being too hard on you that the ink would be even throughout the letter. ... Miss Delaney was meticulous and I did a lot of writing for her. She called me "her secretary." We wrote letters to a lot of people all over the U.S ... She finally got enough money to go back again to Africa.

Clara Floyd and sister Amanda Huggins, Fernandina Beach, FL, November 19, 1972:

We do remember her telling us how strange the natives were over there in Africa. ... She said she found them throwing away the potatoes and eating the vines, not eating the peanuts but eating the plant. She said when she finally got them to roast potatoes in the hot ashes and to roast or eat peanuts raw—oh how they enjoyed them...

Daniel Delaney, Fernandina Beach, FL, September 1984:

Cousin Emma said she had a monkey to bring home with her from Africa. She brought that monkey all the way to the ship, but when she was making preparations to board the authorities would not let her bring the monkey on. ... Yes, that monkey ended up being cooked by the chef on board the ship where she sailed.

Cousin Emma's middle name "Beard" came from a family member. Her uncle's name was Henry Beard Delaney. ["H. B.," as he was affectionately known by family and friends, was born in 1858. He graduated from St. Augustine College in NC and later was a professor there. At an early age he was ordained as an Episcopal deacon and became a priest in 1892. Henry Beard Delaney became the first Black Episcopal bishop in the U.S.]

From Chapter VIII - Suehn Today—A Mission in Action
Willie Mae Ashely—

Emma B. Delaney's childhood commission was not completed with her work in East Africa through the Providence Industrial Mission. This God-fearing spirited Christian soldier had a greater mission to fulfill in Liberia, West Africa, a country fertile for missionary work.

The following accounts written by Rev. William J. Harvey, III. "Emma Delaney, an Indomitable Spirit"[17]

In 1912, another human drama unfolded to give Liberians the present work at Suehn Station in Montserrado County. The woman responsible for this distinguished work must have had incredible vision and determination for she literally carved the Suehn Industrial Mission out of the bush country with her bare hands. Rev. Horton tells how she drove stakes herself to begin the work which resulted in the third mission station of your Foreign Mission Board. Previous to this she had blazed a trail around America raising thousands of dollars for the project. Someone had said, "Put feet to your prayers." Emma Delaney was willing to put everything she had into the outworking of her prayers and countless people throughout a Century of Mission have benefited from her unselflessness.

By 1922, there were three buildings; a 10 room house used as a girl's dormitory, a 7 room cottage for the boys' home and a 1 room combination chapel and school. One of the most used native trails in the Republic cut across the campus providing a great opportunity for a medical clinic. ... Hundreds of men, women and children passed the mission station daily, day and night, with sores and illnesses indicative of that area and social conditions of those times.

---

[17] William J. Harvey III, *Sacrifice and Dedication in a Century of Mission* (Philadelphia, PA, The Foreign Mission Board 1979), 88–89.

By 1938, the Suehn Industrial Mission had an enrollment of 165 students. A record number, at that time. Instructors in the school covered a broad spectrum of trades ... engineering, cement worker, blacksmith, agriculturist, carpenter, woodwork instructor, boat builder, saw mill worker, seamstress, housekeeper, musician, teacher. These instructors and others following in their path have helped raise the standard of living for aborigines and civilized alike.

Primarily a high school for boys and girls, Suehn's high academic rating has been commended by the Liberian Ministry of Education. Evangelistic teams from this Mission have brought many people of the surrounding area into Christian life.

One of the most important and interesting features of the Suehn Mission is its church development program. There are 14 native Baptist churches in the Suehn district. The missionaries work these churches assisting them in developing Sunday Schools and Women's Missionary Societies.

1999—Emma B. Delaney acknowledged as one of Florida's African Americans represented in the Great Floridians 2000 program, which the Florida Legislature established in 1997. The state's Historic Marker Program issued a plaque honoring her, paid for by the city of Fernandina Beach, and placed at First Missionary Baptist Church.

R. S. M Kpahaye-Stewart—

Paul makes an important point in 1 Corinthians 9:22b that is equally descriptive of Christ. Christ was indeed all things to all men. The essence of this message characterizes the Suehn Mission many of us came to know. Suehn bore a message of hope. ...

In this way many today reminisce of Suehn in the words of its Ode, "Suehn, how we love thee, we thy children sing to thee ..." Indeed, we are the children of Suehn. Suehn was more than an academic community. The mission was foster home for the homeless, a mother for the motherless, a clinic for the children and adults of the surrounding villages and spiritual center where each experienced the presence of God in a personal way by direct contact with the redemptive love of Christ.

Those that bore that message of love are many, beginning with Ms. Delaney..., Mrs. Mattie Mae Davis, Ms. Gladys V. East as principals and a number of supportive co-workers.

K. Ntem Agrey, Instructor—

Suehn Industrial Academy is a Senior High School meeting the standards required by the Ministry of Education of the Republic of Liberia and is operated by the Foreign Mission Board, National Baptist Convention, U.S.A., Incorporated ...

Motto: "Go through, go through the gates, prepare ye the way of the people; cast up, cast up the highway; gather out the stones; lift up a standard for the people" (Isaiah 62:10 KJV).

Many students have passed through the walls of the Academy who are now holding responsible positions in either government or private sectors. Others are pursuing various academic disciplines either at home or abroad.

School Ode: Suehn, how we love thee, we thy children sing to thee, Thy leadest ever upward, we will follow onward forward is thy watch word, we will faithful be. Through ignorance dark as night has been our beacon light. Suehn, we do love thee, we will faithful be. Suehn, how we love thee, children of thy foe— we thy sons and daughters thy name upward.

From the Appendix

Living Missionaries Who Served at Suehn Industrial Mission 1924–1986: Missionary Sarah Williamson Coleman, Missionary Ruth Morris-Graham, Missionary Winifred Burrough Holmes, Missionary Virginia Antrom, Missionary Charles Levi, Missionary Gladys V. East, Missionary Erma E. Bailey Ethridge.

Presented as a choral reading by the Sunshine Band of the Missionary Society at the E. B. Delaney Memorial Hour ... First Missionary Baptist Church, Fernandina Beach, FL.

Speaker Four: Today we pause to remember Emma B. Delaney!

Today we give honor and sing her praise!

She left a message of love for ALL to carry

Each Christian must be a true missionary!

[All repeat with emphasis]

She left a message of love for ALL to carry

Each Christian must be a true missionary!

Taken from Humanitarian, Emma B. Delaney, 1877–1922:

Ms. Ashley feels if this outstanding woman was alive today she would have this message for today's youth … "dream, set your goals early in life; prepare and work daily serving all mankind. Be faithful, kind and caring and allow God to direct your path."

Chapter 22

The Life and Work of Rev. Landon N. Cheek
Excerpts from The Bones of My Ancestors

by Margaret J. Durham

Margaret J. Durham is the great granddaughter of Rev. Landon N. Cheek. She is the founder and President Emeritus of the Landon Cheek Chapter of the Afro American Historical and Genealogical Society in St. Louis, MO. She teaches genealogy at the St. Louis Community College and holds genealogical seminars.

She has conducted genealogy seminars for the Missouri Secretary of State in Jefferson City, MO; at Howard University in Washington, D.C.; for the U.S. Army Troop Support Command in St. Louis, MO, and various other agencies throughout the St. Louis metropolitan area.

Margaret has a Bachelor of Science Degree in Business Administration from Columbia College and a Masters of Management Degree in Business Management from Fontbonne University.

When Margaret knew her great grandfather, Rev. Landon N. Cheek, he was a very old man and she did not realize his accomplishments on the continent until she was grown. She has since traveled to Malawi, met with distant relatives, and has been tracing their family lineage. Her complied work will be released as *The Bones of My Ancestors*.

Excerpted from "The Life and Work of Rev. Landon N. Cheek." Used by permission.

Rev. Landon N. Cheek, was a MS born minister who took the great commission to the continent of Africa in 1901. He was a hero, freedom fighter and civil rights activist in Nyasaland (present day Malawi). He sacrificed his own freedom to preserve the freedom of his African brethren.

He was born in Canton, MS, in December of 1871. His parents were Frank and Ada Cheek. Landon was the oldest of their three children. His brothers were Edgar and James. Landon grew up in Canton in an atmosphere of prosperity and congeniality. He expressed an early interest in the work of the Lord and confessed a hope in Christ at the age of 17.

He became a school teacher at the Pleasant Gift School and was also a Sunday School teacher at the Pleasant Gift Baptist Church. The Cheek family donated two and one half acres of land to the Pleasant Gift Baptist Church in 1919. The church still stands on that land today.

Cheek attended Alcorn in MS and matriculated at Natchez Seminary in Natchez, MS. He left Canton shortly after the completion of his studies at Natchez Seminary.

It is difficult to ascertain exactly why he chose the African mission field, but early in his life he was exposed to the work of the Northern Baptist Mission Society in Jackson, MS. It was there that he met E. O. Stillwell, a missionary. She informed the people about the plight of their sisters and brothers in Africa, who were still worshipping idols and knew no gospel light. Stillwell was probably Landon's first exposure to the need for missionaries in Africa.

Landon, like his brother Edgar did not spend much of his adult life in Canton. They were born at a time when Jim Crow laws and racial discrimination ran rampant in the south. Edgar chose the east coast states. Landon chose the mid-west and ultimately the continent of Africa as his home. He left Canton in 1896 to live in MS.

Cheek continued the study of Theology at Western Baptist College in Macon, MO. He matriculated there as a prospective YMCA Secretary to Africa. Western Baptist College was a unique institution of education for its time. It had the distinction of being the first and only Christian school in the northwest founded by Negroes exclusively, without the incentive of land or money.[1] It was at Western that he became associated with the Berean Dis-

---

[1] David O. Shipley, *History of Black Baptists in Missouri* (Kansas City: David O. Shipley, 1976), 82.

trict from which he received financial support to attend the college.

Cheek continued his association with the Berean District after his graduation from Western and he settled in St. Louis, MO, where the district was most active. The greatest interests of the District, which was organized in 1878, were the Home and the Foreign Mission. Cheek served in many capacities in the District. One position which he held from 1899 to 1900 was that of Chairman of the Committee on Corresponding Bodies. Its function was to recommend representatives from the Berean Missionary Association to attend meetings of the National Baptist Convention [N.B.C.], the MO Baptist State Convention, and eight or ten other Baptist association meetings in the midwest. In his capacity of Chairman, Cheek would have heard the appeals made by the Foreign Mission Committee for workers in the foreign mission field.

He was aware of the effort to recruit missionaries because it was consistently on the agenda of the Berean Missionary Association. In Report #14 of the Twentieth Annual Session of the Association's minutes, dated August 1897, the Committee on Foreign Missions stated that Rev. L. G. Jordan, the Secretary of the Board of Missions of the N.B.C., had sent one Missionary to Africa, Bro. F. A. Johns. It submitted its report from him as follows:

> [W]e recommend the pastors belonging to the Berean Association urge their congregations to raise all they can during this year for foreign mission work. There is a great demand for help. In Central Africa there is a population larger than in the United States of America, that has no missionaries. These people are still worshipping idols. They worship the crocodile, as their god. It is reported by some of the late missionaries, that it is sad to see the mothers of the some of the tribes take up their babes, pressing them to their breasts, then dash them in the sea. We may see from this report, that there is much work to be done.[2]

An added stimulus for the African continent was the fact that Cheek, perhaps like many African Americans realized the futility of their efforts to attain equality in the U.S. and sought consolation in the Back to Africa dream. It was during this same time that European imperialism was spreading throughout Africa creating havoc for its people. This served as an even greater reason to render service in Africa to their own people. It was also during this time that the most potent pleas for workers were being published from African-American missionaries in Africa.

Rev. R. H. Jackson, an African-American missionary stationed at the Qanda Mission in Middle Drift, South Africa, wrote to the Editor of *The Richmond Planet* newspaper that white missionaries had gone among the heathen and in the name of God, the Bible and Christianity [and] successfully robbed them. First, of all moveable property such as gold, diamonds, cattle, sheep, fruit, etc.; and next the red coats came to seize the land.[3]

In addition, Mame Branton Tule, and African-American Baptist missionary stationed in Captetown, South Africa, wrote to the same newspaper as follows:

> *Allow me space in your column to insert a plea to our Baptist Family, who I fear is sleeping the golden harvest away. Baptists awake, why slumber so long? ... I wonder when will our Baptists awake to the great necessity of sending the torch-light of salvation to those who are in darkness. ... there are hordes who are in need of salvation and decent morals.*[4]

Rev. Charles S. Morris, an African-American missionary stationed in Queenstown, South Africa also wrote articles concerning the work in Africa to the editor of *The Richmond Planet*. He wanted to set up a chain of self-supporting and self-extending, industrial mission stations with a non-industrial college or training school to supply the stations with teachers. In his letter to *The Richmond Planet*, he wrote:

> *This I believe is God's plan, and as I stand here on the tip end of this great continent of my fathers and look up at it with is ultimate*

---

2 Committee on Foreign Missions, "Report #14," Minutes of the Berean Baptist Association, Third Annual Session (August 2–8, 1897): 37.

3 Rev. R. A. Jackson, "Prejudice in the Dark Continent," *The Richmond Planet*, March 18, 1899:1.

4 Mamie B. Tule, "A Voice From Africa," *The Richmond Planet*, August 19, 1899:1.

area, with its vast interior population, with its woes and wrongs and with the devil high on a throne of royal state—majestic though in ruin, brooding in hellish satisfaction over the havoc he has wrought here in ages past, I long to lead the Christian forces to assault and drive him out and give Jesus Christ a continent he took possession of when a babe and which He purchased with his own blood as a man.[5]

These pleas from missionaries in Africa seemed to inspire Cheek to prepare himself for work in the African missionary field. His religious, educational and family background slid easily into the profile of black missionaries of that era. They were a diversified group of evangelists, which included blacks from both free and slave backgrounds and form both rural and urban areas. They came from thickly black populated areas of the country such as VA, AR, MS, SC, and GA.

Although there were variations among these African-American missionaries, there was also some common ground; such as the fact that they had fairly comfortable childhoods in families that were relatively well-to-do. As a rule their families were not wealthy, but they were not severely affected by the cloud of poverty that hung so heavily over much of the black community. Life in their families centered around religion and the church. Education was also heavily stressed in their homes. A measure of their educational expertise is the high quality of grammar depicted in their letters from the field. In a time of mass illiteracy in the African-American community, their educational level was exemplary. Prior to becoming a missionary, Cheek, like most of these evangelists, was a minister and a teacher. Even though these ministers enjoyed positions of respect in America, they still felt it necessary to render service to their brethren in Africa.

In 1899, Cheek decided to try the foreign mission field and contracted with the Foreign Mission Board (F.M.B.) of the N.B.C. He was commissioned by the board to assist Rev. John Chilembwe in the opening of the P.I.M. in Nyasaland, British Central Africa. Rev. Chilembwe was an African of the Yao ethnic group. He had been educated in America and subsequently returned to Nyasaland to open the mission.

Cheek gave up pastoring in St. Louis in September of 1900 and departed first for Richmond, VA, where he was introduced at the N.B.C. as one of five missionaries bound for Africa. *The Richmond Planet* newspaper billed the convention as "A Great Baptist Gathering Here." The other missionaries introduced along with Cheek were Rev. C. S. Morris of West Newton, MA; Miss E. B. Delaney, of Fernandina Beach, FL; Rev. T. W. Longwood of Hot Springs, AR; and Rev. E. B. Koti of Queenstown, South Africa. The missionaries held a workshop at the convention to inform the public about their work on the Dark Continent.

Although they were supposed to depart for the continent immediately, Cheek was unable to afford the passage to Nyasaland in 1900. Once again, he enlisted the aid of the pastors in the Berean District in St. Louis, MO, for financial support.[6] By January of 1901, he had collected enough funds and was able to book passage on the Steamship Southwark, bound for London. In London he booked passage on a vessel to Nyasaland in British Central Africa.

Cheek traveled with Rev. E. B. Koti, who was on his way to Queenstown in South Africa. In a letter he wrote from the ship to the F.M.B. he stated that he would arrive in London on February 3rd. In a letter from London dated February 5, 1901, he wrote that he and Rev. Koti had met with Dr. Guiness of the Zambezi Mission. He stated that a Rev. Caldwell had assisted them in getting tickets and baggage and that he would arrive in Blantyne, Nyasaland about the first of April. He stated that he would have to wait at Chinde to get a boat up the Zambezi.

He also stated that Mr. Caldwell's farm at the Zambezi Industrial Mission had cleared $15,000.00 in the previous year on their coffee project. Inasmuch, as Cheek was well versed in the operations of farming, the news about the success of the coffee project must have been very encouraging to him. He concluded the letter by stating that he thought the men of the Zambezi Industrial

---

5 Rev. Charles Morris, "He Likes Africa," *The Richmond Planet*, December 2, 1899:1.

6 "History of the Berean Missionary Baptist District Association," July 1989, Commission to Write History, Rev. J. Brown Moderator, 4.

Mission would cooperate with those of the N.B.C. in the creation of a great work in Africa.[7]

It is plain to see from his letters that Cheek felt that he would be able to accomplish a great work both spiritually and financially in Africa. He would lead souls to Christ on the one hand and on the other hand, a good coffee crop would bring the needed finances to support the P.I.M. and for the N.B.C. to continue the black foreign mission thrust into Africa.

Cheek arrived in Blantyne, Nyasaland, British Central Africa on April 14th, 1901. He wrote back to the F.M.B. in America that he was on the Lord's work, 15 miles from a physician, in case of fever or other sickness, and almost penniless. His living expenses in London and in Chinde had taken the bulk of the funds given to him for travel. He also reported that many of his goods had been confiscated by British Customs. He emphasized the fact that the prejudice there was strong or stronger than at Cape Town or Durban.[8]

He sent word of his arrival to Rev. John Chilembwe at the mission station in Chiradzulu and Chilembwe sent men to greet him. They carried Cheek to the mission station in mechilla, a type of hammock in which the traveler reclines and is carried by four men, two in back and two in front Three or four miles before they reached the station a horn was blown to announce their arrival. By the time they reached the mission a large group of men, women and children had gathered and they swarmed out to meet him. Chilembwe was very glad that Cheek had finally arrived. He greeted him with great enthusiasm. On April 16, 1901, he wrote the following to the board regarding Cheek's arrival:

> This will inform you that our brother, L. N. Cheek, safely arrived at this station last Sunday at 10 a.m. We heartily welcome him to our country and pray that he will prove to be a good man and assist us to build up a church in this part of Africa against which the gates of hell cannot prevail. We are proud of his prudence and good sense. He seems to be fitted in every way to make an educational leader.[9]

This meeting of Cheek and Chilembwe was a joyous occasion for all. Cheek wrote that the location of the mission was beautiful. He said that it was situated between two mountains and that the weather was lovely at that time. He warned however, that it would get worse when the rains came from November to February. He also warned that fever of the dangerous type often raged on Zambezi River and in Blantyre. He requested funds to carry him through the rough times.

Cheek was full of enthusiasm and ready to make his mark in the annals of "redemption." His joy however was short-lived. The British Colonial Government, as well as the white religious leaders regarded his arrival as a threat. They felt he would interfere with their administration and control of the Africans in the Protectorate. Cheek became acutely aware of this hostile environment almost immediately. The administration functioned primarily to supply the needs of the British while it disregarded the rights of the indigenous people. It was content to leave the natives mired in positions of servitude while they continued to rape and plunder the land for their own gain. In view of this, Cheek's arrival in the Protectorate was viewed with suspicion and distrust. They didn't know quite what to expect from him and they feared the worst.

It was Cheek's gross misfortune to have arrived during the time when the Ethiopian movement was on the rise in Chiradzulu. On April 20, 1901, the Central African Times in referring to Cheek's arrival stated:

By the S. S. Induna there arrived in Chinde an American Negro who comes to B.C.A. as a sort of emancipator of his people, and we learn that he has settled in that hornet's nest in Chiradzulu. What can the advent of that free Ethiopian religion mean to this country?[10]

Cheek had scarcely arrived and already he was being called an emancipator of his people. Cheek's efforts toward the spread of the gospel were severely hampered by the fact that he had arrived during the "Classical" period of Ethiopianism. The statement by the Central African Times was a reflection of the sentiments of many Nyasaland Europeans regarding the anxiety caused by the Ethiopian movement.

---

7 L. N. Cheek, "From the Sea," *Mission Herald*, February 1901:2.
8 L. N. Cheek, "From the Sea," *Mission Herald*, July 1901:2–4.
9 John Chilembwe, "From the Field," *Mission Herald*, July 1901:2.

10 Unknown, "From the Field," *Mission Herald*, August 1901:2.

In mid-1901, there was great fear that Ethiopian American Negroes might cause a "general native rising there." During this classical period, the movement had its greatest political visibility and appeared most often in the American and European press. It was an expression of the general assertion of African rights. Robert Laws in the British Legislative Council attributed the growth of the Ethiopian movement in South Africa to the fact that the white missions had been too slow in encouraging African leadership and assumption of responsibility within the Church.[11]

Africans in Nyasaland preferred to receive religious instruction at the P.I.M. rather than the Blantyre Mission, where Drs. Heatherwick and Scott were in charge. At. P.I.M. converts were baptized upon the profession of their faith in Christ and received full membership in the church. The Church of Scotland Mission on the other hand kept them in classes ten or twelve years before they could have full membership. Cheek wrote that "Phillip baptized the eunuch immediately and this was the bible way."[12]

The length of the religious instruction offered by the church of Scotland added to the African's disillusionment. These measures were placed in motion to keep the Africans from having full membership in the church and prevent them from having a say in its workings. Thus, the Church of Scotland, whether knowingly or unknowingly was adding to the dreaded Ethiopian movement by the manner in which it treated its religious converts. They bitterly resented Cheek and Chilembwe for baptizing and offering full membership upon the confession of faith in Christ.

Cheek spoke about the dreaded Ethiopian movement in a letter to the editor of the Richmond Planet newspaper. He said, "The Union Jack (British Flag) waves over us, but I think they who hoisted it often tremble when they hear Africans reading the Holy Bible in which it states that God made of one blood all nations that dwell upon the face of the earth and has fixed the bounds of their habitation."[13] They don't want to see the African's kin telling them the whole truth. They call us "Black Dangers," "Ethiopians," "Emancipators of the race," and even class us with "Islam."

Africans in the Protectorate labored under their white rulers in both Nyasaland and Northern Rhodesia. Sanctioned by their government, settlers occupied choice terrain in the productive Shire Highlands. In Nyasaland, whites had purchased large estates for practically nothing. This was due to the fact that Africans knew nothing of Western ideas about the ownership of property. They sold much of what later became the municipality of Blantyre-Limbe for trifling amounts; a coffer planter purchased more than 3,000 acres for " a gun, 32 yards of calico, two red caps, and several other things." A missionary obtained more than 26,000 acres for seven trusses of calico measuring about 1,750 yards. A district officer later stated that the Africans could not possibly have understood the meaning or function of a commercial firm and they could not have realized that the agreement they made was a sale and that by this act they disinherited their tribe and deprived them of the prosperity of the rights to their land.[14]

By the time Cheek arrived the ownership of more than half of the best part of the area had passed into European hands and whites controlled about 15 per cent of the total land and water area of the Protectorate. In view of these facts, it is not difficult to understand why the whites were suspicious of Cheek and called him an emancipator of his people. They directed a great deal of hostility towards him, hoping that he would become disgusted and return to America. He spoke of this hostility as follows:

> *My English friends (?) were eyeing me as a veritable hornet who within 30 years would incite the natives against English rule. To the last day of our long and weary years they tried to trump my every move, even to build up our station, hoping that any day I would be discouraged and return to the U.S.A.*[15]

---

11 C. P. Groves, *The Planting of Christianity in Africa, 1914–1954* ed., vol. 4 (London: Lutterworth Press, 1964), 63.

12 Letter to George Shepperson from L. N. Cheek, dated June 4, 1953.

13 L. N. Cheek, "Voice from the Dark Continent," *The Richmond Planet*, December 20, 1902:1.

14 Robert I. Rotberg, "The Modern Emergence of Malawi and Zambia," *The Transformation of East Africa*, Stanley Diamond and Fred G. Burke (New York: Basic Books, Inc., 1966), 343.

15 George Shepperson and T. Price, *Independent African* (Edinburgh: University Press, 1958), pg 137.

Cheek's description of their opposition to his presence makes it clear that whites in the Protectorate were not content with just to exist side-by-side with him. His statement that they tried to trump his every move amplifies the fact that they used whatever means necessary to prevent him from establishing a firm hold in Chiradzulu. There was no justice or mercy from the white missionaries of the Church of Scotland. They were particularly hostile to Cheek.

Perhaps angered by the loss of their converts, they attempted to thwart Cheek's efforts to spread the gospel. They refused to sell books to him or help him in any way to establish a mission school. They wanted the Africans to continue to come to them for religious instruction. Regarding the actions by these missionaries Cheek wrote:

> *I have taught and preached to thousands, fought my way onward amid prejudice from the government (English), heathenish kings, and even white missionaries, who seem to take exception because the Lord sent us here.*[16]

Another reason the white missionaries resented him was that his education and theological training may not have been the best by some measures; but, he was better educated than many Europeans in the Protectorate. As an African-American missionary, he was knowingly or unknowingly contributing toward the spread of discontent by his very presence in Africa.

Cheek symbolized the height Africans could attain if education were made available to them and what Africans could accomplish if their opportunities were not restricted. He had taken no part in the dreaded Ethiopian movement, but he was an educated, black American minister, and to the Europeans that fact had many negative connotations.

Added discontent in Nyasaland during Cheek's tenure arose from the fact that there were no public schools in the area. There were only church schools. The system of church schools was another means of discrimination against Africans. In order for an African to receive an education, he had to enroll in a church school. The church schools discriminated against the Africans by preventing them from having full membership in the church. In addition to the lack of public schools, the village hut tax was another strike against the Africans in the Protectorate.

The British charged a tax on each hut in which the Africans lived. The necessity to earn funds to pay the tax kept them in positions of servitude. They had to work for the British in order to earn money to pay the tax. To add insult to injury, the taxes paid by the Africans were used by the British to pay the salaries of the soldiers in the army. The soldiers were used to quell any actions by the Africans to protest their predicament. Cheek wrote concerning the effect of the hut tax and lack of educational opportunities in the Protectorate as follows:

> *When the village hut life is broken up and the government will run schools with some of the tax money used for standing armies and imperialism, we can hope for great change. Will we really hope for this change form any other race [but the Negro]? Can we expect the foreigners in Africa to plead for higher wages and more education while we still sell barter goods to natives and get the majority of them for 75 cents per month? Is there no power to save? Who will make a move for justice and mercy?*[17]

The British government made it difficult for Cheek to transfer the ownership of the 93 acres of land on which the P.I.M. stood, to the F.M.B. in America. Although Chilembwe had deeded the land to the F.M.B., the government claimed that the power of attorney was lost in their office. It was well over a year after Cheek's arrival in Africa before the transfer could be officially made to the board.[18]

Racial tension in the area served to hamper the efforts of Cheek and Chilembwe toward progress and growth of the Providence Industrial Mission. The Foreign Board was acutely aware of this tension. Regarding the treatment of the workers in the field by the white colonial government, Rev. L. G. Jordan, Secretary of the F.M.B. reported to *The Mission Herald* as follows:

> *Brother Jordan reports communication between himself and the Colonial Secretary with*

---

16 L. N. Cheek, "From the Field," *Mission Herald*, October 1903:4.

17 Shepperson and Price, *Independent African*, pg 137.

18 Letter, June 4, 1953, from L. N. Cheek to George Shepperson.

reference to the proper standing for humanity. We are sorry to say it seems that our White Baptist in South Africa are unwilling that Negro Baptists should preach to their own brethren. Our Lord has a special settlement with those "who go not in His name, but for themselves, and hinder those who would enter."[19]

Although faced with opposition, Cheek continued his work for the Lord. His principal students of the Gospel were the Yao and the Ngoni. He referred to them as being "a most thoroughly peaceful, hospitable and amenable people." He said, "they were the most thoroughly moral people in the world, as honest as they were moral, and that there wasn't a lock or a key in any of the native villages."[20]

The Yao Chiefs became devoted to Cheek and visited him often. These visits made the Europeans in the Protectorate uneasy because they knew the chiefs bitterly resented them. The Europeans would have been even more disturbed if they knew the chiefs were attempting to persuade Cheek to become their leader in a rebellion against them. He described their effort as follows:

The paramount chiefs of our time at the P.I.M. were Kumtaka and Malika. They have a minor power amongst their subjects, jealously guarded by the English since they established the Protectorate. They were friendly with me and often exchanged visits with us, even with the hope of having me to become one of their chiefs and lead them into autonomy.[21]

Cheek attempted to influence the course of events in Central Africa by speaking out critically of what he saw of race relations in the Shire Highlands, the part of Nyasaland that was most desired by the Europeans. It was clear to him that the Africans were being misused by the Europeans, who intentionally kept them in poverty and ignorance.[22]

The colonial government became even more wary of him when his criticisms of their governing practices were published in the Richmond Planet newspaper in America. Drawing attention to injustice through publication, was essentially the only weapon available to Cheek and other missionaries on the mission stations of Africa.

It was the same method used by William H. Sheppard, an African-American missionary in the Belgian Congo. He publicized the atrocities levied by King Leopold against the Belgian people. Sheppard suffered incarceration and ejection from the Belgian Congo as a result of his actions.[23]

Cheek's consequence was not as severe as Sheppard's however, as a result of his being so outspoken; although he did all in his realm of authority to help Chilembwe and his followers, his efforts were consistently thwarted by the hostility and bias of the neighboring Scottish missionaries and British colonial administrators. The following passage written by Cheek shows the kind of adverse published comments which the British so bitterly resented.

The Negroes are looked upon with suspicion. These brethren here need a start in civilization, and that at most is a few ploughs and farming implements. The plough and mule are unknown. While the native bends down with a hoe-handle about one and one-half feet in length and digs in the earth, making his hills for corn and beans, we cannot expect him to dream of heaven and a higher ideal.

Cheek continued publication of articles of this nature because they served to garner financial support for his effort at the P.I.M., as well as to keep European oppression in Central Africa in the public view. African Americans, like him, serving as missionaries in Africa were in an excellent position to influence ideas about it. This was due to the fact that few African Americans had been there and publicized their impressions in America. Intelligent, well educated missionaries like Cheek, exhilarated by the Gospel were fully qualified to convey their opinions to the American public. The continued financial support for the spread of the Gospel was contingent

---

19 L. G. Jordan, "From the Field," *Mission Herald*, August 1901:3.
20 E. G. B., "Adventures of a St. Louis Missionary in Darkest Africa," *St. Louis Globe Democrat*, July 12, 1908, sec. Magazine, 6.
21 George Shepperson and T. Price, *Independent African* (London: University Press, 1958), 137.
22 Joseph E. Harris, *Global Dimensions of the African Diaspora* (Washington: Howard University Press, 1983), 254.
23 Walter Williams, "William Henry Sheppard, Afro-American Missionary in the Congo, 1890-1910," in Sylvia Jacobs, ed., *Black Americans and the Missionary Movement in Africa* (West Port, CT: Greenwood Press, 1982) 147–148.

on their ability to convince their churches that they were accomplishing something on the mission field. Their continued existence as missionaries depended almost entirely on voluntary contributions; by making their work as widely known as possible, they hoped to increase the amount of contributions and support received.[24]

Cheek's living conditions, health problems, and local opposition to his work were not overlooked by the board in America. L. G. Jordan, the Corresponding Secretary of the F.M.B. of the National Baptist Convention, journeyed to Africa to offer his assistance to the workers in the field. The following was published in an American publication concerning his visit:

> The corresponding secretary recently went to South Africa to set the work in proper light before the ruling power of that country, and seek a closer fellowship between the Baptist Union of South Africa (English) and the workers of the N.B.C. (America). Despite the so called "Ethiopian Movement" in South Africa, their workers have tried to keep in close touch with their English brethren of like faith, and have, in a measure succeeded. The board is now making all possible efforts to correct any irregularities that may exist, or to remove any cause of objection made by the South African Baptist Union or the British colonial government.[25]

Along these same lines, the Baptist Argus, KY, made comments as follows:

> American Baptists are watching with great interest and concern, the efforts of our black American brethren to evangelize their native land. Their efforts in this work need to be carefully directed, and the foundations laid with wisdom and skill. It will be difficult indeed for them to develop a native ministry, and it would take large sums to send over enough of their strong men to do the work adequately. We are sure that the N.B.C. feels the need of educating thoroughly, and of keeping a wholesome and strong directing had upon their native workers.[26]

The missionary flame had grown to a huge blaze during this period in our nation's history, but it was short-lived. Ecstasy soon turned to apathy and many of the fundraising efforts initiated for missionary expenses were thwarted by those who grudged the expenditures on missions and refused to aid them. Funding from America became a particularly huge obstacle for Cheek in Africa. In many of his letters to the board he referred to the indifference displayed by many churches and their leaders to the foreign mission effort. The continued existence of the P.I.M. often dangled precariously while he waited for its financial obligations to be rectified by the board in America. In one letter regarding these financial obligations, he wrote:

> We hope you will not delay in putting into Mr. Allen's hands the means to liquidate the balance due the African Lakes Co., who have helped us so faithfully to keep our work going on. There can be no delay if you want to save the property. The company is strict in business and any slackness on the part of the board will close us out …[27]

Despite financial hardship and colonial opposition to his work, Cheek's zeal to spread the gospel spurred him on and he was able to make many improvements on the missionary station started by Rev. Chilembwe. He continued his efforts to cement the foundations of the mission. By 1907, he felt that they were secure and he packed up his family and prepared to return to America.

The Cheek family arrived on Ellis Island on September 27, 1907, on the stream ship New York. Their port of departure was listed as Southampshire, England. Cheek brought two African boys to America with him. Their names were Frederick and Matthew Nijilima. The F.M.B. of the N.B.C. sent Frederick and Matthew to schools in the south to be educated.

After a brief stay in Philadelphia Cheek and his family returned to St. Louis, MO. An article concerning his foreign missionary work was published in the "Everyday" section of the

---

24 Walter Williams, *Black Americans and the Evangelization of Africa 1877–1900* (Madison, WI: University of Wisconsin Press, 1982), 85.

25 L. G. Jordan, "What the Brethren in Black are Doing in Missions," *Missionary Review of the World*, 1905: pg 601.

26 Ibid.

27 L. N. Cheek, "From the Field," *Mission Herald*, October 1903:4.

St. Louis Globe Democrat in August 1908. By 1910 Cheek had returned to Madison County, Canton, MS. He remained there until he was called to pastor the Central Baptist Church in Charleston, SC.

Rev. John Chilemwe remained at the Providence Industrial Mission. Tension between Chilembwe and the British continued to escalate after Cheek's departure. In 1915, he grew tired of British opposition and discrimination and led a revolt against them. The revolt was triggered by the fact that the British were conscripting Africans into the British army but if they were killed or wounded in battle their families were not compensated. This angered Chilembwe and he called on all the tribes in the area to rise up against the British. Chilembwe was captured and killed shortly after the uprising.

In America, news of Chilembwe's death reached Cheek and he was greatly saddened. He planned to return to the P.I.M. to continue the work, but due to financial constraints and hostility by the British Government against African-American missionaries, his plans never reached fruition.

By 1910, Cheek and his family were back in MS. Shortly thereafter, they moved to Charleston, SC. They are listed in MS in the 1920 U.S. Census. Cheek's wife, Lydia, died of consumption in Canton in 1917. He was living in Nashville, TN, in 1921, where his son Frank died in a drowning accident.

At some point Cheek returned to St. Louis. He was the pastor of the North Galilee Baptist Church and his son Edgar was a graduate of the Summer High School. Cheek lived on Finney Avenue in the Ville area of St. Louis.

Cheek later moved to Chicago and remained there during the waning years of his life. He lived for a while at 4811 South Calumet Avenue and he was a member of the Monumental Baptist Church. He later moved to Drexel Boulevard where he lived with his daughter Ella Mae. It was there that he met Professor George Shepperson, author of *Independent African*. Professor Shepperson, a Scotsman, became interested in Africa while serving with the King's African Rifles during World War II. In 1959, he was teaching at the University of Chicago as a loaned scholar from the University of Edinburgh. During a series of lectures on Lorenzo D. Turner at the University, Professor Shepperson published an appeal in the Chicago Defender for information regarding Cheek. Shepperson knew that Cheek was living in Chicago, but had not had success in locating him. Ella Mae, Cheek's daughter saw the appeal and allowed Shepperson to visit the aging missionary at her home on Drexel. It was at that time that Shepperson presented Cheek with an autographed copy of *Independent African*.

At the time of his death, he was a resident at the Fullerton Convalescent Home. His daughter Ella Mae, still lived on Drexel Boulevard, but Cheek was too much for her to take care of, so she put him in the home so that he could receive professional care. He died on June 23, 1964, from arteriosclerotic heart disease.

Cheek's eulogy was delivered by Rev. Morris H. Tynes. He was buried in the Burr Oak Cemetery in Worth, IL.

Cheek and Chilembwe have passed away but the Providence Industrial Mission continues to thrive under the leadership of Rev. MacFord Chipuliko. Malawi President, Bakili Muluzi visited the Providence Industrial Mission on January 15, 1995, to declare that from that date on that date will be known as "Rev. John Chilembwe Day." In his speech delivered during ceremonies at the mission, Muluzi called Chilembwe, "Father of Malawi Politics!" "Originator of the idea of African Independence!" "Freedom fighter and martyr in the cause of liberty!" These are just some of the many appellations that President Muluzi spoke in praise of Reverand John Chilembwe.

In declaring January 15th the annual "Rev. John Chilembwe Day," the President also paid great tribute to the P.I.M. itself. In his speech, he called attention to the fact that in addition to health and spiritual care, over the years P.I.M. has provided education and technical skills to thousands of people.

President Muluzi said the mission is a living testimony of the vision of Rev. John Chilembwe. He called on them, therefore, to feel proud of P.I.M. and the achievements of all who have served there. He also promised to make P.I.M. a historical landmark. Visiting clergy and choirs joined with high ranking government officials including both Malawi's First and Second Vice Presidents and a Regional Governor to worship God and give thanks for John Chilembwe. Among the dignitaries attending the ceremony at the Providence Industrial Mission was Sister C. MacDonald, representing the National Baptist

Convention, U.S.A., Inc. She joined Chairman, Rev. MacFord B. K. Chipuliko in greeting President and Mrs. Muluzi during the worship service. In addition, the face of Rev. John Chilembwe will appear on Malawi currency.

Cheek and Chilembwe are somewhere around the throne of God and their spirits are happy that the sacrifices they made to establish the Providence Industrial Mission were worthwhile.

Bibliography

Adams, C. C. and Marshall A. Talley. *Negro Baptist and Foreign Missions.* Philadelphia, PA: The Foreign Mission Board of the National Baptist Convention, U.S.A., Inc., 1952.

Cone, James H. *Black Theology and Black Power.* New York: The Seabury Press, 1969.

Drake, St. Claire. *The Redemption of Africa and Black Religion.* Atlanta, GA: Third World Press, 1977.

E. G. B. "Adventures of a St. Louis Missionary in Darkest Africa." *St. Louis Globe Democrat* (July 12, 1908), 6.

Freeman, Edward A. T*he Epoch of Negro Baptists and the Foreign Mission Board.* National Baptist Convention, U.S.A., Inc. Kansas City, KS: The Central Seminary Press, 1953.

Glicksburg, Charles I. "Negro Americans and the African Dream." *Phylon* (Atlanta, GA), VIII no. 4: 323–30.

Harris, Joseph E. *Global Dimensions of the African Diaspora.* Washington, D.C.: Howard University Press, 1963.

Jones, Griff. *Britain and Nyasaland.* London: George and Allen and Unwin Ltd., 1964.

MacDonald, Roderick. *From Nyasaland to Malawi, Studies in Colonial History.* Nairobi: East African Publishing House, 1945.

McGuire, John M. "Back to Africa." *St. Louis Post Dispatch* (January 29, 1988), 1, 9.

Meir, August. *Negro Thought in America, 1800–1915.* Ann Arbor, MI: University of Michigan Press, 1963.

Price, Thomas. "Yao Origins." *Nyasaland Journal* (Blantyre), XVII (1964): 11–16.

"Reminiscence of a Missionary." *The Mission Herald,* Vol. 44, September–October, 17–18.

Shepperson, George and Thomas Price. *Independent African: John Chilembwe and the Origins, Setting and Significance of the Nyasaland Native Rising of 1915.* Edinburgh: The University Press, 1958.

Shepperson, George. "Ethiopianism: Past and Present." In C. G. Baeta, editor, *Christianity in Tropical Africa,* 249–268. London: Oxford University Press for the International African Institute, 1968.

Shepperson, George. "Notes on Negro American Influences on the Emergence of African Nationalism." *Journal of African History* I, No. 2 (1960): 299–312.

The Mission Herald. Volumes 1–12, 1901–1907. Letters from Rev. Landon N. Cheek.

Williams, John A. *Africa, Her History, Lands and People.* New York: Cooper Square Publishers, Inc., 1969.

Williams, Walter. *Black Americans and the Evangelization of Africa, 1877–1900.* Madison, WI: University of Wisconsin Press, 1982.

1920–1954 Era: Hindrances [Time of Garvey]

Chapter 23
1920–1954 Era: Hindrances [Time of Garvey]

by Robert J. Stevens

During the 40-year period between 1920 and 1960, few black American missionaries not already in Africa were assigned there by white boards. One exception was the establishment of the ABCFM Galangue station in Angola in the early 1920's, manned by African-American missionaries. Black American churches continued to send African-American missionaries to Africa, but even they were restricted to certain areas for mission work.[1]

Marcus Garvey, a Jamaican, wanted the British to leave the West African colonies. His campaign was "Africa for Africans." The colonizers feared that African-American missionaries would promote the philosophy of Garvey and thus upset the colonial status quo. For this reason, the colonists restricted the activity of black missionaries.[2]

In 1920, the Portuguese government changed its missionary regulations, insisting that all future missionaries serving in its colonies know Portuguese (as taught in Portugal) and be assigned by the colonial government. Another hindrance came from the refusal of white missionary organizations to utilize the African-American in world evangelization, so as not to offend the colonial governments. The American government complied with the colonial governments' preference by not granting passports. The colonial governments refused to grant visas to certain areas.[3]

The Great Depression of 1929 had a devastating impact on black communities and its repercussions were felt throughout the decade of the 1930's in the dwindling social outreach activities sponsored by black churches.[4] Due to the depression of the 1930s, many undesirable adjustments had to be made in the economic policies. By mid-1930's the African-American missionary was virtually absent from the field. Several were still serving—including

---

1 Sylvia Jacobs, "Black Americans and the Missionary Movement in Africa," *Contributions in Afro-American and African Studies*, Number 66, (Westport, CT: Greenwood Press, 1982).
2 Vaughn Walston, "Mobilizing the African-American Church for Global Evangelization," *African-American Experience in World Mission: A Call Beyond Community*, edited by Vaugh J. Walston and Robert J. Stevens, Pasadena, CA: William Cary Library, 2002 by Cooperative Mission Network of the African Dispersion (COMINAD).
3 Marilyn Lewis, "Overcoming Obstacles, the Broad Sweep of the African-American and Missions," *Mission Frontiers*, April 2000, Pasadena, CA: U.S. Center for World Mission, 27.
4 C. Eric Lincoln and Lawrence H. Mamiya, *The Black Church in the African-American Experience* (Durham, NC: Duke University Press, 1990), 209.

Montrose Waite—but for the most part, African Americans understood that they were not welcome.[5]

Eventually African-American missionaries were banned from parts of Africa.[6] Officially, the mission arena closed for African Americans in the late 1930's, so it is not surprising that we find the civil rights interest in this country started in that era.[7]

During this time denominations split and began new ones. Mission societies did the same. Mission organizations did the same. Mission organizations did the same. Churches did the same. It was a time of freedom to practice democracy and political power within the church for the first time.

Somewhere in the struggle, the vision for world evangelization that many of the early black Christian leaders had exhibited became blurred. As a result, a large scale neglect of the international mission enterprise was experienced among African Americans. Inspite of this, neither the interest in nor the sense of responsibility for a lost, dying world was diminished.[8]

However, the impact of missionaries in Africa before 1960 was profound. Missionary accomplishments were in five areas: (1) language translation; (2) education; (3) medical work; (4) industrial and technical training; and (5) social reform. In the final analysis, when we attempt to stress American Protestant missionary activity in Africa we must recognize, first of all, that American missionaries before 1945 played a minor role in the development of the African church. European, and particularly British, missions took the lead and supplied most of the personnel. European Catholics predominated in French, Belgian, and Portuguese colonies; British and Canadian Protestants in British territories; and German Protestants and Catholics in German colonies before 1920. Nevertheless, the American missions did have an important impact on African education, through their schools. In the 1950's missionaries provided most of the primary and secondary education available in Africa south of the Sahara. American missionaries also made a significant contribution to African culture by reducing many African languages to writing.[9]

---

5 Marilyn Lewis, "Overcoming Obstacles, the Broad Sweep of the African-American and Missions," *Mission Frontiers*, April 2000, Pasadena, CA: U.S. Center for World Mission, 27.

6 Marilyn Lewis, "Independent Study Assignment: The African-American in Christian Mission," Th.M. Candidate, Dallas Theological Seminary, #788, 1993, 82.

7 Ibid., 85.

8 David Cornelius, "A Historical Survey of African-Americans in World Missions," *Perspectives on the World Christian Movement, A Reader*, edited by Ralph Winter and Steven C. Hawthorne, Pasadena, CA: William Carey Library, 3rd edition, 1999, 291.

9 Sylvia Jacobs, "Black Americans and the Missionary Movement in Africa," *Contributions in Afro-American and African Studies*, Number 66, Westport, CT: Greenwood Press, 1982.

Chapter 24
Montrose Waite: A Man Who Could Not Wait

by Eugene Seals and John McNeal, Jr.

Montrose Waite received the call to be missionary at age 17 in Jamaica where he was born. "A missionary from Jamaica had gone to England to be trained for missionary work in Africa. While home on furlough, he said to me by the Holy Spirit that I would be a bearer of the Gospel to some place where there was a need."

Montrose grew up in a Christian, but poor, family with 11 children. Life was not easy. His five older brothers went abroad and he stayed to care for the younger ones and to help his aging parents.

When I began school at age six, I had to walk three miles one way. It was not a pleasant trip, but I loved school. A year after I started school, I was in an accident which kept me home for six months. I didn't have much pain, and each evening I would ask my older brother to help me learn the lessons he had had that day. When I returned to school, I was promoted to a higher class than the one I was in when the accident took me out of school. The nearest high school was 14 miles away, and it was a boarding school. My parents could not send me there because of lack of funds. Some provision for further studies after the eighth grade was made possible by the Jamaican Educational Department. I took it for two years, but at age 18 I dropped out. I tried to get employment in different places without success.

I also remember the Wednesday night when I received Jesus as my Savior. I can't remember the year; but it was before I received the call to serve the Lord. His salvation freed me from bondage to sin and also from a bondage to worldly pursuits.

When the war in Europe broke out in 1914, his father thought he should enlist in a volunteer company organized in Jamaica. His father was an evangelist and their church was associated with the Christian and Missionary Alliance (C&MA) which had its headquarters in NY. A white American friend of their pastor (also white) helped arrange for him to go to America.

Father held prayer meeting every Thursday morning in our home. ... On one visit our pastor brought his friend with him. I asked this gentleman about America. He told me they were busy making arms and ammunition for Britain. He then asked if I would like to go to the States. My answer was a prompt, "Yes."

Condensed from *Waite: A Man Who Could Not Wait*, Carver Foreign Missions, Inc., edited by Eugene Seals and John McNeal, Jr., 1988. Used by permission.

That American provided $50 needed by each passenger landing in America. "I made up my mind that I must succeed in the U.S. I had a cabin mate from Jamaica to New York. I told him that my desire was to enter the ministry. He thought I would change my mind after I started making money."

In 1916, after arriving in New York City, Montose Waite made his way to New Haven and stayed with his brother and then began working for the Winchester Repeating Arms Company.

In the fall of 1916, after I felt secure in the U.S., I wrote to Dr. A. B. Simpson, founder of C&MA and asking about entrance to Nyack Missionary Training Institute. He encouraged me and recommended that I take his correspondence course which would polish up my study skills since I had been out of school so long. I took this course for a year while I tried to save some money to go to Nyack the next year. There were many temptations to forget the ministry, but the Holy Spirit kept urging me to keep my mind on it and to do all that was necessary to get prepared.

Montrose then had to use his savings for an appendectomy and worked an extra year to replace the funds. A friend came from Billy Sunday's crusade in Boston, having become a Christian there, and the two took off for Nyack together in 1917. Montrose requested, and was allowed, to work part time and was protected from the flu which killed a number of people that winter. God kept providing funds as needed for food, clothes, etc.

Dr. Simpson died in the fall of 1919, and for some reason I was selected to be a pallbearer at his funeral. I prayed that God would let a little of the blessings He had given Dr. Simpson fall on me.

Montrose graduated in 1920 when the Marcus Garvey movement had started. The colonial powers, especially Britain and France, were alarmed over this man's program because their African subjects had heard about Garvey and wanted to welcome him to Africa. These colonial powers decided that no black Americans would be permitted to land anywhere in Africa.

Montrose had applied to go to Africa and had been accepted. The C&MA was the only white society of the fundamentalist groups who had decided to use blacks. This was chiefly because black churches contributed to their missionary fund.

While waiting to hear from the C&MA, Montrose proceeded to apply for his passport—he was still a subject of Great Britain and was, therefore, entitled to one. The passport came. He took it with him to the annual C&MA convention and showed it to Dr. R. H. Glover, the Foreign Secretary. He took the passport to validate it. Montrose later went to his New York office to find out when he would be going to Africa. There were others waiting to be sent as well.

The C&MA had a work established in Sierra Leone for 25 years, but the white missionaries on the field did not want black coworkers even though they were missionaries to the blacks. Collette:

It was all right for them to minister to Africans, but American blacks were a different people in the eyes of the veteran white missionaries. I was greatly disappointed when I received the letter from the secretary giving me the decision of the board. To me it meant that my patience would wear out, and I would turn to something else, as many people thought I would. ... Just prior to graduation in May, the Rev. Emory Collete (whom God had used in the South as well as in the North to lead many people to make decisions for Christ) had visited the Bible Institute at Nyack. ... He seemed to know the difficulties other blacks had had going out as missionaries to Africa. He suggested that if I did not get out, I should visit him in Philadelphia. After the disappointing letter from the board reached me, I felt the next best thing to was to visit Rev. Collette.

Rev. Collette approached the C&MA board on his behalf without results. So, he offered to help Montrose Waite with a missionary preaching position in the south with a church whose members were illiterate.

I still had a little change [money] left from my savings. Clothes were cheap. I went to a thrift shop and got a new suit, a new pair of shoes, and other garments that I would need. I decided to return to my brother's home in New Haven to get my trunk and some books. I told my brother and one of my younger sisters that I was going south. My brother expressed foreboding for me because he had heard so much that was against black people in those parts.

Montrose still gladly went, stopping back in Philadelphia for two weeks and leaving at night to arrive in the daylight. In Lenoir, NC, there were about ten people at his first Wednesday night prayer meeting.

> I gave my testimony. I later learned (by the confession of the member who was assigned to board me) that nobody understood what I said. My Jamaican accent at that time sounded like an African dialect to them. They thought I had been born in Africa and had not yet mastered English. ... I was out of touch with the mission board for one and a half years. In February, 1922, I received a letter from New York informing me that plans were under foot to send three young men out, and I was one of the three. I went around to my members' homes and informed them of the good news. Some felt sorry. We had learned to appreciate one another; and even though the membership had not grown much yet, they wanted me to stay.

Montrose was excited and embarked on visiting and preaching across the south and north where he was invited by pastors and friends. During these travels he met Ella Hamilton who had also been called to missions. She decided to go to Nyack for training and he continued to preach and raise his support.

> "What's next?" was the question I must answer. At the same time all I could do was to remember that God's calling was sure. ... There was a light recession and many people had no jobs. Besides, in those days, blacks were the last to be hired and the first to be fired. ... One day, Walter, my expected brother-in-law, asked me to go with him to the Sunday School Times office. ... Walter told them that I was a missionary candidate waiting to sail to West Africa. The only black missionary they had known was Amanda Smith. ... The men of the Sunday School Times told me that I could earn something by introducing the Times to Sunday School teachers in black churches. I was happy about this. ... I took long walks to canvass. ... I recall walking from 16th and Thompson in North Philadelphia to 17th and Christian in South Philadelphia. Car fare was five cents, but sometimes I couldn't spare even the five cents.

> The news came in March that we would sail April 4, 1923, from New York City. ... God had blessed me so that I had a foot locker trunk full of clothes and $100 in cash. When I got to New York, I was informed that the church in which I grew up had sent $200 toward my fare. I had to wonder at God's power in enabling those poor people to contribute so much.

This was seven years after his first call to missions in 1916. His baggage was two foot lockers, wooden cases weighing about 80 pounds each, and a canvas bag containing a camp bed on which he slept for several years on the field. At last, after spending 32 days traveling, he landed in Sierra Leone in 1923.

The C&MA had missionaries in two of the tribes: Temne and Kuranko. There were at least 11 different dialects in Sierra Leone. Each dialect was essentially a different foreign language. The capital city was Freetown, the city where the British were urged to send those from Canada who had come up from America through the underground railroad. After they arrived the British were urged to send a missionary to them. Missionaries traveled on foot and canoe to the interior tribal people. They found Anglican Bishop Taylor Smith and also English Methodist and United Brethren from America active in Sierra Leone.

> Upon leaving customs, we were advised to obtain mosquito netting and some commodities that we would need inland. We were to use the railroad to get where Mr. Rupp was located.

It was mandatory that each missionary study to get a working knowledge of the tribal language within one year. Montrose went with another veteran missionary, Mr. David Rupp, to the Sumbuya tribe.

> This distance of 65 miles had to be made by foot and would take four days. None of us

> had done more than 14 mile walks before. Our journey took us over a very high hill. ... We were met at the entrance of the village by a large crowd headed by the chief. They had annual visits from British officials to collect taxes. ... We had come to live in their village.

The people practiced ancestor worship. These ancestors were called upon to help oppose evil spirits. After a missionary learned the Meneka language which they spoke they preached and taught them. They became their doctor, lawyer, as well as father, who had money to lend and give to those who needed help. They were built a hut by various tribes.

> We made good progress with language study and took our first test in December, of 1923, eight months after we arrived. ...

> We had gotten word in October that Ella Scott and Anita Bolden were coming to Sierra Leone. Anita had graduated in the same class with us at Nyack. ... There were two elderly ladies who came along with Ella and Anita. Both were former missionaries: Mrs. Rose Hart, a widow, and Miss Kate Driscoll. Ella and I were glad to meet again. We thought it was time for us to unite in matrimony. But the field director stated that it was advisable that Ella study the language for at least nine months first. ... Ella and I married on December 16, 1924. By that time I was 33 years old and she was 29.

Much of the preparations for their home took place with about 20 men carrying over 40 miles by foot supplies of roofing and pieces of a former missionary home they dismantled. Nearby they obtained mud, sand, stones and hard wood and ordered in cement for the floors. Sounds simple but "plastic" mud was needed and had to be obtained from ant hills which were dug ten feet deep and 100 feet in circumference at the bottom. This they carried up the mountain. Before the house was completed, Ella became very ill and had to be carried in a hammock 38 miles to the train by Marcus and by the same 20 men. His evangelistic work was not neglected. He continued Wednesday and Sunday services during its preparation and was able to compete the home one day before the rainy season.

He also started a school with two leading "moslem" men, a leader in their superstition as well as one of his servant boys. They all became believers. One white missionary (with only an eighth grade education) wanted to curtail this school because they were taught in English. The missionary told him he didn't think it was wise to educate the African because you couldn't control him after he got an education. As a result they didn't have the opportunity of reading the Bible, however, Musa Kaba, who had been the leader of superstition became a great witness.

When Ella became pregnant with their first child they had no training, no midwife, no provisions.

> We didn't know the time the baby was due, but in early September we felt led to make preparations. We decided to go down the mountain of Magburaka and if we didn't find a doctor, to go to Freetown.

They traveled 22 miles their first day on foot, staying overnight in a local chief's hut who had become a friend. They carried their own cots with them since the nationals slept on mats on the ground. The next day they began to walk again, carrying Ella in a hammock. It began to rain mid afternoon and she had to walk because the men couldn't carry her in the rain. [Each day they drank coffee in the morning, and stopped to cook whatever they had about 11 a.m. Someone had given them a cooked chicken so they heated it every day to keep it fresh and had rice with it. It lasted three days.] They reached the next village at 6 p.m. in the rain. That chief gave them his best hut with some dry wood. Flooding the next day slowed their progress but they reached Magburaka at 6 p.m. Ella took the train from there to get assistance. She was eventually taken to a hospital and safely delivered a girl, Ruth, one week later.

On the trip back home, while they were sleeping one evening, the baby cried out in pain. She was almost covered with driver ants. They were able to take the ants off her and drive them off by fire. Thankfully she survived these bites.

In February, 1926, Montrose set out for the first conference in French Guinea at Kankan near the Niger River. Along the way he had a problem with one of his teeth. In his possession were dental forceps he brought from America and had used numerous times to extract other's teeth. No one else had used them and when they tried to help him the tooth broke and he felt worse but continued the journey. Along the way several people tried to help but were not able to remove all of the tooth.

The only relief I had was to mix a weak solution of carbonic acid and cook the gum, then spit it from my mouth afterwards. It was dangerous, but it helped. ... Before reaching Faranah one evening, I administered the carbonic acid solution to the tooth. It soothed the pain. However, being so weary from walking over 150 miles, I dozed off and swallowed the solution. The next morning I was a sick man. ... Mr Wright gave me some medicine. It helped temporarily.

They traveled by Model T Ford for 66 miles to Dabola, French Guinea and then took a two day train ride to Kankan.

I was so sick with my bowels I thought I would have passed out. Somehow the Lord undertook. I had no medical aid, but my stomach didn't hurt too much.

The conference was for ten days. There they met some old school mates from Nyack. Ella was with him and Ruth. They enjoyed the messages and fellowship. After the conference they began the long return but took a route from Faranah to a place called Kenifiya where an independent mission had spent about two years, but only saw one convert. After leaving there, Montrose's appetite left him.

I tried to eat, but my stomach couldn't take the food. It seems the solution had hurt the lining of the small intestine. There was no doctor and no medicine. ... When I began to pass blood, the folks gave me up. I had strength enough to tell Ella to take the baby back to America; for I was sure that, without medical care, I would not survive.

God supplied help through runners on foot six days obtaining medicine. With no one with knowledge of using a hypodermic needle he decided to receive the shots in his stomach by one of their companions, Mrs. Thornley. Amazingly after five shots and five days he felt better. They carried him 30 miles back to Sumbuya.

When baby Ruth was seven months they let her sleep in a cool room with a mosquito net over her four-sided wooden crib. The chief had given them a chicken which they kept in that room under a basket at night. One evening after hearing the chicken squawk they discovered a leopard had come in and eaten the chicken. The Lord watched over Ruth but Ella kept her close to her bed after that.

The Africans in the jungle suffered many inconveniences in the areas of agriculture, their own politics, as well as outside pressures—economics in general. They all worked together through these things. The Waites had to maintain their own small farm and were not to grow extra food so that the chief would not be jealous. The Waites had their second child in 1926, a third in 1928, and returned home on furlough both to Jamaica and America. Montrose had not seen his father in 13 years.

They came back to Africa in 1930 and were assigned to the Mongo field in Sierra Leone. On the way there they learned that Ella was again pregnant. She was sick from the beginning as usual.

I wrote to Dr. Peaston describing as clearly as I could the symptoms. He sent some medicine and advised if there was no change to come to Kabala. Since he was a government employee, he could not come to us without permission from Freetown (which would take two weeks to know if it were granted.)

In the meantime, I sent another messenger to Faranah, Guinea, where the Ellenburgers, Sallie Botham (a white missionary), and Anna Marie Morris (a black missionary) were stationed. ... The messenger returned on the fourth day, reporting that the missionaries had not returned from the conference.

I had assumed that if he didn't find them that there would have been someone to send word to Kankan since the French have a telegraph system between their administrative posts. However, this didn't happen. By this time, we had a few nationals who had accepted Christ and a church was loosely organized. One dear member, Ma Simbiri, ... called together some of the other believers.

... They suggested we bow in earnest prayer for recovery. We did and that encouraged me some. Ella was constantly failing.

Again, I sent messengers back to both places, Kabala and Faranah.

The doctor sent a hammock and advised Montrose to bring Ella to Kabala. The Faranah messenger came back with Miss Morris who took care of the children. They carried Ella for five days in the hottest, driest season of the year with 130 degree heat. By this time Ella could not sit up.

We reached Kabala at 10 a.m. on the fifth day. As soon as the doctor examined her, he told me it was too late. How could I ever forget that day? Two days later, she laid her hand on my head and said, 'Take care of the children. I am gone.' She never spoke again.

They buried her in a coffin of boards in a grave where there was no civilization.

In April I received word from Rev. Roseberry advising me that the field committee had met and had suggested that I return to America with my children and wait further on the Lord for healing.

Montrose Waite, after much deliberation and prayer, decided to stay on the mission field with his three young children.

The next year, Anne Morris arrived in Mongo. She and Ella had met at Nyack while they were home on furlough. Miss Morris took care of the children while Mr. Waite ministered on the field, sometimes he was gone up to 15 days telling of Christ to the nationals.

Each time I returned, Ruth would praise Auntie Morris (as the children called her). About that time, I began to wonder whether it was in order to ask Anna Marie if she would like to have the children always. She thought I meant she could adopt them. I told her that the only way she could have them was to consider taking the father, too. Her reply was that she had never given her heart to a man and she didn't think she cared to change her name. As time went on and with Mrs. Wilson helping her to make a decision, we were married in November, 1931.

They remained in Mongo until 1934. Then they were called to Kamaduga where they never had a missionary before and stayed until 1937. A number had expressed faith in Christ. By 1937, they had two more children and went back to America on furlough under the care and support of the C&MA. This was during the time of the depression.

Even though the depression had struck us hard like everyone else, God still made it possible for me to save a few hundred dollars. I had sent it ahead from Freetown to Mother Morris to put it in a bank for us. When I saw how things were, I decided to start buying a small house.

The C&MA did not keep their promise to care for them for the two years. After one year they stopped payments. Montrose did not question the decision. They were white and he was black and they felt he was not supposed to know God as he did. He was able to sustain taking care of his family by using the two extra lots that came with the house to raise chickens and a small garden. In 1937, they had their sixth child. In 1938, he felt he should join his wife's former church, Anitoch Baptist. He never thought he could return to the mission field with this large family during these hard times.

Shortly after Germany surrendered to the Allies, I surrendered to the Lord. I went to the foreman of our department. I told him I was resigning. He looked at me, then asked, "What is your trouble?"

I answered, "God is speaking to me. I must obey." I was then 54 years of age. ... I had one thing in my favor: Anna Marie was 100 percent with me.

God moves in mysterious ways to show His own great power. ... I had thought that when I related my case to ministers of the Gospel, they would encourage me. ... Instead, they thought I might be losing my mind.

After a few weeks in 1945, things looked gloomy. The little savings were going and nothing was coming in. I was persuaded by a Jewish friend to engage in a small business. No sooner did I take that up than the conviction became more severe. ... I stretched out on the bed, but I could not sleep. I was aroused by a voice which said, "These children, of whom you are so concerned, can be supported even if you are dead." A great fear came over me. I began to perspire. I cried almost in a loud voice, "Please, Lord. Don't kill me! I will obey."'I sat up on the bed. The Holy Spirit spoke to me to go downstairs and said, "Write to John Bell, a wonderful servant of God." ... He answered immediately, expressing joy. Then he said, "I can't offer you anything until April 7, 1946, when I will have a conference in Winston-Salem. If you can wait until then, I will have you as one of the main speakers."

This began a number of months on the road raising support and making contacts with numerous churches, friends, and mission agencies such as: Lott Carey, WEC, Presbyterian Church, and the Open Door Church. The Evangelical Young Peoples Union (EYPU) asked him to come to do a broadcast on radio. They discussed opening an independent mission board. Prior to this all mission boards had been denominational. The National Baptists, Lott Carey Mission, African Methodist Episcopal Church, United Holy Church of America, Church of God in Christ, and United Pentecostal Church.

Montrose felt sure he would go back to Africa under the National Baptist. The war broke out in 1939 and he found he had to work as a porter for Sears until 1943, later he worked in a factory where war efforts were going on. He then became an American citizen. Just prior to his support raising trip his wife had become pregnant. Mission agencies already were not happy that he wished to take five of his seven children on the mission field. Now, they were to add twins. One English board was new in America and said they just didn't understand American blacks.

After a year these young men of the EYPU along with Montrose Waite started the Afro-American Missionary Crusade (AAMC). Most members were still in Bible college and they needed to send a missionary now under government rules. Montrose and his family had to be the ones. Now he needed to go to his supporters to let them know he was going under a nondenominational board.

Some of the people from other boards that had turned him down, now, as individuals, help direct him to others for support. Again, as before, each step of the way was miraculously provided by God within America as well as travels to Africa.

In Africa he felt called to go to Bopolo but stayed a year in Suehn, a National Baptist Mission station started in 1914. They offered them a home and salary to stay but Mr. Waite knew he needed to go to Bopolo.

In August, a young Christian from Sierra Leone came to visit me. He had not known me in Sierra Leone, as he was from a different tribe than the one in which I had worked. ... I suggested to him that he should go to Bopolo and ask the chief if he wanted a missionary. He went and met a happy welcome. ... I found a district administrator at Bopolo trying to set up a permanent headquarters (similar to our counties in the U.S.). He advised the chief to give me assistance to get a place to build and a lot to help me erect a grass roof mud house. We were the first messengers of the Gospel to reside in Bopolo. The Chief told me he had been in office 25 years. All this time he had asked for missionaries, but none came. ... By November 30, I was back at Bopolo with tools ready to go to work. The chief expressed joy and surprise. It was then that he told me he had not expected me to carry out my promise.

Montrose was not only allowed to choose his own land but also to build a good sized hut and a school. God again provided all their needs while having little or no funds. The beginning school had 20 boys, a few sheets of 8x10-inch paper which Mr. Waite wrote the alphabet on to begin class.

While we taught them to read, we emphasized each day the need to be saved by accepting the Gospel and Jesus Christ as the only way to God. After about a year, a number of the boys asked for baptism. We examined them and found that they understood what water baptism meant. We baptized all eight of them.

After baptism, a number of the people from the village, to whom we had been preaching each Sunday, began to take interest in the Word. Before I left to return to the U.S. in 1954, I had baptized 108 people. In addition, our ministry had spread to other villages, some as far as 30 miles away."

One of these boys ended up a member of the House of Representatives in the Liberian government. All this took place before there was a road for the 50 miles between Suehn and Bopolo—all transportation was made on foot.

In Bopolo, he received a letter from a woman in Philadelphia who had heard of them after mentioning a vision she had for building a house in Africa. He sent her the amount needed and it was raised. By the time the house was built, two more missionaries arrived to be trained to take over the work. In 1954, they were able to go back to America on furlough where Montrose Waite sought new recruits for the mission field.

Seeking recruits for the mission field, I went on the trail to contact supporters who had helped to send us out. I went to see Rev. Talmadge Payne who had stood by me loyally during our tour in Liberia. Rev. Payne was founder of Carver Bible Institute (now Carver Bible College).

I referred to a young woman earlier named Naomi Doles whom God had called in 1946. She had attended Prairie Bible Institute in Canada for five years. I knew she had graduated some time in 1953, but our AAMC never said anything about her in their letters. I made inquiries about her and was told she applied but they didn't consider her to be of missionary caliber. ... (None of the AAMC members had been missionaries, and none of them had any desire to be.) ... God had led me by faith to begin the work, to take my large family to the field, and establish a station, but the board consisted exclusively of working people who used only spare hours to meet once a month.

I tried to show them that there was much to be done, but they were not interested in knowing what was needed to make a strong work. In Atlanta, where I met Naomi, Mr. Payne informed me of his observation since I had left for the mission field, the men were not the caliber to make a successful work. He, therefore, suggested that we needed a new effort and that we should go right ahead and establish a board in Atlanta.

I had attempted to force the AAMC to reconsider Miss Dole's case. I was then the General Director of the AAMC. My attempt caused such a furor that I had to resign from the board. Shortly after that, Rev. Talmadge Payne, Dr. William Hungerpiler, Brantly Knight (a white missionary formerly under TEAM in Japan), and another brother and I organized Carver Foreign Missions, chartered under the laws of the State of Georgia.

When he returned in 1957 to Africa he did not go to Bopolo because there were two single ladies working there and Mrs. Waite had stayed behind in America with the children to care for her mother. He went to Buchanan were he supervised the Bassa speaking people. There were several churches with services in English: Episcopal, Methodist AME, and Seventh Day Adventist. Finding he had extra time he began a Bible and tract ministry. Then one of the missionaries in Bopolo became ill and in spite of the fact it was still an AAMC mission and they had written terrible things about him when he left, he felt God's leading to return. Much was in disrepair and he again helped to build up the homes, the school, and now an orphanage.

The mission work had him separated from his children, and God, by miraculous intervention, put him in touch with each of them, no matter which country they had gone to live, so that he could meet with them face to face and renew fellowship.

In 1962, he again left for America and returned with the AAMC. He saw a need for a building and was able to procure a down payment and mortgage at age 71 without a paid job. God helped to establish this building and to pay it off by 1966 without solicitations. He had to suffer much abuse by his co-laborers but God gave him the grace needed to accept it and continue in his work. In 1967, he was able to take his wife back to Jamaica and then went again to Africa.

In Africa he visited his mission stations. The Christian communities had become widespread. There were hundreds of well-traveled men and women of various tribes who were ministers and laymen in many African states. In some areas where fighting took place it was difficult or impossible to visit. In Yifing, he spoke to the students at the Bible school for a week after their conference. At 78, his heart was still there and he wept with the people about having to leave them at each location. He returned to America and shared the house with the AAMC board. Working together again did not work out well. In 1974, after an operation, upon special request he visited Tanzania and stopped again in several mission posts.

Montrose Waite walked with the Lord and had many friends of different denominations and mission boards. There are too many to mention but well worth learning about. He spoke a number of native languages and ministered to many tribes in a number of African countries.

Montrose Waite stated,

> For 55 years I have made it a rule to tell others about the mission fields of this world, especially those in Africa where my family labored for many years. It has been my fervent prayer that some young people would hear the Lord's call and be willing to go. I have especially hoped that young American blacks would recognize the unusual credibility that is seen in them by Africans and peoples of other mission fields.
>
> As I look back upon my life, I can see the hand of God at work. He said in His Word, "I will never leave you nor forsake you." Over and over He proved Himself to be a God of his word. When things were good, He was with them, when things were going slowly, He provided. When I failed to depend on Him, He was yet faithful. I agree with the hymn writer, "Great is thy faithfulness, Oh God our Father."
>
> I sincerely appreciate how my family gave up so much for the Lord. It does not matter that I suffered hunger, discomfort, disease, or mistreatment. I am a man—God's man.
>
> People today complain about the schools in their cities. Our children received no formal schooling during their early years. For most of my missionary career, we were not close to any mission schools, certainly not close to any public schools. Yet, their mother taught them at home—with my help—enough to enable them to enter school in the States and do well. Sure, they had to work to catch up with the others in their age bracket, but it was a small price to pay for the opportunity to share the Lord with thousands on the great continent of Africa.
>
> What is more, my children made me proud of them as they went on to better than average achievement in engineering, business, medicine, and so forth. They have become world citizens and have been welcomed by people of all races in America, Europe, and the isles of the sea. The lives of Robert, Marie, and the others show that God can take better care of his own in adverse circumstances than you and I can do in the land of milk and honey. If I could have known in advance how God would bless the children, I might have had more of them.
>
> As for me, I was amazed about many things. One mission board closed its doors—but another opened its doors. I marveled how one white brother encouraged me to go to America for schooling—while other white brothers tried to prevent me. Even when several black churches declined to provide support, several others supported the work sacrificially. I concluded that God is not slack concerning His promises. The failure of the brotherhood is a result of yielding to the temptations of the world, the flesh, and the devil.
>
> A whole lot of people need to catch the vision. We are to work for God—not against one another. Our enemy is Satan. Our mission is to assault the very gates of hell itself. We must do that together. But even if no one else will, I say like Joshua, "But as for me and my house, we will serve the Lord."
>
> In spite of adversity, I have no bitterness—no remorse—no regrets. If anything, I would wish I could have been more faithful. Nevertheless, in my waning years, I feel like Paul, "I have fought the good fight. I have kept the faith. I have finished my course. I believe there is a crown of righteousness awaiting me—and not me only but all those who call on Him."

How about you and your house? Will you serve the Lord? Will you step out on faith? Are you ready to join God's front line offense where you are guaranteed to be more than conquerors? What have you got to lose? More importantly, what do you have to gain from exercising more faith in God in the here and now?

Some of the people to whom I ministered believed that they would have a second chance in another life to make amends for anything they missed in the current life. I had to inform them that it is appointed to man once to die—after that the resurrection either into an eternity with God or into an eternity without God. That latter state we know as hell. Eternity is too late to begin doing that which must be done in the here and now. I pray that God will bless you in your decision to become more active in ordained or lay ministry, whether in this country or abroad.

Chapter 25
Efrain Alphonse: Translator

edited by Jim Wilson,
Wycliffe Bible Translators

Efrain Simeon Alphonse—Minister of Religion and playwright; Born Carenero, Bocas del Toro, Republic of Panama, circa 1896. Educated Bocas del Toro Spanish School 1903–1920; Calabar Theological College, Kingston, 1924-26; reduced Valiente Indian Language to writing; wrote first grammar and vocabulary in Hindustani, Spanish, and English; also translated four Gospels in Valiente Tongue and became Translator of Scripture for the American Bible Society, 1928 and 1929; composed and compiled hymnbook and catechism; also wrote and staged the following plays in Jamaica, "Youth-time and Eternity" and "The Gospel Ship"; was the author of "Among Valientes" and "The Pageant of the 4th Force"; traveled to Costa Rica, France, and England, 1938, where he gave missionary addresses on the Valiente Indians.

From "Who's Who Jamaica 1941-1946" http://www.jamaicans.com/culture/people/jamaica.htm.

God's Word in Man's Language, by Eugene Nida, edited for Wycliffe Bible Translators by Jim Wilson: http://www.wycliffe.org/history/blackmissions/ealphonse.htm.

Used by permission.

Elfrain Alphonse is a name we should hear more often, although he would be the last one to think so. In his own quiet way, Mr. Alphonse is one of the great missionary pioneers of this century.

Efrain S. Alphonse was an African-American boy who lived in Panama while his father worked on the canal. He was an adventuresome lad, devoted to God. One day, when he was 19, Efrain escorted a Methodist missionary through the dangerous reefs and treacherous streams along the northeast coast of Panama. While piloting this small boat and chatting, the missionary was so impressed with Efrain that he asked, "How would you like to teach school in one of these Valiente Indian villages?" Efrain knew the Valiente Indians' reputation. He knew they earned the name "Valiente" which means "brave and warlike." He knew they did not speak Spanish and he knew not a word of their language. But the missionary's question and his love for Jesus Christ stirred his heart. He wanted to do whatever he could to help these neglected people.

So Efrain Alphonse accepted a teaching post and went to live in one of the Indian villages. His teaching actually began with learning. Efrain knew to be an effective teacher he needed to be able to communicate well with the people so he began the laborious task of learning an unwritten language, one word at a time. He learned quickly and before long Efrain began offering five cents to anyone who could introduce him to a word he didn't already know. For 12 years, Mr. Alphonse lived among the Valientes, learning not just their language, but also their rich heritage of folklore, legends and tribal history. He developed his own system of putting together consonants and vowels to form root words and slowly built up a written form of the local language. Efrain knew the only way the Valiente Indians would know God loved them personally is if they could hear it and read it in their own language. Spanish wouldn't work. So, prompted by his love for the Indians and his love for God and His Word, Efrain Alphonse tried his hand at translating two gospels from the New Testament into their language.

This whetted his appetite for translation work and evangelism. Mr. Alphonse left the tribe to seek out further training. He studied for several years, attended seminary and became well-versed in Greek. At last he was ready to tackle the translation of the entire New Testament so he eagerly returned to the Valiente people. He revised his early work and completed many more passages from the New Testament. Although he was not supported by his superiors, he pressed on. Eventually several books of the New Testament were completed and published by the Bible Society.

Despite a serious heart ailment which would have hospitalized other men, Alphonse carried on his work among the Valiente Indians, translating the rest of the New Testament, directing five schools and shepherding many new churches in the area and throughout the Carribean. Eugene Nide says of Efrain Alphonse in his book, God's Word in Man's Language, "Of all the missionary translators in the Western Hemisphere probably no one has entered more fully into the rich realms of aboriginal speech than this humble African-American servant of God who (worked) untiring ... among a needy people."

One African-American man saw the need for Bible translation and gave himself to the task for the glory of God. We pray many others will see the need today and join in the task of Bible translation so, like the Valiente Indians, people groups all over the world will soon be able to read ans know of God's love for them.

Chapter 26
Gladys East: A Missionary Daughter With Vision

by Dr. Benjamin W. Johnson, Sr.

Dr. Benjamin W. Johnson, Sr., Christian Creative Ministries, Inc.. — Temple University, Philadelphia, PA; New School of Music; Philadelphia Conservatory of Music; Philadelphia Biblical University, B.S.; Wheaton Graduate School, M.A., Wheaton, IL; Great Commission Theological Seminary, D. D., Bowling Green, KY. Founder & Pastor of Christ Baptist Church, Philadelphia, PA (13 yrs); Taught at Manna Bible Institute, Philadelphia, PA (18 yrs); Adjunct Professor at Eastern Baptist Seminary, Philadelphia PA (4 yrs); Exec. Dir. of Urban Ministries, American Missionary Fellowship, Lancaster, PA (5 yrs); Taught at Moody Bible Institute, (20 yrs); Pastor, Emmanuel Reformed Church, Chicago, IL (5 yrs); Founder and Pastor of Christ Community Church, Chicago, IL (9 yrs/8 yrs Brethren); National Black Evangelical Assoc. President (4 yrs) & member (over 30 yrs); President of Ambassadors Fellowship since 1988, Colorado Springs, CO; Dean of Franklin Bible Institute, Franklin, TN (3 yrs). Preacher, teacher, educator, singer throughout America, Canada, Spain, Liberia, Kenya, Nigeria, South Africa, Mexico, Haiti, Jordan, Israel, Gaza, Nova Scotia, and Japan. Concert artist singing Negro Spirituals, sacred classical concerts which include some oratorical and some opera arias. Active in missions over 45 years and worked with COMINAD and promotion of Perspectives.

"Reflections on the Life of Gladys Virginia East," *Mission Herald*, July/August 2002, 15, National Baptist Convention, U.S.A., Foreign Mission Board, P.O. Box 15783, Philadelphia, PA 19103. Used by permission.

Family Heritage

Often it is asked, "But what about the children of missionaries? How do they turn out?" This is one daughter of a missionary who returned to her parent's mission field knowing the opposition but having experienced the love of Christ Jesus among the people.

Gladys Virginia East was born into mission. Her father, James Edward East was born January 27, 1881, at Huntsville, AL. He was the third child and only son of James and Georgianna Bonefield East. He was converted at an early age to Christianity.

James attended the Missionary Training Institute at Nyack, NY, in 1904. He later became a student in the Virginia Seminary of Lynchburg, VA. He graduated from the Seminary and was engaged to marry another student, Lucinda Thomas. They married on October 18, 1909. She mothered his seven children, six of whom survived.

In 1909, the Easts felt a desire to journey to the mission field. They traveled to South Africa and served 11 years. They worked under the National Baptists and served at the station at Middledrift, South Africa.

Lucinda assisted with the education of the Africans at the Buchannan Mission and Industrial School. James Edwards worked in the evangelization, preaching, and teaching the Word. Their work was so successful that Minister James E. East was affectionately called one of the "greatest missionaries" ever sent out by the Baptist Board. The Easts established a church with 600 members at Rabula, South Africa. The church was well attended.

Birth Away From Family's Homeland

Born September 14, 1910 on the Buchannan mission in Middledrift, South Africa, Gladys was the eldest of the seven children born to the Easts.

The Easts felt the discrimination from the racist government of South Africa and those who supported the colonial regime. James Edward wrote that African Americans were at a point in which the only country that is open to the African-American missionary is that of Liberia.

By 1920, he maintained that the entire continent was closed to all African-American missionaries. Continuing further he stated that the colonial African governments have notified their consuls not to sell tickets to any colored missionaries wishing to come to parts of Africa unless they produce a permit from such countries.

Missionaries Not Wanted

In 1920, the Easts returned to America and settled in Philadelphia. He was selected as Corresponding Secretary of the Foreign Mission Board [F.B.C.] of the National Baptist Convention [N.B.C.]. Gladys was now 10. At this age she began her preparations to meet her future calling.

She was enrolled in the public schools of Philadelphia and after completing Overbrook High School, she attended the University of PA, graduating in 1933. Ms. East also attended the Women's Medical College of PA and the PA Bible Institute.

Gladys helped to organize and conduct several vacation bible schools in coal mining towns of Western PA. For two years she worked as a medical technician at the prestigious Homer G. Phillips Hospital in St. Louis, MO.

Ms. East was a member of the Alpha Kappa Alpha (AKA) Sorority where she served as Basileus of her University of PA chapter. Later she joined her sorority sisters in their widely acclaimed MS Health Project, serving at the Taborian Hospital in Mound Bayou, MS, as an anesthetist, as well as in the mobile clinics traveling through the various counties of MS.

Second Generation Returns

In 1944, Ms. East answered an urgent call to serve as a missionary to Suehn Mission in Liberia, West Africa, under the Foreign Mission Board, N.B.C., U.S.A., Inc., and continued to give dedicated service until 1976 when she retired. She had worked tirelessly as a teacher and principal to improve the lives of thousands. She organized the Dorcas Club, which cared for motherless babies, taught child care and improved health practices in homes, villages and communities. She also adopted a Liberian infant, Carolyn, and raised her as her own.

Ms. East was instrumental in organizing the Suehn Native Baptist Convention for evangelical outreach and church planting. She started several primary schools in remote villages, and also established many small clinics in the "bush" where her college medical training was put to good use. Using penicillin and other wonder drugs, she was able to successfully treat and cure persons ill with the highly infectious "yaws" disease.

Gladys Finishes Well

She was the founder, in 1951, of the Missionary Women's Fellowship, and interdenominational women's group of missionaries working in Liberia. Many of those retired missionaries still meet annually in America at national conventions under their new name, "Women Christian Workers and Foreign Missionary Fellowship (W.C.W. & F.M.F.). She also organized one of the first international chapters of her A.K.A. Sorority in Monrovia, Liberia, and traveled to Washington, DC, to receive the chapter's charter at the National A.K.A. Boule.

Ms. East has been the recipient of many honors and awards, including: The Links International Service Award; the Sojourner Truth Meritorious Service Award of the National Association of Business and Professional Women; The Grand Opening and Dedication of the newly-built "Gladys East Edu-Care Center" in Middledrift, South Africa; the New England Workshop Exemplary Stewardship Award; many "Gladys East Missionary Societies" around the country named in her honor including two in Philadelphia, one at her own Mr. Carmel Baptist Church where she has been a member for 80 years; and most recently, in August of 2002, she was honored by the Suehn Association of the Americas at an elaborate banquet in Philadelphia. In 1979, Ms. East was installed in the International Women's Hall of Fame in Seneca Falls, NY.

Gladys has written often to the U.S. State Department of Immigration on behalf of many of her former Liberian students facing deportation to help them stay in this country to continue their education.

Her many successes at Suehn are evidenced by hundreds of graduates worldwide who have risen to many professional levels.

At sunset on the last day of summer, September 22, 2002, our Heavenly Father in His infinite wisdom reached down to His vineyard to lift His faithful and dedicated servant, Gladys Virginia East, from labor to rest, eight days after her 91st birthday.

She is survived by her two brothers, James and Melvin East of Philadelphia, a sister, Inez and her husband, Raymond Dones of El Cerrito, CA, a daughter, Carolyn and her husband, Moncure Logan of Cherry Hill, NJ, and a host of nephews, nieces, cousins, and other relatives and friends.

Letter of Remembrance by Dr. Benjamin W. Johnson, Sr.[1]

While attending Philadelphia Biblical University in the early 1950's a classmate, Virginia Amtrom, shared with me that she was supporting a missionary in Liberia, and that she was going to be a missionary serving with Gladys East. She asked me would I like to support Gladys East and I responded, "Yes, indeed." My wife and I did support and pray for her.

In 1958 we attended the annual meeting of the Keystone Baptist Convention in Philadelphia. We sat down beside a lady and introduced ourselves. The lady told us her name—it was GLADYS EAST! What a thrill it was for us to meet the missionary that we were supporting and praying for. We visited her several times until she returned to Liberia.

I was sent in 1963 to Liberia as the correspondent secretary of the Afro-American Missionary Crusade to visit Bopolu Mission in Liberia. It was a joy to visit Suehn Industrial Mission and meet my classmate, Virginia Amtrom and the missionary, Gladys East. I spent a week there as a Bible Conference speaker. It was a wonderful experience for me. This took place in 1963. There was a wonderful time of meeting other missionaries that I had heard about.

We continued to write and support them until they retired and came back to Philadelphia. When Sister Gladys East came home, we visited many times. She taught me much about missionaries and their good times and difficult times. She did impact my life in relation to missions and missionaries.

---

1 Dr. Benjamin W. Johnson, Sr., passed away in August 2006 and was joyfully married to sweet Louise for 56 years, having 3 children and 12 grandchildren.

1955–1974 Era: Redefinition
[Time of Civil Rights]

Chapter 27

Redefinition [Time of Civil Rights]

by Robert J. Stevens

There was a "Period of "Redefinition" of mission that occurred in the African-American church. Maybe in part a response to racism and discrimination, the leadership of the church developed a "protective mechanism" for missionary participation. The church changed the definition of missionary. Missionaries were no longer those who journeyed to another country or culture to take out the Gospel. Now, the missionary was defined, essentially, as "a woman who did good works, and who taught the Bible in small women-led groups." Missionary work included all the things that women did in the church—visiting the sick, cleaning the church and feeding the homeless. White missionaries traveled, but African-American missionaries worked in the community because "the needs are so great here."[1]

In the early sixties, another redefinition occurred in the African-American community: the formation of black-led missionary organizations outside of the church denominational groups. These new organizations restored the Biblical perspective and ignited vision for missions.[2] William H. Bentley began the National Black Student Outreach in the early 1960's and later wrote *The Meaning of History for Black Americans*. Carver International Missions was a forerunner in the modern African-American efforts at sending missionaries. Rev. Virgil Amos began his missionary service in 1962 with Operation Mobilization, working for 10 years in Mexico, Europe, India, Sri Lanka and Iran. Upon graduation from Talbot Seminary in 1979 he went on in 1982 to found Ambassador Fellowship.[3] Reuben Connor began the Black Evangelistic Enterprise which would later be called Urban Evangelical Mission.

Ruby Clark received her call to missions in 1964 at an interracial nondenominational church with a thriving missions program. Her pastor suggested applying to United World Mission. She was accepted as their first African-American missionary. She spent 30 years working with Muslims women in Mali and Senegal.[4]

Other Changes in the Black Church

There is some evidence that the present and past central importance of the Black Church may be threatened by the virtual

---

1 Vaughn Walston, "Ignite the Passion," *Mission Frontiers*, April 2000, 28.
2 Ibid.
3 Virgil Lee Amos, "Today's Leaders," *Mission Frontiers*, April 2000, 18.
4 Ruby P. Clark, "Today's Leaders," *Mission Frontiers*, April 2000, 20.

explosion of opportunities, which are now becoming available to recent black college graduates. ... Even with some decline in black college enrollment during the Reagan years, the total number of black college graduates since the 1960's will still represent an unprecedented phenomenon in black history.[5]

The resurgence of Islamic fundamentalism has been a worldwide phenomenon in recent years and it has implications for the general religious situation in the U.S. and for black Christian churches. ... It is already clear that in Islam the historic black church denominations will be faced with a far more serious and more powerful competitor for the souls of black folk than the white churches ever were. This challenge also brings opportunities for ministry in mission here and abroad. Max Muller, the founding father of the academic discipline known as comparative religious studies ... believed that most people have never examined their personal religious faith compared to another world religion. Most have never been challenged to the core of their being regarding their own beliefs. I agree that learning the beliefs of a Muslim, Hindu, Buddhist or some other religious person is essential for Christians to deepen their understanding of the biblical view of God. ... There are, however, an increasing number of Christians who are learning the languages of Muslims, studying their literature, history, doctrine and practices, and getting to know them. As opportunities have arisen, they have witnessed for Christ as much as possible.[6]

Ready For World Evangelization

As the African-American church is involved in the community, we often deploy our gifts to aid our neighbors in community development. This same energy can be developed and channeled to the world. ... Before we can effectively make disciples of the nations, we must learn to be disciples and to make disciples of our neighbors. ... The greatest motivation is a Biblical one. The African-American church must walk in obedience to the Biblical mandate to fulfill the Great Commission.[7] African Americans now have missionary organizations with dedicated missionaries and missiologists focusing upon the task of world evangelization.[8]

---

5 C. Eric Lincoln and Lawrence H. Mamiya, *The Black Church in African American Experience* (Durham, NC: Duke University Press, 1990, 1991), 383.

6 Larry A. Poston with Carl F. Ellis, Jr., *The Changing Face of Islam in America: Understanding and Reaching Your Muslim Neighbor* (Camp Hill, PA: Horizon Books, 2000), 9–10.

7 Vaughn Walston, "Ignite the Passion," *Mission Frontiers*, April 2000, 18.

8 Marilyn Lewis, "Overcoming Obstacles, The Broad Sweep of the African-American and Missions," *Mission Frontiers*, April 2000, 28.

Chapter 28
Andrew Foster

by Rhoda Rynearson and Berta Foster

Shortly after arriving in Accra, Ghana, West Africa, in the spring of 1989, my husband, Rev. Rodney Rynearson, and I entered the office of the Ghanian National Association for the Deaf and were surprised to see a large photograph of Andrew Foster.

My husband had met Andrew Foster at the Ephphatha Conference in Chicago in 1957 and had not seen him since. At that time Andrew Foster had asked a number of missionaries to the deaf how he might become a missionary to Africa to work among the people who are deaf there. In 1957 the Lutheran Church-Missouri Synod (LC-MS) did not have any missionaries to the deaf who were deaf themselves. The members of the Ephphatha Conference suggested he try elsewhere to get certified as a missionary and gave him several suggestions of where he might apply.

While visiting with the deaf man in the office, who signed American Signed English, we learned that Andrew Foster had indeed come to Ghana and opened the first schools for the deaf in that country and had spread the wonderful good news of Jesus to the deaf people in Ghana.

We had come to the country because missionaries there had a need to communicate with deaf people. We did not know whether we would be able to understand this people's sign language. As the deaf man was using American Signed English we knew we had no real problems. This was the language Andrew Foster learned after he became deaf, and he taught this language to the deaf people in Ghana. Also upon questioning them, we learned they were well grounded in the Bible and its truths.

After Andrew Foster had died in 1987, there was no one coming to visit them anymore. LC-MS then became involved in bringing the saving Gospel to these deaf people.

Who was this Andrew Foster who went to Ghana and why was he so important to the mission work in Kumasi? In order to understand him better, we needed to do some research. First, we contacted the other deaf missionaries at the Ephphatha Conference in Pittsburgh, PA, in the summer of 1992; and in October 1993, we had an opportunity to visit Gallaudet University and were able to scan their files about Andrew Foster, and we were able to learn more about him.[1]

Rhoda and Rodney Rynearson spent all their years in the U.S. developing the mission field here. They made trips to help LC-MS missionaries overseas from time to time. Her *Missionary Profile* article was taken from *Journal of the Lutheran Society for Mission*. Used by permission.

Berta Foster, Andrew Foster's wife is the current Administrator of Christian Mission for the Deaf, Detroit, MI.

---

[1] Rhoda Rynearson's article, "Andrew Foster (1925–1987): Pioneer Missionary to the Deaf in West Africa," prompted the USCWM to research Andrew Foster's life story. COMINAD's president, Brian Johnson, knew the Fosters in Africa and put us in contact with the Christian Mission for the Deaf in Detroit, MI, and with Mrs. Berta Foster, his wife, for a complete and accurate life history.

Here is what Andrew Foster wrote in "How God Saved a Deaf Youth" in 1977, renamed "Deaf Ears which Hear" shortly after his death, accompanied with edits about his life and work by Berta Foster.

Andrew Foster was born in Ensley, AL, on June 27, 1925. His father was a member of the Church of Christ and his mother a member of A.M.E.Z church. Andrew and his siblings went either with father or mother to church on Sundays. At age 11, he became deaf through spinal meningitis.

In the hot southern summer of 1936, polio was raging like a storm. Fortunately, the press and radio were able to put most people on guard. Reaction was typical in Fairfield, AL, then a growing steel and wire mill subdivision of Birmingham. Sunday School attendance fell. The park and amusement places were deserted. And though the great economical depression was just behind, most people managed to buy immunizations.

Luckily or unluckily, "lightning" struck, to our knowledge, only one house in the colored community: our home. My three years old brother was "hit." Preventive measures were stepped up. My two sisters and I, then just past my eleventh birthday, were quarantined. Still, about a week later, another "bolt from the blue." This time I went down with spinal meningitis. Upon recovering, the diseases left no crippling defects. But the high fever destroyed my hearing nerves, as well as my brother's. This must have been a terrible blow to our hard-working parents—Dad was a chesty coal miner. But as I was to learn years later, " ... all things work together for good to them that love God, to them who are the called according to his purpose" (Rom 8:28).

Naturally, parents of physically impaired persons do not readily accept their "fate." The advice of one physician or specialist is hardly convincing. Therefore, most parents are willing to sacrifice money and time seeking a cure from other doctors, faith healers and even quacks! Our dear parents were little exception. So around and around we went with Mom— all to no avail. God had better things in store!

Meanwhile, my brother and I were adjusting to our new silent world. We resumed our merry adventures with the neighborhood kids at Sunday School, camp, the park and in the nearby woods. Also I spent almost five years at a school for the deaf children in Talladega. There, I believe God distinctly spoke to me in my second year. During the daily devotion period, a Bible verse would be taught from the blackboard. All would either gather wool or just escape out the back of my head, so to speak. But somehow Matthew 6:33 struck, and has always stood out vividly. It promises, "But seek ye first the kingdom of God and His righteousness; and all these things shall be added unto you."

To seek, I thought, meant more than just going to Sunday School. So I tried to "turn over a new leaf." In addition, I began a habit of daily Bible reading—which today, after nearly 40 years and about the same number of readings from cover to cover, I find true to Acts 20:32, also a most wonderful enjoyment of "the deep things of God" (1 Cor 2:10–12).

Since first walking from the hospital into this silent world, I had wondered what a deaf person could do. How could one get ahead in life? With childhood ambitions swept away, and education for the deaf being what it was in the South then, I set out for Detroit on my own at seventeen. This coincided with the flood of war workers to the industrial North.

God enabled Andrew Jackson Foster to overcome his physical and spiritual handicaps as well as educational and racial barriers. He moved to MI for further education, but since he was a minor (17 years old) and his parents were residents of AL, he was barred from the Michigan School for the Deaf. Unable to go to school, he took job after job, like in a restaurant, etc., and then at Ford Motor Company and Motor Products in Detroit. His draft classification during World War II was 4-F, due to his deafness. There was such a demand for civilian workers that he had no difficulty in finding jobs. Undaunted, he eventually took a night factory job, attended the Detroit Institute of Commerce by day, and studied high school correspondence during odd moments.

In Detroit, one of my first objectives was to find a church for the deaf. Their meeting place turned out to be a small, aging brick house. The minister resided upstairs. Downstairs walls had been removed to make an assembly room. Yet it was God's choice for my rendezvous with Christ.

The Christians there had a tremendous burden for the hearing handicapped. A front section of the hall was reserved for them. Several persons took turns interpreting the service in the sign language, by which the deaf also joined in the singing. And the deaf were often mentioned publicly and prayer by the smiling Bahamian minister, B. M. Nottage.

But my greatest impact came on Sunday afternoons when the entire hall was used for deaf people. Here a short stocky jovial hearing brother, Walter J. Lyon, regularly made his way from across town. Though a full-time factory worker, ministering to the Black deaf was his first love. "Bro. Lion," as he was affectionately called in the sign language, faithfully labored with this group for about 45 years, until shortly before his Home-going in 1966.

The message emphasized by both preachers was essentially the same. "God so loved the world that He gave His only begotten Son …" "Christ Jesus died for our sins." And so on. It was mid-summer. To one accustomed to formalism, it seemed that their themes were "out of season," more appropriate for Christmas and Easter.

One Sunday I decided to give them a piece of my mind—and received a piece of theirs! When Bro. Lyon gestured for anyone to sing, pray or give a word of exhortation, I raised my hand. Then followed reflections of my upbringing: "Vain repetitions," the Ten Commandments and so on. This I did for a number of Sundays. In fact, unwittingly, I was becoming a boy preacher. Most of the deaf always seemed pleased by my "fair speech" and "much saying." Bro. Lyon's gentle face would beam too. But afterwards, using the Word of God, he would quietly try to get me straight on Biblical Truths, though I was not always very "teachable."

I knew the law, but not grace. I possessed a head knowledge of Jesus' birth, life, sufferings, death and resurrection. But the essence of believing about (historically) and believing "in"(saving faith) had never been stressed to me. So Law vs Grace became a long-drawn battle between the two of us. Each week I would arrive at the hall early for our friendly debate, which would be resumed after the service—and often made Mr. Lyon late for meetings elsewhere. No doubt I, like other legalists, was a fitting description of Paul's in 1 Timothy 1:7—"Desiring to be teachers of the law; understanding neither what they say, nor whereof they affirm."

Bro. Lyon was a humble Bible teacher and apt illustrator. I well remember some of his points. The law condemns, but Jesus saves (Rom 7:10, 11, 25). Like a mirror, the law reveals sin (Rom 7:7); but neither a looking glass nor the law can cleanse—only the blood of Jesus Christ can (1 John 1:7, 9), Colossians 1:4). The law was our schoolmaster to bring us to Christ, then we are no longer under a schoolmaster (Galatians 3:24–25). The law bounds, but Christ frees (Gal 4:24; 5:1). You are complete in Jesus (Col 2:10).

Occasionally, these points would reach home. They corroborated with truths I had been learning in the morning services and through Gospel literature. But somehow I would lean back upon the law. And just as 2 Corinthians 3:14, 15 affirms, the legalistic minded person cannot apprehend these Truths. He is spiritually blinded. "The veil is upon their hearts." One day Bro. Lyon's long patience ebbed a bit. Gesturing emphatically, he said, "Andrew, forget the law! Forget the law! Look to Jesus only! Look to Jesus only!"

That was enough. I decided to give Mr. Lyon's idea a better trial. As the days went on, I noticed that "the veil had been taken away (2 Cor 3:18).

Oh, what a glorious transformation! How thankful I am to God! Also to Bro. Lyon and Bro. Nottage! The message and songs at the chapel became more meaningful, such as this favorite:

At the Cross, At the Cross

Where I first saw the light,

And the burden of my heart rolled away:

It was there by faith I received my sight,

And now I am happy all the day.

This testimony, I trust, will give you a little glimpse of what the Lord can do when we fully yield our heart and life to Him. Matthew 6:33 ought to be everyone's motto. Unless you are already truly born again, may I invite you to receive Jesus Christ as your personal Lord and Savior today?

Andrew later zoomed through colleges, earning three degrees in five years. He entered Gallaudet College in 1951. He was the second black student and the first one to graduate in 1954. He received a B.A. in Education. According to Rev. William Ludwig, a classmate at Gallaudet, he went around the Washington, D.C. area, MD, and especially around Newport News, VA, spreading the gospel while he was a student. Pastor Ludwig stated that Andrew was a very independent person. While he was at Gallaudet College, he was looking at an almanac and was astonished to learn that there were no deaf schools in most of the countries of Africa. From then on, he felt compelled to go to Africa to establish schools and at the same time to teach the students about Christianity. He attended summer sessions at Hampton Institute.

Andrew Foster was the first black person to receive a master's degree from Eastern Michigan University in Ypsilanti in 1955. His degree was in Special Education. In 1956, he received a bachelor's degree in Missions from Seattle Pacific College. Furthering his studies, he took some post master's classes at Wayne State University in Detroit, which had a famous oral deaf education program at the time.

In 1955/1956 he contacted a number of mission organizations to apply for work among the deaf in Africa. Though well qualified spiritually and educationally, he discovered the doors of most mission boards closed to Blacks. Undeterred again, Andrew founded the Christian Mission for Deaf Africans on February 24, 1956. He arrived in Ghana, a newly independent country, in 1957, and opened the Ghana Mission School for the Deaf on September 10, 1956, in a Presbyterian public school building in Accra. After the hearing students had gone home, he held classes in the afternoons for 13 children, and in the evenings for 11 adults. The first courses taught were vocabulary, arithmetic, recreation, physical education, child evangelism, fingerspelling and writing. He had the help of two teachers. In January 1959, the primary school was moved to Mampong-Akwapim where a large house was leased for a temporary boarding school as more students continued to arrive. By 1962, there were 85 children enrolled in the school and there was a waiting list of 250. The government of Ghana took over the school on May 11, 1962, and made him the headmaster and manager.

Andrew met Berta Zuther, a German deaf girl, at the World Congress for the Deaf in West Germany in 1959. Born in Berlin, Germany, shortly before World War II, Berta Foster could hear until age of four. She heard her parents telling her fairy tales. Like many parents in Germany, they did not tell any Bible stories. When becoming totally deaf through measles at age of four, she lost all her speech and almost all vocabulary within one year due to lack of practice. Her parents did not know how to communicate with her, except for about ten home made signs.

Although not learning the normal way like hearing children do, she was able to observe, think, imagine and dream. It was in a small village near Russia, to which her mother with three children were evacuated during World War II, that something happened which started her in the direction to God. One morning, her mother got onto a horse-drawn coach, going to a place to buy things. Berta was standing in the house door and watching how the coach became smaller and smaller as it went into the distance. It then disappeared behind bushes. Being about five then, she asked herself how far is the way and what does it lead to? Her own answer: it is very far, far, and ends at a wooden fence. Then how high is the fence? Far, far up into the clouds. No end. Then what is behind the big wooden fence? Lots of clouds and a big man sitting up there. That way, Berta got the concept of endlessness and a heavenly Ruler. She could not tell her mother about that nor ask her questions—because they did not know how to communicate.

A few years later, back in Berlin, Berta was delighted to find in her father's bookroom several books with picture Bible stories, which she enjoyed looking at so often. At age of ten, she went to a school for the deaf, where she finally could start to really learn about many things, thanks to the special teaching methods, which included the sign language. Before that she did not do well in a one-room school for the hearing children in a village in Central Germany and then in a school for hard of hearing children in Berlin.

There was in that deaf school also the weekly one-hour religious instructions, but she was excluded. Berta then learned that she needed parental permission, so she tried to get it. For some reason her parents thought it to be not needed, but she persisted and got their permission. She was glad to learn more Bible stories, but the salvation plan was not explained.

At age of about 15, Berta read different religious books and got confused. So she established her own religion, and was trying to do what she thought would please God. She also read some occult books, even about how to talk to the dead—as she wanted to find out how the life hereafter would be. But soon she left the occult books alone because her trying to follow their instructions brought no result. As she later looked back, she thanked God for not letting her get entangled deeper into occultism.

In 1959, Berta attended World Congress for the Deaf in West Germany. It was exciting for her to talk with the deaf from different countries through international signs. As she also learned English from some books, she was glad to have the opportunity to practice it by communicating (in writing) with some of the English-speaking deaf persons. One of these was Andrew Foster, the first deaf missionary-educator to the deaf in Ghana, Africa. When they talked about his work, she asked him whether she could work in his school in Ghana. He switched the subjects. Some time later she repeated the same question, and he again switched the subjects. She thought he had enough African staff and didn't need any foreign outsiders, and also that God closed the door for her.

However, they continued to keep in touch by correspondence, at first sporadically and then more often. Andrew encouraged her to study the Bible with a correspondence school. She found some in the German language but she chose to study them in English. That helped her to understand more about God and His dealings, but because of her struggling with English as a second language, she was not sure if she understood correctly the explanation of God's salvation plan. It took some time for her to be sure to have her questions answered. Then when she finally understood, she was glad to accept Jesus as her Savior and Lord. How wonderful God's grace is that sinners can be saved by repenting and asking Jesus to forgive their sins, they are saved by what Jesus has done for them, and not by their own "good works."

In 1960, when Andrew was working with his second school in Nigeria, he invited Berta to work in his first school in Ghana. As time went on, they found that they understood each other so well, that they saw that the Lord led them for each other. They were married on January 29, 1961. They were blessed with five children: Andrew, Jr. (12/11/61), John (2/17/63), Faith (6/27/65), Timothy (3/27/67), and Daniel (10/19/69), all hearing.

Andrew was named the "1962 Man of the Year" by the Alpha Sigma Phi Fraternity of Gallaudet College.[2] In 1970, Gallaudet conferred upon Andrew a Doctor of Humane Letters degree. In 1980 he received an Outstanding Alumnus Award from Eastern Michigan, and in 1982 an Alumni Medallion Award from Seattle Pacific.

In 1960 he established a school for the deaf in Ibadan, Nigeria, and two more in 1962: Enugu and Kaduna, also in Nigeria. Then in 1974 the first French-speaking school for the deaf was started in Ivory Coast.

In 1975, Andrew, Berta, and their family came to Flint, MI, for furlough of a year. However, Berta had a bout with cancer in 1976. Berta stayed home in the U.S. where she worked in their mission's office. So, Andrew made his trips to Africa for about six months every year. During this time, he began work in other parts of Africa by establishing schools for the deaf in: Togo and Chad in 1976; Senegal, Benin, Cameroon and Central African Republic in 1977; Zaire (now Democratic Republic of Congo) in 1979; Burkina Faso in 1980; Burundi in 1981; and Gabon in 1982. So, 31 schools and 2 centers were established, and about the same number

---

[2] As was noted in a news release from Gallaudet College, May 18, 1962.

of Sunday Schools and Bible study groups in those countries and four others (Kenya, Sierra Leone, Congo and Guinea in the 1980's). In the last year of his life, he also did his research and efforts of development in other countries: Mali, Uganda, Ethiopia, Zambia, Zimbabwe, Tanzania, and Rwanda.

Andrew Foster was instrumental in sending a large number of African students to American colleges to receive further education. The first student, Seth Tetteh-Ocloo of Ghana, arrived at Gallaudet in 1961.

Many of the Bible study groups in different countries were started by former students at the schools which Andrew began. These deaf students knew how to read and teach from the Bible. Andrew would visit the various groups and also the schools and preach one sermon or more until he could come again.

Andrew Foster made numerous fund raising trips to both the North American and European continents. Rev. Robert Bauer of Edmonton, Alberta, Canada, said that he heard a presentation Andrew made to the Wycliffe Bible Translators, who gave him Bibles and finances. Pastor Bauer invited him to speak at his church on Good Friday. He remembered watching him describe in sign language how he would walk through immigration and customs in various countries with proper visas and credentials. Some officials used to make additional requirements, in the hope of getting bribes. Since the officials could not communicate with a deaf individual, they just let him go through. He even brought religious materials with him, which was not allowed in some of these countries. He also described how he would obtain transportation from one city to another by riding local buses, often fearful to travel and holding on for dear life. He also told of having to sleep at the airport overnight, praying for the next plane to take him to the right destination.

Needing to get to Nairobi, Andrew Foster accepted a seat on a Cessna 404 plane with a number of Americans bound for a safari in Kenya. On December 3, 1987, the plane crashed in the village of Gisenyi, in western Rwanda, and all on board died.

On October 22, 2004, Gallaudet University dedicated an auditorium in Andrew Foster's name, calling him "Father of Deaf Education in Africa." It was his privilege to see a number of deaf souls saved and become Christian leaders. God certainly used one deaf man in a most marvelous way to lead many to His saving love.

Christian Mission for the Deaf is looking forward to establishing more schools and churches in other unreached areas as the Lord leads and provides the means and the workers.

More can be read about Andrew Foster, Christian Mission for the Deaf, and his important articles and reports about deaf ministry at CMD's web site: www.cmdeaf.org.

Chapter 29

Take A Giant Step: The Life Story of Elgin and Dorothy Taylor

by Elgin Taylor

Elgin Taylor, is President of Christians in Action Mobilizing African Americans for World Mission, located in Woodlake, CA. He is a 40-year plus veteran missionary with CinA, and has served as President for the past 20 years. He is a consultant to churches on evangelism, missions, and church planting. He received his Master of Theology degree from the international Bible Seminary in Orlando, FL, in 1982. In 1992 he authored the booklet, "Black History of Missions," which has become a primary source of information for churches and colleges studying missions. Currently, he ministers to over 300 missionaries and national workers in 20 fields of service. In 1992, Rev. Taylor was placed in Who's Who International for excellence in leadership.

A Mission History

A lot of people will not realize that going all the way back to the late 1700's there were people of African descent who was called to missionary work. What I mean by missionary work, I'm thinking of those who are called to do cross-cultural ministry, go outside the boundaries of their own ethnic community and reach cross-racial, and ethnic, and cultural lines, to others who have not heard. Other gentlemen, such as African American, George T. Liele, who in the late 1700's was really the first American to leave these shores to do cross-cultural ministry. He went to Jamaica, West Indies, having indentured himself as a servant on a ship to a British captain for the period of the voyage and did his servitude, as it were, and landed in Jamaica. And, had such resounding success in ministry that he had to call back to GA and appeal for other ministers to come over and help him because of the tremendous response to the gospel he received. I know that William Carey is the father of modern missions, but George T. Liele actually started his ministry at least 10 years or more before Mr. Carey ever left the shores of his native land in order to go overseas as a missionary.

Subsequent to that time, by the dozens, I would say, if not more, people of African descent were sent into Africa, in particular, on the behalf of the Presbyterian church and other denominations at that time, simply because those of European descent could not sustain the harsh conditions, malaria, and other diseases that they contacted in West Africa, in particular, at that time. So, people of African descent were chosen and sent out. And for almost 100 years those folks were very much involved in missions. Then when they found the cure for malaria and other such diseases, then there was a less focus, in fact, the focus was taken completely away from African Americans, and Caucasians then were sent out because they found a way for them to go out and survive. So, the support stopped, the missionary flow stopped, and for the next 50 years or more, the prevailing attitude with those of African descent was that, "You don't really have a message even for Africa. The Africans will not accept you. So we will not send you." So the doors were just closed completely to those of African descent.

The Four-letter Man from Hubbard, TX

I was raised on a farm in Hubbard, TX; 38 miles east of Waco, TX, and about 72 miles south of Dallas, TX. I was the youngest of 12 children. My parents were good godly Methodist Christians, so I was raised, as it were, "on the church bench." That's the term I use often times because every Sunday, from Sunday school at 9:45 in the morning until the Sunday night service was over on Sunday evening, and during the week, I was involved in church. That was my culture; that was where I could be found. However, for the first 17 1/2 years of my life, though I was in church every Sunday, I didn't know Christ personally.

I had aspirations, and an opportunity to try out as a professional baseball player with the then, Brooklyn Dodgers farm club, and instead, I signed on and became a Marine for two years thinking that I need a couple of years to mature a little more, and during that period of time was when I accepted Christ. I knew about Him and I had a healthy respect for God and a type of human love for Christ, and an appreciation for Christ. but I didn't know him as Savior until at the age of 18, while serving in the military, that I came to experience what it means to know Christ personally.

I embraced Him by faith in the city of Oceanside, CA, at a servicemen's center where I happened to be sitting and listening to the gospel one evening. They showed a film of Dr. Billy Graham, depicting his crusade in Harringay, England in 1954; and this was one of his early crusades. I witnessed people who's lives were touched, effected and changed by the power of God and by the living gospel that he preached. My heart was touched, and that evening through many scenarios, that I won't go into at this time, I came and embraced the Lord Jesus Christ as my Savior.

Let me state first of all, the verse that really convinced me to yield was the verse that many people come to Christ on, John 3:16. I was overwhelmed with the sense of God's love. Just an awesome sense of the fact that God loves a TX boy called Elgin Taylor, a nobody. God loves him so much that he was willing to invest Himself on the cross for me. And it was that sense of profound love that I responded to, not some sort of mystical clouds that hung in the air or some thunderbolt that hit me and caused me to awaken to some dramatic response, but just an awesome sense of God's love.

This step forward was not so far, but it became the most important "Giant Step" of my life. From now on I would become a changed man. That was a life-changing experience. Not only my relationship with God underwent a tremendous change from just a response to a vital, loving, relationship; but also my life in other areas was changed. He came in. And, after He came into my life He began to alter my plans. He challenged my career with a career of His own and in 1957, I responded to that challenge and just said to the Lord, "I am willing to go and I am willing to be a missionary if that's what You want." I didn't know what I was saying and I didn't know the implications of that type of commitment because the word "commitment" as a Christian was still new language to me.

My Discipleship
I craved to be discipled after I accepted Christ—within two weeks after I landed on the island of Okinawa, I met a group of servicemen—one has become a lasting friend of mine. In fact, he's the Chairman of our Board of Directors of Christians in Action today. His name is Bishop George W. Thornton. So, I met George. We both were in the Marine Corps, stationed on the same base, and attended the same chapel services there. Then he introduced me to a gentleman (who went to be with the Lord a few years ago) named Bill Quisenberry who had just arrived there on the island of Okinawa with his family of a wife and six children. Bill discipled us as GI's at that time and then challenged us to share our faith. He even had a night school that we were able to attend for several months. So we started not only discipleship, but also our Biblical training there.

We got involved in running the worship service—the English speaking worship service—for the other GI's, and got involved in actual ministry. And because I was a singer, (I sung in a quartet at a younger age), I got involved in doing that—leading the singing as the "minister of music" as they would call it today. Through that I was challenged to go out into this village.

I believe that it is certainly true that God, when He gives us birth, when we are born into the world—I believe it is true that God gives us certain gifts and certain abilities. However, some of these things can be secret to us. We don't know them. As a growing up lad I was heavily involved in sports. I was a four letter man in high school—right through the entirety of my high school, so I was quite an athlete. But, I was absolutely shy. I had no visible leadership skills. I didn't like to talk. I was not a public spokesman. At banquets, given in my honor sometimes, they'd ask, of course, the honoree to say a word of some type, and I would freeze. My voice box would freeze. I could not speak.

I Did Not Speak the Language

While I was stationed in Okinawa, Japan, I was involved in a ministry outreach to a village. I spoke no Japanese except, "Ohayo Gozaimasu" which means "good morning"; "Konnichiwa" which means "good evening"; and "Sayonara" which means "goodbye." Those were basically the four words that I knew. But, I was challenged to go into a village and witness for Christ. I was trying to figure out "How am I going to do this?" I went into that village and I thought that the best person to start with was to go to ask the person who was the head of the village, the village chief, or the village mayor, to allow me to come in and share my faith. So very boldly—I did not know the language—I went to and made inquiries as to where the head of the village's house was.

A group of kids took me to his house. He couldn't speak English. I couldn't speak Japanese. So we bowed and we smiled, and we smiled and we bowed and that is as far as we got. Then all of a sudden he felt, "I have a solution to this." He sent to the local school and a gentleman came with this particular young person who spoke very good English. He was a Japanese school teacher who taught English at this particular school. He spoke very good English so he asked me why I was here. I said, "I am a Christian from America and a serviceman here on the island—I am a Christian and I want to share my experience, my faith, with the people of your village." The mayor, through this translator, said, "Well, I am not a Christian. I am a Shinto, I am Buddist. However, I would welcome you to come and share your faith with my people." So, he gave me an open door. He said in fact, "I will allow you to use my village meeting hall and when you decide what evening you want to come, I will announce your coming on what they called in those days *eriaku rajio*. It was a transmitter that had a speaker in every house in that village and you could get on that microphone and literally speak to everyone in that village. So the night that we had set for me to come, he announced my coming and the people came out in considerable numbers.

I was very surprised. This school teacher who spoke English agreed to interpret for me for that evening. I gave my testimony. I think it was the second sermon that I had preached. I gave my testimony about how my life had been changed. Three young people, teenagers about 15–16 years of age, came to Christ, as well as a number of children accepted Christ. For the next year I would go every week to that village and we would have services using a tape recorder, a slide projector that depicted the life of Christ, and some song books. They would sing and then we would put the tape recorder on and we would have a narrated worship service for the rest of the evening. They would narrate the slides and there would be a little bell letting me know when to change slides. It was a very interesting experience. We called ourselves "mechanical missionaries" because we couldn't speak the language but we had the message with us. That's how we conducted the church services for an entire year until I was able to get a translator to go along with us.

So everything that happened in my life as far as ministry, or as far as any form of leadership, started on Okinawa when I was there as a young serviceman. As far as going into that village and contacting the mayor, that had to have been from God because it was not naturally Elgin Taylor. It was only the years following that experience, and after I had an experience with the Holy Spirit, that boldness was given and I was able to discern the giftings that God had given me that had lain dormant in me until the Holy Spirit touched those and brought me alive and brought those gifts to the surface. And that has been an exciting discovery. And still I am discovering that, because still, basically, I am a reticent by nature.

Only One Convert to Missions

I finished my military tour of duty there on Okinawa, and I was still single at the time. Then, I was almost immediately released from the Marine Corps and went into Bible training school, Christians in Action (which was not under that name at that time) had also evolved its own training program—its missionary prep program in CA. So I joined that in August of 1958 and went through that six months—well, actually it was a year's program.

Dorothy had gotten converted when she was about 12 years old and at the age of about 13 she got a call to the mission field. For eight years she tried to find ways to express that call but there was no open doors until the Lord allowed me to come along and speak in her church.

Dorothy lived in the city of Waco, TX, ran her father's fish market business, and also was a school teacher. She graduated from the university at the age of 19 with a bachelors degree in English and mathematics and was a young school teacher.

I gave a challenge on missions and at the end of my message. I offered to pray with anybody who wanted to respond to God's call on their lives. And, Dorothy, my wife, was the only person that responded. So I said I preached a whole sermon and got one convert, as it were, to the cause, and what a convert she's been over the years. So I married my precious sweetheart, June 10, 1959.

Raising Missionary Funds Took a Miracle

I have been with Christians in Action since I first took the initial training program back in August of 1958. When I came home for furlough for one year, I actually taught missions at the school and I also taught missions at an inner city Bible school that J. Vernon McGee helped to found. [It is still going on today. It is called LA Bible Training School. Alonzo Lavertte is the leader of that and still doing a fine job, and we taught there at some of the evening sessions at the outset of their training program in 1964.]

Christians in Action is a faith based organization so we have to raise our own support. Which we did that. That was a miracle in itself. In those days the mission sending agencies were not as rigid in their requirements as they are today. They went more on the basis of faith and if you felt your faith was strong enough to go with five dollars in your pocket, then some of them would let you. But, it is an interesting story.

My wife and I had been working on our support. When I came towards the end of 1959 and we were looking to go to the mission field, we had ten dollars pledged to our support, and not that much coming in. I think we had two dollars a month coming in from our donors. As we prayed about the matter, however, we kept getting the sense from the Holy Spirit that it is time for us to go. "It is time for us to go." So December of 1959 we said our farewell to our various church friends. We did some radio broadcasting and we said goodbye to our radio audience and we just happened to mention in an interview in which I was asked, "How is your support?" I said that we had about ten dollars a month but we are convinced that we are to go.

That last night in the U.S. we had dinner with an African-American pastor and his wife, (he just went to be with the Lord the year before this article was written) Rev. Starks of Unity Baptist Church in South Central Los Angeles. They had us in their home for our final meal because they were going to give us a good wholesome meal for they figured that we were going overseas and starve to death. So we went to their house, had a great diner, and had a great time of fellowship and prayers. That night we went back to our apartment and I had a message waiting for me to go and see Dr. Dalton, who had become a friend of ours. He wanted to say good-bye to me. So I went to his office that night. He was working late seeing patients there in Compton, CA. When he finished seeing his patients, he asked me to come into his office. He said, "You know what? I was driving up from Laguna Beach the other night and I did something, Elgin, I never do. That is, I turned on the radio station KGER—the station out of Long Beach, CA—and who was talking on the radio, but Elgin Taylor." And he said, "When you said you were going to Okinawa in just a few days and they asked you about your level of support and you said that you had ten dollars a month pledged that was not coming in on a regular basis, it was as if God, Himself, spoke to me and said, "You are to support that family."

So that night Dr. Willis B. Dalton gave me a check—in those days you just didn't see a check that size—for $100. That was like more than $1,000 today. And he said, "Elgin, I want to send you this amount of money every month." So we got our support in, enough to live on, the very last night that we were in the U.S. before going on to our assignment—just within hours of getting on the plane. And the wonderful thing about it was that when we arrived some months later and my wife delivered our first son, Elgin, Jr, we got the next month's check. It had been raised from $100 to $150. And then the following year he increased it to $200 a month. And he became our sole support, practically, for the entire four years of our ministry there on the island.

Okinawa was our first mission field and we served there for four years. Dorothy helped to organize and to build up the Okinawan Christian school which was a school set up for missionary kids there on the Island and that has evolved to a major school with their own very large campus and with, I think the last I heard, over 1,000 students at that school. Reaching not only English speaking people from various parts of the English speaking world, U.S. and other areas, Britain and other countries, but also many English speaking Japanese, Filipino, Chinese, and people of various Asian extraction are being reached at this school. It is just an exciting ministry.

I worked with the university students at the one and only university there in Naha, Okinawa, at the time, and had a club there with some 30 students. I held an English class and we used the Bible as our textbook and a number of those fellows came to know Christ through that exposure and experience. So, it was a wonderful time of ministry. We also went into the villages and I didn't realize it at the time but we were reaching unreached people groups. It was not an unusual experience for me to go into a village where there was no electricity in those days. I would take a generator and an evangelistic film unit and we would have gospel films in those villages and people would respond to the gospel. But there was always one question that many of them would ask and that is—"Sensei," which means "teacher," "What is the Bible?" "Who is Jesus Christ?" "Is He an American?" "Is the Bible an American book?" They literally knew nothing about the message of the Gospel. I guess that in those early years was the time that God began to birth into my heart the need to reach those who haven't had a chance to hear.

Interestingly enough, a year and a half ago, my wife and I spent two months on the island of Okinawa where we were as missionaries. I had the occasion of meeting two of those teenagers and of course now they are 60 and 61 years of age, grandparents, established in their home. The delight in my heart was to hear that those two men, who are both businessmen (and very successful) are still going on with Christ and are still living for him. So, that is one of the experiences that I had in those early days.

A Heartbreak in Africa

Then in January 1956, my wife and I and our two sons—we had two sons born on Okinawa—we headed out to Africa. We felt that we must respond to a call that we sensed that God was putting on our hearts for Africa. We went into Africa, into Liberia. We were in Sierra Leone—every place we stopped—we would ask the Lord to give us the nation. We would pray asking Psalms, chapter 2, I think it is verse 8, where the Lord says, "Ask of me and I will give you the nations—I will give you the nations for an inheritance and the uttermost parts of the earth for your possession." We would pray and ask God to give us those countries never knowing that we would go back there again. We did that in Sierra Leone, we did that in Liberia, we did that in Ghana, West Africa. And finally we landed in Nigeria, the largest African nation on the continent.

We spent four glorious weeks, and yet, in a sense, they were heartbreaking. Because we went to do ministry, we went there to live, but at that time there was a political disturbance. The Prime Minister was assassinated. A civil war broke out and we had to flee. We had to leave the country. We decided to go up to London, England.

London Opens Its Doors

We knew no one when we landed in London, by the way. We landed there with $60 in our pocket. There was four of us—my wife, Dorothy, and myself, and our two sons, Elgin, Jr., and Willis; he was a baby. The immigration official looked at us and he says, "How long do you plan to stay in England?" And, I said, "Indefinitely." And he says, "How are you going to live? What money do you have? How much money do you have?" And, I said, rather sheepishly, "Sixty-two dollars." And he looked at me saying, "Well, that's not much money to live on here in London. And, I said, "Well, sir, I realize that." And he said, "Well, I am going to give you approval to land in our country and at the end of three months we are going to have to decide whether or not you can stay." Well, before the three months were over, we were given approval for one more year and after that, and of course year after year.

Christians in Action had one other missionary couple that had come over from Northern Ireland to open up a training school in London. We were going to go up and just give them some assistance until the conditions in Nigeria quieted down. When we arrived there we found them very discouraged. They had been given promises of opportunities and assistance and help and they did not find that. They came to see me in the home where we were staying. In fact, we didn't know them.

We were going to go up there for six months and interestingly enough we spent 15 years in London. From London we started a church, we planted a missionary training college there. One of our first graduates was an executive with the British American tobacco company. He came on leave, got gloriously converted, was discipled, came into our training program there in London. When it came time for his missionary assignment to the mission field as a missionary, he chose to go back to Africa. He went out and in January 1969, he opened up the field of Sierra Leone and we have 25 churches in Sierra Leone today because of the early efforts of that young man, David Hall, that we sent out to the mission field.

Fifteen years later, we had raised up a church that was over 200 strong. We had planted a school that had by that time trained and sent out over 50 missionaries and we had trained in our school, in the region of 300–500 people, who are today, many of them, involved in various churches as pastors and full time workers throughout the British Isles and other parts of the world.

Dr. Dalton continued support in England until we were able—while we were home on furlough in 1964—to build our support from a variety of sources and he gradually decreased the amount of support.

I've gone back to England every year. We started our work in 1969 in Africa, with David Hall and I began to visit Sierra Leone on a regular basis. So, over the years we have made numerous trips to West Africa.

Taking Others to the Mission Field

Years ago, we would go alone—my wife and myself. We would go and visit our mission fields which I have been doing, as the International President of Christians in Action for the last 20 years, and conduct the crusades with our resident staff in those countries. However, some seven years ago the Lord put in our hearts the desire to travel across the U.S. and build relationships with pastors within the various churches that we would minister and seek to take not only people from within those churches with us on the mission field, but to start by taking the pastors. We felt that once the pastor caught the vision of missions, they would be the most influential in bringing that vision back to their church, thereby convincing their people to go on the mission trips.

Such as Raleigh, NC, where we have Pastor L. Foday Farrar of New Canaan Baptist Church, who has been traveling with me to the mission field since May of 1994. His church now is on fire for missions. We set up a missions campus, as it were, on his church grounds. And every year we have a mission orientation training program. At the end of that program we then take people that we have trained out on short term mission operations. March 2001, we took 20 people from his church out to Ghana, West Africa, with me. They were to be engaged in medical outreach. There were two scientists who went with us; nutritional scientists went on this trip. There were people with experience in nursing, there others with drama experiences, carpentry experiences, and others such as that who went, using their skills and their trades to foster the cause of outreach and evangelism, to reach people for the cause of Christ.

And so this has been repeated numerous occasions throughout the last seven years. Over that period we have seen several thousand, I would say, go to various countries where we are working and with many teams going out each year. The momentum is constantly building and that excites us a lot because we realize that we can't, as a mission agency, do this job alone. The local church need to be involved and we feel that by bonding a relationship with a local church and convincing them that we are their extended arm and without them we can't really get the job done, they will go. The pastor comes along side, he catches the vision, his heart is ignited for missions, he takes that fire back to his church; the church gets involved.

Such as the case with Rev. Farrar. When he came back from the mission field in 1994, he stood up at his church after preaching his sermon and began challenging his people about what he had experienced. He said, "Now, I want to encourage every one of you in my church to do"—and they are over 1,000 strong in his church—"I want to encourage you, everyone, to go and get your passport applications and apply for your passports cause you don't know as to when God might be leading you to go out to the mission field. And hundreds have gone out from his church over the last seven years into short term mission. And there are at least two or more people on the mission field today serving full time because of the program that started in Raleigh some seven years ago.

Responding to the Call of God

I would say, first of all, that in responding to the call of God on my life as we were blessed to do in 1957 and the successive years, there has not been a moment that I can truthfully say that I regretted having made that commitment to Him. It has been a wonderful and exciting journey with God.

I came along in the late 1950's where things, I suppose were still somewhat closed, but I was fortunate enough to get involved with an agency which allowed me to respond to the call of God on my life. But I know many, many others, who, say a decade before me, or even five years before me, tried many doors that was just simply closed to them because of their color.

I thank God that I made the commitment, and when I look back on it 44 years later, I rejoice that commitment has led me through a lot of exciting exploits down through the years. Ninety countries later, having traveled to all those lands and ministering to many people groups, I can see where the Lord has taken what was always there inside of me and brought it out to the surface and He is still maturing it in me.

My passion has been over the last 42 years (and more since I have been involved in missions) is this driving and compelling passion to reach out to those of my community. It is because of the convincing that was done on the African-American community was very very thorough and, even today, very few African Americans in the average church across the U.S. are convinced that they have a part in global evangelism. They feel that their task is to reach those within their community and that's the end of that. They don't think cross-culturally and they don't even dream about the possibility of their becoming missionaries because that has become a foreign word to them. Whereas back in the late 1700's and 1800's it was a very common term used to describe those of African-American descent involved in cross-cultural ministries. So, our job and our challenge is to bring about restoration. And, thank God, we are beginning to see that happen, such as the case in Raleigh and other places across the U.S. and that excites me tremendously having been involved for four decades myself.

Chapter 30

Bob Harrison: When God Was Black

by Bob Harrison

Introduction

Not too long after our Lord's ascension, an Ethiopian believed on Jesus Christ and was baptized. And God became black. In the 19th century white missionaries went to parts of Africa knowing that their life expectancy was only a few months. They came and they died as many Africans put their trust in Jesus Christ. And again God was black. In a rough-hewn, crowded shack in America, a black slave, having nothing in this life but hopelessness and chronic, bone-weary fatigue, found his release in Jesus Christ. From being a miserable slave he became the child of a King. As the Scripture had promised, the lowly slave was filled with the Spirit of God. God took up His residence in the black slave. The black body became the temple for the Holy Spirit of God. God's exterior was black. What's it like when God is black? Are the prejudices swept away, the doors flung open, the awesome power of God just as effective? I think I can tell you because I am black and God lives within me, too. I'd like to tell you my story of what it's like when God is black.

Growing Up Wasn't Easy

Mom says I was only two when I came down with double pneumonia. "I'm sorry, mam, but I can't make any promises. Even if he does pull through it will be a miracle if he grows up to be a normal, healthy boy." It just so happened that my mother did believe in miracles. Mom and dad prayed. I quickly mended after that. The place I remember best was a musty little basement apartment my sister and I and my mother and dad shared with the rats and roaches. We all suffered from severe colds, and tuberculosis was constantly nipping at our heels. I can remember living in seven such flats in my childhood.

Mother was born in New Orleans to a Creole father and Negro mother. Dad's parents were mixed racially—his father was one-half English but he grew up in the West Indies where the black was kept "in his place." He started out as a cook on ships going to South America and his blackness never let him out of the kitchen. He later cooked for a university in South America and then spent 40 years as a chef with the Southern Pacific Railroad in CA. Because of his job, dad was gone much of the time and his paychecks were miserably small ... Mother took in foster children and did sewing.

During rainy seasons we had to cut out a new sole from those carefully hoarded Shredded Wheat boxes. We went to school

Bob Harrison is founder and president of Bob Harrison Ministries International, Inc., Concord CA ©1978.
Used by permission.

with white kids. We even made friends and played with them. Even in those boyhood days we knew that dreams could come true if you had white skin but not if you were black. So we blotted it all out by going back to our streets and getting into a fight. One thing led to another and pretty soon I found myself in a series of gang wars. About this time I entered junior high school where they had an organized athletic program. I soon found that my greatest abilities were in track. In high school I continued as a successful runner and I also developed into the top halfback on the football team.

It's hard to be the neighborhood tough and the best pianist on the block at the same time. How my mom scraped enough money together to buy a piano I'll never know. But when I sat up to it I could pick out the melodies that were running through my head. When I was in high school I was even able to study at the San Francisco Conservatory of Music. Music didn't turn me into a saint, of course. In fact, for many years I believe it kept me from the Lord. In more ways than one, music eventually would turn my life around, but in those high school days it just wasn't enough to blot out the curse of being black. The whole load was becoming too much for me. So after my junior year in high school, I dropped out and joined the army … this was quite likely the salvation of me as a person. The army taught me to be a man.

In those days the service was still segregated so my officers and buddies were all Negroes. "Man, if you're going to have any chance at all, you're going to have to get education," they said. They were so convincing that … I actually earned my diploma … I couldn't wait to get out and start college. I managed an early discharge and it was with a sense of elation that I enrolled in San Francisco State College as a music major. The world was going to be my oyster after all.

When God Was Sneaky

The army has been good for me and good to me. I could believe that Uncle Sam was black. Music treated me well, too. Whatever I invested in it, it repaid me handsome dividends. Maybe music was black. I was sure that education was going to do a lot for me. And anything that was going to help a Negro must be black. But was God black? What had he done for mom? For years my sister Florence and I had perfect attendance in Sunday school. Later on I was a leader in the youth group and I sang in the choir. But what had all this gained us? We didn't have a car, we didn't have fine clothes, dad couldn't get a better job. If He were black, would not He be doing something for us, too?

Johnny Mathis, who really made a big name for himself, was one of the guys in the neighborhood with whom I spent a lot of time. When we appeared together everyone said that there were two boys who were really going places. I began to make some of the money I had my eye on … But before I could get my jazz career off the ground, Someone interfered. It was all kind of sneaky.

"So Bob likes music," the Lord must have said to my mother. "There's this Spanish musician who made quite a name for himself in the entertainment world. Now he belongs to me. You get your son down to the church when my musician is there and we'll see how strong a hold jazz has on him." I was still living under my mother's roof and I was still very close to her in spite of the fact I had not yet trusted the Lord. Not for one moment had I tried to give anyone the impression that I was a Christian. I guess there was this much fear of God in me.

But for mom's sake, I didn't hesitate when she asked me to attend an evangelistic rally on a Sunday afternoon in a few weeks before graduation. My plan was to attend the rally, sit in the back, and then leave when everyone was absorbed in the meeting. The rest of the afternoon I just can't explain. My mind was on the four-hour jam session planned for that afternoon. But suddenly I found my attention riveted to the service. The hymns I had heard and sung hundreds of times without noticing before became very personal. They all seemed to be aimed directly at me. They pointed to the love of God, to the patience of God, to the forgiveness of God. In return for all these, I realized, I hadn't been willing to give God the time of day. I had not even said "thank You" for a breath, much less anything else.

A final blow was struck by George Morales, the Spanish soloist who had been converted from the entertainment world. Using his guitar as accompaniment, he got up and sang, "I trust in God, I know He cares for me." During that first verse it seemed that my whole life up to that moment flashed before me. It added up to a big fat zero.

I had drawn everything on the bank of heaven, but had deposited nothing. God had given me a godly home. He had given me loving parents who sacrificed for me. He had given me a fine Christian background and a good education. It struck me also that He had given me my musical talent. He gave it to me but I was planning to use it only for myself. George sang the second verse. I began to realize that God did care for Bob Harrison. I realized that I had found God's Son in the church building. I found His Son in the hymns being sung, I found His Son even in the solos. But His Son could not be found in my heart. About the third verse of that song the Holy Spirit came with great convicting power.

Before the last verse, I knew I had to accept Christ personally. Without a counselor, without a message, I accepted Jesus as my Lord and Savior. I stayed the rest of the service—uncontrollable tears rolled down my cheeks. First they were tears of repentance and then tears of joy. God loved me and now He dwelt within me. God was black! I told the agents that I had accepted Christ into my life and didn't feel that I could take Him into theaters and night clubs. The more I said "No," of course, the stronger I became. By the time five or six months had gone by, I had the strong conviction that God wanted me in full-time ministry. Now, life would be beautiful.

A Little Black Boy Going Nowhere

Just to show you how naive I was, I was over 20 years old before I realized it made any difference among Christians that I was black. I don't mean in the secular sense, of course. If I just heard someone speaking with a Southern accent I immediately hated him. It was the walls of prejudice in evangelical circles which really threw me when I encountered them. I guess it was my church and my family that had sheltered me. We sang and praised the Lord and clapped our hands with other Negroes, Japanese, Chinese, Scandinavians, and a sprinkling of Filipinos and Mexicans.

Black Christians at that time, and for the most part up to this moment, were almost completely unaware of the things so familiar to the white Christians. We knew little about Christian conferences, about foreign missions, about white Christian organizations, about evangelical leaders or about Christian schools.

Bob Jones, Bob Jones, Bob Jones—I heard the name so often that I came to believe that it must certainly be one of the most outstanding Christian schools. So when I began to feel the Lord leading me to go to a Christian school, I inquired at B.J.U. in SC first. I guess you know what Bob Jones had to say back then. "Under no circumstances will we accept a black as a student at Bob Jones University." I was more or less able to rationalize racial prejudice at BJU. They were right in the South.

The independent church I had grown up in leaned toward the Assembly of God denomination and their Bethany College was right in the city. It seems ludicrous now, but grandma took me by the hand and off I went to enroll in Bible college. We were ushered into the president's office ... " You realize that when you enroll you'll be our first Negro, don't you?" So, I am the first Negro, I thought. Hurrah. The first wall in my life started to crumble. Bethany was moving to its new campus in Santa Cruz some 78 miles south of San Francisco for the second semester. A Filipino brother was enrolling as a freshman that year—and they decided that since his skin was brown he probably wouldn't mind living with a Negro. Later, I would be victimized by other racial issues in the denomination.

I was elected to the student advisory committee and was also elected vice-president of my class. I was also busy arranging music for trios, for the choir, for our quartet and for other small groups. Perhaps, surprisingly, the two faculty members who meant the most to me were from TX. "Bob," they said, "there will be people who cannot accept you as a person and as a Christian."

As we traveled, I became more and more aware of a certain uneasiness that hovered around me. The pastor or leader would acknowledge and greet the quartet. "And we are so glad to have our dear colored brother with us," they would say. "And we know there is no difference in us. We want our dear colored brother to know we feel there is no difference."

They were simply making it quite clear that there are white Christians and there are black Christians. I honestly feel that the apostle Paul wanted us to get over the idea of feelings of racial superiority when he kept emphasizing the oneness in the body of Christ. By this point I thought I was at the place where racial incidents would not bother me. I couldn't have been more wrong.

We seniors had finished all our classes, had turned in all our papers, and had taken all our exams. All of us were planning on full-time ministry with the Assemblies denomination and were on our way to meet the District committee. Earl and Eddie and I were talking about our evangelistic plans. Earl and Eddie were good musicians who had been in our school quartet. I would provide added music as well as the preaching ... the school had used me to present them all over the State.

As we all got in line to wait our turn to go before the presbytery, I saw that my mother, along with my sister and godmother, was already waiting for me in the car. I think there were four examiners in the room. They represented northern CA and NV. "Well, Bob, we're proud of you, and we're glad for the grades you have and we've enjoyed your being in the school," ... "I see that you have made application for credentials." Then he looked me square in the eye and said, "I'm sorry, my brother (sic), but is not the policy of our denomination to grant credentials to Negroes." The bottom fell out of my life. I was so shocked there was nothing to say. I didn't question the statement, I didn't ask, "Why?" After a few tense moments he quietly said, "You can step into the office and get your fee back. We're sorry." I just rushed out.

After I had walked about a quarter of a block, uncontrollable tears began to roll down my face. I rushed straight for the car where my mother was sitting. The bitterness welled up in me and finally I turned to my mother and said, "Well, I'm just not going back. I don't even care if I don't graduate." "Son," she said, "you think about this and pray about it. Remember, if you don't go back and graduate then you may be further hurt and hindered in what God has for your life. This is one of the severe testing grounds that God is allowing you to go through. What has happened is not right nor can it be justified. But you're not the first to have something like this happen and you'll not be the last. Now you must prove your strength in God and the reality of Christ in your life." The bitterness engulfed me. It was eating me up.

Up Off the Floor

I was ready to forget Christianity and all it stood for. I had a year in the army, a degree from San Francisco State, an exhilarating experience with the Lord, and Bible school diploma behind me. But nothing ahead of me. I was ... disgusted with Christianity, disgusted with my black self. I was disgusted with everything.

I was moping around the house one day when the mailman came. "This black reject is invited to preach at an evangelistic service," I snarled. In those first weeks mom encouraged me and prayed for me and took me to church. I accepted the invitation and a couple of weeks later I found myself in the pulpit again. I felt like an intruder. But as I spoke, some of the old fervor came back. At the invitation, several came forward. With this encouragement, I began accepting other invitations ... In spite of my denomination, and—more significantly—in spite of myself! I had suddenly become a member of a two-man evangelistic team ... accepting invitations which took us up and down the coast of CA and OR.Besides putting me back on my spiritual feet, that first summer spent as a traveling evangelist brought a couple of other things that would have life-time consequences. For the rest of my life it would be my singing as much as anything that would open doors for me. The second resulted from the fact that we began to receive as many invitations to black churches as white. Pastor Miller had in his black church in Pasadena, CA, a beautiful daughter ... As subsequent meetings took me to Southern CA I managed to meet Marilyn again and again. Eight months later we became engaged and a year after that, on July 6, 1952, we were married.By this time I accepted the invitation to become associate pastor of a little ghetto church in San Francisco, "Emmanuel Church." My salary was $55 a month. I took a job at the post office. The project where we finally found an apartment to match our pocketbooks was an eyesore. It was hardly the place to bring up three children who were born to us here. Among our immediate neighbors were winos, prostitutes, and other ne'er-do-wells groveling through life on various forms of government aid. We survived, of course, and the children grew up normal and healthy. I had kept in touch with many of my school chums and we were invited to their homes on occasion. Most of them had become pastors of good churches and lived, if not elegantly, at least quite comfortably. The old bitterness was not too far from the surface.

Looking back on that period of my life, I get a completely different perspective. Living in the ghetto, scrimping on food, tripping over winos, all these played a tremendous role in preparing me for a future ministry of which I wasn't even thinking at this time. The lack of official denominational recognition didn't hurt much either. It was the call of God on my life. The Lord didn't mind that I was only a black—because He was black, too. Another thing they couldn't take away from me—Bethany really was a good Bible school.

Pre-fab Walls

Some of the walls holding back evangelical blacks have been pre-fabricated. One of these is the notion that blacks can have an effective ministry only with other blacks. If an enterprising black Christian feels called to foreign missionary work, or wants to minister in white churches or join any number of evangelical organizations, this pre-fab wall is hastily set in the way.

The ministry at Emmanuel was fully satisfying and the Lord had taught me some big lessons about pride. But the desire to be an evangelist had never left me. Then came the day in 1958, when I was invited to sing and give my testimony at a huge Fourth of July camp meeting held by the Assemblies of God in Santa Cruz. Among the four or five thousand who attended was Dr. Ben Kumerfelt, a former professor of mine at Bethany. He had returned to his native Germany and now was visiting just briefly in the States. "Have you ever given any thought about coming to Europe for a time of ministry?" After the conversation I forgot about it. But about four months later I received a letter from Dr. Kumerfelt and two other evangelical leaders in Germany. "Your singing and speaking coupled with the fact that you would be the first Negro ever to have a public ministry here would draw great crowds and result in many conversions." The white propaganda that I would not be effective overseas had already brain-washed me, and, as we'll see later, most other black evangelicals. I really had never thought of making such a trip.

It was a nervous Negro at his window seat as the plane came in for a landing in West Berlin. I stepped off the plane and was greeted by a crowd welcoming me not with polite handshakes but with enthusiastic bear hugs. I chose to stay with a German family and used my Berlitz book on conversational German. We got along famously. I could sense that God had used my ministry to touch their hearts. I don't know exactly how many came forward that week, but there must have been at least five or six hundred who made first time decisions for Christ.

I began to receive invitations from all over Germany and Switzerland as well as England. I was soon ministering at Warner Concern, the American military base in Munich. It was Germany, at least for me, that exploded the myth that a Negro can have an effective ministry only among his own people. And it was in Germany where the revolutionary thought that it might be an advantage to be black first popped into my mind. This bold idea would ultimately redirect much of my energies for the rest of my life.

Africa the Beautiful

I was just beginning to come down out of the clouds and back to the realities of my pastoral duties at Emmanuel in San Francisco when another letter arrived that sent me through the same emotional changes as that first invitation from Germany. This one was from Dr. V. Raymond Edman who was writing in his capacity as Chairman of the Board of the Billy Graham Evangelistic Association. The Association was asking me to join with Dr. Howard Jones in representing them in a ministry in Africa.

Marilyn and I were astonished and overwhelmed. We were deliriously happy. We were scared to death. But Dr. Edman had asked us to spend much time in careful prayer before we made any decision. With our positive answer, the Graham association then made detailed inquiry into my educational background and spiritual experience and ministry. The trip was made with Dr. Howard Jones, who by this time had become the first black associate with the Billy Graham team.

Jones worked with Billy in an unofficial capacity in New York and then in the Cow Palace in San Francisco in 1958. As a pastor in San Francisco at that time, I became involved in the Cow Palace crusade and worked especially in getting black churches involved. This undoubtedly played a large part in my being contacted by Dr. Edman. This was my second international trip—If our plane had crashed on leaving Africa, I would have died a happy and contented man. The national workers greeted us with glee and joy written all over their faces. Just the fact that their black brothers had come from America was enough. Our ministry began with a city-wide crusade in Monrovia ... while there I was invited to speak and sing for some other meetings in Kenya. The crusade, by the way, was sponsored by the Anglicans, Southern Baptists, Methodists, and the

African Inland Mission—a pretty interesting bit of integration in itself. From there, Howard and I went to Ethiopia and Uganda in East Africa, and then back to the west coast and Ghana and Nigeria and finally back to Liberia. With tears in their eyes, the folks would ask us through their interpreters, "What has taken you so long to come? We heard that we had black sisters and brothers in America and we wondered why they never came over to tell us about Christ." We learned, by the way, that the African had been told that American Negroes did not want to come to Africa, that he was ashamed of Africans.

We'd be in one meeting and they would want us to go to another meeting in another tribal area. "There are many many more members of our tribe who have never heard the Gospel. Can't you please stay longer?"

What a sight it was when these Africans gathered by the thousands in some of our meetings. They rocked back and forth while singing the great hymns. The American Negro has this same custom of swaying back and forth during congregational singing. I had assumed this came from slavery days, for a people mourning their fate and longing for that day of release. It comes from Africa, from people expressing their faith and their joy in a living God. In one meeting in a later trip to Sierra Leone there were 18,000 people singing a spiritual with me in six different dialects at the same time.

I was singing and speaking before greater crowds than I had ever dreamed of. I was seeing and doing and experiencing things far removed from the gutter fights of San Francisco as could be imagined. It gave me identity. There was a time when I was ashamed to admit even to myself that my ancestors had come from Africa. ... I grew up with a mental picture of the African as ... a cannibal boiling a missionary in a newspaper cartoon. I imagined myself growing up in a heathen tribe in the jungles of Africa. I imagined it and for the first time I thanked God even for slavery. Man's inhumanity to man was ugly, but God used it for good.

With Billy Graham in Chicago

The invitation to join as a full member of the Graham team came as Howard Jones and I were still up to our elbows in ministry in Africa. In 1951, I couldn't become a minister because I was black. In 1961, I was sent to Africa because I was black and in 1962, I was invited to join the Billy Graham team because, among other things, I was black. The cynical, of course, will say that Howard Jones and then myself and later other blacks were put on the Team as a token of gesture. It just isn't true. In the years that would follow I saw full evidence of his real love and concern for all minority peoples.

Marilyn, who has always had a tremendous spiritual perception, felt that the Lord was giving us this opportunity for a special purpose. "Bob, I believe God has placed you on the Graham team to prepare you for an even greater ministry," she told me. By now there were four Harrison kids: Keith, age 10, Carol, 8, Adrienne, 5, and little David, 3. The family would remain in San Francisco while I traveled all over the continent with the Graham team. I vowed then to be as close to the family as I possibly could when I was at home.

On the platform I was involved in reading the Scripture and praying. Behind the scenes I was involved in such things as coordinating the counseling and follow-up, taking charge of advisors and counselors, watching for overflow crowds and so on.

When we were invited on the team, Howard and I were assured that our ministries would not be just to the black community. They really kept their promise and our ministries took us everywhere. I was in many white churches and ministerial meetings and spoke at a number of the evangelical colleges in the area—Wheaton College, North Park College and Seminary, Trinity Evangelical Divinity School, Moody Bible Institute. One of my invitations was from Rev. Louis Brodie, pastor of Greater Harvest Baptist Church. This is one of the leading black churches in Chicago and Pastor Brodie had a tremendous influence on all the black community through an extensive radio ministry. Pastor Boddie invited me to speak three different times on his radio broadcast so that I might have a ministry with many thousands more. The Chicago crusade was a thrilling and satisfying adventure. Among other things, I was helping to bridge the gap between black and white Christians and also helping to get the black church concerned about, and involved in, evangelism.

Five Fantastic Years

In all, I was to spend five fantastic years with Graham during which time I would participate in six major crusades including Chicago, Fresno, Los Angeles, Omaha, Boston, and Denver. I remember several times when just Billy and I talked together. He emphasized and reemphasized the importance of making certain that I remained humble before the Lord. "You must realize that everything you have, God has given you. No matter how people might applaud your musical talent or your speaking ability, you must always give the glory to God because God will not share His glory with another. As long as you remain humble, God will always use you. I feel that God has a great ministry for your life and this is just the beginning."

During the Omaha Crusade, Billy and I were talking together again. At this time, racial strife was the number one topic in the nation. The need for more black voices in the field of evangelism weighed heavy upon me. I stayed with Graham through two more crusades (Boston and Denver), but the feeling grew in me that the time had come for the "greater ministry" Marilyn had believed in. So, by mutual consent, and certainly under the leading of Almighty God, those five fantastic years with Billy Graham came to an end.

Joseph in Egypt

Eleven years had passed since the Friday afternoon when the sky fell. In the intervening years I had been a pastor, an evangelist in Europe and Africa, and finally a member of the Billy Graham team. All this without being ordained. I can't say I really listened to my mother, either. "The very ones who are putting you down," she said during those dark days after Bible school graduation, "will someday be the ones who will honor you."

The injustice of my case smoldered in the hearts and minds of my school buddies and friends among faculty members and pastors in the denomination. Five years later at the national convention in Springfield, MO, attended by some 3,000 Assemblies of God delegates, the embers were fanned into flame. The case of Bob Harrison, first Negro to ever apply for credentials in the denomination, was brought to the floor. After an impassioned debate, the problem of what to do about blacks applying for credentials was given a half solution—the kind that committees everywhere are so disposed to. It was decided that the granting of a license to preach was a district function and that the national body could not dictate this policy.

With this decision, a black could now be granted a license from his district, if it was so approved, but he still could not be granted an ordination. The superintendent who had presided over my application refusal was dead. A younger man, a personal friend of mine, had taken his place. "Bob," he said, "what happened to you was totally unjust and we are making many efforts to correct the situation." What he was saying amounted to this: Would I give them another chance? He asked me to come down and make another application for license, which I did. The license was granted, the first to a Negro in this 600,000 member denomination.

The "Very Ones" My Mother Had Said

This was but the very beginning. Five days later I flew down and met many of the officials of the denomination. After the tour I was given a private audience with the head of the missions department. "You can write your own ticket, Bob, if you'll come and minister under our banner," he said. He promised an extensive expense account, travel to Africa, the Caribbean, the Fiji islands and other exotic places. "This all sounds great," I said, "but how can it be possible when I don't even carry ordination papers with the denomination." He inferred that this might be arranged if I would just come with the organization.

Humanly, I wanted to mock the hypocrisy of the denomination that had excluded Negroes for generations only to change their minds when public opinion was changing and when they found a black who was "not like the rest." In my heart, however, I knew these men were human, too, and that they were sincere. Also, I couldn't lay 60 years on sin of a whole denomination on their backs. The Assemblies did even better than their word. Without my leaving the Graham team, they granted my ordination.

It was no longer so important that I was being ordained. But I could see my mother waiting in the car for me those 11 years before, expecting that I could walk into the committee and be ordained like anyone else. Since that day in 1962, the Assemblies of God have continued to take important strides in reaching and accepting the black man they had shunned. The results have been well worth the humiliations I had to experience as the vanguard of this force.

How Could It Have Been

I've been saying all along that black Christians represent a vast potential for effective service in worldwide evangelism and missions.

It happened while forty million white evangelicals were making themselves comfortable behind the stained glass of their all-white segregated churches. Black Christians were weak when they could have been strong, but this was at least partly because white Christians found it less unsettling to their nerves to be concerned with correct doctrine and keeping themselves "separated from the world." The liberal church, however patronized and paternalistic it was, paid attention. They saw discrimination, they saw poverty, they saw joblessness and hopelessness and did something about it. They came with a social gospel, but at least they came. So the black church, by and large, became liberal. However ... I know of few black churches anywhere that deny such basic Bible doctrines as the deity of Christ, the virgin birth, the miracles, the resurrection of Jesus and the inspiration and authority of the Scriptures.

How different it could have been. I was at the Los Angeles crusade in 1964 and inundated in the usual rounds of luncheons, press conferences and miscellaneous meetings. Driving 70 miles to Forest Home to sing and speak and then return in time for the evening crusade meeting didn't appeal to me. When I arrived I was amazed at the size of Forest Home. An unusual anointing and deep burden came upon me as I was ministering to these kids. At the end I gave an invitation for those who had never committed their lives to Jesus Christ to come forward and do so. But in the crowd of 900, more than a third came forward at this invitation. I gave a second invitation for those who would like to surrender their lives to full-time Christian service and more came forward. Just one day at Forest Home and I could immediately see why the white church of North America had 28,000 foreign missionaries overseas and was turning out hundreds of pastors, ministers of Christian education and youth directors every year.

Where will our young people exchange their inherited, second-generation religion for a deep personal experience with Jesus Christ? The possibility of bringing blacks on the grounds brought up a whole kettle full of questions which I tried to answer. I told them they had to learn to think black. Our culture, our thought patterns, our frame of reference are different from the white man's. I emphasized the point that the blacks had not only something to gain but something to give. The part of God that was black was as vital to the whole as was any other part. For it, tens of thousands of blacks had these experiences year after year; who can say what great advances would have been made in foreign missions, in revival and evangelism in black churches and perhaps even in a greatly changed complexion of the whole scene in America? My vision of how it could have been is now turning to what it might yet become.

What Do Blacks Really Want?

When I walked into the office of Dr. Dick Hillis of Overseas Crusades, Incorporated, one day in August of 1965, I got what blacks really want. I had first met Dick Hillis in Fresno, CA, at a ministers meeting held in connection with the Billy Graham crusade there. By this time I was on my own and was still casting about for the right way to develop my ministry. He simply greeted me as Dick Hillis, my brother. We talked about the racial problems of our country and I saw that he was a sensitive man. "Bob," he said, "I really believe that a man of color can have a tremendous ministry in Asia. Have you ever given it a thought?" He had a tremendous burden for the people of the world. He saw my specific talents and concern and realized how this could be used in world evangelism. This is what the black of America really wants—to be accepted for his actual value.

After much prayer, much preparation and a whole lot of fund raising, Norm and I left for the Orient in December of 1965 ... In Formosa (now Taiwan), and then the Philippines, we plunged into our schedule of meetings in schools and universities and indoor and outdoor crusades. In one unbelievable experience in a section of Manila known as Plaza Miranda, we saw crowds of as many as 20,000 miraculously gather from the streets and shops ... In Dalat, Vietnam, we were warmed and humbled as we ministered to Montagnard ("mountain" in French) tribal people whose heroic spirit in serving the Lord in spite of tremendous persecution and death I had read about in the book, *Bamboo Cross*. Our crusade in Huie, the old imperial capital of French Indo-China, was particularly poignant. We arrived in Singapore during the Chinese New Year. At each invitation, the altar was jammed—mostly with young people. It was my first opportunity to minister in Asia and I found as I had in every other place that thousands and thousands of people were responding to the gospel message through the preaching and singing of a black man and—in this case—his white companion. One Chinese leader said, "This is our first Negro evangelist in the 103-year history of our church. The sufferings and disappointments that his people suffered in the past are similar to our experiences, and this made him able to communicate so effectively to our people."

Who, Me, Lord?
Of the 28,000 missionaries sent out from America, I have been able to find only about a dozen or so who are black. When God was black He could speak to brown hearts and black hearts and white hearts just as effectively as He could when He was white. If one in 1,000 black Christians went overseas, I reasoned, we would have a missionary force of 10,000.

On my return trip to the States in February of 1966, Dick Hillis asked me to meet with the board of O.C. We came to a pretty quick agreement that I should become one of their associate missionaries. It came as a bit of a surprise to me, then, when Dr. Hillis called me a couple of months later asking me to consider moving to the Philippines with my family. The logic wasn't there, and Dick, uncharacteristically, wasn't very convincing. But I agreed to pray.

I met with Dick sometime later. "You know, Bob," he said, "you have told me that one of your burdens is to see the field of foreign missions opened to the Negro. You've convinced me that this is one area where the Negro has not had opportunity to serve. Are you willing to let God make you the first black missionary O.C. has had and possibly one of the first with an evangelical organization?"

But there were still some pretty strong resistance factors in my life. One of them was South America. By now this little black boy from the streets of Filmore had preached and sung on every continent in the world with the exception of South America and Australia. There were some personal factors. Marilyn and I had come a long way from the ugly tenement housing projects of those first years as a struggling pastor. When I went with the Graham team my salary was such that I could devote my full energies to the ministry. Being with Graham had also launched me into a recording ministry. We were able to buy that nice home which most blacks just have to go on dreaming about decade after decade. My children were able to go to fine schools. We had a new car for the first time. Every cent that I would spend for travel, for equipment, for moving the family to the Philippines, for my ministry expense as well as for my monthly allowance would have to be raised in gifts and monthly pledges. This, of course, is true for all missionaries going out with Overseas Crusades and not just for this black man.

Jumping ahead ... when we walked out of the air-conditioned plane and hit the thermal barrier outside, I wondered if the family would even make it into the airport, let alone make it for a whole year. We reached the mission compound and moved into the World War II quonset hut which was to be our home. It was almost like reliving those first years in the housing projects. I must say, however, that the missionaries had really fixed up the quonsets nicely and we really enjoyed living in them. And so did the rats, mice, lizards and roaches, they were ugly monsters with armor plated bodies and creepy antennae.. the rats and mice were relatively bigger too ... it was impossible to completely control these pests.

The drinking water had to be boiled, flour had to be sifted to remove the uninvited guests, and nothing could be left out of the refrigerator without attracting an army of ants. It was a new culture, and the kids had to get used to a new school—albeit a good missionary school. Keith was now 14, Carol 12, Adrienne 9, and David 6. Marilyn hardly had a single day free of tropical parasites in her intestines. As I have intimated, we learned to love the Philippines very much in spite of these circumstances, so much so that we stayed an extra year. So now we had become one of the first black families to go out with an evangelical mission as foreign missionaries. Another wall had come tumbling down.

It's a Brown World After All
Those wonderful Filipino people who instantly became our life-long friends provided some real insight into why our ministry was so well accepted all over Asia. "We've heard so much about the black problem in America," a young

Filipino said to me one day. "But you're not black, you're brown." He put his arm up to mine and sure enough, his skin was about the same shade as mine. It began to dawn on me that two-thirds of the world's population lives in Asia and the islands of the Pacific where skin colors vary in shades of brown. Add to this 325 million blacks in Africa and the dark skins of much of Latin America and one must come to the conclusion that it's not only a small world but a brown world after all.

But skin color was just the beginning. I soon found an identification on a real gut level. Many of these brown and black peoples of the world have been exploited and subjugated by the white Westerners for centuries. They could easily identify with the problems that discrimination brought to the American black. The American Negro and the Filipino are alike in their love for music. We had planned to be in the Philippines for only a year, but we ended up jamming two fantastic years full of ministries in Okinawa, Taiwan, Singapore, Malaysia, Indonesia and Ceylon as well as a dozen cities in the Philippines. During this period I even participated in a crusade in the Democratic Republic of Congo where we saw over 7,000 of the 87,000 attending come forward in the final meeting.

Day after day and month after month I was proving to myself that the black Christian was wanted—even desperately needed. And day after day, month after month, I was praying and longing for the time when hosts of my black brothers in Christ would discover this fact and act upon it.

The Devil Didn't Like It

I suppose that one test of a good idea is to see how strongly an enemy fights against it. The idea came to me after we had completed our first year as a family in the Philippines. As I traveled from city to city, the Lord wouldn't stop bothering me with the concern of getting black Christians to the mission fields of the world. Christian camping centers, missionary conferences, evangelical schools, all these, I believed, would someday provide an answer. Would we have to wait years for a trickle of blacks to come in contact with white missionary work, to be accepted by and trained in white schools, and to be sent out by white organizations?

Why not organize a tour of leading black ministers and let them see the opportunities firsthand? I was scared of the idea, but I couldn't let it go, either. Feeling a little foolish, I flew down to L.A. to see my good friends Rev. Earl Pleasant, pastor of Mt. Moriah Baptist Church, and Rev. E.V. Hill, pastor of Zion Baptist Church. Both of these churches are large and influential in the black community and are two of the few who have any significant foreign missionary program. "What in the world can we do to get our people involved in foreign missions?" I asked Earl. "Well, Bob," he said, "you've traveled quite a bit and are knowledgeable about mission activity. Why don't you formulate a minister's tour to a mission field?" We talked with Ed Hill who quickly became enthused with the idea. By now, I had only a couple of days left before returning to the Philippines, but I wrote letters to pastors in Southern CA and TX ... we quickly filled up our quota of twenty-five.

The enemy had pulled out his big guns: illness, riots, floods and death. We were down to six. Should I forget it? On top of this, my own body was screaming for mercy.

About two weeks later, I received four letters almost simultaneously from key ministers assuring me that they would be part of the tour. Two of them said they were bringing one other minister with them. They had already taken their shots, they had paid part of their tickets, and they were looking forward to the time with great anticipation. I had a new problem ... As tour director for 25 ministers, I could receive a free round-trip ticket to San Francisco to meet them and bring them back. The bank balance was low, but I scraped all the way to the bottom of it and flew to San Francisco. Even then Satan didn't let up. In San Francisco I received a long distance call from Dr. Robert Wilson of Dallas, TX. He said that he had been on the way to the plane when a death took place in his family. His companion canceled out with him.

We had been through a slugging match with the devil, and I'll have to admit that he all but had us whipped. When five of us met in San Francisco, for instance, I found that two of the ministers somehow didn't have visas for the Philippines. We had just one day to get them—the Lord pulled this one off, however, and we left for Tokyo on the first leg of the tour.

There was one last desperate lunge. En route, the pilot was notified that the worst snow storm in 100 years was sealing off Tokyo and that we wouldn't be able to land there. The plans for ministry in Tokyo were canceled. The next day, March 12, we took off for Taiwan and it was as if God said, "Okay, devil, you've had your licks. From now on I'm taking over." And He did.

Gideon's Army

The comparison with Gideon is not inappropriate, I feel. The four pastors represented a good cross section of a vast majority of the black church in America, and two of them held top positions in their denominations. Besides having these leading men on the tour, we were also making a 16 mm color film which ultimately would be shown in hundreds of black churches. Two hours after we landed in Taipei, Taiwan, we were hustled into a T.V. studio for the first of many, many appearances during a seven-day stay. The next day each of us was assigned either to a Chinese or American missionary and we headed for five different parts of the island. What stories these men had to tell when we assembled back in Taipei five days later!

Hong Kong, our next stop, provided and entirely different type of experience. We checked into the Hong Kong Hilton … we, therefore, saw the glittering face of Hong Kong first. One the second day, we stepped into a different world, one these ministers hardly knew existed. An FEBC missionary, the Rev. Bob Larson, and a Chinese national took us into the walled city of Kowloon. Its filth, its depravity, its inhuman living conditions are almost indescribable. On this same day we saw other parts of refugee-choked Hong Kong. We saw the boat people—hundreds and hundreds of them. Amid these terrible living conditions we saw the white American missionaries struggling to reach these people with the Gospel. It was a different group of black pastors who returned to their plush Hilton Hotel that night.

"We've got to come back and bring many more ministers," said one of the fellows. "We've got to bring some laymen, too."

In the Philippines, we were overwhelmed by the eagerness with which we were received as blacks. The city sponsored a panel discussion in the 7,000-seat auditorium of West Negros College. Included in the group were publishers of two local newspapers, a high school principal, a university professor and a sociologist. "We were told that we weren't wanted," said one of our blacks. Then someone stood up—it must have been a Christian—and asked point-blank if we were planning to send a black missionary back to stay. We said this was definitely what we wanted to do but the young man wasn't satisfied. "Are you really going to send someone or are you just being polite?"

My minister friends said not only that they were coming back but that they wanted to bring others with them. As God would have it, at that very moment Jim Montgomery had on his desk in Manila a letter requesting that we sponsor a black graduate student from Wheaton College for the summer. Within a few weeks, then, we had a black short-term missionary living in Bacolod.

Before leaving, Dr. Branch summed up what all the men had been saying: "The time is ripe. I feel black missionaries must go to every nation."

Once Around Jericho

I think we have to change our attitudes. We must come to the full realization that when God is black, God is God. He can do the same mighty exploits through us that He can through anyone else. The time has come for us to stop using the excuses that we can't go to the white Bible school or to the white conference grounds or go out as missionaries with white societies or join other white evangelical organizations, or even attend a white church if that is the place where you can get the best training to serve Jesus. The point is that He can and wants to develop your abilities to the very highest for His glory.

In this last word I've been addressing my remarks to "white Christians" and to "black Christians," and thereby perpetuating the very idea I abhor. Paul speaks of Christ's followers as making up a body. This body of Jesus Christ is made up of black parts and white parts and brown parts and red parts and yellow parts. The white parts of the body of Christ cannot say to the black part, "You are only black, I have no need of you." Neither can the black part say, "Since I am only black, I don't have to take my responsibility in the body of Christ." This cannot be any more than the eye can say to the hand, "I have no need of you," or the hand to the feet, "I have no need of you" (1 Cor 12:21, RSV).

But my dream and my prayer is that someday we will be able to say these words about "black" and "white" Christians:

On the contrary, the parts of the body which seem to be weaker are indispensable, and those parts of the body which we think less honorable we invest with the greater honor, and our unpresentable parts are treated with greater modesty, which our more presentable parts do not require. But God has so adjusted the body, giving the greater honor to the inferior part, that there may be no discord in the body, but that the members may have the same care for another. If one member suffers, all suffer together; if one member is honored, all rejoice together. Now you [black, brown, white] are the body of Christ … (1 Cor 12:22–27, RSV)

When Christians everywhere finally realize that we are one body, we won't have to talk anymore about what happens when God is black.

The walls have come tumblin' down for me, for which I can only praise God. But for hundreds of thousands—even millions—of my fellow black American Christians, the walls are still there … we've only been once around Jericho. We have 12 more laps and a great shout to go before the enemy is defeated. For the enemy is not the white man or the black man but the devil himself. What is really significant is that millions of black Christians in this country represent a vast potential for the cause of Christ … a vital and significant part in the evangelization not only in America but also of great throng of people around the world. Let us together be more than conquerors for Christ.

Chapter 31

The Life and Work of Daisie Whaley

by Nene Bi Tra Albert

If we know Jesus as our Savior, He also becomes our Lord and Master. As our supreme Master, we must know how to serve Him. To want to serve God doesn't mean that He is there to do what we want, but He gave us His Word and His Spirit as our guide. By following these two guides, Daisie accepted the call to serve God in missionary service. We see that since the beginning of the church until our time, there have been people who understood and accepted to sacrifice themselves for the Christian cause. They abandoned their social status, their professional future and their country to go to an unknown land to announce the Gospel. It seemed important even imperative to me to give a concise history of Daisie's missionary ministry in the Ivory Coast since she has sacrificed in this way.

Early Life and Call

Daisie Whaley was born March 3, 1939, at Philadelphia, PA. She had the grace to be born in a family that went regularly to church. She is the oldest of nine children. Although her family attended church regularly, it did have a solid biblical base. Her father, George Whaley, and her mother, Elisabeth, gave their children a home so full of joy and love that the children were not aware of being poor. After graduating from the William Penn High School for Girls in 1957, Daisie studied at a university from 1958 to 1960.

Since her parents had her attend church, Daisie was able to profit from biblical teaching in Sunday school from a young age. When she was 12 years old, she truly received the Lord in her heart as her Master and Savior thanks to her Sunday school teacher. At the age of 14, during a Vacation Bible School, her teacher spoke about missionary service. During the lesson she spoke about her desire to "GO" to another nation to share the message of salvation to those who have never had the chance to hear it. That message motivated Daisie to dedicate her self for missionary service. After her Sunday school teacher left, Daisie took over in the Sunday school ministry. She remained faithful to this ministry until God permitted her to attend Manna Bible Institute. Keeping her missionary vision in her heart, she received biblical training without knowing "the land that God wanted to give her as a heritage." After studying the needs for missionaries, she felt a call to Africa. After four years of biblical training (1960–64), she became a candidate at WEC International, Camp Hill, PA, 1965, in keeping with her missionary call. During this time she met the Rieders, who helped direct her, as well as other contacts, to the Ivory Coast to work among the Gouro people. After being

---

Nene Bi Tra Albert is a spiritual son of Daisie Whaley whom she had trained and had much influence in his life on the mission field in the Ivory Coast. He lives there now with his wife Elizabeth and heads the literacy program for WEC. He also is head of a team doing a revision of the Bible translation work for the Gouro language. He also translatated the JESUS film in Goro and Bete languages and played the part of Jesus. He and his wife are the right hand people for Daisie's work in the Ivory Coast and channels the support from her to the girls whom she had trained. He also heads up children's ministries. Nene Bi Tra Albert seeks to take more theological training for his ministry work.

Daisie Whaley passed away in March 2007.

accepted by the mission, she went to Canada to study French for two years from 1966–67. After that, she returned to leave for another adventure in the Christian life, taking a ship from Brooklyn, NY, on December 7, 1968, to go to the Ivory Coast, land of her vision. After a voyage of three weeks, she landed at Treichville (in Abidjan).

Arriving in the Ivory Coast for the first time, she was welcomed by John and Grace Rieder (church elders), Mr. & Mrs. Bolou Alphonse and Mr. Salomon of Abidjan. These weren't the only people waiting for reinforcements; there was also Mrs. Staniford, Misses Dicks Sandersan and Barbara Rowe, as well as Mr. Ian Crowe and Pastor Jeremie, an Ivoirian Pastor.

Ministry in Ivory Coast

Daisie's first impression:

> When I first arrived in the Ivory Coast, my vision was children's ministry. In the bus stations, in the market places, along the streets, all I saw was children. Children and nothing but children. Some sold merchandise, other shined shoes, others carried bags for a few coins." This statement showed me that from the time that her feet touched Ivoirian soil, it was the children that impressed her. She asked herself how to reach these children with the Gospel, how to touch their lives to lead them to Christ. "For me," she said, "these children who wander like sheep without a shepherd are the political and religious leaders of tomorrow. If only the church could help them to reach them for Christ."

When she arrived upcountry, she was assigned to work at Zuenoula by the Rieders. As she visited the villages, she was moved by the living conditions of the women and children. They were tied down to their village life, working seven days a week, working in the fields, returning, eating, playing without any concern for their eternal destiny. While laying in bed, as these scenes kept coming back to her, she asked herself this question: "How can I possibly reach these children with the Gospel?" During this time, she was already engrossed in learning the Gouro language, having started her studies from her second day at Zuenoula. To better learn the language, she put herself in the middle of this unknown people in the village of Zuenoula. She adapted quickly because she was able to adjust easily to the Gouro culture and food. She was also helped by Pastor Jeremie, Mrs. Staniford, and Pastor Zre Emmanuel.

Before the challenge of ministry to children and women, the Lord showed her a ministry with three dimensions: teaching religious courses in the primary schools, teaching the children in the village with pictures to learn Bible verses, teaching women in their villages and having meetings with them. By the grace of God this plan worked well. During this time, the Ivoirian government allowed missionaries to teach in elementary schools. She always asked herself how to have all of these activities and teachings work together to be able to evangelize the village children. When she became fluent in Gouro, she started teaching children in the Gouro villages. According to Daisie, if you want to reach these people, you can't wait around. You must go where they are, give them biblical teachings, whether open air, or in the tree shade. And that is what she did.

After a while, she saw the need to organize a children's camp in several Gouro villages as well as in several towns. In 1989, during a furlough, she presented her plan to hold Vacation Bible Schools in the Ivory Coast to her church and asked for volunteers to help her. They responded by sending a team led by Pastor Norman Griffin to hold a Vacation Bible School during summer vacation. The project was supported by "The Abundant Life Bible Ministries Missions." The Pastor and his wife are the founders of the mission, which had worked for over 20 years in urban ministry. Since they wanted to expand their horizons of ministry, they decided to support this ministry. They started in 1990 with a team of four persons and two suitcases of teaching materials. During this year, they worked in villages among three different ethnic groups, sharing the Word of God with 499 children. In 1991, 713 children heard the Gospel. In 1992, 1,729 children were touched by the Gospel. In 1993, 3,732 children were reached. In 1995, they worked in 24 villages, preaching to 6,619 children.

In 1996, she had three friends from PA visit her who helped her evangelize children. In 1997, they targeted the region of Oume. This time of ministry ended with the first nation children's camp of AEECI at the capital of Yamoussoukro. In 1998, a team of 26 persons, composed of seven ethnic groups, targeted the North of the Ivory Coast, a strongly Muslim region. During six weeks, 7,989 children heard the Word of God. They came with 26 carton of teaching materials and rented two 18 seat mini-buses. The help given by this missionary project was enormous. They had children's meetings throughout the Ivory Coast from Abidjan in the South to the Booko in the far North. As she ministered, Daisie noticed something—since there were no junior high or high schools in the villages, the students who were active Christians suddenly found themselves in large cities after passing the exam to go to junior high school. The social life there made it very difficult to live a Christian life. She wondered if the church couldn't do something for these young people. "Could they have a program to help these youth? Why not allow these young people to stay in one of the mission guest houses to help keep them in the faith." These questions kept coming to her every day. Daisie decided to help out these young men and women in a practical way. As her finances allowed, she took in several youth. She fed them and took care of their needs (clothing, money, shoes, etc.). I remember one year she had 22 persons, boys and girls, that she was taking care of, but every day that God gave, there was always food. During four years that I was under her care, I saw the Word of God lived out in seeing how she gave. In Proverbs 11:24 we read, "One man gives freely, yet gains even more; another withholds unduly, but comes to poverty." I am not saying that her gifts made her richer than other people, but she never was without. If there was a need, the Lord provided at the right time.

She shared what she had with the people, even to her last cent. According to her, as far as money and helping others is concerned, "Money means nothing to me. If I receive some, I use it for God's work. If it's all gone, God will provide because I live by faith." Isn't that a good example of biblical faith that all of us should learn from Daisie?

Difficulties in the Ministry

In doing her ministry Daisie had difficulties as all is the case with every servant of God. Having left her family to serve God, her preoccupation was to accomplish her vision. One day, when she was deep in thought and prayer about other leadings for ministry, the telephone rang. Someone wants to speak to "Tantie" (our name for her—meaning Auntie). What's it about? Her father passed away. What a shock! It was March 19, 1975. After several words of consolation from several people, she packed her bags and went to see her family. Twenty years later, to be precise, December 29,1995, a second death. One day, when we were working on developing strategies on how to pay for a new printing of the Gouro Bible, how to correct and edit other Gouro books as well as to translate other booklets, she received another shocking call—her brother George passed away. I saw her tears flow as she said, "I can't understand it." When we went to the airport with Mady Vaillant, a fellow missionary, I then realized that a missionary's life is one of sacrifice.

Three years later, another sad news about the death of her young sister. On April 27, 1998, Ellen Whaley left us. What sad news! It was hard for the family to lose two members in three years. She just talked with her the week before her death. Daisie asked her how her mother was doing. In all of that, she was not distraught nor did she leave the field, but she was submitted to God's Spirit to stay until it was His time to go.

The Goals Realized: Joyful Subjects

Even though she had these difficulties, Daisie didn't let up one bit, but she worked with all of the strength that the Lord gave her. Being at the end of her ministry in Ivory Coast, she felt like she can return with her head raised high because she didn't minister in vain. She had a vision of ministry like that of the Apostle Paul, who also didn't count his life as precious. This produced fruit. Unlike in 1969, when children's ministry was unknown here, this ministry has really taken off. Our church leaders, who weren't aware of the importance of this ministry, now see its value since the children form the church of tomorrow. This ministry has been well organized and she says, "I have placed it completely in the hands of the national leaders. I rejoice enormously over that." Secondly, women's ministry has become one of the pillars of the church.

Women I see teaching. I give glory to God because He has answered the wish of my heart. My last subject of joy is the evolution of the youth ministry in our churches. The young men and women are discipled and taught according to God's word. As far as the Gouro Literature ministry is concerned, the storage building is built, the Gouro Bibles are printed as well as several other books. I am gratified. I thank God because I can leave everything knowing that the church AEECI will have some very good leaders.

We see in the life of Daisie that she did not spend her life wisely according to the world. However, she abandoned control of her life to the Holy Spirit and her ministry has left rivers of living water that will last. She lived her life according to the will of God, which permitted Him to accomplish His desires and enabled her to put all of her strength and talents into the ministry. Can't she say that she has fought the good fight? Here is her testimony:

> I started discipling young village girls. They came to learn to read the Bible, whether in French or their native tongue. I also helped some young boys. I also worked with orphans as well as others who were sent away from their parents because they couldn't deal with them. By the grace of God, I was able to teach them to follow the Lord. I still saw the importance to enlarge my vision. There were girls who never had the opportunity to meet Jesus in their life. But in taking care of them and teaching them, they were able to become Christians. Before starting such a type of social project, I had to have the approval of the local church of Zuenoula. I also needed local help with all of the needs. God helped me in all of these projects. Thanks to the support of this church, I was able to exercise this ministry.

> After these young people became mature Christians, they needed to be involved in a ministry themselves. I suggested that they train others who, according to me, had made progress and could be used by the Lord. That was the reason why I sent several of them to the Discipleship School of Youth with a Mission (YWAM) in Burkina Faso. Thanks to that training, Sylvain and his wife went on to missionary service in Guinea Bissau. Two other youth, Modest and Moises (Moses), went to YWAM, camps which had a positive spiritual influence on their lives. By God's grace, my dreams in this area were realized. Today "my girls" are Pastor's wives, elder's wives and leaders in the church. I thank God that several of "my children" are in full-time ministry. This was the wish of my heart, and it has been perfectly realized. These are people who lived with me for years. Thanks to the churches that support me in America, I could take care of them and enable them to stay pure until their marriage. My sisters gave wedding gowns for these girls. They were originally intended for the girls that I raised, but as time went on I saw that I needed to let any girl who stayed pure until her marriage use it. Thanks be to God, I was able to leave these wedding gowns to the women's ministry of our churches (Women's Union of AEECI—UFAEECI).

> I'm leaving the Ivory Coast on December 7, 1998, to work in another ministry in the U.S. As Paul said, I am with you in heart and in spirit. Our Lord sent me to another assignment, always in His service. My most fervent wish is to be replaced by those I trained. I must also say that I thank God for my son, Nene Bi Tra Albert and his wife, Elizabeth. If you see them serving God today, I see in that how marvelous God's grace is.

> I wish and recommend to all those who have lived with me, who have benefitted of my aid and of my training to be open, and to open your doors to those who are in the same need.

> To my fellow missionaries I say this: From now on, work at committing your ministry into the hands of the national Christians. Your job is to be there to support them morally, materially and financially.

As an Ivoirian and a full-time Christian worker, the challenge is before us. Daisie has come, she has worked, sown the good seed. Her time here is at an end and she has left it up to us to continue what she has started. What will we do? Drop the ball or simply squander what has been brought to us? As Charles Studd, the founder of WEC, said one day, "True faith is like smallpox. When one has it, he passes it on to others and it is spread." Daisie did what she could do. We need to permit ourselves to be contaminated by her life full of zeal, faith and ardor for the Lord.

Chapter 32
The Mable McCombs Story

by Dorris E. Ngaujah

Dorris E. Ngaujah recently joined the adjunct faculty of Atlanta Christian College. She was professor of Missions, Evangelism, Urban Ministry, and Old Testament Survey at West Angeles Bible College in Los Angeles, CA, while pursuing Ph.D. studies in Intercultural Education at Biola University. Her work, in cross cultural missions spans four decades—beginning as one of Christians in Action (CinA) International's youngest licensed missionaries in 1971. She served a team in Sierra Leone, West Africa, and has led several short-term teams to Zimbabwe, Kenya, South Africa, and inner cities of the U.S. Dorris is passionate about students and missions; therefore, she has given many years of volunteer service to such organizations as InterVarsity Christian Fellowship (Atlanta, GA); Campus Crusade for Christ (Atlanta, GA); Adventures in Missions (Gainsville, GA); and Pathfinders International (Chicago, IL). Her two-fold goal is to develop culturally informed and sensitive communicators—especially cross-cultural Christian workers and to write life stories of missionaries of the African Diaspora.

Dorris has a grown son and daughter-in-law, Sahr and Ayesha Ngaujah. Parenting, however, began again for Dorris most recently as she became the legal guardian of her ten-year old goddaughter, Desiree Ngaujah, after the sudden death of her 41-year old mother, Denise, on July 3, 2005.

Spreading God's Word Among the Sick

The Muslim young man had been a hospital patient for some time and had pondered the message he had heard from the missionary each time she came to them. Finally, when she came that Thursday, he was ready. He began his prayer, "Mohammed, I ... " Mable McCombs interrupted him, "Un uh, not Mohammed." The man continued, "Mohammed, I'm leaving you today. Jesus, I'm coming to you, today, Thursday. Jesus, I'm coming to you today, Thursday."

Sharing God's Word with the sick and with those caring for the sick was one aspect of Mable's Liberian ministry that she immensely enjoyed. For 32 years, she weekly went to the government hospital and/or to the hospital at the ELWA (Eternal Love Winning Africa) compound. At 78, Mable McCombs says, "I was very timid at first. I would just quietly leave tracts here and there." People, however, were watching her and one day someone boldly confronted her with the question, "Ma, is this for me?" "Yes," she replied. "Oh, thank you, Ma." Immediately others started to gather the tracts, thanking her profusely. She discovered that the people would readily gather and listen attentively as she explained the Gospel message. She always had a receptive, though captive, audience at the hospitals.

This surprised her. Initially, however, what surprised Mable most upon her arrival in Liberia in 1962, was the fact that Liberians already knew about God. During her first week in the country, she heard a village chief pray thanking God for sending the missionaries to tell them more about Him. She thought they did not know. God had sent her and others there to make known God's plan of salvation through Jesus Christ. This knowledge comes from knowing the Word of God, the Bible. The Liberians she met were eager to receive the printed Word. They really wanted to know what God, or as they put it, "the Holy Bible" had to say.

One day, in the capital city of Monrovia, a young man walked up to her and said, "Ma, I want you to know that I am a Christian now." "When did you get saved?" She asked. "When you preached to me in the hospital, remember?" Mable could not remember, but she was tickled by the use of the word, "preached." She never considered herself a preacher. "I'm not a preacher," she told the young man. "I'm a missionary."

Called to Teach

Becoming a missionary was not a childhood dream of this 78-year-old veteran missionary. As I interviewed her, she told me that the very idea of people being in this world without knowledge of Jesus, the Savior was an unimaginable concept. "I had known about Jesus all my life. I just assumed everybody else knew about Him, too." At the mature age of 40, she understood the need for missionaries. Before this, Mable had spent her life pursuing varied opportunities. After graduating from Allen University in SC, she lived and worked in Atlanta, GA, for a while then moved on to New York City. After a time there, it was back to SC. In SC, she landed an elementary school teaching job. It was a secure position, though contracts had to be renewed each year. For ten years, teaching in America was, so it seemed, the career position she would keep for life. Well, she would be teaching for the rest of her life; but she would have a different employer. God had a bigger classroom in mind for her.

Mable was born November 17, 1921, in the town of Mt. Carmel of McCormick County, SC. She was the youngest girl and the seventh child of the nine born to William and Carrie Bell (Banks) McCombs. The McCombs, like most blacks in McCormick County, were farmers. Girls had to work as hard as the boys did. Cotton had to be planted and picked, vegetables had to be harvested and sold. When the family added cattle, the chores for everyone increased. Mable remembers the hardship of having to carry water from the fresh water springs. It was a strenuous job. "We didn't have a well, so we had spring water which we had to go and bring in." Because of chores, black children were only allowed to go to school four months of the year. Subsequently, most of them did not finish grammar school. Those that did complete grammar school were considerably older than today's eighth graders.

All the McCombs' kids finished grammar school regardless of their age. However, they were exceptions in another way. They went to high school and some, like Mable, went to college. Carrie Bell McCombs was determined to have all of her nine children get an "education." So, as each child finished grammar school, Mrs. McCombs sent that child away to high school. (There was no high school for black children in their area.) The four girls were sent away to board with families willing to house girls. The fee was $1 per month. One daughter continued her education with a family in Chicago, IL. All five of Mable's brothers were sent to boarding schools in SC. Mable proved to be a mature and focused learner. She graduated from high school on D-Day, June 6, 1944.

Having become a member of the Rockford AME Church when she was 12 years old, she had the opportunity to attend the Methodist's Allen University in Columbia, SC. She majored in English and graduated with a bachelors degree in three years.

Teacher Learns A New Lesson

She moved to Atlanta, but her stay was brief. She lived with cousins. When the rumor of "jobs up north" beckoned her, she went. She had no relatives in New York City, but she found lodging in a boarding house for single female workers. A few years passed, then Mable became seriously ill. She returned home to recover. As she improved she became involved in the Sunday school ministry of her church. In 1951, she started teaching at the grammar school.

For nine years, teaching at the school and being active in her church were routine for Mable. One day in 1960, just before school closed for the Christmas holidays, Mable received an unusual envelope at school. She opened it and discovered a tract from the Back to the Bible Radio broadcast. At first she felt insulted that someone would send her a tract when she was already a born-again Christian. However, she read it and the words pricked her heart. There was a series of questions on the little brochure—questions that were unfathomable to Mable. "Suppose Christ had not been born? Supposed the shepherds had only dreamed? Suppose? Suppose? Suppose? So far as the heathens are concern, all that I have supposed is true." Mable pondered the thought, "Do you mean there are people in the world that have never heard of Jesus? 'I'll tell them,'" she said to herself.

She went to church the next Sunday and asked God to make her a missionary. She had no idea how a person becomes a missionary, she just knew that since reading the tract, she had a strong desire to go to the heathens, the people who have never heard, and to tell them about Jesus.

The New Year came in and children returned to school. Mable taught class as usual but often her mind wandered as she daydreamed about going to Africa. While the children were at recess one spring day, Mable picked up the *Upper Room*, a devotional guide, and began reading. She still remembers the words, "Have you ever seen a grain field when it is fully ripe. It is a beautiful sight. But if they do not harvest it, it will fall to the ground. So is the mission field." Mable says, "My heart was just so burdened to think of all the people just falling the way grain falls." She felt the ache in her heart, but as the children returned to the classroom and as the rest of the day unfolded, she forgot about the grain falling to the ground.

The next day, again, while the children were at recess, she picked up the *Upper Room*, and opened to the same page as the day before. The accompanying scripture to the grain poem was, "Say not ye, There are yet four months, and then cometh harvest? Behold, I say unto you, Lift up your eyes, and look on the fields; for they are white already to harvest" (John 4:35 KJV). From that day onward, the rest of the school year was an emotional and spiritual struggle. "At times," Mable said, "I'd be tipping around the classroom, hoping no one noticed, with my mind far away—away across the waters to other children just looking for someone to tell them about Jesus."

A Broken Contract; A Commitment to Go

As the school year came to an end, the teachers were handed their contracts for the coming year. Mable had already decided not to sign hers. Instead, she had followed her cousin, Joshua Dunlap's advice and had applied to Carver Bible Institute, in Atlanta, GA. Hoping to hear from Carver shortly, she put off signing the contract as long as she could hoping Carver's acceptance would confirm her "call" to go to Africa. Fellow teachers told her that she should not refuse to sign the contract. They said, "If you are serious about going to Africa, you should sign the contract, then break it later." Jestingly, however, they continued to taunt her. They would say, "Girl, you know you will be the first one back in her classroom come fall. (By this time all children were going to school for the entire nine-month school year.)

Carver did not answer right away. She was forced to take a step of faith. So before the school year ended, Mable wrote the letter, breaking the contract, though she had not been accepted into Bible school. She felt such a sense of relief when she turned it in to her principal. She then went off to Atlanta, hoping her acceptance would soon follow. It did.

Initially, Carver used Ms. McCombs as a typing instructor. When school started in the fall, she went to class both night and day and took a correspondence course. "I wanted to get to the field fast." She finished with classes in a year's time and applied for missionary candidacy. When she asked Rev. W. D. Hungerpiller how long it would take to get to the field? He told her, "Maybe six months." She said, "I was so sick, I went home and went to bed." The fact of the matter is that for most missionaries it takes a year to raise support and complete the necessary processing for overseas ministry. Mable, however, was determined not to prolong the process. By late October 1962, Mable McCombs was on her way to New York to board the ship that would take her to the land she had dreamed of. She arrived in Monrovia, Liberia on November 16, 1962. It was most memorable for her because the following day was her 41st birthday. "My heart was so happy," she said as she recalled that day. The Carver missionaries that met her that November day, were Cora McCleary, Naomi Doles, Henrietta Herron, and Mary Faucett. The activity of that first day included a trip to the ELWA (Eternal Love Winning Africa) radio station and compound and a five-mile trip to the mission station. Not without car trouble, though. The new missionary would be living with other missionaries five miles from the ministry site located on Randall street—a facility that could only house two of the missionaries since the rest of the house was used for classrooms.

Challenging Students Further

The teams' main ministry at that time was in King Gray Village. Carver Foreign Mission had opened up a school there. It was 12 miles from the Randall Street place. Mable did not start teaching immediately, as the school year would soon to be over. However, she did embark on her hospital ministry and it became her "baby." When the new school season opened Mable taught the youngest of the children—those learning their ABC's. Because so many children and adults wanted to "learn book," Carver Foreign Mission conducted morning, afternoon, and night school, to accommodate. The adults came to night school. When Carver opened the Monrovia Bible Institute,

Mable served as one of the instructors there as well. The schedule was demanding but the variety was refreshing. Each missionary taught one night a week at MBI and four nights a week at the evening classes for adults.

Mable's greatest joy in teaching was seeing how readily the student's engaged in memorizing Bible passages. The missionary teachers had a hard time keeping assignments for the avid learners. Once, Mable went to the principal for a suggestion of what to give a star student to memorize. He had completely learned everything she had given him. The principal suggested 1 Corinthians 15—all 58 verses. Not only did that student learn them, so did another and another and another. Girls and boys took up the challenge and they learned 1 Corinthians chapter 15. Many of the King Gray students became lead quizzers at the Saturday night Bible Quiz held by Youth for Christ. The competition was aired on the ELWA radio station. The first young man to request more passages to learn is now an executive with the World Bank. The Liberians' reception of the Word of God was the impetus that kept Mable and her team going even when they were very tired. They could work everyday, all day, and still there would be people that would want a Gospel tract or want to know if there is a scripture addressing some issue.

Mable seemed to handle weariness quite different from the other ladies. She could work endlessly, it seemed; but she would get her rest. Whether it was strategy or narcolepsy, Mable had the unique ability to sleep instantly anywhere and any time. She would be refreshed and ready to go when duty demanded. Once, after a late night of ministry and conversation, Mable recalls going to the hospital the next day. She went by to visit a man who had been given a Bible. The man was still an inpatient and a friend was with him. The sick man welcomed her to his bedside and proudly told her, "Ma, I can read it to you." She listened. Then she pointed out that he had made a mistake. He continued reading. When he stopped, she told him that he was making the same mistake all the time. He tersely replied, "Ma, I learning it." The man attending him followed with, "Ma, I teaching him." She was encouraged and humbled to see that this man was spending his time in the hospital learning (memorizing) scripture, word-for-word and to see that his friend was committed to being there and teaching him. Sometimes, Mable would know that the person begging for a Bible was illiterate. She would ask, "Can you read?" "No, Ma," the person would reply, "but somebody will read it to me."

Mable could not get over how the Liberians loved the Word. If she took a basket of tracts to the hospital the people would throng her begging for Bible literature. On another tireless day at the hospital, a patient told her that he had been in Sierra Leone and he had seen a Study Bible. "Ma, I want a Study Bible," he told her. "Son, you gonna have to pray," she told him. The next time she saw him they had the same conversation. This went on for several weeks. Some friends of Carver came from Atlanta to visit the missionaries. One of them, a Mrs. Cornelius, gave Mable some money. She immediately went out and bought the Study Bible. When she returned to the hospital, the young man, not knowing that she was coming with the Bible, complained, "Ma, I been praying for the Study Bible. I want my Bible, Ma. I been praying." She was please to tell him, "Well, you got your Bible."

War Ceases Teaching Work

How long Mable would have stayed in Liberia is hard to say. She was not ready to come home and retire in 1996, when the war broke out again. She had come home for an emergency health evaluation. It was to be just a month-long visit. At the time of this writing, she has been home for four years. She currently lives in a high-rise for senior citizens on the west side of Atlanta. She continues to "preach" at churches and to encourage others.

1975–Present Era: African American Rise in Mission

Chapter 33

AFA Rise in Mission: 1976–Present

by Robert J. Stevens

Mission Awareness

By 1976, African-American college and university students became unrelenting in their demand for courses dealing with the experience of African Americans. During the 1980's and 1990's more books by African Americans were written and published than ever before. This included research and writing on missionaries. Many major themes of missionary work in the fields of education, medicine, social welfare and politics still await detailed investigation.[1] This is still true today.

What had missions in Africa accomplished? In 1900, there were a little over half a million Christians in Africa; by 1960, that figure had grown to almost 35 million and by the early 1980's, almost 130 million. By 2001, it was estimated that total population of Africa was 867 million, and the continent had become the second most populous in the world (exceeded only by Asia), with a Christian population that almost doubled since 1980. By 2000, the Christian community was to represent approximately 31.2 percent of the world's population. In 2010, the population was 1,033,042,510 with 41.2 percent under 15 years of age with an overall life expectancy of 59.9 throughout the country.[2] Africa may well be the home of one of the largest Christian communities in the world.[3]

This new interest in cultural history and finding your "roots" among African Americans began a new surge of interest in missions. Many more began to start their own missionary groups and increased knowledge of world missions was made available. But, still, many continued to be "community-minded" in building up the African Americans at home.

A New Vision

God is raising up a new generation of pastors in the African-American church: pastors who are being led to seek opportunities for their own involvement and that of their congregations, in

---

1 Sylvia Jacobs, "Black Americans and the Missionary Movement in Africa," *Contributions in Afro-American and African Studies*, no. 66 (Westport, CT: Greenwood Press, 1982).
2 Jason Mandryk, *Operation World*, completely revised 7th edition (Colorado Springs, CO: Biblica, 2010), 30.
3 Patrick J. St. G. Johnstone, *World Handbook for the World Christian* (South Pasadena, CA: World Christian Book Shelf, 1976), 17–18, 111, 118–119, 122; and David B. Barrett and Todd M. Johnson, *World Christian Trends* (Pasadena, CA: William Carey Library, 2001).

international missions. International partnerships between African-American congregations, associations, state conventions and fellowships in the U.S. and overseas entitles the developing trend toward ever-increasing numbers of African Americans giving their lives overseas, and serving long-term as Christian missionaries.[4]

While studying for her doctorate, Shirley Wright came into contact with Campus Crusade. Through this contact she gained a vision for missions and began serving with Campus Crusade in Nigeria in 1983 as a teacher and campus ministry leader. When denied a visa, she began working with the Campus Crusade ministry, Here's Life Black America. With a passion burning for the Hausa people in her heart, Shirley began working with the Hausa people in Cameroon in 1990 through the Baptist General Conference. It was here that she met her husband Wilondja. They are serving the unreached Hausa people.[5]

Opportunities

The African-American church has both the resources and manpower to lend a strong voice in the missions world. Indeed, many say that African Americans are in a position to become one of the most effective mission forces in the world today.[6] Despite the many historical, cultural, and spiritual challenges, the African-American church has never been closer to rousing herself to the Great Commission. In fact, at least 12 factors combine to give great, but sober, optimism: (1) Africa and other nations are wide open to African-American missionaries; (2) Civil rights legislation is in place in America; (3) White mission agencies and schools welcome African-American candidates; (4) Evangelical Christian Bible institutes and colleges not only welcome minorities, but some provide special funding for minority attendance. Thus, proper preparation for the field is far more available today; (5) New African-American nondenominational mission agencies have arisen; (6) Racism is newly and increasingly unpopular among white Christians, as illustrated by the pledge of the Promise Keeper movement; (7) The necessity of the African-American church serving interculturally has a higher profile through indigenous efforts such as The Destiny Movement (especially through 1992) and the Cooperative Mission Network of the African Dispersion (COMINAD); (8) Independent and other churches are committing to a foreign missions program; (9) Black income has risen in the past 20 years and black church income is fully sufficient to fund missions; (10) Black clergy also have access to the aforementioned schools, which hopefully impacts their pulpit teaching and preaching ministry, including evangelical missions theology; (11) The world is getting over, in Crawford Loritts' words, "white idolization," and other ethnic groups are both accepted and are picking up the mission torch; (12) Opportunities for short-term mission exposure abound—a very potent recruitment tool.[7]

---

4 David Cornelius, "A Historical Survey of African-Americans in World Mission," *Perspectives on the World Christian Movement, A Reader*, edited by Ralph D. Winter and Steven C. Hawthorne (Pasadena, CA: William Carey Library, 3rd edition, 1999), 291.
5 Vaughn Walston, "Today's Leaders," "Ignite the Passion," *Mission Frontiers* (April 2000), 17.
6 Rebecca Walston and Robert Stevens, "Moving Beyond Community," *African-American Experience in World Mission: A Call Beyond Community* (Pasadena, CA: William Carey Library, 2002) by Cooperative Mission Network of the African Dispersion (COMINAD).
7 Jim Sutherland, "How Black is the Harvester? A Profile of the African-American Intercultural Missionary Force, The Extent of the Problem," *African-American Experience in World Mission: A Call Beyond Community* (Pasadena, CA: William Carey Library, 2002) by Cooperative Mission Network of the African Dispersion (COMINAD).

Chapter 34

Reconciliation in Mission— Brian Johnson's Story

edited by Miss Jean and Dorris Ngaujah

Brian Johnson is the national coordinator for the Cooperative Missions Network of the African Dispersion (COMINAD). He served as pastor, Bible college professor, Christian schoolteacher, and a foreign missionary and has worked for Carver International Missions, World Relief Cooperation, and the International African-American Mission Mobilization project. While in Africa, he was principal of the Monrovia Bible College, field supervisor of Carver Missions of Liberia, secretary general for the Association of Evangelicals, and the country director for World Relief Corp in Liberia where he was tasked with microenterprise development, war trauma counseling, facilitating for reconciling ethnic groups, and relief assistance. World Relief honored him with its Helping Hands Award in 1997. Brian continues to do ministry in Africa.

This chapter was edited by Miss Jean, projects manager for the Southeast Regional Office of the USCWM. She has served administratively in mission work with ISI, ELIC, CMI, and USCWM.

Dr. Dorris Ngaujah, a former African-American missionary to Sierra Leone, West Africa, is now a missionary in Kenya.

Taken from the article "Escape from Liberia" by Bonne Steffen, *Christian Reader* (currently known as *Today's Christian*), November/December 1996. Used by permission. Also used by permission are excerpts from Brian's teaching lectures for Perspectives on the World Christian Movement for USCWM SE.

Helping Hands Award

In March 1997, World Relief honored Brian Johnson with its eighteenth annual Helping Hands Award for his dedication to the people of Liberia. It was while Brian was in Liberia (a country about the size of SC) that he faced continued personal risk. "Brian worked tirelessly to promote reconciliation among Liberia's warring ethnic groups," said Bas Vanderzlam, World Relief's vice president of International Ministries. The same ethnic divisions that pulled the country apart in civil war also pulled the church apart. God used Brian to help bring unity among church leaders, to the various people groups, and within the Association of Evangelicals (AEL) in Liberia. They were able to work together to help the hurts of the Liberian people.

Johnson, a native of Detroit, Michigan, first arrived in Liberia as a self-employed missionary in 1973. He met and fell in love with Ruth, a beautiful Liberian girl. He first noticed her when he was washing his clothes by hand in a bucket. All the other girls were laughing at the way he was washing his clothes because he didn't know how to wash by hand. He just put his clothes in the bucket, soaked them and rinsed them out. Ruth was the only one who did not laugh at him. She walked up to him and with a sweet voice asked if she could help. Her sweet spirit won him over and they got married that same year. They married in Liberia and there they raised four children, Tangie, Nyutu, Keyshia and Kristina, and enjoyed peaceful times in Liberia. Johnson's first work in Liberia was as a liaison between Liberian church leaders and American pastors. This helped to prepare him for the difficult task of bridge building that was yet to come.

From 1983 to 1989, Brian Johnson worked under Carver Foreign Missions in Liberia and dedicated himself to teaching and training Liberians for Christian leadership through the Monrovia Bible Institute and College and the Carver Christian Academy. When civil war erupted in December 1989 the Johnsons were scheduled to leave Liberia for their furlough, which was to last for one year. They could not imagine that that time home would be extended for three years. While they were in the States, Brian pastored a church in Detroit. He could hardly wait for the time when he and his family could go back to Liberia to continue his mission work. The Johnsons, as well as other people, believed that the war would not last long, but after the unsuccessful attempt by rebel Charles Taylor to speedily overthrow Liberian President Samuel Doe, the war dragged on. Eventually, another rebel leader killed President Doe but that did not bring the war to an end. Waiting for the war to end was not an option for Brian, so he went back to Liberia in 1993 to participate in a reconciliation conference sponsored by World Relief Corporation and the AEL. The conference was so inspiring that Brian returned to Liberia with Ruth and his two younger children in 1994 to help with peace building and development.

Upon their return, hope for a unified country was strong. Brian's new role as World Relief's country director was dangerous. His task was to bring healing to the fractured evangelical church in Liberia and develop a ministry of assistance for people's physical needs. Because of the respect Johnson had earned from the Liberian Church over the years, he was asked by the leadership of the evangelical churches in Liberia to assume the position of secretary general for the AEL. His job would be to guide them in reconciliation and in meaningful relief development work. They also wanted him to help develop the association's capacity to do missions and to establish programs geared toward church renewal. The reconciliation work soon went beyond the evangelical churches as warring faction leaders were drawn to the associations' biblically based workshops on healing for broken people.

Though Brian Johnson rejoiced at the changed lives witnessed at the reconciliation conferences, he knew his work was facing a formidable foe—the business of war. He sought opportunities to speak out on American radio stations and write to American public officials about the United States' arms that were in the hands of child fighters in Liberia and Sierra Leone and about the use of arms from France, Briton, Israel, China and Russia. Arms dealers were supplying arms that were fueling the wars. The trade in arms was so formidable and so many people were making money off the commercial trade in arms that Brian gave up trying to work toward eliminating the commercial interest in arms and just continued to work toward the reconciliation of the people that were fighting the war. "When you have governments sanctioning their weapons that are going to warlords, and when big money is involved, you can't get very far without massive groups of people speaking out against this injustice," said Johnson. Politically, in 1990, ECOMOG, a West African military peacekeeping group, stepped in to quell the hostilities in the country, but violence continued randomly throughout the country.

In May 1994, Ruth's father, aunt, and two cousins were murdered in a raid, along with most of their village, 200 miles from Monrovia. This horrific event occurred three weeks before a major reconciliation meeting sponsored by the AEL. Johnson pushed the conference on, and he and Ruth joined other groups in praying for personal freedom from bitterness.

Leaders from other West African nations proposed a new strategy in March 1995. It entailed asking factional leaders, whom had been the warlords leading the people into the civil war, to move to Monrovia and work together as the country's collective leadership for a year. They thought that this move would lead to peace. The goal was to have, at the end of that year, a national election to determine who would run the country as its next president. Johnson admits the proposed political change seemed strange. The idea of putting warlords into leadership roles didn't seem to be a step in the right direction. His hunch was right.

As each warlord arrived in the capital, each gradually brought heavily armed fighters into the capital city. Monrovia swelled with young fighters—some only eight or ten years old. They were made to feel grown-up with a steady supply of drugs and weapons. It was only a matter of time before violence would be ignited.

Less than a year after the six-member State Council was established, men were killed near the house of one factional leader. The others in power tried to arrest the warlord who lived near the killings on murder charges, but he wouldn't surrender. His claim was that all warlords were guilty of murder. If he was arrested, every warlord should be arrested. When they attacked his house, he escaped and then the struggle for control intensified.

Terror by Day and Night

Early in 1996, war erupted again and engulfed Monrovia, trapping the Johnson family in their home on the outskirts of town. At first, the fears were mentioned only in discreet conversations as the atrocities in the country's interior were reported on the radio. But in March, a warlord's son (a long-time family friend) visited the Johnsons at their home, seven miles from Monrovia. When daughter Tangie (visiting from the U.S.)

came out with water for him, a teenage boy ran over from a nearby basketball court, knocked the pitcher out of her hand, and said angrily, "You didn't give me a drink why are you giving water to a murderer's son?" Trying to remain calm but shaking inside from the vicious verbal exchange, Tangie explained, he was a friend before the war as was the case with many people before the civil war. That's the tragedy of civil wars, some people were friends before the war, but because in some cases the war is along tribal lines or according to economical status, people gravitate to people who are of their own ethnic groups or status and begin to fight those who were friends before. Nothing more happened between the young man and Johnson's daughter.

Tension was rapidly building. The Johnson's short-wave radio tuned to the embassy station continually repeated, "All Americans stay home today. Don't go into the streets." But there was work to be done. The first week of April, Brian was helping unload 12 World Relief food containers that had just been released from the port, supplies which would be looted in the next few days. With the faction leaders announcing over the radio that everyone should remain calm, Brian hoped the city would avoid violence. Then, as hundreds of rebels poured into Monrovia's streets, shooting erupted and anarchy ruled. Brian managed to get safely back to his house. Young rebels with familiar faces—children and teenagers whom the Johnsons had fed and clothed—now began to harass the neighborhood. First, they came for vehicles. Carrying AK-47s and huge knives, they called each other by Hollywood names like "Rambo" and "Commando." To the Johnsons' horror, the rebels seemed to be playing a game, boasting of how may people they had killed. Most of them were high on drugs. Over the next three days, different warring bands came to the house ten times to demand possessions. Day or night, the Johnsons never knew when the next band of rebels would appear.

Meanwhile, missionaries and people from different tribes sought shelter in the Johnson home, including some from the tribe that murdered Ruth's family. When a gang of rebels came to the house, Brian would step out of the front door of the house to hear their demands, knowing that if they discovered who was inside, everyone could be killed. Befriending people from other tribes and factions was now a compassionate, but deadly consideration.

Over their short-wave radio, the Johnsons could hear people throughout the city pleading for help. All the people in the Johnson house were praying and trying to keep the children quiet so the rebels would not come in the house and start killing. There were missionaries, people that they did not know and friends scattered in every room and in the hallway, away from any windows. Without weapons, everyone in the house knew they couldn't resist the rebels' demands. After everything had been looted, one gang made a more frightening threat, "We'll be back for your women," he said. That night, Wednesday, April 10, three rebels, each about 18 years old, came to the Johnsons' porch. Brian, as he had done previously, came out and sat down. He didn't want the gunmen to simply walk into the house.

For forty-five minutes, no one said anything. One rebel was smoking marijuana; a second stood with head down, exhausted; the third was sitting near Johnson. All cradled AK-47s on their laps. Johnson closed his eyes and silently prayed. After an hour, he couldn't stand the strain any more. He slowly stood up and went inside the house. No one moved. At first, Johnson stood behind the door, thinking the gunmen would try to break it down. Then he lay down on the floor, praying for four hours. At daybreak, to Brian's surprise, the gunmen simply walked away.

A Ten-Minute Window

Brian knew he had to get everyone to move and move quickly. On the mission compound, there was an old bus. Groups of rebels had noticed it, but though each group had talked about stealing it, none had. The tires were near flat, and Brian knew it took a half hour to warm up, but it was their only hope. Approximately 20 people jammed into the bus. Amazingly, when the driver turned the ignition key, the motor started right up. He drove across the street to the Sudan Interior Mission (SIM) and radio station (ELWA) compound. Brian told the driver to go around to the mission's air pump and fill the tires. Brian wondered why he told the driver to fill the tires up with air because it was discussed within the mission circles and the U.S. embassy that if missionaries were in danger, the U.S. military would rescue the missionaries by helicopter from the radio station compound so all we needed to do was wait there. Just when they got out of the bus and greeted other missionaries and friends, the American embassy radioed a message to SIM: "You have ten minutes to prepare for evacuation. An armed convoy, employed be the American embassy, will arrive at the mission to get any foreigners out. If you're not ready in ten minutes, you'll be left behind."

Brian couldn't believe God's timing and provision—the prompting to leave early that morning with bags packed, the "miracle bus" that started, and now tires filled with air, praise God for His faithfulness. God, Brian believed, had not allowed the rebels to take the bus so that he would be able to take other missionaries also. Without the bus the other missionaries would have been stranded. Within ten minutes the embassy convoy arrived. "We're going to drive very fast and you must keep up with us," the embassy personnel told Brian. "If you don't keep up, we can't wait for you." They told Brian this because the bus he was driving was old and filled with people.

Brian placed the old bus with all the people in the middle of the 20-vehicle convoy. He felt that if he was going too slowly others would not leave his group and maybe the convoy would slow down. They careened through the back streets of Monrovia amid heavy shooting and the smoke from burning buildings. Although the ride to the military base was only seven miles it seemed to last forever. Arriving unharmed, they waited until the next day before a helicopter arrived to make the final evacuation to Sierra Leone. The Johnsons were among the last Americans to be airlifted out of Liberia. From Sierra Leone, the evacuees were taken to Senegal where it was peaceful. Nevertheless for Brian, his thoughts were turned toward his return to Liberia's border areas to continue World Relief's work from there.

Ruth thought of the homeless, the starving, of those who lost family members and of the many friends left behind. Months later she missed the family photos and drawings the children had made. Important documents that were stolen were impossible to replace. There were moments when Keyshia and Kristina could laugh over the absurdity of what they went through, but they also missed their Liberian friends.

Brian did return shortly thereafter and several times after that to assist with relief projects. Faced with the enormity of the country's losses, he wanted to do what he could to relieve the suffering. Brian continues to facilitate reconciliation efforts in Africa and to advise African church leaders and to give assistance in community and economic development. Most of his current ministry is in cooperation with the Cooperative Missions Network of the African Dispersion (COMINAD). Each time he returns to the United States from Africa, it's a culture shock from the painful reality of what he has seen in Liberia. Trying to get back to a "normal American life" evades him.

Brian Speaks On Reconciliation in Mission

I went to the mission field in 1973, traveling long distances by airplane, cars and on foot. I met many people who had many problems. What I have realized over the years is that if Christians communicate Jesus—He died for us, He was buried, He rose again—without being reconciled to each other, the Gospel message we proclaim is not believable. The Bible says, "By this shall all men know that you are my disciples if you have love one for one another" (John 13:35 NKJV). God has armed Christians with a message that promises reconciliation if believed (2 Corinthians 5:19b). This message that is communicated to others is the message that reconciles sinful mankind to a loving God. Christians must concentrate on proclaiming the message but they must also concentrate on making the message believable. In the United States, we are very individualistic. When a non-Christian would ask a Christian a question such as, "How do you Christians know that Jesus is real?" Or "how do you Christians know that you have salvation?" Normally, we will answer these questions in an individualistic way. We American Christians normally will answer, "Well, I know I have salvation because ... " and it will all relate to what Christ did for me, and what I am doing for Him. But what's the answer when someone asks God the question, "How can you prove that your power is real?" Paul said in Romans 1:16, "For I am not ashamed of the Gospel of Christ for it is the power of God unto salvation." So, the idea of "power" is very important. The question to God is, "How can I be sure your Gospel has power?" While I am sure God will point to the transformed lives of believers, I believe He will also point to His church. The Gospel's power is evident when the reconciled nature of His body is clearly seen.

It is important for Christians to understand their role in making the Gospel believable is proclaiming Christ by the power of their unity. Now He has reconciled us by His blood through organically making us His body. All He did was put us in an environment (the church) and lets us know, through His word, that we are one.

We know that we must endeavor to work at being like Christ (holy), but it hasn't been so clearly proclaimed that we must work at becoming visibly reconciled to each other so that the reconciling Gospel message can be believed.

Reconciliation is one of the goals that we are working toward through the COMINAD network. The network reconciles church denominations, local churches, individuals, mission agencies and other ethnic groups. The goals through reconciliation are to produce greater resources for global missions and to strengthen the presentation of the Gospel message in the world. The initial targets are Christian descendants of Africa and bringing them into a reconciled relationship with Christians of other ethnic groups so that we can accomplish the task of global missions together.

COMINAD harnesses, within its network, people that have a real heart for missions and for the church of Jesus Christ. These faithful people concentrate on educating other Christians about missions and developing resources to help get the Gospel to the world. We create tools for pastors to help them develop a global vision for their churches and mediate when churches or individual Christians are having difficulties with each other both in the United States and in other countries.

Besides developing tools for missions training, we expose Christians to unsaved people around the world that need to be reached with the Gospel. There are many trips scheduled throughout the year that Christians are encouraged to take so that they can have a better understanding of the needs of people around the world and how they can get involved.

We believe that it is only through a network such as COMINAD that we can mobilize churches with all their differences to work toward the common goal of the great commission. The network allows for communication between groups and churches. This communication allows us to pray for common concerns together, cooperate on mission endeavors together and train others together.

COMINAD is very much needed by the church in the African Diaspora, because the network name, Cooperative Missions Network of the African Dispersion, creates unity and harnesses all descendants of Africa. African descendants are scattered throughout the world but they are called by various names. For example, in the United States they are called African Americans. In the Caribbean they are called Afro-Caribbean and in Brazil they are called Afro-Brazilian. Through developing a common network name that unites our people, some of the walls that divide us are automatically broken down.

The greatest enemy to God's mission work is division among His followers. As was stated earlier, a reconciled group of believers make the message of Christ more believable, but also the lack of reconciliation hinders the development of resources necessary for the task of the Great Commission.

The Church's Response to Division

While overseas, I worked with African tribal groups that needed and still need reconciliation among them. Some of the tribes that have, in the past, been fighting and killing each other through warfare requested mediators to help. Doing the work of a mediator with warring groups is probably the hardest work I have ever done. Plus it is so dangerous. In fact, my family and I were evacuated out of West Africa by the American military in 1996, after being in a terrible situation for a long period of time—guns pointed at our heads and other dangers related to war which created tremendous hardships. But, through that process, I was able to see the importance of God's church speaking with one voice through the world media about the plight of us as Christians suffering in a country far from their own. This is another reason to motivate the church worldwide to work toward reconciliation. God desires His church, as a whole, to be able to speak with one voice, so that the voices of persecuted or suffering Christians can be heard worldwide. Therefore, another goal of reconciliation is advocacy.

When most people think about the nations of the world they think of countries as nations. But, the other way of looking at nations is to not think about geopolitical boundaries as nations at all. Countries, nowadays, should be seen as countries containing nations. According to Scripture the nations are the people groups or language groups that are within countries. These are the nations that the Lord is talking about in Matthew 28:19. What you see within countries are nations that are sometimes at odds with each other. The Lord is asking us as His body to help facilitate through the message of the Gospel these people coming to Him. Satan might not have created the divisions between peoples but he certainly adds sinful stimuli to ferment discord between peoples. Matthew 28:19–20 seems to be saying that the goal of the Great Commission is to target people from the various people groups around the world to become disciples of Jesus Christ. If this is the case, the Holy Spirit seeks to deploy an army of believers that make up people from these groups and equip them with the skills to communicate Jesus to the world and at the same time equip them with the skills to reconcile people within these groupings so people can draw people to Christ.

I remember when I was in South Africa at the Global Consultation on World Evangelization (GCOWE) conference in 1997, while we were discussing how to reach the rest of the world with the Gospel, spontaneous requests for reconciliation could be heard from people who had been at odds in the past. One American church denomination confessed their pride by requesting forgiveness from everyone at the conference because they thought they could reach the world themselves and didn't need the rest of the church of Jesus Christ. They had finally come to the conclusion that, because of the magnitude of the task, they really needed the rest of the church. But, I believe it was God's intent that the whole church working together should bring the lost to Him. It is not just because of the greatness of the task or the chaos and divisions in the world, but God intends for us to work together so that the church reflects what He intended from the beginning, that people from every tribe, peoples, nation, and tongues be in heaven.

At almost every meeting during the conference, God motivated someone or a group of people to reach out and appeal for forgiveness from someone that they might have had problems with in the past. Although it might not have been the person asking for forgiveness who was responsible for the problems, in some cases they apologized for their ancestors who were responsible. For example, White American Christians would ask African-American Christians to forgive their ancestors for the brutality their ancestors had inflicted on the ancestors of African Americans. The Tutsis and the Hutus would ask forgiveness for their longstanding tribal differences. The Palestinians and the Jews, who were Christians now, asked for forgiveness for their respective peoples and voiced their desire to work together on getting the Gospel to the world. Even though the conference did not have a segment in the program for reconciliation it was as if God knew that He could not reach the world through us unless we were first reconciled to each other.

Under God's Mandate for Mission

"Mandate" means to pursue and accomplish a task. God's mandate to Christians is to fulfill His purpose for all history. It is very important for us to realize that we are under mandate. God is trying to do something that He has planned before the beginning of the world. The rebellion of Satan and his fallen angels was not a surprise to God. Furthermore, the conversion of people around the world was also planned. In Ephesians 1:4, it says, you,(the believers, and all the believers around the world) were chosen before the foundation of the world in Christ Jesus. God doesn't see events in the past, present, or future. He sees things in the NOW.' He sees you and me sitting in the heavenly places right now.

The mission endeavor is not the goal. It is not an end in itself. Mission leads to something—there is a purpose in it. God had lost the intimate relationship He had with human beings in the sin that Adam committed. Before Adam and Eve sinned, God and Adam used to have a good time together. There was good conversation, there was good relationship and everything was so wonderful. Then one day God came to Adam and found him hiding. Adam had never hidden from God before so God said, "Where are you Adam? Where are you in relationship with Me?" was his question. By the way, that is the question to all humanity who is not rightly related to God. The losing of God's intimate relationship with man troubled God and hurt Him very much.

The Lord impressed upon me that the whole Christmas story was as much a blessing for God as it was for us. God, who had lost His intimate relationship with man, saw in this little boy

(Jesus), the beginning of the cessation of hostility that existed between human beings and Himself. He pulled the veil of heaven back and let the angels be seen by human beings. When the shepherds saw and heard the great praise in the sky they were dumbfounded. The shepherds probably told Mary and Joseph what had happened and they were dumbfounded. God's excitement can be seen in how He orchestrated the appearance of the angels with the wonderful praise they were saying. It meant that now through His Son, mankind could be drawn back to Him. I think that that is why the angels said, "Peace on earth to men of goodwill." Now through a relationship with Christ—that is what Christianity is—mankind can now give Him worship and have fellowship with God again.

We Shall Gather Around the Throne

We don't seem to be in much of a hurry but I think God can hardly wait to have three groups of beings in heaven having a good time with Him. Actually, I think, God envisioned this good time in heaven and put everything in place in order to accomplish His plan. So you can read the Bible backwards from the book of Revelation to the book of Genesis to get a better understanding of the plan of God instead of reading the Bible forward.

According to Revelation 4:4 (NKJV), the first group to be identified at the party in heaven is the twenty-four Elders: "Around the throne were twenty-four thrones and on the thrones I saw twenty-four Elders sitting, clothed in white gowns, and they had crowns of gold on their heads." First of all, we see a group of people in heaven, but who are they? There is some debate among Bible-believing Christians on this issue. Some say these Elders are representatives of the church of Jesus Christ, which is on the earth now but will be in heaven in the future. Others say it is the church of Jesus Christ, represented by the twelve apostles, and the Old Testament saints represented by one elder for each of the twelve tribes of Israel. It is my belief that these twenty-four Elders represent the Church of Jesus Christ and possibly the Old Testament saints. If there are 12 elders representing the church and 12 elders representing the Old Testament saints then it means that the Great Commission did not start with the church but way back in Genesis.

The church of Jesus Christ, I believe, started on the day of Pentecost and ends, as far as the earth is concerned, when the church is raptured to heaven. For one thing, in Revelation chapters 1, 2 and 3, we see that church of Jesus Christ on the earth. But in chapter 4 we see a different scene: redeemed people from the earth around the throne. Even if there is some controversy over whom these twenty-four Elders are, most Bible scholars believe these are redeemed people from the earth. The Elders are clothed in white robes and have crowns of gold on their heads. The robes represent purity and the crowns represent exaltation and rewards. We are not told here the reason for their exalted position in heaven but we do see them casting their crowns at the feet of Jesus and saying Jesus is worthy, not them, to receive exaltation. This seems so much like the attitude of Christians who are now on the earth who understand the significance of salvation by grace alone. Christians receive salvation which they don't deserve and an exalted position in heaven according to other scriptures beside this one in Revelation 4:4 for nothing they have done. They are not just doormen in heaven but they are exalted. This group is always falling down and worshipping. There seems to be a difference, according to other scriptures as well as this scripture, between praise and worship. The difference is in the posture of the ones doing the praising or worshipping. Praise is generally done with uplifted hands and heads, singing, or praying and telling God and others of His greatness and His accomplishments. Worship, on the other hand, is usually done from a prostrated position. Judging from the worship position that the twenty-four Elders in heaven, it seems to me that God wants those who receive Christ to have a life of prostration or submission to the lordship of Christ. This prostrated life starts at the time of salvation and continues throughout eternity. The great rebellion in heaven that Satan masterminded in the past will never happen again. Neither will it happen from redeemed human beings because the lordship issue is completely understood by those who are redeemed from the earth.

We see another group of beings at the heavenly party according to Revelation 4:8 (NKJV), "The four living creatures, each having 6 six wings were full of eyes, around and within, and they did not rest day and night saying, "Holy, Holy, Holy, Lord God almighty, who was and is and is to come'." Whenever the living creatures gave honor and thanks to him who sits on the throne who lives forever and ever, the twenty-four Elders fall down before Him who sits on the throne and worshipped Him who lives forever and ever and they cast their crowns before the throne saying, "You are worthy O Lord to receive glory and honor and power, for you have created all things and by your will they exist and they were created."

These beings worshipping God at this time are angels with six wings. According to the way they are described they seem very much like the Seraphim's in Isaiah 6. The Seraphim's were huge six-winged angels always committed to worshiping God. They fly around calling to one another, "Holy, holy, holy is the Lord Almighty; the whole earth is full of his glory." With two wings they cover their faces, with two wings that cover their bodies and with two wings they fly. Other Bible scholars believe that these huge angels are cherubims, another type of angel that guards the mercy seat in heaven. There are also other angels mentioned, of which we humans cannot count, at the party, also.

If it is true that the first group, the twenty-four Elders, represent the church, then every time these angels cry "holy, holy, holy" we fall on our faces, worship, and take the crowns off our heads and throw them at Christ' feet.

In Revelation 5:8, when He had taken the scroll—that is Jesus—the twenty-four Elders fall down and worship and also the angels fall down before the Lamb and worship. Every creature seems to be falling down before the Lamb. The group represented by the twenty-four Elders seems to represent redeemed people from every tribe, every tongue, and every nation. God seems to want, and He gets, people from every tribe on the earth, every people group on the earth. So now we get a clearer picture through the scene in heaven of who is invited and what they are doing. Revelation 7:9–17 (NKJV) says:

> After these things I looked and behold a great multitude which no one could number of all nations, tribes and tongues, standing before the throne and before the Lamb, clothed in white robes, and palm branches in their hands. And crying with a loud voice saying, salvation belongs to our God who sits on the throne, and to the Lamb. And all the angels stood around the throne, and the Elders and the four living creatures, and fell down before the throne on their faces, and worshipped God, saying, "Amen: Blessing, and glory, and wisdom, and thanksgiving, and honor, and power, and might, be unto our God for ever and ever. Amen." Then one of the Elders answered, saying to me, "Who are these in white robes, and where do they come from." And I said to him, "Sir, you know." So he said to me, "These are the ones who came out of the great tribulation, and washed their robes and made them white in the blood of the Lamb, therefore they are before the throne of God and serve Him day and night in his temple: and He who sits on the throne will dwell among them. They neither hunger, neither thirst any more, the sun shall not strike them, nor any heat. For the Lamb, that is in the midst of the throne, shall feed them, and will shepherd them and lead them to the fountains of living water. And God will wipe away all their tears from their eyes.

According to this passage, God is inviting another group of people to His heavenly party. They seem to be different from the other group. The question to John seems to indicate that these are different people from the twenty-four Elders. One of the Elders say to John, "Who are these and where do they come from?" (Rev 7:13). The indication that these are different groups are not just because of the question to John but this group does not have golden crowns on their heads like the twenty-four Elders do and they have palm branches in their hands. They also, come up through great tribulation and wash their robes and made them white in the blood of the Lamb. There is no mention of the group represented by the twenty-four Elder as coming up through great tribulation. They are before the throne doing service to God. I am sure this includes worship but it might include other service. Although this group seems to be different from the first group they have several things in common. They both have white robes, they both worship and they have representatives from every nation, every tribe and every tongue.

Every nation, tribe and every tongue must have representatives in heaven according to God's plan. This could mean that maybe He has enough white Irish people and enough black Zulus for His heavenly party. He might not have enough Curds but He may have enough Arabs for

His party. If God is targeting people groups we should be open to going anywhere in the world to preach the Gospel and not just proclaim Christ in our own home countries. God doesn't let us know whom specifically the individuals within people groups He is receiving but we do know He is targeting individual people groups. As was stated earlier, the Greek term *ethnos* translated to "nation" in the English Bible, and in Matthew 28:19, it refers to people groups or language groups, not geopolitical countries of the world. Since we don't know who the individuals are within people groups, God commands all Christians to "Go ye into all the world, and preach the gospel to every creature" (Mark 16:15b). Now that we understand what God is trying to do, having all ethnicities represented in heaven, church leaders around the world can broaden their ministry trust to the world and this is possible even in some churches' local areas because some of the people groups from around the world are right hear in our country. So now our local churches can represent peoples from every flavor of peoples within our communities.

It seems like a nice thing that God is trying to reach out to all people because He created all of us. But, why is He keen on displaying these saved targeted people from each people group? I am not sure why but I can say, according to Ephesians 3:10-11, who He is doing it for. Ephesians 3:10-11 (NIV) "His intent was that now, through the church, the manifold wisdom of God should be made known to the rulers and authorities in the heavenly realms, according to his eternal purpose which he accomplished in Christ Jesus our Lord." The term "manifold" means multiethnic, which could also mean multicolored, because multiethnic groups display multicolors. The New Living Bible reads: "God's purpose was to show his wisdom in its rich variety to all the rulers and authority in the heavenly realm."

This whole thing of bringing in every culture, every tongue, and every tribe is displayed for the angels. We know there is warfare going on above our heads; in the heavens there are the good angels and the bad angels doing battle. The goal of the battles seems to be "worship." Satan's angels are trying to get people to bow down and worship him and God's angels are trying to get people to bow down and worship God. We know from scripture who is going to win the war because according to Philippians 2:10-11, when the Lord comes back, every eye shall see him and every knee shall bow to him and declare him to be Lord. Satan's whole revolt in heaven was over his desire to be like God and to enjoy the worship of his subjects. He even tried to get the Son of God to bow down and worship him. So the prize God and Satan receives from the battles of the war is worship from angels and people. Satan's ultimate enemy is God, but Christians are his enemies also. We are his enemy because we can offer up worship to God. This he cannot stand. We also can bring others to worship God. So he tries to nullify the life of Christians by keeping them from being missionaries. He does this by destroying their characters through luring them to sin and unfruitfulness. When Satan and his angels are victorious over a Christian, they give each other high fives. When a Christian sins or neglects God's mission, they do not just hurt themselves, but demons laugh in excitement because they are successful in keeping worship and worshippers away from God.

I previously said that I could tell you to whom God was presenting this multiethnic and multicolored church, but I could not tell you why. I can tell you that ultimately all things lead to God's glory. The term principalities and powers in heavenly places refer both good and bad angels (Eph 3:11).

The good angels can neither figure out why the mysterious multiethnic nature of the church is so important nor can they appreciate the exalted position given to redeemed sinners. Bad angels or demons are just simply bent on deceiving people so that Satan will be worshipped and not God. Satan's modus operandi is to create as much divisiveness as he can. The important action to watch for when observing Satan's work is his ability to create division among people. God's modus operandi is reconciling people to Himself and to each other through the power of the Holy Spirit within his body. Satan is trying to create the greatest amount of destruction that he can and God is trying to bring about as much peace as He can. Satan's message to create as much destruction as he can is centered in the term "selfishness" (you can be like God). But God's message to the world, which brings peace, is a message of reconciliation—the Gospel. The Gospel is a message that reconciles people to God, but it cannot be preached with authenticity unless people, who are reconciled to each other, preach it. This would mean that if God is going to win the war with Satan by getting a multiethnic group of people in heaven, He has to have a church that understands what the goal is (every tribe, nation and tongue), reflect that multiethnic mission force that goes throughout the world and lives harmoniously with each other so that the reconciliation message that brings people to God can be believed.

Mission Enterprise

In order to ensure the goal of having this great eternal party of worship and praise by multiethnic groups of people in heaven God put His plan into operation. He called out a man named Abram from a city in Mesopotamia called Ur.

If I were God, and thank God I am not, I would not have made my mission of redeeming people a human and divine effort. From what I see of the human contribution to reaching the world for God's planned heavenly party gives me great cause for concern. But, God is still inviting believers to join Him in His enterprise of global missions.

God first called Abram to join Him in reaching people for His redemptive plan according to Genesis 12:1–3. He was told by God, to come out from the place he lived, leave his extended family and go to a place that He would show him. He did not do exactly what he was told. First of all, he left his city and his father's house, but he took his father and his nephew Lot with him and went to the city of Haran. He stayed in Haran for some years until his father died. Abram was disobedient right from the start. So you can see what I mean when I say that, "If I were God and thank God I am not, I would not have made my mission of redeeming people a human and divine effort." Human beings are just so unreliable. But, Abram was God's chosen man and He tells him that through him and his posterity all of the nations of the earth will be blessed. God's plan seems to have been as Abram and his descendant went around from place to place their faithful holy blessed lives would bring light to the world and people would be drown to God and be saved. Also, it was through Abram and his descendants that the Savior of the world would come.

Right from the beginning God was very intentional in allowing the radiant light of Himself, though Abram, be seen by all peoples. There were many people who believed in the God of Abram (who became Abraham), because of God's power and the righteous example that he and his descendants displayed to the world; people such as Joseph, David, and Moses.

God's light to the world was clearly seen through Abraham and his descendants, but when they became disobedient the light began to diminish. People were not being blessed because Abraham's descendants (Israel) became idolatrous. Instead of God being worshipped because of Israel, Israel had been drawn, either by their lust or by other people, into the worship of other gods. The gods that they worshipped were heavenly bodies, man made images, images of human beings and human parts and animals. They also worshipped at the altars of their own sensual appetites. It was because of their idolatry that the spotlight was directed away from God and His goodness. So God sent judgment on Abraham's descendants.

One of the consequences of God's judgment on His people was the pagan lordship of their nation. They were taken captive by the Assyrians, the Babylonians, the Medes and Persians, the Greeks then the Romans. While God was bringing judgment upon them because of idolatry, He still was faithful to his promise to Abraham. He still used Abraham's descendants to reflect His glory and message to the world. The world saw through God's judgment of His people that He is a holy God and serious about His people being faithful to Him.

Not only through the judgment of His people did God reach others for Himself but He also used men like Daniel, Hananiah, Mishael and Azaria to be a blessing to all the people on earth. All four of these men were taken captive by the Babylonians and became instruments for God by resisting the idolatry of their pagan rulers. Although, they were condemned to death by these rulers, God miraculously delivered theme from death, which in turn caused the rulers to proclaim the message of the true God to all the people of the known world at that time. God got the message of His power and sovereignty over the world to every person on earth through the Babylonian king, Nebuchadnezzar. He was God's missionary voice to all nations, peoples, languages and tongues (Dan 3:29–30). The facilitators to get the message out through the king were Hananiah, Mishael and Azaria. God used Daniel to get the message of His power and sovereignty over the entire world to a much larger group of people than Nebuchadnezzar ruled. Darius, the Persian king that ruled the known world after defeating the Babylonians, proclaimed throughout his entire kingdom that the God of Daniel is the God to be worshipped and served above all gods. His decree went out to all nations, peoples, languages and tongues (Dan 6:25–27).

I am amazed that God would put His trust in these four men. If they had not played their parts well as faithful servants, the message about the power of God would not have been proclaimed at this time. Daniel had to be willing to go into the lion's den and the Hebrew boys had to be willing to go into the fiery furnace rather than disobey God. Their obedience, to God alone, lead to God's message being proclaimed throughout the whole world. The alliance between the divine and the human in order to reach the world is a risky proposition but in this case it worked well. It is risky if the human participants are not committed, obedient servants of God. I can see why our Lord said to His disciples that if they wanted to follow Him they must hate their families; that their possessions must not posses them; and they must take up their crosses and they must die to themselves in order to follow Him. God's work depends on Christians who are willing to sacrifice for Him by laying down all they have, even their own lives, for that is the message He is giving to the world. The message is rendered less powerful when Christians do not live the message.

Everything was going well for God, but not going well for the Israelites. The expansion of God's kingdom was on schedule but the Israelites were still experiencing national domination. First, it was by the Assyrians, second the Babylonians, third the Medes and the Persians and after these groups the Greeks. In 334–331 BC the Greeks began their rule of the world under their leader Alexander the Great. Alexander permitted the Israelites to observe their laws and be exempted from taxation. But, Alexander sought to Hellenize them.

The imposition of the Greek language and culture on the nation of Israelites was called Hellenization. The Greek language was not bad but the Israelites didn't like the Greek culture. The Greek culture was very much man centered. You can see this in the statues they carved. The gods they worshipped were glorified humans and not the true God of the Jews. The Jews had real problems with the idolatry and immorality of Greek culture, but for over two hundred years the Jews were allowed to practice their religion and they prospered.

After Alexander died his empire was divided among four of his generals. These generals fought each other for control of all the empire and eventually one prevailed. His name was Seleucus. Seleucus and his descendants created what is called the Seleucid Empire. The Seleucid Empire dominated much of what had been Alexander's domain. Eventually, the Jews found themselves controlled by a Seleucid emperor named Antichus Epiphanes IV who wanted to be worshipped as God. He forbade the Jews from circumcising their male children under penalty of death. The Jewish religion was declared illegal, which meant that there could not be worship on the Sabbath and no reading of the Torah.

The Jews rebelled and eventually their rebellion escalated into all-out fighting when a priest named Mattathias and his five sons started what is called the Maccabean Revolt. It was named after one of the priest called Judas Maccabeus. The Maccabean Revolt started when in 168 BC Antiochus marched into Jerusalem, put an altar to Zeus over the temple altar, offered a pig on it then made the Jews eat it. After some time the Jews were successful in defeating Antiochus, allowing Judas to rebuild the altar and restore the worship of God.

God's promise of blessing, given to Abraham and his posterity and then extending to all the earth, had been proclaimed in various ways through the Jews, but it was at this time in history that the message was in its greatest danger of ceasing. As long the Israelites were showing the world who God was and proclaiming the message that God should be worshipped by all the peoples of the earth, God was pleased. It was at this time in history that they stopped proclaiming God to every tribe, peoples, nations and tongues because they became ethnocentric. The biggest danger to God's plan—of reaching every tribe, people, nation and tongue—is for His people to shut off the light to the rest of the world by becoming ethnocentric. There are many reasons why the Jews became ethnocentric and we would do well to learn from their downfall so that we don't make the same mistakes they did. It is through the church that God's plan and promise is to be carried on.

What is ethnocentrism and how does a group of people become ethnocentric? Ethnocentrism is the belief that ones own ethnic group is superior to any other group of people. The Jewish superiority complex, which rendered them useless to God's plan, came from their forgetting who they were and why God chose them. They remembered and took pride in their family line going all the way back to Abraham. They remembered that they were special to God but they forget that they were special because God wanted to use them to be a blessing to the entire world and not just be receivers of His blessings. There was not very much for them to boast about during the captivities by the Assyrians, the Babylonians or the Medo-Persians, but under the Greeks they had fought and won the right to practice their religion. They translated the Bible into Greek, they built places of worship called synagogues, new groups of teachers called the Pharisees, and Sadducees and the Scribes together with other more radical groups appeared during this time. The pride they possessed because of their accomplishments caused them to focus God's light inward on themselves only, which closed the door for their witness to the world. Therefore, by the time they were dominated by the Roman Empire, God was ready to do something new and different from what He had done in the past.

Jesus' Ministry Was Universal in Scope

Right from the opening of the New Testament we see the universal scope of the God's message. It was a few days after the birth of Jesus Christ that we see international significance proclaimed. Do you remember what Simeon said when he had the baby Jesus in his arms in Luke 2:25–33? "Now I can depart in peace for I have seen the Messiah, God's salvation for the Gentiles." It is interesting to note that the genealogy of Christ included gentiles such as Ruth (a Moabite), Tamar (a Canaanite) and Rahab, and some in the line of Christ were half Jews and half Gentile, such as Solomon, David's son by Bathsheba Uriah's wife. Matthew's genealogy of Christ, charts the family line through which God presented the gift to the world that would be a blessing to all who would receive Him. God's gift to the world, given through Abraham and his descendants, was His Son.

Jesus' baptism also had universal significance (Luke 3:4–6); all flesh shall see the salvation of God. The starting of our Lord's ministry in Capernaum outside of Jerusalem was strategic to His plan (Matt 4:13–16). His plan is clearly seen in these verses, "The land of Zebulun and the land of Naphtali, by the way of the sea, beyond the Jordan, Galilee of the Gentiles: The people who sat in darkness have seen a great light, and upon those who sat in the region and shadow of death Light has dawned" (Matt 4:15–16 NKJV). His ministry first influenced Gentiles in Syria and went everywhere (Matt 4:24–25).

From the beginning Jesus prepared His disciples for an international ministry when He allowed them to be a part of His evangelism trust into Samaria, where they met the woman at the well in Sycar (John 4:5). Jesus said that He needed to go through Samara because God had to get some Samaritans for His heavenly party. This trip through Samaria was also for his disciples to observe first hand his plan because they were going to be the foundation for what He wanted to accomplish—the church.

The Multiethnic Makeup of the Church

The church was something new and at this time in history, just something in the mind of God. The church of Jesus Christ was not mentioned before the first mentioning of it in Matthew 16:18. We know it was in the future because our Lord said, "Upon this rock I will build my church and the gates of hell shall not prevail against it" (KJV). Neither the disciples nor the woman at the well nor the believing Samaritans knew that they were going to be a part of His new body of believers in the earth.

The church actually started about 50 days after the resurrection of Jesus Christ. It was on the day of Pentecost, according to Acts 2, that God sent the Holy Spirit to do something new by bringing many people to Christ starting with the Jews who had come to Jerusalem on the day of Pentecost. The Holy Spirit continued, according to other passages in Acts, to reach out to other distinct groups of people. This followed God's plan going all the way back to Abraham.

The Holy Spirit was on the move, bringing believers into the church. It is noteworthy to see when and where God decided to start the church. His plan was to start the church in Jerusalem on the day of Pentecost. The day of Pentecost was 50 days after Passover on the Jewish calendar. Pentecost means "fiftieth" and refers to the feast of Weeks (Ex 34:22,23) or Harvest. I believe the Holy Spirit chose this day because this day offered the way for the most effective avenue to harvest people from every tribe, people, nation and tongue. Acts 2:5 (NKJV) says, "And there were dwelling in Jerusalem Jews, devout men, from every nation under heaven." Then the passage goes on to list where these Jews were from because, I believe, God wanted some from each area of the world to believe in Him but also so those at the feast could take the message back to their own home areas which would result in others believing in Him.

On this day three thousand people were saved according to Acts 2:41 and the Lord continued to add to the church daily those who were being saved (Acts 2:47).

The Holy Spirit was not moving among the people randomly according to the book of Acts. He was following the plan, targeting and drawing Jews and proselytes, then reaching out to Samaritans (Acts 8), then Gentiles (Acts 10) and last of all, those who were baptized unto John's baptism (Acts 19). Through following this plan of targeting these groups the Holy Spirit knew He would get some people from every tribe, people, nation and tongue.

The church's greatest appeal to the world was the love that Christians had for each other. This love was how unbelievers recognized who were real followers of Christ. The Christians were all of one heart and shared what they had with each other so that all of their needs were met (Acts 4:32–35). This type of love was unheard of in that day so this was a powerful force in winning people to Christ. The oneness of the body of Christ was brought home to everyone by the method the Holy Spirit used in harvesting the four groups: Jews and proselytes, Samaritans, Gentiles and those baptized unto John's baptism.

The Church of Jesus Christ

The body Christ began by the pouring out of the Holy Spirit on believers as Joel the prophet predicted (Joel 2:28–29). God used the idea of speaking in tongues to draw the attention of all who were at the feast of Pentecost. Those who were in the upper room began to speak in languages not their own but in the languages of the people who were in Jerusalem for Pentecost. They were, according to Acts, talking about the wonderful works of God (Acts 2:11). We know from 1 Corinthians 14:22 that speaking in tongues is a sign to unbelievers and that was the case on the day of Pentecost. The tongue-speaking ability of the disciples amazed the people and caused them to listen to the Gospel message proclaimed by Peter. Many of the Jews did not believe Peter's message about God's Messiah but some did believe and were saved.

The next people group the Holy Spirit went to was the Samaritans according to Acts chapter eight. The Holy Spirit fell on the Samaritans differently than He did on the Jew on the day of Pentecost. As the Jews were praying in the upper room the Holy Spirit simply fell on all that was in the upper room, but in the case of these Samaritans the disciples laid their hands on them, then the Holy Spirit came upon them. It was also different when the Holy Spirit came upon the Gentiles in Acts chapter ten without any hands being laid on them. Cornelius and his family were just listening to Peter, and the Holy Spirit just fell on them. The last group the Holy Spirit targeted was those baptized unto John's baptism in Acts chapter nineteen. These people were not around to experience the events in Jerusalem but they had traveled away from the area where John the Baptist had baptized them and had preached. Paul found them and laid his hands on them and they received the Holy Spirit.

I believe the Holy Spirit was teaching a profound truth in the way He filled the lives of these groups of Christians. The Holy Spirit falling on the Samaritans came only when the apostles, being Jews, laid their hands on them. Historically, the Jews did not like the Samaritans and thought they were better than them. But, also the Samaritans did not like the Jews and thought they were just as good as or better than the Jews. I can see this from the conversation Jesus had with the woman at the well in Samaria. She said Jews don't have any dealings with them. She was right, as seen from the surprised look of the disciples when they saw Jesus talking to the woman. How arrogant the Jews were. But the woman arrogantly said, "Are you greater than our father Jacob who drank from this well and his cattle?" The Samaritans' pride came from their claim of descendance from Jacob. I believe the Samaritans were humbled when Peter, a Jew, laid hands on them and they received the Holy Spirit. In the case of the Gentiles, the Holy Spirit fell on them before Peter could lay his hands on them. This must have humbled the Jews who thought they were better than the Samaritans but thought they were much better then the Gentiles. In the last case, it was Paul who laid hands on John's converts. Somehow, I believe, the Lord dealt with the pride in John's disciples by using Paul whose authority, as an apostle, was challenged on many occasions. I think all of these four groups got the message that in the church of Jesus Christ everybody is equal. Peter echoed this when he said in Acts 10:34 (KJV), "Of a truth I perceive that God is no respecter of persons: But in every nation he that fears Him, and works righteousness, is accepted with Him." This was quite a revelation to all, no more Jew and Gentile, slave nor free, intellectual and illiterate, ruling class and underclass, rich and poor, but everyone has equal access to God and everyone in the body of Christ is related by the new birth.

It seems like the Holy Spirit was accomplishing His goal of setting the stage for a church that would reflect the multiethnic make up that He wanted.

The Holy Spirit was doing His part by drawing people to God but, as you remember, the task of world evangelization is a human and divine effort and it was the human witness to the world that could have caused God's plan to lose steam. The discrimination and prejudice recorded in Acts chapter six could have hindered the witness of the church if the apostles had not acted quickly to prevent Satan from gaining a foothold in the church.

In Acts chapter thirteen, we see a very mature church. The church had godly officers serving God and His church who were committed to prayer. The church was mature enough to send out missionaries. It is important to note that its leadership was made up of different ethnic groups and those of different social status.

One of the biggest treats to the multiethnic makeup of the church was recorded in Acts fifteen. The problem came from a group of believers, who were of the sect of the Pharisees, and spread throughout the church. Their contention was that although the Gentiles were saved, it was not enough to make them right with God. They said that Gentile believers must be circumcised and keep the Law of Moses in order to be fully saved. Paul and Barnabas went to Jerusalem to confer with the apostles and Elders so that this matter could be settled as soon as possible because Paul's ministry was to the Gentiles and there was a lot of dissension among Christians. This dissension could have caused great harm to the health and witness of the church.

After a long time of debate, Peter stood up in the midst of them and said, "Brothers, you know that some time ago God made a choice among you that the Gentiles might hear from my lips the message of the gospel and believe. God, who knows the heart, showed that he accepted them by giving the Holy Spirit, just as he did to us. He made no distinction between them, and us for he purified their hearts by faith. Now then, why do you try to test God by putting on the necks of the disciples a yoke that neither our fathers' nor we have been able to bear? No! We believe it is through the grace of our Lord Jesus that we are saved, just as they are" (Acts 15:6–11 NIV).

Maintaining a Reconciled Testimony

Peter's words seem to have settled the issue but James added something I think he felt was necessary for maintaining unity among believers. James stood up and said, according to Acts 15:19–20 (KJV), "Wherefore my sentence is, that we trouble not them, which from among the Gentiles are turned to God: But that we write unto them, that they abstain from pollutions of idols, and from fornication, and from things strangled, and from blood." James was aware of the negative feelings the Jews had toward the Gentiles. The Jews even called the Gentiles dogs and they avoided them at all cost. Now God was including the Gentiles in His church, of which many Jews had already become a part. James was trying to make the Gentiles more acceptable to the Jewish Christians. He knew the Gentile ate different foods than the Jews and some of their food was just not acceptable by the Jews. He had four demands that he hoped the Gentiles would accept to do. Not to be saved, because they were already saved and God had already accepted them, but these suggestions about lifestyle customs would bring about less interpersonal problems in the church.

The first suggestion was that the Gentiles stop eating meat offered to idols. This first suggestion probably disturbed the Apostle Paul because he felt that an idol was nothing in and of itself, and the meat was the best meat you could find, so he enjoyed collecting and eating the good meat offered to idols. The second suggestion was that the

Gentiles abstain from fornication. The term fornication mentioned in this passage means "sexual immorality" of any kind. It included having sex with someone you are not married to and having sex with someone who is married. This could be sex before marriage and sex after marriage. It also included people having sex with animals. Sexual immorality was a part of Gentile pagan religions, so it would seem proper for James to suggest this right from the beginning so that the church would remain pure, but would also limit sexual relationship between Jews and Gentiles. There was more to this idea of fornication from the Old Testament that James might have been thinking about. In Leviticus eighteen Moses records God's prohibition of marrying near kin. The Gentiles practiced incest, and the Jews also had a history of marrying near kin before God issued His command against the practice. With all this Christian love to share I am sure James was thinking of the day when there would be interracial marriage among Jews and Gentiles so if the biological problems (birth defects) that might be caused by marriages to near kin was eliminated, things would be better for all of them. The third suggestion was that they abstain from things strangled. This was the avoidance of eating the flesh of strangled animals, which therefore still contained the blood. The fourth suggestion was that they abstain from drinking blood. The drinking of animal's blood was a common practice among pagans in that day.

Gentile Christians are to be exempted from circumcision, but for the sake of Jews living among them they too must be prepared to make concessions and abstain from offensive practices, if Gentiles and Jew are to enjoy full social intercourse together in a united church. James was trying to avert confrontation between Jewish Christians and Gentiles Christians over the practices that go against the scruples of the Jews. James needed to get these rules voted on and accepted as soon as possible because just before Christians celebrated the Lord's Supper they enjoyed a love feast. It was called a "love feast" because everyone would bring a potluck plate from home and share with all who were there. At times there was not much love shown because when some wealthier Christians would come to the feast with a lot of good food on their potluck plate and the poor Christians came with little to share, the poor people ate well but did not contribute much. This was a problem that could have gotten out of hand. The wealthier Christians came up with a solution but it only caused more stress among the body of Christ. The wealthier Christian came to the love feast early and ate up all their food before the others came. The problem was not really solved by this action, so Paul had to deal with this problem by telling the Christians that if they could not share equally they should stop having the feast altogether. There would have been other major problems during the love feast if the Gentiles brought meat offered to idols, strangled animal meat, and a large jar of blood. I think James was trying to maintain harmony within the body, but I don't think it was fair that the Gentiles should have to give up their eating customs just to satisfy the inflexibility of the Jews.

We understand that God is trying to get people from every tribe, people, nation and tongue in His body, the church. He knows that when He calls us into His body we become one. He gets us into His body when we are reconciled to Him by believing the Gospel, which is a message of reconciliation. The draw back to this process is that the Gospel message, as was stated before, is not believable unless Christians are reconciled themselves. That is why our Lord said in John 13:35 (NIV), "By this shall all men know that you are my disciples if you love one another." James understood this so he suggested a formula to avert confrontation and, thankfully, the Gentile Christians accepted the suggestions. Sometimes Christians don't understand what God is trying to do in His body and what He is trying to do with His body. I think we should understand that God is always trying to do something in us (the fruit of the Spirit) and also trying to do something with us (communicate a reconciling message to the world).

I admit that I don't understand why a multiethnic-loving church body communicating Jesus to the world is so important to God, other than that is multiethnic people who He is trying to draw to Himself, making the job flow much easier if they love each other. So the drawing power of this multiethnic composition is the love they have for each other. I can understand how this would be so effective and so powerful because this type of love is so rare.

There seems more that the Lord is after by using love to win people to Himself. Because when we read the passage in Ephesians 3:10 we see that God had others in mind (principalities and powers) to whom He is displaying His reconciled church. I can't begin to understand why this is so important to God, but ultimately I am sure God will receive greater glory from His Angels and Satan and his demons will experience greater humiliation. It could be that Satan observed what God was doing from the beginning and sought ways to defeat His plan and God is showing him that His plan is still working. One way Satan tried to hinder God's plan was by creating multi-ethnic unity at the Tower of Babel, but with him as the head.

Movement of Power and Authority

Matthew 28:19–20 is generally referred to as the Great Commission. The Lord told the disciples to "[g]o therefore and make disciples of all the nations (ethnos), baptizing them in the name of the Father and of the Son and of the Holy Spirit, teaching them to observe all things that I have commanded you; and lo, I am with you always, even to the end of the age" (NKJV). It is through this command to our Lord's disciples and us that He desired to mobilize and direct His church to harvesting people from every tribe, people, nation and tongue for heaven. It is also through this command that He desired to prepare people from every tribe, people, nation and tongue for what they will be doing (worshipping) in heaven.

He starts out His commission by letting them know that He has the authority from God the Father to command them to make disciples of every nation. Also, when the disciples heard that He was in charge of everything in heaven and in earth they understood what they must do and when they would know they had completed their task. By stating His position over everything in heaven and earth the automatic response of the disciples is submission and obedience. I know the definition of the term "disciple" is one who follows or one who is a learner. There are many people today constantly learning about Christ, which was the case when our Lord was here on earth, but there is very little change in their lives towards being like Christ and serving Him. The only ones who became like Christ and served Him with all their hearts were those who acquiesced to His domination of their lives.

It is my belief that Paul became a disciple of Christ on the road to Damascus. As he was on his way a light shined suddenly from heaven round about him and those who were with him. They were all knocked from their horses to the ground but only Paul experienced blindness. The words that came out of his mouth lets me know that he was a disciple at that moment. His first question was an acknowledgement of Christ' sovereignty over his life: "Who are you Lord?" (Acts 9:5) His next question, "What would you have me to do?" began the process of learning and following Jesus without complaint or retreat. The issue of lordship and mastery over Paul's life was established on that road.

It was not long after this that Paul began to address himself as a slave. I saw this tactic used when I was drafted into the U.S. Army in the 1960s. The Vietnam war was raging and many young men of my age group were trying to get out of going into the Army. We were afraid of going to the war because we did not want to die. Some guys escaped to Canada before they were drafted, but I chose to obey the law and submit my life to the Army. As we traveled to Fort Knox in Kentucky, the fear was difficult for some of the young men to bear. When we got off the bus they lined us up and we went into an auditorium to be processed in. We sat in chairs waiting to see what was next. All of a sudden a man with a Smokey the Bear hat on his head came walking out from behind the curtains above us on a high stage. He seemed eight feet tall with shoulders about forty inches across with a waist size of twenty-four inches. He wasn't really that big, but somehow our eyes were playing tricks on us. The first thing he said to us was, "You punks, from now on I am you mother, father, grandfather and grandmother." One of the guys fainted just by the sight of the man and his declaration. Our Lord, in His great commission, started out the same way. He stated that He is in charge of everything in heaven and earth. I understood later that if the Army was going to be able to send us into battle where we might lose everything, they must establish a position of authority over us right from the beginning. They needed submission from us so they established a position of authority. Submission is a natural response on the part of a person when faced with someone who has absolute authority over him or her. The English term "power" used in Matthew 28:18, in the Old King James Bible is the Greek word *exousia*, meaning authority. Another word for power is *dynamis* as recorded in Romans 1:16. This term means force, ability or might. This term shows God's omnipotence or strength. Exousia or authority is a different kind of power receiving its dominance from position or status, such as a king. The position of authority that our Lord has should produce voluntary submission on the part of everybody on earth in order for it to be a true declaration. But, there are some who will not bow to His authority voluntarily, but one day they will bow to His authority (dynamis) but it will be because they experience His power on them. Dynamis does not require voluntary compliance because the Lord's omnipotent power is enough to cause people to submit even if they do not want to. One day our Lord will come back and every eye shall see Him and every knee shall bow and every tongue shall confess that He is Lord (Philippians 2:10–11).

In the days of the disciples and until our Lord comes back, Jesus seems to be asking His disciples (ones who have bowed) to make people from every ethnos voluntarily submit to Him as Lord. I know this sounds contradictory "making people voluntarily submit" to Jesus as Lord. How does one "make" someone voluntarily submit? I think by the term "make" he is asking the disciples to make them want to submit to Him as Lord. I realize that it is impossible, if someone does not want to submit, to submit to someone as the authority over his or her lives without demonstrating physical power over that person, but the Lord wants a submissive heart and not just physical submission. The heart of the person has to be changed where they will see the Lord Jesus as someone they want to submit to. I think that was what He was asking the disciples and all true believers to do as they travel throughout the entire world.

Our Lord asked the disciples to baptize converts in the name of the Father, the Son and the Holy Spirit. The name of the Father, Son and the Holy Spirit is not a formula for baptizing converts. It is an outward demonstration to the world of a change of allegiance. God wanted His disciples to make people want to change allegiance from what they are aligned to before coming to Christ and transfer their allegiance to the totality of the Godhead. The outward demonstration of their change of allegiance is being baptized in water, being seen by others, so that the world can know whose side they are on. If you notice in the book of Acts some converts were baptized in the name of Jesus Christ. This was because all of those people, including Cornelius, a devout man and the Ethiopian eunuch who had come to Jerusalem to worship, had no problem showing to the world their allegiance to the Father and the Holy Spirit but they did have a problem openly declaring allegiance to Jesus. As the church progressed through the second century, declaring open allegiance meant certain persecution for them.

Last of all, our Lord asked the disciples to teach people to obey or observe everything that He had commanded them. He did not ask the disciples to teach prospective disciples everything that Jesus had taught them, although teaching everything that Jesus taught is involved in being an effective disciple. He asked the disciples to teach obedience to Him as Lord. In a world with so many competing voices, this submission to the voice of the Lord alone is absolutely necessary to be a follower of Christ. Mary told the servants at the wedding of Cana, "whatever He says do it." How does one teach a person to obey? When I raised my children, I had to teach them to obey me. This had to be done long before they got into a situation that could harm them. They had to understand that I had authority over them and if I wanted voluntary compliance to what I told them, they had to know that I loved them. They also had to believe that I knew what I was talking about when I advised them. These three things have to be communicated to people about Jesus if they are going to grow as followers of Christ. The most important thing in making disciples is for the prospective disciple to see the disciple maker to be one who submits to Christ. Without this submission on the part of the disciple maker, it is very difficult for people to become disciples of Christ.

The Lord was asking the disciples to make people willing to submit to His Lordship, change allegiance and obey Him. I think if we get people to do this, God will have a good hold on the person then we can go on to someone else and disciple them.

The Problem of Idolatry

God knows that man's greatest problem is idolatry. It is from idolatry that all other sins flow. What our Lord was asking the disciples to do was to vanquish all other gods in a person's life by inserting Christ as the only God over their lives. This seems to be what God was doing when He used the declarations of King Nebuchadnezzar and King Darius. The kings declared to the world that the God of the Hebrew boys and the God of Daniel was in charge of everything. The natural response to their command should have been for all the people on earth to submit and obey the God of Daniel and the Hebrew boys.

When we see idolatrous practices in the scriptures it is usually someone bowing down to animate or inanimate objects. But idolatry can be the worship of man himself as was recorded in Romans 1. The Bible also states that some people worship the god of their stomachs (Phil 3:19). This means worshipping at the altar of one's own senses. Their desires come first before anyone or anything. The rich, young ruler rejected Christ and forfeited eternal life because he was not willing to let Jesus supplant his god (money) with Himself. In winning someone to Christ it is important to identify the idols in their life and showing them that Christ is a better God to worship than the god or gods they are worshipping. I am convinced that churches all over the world have people in them who are not disciples of Christ. Many of these people are attempting to worship the true God while still worshipping their idols. It is impossible to do both because when Christ is accepted in one's life He comes into his or her life to take full control of their lives. It is only after the gods of a person are supplanted by accepting Christ as sovereign that a person can become a disciple of Christ. In certain cultures of the world, it is difficult to identify the idols in the lives of the people because many of the people are syncretistic with their beliefs. Although their beliefs are syncretistic, their gods must be identified then challenged as to whether these gods can give eternal life. Idols can provide certain things, this is why people serve them, but real life that is eternal should be the goal.

In conclusion, the Lord is going to have His grand celebration in heaven. The people that He will have in heaven will be from every nation or ethnos (people group). They will all, including the angels, be bowing down and worshipping Him. God is using Christians today to get the right people to heaven and to make sure these people bow down and worship Christ throughout all eternity. There will not be any boasting in heaven unless it comes from God. So Christians are to make sure that people bow down to Christ and present all they have to Him now on earth. This will prepare them for what it will be like in heaven. Making a disciple is the same as making a worshiper. Presenting one's body is our spiritual service of worship according to Romans 12:1b. Disciples are worshipers of Christ and they bring others to worship Christ. Satan is angry with disciples because they worship Christ and they can bring others to worship. Christ is the Lord of all and worthy of submitting to.

The most powerful way a Christian can make a disciple is to, first of all, show the prospective disciple a life that is totally submitted to Christ. They must first see someone who submits to Jesus as Lord, has no other allegiances and obeys Christ completely. Good quality service for Christ comes from a life that has been laid down. Our Lord Jesus Christ said to Satan, "Thou shalt worship the Lord thy God and Him only shalt you serve" (Luke 4:8 KJV). The word for worship in this passage is "prostration" in Greek. Worship is done through laying down one's life for Christ. That is our message to all nations so when a person surrenders to Christ once and for all they are disciples of Christ. It is only through a surrendered life that real service to Christ can be performed.

Now that we understand the extent to where we should go in making a disciple (all ethnic groups), and when they become a disciple (when they surrender themselves to Christ as Lord), all we need now is to do the work. It is important to remember that discipleship does not start after a person gets saved. A person should be discipled to Christ by gradually submitting until they are ready to offer themselves in total submission. This seems to be the way our Lord did it.

Chapter 35
Jacqueline Huggins
by Dorris E. Ngaujah

To meet Jacqueline Huggins is to experience effusive excitement. For the greater portion of 18 years, she had been the only American on a tiny remote island, Cagayancillo, in the midst of the Sulu Sea, southwest of the Visayan Region of the Philippines. Yet she remains today as thrilled with her work as a language consultant and Bible translator and as exuberant over life with the Kagayanens in such an isolated place, as she was during the first initial weeks of her arrival on the island in 1987. She never ceases to revel in the art of making the scriptures come alive in the vernacular language of the people.

Jacqueline's childhood, however, was far different. Dissuading people from Christianity was a worthy and necessary life pursuit, so she thought.[1] Jacqueline's mother had been a victim of spousal abuse and when the abuse threatened the welfare and safety of her three children, Doris Wilson gathered Mark, then four years old, Jackie, age three and baby Janice, just ten months, and went to live with family members. Shortly after the separation, while visiting their father, he voluntarily placed them under the aegis of the Roman Catholic Church to spite their mother, a devout Lutheran, in a scheme to bypass a custody battle after the divorce. Citing Mrs. Wilson's unemployment and dependency on others, the state allowed the children to remain in the custody of the church which placed them in foster care. Sadly, here abuse took many forms: verbal, physical, and psychological; as well as poor supervision in the home resulting in harassment by older foster boys.[2]

At age ten, the move to her mother's own home took place. Both Jacqueline's parents had high regard for the church. Out of fear, Jackie and her siblings never told their mother what went on while in foster care. She did not realize the seriousness of the abuses at the time believing that most homes were similar to hers. Still, as a result of all these experiences in her life, Jackie grew up convinced that people who called themselves Christians were bad people.[3]

Dorris E. Ngaujah recently joined the adjunct faculty of Atlanta Christian College. She was professor of Missions, Evangelism, Urban Ministry, and Old Testament Survey at West Angeles Bible College in Los Angeles, CA, while pursuing Ph.D. studies in Intercultural Education at Biola University. Her work, in cross cultural missions spans four decades—beginning as one of Christians in Action (CinA) International's youngest licensed missionaries in 1971. She served a team in Sierra Leone, West Africa, and has led several short-term teams to Zimbabwe, Kenya, South Africa and inner cities of the U.S. Dorris is passionate about students and missions; therefore, she has given many years of volunteer service to such organizations as InterVarsity Christian Fellowship (Atlanta, GA); Campus Crusade for Christ (Atlanta, GA); Adventures in Missions (Gainsville, GA); and Pathfinders International (Chicago, IL). Her two-fold goal is to develop culturally informed and sensitive communicators—especially cross-cultural Christian workers and to write life stories of missionaries of the African Diaspora.

Dorris has a grown son and daughter-in-law, Sahr and Ayesha Ngaujah. Parenting, however, began again for Dorris most recently as she became the legal guardian of her ten-year old goddaughter, Desiree Ngaujah, after the sudden death of her 41-year old mother, Denise, on July 3, 2005.

---

1 Dorris E. Ngaujah, Lombard, IL, personal collection of prayer letters and correspondence from Jacqueline Huggins.
2 Archives of the Billy Graham Center, Wheaton IL, Jacqueline Huggins, Collection #545, VI, Videotape cassette. An untitled chapel address given at Wheaton College, March 21, 1997.
3 Ibid.

I remember planting a thought in my mind as a young child: "People don't need religion. When I grow up I'm going to help people know that they don't have to believe in God."'

Jacqueline's teen years in the 1960's were very turbulent and included the birth of two sons. She lost the eldest son in a spurious foster care arrangement that only added to her distrust of religious people and institutions. An avid reader and now an adult, Jacqueline was equally convinced that people needed to know about "her religion," astrology, which, to her, held credible substance for spiritual enlightenment.

Astrology was the thing that stayed with me the longest and seemed to satisfy my need of wanting to have a handle on the future. … Astrology became my god. … I'd go all over looking for people to help and I'd ask them, "Are you a Christian?" and if they said, "Yes, I'm a Christian." I'd begin to teach them my philosophy. "If there is no God,"I'd say, "there can't be a book that's called God's Word." If I met people who said, "No, I'm not a Christian," I'd tell them, "I've got good news for you." And I began to help them develop their own well-planned and well thought-out philosophy of life and helped them to live by it via Astrology. I'd show them how to know whom to marry, who to do business with and what people and situations to avoid."[4]

Jacqueline became a self-proclaimed fortuneteller and by age 28, she could boast of a significant clientele on her job with the Internal Revenue Service and among her friends and family.[5]

Over the years her little sister Janice became an ardent Christian. Janice consistently prayed for Jacqueline's salvation. She regularly invited Jacqueline on Monday nights to attend a Tuesday night weekly Bible study. Jacqueline methodically and consistently refused. On November 15, 1977, Jacqueline had surprisingly agreed to attend the Bible study to take advantage of the opportunity to "enlighten" a whole group of Christians. However, she never made it to the Bible study that night. An ominous thing happened as she prepared to go. Just before she was to meet with her best friend and supporter of "the cause," prepared, as they were to crash the Bible study, Jacqueline's beloved cat died, preventing any dissuasion of Christians that night. This was no small matter. Jacqueline was devastated. Her world had abruptly crumbled.[6] "Why my cat?' she thought. It might as well have been a close relative. "God if you are mad at me for wanting to tell those Christians that they are wrong, why take my cat?" That was the inquiry that preceded a revelation night, making the turning point in this young woman's search for truth. Jackie heard the voice of God speak to her conscience. "Why not YOUR cat? What were you about to do earlier this evening?" It worked, HE had her undivided attention.[7]

The Holy Spirit led her to a Bible someone had given her for her birthday the previous month and which she thought she had thrown away. In it she randomly chose and read Romans 2:4 (KJV). "Or despisest thou the riches of his goodness and forbearance and longsuffering; not knowing that the goodness of God leadeth thee to repentance?' I read that verse over and over. I kept thinking, 'What does this mean?' Why do I have to repent? I haven't done anything wrong. I'm not all that bad.' … I started to make a mental list of all the good things I had done, things which I considered good and thought surely would outweigh the wrongs."[8]

Then she read verse 3. That didn't help. Then she read verse 5 and it brought the meaning home "loud and clear."

"But after thy hardness and impenitent heart treasurest up unto thyself wrath against the day of wrath and revelation of the righteous judgment of God."[9]

Immediately Jacqueline felt rebellion melt in her soul. She repented of her sins asking God to forgive her for reading the wrong "books" in her quest for truth. She burned her astrology books

---

4 Cassette tape, Jacqueline Huggins, "Unshackled!," Pacific Garden Mission, Chicago, IL, 1997.
5 Archives of the Billy Graham Center, Wheaton, IL, Jacqueline Huggins, collection #545, T1 and T2, Audio tape reels, interview with Paul Ericksen, March 21, 1997.

6 Cassette tape, Jacqueline Huggins, "Unshackled!," Pacific Garden Mission, Chicago, IL, 1997.
7 Ibid.
8 Ibid.
9 Ibid.

and all other occultic materials, and discovered the relief of forgiveness.[10]

Two weeks later, Jacqueline asked her sister Janice to make an appointment for her to visit Janice's pastor. Responding to her plethora of questions, the Pastor Ben Tolbert explained the meaning of the cross to Jacqueline.

> He began by telling me that Jesus died on the cross for our sins. Then he was buried in a tomb. Then he said three days later Jesus rose from the dead and went back to heaven where he came from. ... Pastor said that those three things—the death, burial and resurrection of Jesus—is known as "The Gospel." Now, that was the first time I heard that. Up until that time I thought that "Gospel" was happy church singing. He said that all people want to go Heaven but what they don't realize is that they must do something with the cross. He then turned to me and asked me if when I had heard the Gospel from him earlier, had I believed it. I told him, "Yes." He continued by saying that when a person believed the Gospel, the Holy Spirit of God, in some miraculous way, and at that exact moment in which the person believed, placed that person in Christ and that person would now experience what happened to Christ about 2,000 years ago. He drew a stick figure of Jacqueline inside the body of Christ on the Cross. "Who died with Him?" he asked me. "I guess Jacqueline did," I answered. Then he drew a stick figure of Jacqueline inside the body of Christ as he lay in the tomb. "Who was buried with Him?" "I did." Then he began to draw the stick figure of Jacqueline as he stood in his resurrected state on the right side of God. "When the Holy Spirit placed you inside Christ, because you believed the Gospel, when Christ was raised from the dead to return to Heaven, who was raised with Him?" "I was ... It looks like he'll see me inside Christ," answered. "It was God's simple plan for all mankind and it was available to all mankind, but not all men will accept this simple truth that will save them."[11]

Overjoyed with this new truth, Jacqueline immediately started looking for her astrology clients and others she had tried to dissuade against Christianity. She wanted to tell them that she had been wrong. She suddenly realized that many people in her city of Philadelphia were misinformed and misled about Jesus and the Bible. She felt duty-bound to share her good news with them all.

Passionately she pursued every ministry opportunity: door-to-door evangelism, prison ministries, juvenile home visitation, nursing home visitation, Bible studies with at risk youth and other church ministries. She was not discouraged by "turn-offs" or "put-downs" for she remembered how she used to be. She never saw the need to venture beyond the borders of Philadelphia, PA, believing that "Philly" was the biggest mission field in the world. One day, however, a man's refusal to accept Christ did profoundly affect her journey into Christian ministry.

When the professionally dressed gentleman completed his astonishing articulation of his prolific biblical knowledge, infused with his adamant and defiant rejection of the Savior, based on, he said, his innate freedom of choice, Jackie had new insight for ministry!

That one encounter caused her to reconsider her passion for ministering in the city of Philadelphia. She thought, "What about people who have never had a chance to refuse to accept Christ? What about the ones who have never heard of, or read, the Bible?" Her sensitivity and desire mounted for people who have never heard about Jesus. Jacqueline remembered that she had been very good in languages as a schoolgirl. She taught herself Spanish when she was 14 and studied Latin for four years in high school. She loved the way language was formed. All the technical issues of language structure had always fascinated her. Subsequently, when she heard about translation work, she was at first shocked to learn that more than 3,000 languages (half of all known languages) in the world do not have a single verse of Scripture translated.

Jacqueline was keenly aware of her lack of biblical knowledge, so she faithfully attended Bible study (the same one she had intended to crash in ignorance), took laymen Bible courses at her church, and then enrolled at Philadelphia College of the Bible (PCB), Langhorne Manor, PA, in 1978.

---

10 Archives of the Billy Graham Center, Wheaton, IL, Jacqueline Huggins, collection #545, T1 and T2, Audio tape reels, interview with Paul Ericksen, March 21, 1997.

11 Cassette tape, Jacqueline Huggins, "Unshackled!," Pacific Garden Mission, Chicago, IL, 1997.

Later, she transferred to Fort Wayne Bible College (FWBC) in IN. In December 1979, Jacqueline went to Urbana, the huge mission convention sponsored by InterVarsity Christian Fellowship and held every three years in Urbanba, IL. It was there that she heard more about Wycliffe Bible Translators (WBT).[12] During her Bible college years Jacqueline had two short term summer missions experiences. In 1981, she assisted a missionary family her church supported in south FL. They had a ministry to Haitian migrant farm workers. In 1982, she served as team leader with Teen Missions International (TMI), taking 30 teenagers to the Philippines to construct a church building for a group of believers of the Evangelical Free Church of the Philippines who had no church building and worshipped outside sitting on crudely constructed bamboo poles.

Because of her experience in the Philippines with TMI, Jacqueline felt a nudging for the work of church planting overseas although she had already sensed that the Lord's clear leading was in the ministry of Bible translation. Still, she wrote five mission organizations she had studied about in Bible college and was turned down five times.

Jacqueline continued corresponding with Wycliffe while finishing her undergraduate studies. Upon graduation in 1983, Jackie felt led to stay in Fort Wayne, IN, and make it her new home base. She finally sent in her application to WBT five years after her initial correspondence with them. The person handling her application noted that it had been 1978 when Jacqueline first corresponded with Wycliffe. She entered Wycliffe's training program at the Summer Institute of Linguistics (SIL) in Dallas, TX, and in December 1984, she was accepted as a member of WBT.

She enjoyed her courses very much although they were not easy and accessed areas of her brain, she felt, had never been used. At that time, the translation track of SIL involved three semesters training. Jacqueline completed two semesters in Dallas and one semester at the University of OK at Norman, and three months of training in Uvalde, TX, which included a month long village living phase in Mexico. Of all her courses, the language survey course was the most difficult for Jacqueline because it involved the study of statistics with the use of the computers.[13]

Her only previous experience with computers had been with the IDRS (Intra-Date Retrieval System) terminal at the Internal Revenue Service where she had been employed as a taxpayer service representative. At one point during the survey course she wondered if she may have missed God's leading in ministry. But a Scripture verse from Jeremiah 12:5 (NIV) encouraged her. "If you have raced with men on foot and they have worn you out, how can you compete with horses? If you stumble in safe country, how will you manage in the thickets by the Jordan?"

It was clear to Jacqueline that there would be hard times but she should just hang in there. She persevered and mastered all her classes. Her previous language knowledge was a big help having had four years of Latin in high school, three years of Greek and one year of Hebrew in her undergraduate program at Bible college. It was during her time at SIL, she was encouraged to lead a short-term mission team to the Philippines. God used this assignment to develop in her a strong interest in Asia and for the people of this continent.[14] Upon finishing her linguistic studies, she had to choose in which part of the world she would be interested in serving.

By now Jacqueline knew that she would welcome the opportunity to return to the Philippines. She and a classmate from FWBC, Carol Pebley, were assigned to the Philippines to do translation work among the Kagayanen. Carol had some sight limitations, so the two of them decided that: a) they needed a place with a flat terrain, and b) they wanted a project that was already in progress but needed the assistance of another team in order to finish. The ideal situation was unfolding for them in the Philippines. A husband and wife team, Scott and Louise MacGregor, who began a project in 1976, were seeking replacements because they had been asked to take up administrative positions. The MacGregors had already completed the translation of the Gospel of Luke, a health pamphlet, a set of easy reader booklets with stories taken from the Book of Genesis, a four-language phrase book with Kagayanen phrases translated

---

12 Archives of the Billy Graham Center, Wheaton, IL, Jacqueline Huggins, collection #545, T2, Audio tape reels, interview with Paul Ericksen, March 21, 1997.

13 Ibid.
14 Ibid.

into a local trade language, the national language and English.¹⁵

After raising their support, the pair arrived in Manila on July 14, 1986, and they began language school. They studied Tagalog, the national language of the Philippines. Earlier translators, such as SIL members, Dr. Dick Elkins and his wife, Betty, had done significant work among the Manobo. They had lived among the Western Bukidnon Manobo people of Mindanao from 1953–1980. Dick and Betty had studied the Manobo culture and language and had facilitated in the production of literature for this mother tongue group, including a dictionary and the New Testament.¹⁶

Jacqueline and Carol wanted their project site to be among people who spoke a dialect of the Manobo language family. Jacqueline had first heard of the Manobo people while a freshman at Philadelphia College of the Bible. It was during Missions' Emphasis Week as she perused the many mission booths set up in the auditorium. It seemed that the topic of the Philippines came up several times that week but Jacqueline wasn't interested because she had Filipino classmates in grade school so she assumed that their country wasn't "primitive"¹⁷ enough if people from this Asian nation could end up in her home town of Philadelphia.

Subsequently, that December of 1986, while still studying Tagalog, they went to visit the predominantly Kagayanen town of Caguisan located on mainland Palawan, where the MacGregors had begun the work and lived among the Kagayanen people. However, the MacGregors, as well as SIL administrators, suggested that it would be better for the two young ladies to begin their project site on the Kagayanen home island of Cagayancillo, located almost in the center of the Sulu Sea in south central Philippines. It was reported that the 3,336 people on Cagayancillo, of the approximately 20,000 total speakers of this language in Palawan province spoke a more purer form of Kagayanen. It also met their criteria. With the location decided upon, they went full swing into the dual tasks of completing language school and gathering supplies and furnishings for establishing a home on that tiny municipal island of the remote Cagayan Islands Archipelago.

Later Jacqueline had this to say about the relationship between the Kagayanen language and the Manobo language. There is no single language called Manobo although speakers of several Manobo languages will refer to their language as "Manobo." Actually, Manobo is the name of a major language family or group of several dozen related languages whose speakers are located mainly on the large southern island of Mindanao. Kagayanen as recent as the 1970's has been considered a member of the Manobo language family.¹⁸ However, it is not considered a Manobo language by mainstream Filipino linguists because its speakers are not located on Camiguin Island off the northern tip of Mandanao. Cagayancillo is some 300 miles northwest of Camiguin Island.

> We did not know any of this when we took the assignment among the Kagayanens. We had no idea that it was considered a Manobo language. We had given up the idea of ever working among this language family. Then we learned about Harmon's comparative study and thought it ironic, or maybe 'Providential' that we were assigned to a translation project that turned out to be among the Manobo after all!¹⁹

Jacqueline and Carol, accompanied by Louise MacGregor, made a preliminary two-week visit to Cagayancillo Island in May 1987. They were told by the OIC (Officer-In-Charge.) mayor that there was no extra land upon which to build a house. They would have to use an existing dwelling. He also mentioned that he knew of an

---

15 Prayer letter from Jacqueline written by her collegues, the MacGregors, dated march 1994, from the private collection of Dorris Nagaujah.

16 "Windows to the Kinagayanen Translation Project," June 1999, vol. 1, issue 1, Wycliffe Bible Translators.

17 The term "primitive" is no longer used in mission circles as it is viewed by many as a pejorative term depicting people who among other characteristics cannot read or write. The nation of the Philippines is approximately 85% literate in at least the national language and English.

18 Based on a comparative study by Carol Jean Harmon (1978) encouraged by Dr. Elkins between Kagayanen and the 22 Manobo languages on the supposition that certain vocabulary items are rarely borrowed from other languages. In other words, relationship within the same language family. There was true similarity between the carefully selected Manobo words when compared with the same words in Kagayanen.

19 Dorris E. Ngaujah, Lombard, IL, personal collection of prayer letters and correspondence from Jacqueline Huggins.

available dwelling which belonged to a member of his family who had moved away 13 years ago. At the same time, some members of the small Baptist Church on the island mentioned that they too knew of an unoccupied house owned by a judge who, together with his family, had moved away many years ago because there weren't enough litigable cases to support their family there on the island. Most legal cases were handled by the village leaders or the mayor and his cabinet. The two ladies first looked at the house that the OIC mayor had in mind and later in the day looked at the house the members of the Baptist Church had in mind. It turned out to be the same house! The judge was a believer and follower of Jesus Christ and his family were members of the Baptist Church. What clinched the deal in their choosing this two-story, three bedroom, wood framed house for their project site was a phrase that had been painted some time ago in large white letters at the top of a wall in the main bedroom. It said, "Jesus Christ Is The Head Of This House." Months later after moving in, when people would ask the two if they were afraid to live in a house that hadn't been occupied for so many years, they reminded them of that assuring phrase.[20]

Jacqueline and Carol completed Tagalog language school in April after seven months of study. The ladies returned to the remote island of Cagayancillo in the JAARS aerocommander twin engine plane to continue a Bible translation ministry among the Kagayanen people. As soon as they arrived, they went to visit with the OIC mayor and the town officials. They were officially welcomed into the community once the purpose of their stay was explained to the people of the communities by the mayor and village leaders. The Kagayanen people had been already preparing for their arrival. In their absence, the previous mayor, a believer and member of the Baptist Church, had taken full responsibility for seeing to it that the house that they had chosen was fully repaired and ready for them when they returned. Of course, the ladies had left behind during their first visit a sum of money that he managed for them to pay the carpenters and other contractual workmen.

The little island of Cagayancillo, though the largest in the archipelago is one and a half miles wide and 12 miles long. Its coasts are contrasts of steep rugged cliffs on one side and long palm swaying, white sandy beaches on the east. Jacqueline spoke of the weather on Cagayancillo:

The climate is tropical year round with the typical two season weather pattern of mild monsoon rains half the year and hot dry weather the other half. However, within the seasons there are two frightening seasons. During the rainy months between May and October, July and August are known as lightening season. Each year something or someone will be struck by lightening. During the hot season between the months of October and April, October to December is known as windy season. The house is not equipped with glass windows, but merely wooden jalousies that don't close all the way. We make a pretty sight sitting at our desks with both hands holding down papers to keep them from flying around the room and our hair standing on end from the wind coming in the windows. When the winds accompany the rains, you could have a real disaster on your hands with buckets of water coming in through the cracks in the walls and windows. School children actually have "wind days off" from school, somewhat like we, as children, had snow days off in Philadelphia.

The good new is that there is no malaria or typhoid on Cagayancillo like the surrounding mainlands to the east and west of the island. Transportation around the small islands was by boat and canoe. However, there is an airstrip cut by on ABWE (Association of Baptists for World Evangelism) missionaries back in the 1950's when the church was planted there post World War II. This was a big help to Jacqueline and Carol.[21]

At long last, the day came for them to leave the "big city" for their new home on the island. A Wycliffe pilot flew them there. A host of excited and anxious children met them as the plane landed that humid August day. They helped unload boxes from the twin engine plane only to reload them into the pump boat that would take them and their cargo of clothes, food and many cartons of books (computers were not

---

20 Ibid.

21 Ibid.

widely used yet) to the part of the island nearest the house where they were to live. The local contractors had done a great job at repairing the two-story wood frame house. Among the "stuff" Jacqueline and Carol brought with them were their two cats, Spunky and Moning.

Language study began again immediately. This time it wouldn't be the national language because the Tagalog is not spoken on Cagayancillo. Now they would begin to learn the language into which they were to translate the Word of God. In her September 1987 newsletter, Jacqueline wrote:

> We can't begin to translate the Scriptures until we have mastered the Kagayanen language. The initial two years is given to language and culture study and building relationships.

The high school principal is the one who requested an SIL team to come and "help preserve their language, [and] culture and provide them with written literature such as the Bible, that would instill a sense of morality in the young people."[22] In those earlier years Jacqueline said,

> The majority of the people thought we're tourists who are willing to take up residence on their island ... or that we've disowned our own country in order to adopt theirs. You can imagine how anxious we are to begin translation because then the people will have more ... involvement in the work with checking all translated verses for comprehension as well as [for] correct cultural wording. Then maybe they will understand more about why we're there. Until that time comes, we struggle with the language and ask the people to hang in there.[23]

Within nine months both Jacqueline and Carol were writing home giving Kagayanen language lessons via their prayer letters. They tried to help us understand the great task and responsibility of the translator. In "Carol's Corner" dated June 1988, Carol explained that there are at least 16 words in Kagayanen for the English word, carry:

> When you are carrying something in a container and you are holding it by the handle of that container it is called bitbit. However, if this thing you are carrying is heavy, than it is bingbing. When you are carrying something like a purse or bag with a long strap and it is dangling from your shoulder, elbow or hand, then it is kel-ay. When you carry something in your fist then it is kemkem ... [24]

Translation work involves many people. First Jacqueline and Carol employed people to teach them the language—from lay persons to professional schoolteachers. But the most consistent helpers were children who don't mind repeating a word or phrase many times. Later, many more people were needed to help read, review and correct their work. One of their teachers was Mr. Javiar Carceler, a retired schoolteacher who also co-authored the Kagayanen phrase book in four languages: Kagayanen, Hiligaynon (a nearby trade language), Tagalog (the national language) and English.[25]

In addition to those people on the island working with them, there is a network of support staff at the administrative center in Nasuli and Manila. Nasuli, located in the province of Bukidnon on the larger southern island of Mindanao, is about 300 miles south east from Cagayancillo. These faithful people see to it that Jacqueline and Carol have the practical assistance necessary to carry on their work. When the ladies have mechanical or electrical problems, need supplies, get sick, need printing done, have business matters to tend to, need to attend workshops or seminars to further their training, or just need some time for rest, they find all the help they need at Nasuli Center. Accountants and computer specialists also serve them, as well as radio technicians, pilots, nurses and a center doctor.

It is obvious translation work is not for the missionary who desires to see conversions right away. Results take time. It is a tedious, painstaking ministry requiring a lot of patience. In one of her personal letters to me, Jacqueline wrote, "As you already know, this is a rough life. I can

---

22 Windows to the Kinagayanen Translation Project, June 1999, vol. 1 (1). Wycliffe Bible Translators.
23 Personal letter to Dorris Ngaujah from Jacqueline, May 15, 1988.

24 "Carol's Corner," June 1988, prayer letter sent by Jacqueline.
25 Ibid.

see that when we talk about a 'calling', 'commitment', 'being led', 'service', etc., one must really have a sense of certainty doesn't one? I don't see how a person could stay on the mission field even for one year without being certain God has sent them."[26]

God does, however, draw to Himself those He chooses. Carol and Jacqueline had prayed that their life style would speak as loud or louder than their words. They desired some spiritual depth in their relationships among those that worked for, and with, them day by day. Beth, one of Jacqueline's language helpers, had been a believer since childhood. However, she did not know that the people who wrote the Bible books were real. Nor did she know that Christians are to share their faith in Jesus with those closest to them. After reading a practice portion of translated Scripture in her language, it convicted her. She went home that day and told her husband that he needed to believe in Jesus or else they would be separated from each other forever after they died. He became a believer in Jesus Christ and shortly afterward asked Beth why she had waited so long to tell him this 'good news' after being married for more than six years. Other language helpers and housekeepers also became believers as a result of their involvement in the work of Bible translation or witnessing the work going on around them.[27]

By the end of their first term, Jacqueline and Carol had mastered the language and had an excellent team of language assistants. These young ladies learned how to type, use the computer, gather good texts for language and culture study, use recording equipment and write and edit their language creatively.[28] A pre-primer and primer for teaching reading and writing Kagayanen had been created, but the actual work of translating the Bible would begin sometime after both ladies returned from their respective furloughs.

The second term brought many changes. The most drastic of which was Carol's transfer to the city of Manilla. She could no longer be so far from medical assistance in relation to her sight limitations and was moved to a community in this major city, leaving Jacqueline alone on the island for the next three, four-year terms. But,

Jacqueline, focused and highly motivated, and very prayerful about the issue of loneliness, discovered that God was already answering all of her prayer concerns. She found some new "American friends" on the island. She was the envy of all the other SIL missionaries living in mountainous regions, because there in the middle of the Sulu Sea, unhindered by mountain ranges, the radio waves from station DYVS located in Bacloud City, Negros, came clear and static-free to the little island bringing the ministry of FEBC (Far East Broadcasting Company) to her. Seven days a week from 5:30 p.m. to 9:30 p.m., she had "fellowship" with the likes of James Dobson, Charles Stanley, Chuck Swindoll, John MacArthur, Billy Graham and, later Franklin Graham, and many others.[29] Classical artists and contemporary Christian musicians stopped in and 'visited' with her on the weekends.

Jacqueline readily testifies to the value of giving liberally to Christian radio programs in faraway lands:

> I was really ministered to during those years. So much so, that in one of my prayer letters I practically 'preached' about the importance of praying for our pastors, inspired from a sermon I heard from Chuck Swindoll.[30]

Another newsletter was dedicated solely to the programs to which she listened. She sent each of them a copy of this newsletter. A host of one of her favorite programs aired from Atlanta, GA, she actually got to meet quite providentially at a missions conference in Atlanta during her second furlough. That radio ministry became financial and prayer supporters of Jacqueline for a time until the host became ill.

Some of the African-American churches, that initially pledged to support Jacqueline, didn't take her seriously the whole first term she was away, but when she returned home and visited them that first furlough, many of the pastors and church members made comments like: "Do you mean to say that you are still out there in the same place doing the same thing for the past four years!" Or "We heard you got married!" Or "We heard you were no longer on the mission field and returned home for good!" One supporter,

---

26 Personal letter to Dorris Ngaujah, May 15, 1988.
27 Dorris E. Ngaujah, Lombard, IL., personal collection of prayer letters and correspondence from Jacqueline Huggins.
28 "Jacqueline's Corner," July 1991.
29 "Jacqueline's Journal," May 1995.
30 Jacqueline Huggins, "The Importance of Prayer," October 1995.

who long ago had discontinued sending funds said, "We heard you got the big 'C' and died!" But most said, "You must really be serious, and we are so far behind in supporting you!" ... "We better get on the ball!"

They had committed themselves to praying and giving, but it ceased until they saw she was really doing what she said she was called to do and was sticking to it. After Jacqueline returned to the field, her support picked up and she has not been "in the red" since.[31]

Although her three translator colleagues worked separately with their respective Kagayanen translation assistants, MacGregors now returned to the project and the work made great progress during the second term. Their goal was to have translated half of the New Testament in Kagayanen (later changed to Kinagayanen) by the year 2000. By the end of 1995, a revision of Luke was completed and published, the books of Acts, the 5 Ts: 1 and 2 Timothy, 1 and 2 Thessalonians, Titus, and James were also published. Carol also translated Genesis which will be included in with the New Testament books. Although all three ladies work on translating the New Testament books, they decided among them to each be responsible for a discipline of their own preference to enhance the project and the quality of the work they were doing. Louise's emphasis would be Literacy related, Carol's would be Linguistically related and Jacqueline's would be Anthropologically related. Each translator would focus on their respective disciplines when checking the other translator's work.[32]

Jacqueline's personal growth over the years has been astounding. Her enthusiasm for cultural information has gained her a reputation in Kagayanen anthropology. She would later become the head of the Anthropology Department of the Philippine Branch of SIL, a position that took her away from the island for a number of months in the year as she filled in for the furloughing head of department. She has been called upon to teach quite often at the SIL Cultural Awareness Seminars whenever there are significant numbers of new personnel to the Branch. Towards the end of her second term, in 1994 and 1995, she also taught Bible Translation Principles at the Koinonia Theological Seminary in Davao City, Philippines. She taught as an invited guest lecturer of graduate students of Divinity and Christian Leadership in what was called the Bible Translation Module Course, a requirement for Master degree candidates. Among with many other things, her students learned that understanding the culture often helps the translator know which book of the Bible to translate first, which book would be most readily understood by the people of the language and which books would present the most cultural barriers to understand the text. Jacqueline's unique model of putting together translation work teams is used by other teams in SIL.So positive was the response to her seminary teaching, which has been followed by many such assignments, that Jacqueline has given serious thought to pursuing post graduate studies to qualify her for what experience has already shown to be a natural gift. About that first seminary assignment, Jacqueline wrote:

> *Many have asked me why I accepted that teaching assignment. I probably would have declined had I not experienced what I did with a seminary student named Eusebio [name changed for confidentiality.] He was a Filipino (non-Kagayanen) pastoral studies major assigned to Cagayancillo as an intern for one year. His work would be to teach Sunday school and preach in the local Baptist Church. Pastor Eusebio didn't know anything about the work of Wycliffe or SIL, nor did he see the importance of vernacular Scriptures. He does now. Before I left Cagayancillo for my second furlough, Pastor Eusebio came to the SIL office and asked, "Can I please have a copy of the Kagayanen Romans?" "It is not done yet," I told him. "In fact, I haven't even started on it yet." "Well, how long will it take to finish?" he asked. "Can you have it ready in about a week?" When I responded that it could take years, he wailed, "Years! How am I supposed to do soul winning here without the Kagayanen Romans?" That's the kind of talk translators love to hear! But how do we reach seminary students and give them the translators' burden for missionary pastors to use the*

---

31 Archives of the Billy Graham Center, Wheaton, IL, Jacqueline Huggins, collection #545, T1, Audio tape reels, interview with Paul Ericksen, March 21, 1997.

32 Kagayanen TEAM NEWS by Louise MacGregor, Phillip Schmuki, September 4, 1994.

vernacular language and Scriptures in places where they will be assigned after graduation?[33]

Jacqueline added, that when she was later asked if she would be able to teach Bible Translation principle module course at an OMF seminary in Davao,

> *I jumped at the chance to encourage Filipino seminary students about the importance of learning the language and using Scriptures in the language of the people if they exist."*[34] Eusebio was later called by the Cagayancillo Baptist Church as their first missionary. He has since married and together with his wife have a thriving church ministry, home Bible studies, a Christian kindergarten and a youth camping program among Kagayanens on one of the outer islands in the archipelago. Why? Because he took the time to learn how to teach and preach in Kagayanen and he's presently using the Kagayanen Scripture portions that have been published to date.[35]

Perhaps Jacqueline's most prestigious assignment came when she was asked to represent the ministry of Wycliffe Bible Translators as one of the keynote speakers at Urbana 1996, InterVarsity's Triennial Student Missions Conference held in Urbana, IL. There was a record number of 19,000 students, pastors, youth leaders and missionaries who heard her compelling story. That assignment lengthened her stay in the states during her second furlough to do a post-Urbana speaking tour at high schools, colleges, universities, churches, and campus groups. But it also allowed for many more opportunities for young people to hear of the great need and the responsibilities of linguists and translators to advance the kingdom of God through the ministry of Bible translation.

By June of 2004, the translation team's status report read: [36]

Genesis	Published (Carol)
Matthew	Completed (Jacqueline)
Mark	Completed (Jacqueline)
Luke	Published (MacGregors)
John	Completed (Carol)
Acts	Published (Jacqueline)
Romans	Completed (Jacqueline)
1 & 2 Cor	Completed (Carol)
Galatians	Completed (Jacqueline)
Ephesians	Completed (Louise)
Philippians	Completed (Louise)
Colossians	Completed (Carol)
1 & 2 Thess	Published (Carol)
1 & 2 Tim	Published (Carol)
Titus	Published (Carol)
Philemon	Completed (Carol)
Hebrews	To be completed in 2005 (Jacqueline)
James	Published (Jacqueline)
1 & 2 Peter	Completed (Jacqueline)
1, 2 & 3 John	Completed (Carol)
Jude	Completed (Jacqueline)
Revelation	Completed (Carol)

God has honored the dedication and the commitment of Jacqueline Huggins and the other members of the team: Scott & Louise MacGregor of Cape Cod, MA, and Minneapolis, MN, respectively; Carol Pebley of Fort Wayne, IN; and Michael Y Josephine Wan of Malaysia and Singapore, respectively; and all the supporting staff of Wycliffe Bible Translators and the Summer Institute of Linguistics. As I write these few words, the speakers of Kagayanen can now take pride in the dignity of having a written language. They can find the truth of God's great plan of salvation as they read, or have read to them, the Holy Word of God in their own mother tongue. Praise God!

Jacqueline's story is not over. In days to come I hope to be able to share more of her extraordinary, solitary, yet effusive life. I will travel to the little island of Cagayancille and spend some time experiencing what God is doing in her life there and learning more about His leading for the next step in the amazing journey of her life.

Jacqueline's forth term in the Philippines began December, 2002. She has now been in the Philippines almost 19 years. Originally, her goal was to finish the Kagayanen New Testament then possibly translate another New Testament in another language project, however, God has more practical plans for her.

---

33 Kagayanen TEAM NEWS by Louise MacGregor, Phillip Schmuki, September 4, 1994.
34 Ibid.
35 Dorris E. Ngaujah, Lombard, IL, personal collection of prayer letters and correspondence from Jacqueline Huggins.
36 Windows to the Kinagayanen Translation Project, June 2004.

Some next steps:

Training national Bible translators (NBT) so they can translate the Scriptures into their own languages.

But first, finish a study program at Fuller Theological Seminary, Pasadena, CA, qualifying her to teach on a seminary level.

She is currently in an MA study program at Fuller with plans to bypass the MA degree and just do the course work.

She is hoping to continue on into a doctoral program in Intercultural Studies with an emphasis in Translation.

The dedication of the Kagayanen New Testament took place in early 2006.

(It's time to sing the Doxology like we do whenever we finish a Scripture book! Praise God from whom all blessings flow!)

Bibliography

Archives of the Billy Graham Center, Wheaton, IL. Jacqueline Huggins, Collection #545, V1, Video tape cassette. An untitled chapel address given at Wheaton College, March 21, 1997.

Archives of the Billy Graham Center, Wheaton, Illinois. Jacqueline Huggins, Collection #545, T I and T2, Audio tape reels. Interview with Paul Ericksen on March 21,1997.

Ngaujah, Dorris E., Lombard, IL. Personal collection of prayer letters and correspondences from Jackie, Carol and the MacGregors. "Jackie's Comer," "Jackie's Journal," "Carol's Comer," "TEAM NEWS," and "Windows to the Kinagayanen Translation Project" were the respective headings on prayer/newsletters mailed by Jackie to prayer supporters, friends and family.

Story Documentation from Jacqueline Huggins to "Unshackled!," Pacific Garden Mission, Chicago, IL, June 23, 1997.

Chapter 36
David Cornelius: My Missionary Experience

by David Cornelius

Early Life

I was born on August 28, 1944, to David and Georgia Mae Cornelius. Though my parents were residents of Texarkana, TX, due to restrictions placed on service given to black patients in the hospital administered by whites during those days, my parents used the services of a small hospital owned and operated by black doctors in Texarkana, AR. Thus, I have an AR birth certificate even though I never actually lived in the state.

I had one sister (slightly more than one year younger than me). I have very vague memories of our mother, for she died while we were still toddlers. I do recall missing her after she died. Our father remarried some time later. During the time between the death of our mother and the remarriage of our father, we spent a great deal of time with our maternal grandparents (Alfred and Mary Bridges). After our father's remarriage, we moved from our rural home just outside of the Texarkana, TX, city limits into an area of Texarkana called "New Town." The house we lived in on Ball Street (later renamed Bell Street) became home until I left for college. This had been owned by my stepmother, Florence. I never thought of her as stepmother, always just mother. In addition to my mother, father and sister, my mother's niece and elderly aunt lived in the four-room house with us. Later, her father also moved in.

Mamma and daddy were very active members in the New Town Baptist Church. For nearly 30 years, my daddy was Sunday school superintendent and has been a deacon for as far back as I can remember. Mamma was church clerk, mission board leader and usher. They carried us to church for both Sunday school and worship every first and third Sunday, and just Sunday school every fourth Sunday. (Our pastor was the pastor of two congregations. He attended the other congregation on the second and fourth Sundays.) Fifth Sundays were mission Sundays. Our pastor preached every other fifth Sunday at our church. We children were not always required to attend Sunday night services.

I liked first and third Sundays because we could go home after Sunday school and not have to endure two to two and one-half hour worship service. Really, I loved the Bible study and discussions that went on in Sunday school and was glad we did not have to rush to finish in order to begin morning worship. We could spend a little more time in Sunday school.

David Cornelius is the Director of African-American Church Relations and Co-Director of the International Volunteer Fellowship of the International Mission Board, Southern Baptist Convention, Richmond, VA.

Two Life-changing Events

When I was ten, two events changed my life forever. The first had its genesis when I was approaching my ninth birthday. A friend, who was just 16 days older than me, was baptized. I went to my mother and told her that I wanted to be baptized. She asked me why. I told her since my friend was being baptized, I wanted to be baptized. She said, "NO!" When I asked, "Why?", she said, "Because you ain't got nothing." I didn't know exactly what I was supposed to get, but she did. She recognized this as a critical moment in my life and over the next year, step-by-step, she led me to the point where I was ready to receive Christ as my Savior and Lord. I took this step during our annual summer revival and was baptized just after my tenth birthday.

The second event took place just a few weeks after my baptism. My sister (named Lois, nicknamed "Sister") who was just a year and eight days younger than me, died. We had been very close over the years. (Even today, nearly 50 years later, just thinking about those days and our closeness causes tears to well up in my eyes.) This event changed our whole family forever. The things that we did as a family (going to town and to the movies every Saturday, going to church and visiting relatives) seemed to have something missing. It wasn't long before we stopped going to the movies. My parents bought their first television set. For better or worse, this became our replacement for the movies.

For me, it was no longer the two of us who went to spend weekends and summers with our maternal grandparents in the country just outside of the Texarkana city limits. Her death occurred early in the school year and it was tough getting back into the swing of school. My teachers and principal were concerned and very helpful to me during that period. Family and neighbors stood by us and I came to understand the difference that knowing Christ could make in difficult times even at that tender age. Years later as a pastor, reflecting back on those days (how I felt and how my parents moved through the grief process and continued life) helped me to understand how to minister to parents who had lost children, and children who had lost siblings. By God's grace we got through the death of Sister.

For me, deep impressions and the lessons learned remained. One occasion when I was 12 years old, my (step)mother became very ill. The doctor came out to the house to see about her and advised that she go to the hospital for the removal of a tumor. I recall that on the day of surgery, I wanted to stay out of school in order to be with her. However, she and dad insisted that I go to school. I was in the seventh grade. I was so upset at school—I couldn't stop crying—that the school called my dad and had him come and pick me up right after lunch. I had told them that I was afraid that my (step)mother was going to die. They explained to dad how the loss of my mother and sister had affected me and contributed to my fear of losing another person who was close to me. He then took me to the hospital where the doctor had finished the surgery. When I saw that mother was alright, I was fine.

Leaving the Nest

It was May 1962. I graduated from Dunbary High School (as an honor student) at the age of 17, at the top 25 percent of the class. However, I had neither plans nor desire to go to college. A first cousin of mine and I had made plans to volunteer and enter the U.S. Army on what was called their "Buddy Plan." They would keep us together through basic training, career training, and on to our first assignment. We were as close as brothers (Samuel Jr. or "Sonny," was the oldest son of my dad's oldest brother). Our plan was to learn auto mechanics, finish our tour in the Army and get out, return to Texarkana, and start an auto repair business.

Our plans failed to fall into place when I failed my physical in Shreveport, LA and was sent back home. Within two days, my cousin had found a way to get out of the Army and was back home with me. (He later volunteered again and served in Vietnam.)

When my dad saw me back home only two days after leaving, naturally he wanted to know two things: what had happened in Shreveport, and what were my plans now. The answer to the first question was easy. The second was a bit more difficult. After I spent 15 minutes sharing my "plan" for the future with him, he realized that I really didn't have a plan. So, he helped me to formulate one.

He said, "First, you are going to get out there and get a job. Then, you're going to start paying rent here, you're going to have to help put food on the table and eventually, you will have to find your own place because two grown men can't operate the same household." By then, I was wondering what I had done to make him angry with me. He had never talked this way before. However, as he continued talking, my ears perked up when I heard him say the word "but." I knew that something else (possibly better) was about to come out of his mouth. He said, "But, If you want to go to school, I'll do all that I can to help you." I knew right away that my best option was to go to school. The problem was that it was mid-June and I had not applied to a single college or university anywhere. I would probably have to end up getting that job that he had mentioned and finding myself a place to live. My life plans were in ruins.

A few days later, while talking with a former schoolmate who had finished high school a year before me, I mentioned my problem. He encouraged me to apply to the school that he was attending, Jarvis Christian College in Hawkins, TX. I did and was accepted for the fall 1962 semester. I eventually decided to major in chemistry. It was at Jarvis that another life-changing event happened: I met the young lady who would eventually become my wife, Elwanda Brown.

Move, Marriage, and Ministry

After three years at Jarvis, I transferred to Texas Christian University (TCU). I graduated from TCU in May 1967, took a job with a food company in Dallas, TX in June of the same year, and got married on December 9, 1967. We bought a house just prior to getting married, moved in on our wedding day, and united with Greater Saint James Baptist Church in Dallas. I worked as a chemist and Elwanda continued her work as a medical technologist. Within a few months, both Elwanda and I were deeply involved in the church's various programs. The church affiliated with the Southern Baptist Convention shortly after we united with it.

By 1969, the church was moving toward ordaining me as a deacon. I had been active in the men's program and served as Sunday school superintendent, and later as Religious Education director. I was also sensing a call to the ministry. God was reminding me of a promise that I had made to him during my last semester at TCU. I had promised him that if he allowed me to finish school, get a good job and work a couple of years, I would do anything he wanted me to do. I had sensed this "calling" as a teenager, but didn't want to be a preacher (the only thing that I knew God called men to do). I had pursued other avenues when I finished high school in part to get away from that calling.

After talking with my pastor about this "calling," plans to ordain me as a deacon were dropped and he proceeded to make plans for me to preach my first sermon, which I did on May 30, 1969. I was licensed as a preacher on that same day.

In 1971, there was a Billy Graham crusade held at Texas Stadium. I had the opportunity to work with and get to know his crusade team leaders, Charlie Riggs and John Corts. About a year after the crusade was over, John called me one Saturday morning to talk about the possibility of joining the team to work with crusades all over the world. My first assignment would have been in South America. I ended up not going with the organization, however, the event was a hint of where God might be leading me in the area of ministry. It was the first serious consideration that I gave to ministry other than a pastorate.

It was not until 1977 that I left my work as a chemist to pursue seminary full time. During my seminary years at Southwestern Baptist Theological Seminary, I worked as an assistant janitor at First Baptist Church of Oak Cliff, and later as BSU director at El Centro Community College in downtown Dallas, TX. I later served on the ministerial staff of First Baptist of Oak Cliff as assistant to the pastor. I went from that position to become pastor of the Fruitdale Baptist Church, Dallas.

Missions

I had first understood that mission calling clearly during the four and a half years that I served as BSU director. Working with students and encouraging them to be open to God's calling on their lives to go anywhere made me realize that I was not completely open. I had been approached on numerous occasions by international students on campus (mostly from African countries) and challenged to consider going to their countries to serve as a missionary. The turning point came in 1978, during Student Week at Glorieta, NM. It was several years later before Elwanda had her calling clarified. In 1984, I left Fruitdale as Elwanda, our two children—Michael and Wynelle—and I prepared to go to Abua, Nigeria, as

Southern Baptist missionaries, to help begin our Baptist work in the new capital city of Nigeria.

Neither of us had ever been outside of the U.S. before leaving for Nigeria. For our first three and a half years, we lived in a place called Kefe and we lived on an old-time mission compound. We were the only family on the compound, but it was a huge amount of property for one person to try to keep up—five or six acres. I had a 21-inch push power motor. During grass-cutting season I wore cowboy boots because I would run over at least one snake each time I cut the grass. We mainly saw spitting cobras.

It was a big deal sometimes just making a living. For example, getting your wash out during rainy season and getting it dry without electric dryers. Sometimes it would take several days to dry. And when we did have a dryer, the electricity wasn't always reliable. These difficulties were a part of the ambiance of living in Nigeria.

Nigeria became home for us and in many ways is still home. I hated to leave. It was probably one of the most difficult things I have ever done in my life. And it wasn't so much that life was so easy there. In fact, some of the most difficult years of my life in terms of making a living were in Nigeria. I spent a great deal of time doing things that were necessary to stay alive, in addition to doing the job I was sent there to do. I would just like to get back with the people. We didn't have to search for entertainment there. There was plenty of adventure every day. You got up in the morning and you never knew what was going to face you. Very often the plans we laid out didn't even come close to being fulfilled because other things popped up. Our Nigerian family had a tendency of coming to the house very early if they needed to talk business over with us. And the more serious the business, the earlier they would come over.

Welcome to Nigeria

About two months after we got to Nigeria, I ended up in jail. We had been in language school only a month and I got a call to go to Lagos because our household goods had come in. They wanted me to go down there and clean the ship. Among our household goods, we had hospital supplies and electronic media equipment that the mission had asked us to pack in our crate. I got down there and discovered that they had my itemized packing list and couldn't find the two B.B. guns that I had listed. When I showed them where I packed them, they arrested me and said "You have smuggled guns into the country." They really wanted me to give them money and all would be forgotten. I didn't do that, so they arrested and charged me with smuggling guns and drugs into the country. The "drugs" were hospital supplies, the chemical agents for testing blood, etc.

By the time they put me in jail, it had been two days since I had eaten anything. I wasn't about to eat the food in the jail. Still, I became sick. They took me to the hospital, which was full, and the doctors were on strike. I checked in and laid on the floor. Later that night a gurney became available. Around 2 a.m., I was given a bed in the emergency room, then moved to a bed in the men's ward. It wasn't the finest bed. It had a hole in the middle and was out in the aisle. A nurse took a couple of pillows and stuffed the hole.

By the next day the U.S. Embassy heard that one of their citizens had been arrested for smuggling drugs and they sent a person to see me and to see what he could do. I thought the mission could take care of it. However, no one from the mission knew where I was. The guy that accompanied me to Lagos ran off when I was arrested. Eventually, I did get in touch with them.

I spent a better part of the week under arrest before the police finally released me into the custody of the Missions Executive Secretary, although I couldn't leave the area. At this point my problem was that the hospital wouldn't let me check out because there was no doctor to sign my release. After a very long conversation with a nurse she said, "Let me go get some papers and you can sign yourself out." After an hour passed, we finally figured out that she was giving me a chance to leave. I ended up having to climb over a wall to get out.

There were people praying that this experience wouldn't discourage me. They felt that after this incident, I would be anxious to get back home. But in this process I had time to reflect, and as I prayed, I became aware of the fact that this was Satan attempting to discourage me. I made up my mind and said, "If the devil wants me out of Nigeria that badly, then I need to stay here." So it actually had the opposite effect. It made me more determined than ever to stay.

Power of Prayer

Armed robbers came to our house about 3 a.m. one night. It was the Sunday before Thanksgiving. I heard a commotion outside. I got up and went outside and the watchman told me thieves had come onto our property and that he had chased one away, but there may be another one hiding on our property. We shared a relatively small piece of property, so we looked around his house, and our house, and found another man and chased him over the fence. I went inside to get my B.B. gun and went to the gate to let them see the gun and to chase them further away. About the time I got to the gate, a shot rang out. I was standing next to a pile of concrete blocks and dust blew. I rapidly made my way back behind the wall and inside the gate. For the next 2 1/2 hours the thieves bombarded our place with large stones and gun shots. At one point we could see one of the thieves trying to get into the washroom. We brought our night watchman's family into our house and began to pray in the midst of all this noise.

Around 5:30 a.m., for no apparent reason, the thieves ran off. I mean, they literally ran off. Later, the night watchman stationed across the street from my property told me, "They ran like there was something after them. I didn't see anybody or anything behind them, but they were running." We decided that the Lord sent His messengers to scare the thieves off. I became very much aware of the power of prayer because it happened during the time that we were actually praying that God would show Himself and take care of us in that particular situation. God takes care of His own. This doesn't always mean that your life is going to be saved, but you're still in the best hands when you are in God's Hands. He just chose to take care of us by keeping us safe from those robbers.

That home has had no more problems with thieves to this day.

"Did you bring a curse?"

A few years before we left Nigeria, Elwanda and I were selected with a team that consisted of missionary physicians and dentists and some of our Nigerian colleagues to go to a village of several hundred people outside Ogoja, which is in Southeast Nigeria. We were sent to establish a church there.

The first thing I noticed was a little house surrounded by figures—some carved out of wood. I asked about this house and was told that this was the house of their ancestors. This was a house built in honor of their ancestors and the carvings, as I understood it, were meant to represent their ancestors.

Our team's plan was to do dental and medical treatment during the day and have evangelistic services in the evenings. At the end of the first day, we were all tired. It was getting close to start the service, and I was sitting on a log looking at the passage I was going to preach on that night. Out of the corner of my eye, I noticed a young man walking back and forth. When I realized he wanted to talk to me I made eye contact and beckoned him to come over. He did, and we began to talk. His reason for coming was to share with me the fact that some people in the village had some concerns about my being here. I wanted to know why. He reluctantly told me that they had been told by means of their storyteller that many years ago their people had a conflict with some people in a village not far away. In the end, their people had been victorious and had taken some of the other people captive. Soon after this, some Europeans came to the village and these ancestors sold the people they had enslaved. He said those people had not been seen or heard from since.

Now the people had been told that my wife and I had come from that place where the Europeans took those people and they are afraid that I had come back to bring a curse on them. According to their tradition, it was the responsibility of the descendent to take revenge for wrong done, even if that wrong was done to their family before their lifetime. Therefore, I was to be responsible for taking revenge.

I can't tell you exactly how I felt about this. I felt that I couldn't preach that night because I felt like the people were afraid of me and didn't want to hear what I had to say. I began thinking of who I could get to preach, and as I contemplated and prayed, I was playing with the pages of my Bible. My eyes fell on the 50th chapter of Genesis.

This is the story of the events that took place after Jacob's death. Joseph's brothers sent messages to Joseph to ask him to forgive them. Later, they went themselves and Joseph assured them that he was not there to take revenge on them and that he was not in God's place. He told them that they meant what they did to him for evil, but God meant it for good in order to save many people.

That evening I preached from that passage. And when we left, we left a fairly strong church in that village.

The World Asks

One thing I became aware of after I became a missionary was that there are very few black Americans who are involved as missionaries overseas. This was a need the foreign mission board of the Southern Baptist Convention recognized. We served there for nine years before being directed back to the U.S. to focus attention on encouraging other African Americans to consider the possibility of God calling them to international missionary service. I was offered a position to encourage other African Americans to consider international missions and accepted this position after my wife and I prayed about it. My assignment was to enlist and nurture African Americans for missionary service. After my wife and I left the field, and the only other African-American missionary resigned from the field, we were left with zero. Well, there's only one way to go from zero, and that is up.

God clarified my call to international missions over a period of years. Among other things, he used my wife to help me understand His timing. In looking back, I can see how a number of turning points in my life served to direct me toward the mission field, most often without my understanding what was going on. I can say that the key to understanding that call was a desire to be obedient to my Lord and a willingness to go anywhere He wanted to send me.

One of the most important things I do is to educate people to the fact that foreign missions is not optional according to Scripture. As Christians we have an obligation to share the Gospel with all the peoples of the world not just our friends and neighbors.

Involvement in carrying out the Great Commission is not optional. It is not regional. It was not given to one specific segment of Christendom, but it was given to, in my opinion, the Church as a whole. We are responsible for making disciples of all nations, and all Christians are to be involved in this.

At the present time there is a tremendous cry coming from overseas for more Americans of African descent to come as missionaries. People around the world are beginning to ask the question, "Where are the black missionaries?"

Chapter 37

Michael Johnson: What Does it Cost to do Missions?

by Michael Johnson

I Didn't Want to Be That Good!

The author and radio personality, Garrison Keilor, was heard to relate the story of holding his newborn baby daughter in his hands. He tells of the joy of holding new life. It was such a joy to behold a soft and innocent baby in his arms. He knew his daughter would forever change his life. She would require constant attention. She would require sacrifice. She would require him to change. She would require him to be a better person. He would have to be good. Then he goes on to admit, "I didn't want to be that good!"

I guess when it comes down to it, I really don't want to get too close to Jesus. I don't want to be that good. We all wrestle with this somewhat. The more the Holy Spirit becomes real to me, the more I'm inclined to have second thoughts about this burden for missions.

You see, I became a Christian reluctantly. I was really enjoying all of the things in which I found myself involved. I enjoyed smoking dope. I enjoyed having any woman who would be willing to spend a little time with me.

I enjoyed the attention of being among the elite intellectuals within my small congregation of a black Baptist church. I enjoyed buying new expensive suits and shoes on a whim.

I enjoyed a life without real sacrifice. I enjoyed giving what was left over out of the abundance God had given me. I enjoyed going out to dinner for any occasion, spending whatever it would take to keep my wife happy, and impress my friends. I enjoyed buying those four new cars in five years.

I enjoyed having a beeper, a phone in my car and the ability to hire two staff members in the office to manage my growing patient load. I enjoyed the new computers we had purchased for the office and being able to dictate letters to the referring physicians detailing how I removed the skin tag from one man and the gall bladder from his wife.

Why did I need to do overseas missions? I really don't want to be that good!

Comfortable, Well-adjusted Negroes

Martin Luther King Jr. is quoted as saying he intended to "comfort the disturbed and disturb the comfortable." It is in this same sense that he went on to describe himself as a maladjusted person in one of his essays on nonviolence. In this essay, Dr. King writes thusly:

Michael and Kay Johnson sold their home and cars, closed a busy and prosperous surgical practice, and moved to Kenya with their four children in 1990. The Johnsons have since been involved in a variety of ministries in Kenya. Most of the ministries have revolved around hospital administration, surgical care for the extremely impoverished people of Kenya, work with street children, providing health care to more than 30,000 children of Nairobi, and the training of Kenyan physicians.

For a more detailed look into their personal triumphs, tribulations, joys, and sorrows in missions, read their book, *Making the Blind Man Lame*.

Modern psychology has a word that is probably used more than any other word. It is the word "maladjusted." Now we should all seek to live a well-adjusted life in order to avoid neurotic and schizophrenic personalities. But there are some things within our social order to which I am proud to be maladjusted and to which I call you to be maladjusted ... I call upon you to be as maladjusted as Amos who in the midst of the injustices of his day cried out in words that echo across the generation, "Let judgment run down like waters and righteousness like a mighty stream."

Our problem with regard to reaching the world for Jesus Christ is that we are too comfortable and too well adjusted to the world. We are comfortable, well-adjusted Negroes. Our churches are getting bigger. We are on television preaching, teaching, and reaching our own. We have our own brand names of clothes, magazines, television shows, and even take home Oscars and Grammy awards every year. We are so comfortable and well adjusted that we have completely forgotten that we live in a world that is in desperate need of food, water, clothing, and shelter.

That's the problem with Christianity. The more I read the Bible, I find that there has to be something to the admonition Christ lays out about "seeking the kingdom first" and having the needs of life met in the process (Matt 6:33). I don't want to be that good, however, because it will cause me to live out this goodness. It will cause me to "sell all I have and give to the poor and follow Him" (Matt 19:21).

I don't want to be that good because it will not allow me to store up treasures in this life, but cause me to think more about the life to come. Who needs that? I really want to enjoy life here, Lord. I told Jesus this on several occasions. This idea of bringing every thought captive to Christ (2 Corinthians 10:5) means that I can't even think bad thoughts, watch bad movies, tell dirty jokes or keep bad company, at least not for pleasure.

What good is this sterile life? How can I be of any use to God if I don't enjoy life? I don't want to be so good that I have to be that weird thing called "holy." Holiness and godliness are attributes for losers who wear out-of-date clothes, drive old cars, and watch dull movies in black and white. I don't want to be that good. Just let me be good enough to appear to be good. Just let me wear the cross around my neck without carrying the burden in my heart. "I promise I wont' stray too far from you, Jesus!"

Well, as we all know, God never does things halfway. I came to know the Lord as my Savior as a young boy. I didn't truly allow Him to be Lord of my life until I was in my junior year of college. There, after having done all of the wrong things, I knelt down and opened the Bible my mother had given me my freshman year. I asked the Lord to prove He was truly who He claimed to be by coming into my heart and doing what He said He could do.

Weeks later, I was on a date. I had one thing in my mind for this young lady. I would amuse her. I would overwhelm her with my charm. I would then do what everyone else was doing in those days of "do your own thing." As I laid out my plan on the date, I found something kept bothering me. I would want to say little nothings in her ear and it came out as spirit-filled somethings. Someone was interfering in my game plan. If I had known this was going to happen, I would never have invited Him into my heart!

The young lady looked at me in amazement. She asked, "What are you? Some kind of fanatic or something!" Well, needless to say, the night was only downhill from there. I did not get what I wanted because God answered my prayer. He did what He said He would do and started "giving me the desires of my heart" which He promised in Psalm 37:4. As I understand this verse, it means God would actually change the desires of my heart. He would actually make my heart desire other things than it would normally. In that sense, He would give my heart the things it should desire.

When I was in medical school at the University of Michigan, I attended New Hope Baptist Church. Dr. A. J. Lightfoot was my pastor there. He was my mentor and my friend. I admire him greatly for the tremendous influence he had upon me. One day he was preaching and he threw the Bible on the floor and put one foot on it. The he proclaimed, "You must be able to stand on the word of God!" It was the most vivid illustration I have ever had of how much I must learn to depend on God. I didn't have to make myself good.

God Could Do It if I Would Yield to His Word and Depend on Him

I still struggle with being good. God has built a hedge around me. I have my wife to remind me of my tendency to err and, of course, my kids constantly keep me in check, as I must be what I want them to be. I do believe that "He is increasing as I am decreasing" as John states in John 3:30.

I neglected her needs. I watched her cry. I have never known her to cry that long. I felt hopeless, yet when our kids were driven away for boarding school in Kenya for the first time in September 1990, I saw a side of my wife that still shakes me. It was at least a five-hour drive and we stayed behind, entrusting our kids to other missionary parents. Kay cried.

She cried more than eight hours straight. The following day, she went to work. She wore sunglasses to hide her swollen, bloodshot eyes from her Kenyan and missionary coworkers at Tenwek Hospital. I still wince at the thought of this pain she endured as she saw our kids driven away. My wife is God's second best gift to me.

I believe that if God had not heard my cry and sent me this beautiful woman, I would be in the same drunken stupor I was in the night the Holy Spirit came to me and revealed His salvation plan for my life—which is my first best gift from God.

I was in my junior year in college. I had done all of the things that my mom had told me not to do. Well, at least many of them. I recall my mom crying, too, as she looked at me as I sat in a drunken stupor during one college visit she made to encourage me. College was such a lonely time for me. I was in a college town in upstate WI. Black people were warned not to stay out late in the town. There was reportedly still a law on the books of the town that said that Black people could not stay overnight in town.

In the midst of my fear, loneliness, and anxiety, I took to partying with the "fellas." It took my mind off all of the reminders of my inferiority constantly around me. It didn't fix the problem, but it dulled its influence. No fraternities made us feel comfortable.

No societies or fraternities welcomed us. This was in spite of this being the mid-1960's liberal, freedom era. The Lord God spoke to me one day in the midst of all this insanity. He bade me open the Bible that my mom had sent me three years earlier. He showed me in Psalm 1 that He could cause me to prosper. I told the Lord that I needed a soulmate in order to make it.

I told God that I could not be the kind of Christian He wanted me to be, unless I could have a woman that loved Him more than she loved me. He promised me that He would provide me such a woman. One and one half years later, I met Miss Sandra Kay Hugan in New Hope Baptist Church in Ann Arbor, MI, where I attended medical school.

This was not really love at first sight. It was more of my lust at first sight. Kay was a beautiful girl. I say "girl" because she was all of 17 when I met her. I could not take my eyes off her. I was a freshman in medical school, dating a senior in high school. I even took her to her prom. I was so afraid I would meet some of my classmates en route to the banquet. It was a challenge to both of us as I hid behind posts and columns at the hotel in an effort to remain incognito. I am sure she wondered if I was on some hallucinogen that night as I dodged real and imaginary colleagues.

We were married two years later. Kay was attending Eastern Michigan University in Ypsilanti, studying accounting and I was in my junior year of medical school at the University of MI.[1]

There were many naysayers. Many in my family thought I was marrying "beneath myself." This was a young girl whose family had no professional people. She had never traveled. I introduced her to her first taste of something as common as Chinese food. That was considered a novelty. How were we going to make it?

That was a good question. Our first year of marriage was a challenge. During the summer of 1977, I could only find work as a dishwasher in a restaurant, so we were on welfare for two months to supplement the income.

It Cost My Wife to be Obedient

My new bride had gone from the comfort of her mom's home to the life of a poor college student in less than one month. She was less than happy. What had she gotten herself into? When she became pregnant with Elijah a few months later, we had to depend upon government assistance

---

[1] We now have more than 20 years of marriage and I find her more beautiful and I love her even more. I no longer hide when people come up to us unless I can't remember their names. She helps me then.

for dairy products under the Women, Infant and Children program, or WIC.

I was still doing some of the bad habits of hanging out with the "fellas" and this was not to her liking. Right away, she started to put her foot down. I had to determine my priorities. I think this was what I asked the Lord to do, wasn't it? Kay was an answer to my prayer. I began my clerkships in the hospital and Kay was full time in school. Right away, the mistress of medicine entered into my life. This mistress was so demanding that she would not even allow me the comfort of being at home without thinking of her. Medical school and the years which followed were some of the loneliest years for Kay.

I know she cried many times. I bought her a small puppy to keep her company and we named it Tasha. One day while we were away shopping, Kay got a sense of urgency to return to the house. When we got home, we discovered Tasha had jumped from the porch with the leash and collar still on and had hung himself. Kay cried. My attempt at comfort had failed. I bought her another right away and we named it Dina.

Upon my graduation from Ann Arbor in 1979, we moved to Philadelphia in order for me to train in surgery. Kay had never lived away from home. We loaded up a U-Haul truck with furniture from my mother and some old pieces from our little place and moved. Elijah, our eldest child, was just about one year old. He got car sick in the truck just a few miles from Ann Arbor and Kay got upset because I wouldn't stop and take him to the doctor. In my typical male "hunt it down and kill it" attitude, I rebuffed her and told her we had to reach our destination. Now in retrospect, I realize her real cry was that she was leaving home.

I was taking her away from all the comforts she knew. Moving was no big thing to me. We had moved over a dozen times while in Chicago, where I grew up. Traveling to a new city was no big thing as we had traveled from coast to coast and made numerous trips to East and West Europe and Mexico while I was still a boy. I was insensitive to why she was near tears. I was insensitive while we settled into a rooming house with a motorcycle gang living above us. I would leave for work at 5:30 a.m. and return at 8:00 p.m. the following day. Kay was alone in that house with Dina. The surgical residency attitude is that "the only thing wrong with every other night call is that you miss half of the good cases." My mistress of medicine became more and more demanding and unforgiving, as I needed to impress my seniors in order to keep my job and advance in the program.

I left Kay alone in Philadelphia. She had no job, no friends, and she had left school mid-term to move to Philadelphia with me. She had left her college career, her family, and all she knew to be with me. We finally made it out of that rooming house as Kay continued to cry in her loneliness. I needed to find a way to make my mistress of medicine get along with my wife. It is still a task I haven't mastered.

Over the next few months the strain on our marriage continued. Kay found herself getting lonelier and more in need of companionship. We moved to Sharon Hill and joined First African Baptist Church. Kay found friendship and fellowship there. Before she was finally settled, however, she got ready to leave me. She bought a plane ticket to return to Ann Arbor. She was so lonely. I thought she would not survive our move, and certainly our marriage would fail.

As she called me at the hospital (I was too busy to take her to the airport) and told me she was leaving, I told her I loved her and would stay in touch. She told me that when she got to the airport she cried so much in front of the checkout counter that she could not get the man to understand that she had changed her mind. She says she knew that if she had left, she would never return to me again.

Kay stuck with me though my residency. She worked full time at St. Agnes hospital in Philadelphia in the Billing department and learned the medical insurance lingo and became proficient in medical terminology. She began to build her own life and came out from under the shadow of "Dr. Johnson'" as time went on.

Kay gave birth to Christina, our second born, in 1980, and then Emmanuel in 1983. She chose and bought our home in Upper Darby. I worked overtime, double time, triple time, to make the payments. I was rarely home for more than one day a week, and just for a chance to sleep and complain. Kay stuck with me. We never went anywhere for vacation during those years. I worked during vacation.

Kay would occasionally take the kids to Ann Arbor to visit family, but I would stay and work. At the end of those hellish five years, I told Kay

I would take her on a vacation adventure. It was not exactly the vacation she envisioned, but being a dutiful wife, she went along for the ride.

Real Missions: A Passion for Whores and Lepers

We cannot develop a passion for missions until we develop a passion for whores and lepers. Until we feel the desperation of people who are considered untouchable, undesirable, completely rejected and completely dejected by the world, we will never have a passion for missions.

We must learn to touch the filthy, embrace the smelly, look at the ugly, and welcome the completely unwholesome into our midst if we are going to impact the world for Jesus Christ.

Unfortunately, for most African-American churches, the closest we want to get to the disgusting things in our world is what we see on television when we hit the wrong remote button. We feel that we have somehow earned the right and privilege of not looking back from whence we came. It is this belief that we are still amongst the most downtrodden of the world that prohibits us from truly identifying with them. We carry the badge of honor of having "survived" the brutality and inhumanity of slavery, but dare not impart our experience and survival techniques to the billions of rejected in today's world.

Jesus constantly exhibited such a passion. As he reclined at table of Simon the leper in Mark 14, he felt perfectly comfortable as a woman came and anointed his feet. He did not withdraw from the people who most would have counted as untouchable either by reputation or disease. Quite the contrary, Jesus set the example for us by meeting the needs of those who received neither compassion nor counsel from the religious leaders of the day.

This was our introduction to missions in December 1984. We left the kids in the care of Kay's sister Brenda, who volunteered to come to Philadelphia for 7 weeks. We had no prospect of a job upon our return to Philly. We had a few checks coming in from the work I had done which would cover the mortgage and groceries for those few weeks. We were heading for Africa!

The Cost Brought a Life-changing Experience to Kay and Me

Our values and worldview changed. We had one thing in mind when we went. I at least thought I could do short-term missions. Kay was just being a beautiful, submissive wife.

We came back from Zaire and determined we would never do anything so foolish again. Missionaries in Zaire had to take everything for four years. Four years of shoe sizes, corn flakes, and toilet paper, and hard things to calculate. We were determined that we had suffered enough from medical school and residency. Why should we do anything like missions?

I did not want to make my wife suffer anymore. I was tired of seeing and making her cry. I was determined to reward her for her faithfulness and her support all of those years. I would do anything possible to keep her happy. I didn't have to make her cry again. She made herself cry.

Kay showed a determination to love Christ more than she would love the world. She made a determination to love the Lord so much that she would give up her own aspirations to serve him anywhere. In 1987, she heard the Lord tell her we needed to make another trip to Africa. I had heard Him as well, but I did not want to bring it up. I did not want to make her cry again. Kay was determined to do God's bidding no matter what the cost.

We took our kids to Africa for the first time in December 1987. We served at Tenwek Hospital. It was here the Lord confirmed our call to missions. Kay used the skills she had mastered in computers, which she had learned in putting together her physician's billing service in Philadelphia. She used the managerial skills she had honed as she managed my very busy private surgical practice.

As we returned from Kenya in January 1998, where we had served for seven weeks, we determined to close the practice. We sent all our patients letters to tell them of our intended move. We sent letters to all of the referring physicians to let them know of our plans. We let our two office employees go. We sold some of the office equipment. Much of the equipment, like computers and phones, we gave to friends and to the church.

We began selling our house furniture and giving away clothes and toys. We gave away Kay's car to my mother. It was a car I had given her for her birthday. We made our wills. The mission had made it known that we had to specify what we wanted done with our bodies should we die overseas. It was the mission policy in the past to have the body buried in the foreign field.

What would we do if our kids were kidnapped? We had to prepare ourselves for this because it was in the mission policy not to pay kidnappers. If we were held in some jungle in Africa that would mean we would either be released or found by interested parties. To underscore this threat, we recently were required to have all of the family's hand and fingerprints placed on file with the mission.

We checked out our new insurance policies: life, health, and dental. We resigned our positions on boards and committees. I sent notices to the hospitals that I was no longer going to be in attendance as a surgeon. This move cost us a lot. It cost us friends as we searched for churches that believed we were truly called into missions and did not see it as an affront to their home mission activities.

I had not yet paid off my student loans, as I had the kids in private schools and was paying Kay's student loans, the house note, and two car loans, not to mention two employees in the office. We went to Kenya with the mindset of using our residual savings to pay off the loans.

Because Kay was such a dutiful wife, I had tried to make life a little easy for her before this call. When she bought our home in Upper Darby, I let her pick it out. I wanted her to be happy. For the seven years we were there, she poured her life into this house. She had decorated, picked out the curtains, chosen which flowers would be planted in which flowerbeds after the landscaping had been furnished.

Kay had now decided that in order to do God's will for our lives, she was willing to do without. If I felt it was necessary to be obedient to the call to serve, she was going to go all the way. All the way meant ridding ourselves of the many things we called "ours."

Kay either saw that it was sold or given away. Since we did not have much time before departure, most of it was given away. I saw my wife give away her crystal glasses, her fine china, and her linens. I saw my wife take the carpets up and the curtains down. I saw my wife give away the beautiful brand new bedroom set of furniture with soft lighting and mirrored matching dressers. I saw my wife give away her gold plated flatware and many of the wedding presents of small appliances and dishes. I saw her give away a lot of things, but I did not see her cry.

One of the things I had done before our decision to visit Kenya for the first time was to buy Kay a nice coat. I did not have enough money to buy her a full-length fur coat, so in the midst of my practice, I bought her a coat with a fur collar. I can still see her cry as she accepted this gift years earlier. Now, as we stood on the back porch of the house we had just sold, Kay cut the collar off her coat. She wanted some memento of the good times. She was trying to salvage something of those good years. Now it was all gone.

Someone else, a Buddhist family, was getting all of the good work she had put into the house. Someone else was using her fine china and flatware and crystal. Someone else was benefiting from her loss of so many things she had set her heart upon. She knew this and it made her cry.

Once again in Kenya, Kay did all the right things. She decorated the kids' rooms. She made them special treats. She put the labels in their clothes as they got ready to be driven to school. She tried to make each of the Kenyan houses a "home," knowing that they would not be there to enjoy them except for one out of every four months, and for a brief visit one weekend out of every six.

I refer to these houses as "homes" because that is what happens. Each time we leave Kenya, we move out of, and back into, a "home." The last house we lived in at Tenwek was in such bad shape that no missionary wanted to live in it. This was for good reason. The walls were in bad repair. The floor would shake when we walked on it, giving the impression that the entire house would fall at any time.

The ceiling boards bowed downward as the rats overhead did the all-night disco (could have been the music). Kay cried the entire first night of our move into this house. I had to assure her that we could fix the place up. After several doses of poison, we were able to remove the rats which died in the open, and tolerate those who died in the ceiling as the stench from their bodies slowly dissipated.

I often times feel I have neglected my wife, but God has given her such strength of character as to forget the things she left behind, that she has truly pressed forward to claim Christ. I have seen my wife "count these things as dung" as Paul admonishes in Philippians 3:8 (KJV), "Yea doubtless, and I count all things but loss for the excellency of the knowledge of Christ Jesus my Lord: for whom I have suffered the loss of all things, and do count them but dung that I may win Christ."

I have seen God bless her with an understanding of His grace and goodness that far surpasses all of the things she has left behind. This gives me cause to cry tears of joy.[2]

Elijah Learned from the Cost

I often felt, and I am still of the opinion, that we have neglected our children for this work. I don't feel we always acted in the will of God. I think we acted many times out of our fleshly desire to see a work completed or a project finished. We neglected our children in order to finish this work. It didn't necessarily have anything to do with Kingdom building. When we first went to Kenya as fulltime missionaries, we felt a great strain within our relationship with Elijah, our first born.

We had adopted the Scripture, 1 Peter 2:9, as our family scripture where Paul notes that "we are a chosen generation," "a royal priesthood," "an holy nation," "a peculiar people." From this was born our motto

"Those peculiar Johnsons."

Elijah was not interested in being "peculiar." He was 12 years old. He was coming into his own. He was the son of a successful black surgeon in suburban Philadelphia. He could see the writing on the wall. He was ready to be different, but certainly not peculiar. Then mom and dad had to get this idea in their heads of going to Africa! Elijah would write letters and notes for us to find. Consider this for instance:

Dear Everybody,

The reason I hate being a Johnson is because I don't like being laughed at because I don't have any Nintendo game. And I don't like having to stand in front of crowds. I don't like going places. I don't like being not able to see my friends. And I don't like missing field trips from going places. I also hate being the only person who has school at home until 5:00 p.m. doing classes over and over. These are the many reasons I am going to run away. I also don't want to be a missionary going to Kenya.

Elijah

P.S. I don't like my little brother.

Elijah would write letters about being a part of "those dumb Johnsons" and deface our newsletters and prayer cards with the same words.

We were doing home schooling for Elijah as he was in the seventh grade, Christina in the 4th, Emannuel in 1st grade. Keturah was learning to get our attention with loud noises. Home schooling is a true test of our love of many things. Do you love your children? Do you like home? Do you enjoy reading and teaching? Mix the three together. It sounds alright when you see it on paper like this. But in reality, it is worse than having your teeth itch—just where do you scratch?

Home schooling, in my humble opinion, was created to punish people who did not appreciate their teachers when they were students. I think the worst lessons were those I had to teach on the "birds and the bees." I tried to make it an accounting course so Kay would be obligated to teach it, but she refused to acknowledge that "multiply and fill the earth" had anything to do with mathematics.

Our kids were hit with the double whammy of trying to do home schooling and raise support for missions on the road. We taught them from the backseat of the car and in hotels and motels as we spoke about mission in a variety of big and small churches in big and small towns. Elijah was not happy.

He would cut his picture out of our family portrait on the prayer cards. The other kids, being younger, Christina 10, Emmanuel 7, and Keturah 3 years old, were relatively oblivious to all of this. They knew we were moving, but it didn't mean a whole lot to them. They just wanted to make sure that we took all of their good stuff with them. Kay made sure of that. I am sure that to my estimation, at least 80 percent of that container we sent to Kenya had stuff like toys, kids clothes, and the like in it (and, of course, the Nintendo). I could be wrong about this.

---

[2] As Kay read this part of the story, she cried again. Being the sensitive guy I am, I ask her, "Now, why are you crying?" She said, "All that time, I never even thought you noticed my tears."

Christina Learned from the Cost

We made a covenant with the kids. We told them that if, at the end of one year, if they felt collectively that this work in Kenya was destroying us as a family, we would come home. We made that promise and we were sincere in it. For the next two and one half years in Kenya, we never heard even a little discomfort in their voices.

True, the day they were driven away to boarding school, the day Kay cried so hard, was traumatic for all of us. For several months we persevered. Kay threw herself into her work in order to forget the pain she felt. I was always used to serving my mistress of medicine. Working hard and neglecting everyone and everything was normal for me. I don't think I gave it a second thought, as I had grown accustomed to a tunnel with no light at the end of it. It is called surgery residency.

One day we received notice that we must keep Christina at home when she returned for semester break. The teachers and dorm parents were in agreement. Christina was depressed. One of them stated she was the most depressed child they had ever seen. We were not sure what to do. We did not want to neglect her emotional state. We thought we would have to do home school again. So we decided we would do whatever was necessary for Christina. After this break, Christina would stay at home.

God had another plan, however. At the end of that month, Christina appeared exuberant and revived and was ready to return to school. It was God's grace in action. It was not the first time we would need God to intervene for Christina. During Christina's last year at boarding school, we receive word that again she was in the dumps. Her counselor thought she was in danger of doing harm to herself. Their advice was that we bring Christina home to Tenwek or take her home to America.

Christina's grades suffered. Her relationships with her friends had soured in addition; she was a terror at home whenever she would visit. It was a very heavy spiritual battle. The amazing thing about all of this is that we were oblivious to just how deep her depression was. Kay and I were so immersed in our work that we had failed to recognize our daughter was in trouble. We had neglected our calling to our children.

We were not able to be with Christina as she confronted a teacher who called an African student a "nigger" in front of the whole class. We were not able to comfort her when one of her teachers would tell her that slavery was a good thing from God and that the American Indians or Native Americans were allowed to be slaughtered in accordance with God's desire because they were an ungodly people.

These issues were handled by mail to the teachers and principals of Rift Valley Academy because we could never get away from work to deal with them. I never really felt totally satisfied at the outcomes. No teacher was ever disciplined or sent home for such insensitivities.

We hurriedly made the necessary move to get out of Tenwek when we finally recognized our failings in ministering to our children. Some grumbling of our fellow missionaries at Tenwek also precipitated this move itself. However, their discontent with our work served to awaken us to our missed ministry to our children. We moved to Kijabe Hospital on the campus of the boarding school. This move was God's healing process in our family. It was His way of helping us keep our covenant with our children that the work of missions would not supersede our obligation to them.

As I write this chapter, Christina is doing phenomenally well in school, a freshman, studying pre-med with an eye to child psychology or psychiatry. She is more in love with Jesus than ever. She has blossomed to be the young woman that God promised us He could make her to be. Elijah is there with her in the same school, studying pre-med, and a junior, with an eye to forensic pathology or plastic surgery. (Go figure. Try to help the dead or enhance the living.) He also likes his brother.

Our Marriage Grew Better with the Cost

It took this same near meltdown to awaken us to the trouble continuing to brew in our own marriage. We were so intent on doing God's will through our lives, that we neglected God's doing His will in our lives. We placed all of our energies into doing and little attention was placed into being. We buried ourselves in work. I would average as much as five major cases per day. I would work two clinics on some days, surgery clinic, orthopedic clinic and do the consults on the wards including covering for labor and delivery ward, doing the necessary C-sections or difficult vaginal deliveries.

I would make rounds, operate and then try to lead a Bible study in the evening. I worked on several committees of the hospital, administrate as medical superintendent, and try to keep up all of the correspondence with our 2,000 plus prayer and financial supporters.

I was working on a variety of projects, including the internship program, the recruitment of missionaries from abroad, the intensive care unit, the intravenous fluid production plant for the hospital, the building of the library for the Tenwek primary school and providing books for that library.

I was frequently called upon to preach at the many churches in the area. I was the "guest of honor" at a variety of special fundraising events. I attended weddings and funerals of my Kenyan friends in order to build our relationships, but at the cost of my own relationships within my family. In the midst of all this, I would try to get to see our kids every third or fourth weekend by driving five hours away to their school.

I missed most of the ball games and special events they had. I would let Kay go to as many of these as she could. When we did come home to the U.S., I was not much better. I would work in order to make up the difference in the money I had not paid toward my student loans. I would visit any church, which would request it in order to raise support and awareness of missions.

We would typically make at least two meetings every week. I would work part-time, sometimes full time. In 1996, while at home, I worked full time as a surgeon, studied for my surgical board recertification, published two newsletters, visited 30 churches, went to basketball games at the kid's school, made trips back and forth to visit Elijah in college, and after 5 months of living like this, returned to work in Kenya exhausted and wondering what was wrong with God.

Little did I know that my relation with my wife was not improving. We were still in love, but we were drifting in our commitment to one another. Kay was no better, when it came to overworking. She returned to Tenwek and immersed herself in work like never before. As the financial comptroller of a hospital with a budget of over one million dollars, she was responsible for finding the holes in the pockets and the hands of the cookie jars.

With over 500 employees, Tenwek depends on donated professional help such as Kay. There are a lot of ways money could get lost. Kay did not make a lot of friends in that position. But she was able to make it possible for the hospital to operate on the income generated from patient fees. The capital development came from oversees still, but the day-to-day operation came from patient fees. Kay worked tirelessly with a staff that was not known for its honesty, efficiency, or talents.

Upon her arrival in 1987, there was no one in computer services. She updated the hospital computer services to function for accounting and inventory. Upon her return in 1990, she oversaw the audits. She oversaw all of the legal and insurance needs of the hospital. She performed the audits for the outlying clinics and dispensaries. She monitored the cash and inventory books for the church bookstores.

These duties required her to spend hours on the road between Nairobi, Kericho, Nakuru and the dirt roads to the outlying clinics. She spent so much time on the roads that her duties at home and at the hospital would conflict. Home was easy to neglect, as everyone understood, she was doing this for Jesus. It is just the way we lived. This all came to a head when we came to recognize that not only was Christina in trouble, but so were we.

We saw that we were not speaking of loyalty to one another, but loyalty to the work. If we did not have the wake up call provided by our fellow missionaries, we would probably have persisted in this madness. In Joel 2:25, God promised He would "restore the years that the locust had eaten." God has proven faithful. Our family and our marriage is stronger now than ever. God has fulfilled His promise.

Early on in our marriage we had begun reading the Bible together. One particular portion has been the solution to many of the problems we have faced. Deuteronomy promises that God would bless everything we put our hands to if we would abide in His will. We have also found that having a "purpose" as a family has made a difference.

Our kids have never really complained about our work. They have been somewhat sheltered. They have gone to a boarding school, the Rift Valley Academy in Kijabe, Kenya. This school is an American "oasis" in many ways. It has many of the trappings of any American school, with sports and entertainment activities suited for the mainly north American students. The school has many students from many countries and this allows our children to have a broad range of experience and a broad view of the world.

Our children have experienced the best and worst of Kenya as they have gone with us to the slums of Nairobi and the resort hotels of Mombasa (at reduced missionary rates). To say they have missed something in the U.S. is not true, unless one considers they have missed the opportunities to become involved in a culture, which encourages them to desire more than they could ever use of "stuff."

The Cost Produced A Johnson Family New "Coat of Arms"

In April 1995, we made a family covenant. It is a document we have placed in our family Bibles and each copy of our personal Bibles. It is what we recite whenever we have our family devotions. It was conceived as our "coat of arms." The Johnson Family Covenant has helped Kay and me remember that our first call is to our God. We could be "peculiar" without being dumb.

JOHNSON FAMILY COVENANT

Our God and Father has given us life and health in order that we as a family may serve Him and glorify Him. We therefore resolve as a family that we will glorify God in our daily lives by:

1. Representing Jesus Christ the Son of God, as we live and how we live. We will do nothing for self-glory or selfish ambition, but in accordance with scripture. 1 Corinthians 10:31 (NIV), "So whether you eat or drink or whatever you do, do all to the glory of God." Bringing others to Christ by our deeds, words, thoughts, dreams and desires.
2. We recognize the world is looking for hope in God and many will only read the scripture that they see written in our daily lives. In accordance with scripture, Matthew 5:16 (NIV), "In the same way, let your light so shine before men, that they may see your good deeds and praise your Father in heaven."
3. Living together in love at home and as a family. We can only do this by dwelling in unity at home as brothers, sisters, cousins, aunts, and uncles, mothers, fathers, nieces, nephews, grandfathers and grandmothers. We recognize it is impossible to show love outside of the family if we cannot show it inside of the family. We also cannot love God if we do not love one another. In accordance with scripture, Psalms 133:1 (NIV), "How good and pleasant it is when brothers live together in unity!" We will share in rejoicing, sorrow, dreaming, hoping, loving, losing, gaining, forgiving, laughing, crying, success and failure. We will share one another's burdens and victories. In accordance with Scripture, Romans 12:15 (NIV), "Rejoice with those who rejoice, mourn with those who mourn."
4. Recognizing that God will honor us as we honor Him. Our individual success must always be successes, which will honor God. In accordance with scripture, 1 Samuel 2:30 (NIV), " … Those who honor me I will honor, but those who despise me will be disdained."
5. Putting aside selfish aim and work only for the Kingdom of God, knowing that all of life's greatest needs will be taken care of by Him.

In accordance with scripture, Matthew 6:33 (NIV), "But seek first His kingdom and His righteousness, and all these things will be given to you as well."

The Cost of Giving Our Talents Back to Jesus, Our Lord

We are familiar with Jesus' parable of the talents. But the passage as I read it lacked a little punch to it. So, in the margins of my own Bible I added one more servant to the passage. This guy was given not five, not two, and not one talent. This servant that I added was given 20 talents. I know I am not supposed to add to the Bible, but it's only in the margins so I think I am okay.

It just so happened that this guy took his talents and did not invest it like the other guys, nor did he hide it under a rock. Instead, he had a party! It was a great party! Everyone who was anybody, or thought he was anybody, came to the party.

At the end of the party, when his master came and asked him what he did with the 20 talents, he told him straight up: "I had a party and you should have been here!"

Then the master asked, "Is that all you did?"

This guy, without shame, says, "Oh, yeah. Here is your change!"

We have been given a legacy as an American people of African descent. We have been given the legacy of having survived being dragged from within the African inland to the shores. A few of us survived the journey that went from the shores of Africa to some of the nations of Europe, North Africa, Southeast Asia, and the Americas. We in North America were better off than many in these other destinations. We actually saw white people fighting and killing other white people in order to free us, when we had no guns, armies or money to do so ourselves. When we did fight alongside them for our freedom, the guns we used, we had to turn in afterwards.

We survived slavery, reconstruction, Jim Crow segregation, lynchings, mob violence, and persistent intimidation from the halls of government to the institutions of higher learning and healing. We were, and in many instances still are, last hired, first fired. We could not vote, had no chance within the halls of justice, and lived in housing similar to that we see in much of the third world today.

We now have an income and disposable wealth equivalent to that of several African nations combined. We literally have billions at our disposal to buy whatever we want. We have been given 20 talents. What are we doing? We are having a party!

No matter where I go in Africa, or the world, the legacy of Martin Luther King Jr. and others like him are known more prominently by others than known or appreciated by those of African descent in America. Why is that? I believe that it means more to them.

It means more to them to know of our history and the struggles we faced and how our Lord and Master helped us to overcome, than it means to us. They are struggling to overcome as we once did. They have embraced our legacy, our 20 talents.

We are preaching the gospel of self-reliance and morality to people who are dying, not from lack of motivation or morality. No doubt there are parts of this in every scenario. This is not the sole cause for billions of men, women, and children who are caught in the spider's web of poverty. This web has many strands, including bad government, bad traditions, and bad policies. However, some of the stickiest strands of this web are our own indulgences in having the best of everything without considering the cost to the nations of the people providing those things.

What have we done with the talent that our forefathers decreed us? What have we done with the mandate within the American Black National Anthem? That mandate states that we will forever be true to our God and true to our native land.

We have been given a legacy of suffering and overcoming. Let us use that to comfort the disturbed and disturb the comfortable. Let us go into the world and make a difference for Christ. He will ask a lot of questions at the end of all this. To find comfort and to be well adjusted for the questions, just read ahead for the test: What have you done to the least of these? (Matt 25:40–46).

When the party is over, where will we go if we have wasted our legacy? The Master is coming and He will require an accounting. There are literally billions that don't know anything about Him all around the globe. That is part of our mandate as the church.

If we want to be invited to the wedding of the Lamb, let's not go to the party of our own making. Let us use the legacy God has given us in a manner which brings Him the glory due His name.

Chapter 38

Hakim Scott Stands Tall as a Missionary to China

by Thomas M. Watkins

In more ways than one, Hakim Scott stands out from the crowd. A tall African American with an athletic build, Scott is a rare sight among the teaming masses of people in China. He is also a unique example of how God is mobilizing, calling, and equipping a new generation of African Americans for strategic missionary service overseas.

Scott's story begins in Detroit, MI, where he was born to Muslim parents. His father was a dedicated Muslim who taught him many things about the Islamic faith. Hakim always considered himself a Muslim, but more on a nominal basis. He did obey many laws of the Koran, including never eating pork. But, as he says, "my heart was empty." There was clearly an emptiness in his life, a restlessness that was present despite following the strict tenets of the Muslim faith.

Hakim's family couldn't afford for him to go to college, so at age 18 he joined the U.S. Air Force at his father's request. Ironically, it was in the military service that he had a life-changing encounter that led him into the service of the ultimate King of Kings. His first assignment was to an air base in the South.

"I became good friends with one of my dorm mates, Samuel Robinson," Scott recounted. "He lived a sinful life, with girlfriends, rap music, and all. I thought to myself that I would never want to be like him. When I turned 19, I felt a profound spiritual emptiness. But as I look back, I know the Lord was working in my life."

It was not too long before the two were separated. Robinson was transferred to an overseas base. One year later, Hakim also found himself stationed at the same base. But a great surprise awaited him there.

> When I got there, all the guys kept saying, "You'd better stay away from Sam Robinson, because he'll invite you to church." He called me after I had just gotten there and asked me to be his roommate. I really didn't want to, but eventually agreed. When I moved in, he was gone for the first three days, but I noticed some really unusual things. He didn't have the same music tapes and all that he did before. I wondered, "What's happened to him?"

When Samuel returned, Hakim described it as "meeting a new man."

Thomas M. Watkins is Director of Foundation and Corporate Relations for Trans World Radio, an international Christian broadcasting ministry based in Cary, NC. He has served as a contributing writer and editor of Christian books and periodicals as well as business trade publications.

Editor's Note: The identity of Hakim Scott, along with some of the names of people and places in this article, have been changed for security reasons.

He invited me to church. Although I was a Muslim, I wanted to see what had happened to him. As I listened to Sunday school lessons, God began to open my eyes, and I decided to receive Jesus Christ into my life. I realized that only God could change a man's life like He had changed Sam's. From the day He saved me, God called me to preach His Word.

While stationed overseas, Hakim met his wife and began serving the Lord, starting with teaching deaf people. After three years, he faced the major decision of whether to reenlist. He told God he could stay in the Air Force and serve Him. He began praying, fasting, and reading his Bible earnestly. It was then that God spoke to him through a passage in Isaiah 50 that he was to leave the Air Force. He and his new wife returned to the States where he attended a Baptist college, graduating four years later.

Hakim says that his heart was always burdened for missions, and he still wanted to help the deaf. His first short-term mission trip was to Mexico to reach the deaf. He also has a desire to reach Muslims and met a number of them on subsequent trips to the Ukraine and to Albania. Then one day a missionary came to his home and asked him to pray about going to China.

"My first reaction was, 'I'm black, and there're no blacks in China,'" said Scott. "But I said I'd pray about it."

As God began to open doors, he made his first trip to China and shot a video that he brought back to show to his wife. A year later they departed for China where they have now served as missionaries for three years.

History records that China expelled all missionaries during the 1949 revolution and the vast nation of more than 1.2 billion people remains officially closed to missionary work today. To keep up with the world, China had to relinquish some of its Communist ways and open up to the West. But Scott is one of many who are allowed into the country as "tentmakers"—those who officially enter the country as businessmen, teachers, students, technical experts, or other occupations—and once inside the country, are able to share their faith and establish secret Bible studies or underground "house churches."

Missions experts estimate there are between 50 and 100 million evangelical Christians in China today, most of whom have been saved and discipled through the underground movement. In spite of great persecution, the Church in China is believed to be among the fastest-growing anywhere in the world, fueled by the efforts of missionaries like Scott, Christian ministries that are able to smuggle Bibles and other Christian literature into the country, and radio broadcasts from outside the country that are evangelizing and discipling believers and ministering to the house churches and their leaders.

Scott joined a missionary-sending organization and started out working alongside another missionary who was already there. However, it wasn't long before the other missionary experienced health problems and had to leave the field. The Lord had put the ministry in Hakim's hands.

Hakim's official status in China is that of a teacher. That brings him into contact with a large number of people whom he has been able to befriend and share the Gospel with.

I try to do the best job I can in teaching, and before I know it I am able to make friends. One of the first things I tell my students is that I'm a Christian and that I am willing to teach the Bible in English.

Hakim has even had some Chinese soldiers who have participated in some of the studies. He tends to receive a slightly higher response to the Gospel from women than men. And his best response is from young people ages 25 to 30.

The Lord has allowed me to get to know and love many Chinese people, most of them young people. Many of them are disillusioned with the government and with the Communist system, and are open to the Gospel. They typically come to faith in Christ much more quickly than the older people; they are not as brainwashed. I began to teach people and started a house church using small group Bible studies, and by refuting evolution. The Lord has begun to add to the church; I was just a vessel.

Hakim has also been involved in the high-stakes smuggling of Bibles into China, and has been caught on at least one occasion. A false rumor circulated at one point among his supporters in the U.S. that he had been jailed.

While being an African American in China has made him stand out, Scott believes it has also been an advantage in many ways:

> One of the big advantages is that when people see you, they instantly wonder why you are here. There are not a lot of black Americans who travel overseas—Africans travel to China more than black Americans. I often get asked if I am an NBA player. People stare at me and nudge each other when they see me. No one's ever mistreated me. There was one instance when I tried to teach English but they said I wasn't what they were looking for. I've always had good rapport with the schools, usually as a back-up to the regular teachers.

Although living costs in China are quite reasonable, still raising the support he needs for himself, his wife, and children has been quite a challenge for Scott. One of their biggest financial needs is for travelling expenses. "I have both white and black churches supporting me," he noted.

He added,

> I have no problem with color. I never look at my color as an obstacle. But sometimes people are cautious—many doubted at first about a black man saying he was going to be a missionary in China. Our support actually went up after we got there. One pastor at a missions conference took me aside and told me that a black man with a foreign-born wife going to China wouldn't work. He said later he had to confess that to the Lord and apologized. Some said we should go to the inner cities. I was reminded that Jonah went to a place he didn't even like. I had always prayed for China.

> Some people told me they didn't like black people over there, but I have not found that to be the case at all. Then there are some churches that don't support me because I have kept my Muslim name. Not everyone has been behind me, but my local church in the U.S. has been very supportive, and that has made a tremendous difference.

Scott believes that now is a wonderful time for evangelism in China because every foreigner is not under suspicion. The proof is in the results of the God-blessed ministry of an African American who was not afraid to take a monumental step of faith: over 50 people led to Christ so far, many of whom have become witnesses themselves. There are so many yet who wait to hear the Gospel for the first time.

Chapter 39

Virgil Amos: Seeing Ourselves as Agents of God

by Virgil Lee Amos

My interesting missions began while studying at Moody Bible Institute, but I was reluctant in some ways. I didn't want to go to Alaska because it was too cold; nor did I want to go to Africa just because everyone thought I should go there. I had to humble myself to the point of saying, "Wherever You want, Lord."

Seeing is Believing

God then spoke to me about Iran, even though I had to go to the library to find out where it was! The same week God spoke to me about Mexico. Operation Mobilization (OM) was about the only mission that welcomed black people, so I went with them on five short-term outreaches before moving with my family to southern Spain. Soon after we went by ship to India, where in Bombay my job was to train south Indian workers en route to ministry in north India.

In 1966 we went to Iran and a year later I was put in charge. We soon saw the team double in size to 24 on five teams. We covered the country with literature. We were in the universities; we used every opportunity there was.

Already by 1970, my vision was to challenge Christians from minority groups about missions, as they were largely overlooked by traditional mission organizations. While finishing a degree in CA after leaving OM in 1975, I began a discipleship group and led them to Mexico for ten days' outreach, OM-style. A church was planted as a result. In 1982 Ambassadors Fellowship was formed and we sent teams back to Mexico. Soon we expanded to Spain and then Turkey, Kenya, Puerto Rico, Dominican Republic, and now Nigeria. We're also planning to work in Benin, Ghana, and Liberia.

African-American History of Mission is Alive Again

Very shortly after emancipation from slavery (1865), the black church in America was strongly involved in missions, sending workers across Europe to China and Africa. Sadly, the colonial realities in Africa led "white" missions to stop accepting black missionaries out of fear that they would identify and align themselves with the Africans and cause trouble for the colonial powers. Then came WWII, followed by a wave of persecution of blacks in the southern U.S. states and a subsequent migration of many blacks to the north. Economic hardship in the South among blacks and the rising civil rights movement turned the focus of black churches away from reaching

---

Virgil Lee Amos was born in Oakland, CA in 1942 and was reared in the heartland of Central CA with a love for the Lord Jesus Christ. In 1961, he boldly entered Moody Bible Institute in Chicago, IL, to major in missions and pastoral studies. In 1962, he enthusiastically became involved in foreign missions with Operation Mobilization (OM). He is the founder and General Director of Ambassadors Fellowship, a missions training and sending agency, which works in Mexico, Spain, Kenya, Nigeria, North Africa, U.S., and various other countries. He is a frequent speaker in churches, on college and university campuses, and in mission conferences. He also lectures in various cities with the Perspectives on the World Christian Movement course.

the world to looking after themselves. They poured their resources into caring for the black community rather than reaching out to the ends of the earth.

It was only in the 1960's that blacks as people began to appreciate themselves. For generations we were told that we were nothing, and we certainly were never in control of our environment. In retrospect, we should accept with shame some of the responsibility for that earlier self-image. We should have seen ourselves as agents for God, and here on earth for His purposes.

In a missionary sense, therefore, the black church was further ahead 100 years ago than it is today. However, in the past 20 years that is starting to turn around again. All of a sudden, we realized our dignity and beauty. This led us to ponder whether we might have something of significance to offer other peoples in the world. Change is happening and really doing so at an amazing rate, especially among the younger generation who perhaps have fewer burdens of history to deal with. Blacks are seeing and accepting responsibility for world evangelism—at least in the short-term, which is where it starts.

Our dream is for 2,000 or more African Americans to be in mission in the next ten years. Seeing that realized will mean major shifts in attitudes and approaches in the black church community.

We Want True Partnership

OM is increasingly becoming a place where minorities can find their calling to serve. But OM—among other missions—does not yet fully understand some of the complexities that black churches face in responding to missions. Little can be accomplished without first establishing a foundation of trust. Blacks have historically been abused in one way or another and thus are suspicious by default. You can't win over leaders by speech alone, you need to expose them to the heart of your message by letting them see for themselves. You might need to prove your sincerity by investing financially to expose them to missions. But once the vision is born, they will become full participants,money and all. This takes longer than your average recruiting meeting!

It's no partnership to come and basically ask to take people from a church to fulfill your goals. Have you sought to get to know the pastor? Do you understand where the church is at and what its own aspirations are? Are you inviting us to join the programme but not the planning meeting for that programme?

Most pastors are overworked, underpaid and underappreciated. A typical pastor can't see how siphoning off some of his energy and resources for someone else's mission is going to help him or his people. Thus, it has to become his mission too—and then can only come about through a commitment to him as a person.

Same Vision, Different Approach

There are other issues that are worth considering not only about blacks but other cultures as well. Not everyone is fond of rules and regulations in the European style of thinking; many cultures exalt relationships over rules. Comfort is another issue. For middle-class white youth on a summer campaign, it might be novel or exciting to sleep on the floor and eat peanut butter. But blacks are determined to move upward in their lives, not downward!

Yet somehow we have to convey the truth that missions does involve sacrifice—that regardless of your cultural and historical background at home, you go to another nation in humility and service. Once blacks get to the field, they do well because they are for the most part people-oriented. But it's the "getting there" that presents challenges. We find that black security-conscious churches yet lack the infrastructures of other churches.

Can black missionaries from the West have a better connection with Nigerians? Certainly there is an initial camaraderie, but we focus on our calling to be servants and partners. It is not for us to come in and tell people what they need. They are the ones to lead the local ministry; we are to get behind them. Consequently, we earn a great deal of trust and respect. This was demonstrated to me by George Verwer. In Nigeria, our task is to work with church leaders to impact solid discipleship principles. They are the ones to influence ordinary Christians.

Most missionaries in Nigeria do not trust Nigerians, at least regarding the handling of money. That was the first thing we did: we gave them our money and asked them to manage it as they saw best. Such a small thing and yet it sent a huge message. In fact they probably did a better job with it than we would have.

The OM Heritage

I believe in OM and its foundational principles: prayer, faith, humility, flexibility, perseverance. Do so and God will continue to bless you. The international model of leadership in OM is an example to the church.

One of the key virtues of OM is its commitment—not only to God but to one another. George Verwer, Dale Rhoton, Jonathan McRostie and others have stuck with one another from the beginning, through thick and thin. As Christians, we ought to rise up in times of adversity, not run and hide. Unless we change, this will result in many people departing from the faith in the days to come.

On the other hand, God is raising up people who are totally committed to serving Him. God has told us that things will get darker, but this will only help his true servants to shine all the brighter.

Chapter 40
The Cal Neighbor Story
by Dorris E. Ngaujah

Dorris E. Ngaujah recently joined the adjunct faculty of Atlanta Christian College. She was professor of Missions, Evangelism, Urban Ministry, and Old Testament Survey at West Angeles Bible College in Los Angeles, CA, while pursuing Ph.D. studies in Intercultural Education at Biola University. Her work, in cross cultural missions spans four decades—beginning as one of Christians in Action (CinA) International's youngest licensed missionaries in 1971. She served a team in Sierra Leone, West Africa, and has led several short-term teams to Zimbabwe, Kenya, South Africa, and inner cities of the U.S. Dorris is passionate about students and missions; therefore, she has given many years of volunteer service to such organizations as InterVarsity Christian Fellowship (Atlanta, GA); Campus Crusade for Christ (Atlanta, GA); Adventures in Missions (Gainesville, GA); and Pathfinders International (Chicago, IL). Her two-fold goal is to develop culturally informed and sensitive communicators—especially cross-cultural Christian workers and to write life stories of missionaries of the African Diaspora.

Dorris has a grown son and daughter-in-law, Sahr and Ayesha Ngaujah. Parenting, however, began again for Dorris most recently as she became the legal guardian of her ten-year old goddaughter, Desiree Ngaujah, after the sudden death of her 41-year old mother, Denise, on July 3, 2005.

Introduction

It was three o'clock in the morning and the streets of Cairo, Egypt, were bustling with people; clamoring with the sounds of Ramadan celebration; and sizzling with the aromas of exotic foods. For 21-year-old Calvin (Cal) Neighbor and his 19-year-old sidekick, Rickie, there was no time to waste. Just minutes before, the 1985 frontier short-term missionary team entered and secured their rooms at a hotel in the heart of the ancient city—a place that would be their home for the next six weeks. The two youngest members of the team of twelve—daring "whippersnappers"—left their team and went out into the glistening night. They were too excited to sleep and too eager to experience firsthand, friendship evangelism in a Muslim country. Their regard for the new "imposed" curfew was perfunctory, at best. They were imbued with evangelistic passion as well as a heightened sense of adventure. In their hands they carried the white "Bible"—a title book of John in parallel English and Arabic.

Thus began the fifteen-year, cross-cultural Christian ministry of the former college socialite, Cal Neighbor. His service in Egypt ended abruptly six months after 9/11. With wife Teresa and two children, Sonja and Daniel, Cal returned to Carson City where he now serves on the teaching staff of Christ Our Strength Baptist Church.

Cal's father began his military career as a Marine during Cal's childhood, leaving his unwed mother to raise him as a single parent in Waycross, GA. Fortunately, Cal had a very close-knit church-going maternal family. When Cal's mother left GA for better job opportunity "up north," she took seven-year-old Calvin with her to Carson City, North. There she landed a job with the Post Office and left her only child with Mrs. "V. J."

Mrs. V. J. believed that little children needed to receive Jesus Christ in their lives and have their sins forgiven. One night, before putting the children to bed, she talked to them about Jesus, about the need to have their bad ways changed and their lives cleaned up. Cal understood that he had a "bad mouth." At nine years old, he said, "I felt like God was washing it out and putting peppermint in it." He and his mother lived down the street from a famous Baptist church in West Carson City. As a small boy, he attended that church faithfully and was a fellow Sunday school student with the pastor's son.

During those early years in Carson City, Cal's mother became friendly with a gentleman that later became her husband, Mr.

Washington. It was decided, sometime after his twelfth birthday, that Cal should go live with Mr. Washington's mother in another district of Carson City. He attended her church often but his enthusiasm waned. While at his grandmothers in GA during the summer months, his church-going practice continued; though mostly as a familial and social obligation. By the seventh grade Cal lost all interest in church and in spiritual matters, ceasing even to attend. Back in Carson City, he was a student at an all-boys multi-racial and multi-ethnic elitist high school, from which he graduated and went on to matriculate at Eastern Harbor University. There he majored in political science with aspirations of becoming a lawyer. His popularity on campus was enhanced by his immediate involvement in student government and by his association with black fraternity brothers, a relational and racial identity he had not known in the past.

The Life-changing Process
As with many freshmen college students, being "away from home and on your own" opened up new opportunities for unchallenged explorations. Though he did not consider himself a "wild" person, the new association influenced him, especially the partygoers. The social butterfly was always ready to go and to dance. He became the "hook-up" for those students looking for information on the next party. He had been told that this was the time in one's life to "sow your oats" and "let it all hang out"—that there was plenty of time later to get serious. Of his freshman year, he recalls:

> It was the first time I actually got drunk. I never drank before … and I had stayed away from it because members of my family in the South were always into alcohol even though they went to church … I was adverse to it. But here in college…you take a sip and the next thing you know, you are drunk … [I]t happened to me one time and you know, that was conviction.

Drinking was not the only liberty of his first semester of college that caused guilt and shame to overwhelm Cal. Conviction replaced guilt and soon Cal found himself longing for peace and for a shameless relationship with God again. He wanted to feel clean again. In the solitude of his heart, he rededicated his life to Christ in the spring semester of his freshman year. When he went south that summer he returned to church and gave public testimony to the life-changing process taking place in his life. He studied his Bible and began sharing Bible truths with his family members and anyone who would listen to him.

When he returned to Eastern Harbor for his sophomore year, he became a little "witnessing machine." As a novice, he got on everyone's nerves. His reputation always preceded him with an announcement, "Here comes Calvin again." He said,

> I would go to the cafeteria, sit down at a table with people I did not know. By the time I finished my meal, I was sharing my faith with somebody at the table. It was something I thought I needed to do. I was just so excited that I needed to do that. I was evangelizing my family to the point … they got sick and tired of me. One relative said, "Ah, boy, shut up. Leave me alone and take that stuff with you to church."

Christ Our Strength was the haven that drew him from Eastern Harbor each weekend. He took the hour-commute on public transportation and occasionally he got a ride into the city by a friend. In that family of believers, he grew spiritually and his love for the Word of God deepened with every visit. He started attending the church in response to an invitation by a girlfriend from his high school days. She had become a Christian and she told him he needed to be saved also.

Christ Our Strength Baptist Church is a church known for its commitment to the teaching of the Word of God and for accountability of members to be active in the advancement of the kingdom of God. It is a church with a strong and consistent history of biblical education, including the training and sending out of missionaries and lay evangelists. Under Pastor Oscar Shellbutt, Christ Our Strength is one of the leading churches for the involvement of African Americans in global missions.

Concurrently, things were changing for him on campus. He saw his friends and associates in a different light as he advanced through his second year in school. Prior to rededicating his life to the Lord, Cal had worked hard at building relationships with his fellow African-American students. He had planned to pledge in one of the black fraternities. Nevertheless, his perspective on his frat relationships changed. He realized that most of the "brothers" and "sisters" in his friendship circles were nonbelievers. Neither were they interested in this "zealot for Jesus" guy called Cal. Subsequently, he had to make some friendship breaks. Soon he discovered his new friends outnumbered the old, though they were predominantly of the majority racial group. He aligned himself with such Christian groups as Campus Crusade for Christ, InterVarsity Christian Fellowship, Chi Alpha and the Friars, a service honor group.

Exposure to Cross-cultural Missions
Through the Christian associations on campus, Cal was introduced to an African-American student who had actually gone over to another country and returned to tell about it. David Damion's story and his passion for returning abroad to the mission field fascinated Cal. Cal became a part of a Bible study group conducted by David. The other members included a Messianic Jew, a Greek, a white Presbyterian, David, and Cal. Thus Cal's on-campus discipleship group was multi-ethnic and multi-cultural. Like his years at the boys' high school, God was continuing to prepare Calvin for intercultural ministry. David introduced Cal to the InterVarsity's student mission conference that is held every three years in Urbana, IL, called simply, Urbana. Cal would later attend his first Urbana conference in 1984.

In the meantime David Damion joined a mission mobilizing group—i.e. a group of mission-minded individuals who organized to bring mission awareness, exposure and opportunity to other Christian students. The traveling Gideon's Band's goal was to instill vision for ministry to the Muslim people of the world. The leader of this group was a second-generation missionary from Irian Jaya. Cal recalls spending a whole day in intense discussion and interpersonal dialogue with this group. The disclosures awakened desire in him to go to the mission field. He attended the Urbana '84 conference and that sealed his passion for overseas ministry and especially for reaching the unreached Muslim groups.

Cal applied to an agency that worked among Muslims for a short-term mission project the following summer. When the planned destination changed from Indonesia to Egypt, Cal was not phased by it. He just wanted to share his faith among Muslims in unreached areas wherever God sent the team.

To go on the six-week short-term mission trip, Cal had to raise his own support—i.e. cost of travel, board and housing, expenses and ministry materials. Embolden with the challenge of letting people know what God was calling him to do, he wrote letters to everyone. His access to the technology lab at school, the place of his part-time on-campus job, provided him with capabilities for multiple productions of letters—something others only dreamed about in 1985. He said, "We had word processors in there and I was just typing them and printing them out. I must have sent out 300 to 400 letters ... to saved and unsaved alike ... I even sent prayer letters to Jewish people I knew ...they sent money in. I didn't have any lack at all."

Cross-cultural Ministry Begins
Out on the street that first night in Egypt, Cal looked up at his hotel, at the surrounding buildings, then at the activity on the street and thought, "They picked the right room in the right three-star hotel to put folks like us in." He realized that they were strategically placed in a locale where they were regarded as foreigners but they did not stick out as different because there were many expatriates in the area. Cal, of course, was none the less conspicuous because he was African American, the only person of color on his team. He was considered an intriguing individual. The young "whippersnappers," Cal and Rickie, attracted young Egyptian men of their own age. Often they were seen sitting for hours at teashops or on the grass sharing their "white Bible." The Egyptians practiced English and the short-term missionaries practiced Arabic. They read to each other.

In a matter of days, Cal saw the power of friendship evangelism. A familiarity developed with two young boys who became Cal and Rickie's companions for the duration of their time there. The four youth took escapades into areas of the ancient city rarely seen by non-Egyptians—from the poorest-of-the-poor neighborhoods of the great Khan-al-Khalili, the 900-year-old bazaar which they toured from one end to the other. The visited 700-year old mosque, as well as many other buildings of antiquity, though still in active use today. The tea shop, where one of the boys worked, became a regular meeting place for interaction with Egyptians and Muslims from other countries as well. Cal handed out over 80 "white Bibles" during those six weeks and he actually had conversations with at least 40 of the individuals who accepted the little book of John in English and Arabic. The final week of their short-term mission trip was spent in Israel. Cal enjoyed walking where his Savior must have walked, reflecting on the scriptures.

Mission-inspired Career Goal—A Change
Cal's life was forever changed after that trip to Egypt. He struggled at first trying to make his legal aspirations fit into his growing passion for overseas occupational ministry. He understood his was to be a missionary career but he mused over incorporating his natural interest and his acquired skills with his calling into mission work. Mission work as he understood it at the time involved church planting and evangelism only. He knew very little, if anything, at the time about tentmaking—using one's profession or trade in cross-cultural environment for the purpose of representing the kingdom of God in that locality. The first action he took was to change his major from Political Science to Speech Communication. This meant he had to take some additional courses. In the process his word continued to expand. He traveled with the speech team and studied International Relations. During the same time he nurtured a growing relationship with a local church in Eastern Harbor, Christ Community Church. In this church he had opportunity to exercise his leadership skills and develop them.

Like most college graduates, Cal had to find a job after leaving Eastern Harbor. With his computer skills he quickly landed a position with a radio station as the trainer for the office software. Eight months into that humdrum, he yearned for a passion-inspired occupation. Deeper to the core of his yearnings however, was the desire to return to Egypt. In the course of events at Christ Our Strength, a professor and researcher came to the church to embark upon a three-year project using the urban church as her study base. In exchange for access tot he ministries of the Christ Our Strength congregation, her institution offered scholarships to several members interested in furthering their graduate school, majoring in business.

Cal's interest in business continued to grow but his desire to learn the language of Egypt was stronger. In the course of that first year in graduate school he began tutoring lessons from a language professor who spoke, among her five fluent languages, Arabic. So strong was his desire for returning to Egypt, that at the end of that first year he boldly approached the Director of his program and requested a leave of absence. Planning to go immediately to the mission field, he asked for a four-year leave so he could serve one term overseas. He would then reenter the program without penalty. His request was granted. The subsequent chain of events, however, would take him far from that plan.

Leaving graduate school put him back into the job market, at least until he left for the field. First he had to find a mission agency. He considered five agencies with work in the Middle East, especially in Egypt. He narrowed his choice to one in particular and in June 1989 he was accepted to candidacy school. His church leadership supported his decision and was actively involved in the process of getting him ready for overseas work. By that time, Christ Our Strength had an Assistant Pastor who was also the Missions Pastor. The Missions Pastor had been a career missionary in Africa and had returned home after 12 years of service. He became Cal's mentor throughout his ministry preparations.

Christ Our Strength Baptist Church holds a mission conference every year in September. During the three-day event, missionaries share their testimonies and report to the attendees about life and ministry in the various global fields they represent. There are workshops in which missionaries discuss more intimately mission life, callings, preparations, etc. At that 1989 conference, Cal met a young lady in one of the workshops who expressed an interest in going to Morocco. He found out that she had just finished an associate degree in business-secretarial services at a local junior college. Not at all thinking about a romantic relationship, Cal spied her as a possible candidate for his stateside secretary. The relationship quickly developed into much more. Cal sought the counsel of his mentor. Not wanting to rush into marriage, and not wanting to be a missionary casualty by marrying and not going to the field, Cal considered a long-term distant engagement while he would go and serve a four-year term in Egypt. His mentor strongly disagreed and recommended marriage.

As the two considered lifetime partnership, Teresa consented to go to Egypt instead of Morocco and was accepted into candidacy in June 1990, exactly a year after Cal joined the Mission. While candidacy school was only two weeks in duration, the process of qualifying for the field can take as long as two years or more. Cal and Teresa were married in November 1990, and together they prepared for the field, doing deputation and fund-raising together.

In retelling the story of his engagement to Teresa, Cal said he tried to be creative. On the day before Teresa was to start missionary candidacy school, and the last day on her job, Cal showed up on her lunch break with a cup of ice cream topped with what he thought was her favorite topping. Under the ice cream in the cup was a small plastic bag with a diamond ring inside. Cal brought the ice cream to her, said his salutations, and then walked away. Down the hall he waited. To his chagrin, Teresa did not like the topping he chose; it was wet walnuts. Instead of eating it, she handed it over to her friend. As the friend graciously ate the prized dessert, she discovered the little plastic bag and then she saw its precious content. To his delight, before exiting the building, he heard Teresa screaming down the hall.

Christ our Strength has a policy for newlywed ministry and missionary couples. That policy requires couples to wait twelve months before going to full-time ministry. His selected mission also had a similar requirement of nine months. Therefore, the new Neighbors had a year to bond as a couple while raising support. The Neighbors found the stipulation to be most beneficial. In that they had only known each other a short time before their engagement, they discovered, among other things, that they could enhance their effectiveness in communication by taking advantage of another recommended stipulation. They were encouraged to utilize professional counseling resources made available through the mission agency's network for help in adjusting to their different communication styles. They attended 12 weeks of counseling. After the first six weeks, the couple realized that even the one-hour drive to the counselor each week was therapeutic.

More than a year past and the couple continued to raise their financial support. It took much longer to raise the required amount for a couple going to the mission field than for a single man. In the interim, the third Neighbor made her entry into the world on April 8, 1992. Four months after her arrival however, the family had all of their support and was ready for Egypt. It had been four years since Cal left graduate school, but he was not disappointed, nor did he ever lose sight of his dream. At long last his passion for Egypt became a reality.

Egypt At Last

From Carson City they flew to New York, but inclement weather delayed the New York to France flight, thus causing them to miss their France to Cairo connection. They spent the night in Paris and flew to Cairo the next day. Two days in Cairo, then they were off to Cyprus for an orientation week. There they met other missionaries from other agencies also going through the orientation for working in the Arab world. A week after returning to Cairo, the Neighbors secured a place to live on the outskirts of the city, found a daycare center for their daughter, Sonja, where the staff would speak Arabic to her, and they enrolled in language school.

The daily routine was grueling. Using public transportation, they traversed the city in the mornings to get Sonja to the day care center. Then, they joined the rush-hour traffic to language school. Every day, they left class 20 minutes before class ended to get to the day care center before it closed. A year of that and the couple decided to study at home with a personal tutor.

Cal's fluency grew steadily because he had more direct verbal contact with other Arabic speakers. Teresa, on the other hand, at home more and unable to practice verbally, excelled in literary skills and became rather competent in reading, comprehension and writing Arabic. During that second year, Cal's verbal skills received another boost. He was invited to work as a paid schoolteacher.

Getting Settled in Cairo

Six weeks into their stay in Egypt, the Neighbors had to be separated for nine days. An earlier arrangement for having their belonging shipped to Egypt fell through. Cal had to return to the states, repack their things and make arrangements for another mode of shipment. This

$1,400-expense left a large hole in their support account. After that first year abroad, with the $1,400 used for shipping and with the drop in support—a common phenomenon after missionaries leave for the field—the supplemental income from Cal's teaching during the second year was a welcomed asset.

Making a home in another country includes finding a church home. For the Neighbors this was especially difficult because their model, Christ Our Strength, was hard to match, even in the States. At best the Christian groups in Cairo were eclectic—a mixture of every sect of Christianity imaginable. Often sectarian theological discourses took the place of Bible teaching. They only hoped for a Bible teaching English speaking congregation. Eventually they settled in with one of the international congregations where there seemed to be a thirst for Bible teaching. Cal became one of the rotating quarterly expositors, teaching the whole congregation at the weekly services. In Egypt, many Christians choose to worship on Fridays because it is a Muslim holiday. While Muslims are at the Mosque, some Christians go to church. The church the Neighbors attended worshiped on Friday. Thus, they adapted and participated in Friday church services.

Conflict in Teamwork

The Neighbors discovered that missionary teamwork affords the strength of numbers, the wisdom of consultation and the comfort of friendship, especially when there is comradeship and where there is a sense of common identity. Sometimes, however, relationships among team members become strained and fraught with misunderstandings and interpersonal conflicts. Such was the outcome of a team meeting early in the team ministry of the Neighbors. It started as a simple taxi ride. The Neighbors learned early to tip taxi drivers generously as was expected for foreigners to pay above the local rate. They determined what would be a gracious tip and had been giving that flat amount each time they traveled from a certain part of town. One this particular day, Cal, Teresa, and Sonja, disembarked from the taxi a block from their home, a custom they had adopted so as not to disclose their actual residential location and not be embarrassed n front of neighbors should the driver make a scene. Drivers had been known to shout at foreigners is they do not pay exorbitant fees. Cal gave the driver—a man of stature over six feet and weighing about 230 pounds—the predetermined rate, and Teresa, with Sonja in arms, started up the street. In a flash, the driver jumped out of the car and cut Cal off as he began to follow his wife up the street with their packages. He mentioned, "He cut me off in my path, poked me in the chest with his pointed fingers and demanded more money. I told him, 'No.'" The man then spat in Cal's face. Cal raised his fist to punch the bully, but just as his arm was moving from one direction to the other, Teresa put the baby in his arm and he caught his daughter instead of hitting the taxi driver.

That afternoon they had a missionary team meeting just minutes after the humiliating incident. Hoping to find empathy and consolation, the Neighbors recounted the incident for their colleagues. To their chagrin, their leader, a white man advised, "Well, you need to learn to give them more money. Even though you gave him what was right, because we are foreigners, we are expected to give them more than they are expecting." Cal felt betrayed. He argued. "You are ignoring the fact that the man pushed me and spat on me." The leader chided him for not adjusting to the culture, and for not respecting the economic advantages westerners have over most Egyptians. Cal was livid. He knew he had not been in the country as long as his leader and he knew that there was much that he had to learn about living in Egypt. Yet he thought, with regard to tipping taxi drivers, he had learned and had adjusted to that aspect of Egyptian culture. He did not think he should encourage greed, nor should he give in to violent threats. He expected his spiritual leader to give him scripture for his position on the matter. Instead he received an opinionated indictment. Over time, the differences between the two men grew into major personality conflicts requiring administrative intervention. However, before an administrative decision could be made, the Egyptian government unknowingly resolved the matter. The leader in question took a short trip out of the country. Upon his return to Egypt, re-entry was denied.

Developing the Tentmaking Ministry

After teaching for a year at one of the international schools, Cal heard about a need for an

Information Technician at one of Egypt's top schools. He worked as an assistant for a short time and then was asked to take the head of the department position as the former head returned to his native home in Britain. Children of very wealthy Egyptians and of various expatriates attended the school. Cal thought the job afforded him opportunity to make friends and share Christ with the parents and family members of his students. Subsequently, he received numerous invitations to their homes and businesses. Through the observation he learned much about the lifestyles and the needs of the élites of Cairo.

Yet, his desire was to make a spiritual impact through his occupation. He surmised that teaching, while it supplemented their income, did not give him the access to the adult population he had longed to impact. He wanted to have a more significant channel through which he could engage Muslims in discussion of spiritual matters and he also wanted a channel to be of greater support to the underground Christian church. His technological knowledge and skills were in high demand. The inspiration to start a computer service business emerged. Cal took the idea home with him when the family went on furlough in 1997. They discussed the idea with ministry partners and found a couple willing to invest in a start-up business venture in Egypt.

By the time the Neighbors got back to the field in late 1997, they were able to see their dream become a reality. He launched the computer service business and hired a new believer as his assistant. One set of clients were leaders in an underground church. They started a business and Cal created a website for them, enhancing their business by adding the Internet exposure. Notwithstanding however, without having more than a novice level of business experience and none internationally, that particular venture was profitable. From a general business perspective, however, his overall business did not turn a profit. It was negatively effected further when,

"I went into debt trying to keep it running while we were away for a year raising support," Cal laments. They had only been back in Egypt six months after that year away when 9/11 occurred. The international impact of that infamous event affected the Neighbors' business and relationships, dampening the debt recovery efforts. Six months after 9/11, the Neighbors were called back to the states. Cal said, "I have learned a lot about my weaknesses in running that venture. I have made adjustments and now know what I did wrong." The accrued debt has hindered their return to Egypt.

Should Others Go?

Cal sees magnificent opportunity for western believers to serve abroad, both short- and long-term, but he believes even more now than at the beginning of his ministry that a new paradigm to missions should be employed—that of business development: to directly finance and support the ministries and the believers local to the target cultures. He believes secularly educated, skilled, and trained Christians who are prepared to teach others their skills will have the most success getting into Arab countries. They should be well grounded in faith and biblical knowledge, "given to hospitality," and have a patient disposition. Young Western Christians with the call of God on their lives for cross-cultural ministry "must be willing to sacrifice the big paychecks they could get at home and go, live, learn, and leave the Gospel with national believers."

Presently, the Neighbors serve faithfully at their home church, Christ Our Strength Baptist Church. Cal runs a technology business in a nearby city. They work with other national and international agencies—mentoring and facilitating missionaries and businesses. Their children, Sonja and Daniel, are twenty and fourteen years of age respectively. The family expects to return to the Arab World someday and for that reason, we have used pseudonyms.

Resources

Aiyeru, Babatunde S.
ACFUSA African Christian Fellowship, USA
6706 Annapolis Road,
Hyattaville, MD 20784
officeat@acfusa.org
www.acfusa.org
301-322-8701

Alexander, Gregory
PACE Pan African Christian Exchange
Rosedale Baptist Church
14179 Evergreen
Detroit MI, 48223
Galexander_1@msn.com
248-557-2499

Amos, Pastor Virgil
Ambassadors Fellowship
P.O. Box 62309
Colorado Springs, CO 80962
virgilamos@gmail.com
www.ambassadorsfellowship.org
719-495-8180
719-332-0435

Ashley, Willie Mae
c/o Mrs. Ruth Terrell
46 Indian Trail
Sanford, NC 27332
919-498-0265

Baker, David
AME Zion Publishing
P.O. Box 26770
Charlotte NC 28221
706-599-4630

Barber, Curtis
Friends of Africa Mission Ministries, Inc.
Barbers19@aol.com
410-679-1215

Bonk, Jonathan J.
International Bulletin of Missionary Research
490 Prospect Street
New Haven, CT 06511
Ibmr@oms.org
Bonk@OMSC.org
www.OMSC.org
203-624-6672

Boyd, Minister Orchidy
African American Mobilization Services (AFAMMS)
20412 Seminole
Redford, MI 48240
P.O. Box 39803
Redford, MI 48239
orchi41@yahoo.com
afamms@gmail.com
www.ywam.org
501-248-7033

Broadman-Holman Press
Copyrights Department
127 9th Avenue N.
Nashville, TN 37234-0114
615-251-2520
800-247-4784

Burrell, Eugene
The Navigators' African-American Ministries
http://www.navigators.org/us/ministries/ethnic/afam
719-598-1212
866-568-7827 (toll free)

Coleman, Richard
Director of Mobilization and Candidacy
The Mission Society
6234 Crooked Creed Rd
Norcross, GA 30092
www.themissionsociety.org/people/coleman_richard
678-542-9040

Cornelius, David
International Mission Board of
Southern Baptist Convention
African-American Relations
P.O. Box 6767
Richmond, VA 23230
Dcornelius@imb.org
804-306-5341

Crummie, Rev. Robert W.
President
Carver College
3870 Cascade Road SW
Atlanta GA 30331
www.carver.edu
404-527-4520

Daniels, Kimberly
Team Expansion
4112 Old Routt Road
Louisville, KY 40299
Kdaniels@teamexpansion.org
www.teamexpansion.org
502-719-0007

Degraffenreidt, K. J.
African Methodist Episcopal Zion Church
Department of Overseas Missions
475 Riverside Dr. # 1935
New York, NY 10115
Domkd5@aol.com
212-870-2952

Dickinson, Rev. Dr. Richard
Black Ministry
Lutheran Church-Missouri Synod
1333 S Kirkwood Road
St. Louis, MO 63122
blackministry.lcms.org
314-996-1349
800-248-1930

Duberry, Rev. Ivor
African American Center for World Mission
1605 E. Elizabeth Street
Pasadena, CA 91104
rev.ivor@aacwm.org
626-398-2205

Durham, Margaret J.
3934 Monsols Drive
Florissant, MO 63034
margaret.j.durham@niduscener.com
314-812-8004

Foster, Berta
Christian Mission for the Deaf
c/o Mrs. Faith Foster Haynes
1207 Surreny Lane
Allen, TX 75013-5313
www.cmdeaf.org
313-933-1424

George, William
CME Church Publishing House
4466 Elvis Presley Blvd.
Memphis, TN 38116
901-345-4120

Goatley, David
Lott Carey Baptist Foreign Mission Convention
LottCarey@Lottcarey.org
www.lottcarey.org
202-543-3200

Hannaman, Jerome
U. S. Center for World Mission
Mobilization Office
1605 E. Elizabeth Street
Pasadena, CA 91104
Jerome.Hannaman@uscwm.org
626-398-2204

Harris, Dr. Esker J.
880 S. Abbeywood Place
Rossell, GA 30075
eskerjharris@att.net
770-518-1141

Harris, Lonnell
5142 Dunnellon Ave.
Memphis, TN 38134
lonricah@aol.com
901-385-3865

Huggins, Jacqueline
jacqueline_huggins@sil.org
215-779-9677

Jeter, Pastor Joseph C.
Have Christ Will Travel
528 E. Church Lane
Philadelphia, PA 19144
215-438-6306

Johnson, Pastor Brian
Johnson, Ruth
COMINAD
608 Warwick Drive
McDonough, GA 30253
bJohnson@COMMNAD.com
313-671-4991
404-343-4172

Johnson, Dr. Leonidas A.
President
Crystal Fountain Ministries
P. O. Box 4434
Diamond Bar, CA 91765
crystalfountainministries@hotmail.com
909-396-1201

Johnson, Dr. Michael
Johnson, Sandra Kay
Out of Nazareth
810 Brand Drive
New Castle, DE 19720
Michael.Johnson@wgm.org
mjohnson@nbnet.co.ke

Johnson, Robert
AME Zion Church
3225 W. Sugar Creek Road
Charlotte, NC 28269
704-599-4630

Loretta, Jackson
WEC International
African-American Mobilization
P.O. Box 1707
Fort Washington, PA 19034
mobilization@wec-usa.org
www.wec-usa.org
443-562-2319

Mason, Glenn
Carver International Missions
P.O. Box 92543
Atlanta, GA 30314
CARVERIM@bellsouth.net
404-522-4000
770-323-0772

Moore, Rev. Olah
Faith Community Church
100 East 30th Street
Norfolk, VA 23504
757-632-0818

Nelson, Phillip
Sudan Interior Mission USA
African-American Relations
14830 Choate Circle
Charlotte, NC 29273
www.simusa.org
704-587-1437
800-521-6449

Nicholas, Kevin
Nicholas, Gertrude
Wycliffe Bible Translators
Gertrude_Nicholas@wycliffe.org
Kevin_Nicholas@wycliffe.org
www.kevinnicholas.net
For more information about Wycliffe
www.wycliffe.org
407-852-3600

Nichols, Doug
Action International Ministries
P.O. Box 398
Mountlake Terrace, WA 98043
www.actioninternational.org
425-775-4800

Ngaujah, Dr. Dorris E.
200 Butterfield Lane
Fayetteville, GA 30214
[Currently serving in Africa]
dorrisngaujah@gmail.com

Perrin, Bishop David T. P.
Great Commission Global Ministries
P.O. Box 780609
Orlando FL 32878
gegm@gegm.org
www.gcgm.org
301-251-7218

Phipps, Dr. William E.
1217 Rennie Avenue
Richmond, VA 23227
805-355-4840

Rapheal, John C., Jr.
Executive Secretary
Foreign Mission Board
National Baptist Convention of America

www.nbca-inc.com/resources/ForeignMission.html
214-942-3311

Scott, Calvin
Good News Jail & Prison Ministries
P.O. Box 9760
Hevrica VI, 23228-0760
info@goodnewsjail.org
1-800-220-2202

Scudieri, Dr. Robert
400 S. 14th Street, Apt. 916
St. Lewis, MO 93103
bscudievi@aol.com
314-703-9729 H

Seruggs, Dr. Julius R.
President
National Baptist, Convention USA, Inc.
Baptist World Center Headquarters
1700 Baptist World Center Drive
Nashville, TN 37207
256-428-1255
Toll Free: 866.531.3054

Sidwell, Mark
BJU Press
1700 Wade Hampton Blvd.
Greenville, SC 29614
800-845-5731

Siryon, Elaine
National Baptist Convention USA
Berrian2sir@netscape.net
215-843-1949

Sprinkle Publications
Copyrights Department
P.O. Box 1094
Harrisburg, VA 22803
800-460-3573

Stevens, Bob
Stevens, Ellen
809 Spring Forest Road Ste. 1000
Raleigh, NC 27609
bobstevens6@gmail.com
919-787-3821

Sutherland, Dr. Jim
Director
RMNI Reconciliation Ministry Network

P.O. Box 2537
Chattanooga, TN 37409-0537
jim@rmni.org
www.rmni.org
423-822-1091

Synan, Dr. Harold Vinson
Regent Univ. School of Divinity
100 Regent University Drive
Virginia Beach, VA 23464
www.regent.edu/acad/schdiv
800-723-6162
757-352-4016

Taylor, Rev. Elgin
Taylor, Dorothy
[Director, Retired]
Christians In Action International
67 Melfort Road
Thornton Heath, Surrey
CR7 7RT, England
TaylorElgin@yahoo.com

TEAM
Church Mobilization Office
Jim Rathbum
Church Connections Facilitator
International Headquarters
team@teamworld.org
www.teamworld.org
800-343-3144
630-653-5300

Walston, Dr. Vaughn
Walston, Rebecca
Impact Movement, Campus Crusade for Christ
2869 Jonas Prophet Trail
Williamsburg, VA 23185
Vaughn.Walston@uscm.org
510-468-6135

Watkins, Tom
Trans World Radio
P.O. Box 8700
Cory, NC 27512
twatkins@twr.org
919-460-3700

Timeline

Chronology of major events prior to, and including African Americans in world mission in the United States

This is a chronology of major events prior to and including African-American events in world mission in the United States. This is not an all-inclusive listing, but one that coincides with this book. There are many more missionaries and denominational history articles that could have been introduced. Much of this book was done by personal contacts, which led to choices of articles.

Pre-13th Century Jesus Christ issued the Great Commission (Matthew 28:19) *Ca. 33*

Ethiopian eunuch converted (Acts 8:36–40) and carried Christian faith to North Africa. *Ca. 34 AD*

Formation of oldest church: The Coptic Church of North Africa (tradition has St. Mark as founder). *Ca 45–60 AD*

First theological college organized in Egypt. *189 AD*

Roman Emperor Diocletian sought to stamp out all Christians on the earth—Many martyred in N. Africa or reduced to slavery. *303 AD*

Church of Abyssinia founded as offshoot of Egyptian Church. *330 AD*

Church of Egypt disestablished until the Arab Conquest. *543 AD* Arabs conquered N. Africa and Christians driven to N. E. Africa. Africans sold Africans as slaves. *640 AD*

13th Century European Christian crusaders reached Egypt. St. Francis of Assisi joined—Sultan already surrounded by Christian subjects. *1216 AD*

14th Century First translation of Bible in the common language—John D. Wycliffe *(1320–1384) 1384*

15th Century Catholic missionaries from Europe circled the globe in an effort to expand the church and encourage believers, but, unfortunately, this was also the time slave trade began. During the next 350 years Europeans invaded the jungles of Africa and over 20 million Africans were gathered from their homeland and sold into slavery.

16th Century Protestant Reformation, Martin Luther. *1517*

William Tyndale Bible translation. *1536*

17th Century Puritan "Separatists" compelled to leave England for Holland because of persecution. *Ca. 1600*

"Separatists" established first English Baptist Church in Holland. *1609*

King James Version Bible translation. *1611*

Baptists returned to England and established first church in London. *1612*

First Baptist Church of England split and formed second group. *1616*

USA Denominational and Mission History

First blacks arrive in North America. *1619*

Pilgrims aboard the Mayflower land near Plymouth Rock. *1620*

Puritan Roger Williams arrived in America. *1631*

Williams formed RI colony and First Baptist Church in America. *1639*

Second Baptist group in England split and formed a third group. *1641*

Second Baptist Church organized by John Clarle, Newport, RI. *1641*

Beginning of spread of Christianity in Africa south of the Sahara. *1652*

RI Baptist Churches (followed Arminian), known as "General" Baptists, organized first Baptist association. *1670*

18th Century

Smallpox kills half the children born in the colonies. *1700*

The Church of England started in the American colonies the Society for the Propagation of the Gospel in Foreign Parts—to spread Christianity—gave new impetus to slave religion in the New World. *1701 (1702)*

Anglican Church established in NJ. *1704*

RI churches known as "General Baptists" formed the first association. *Ca. 1706*

"Particular" Baptist following Calvin, formed Philadelphia Baptist Association (churches in NJ, PA & DE). *1707*

THE FIRST GREAT AWAKENING. *1720 –1750 (?1730–1760)*

Holiness Club led by Charles Wesley at Christ Church, Oxford University. *mid-1720's*

Lutheran Salsburgs began missions to African slaves in GA. *1734*

Jonathan Edwards inaugurated in Northampton, MA. *1735*

Moravians began missions to Africans in SC. *1738*

- John Wesley establishes "united societies" to nurture young Christians. *1739*

Sons of The Propogation of the Gospel founded training school for African Americans in Charleston, SC. *1743*

George Washington with 200 militia attempts to drive the French from OH. Known in America as the French and Indian War. *1754–1763*

First Methodist Society established in NY. *1766*

More Baptist associations organized in New England, VA, NC, & SC. *1767*

Awakening led to Baptist division "New Light" or Separate Baptists in New England area "Old Light" or Regular Baptists Philadelphia association. *1767*

- John Marrant, a free black from New York City, ministered cross-culturally, preaching to the American Indians. By 1775 he had carried the gospel to the Cherokee, Creek, Catawar, and Housaw Indians. *1770–1775*

The Boston Massacre. *1770*

- George Liele, a slave preacher preached to African Americans on plantations in SC and GA. Start of Plantation Missions which led to independent African Baptist Church movement. *1770s*
- Silver Bluff Baptist Church, Aiken County, SC, by George Liele *Ca. 1773–1775*

First Annual Conference of the Methodist innovation. *1773*

American Revolution. *1775*

Articles of Confederation becomes the first constitution of the U.S. *1781*

- George Liele, first black foreign missionary to Jamaica, British West Indies. Sent by Silver Bluff Baptist, SC. *1783–1828*
- Moses Baker and George Gibbons to West Indies. *1783*
- Brother Amos to Bahamas. *1783 (?1782)*

England signs the Treaty of Paris recognizing the independence of the U.S. *1783*

Christmas Conference, a gathering of independent societies, Methodist Episcopal Church established. *1784*

First colored Baptist church organized Savannah, GA, formal beginning of African-American Baptist Church movement. *1788*

Black Revivalists preachers across U.S. *1790–1810*

- Prince William, a freed slave from SC, went to Nassau, Bahamas. *1790*
- Hector Peters and Sampson Calvert, W. Coast, Africa. *1790*

In Britain—Baptist Society of the Propagation of the Gospel among the Heathen formed as a result of William Carey's concerns. *1792*

NY Missionary Society supported by Baptists, Presbyterians and Reformed results of 1792 Society in Britain. *1796*

African-Methodist Episcopal Zion church, New York City. *1796*

19th Century

Washington, D.C., becomes the national capital. *1800*

General Gabriel leads slave rebellion in Richmond, VA. *1800*

United Brethren in Christ. *1800*

- Prince William helped organize the Society of Anabaptist, Bahamas. *1801*

Old Light & New Light General Missionary Convention of the Baptist Denomination in the United States of America for Foreign Missions—Later ABFMU *Ca. 1802*

Albright Brethren. *1803*

Slave trade officially ends. *1808*

Richmond African Baptist Missionary Society. *1811*

American Baptist Missionary Union & Triennial Convention. *1814*

American Baptist Churches in the U.S.A. (ABC, USA) formed. *1814*

- Lott Carey organized (ABFMS) African Baptist Foreign Missionary Society. *1815*

American Colonization Society founded American Society for the Colonization of Free People of Color (ASC) Washington, D.C. *1816–1817*

- African Methodist Episcopal Church organized in PA. *1816*
- John Stewart, Independent, Methodist, to Wyandott Indians. *1819*
- Daniel Coker, Liberia, AME. *1820–1846*
- Lott Carey and Colin Teague, with several other African Americans, Liberia—emigrants of the ASC of 1816 and commissioned by FMB of the Baptist Triennial Convention.

ABMU, supported by William Crane (white) and the Richmond Society (white & black) & Southern Black Baptists. *December 1820–January 1821*

- Charles Butler appointed by deacons and elders as AME missionary but never left U.S. *1822*
- Lott Cary, Sierre Leone. *1822–1828*
- Colin Teague, ABMU, (*1823–1855*), Harriosn Bouey, Liberia. *1823*
- Betsy Stockton, Hawaii, American Board of Missions. *1823*
- John Boggs, AME, Liberia. *1824*

AMEZ completed break from General Conference of ME church. *1824*

- AMEC sent first missionaries to Haiti from the north. *1824.* The church was established in Haiti. *1836.*
- Missionary Department of AMEC organized. *1864*
- Scripio Beans, AME, Haiti. *1827–1835*

Methodist Protestant Church. *1830*

- Andrew Cartwright, AMEZ, Liberia. *1835–1903*
- Francis Burns, Liberia. *1833*
- Melville Beveridge Cox (died after 4 months) and Eunice Sharpe (First United Methodist teacher), to Liberia. *1833*
- James Temple, Presbyterian, (withdrew after 4 months), Liberia. *1833*
- James M. and Mrs. Thompson, Protestant Episcopal Church, Liberia. *1835 (1836)–1865*
- Rev. W. C. Monroe, ABC of NY went to Haiti. *1835*

Providence Baptist Association, OH, organized by free Blacks & slave refugees Buffalo, west to Chicago & south to Cincinnati. Sole objective was African missions. *1835–1836*

Wood River Baptist Association, IL, organized after PBA. *1838*

Pope Gregory XVI condemned the slave trade. *1839*

THE SECOND GREAT AWAKENING. *1840–1860*

Abolitionist movement began. *1840*

American Baptist Missionary Convention, NY, formed. Blacks from New England and Middle West beginning of the national organization of Black Baptists and first regional convention to be formed. *1840*

Amherstburg Association Canada and MI organized. *1841*

Wesleyan Church of America. *1843*

- James M. Priest, American Colonization Society/Presbyterian Church, Liberia. *1843–1883*

Methodist Episcopal Church, South. *1843*

Methodist Episcopal Church. *1843*

First place of worship for use of black Catholics, Pittsburg, PA. *1844*

Southern Baptist Convention formed. *1845*

- John Day Liver, Coloured Society and SBC's first black missionary sent with A. A. Jones, Liberia. (Next 40 years SBC FMB sent 62 missionaries.) *1846–1869*

The Lutheran Church-Missouri Synod (included Norwegian Lutheran Church and Wisconsin Evangelical Lutheran Church). *1847*

- B. J. Drayton, SBC FMB, Nigeria. *1848*

African Methodist Episcopal, Zion Church. *1848*

- Robert F. Hill (started intense revival for missions) with his 1867 address to ABMU convention), Liberia and then with Thomas J. Bowen and Harvey Goodale, Nigeria, ABMU. *1849–1867*
- Reverend and Mrs. John Clarke SBC, West Africa. *Ca. 1849*

Mid-to-Late 19th Century First independent black Baptist congregations last half of the 19th Century

First national convention—Free Blacks and remaining years before the Civil War national and state conventions held to promote a variety of causes. *1850*

Wisconsin Evangelical Lutheran Church separated, but still had fellowship with, LC-MS until 1961. *1850*

- Alexander Crummel, Episcopal (British Anglican Ch), Liberia. *1852–1873*

Black Baptist Convention Western States and Territory. *1853*

- Alexander Cross, American Christian Mission, Liberia. *1854*
- Joseph M. and Sarah H. Harden, SBC, Liberia. *1855 (J. to 1860) (S. to 1875)*
- John R. V. Morgan, AME, Liberia. *1856*
- Wilberforce University, established by Bishop Daniel Payne, AME, first AF institute for higher learning. *1865*

General missionary activity increased after Civil War. Gains made in education, politics, and civil rights began to manifest themselves on the mission field. *1860–1877*

- First Black American Catholic priest, Augustus Tolton, was to be sent as a missionary to Africa but they kept him in U.S. *Ca. 1863*

Free Methodist Church. *1860*

- James Theodore Holly, Episcopal elder, took about 100 church members with him to Haiti. Later became Bishop. *1861–1911*

The Northwestern and Southern Baptist Convention formed (8 states) to serve where ABMC did not have jurisdiction—Second regional convention to be formed. They served together with ABMC. *1864*

National Primitive (Black) Baptists withdraw from white Primitive Baptists. *1865*

- Samuel David Ferguson, Protestant Episcopal Church, Cape Palmas Mission Station. *1865–1916*
- E. B. Topp and wife, NBC, to Vai people, Liberia. *1866–1887*

Consolidated American Baptist Missionary Convention. Merger of Northwestern and Southern Baptist Convention and the American Baptist Missionary Convention. *1866*

- American Baptist Foreign Missionary Union's (ABFMU) Executive Committee seriously considered renewal of assistance to Baptist in Liberia. *1867*

By 1868, 12 of the 13 Presbyterian U.S. staff members in Liberia were blacks.

- D. E. Murff and Mattie E. Wilson Murff, NBC, Cape Town, S. Africa. *1867–1910*

Zion Union Apostolic Church. *1869*

- Consolidated American Education Association, subsidiary of Consolidated Convention of 1866, formed. "Offered and managed by colored persons, and laboring for the education and evangelization of their race in the south, Africa, and wherever found unimproved." *1869*

United Free Will Baptist Church began. *1870*

- Joseph and Mary Green Gomer, United Brethren in Christ, Mendi people, Sierra Leone. *1870–1892*
- Reverend Harrison N. Bouey Liberia, sent by Black SC Baptist Convention. *1870*

Colored Methodist Episcopal Church. *1870*

- Aron T. Gillett, AMEC, sent to Arkansas as missionary to Indians. Others joined: Bishop John M. Brown, George T. Rutherford, Granville Ryles to several Indian tribes. *1870*
- James A. Evans, United Brethren in Christ, Sierra Leone. *1871–1873*

Northern Baptists could claim to support 14 Baptist preachers and teachers in various locations in West Africa. *1871*

- SC Baptist, African Committee of the FMB recommended African field remain open. *1872*
- John Byrant Small, AMEZ, Ghana, W. Africa. *1872–1896*

General Association of the Western States and Territories, organized. *1873*

- Beverly Page Yates, SBC, Liberia. *1873–1893*

New England Baptist Missionary Convention, organized. *1874–1875*

Wisconsin Evangelical Lutheran Church combined with Evangelical Lutheran Church in America. *1874*

- William W. Colley, FMB, SBC West Africa by white and black conventions. *1875*

By 1876 Blacks serving under the Protestant Episcopal Church in Africa outnumbered whites 21 to 5.

- Rev. C. W. Moselle and wife, Port au Prince, Haiti, AMEC. *1876–1884*
- Andrew Cartright returned to Liberia with Rosanna (Anne) Cartright, AMEZ. *1876–1903*
- Thomas Lewis Johnson, British Baptist Mission Society, Liberia, Cameroon. *1877–1879*
- Rev. Dr. Joseph G. Lavalais, LC-MS, called to Africa, but declined due to health issues. *1877*
- Betty Dickens, first missionary, LC-MS, Nigeria. *Ca. 1877*
- Solomon Crosby, FMB of VA Convention, SBC-Africa by white & black conventions. *1878*

Consolidated American Baptist Convention terminated. *1878–879*

- Samuel E. Flegler, AME, and Harrison Bouey, Consolidate ABC, Liberia. *1878–1881*
- S.A. Bailey, Clement Irons, AME, Liberia. *1878–1900*
- Elizabeth Harris Mendi, United Brethren in Christ, Sierra Leone. *1878–1893*
- Solomon Crosby, SBC, Yoruba. *1878–1881*
- Thomas L. Jackson, British Baptist Mission Society, Cameroon. *1878–1879*
- James O. Hayes, Africa by black NC Baptist Convention. *1879*
- Charles Mossell, AME, Haiti. *1879*
- Charles H. Richardson, Consolidated ABMC, Cameroon. *1879*

Beginning of ANTEBELLUM PERIOD and CIVIL WAR *Ca. 1880*

First regional black Baptist conventions formed. *Ca. 1880*

African Foreign Mission Convention organized. *1880*

Baptist Foreign Mission Convention of the United States of America (BFMC, USA) or Foreign Mission Convention organized by Colley, headquarters in VA. *1880*

Regional Baptist Foreign Mission Convention (BFMC), AL, organized. W. W. Colley returned from Africa and hired by Black Baptist of VA. He then canvassed United Baptist & those of disintegrated Consolidated Convention. *1880*

- Rachel Allen, United Brethren in Christ, Mendi people. *1880–1899*
- Kely M. Kemp and wife, American Mission Association, Sierra Leone. *1880–1885*
- Samuel Miller, American Board of Commissioners for Foreign Missions Angola. *1880–1885*
- James O. Hayes, Black Baptist State Convention of NC, Liberia. *1881.* Sent to Monrovia, NBC. *1882–1900*
- Henry McNeal Turner, South Africa. *Ca. 1880*; NBC, Monrovia. *1882–1900*
- Henry Highland Gornet, former slave, Presbyterian pastor/abolitionist appointed ambassador to Liberia. *1881*

Reformed Zion Union Apostolic Church. *1882*

- Theolophilis E. S. Scholes, MD., Congo ABMU, Jamaica, Congo. *1882–1890*
- Ackrell E. White. *1882*
- Amanda Smith, Independent, Liberia, Monrovia, India. *1882–1890*
- Melville Beveridge Cox, Methodist Episcopal Church, Liberia. *1883* (Died in 4 months.)
- Baptist Foreign Mission Convention sent 6 to Liberia. W. W. Colley and wife, Lagos (1883–1879); J. (James or Joseph) H. Presley, *(1883–1885)* and Mrs. Hattie Presley *(1883–died 1884)*; John J. Coles *(1883–1885/1887–1893)* and Lucy A. Henry (Mrs. J. J. Coles) *(1883–1887)*; and Henderson McKenny *(1883–1887)*.
- W. W. Colley and his wife, J. H. Presley and Mrs. Presley, J. J. Coles and Rev. Hense McKenny, BFMC's first missionaries to Africa commissioned by an all black southern national organization. Established Grand Cape Mount. *1883*
- Henrietta Bailey, Benjamin F. Ousley, American Board of Commissioners for Foreign Missions, Mozambique. *1884–1893*
- Benjamin F. Ousley, American Board of Commissioners for Foreign Missions, Mozambique. *1884–1893*
- John E. Ricketts, ABMU, Congo. *1885–1893;* Leticia Ricketts joined him in *1890–1893*

American National Baptist Convention New England Convention and the Baptist African Mission Convention that did not join BFMC—However, BFMC continued doing foreign mission work for them. *1886*

Christian Unions began with a mountain revival. (Later was called Holiness Movement, then United Holy Church of America, then Holiness Church, and later Church of God). *1886*

- Samuel J. Campbell, AME, Zimbabwe. *pre-1890–1895*
- John Richard Frederick, AME, Sierra Leone (later British Wesleyan Methodist Church) *1886–1912*

- William Sheppard, S. Presbyterian, Congo. *1887–1910* (Lucy Gantt Sheppard joined him in 1890)
- Edgar B. and Mattie Topp, James Diggs and wife, Liberia, BFMC. *1887*
- Sarah Gorham, AME, Liberia. *1887–1891*; Later to Sierra Leone, AME. *1890–1894*
- J.J. France, ABMU, Louise Cecilia Fleming "Lulu," ABMU and Womens' Baptist Foreign Missionary Society, Congo with Sheppard. *1887–1899*
- Nora S. Gordon, Spelman Seminary/British BMU, Congo. *1888–1897*
- Nancy Jones, American Board of Commissioners for Foreign Missions, Mozambique/Rhodesia. *1888–1897*
- William A. Hall, ABMU, Congo. *1889–1916*
- L. C. Curtis, AME, Monrovia. *1890–1898*
- L. G. Davis, AME, Campbell. *1890–1899*
- Joseph Gomer, United Brethren in Christ, Sierra Leone. *?1890–1950?*
- Clara Ann Howard, ABMU, Congo. *1890–1895*
- Bishop Turner, Zion AME, Sierra Leone. *1891*
- M. J. Newland, AME(?). *pre-1891–1900*
- T. R. Geda, AME, Liberia. *1892*
- George Henry Jackson, Grace Jackson, Stephen E. Jackson (George's brother), ABMU, Congo. *1893–1894*
- Bessie Gardner, ABMU, Congo. *1893–1895*
- Hagen, Baptist, Grand Bassa, *1893*

Baptist National Educational Convention of USA, founded Washington, DC; primary purpose to train clergy and missionaries. *1893*

- R. L. Stewart, NBC, Monrovia. *1893*
- Fannie Worthington Ridgel, AME, Monrovia, assisted Bishop Turner. *1893–1896*

National Baptist Convention, U.S.A., AL, Foreign Mission Board took over what had been done by BFMC and Education Board took over what had been done by BFMC National Convention. *1894*

- G. G. Vreeland, AME, Monrovia (went with Bishop Turner). *1894*
- J. C. Jacson, Independent/NBC, Cape Town, S. Africa. Called "Father of Missions" in S. Africa. *1894–1899*
- R. A. Jackson, independent/BFMC, Cape Town, S. Africa. *1894–1906*
- Joseph I. Buchannan, NBC, joined Jackson, Cape Town, S. Africa. *1894–1899* (Later joined by daughter Mary Buchanan, 1909).
- Henry P. Hawkins, Presbyterian Church U.S., South, Congo. *1894–1910*
- Alfred Lee Ridgel, AME, Monrovia. *1894–1896*
- Mary Tearing (Fearing), Independent/Presbyterian Church, Congo with Sheppard. *1894–1915*

- Joseph E. Phipps, Presbyterian Church in the U.S. West Indies and later to Congo with Sheppard. (Assisted with translation of dictionary.) *1895-1908*

Reconstruction Era *Ca. 1895*

National Black Convention formed Education Board Foreign Missions Board Home Missions Board. *1895*

BFMC carried over into FMB of the National Baptist Convention. *1895*

- C. M. Manning, AME, Monrovia. *1895-1898*
- Oscar H. Massey, Presbyterian Church, North, Liberia. *1895*

Baptist Convention of Western States & Territories joined the National Baptist Convention, USA., VA. *1896*

- Bishop John Bryan Small, Julia Blair Small, AMEZ, Gold Coast. *1896-1904*

Pilgrim Holiness Church. *1897*

- Reverend J. I. Buchanan, BFMC, S. Africa. *1897*
- John Tule, sent to U.S. by Jackson, NBC, S. Africa and then sent back to S. Africa by NBS. *1897*
- Alexander Priestly Camphor, AME, North, Monrovia. *1897-1918*
- Floyd G. Snelson and wife, AME, Sierre Leone. *1897-1900*

Lott Carey Baptist Foreign Mission Convention (LCC) organized—splintered group from BFMC. *1897*

- Rev. J. O. Hayes, first LCC missionary (formerly under BFMC since1881) sent to Liberia—established church and in 1902 an industrial school. *1897*
- G. F. A. Johns and wife, S. Africa National Baptist Convention, Capetown to Zulu people. *1897-1898*
- Mamie Weathers, ME Church, Monrovia. *1897*

Church of God in Christ organized by Eliza Mason. *1897*

Holiness group–Church of the Living God (or Christian Workers for Fellowship). *1889*

- Julia Foote, AMEZ, first woman missionary. *?—1900*
- J. A. L. Price, America, Sudan Mission. *1898*
- Mamie Branton, NBC, Capetown, S.A. *1898-1900*
- Walter F. Hawkins, Presbyterian Church, North, Monrovia. *1899*
- F. M. Allen, Methodist, Monrovia. *1899*
- Amanda Davis, ME Church, North, Monrovia. *1899*
- Joseph A. Davis, ME Church, Monrovia. *1899*
- Charles S. Morris, NBC, Capetown, S. Africa. *1899-1900*
- Joseph C. Sherrill, ME Church, Cape Palmas, Liberia. *1899-1908*
- J. S. Simpson and wife, ME Church North, Liberia. *1899-1908*
- Ruby Williams, ME Church, Liberia. *1899*

Baptist Young People's Union (BYPU) of NBC formed. *1899*

- Efrain Alphonse, Africa, translator of aboriginal speech, Panama. *Ca. 1899*

NBC education fund for African students in the U.S. who would return as missionaries to Africa. By 1910, 12 of the NBC 19 foreign students came from Africa. *1899*

20th Century

Women's Auxiliary, NBC formed. *1900-1901*

- John Wesley Gilbert, Colored ME Church, Paine College. *1900*
- John Chilembwe, NBC, Nyasaland. *1900-1915*
- Reverend Landon N. Cheek, FMB, sent to Providence Industrial Mission, Africa. *1901-1907*
- Miss Emma B. Delaney, E. Central Africa, first missionary Women's Convention Auxiliary, NBC, U.S., East Central Africa. *1901*

United Free Will Baptist formally organized. *1901*

- Eva Boone (1901-1902, died in Congo), Clinton, ABMU, Congo. *1901-1906*
- Levi Jenkins Choppin and Fanny M. Jackson Choppin, AME. *1901-1904*
- Rev. J. O. Hayes, LCC (former BFMC), Liberia. *1902*
- Althea Maria Brown, Congo Presbyterian Mission. *1902-1937*
- Lucius A. DeYampert, Congo Presbyterian Mission, South. *1902-1915*
- A. W. Anderson, NBC, S. America. *1902-1904*

Church and Kingdom of God in Christ organized. *1902*

- Alonzo Leaucourt Edminston, Presbyterian Church, Congo. *1903-1937*

Holiness group—The Free Christian Zion Church of Christ. *1905*

- A. A. Rochester and Annie Katherine Taylor (1906-1914, Rochester stayed longer), Congo Presbyterian Mission, South, Congo. *1906-1939*

Church of Christ (Holiness), U.S. *1907*

- Lillian Thomas, Congo Presbyterian Mission (married Lucius A. DeYambert), Pres. Church, South. *1907-1930*

National Primitive Baptist Convention, U.S.A., officially organized. *1907*

Church of the Nazarene. *1908*

- D. E. Murff (and wife Mattie Wilson), LCC, Cape Town, S. Africa. *1908-1910*
- Rev. William. H. and Cora Ann Pair Thomas, LCC Liberia— organized a monthly paper, the *Watchman* in 1909 and by 1917 had completed Alexander Chapel with church, Sunday school and day school and work on the "Salle Mile Building" home house for the missionaries. *1908*
- Thomas G. D. Gayles, NBC, Liberia. *1909*
- James Edward East, NBC, S. Africa. *1909-1921*

- Dr. Rosa J. Young, LC-MS missions mobilizer. *1909*
- Clinton Caldwell Boone, LCC, Congo. *1910*
- John Wesley Gilbert, Colored Methodist Episcopal, Congo, Basutoland (today Botswana), Rhodesia (today Zimbabwe). *1911–1912*
- Miss Emma B. Delaney—second trip to Africa after 7 years of furlough. Established Seuhn Mission, West Africa, one of most important missionary outposts sponsored by the FMB). *1912–1920*
- Susie A. M. Taylor, NBC, Monrovia. (Worked with DeLaney). *1912–1913*
- Mother Eliza L. Davis George, NBC USA, Suen Mission, Liberia, West Africa. *1911–1917*; Greenville Sinoe County, Liberia, West Africa. *1918–1949*; Founded and labored with the Evangelical Negro Industrial Mission, Sinoe County, W. Africa. *1949–1973*

National Convention of the Churches of God, Holiness. *1914*

Assemblies of God, organized. *1914*

National Baptist Convention, U.S.A., Inc. (split of 1895 NBC group led by R.H. Boyd). *1915*

National Baptist Convention of America unincorporated (split of 1895 NBC group led by E. C. Morris). *1915*

- G. D. Gayles, LCC, Liberia. *1915–1917*
- D. R. Horton, NBC, Liberia. *1917*
- Henry C. McDowell, Africa Congregational Church, Angola. Taught languages and Christian studies. *1917–1923*

Pentecostal Assemblies of the World, Inc. *1916*

- Delia Harris, L. G. Jordan, Pricilla Byron, Liberia Baptist Convention. *1919*

National Baptist Evangelical Life and Soul Saving Assembly of the U.S.A. formed as part of the NBC of America. *1920*

- Clinton & Rachel Tharps Boone, LCC, Monrovia. *1920–1926*
- Samuel B. Coles, Congregational Church, Angola. *1920*
- Frances B. Watson, LCC, Liberia. (Planted 40 churches). *1922–1934*
- Mother Anita Bolden Fitts, C&MA, Guinea and Sierra Leone, W. Africa. *1922–1929*
- Rev. Eugene Thornly, C&MA, Sierra Leone and Guinea, preacher and Bible teacher. *Ca. 1922–1939*

International Church of Foursquare Gospel began by Amy Semple McPhearson. *1922*

- Montrose Wait, C&MA, Independent-AAMC, Sierra Leone, Liberia. *1923–1974*
- Sarah C. Williamson, NBC, Liberia. *1925*
- Winifred Burroughs, Liberia, NBC. *1925*
- A. P. Brown, Liberia NBC. *1925*
- Hattie Mae Davis, NBC, Liberia. *1925*

- Emma F. Butler, Liberia NBC. *1925*
- Flora Zeta Malekebu, NBC, Liberia. (From Emma B. Delaney's work.) *1925*
- Mildred Griffin, NBC, Liberia. *1928*
- Ruth Occomy, NBC, Monrovia. *1928*
- United House of Prayer for All People. *1929*
- Naomi Crawford, Liberia NBC. *1934*
- Rev. Joseph G. Lavalais, LC-MS, Nigeria, but unable to go. *1936*
- Betty Dickins, LC-MS, Nigeria. *1936*

National Baptist Evangelical Life and Soul Saving Assembly of the U.S.A. became independent. *1937*

- Susan Harris, Liberia NBC. *1938*
- Jonathan Udo Ekong, LC-MS, Nigeria. *1938*

Bible Protestant Church. *1939*

The Methodist Church combined ME Church; ME Church, South; Methodist Protestant Church, and created the Central Jurisdiction for blacks. *1939*

- Efrain Alphonse, Independent, Bible Society, Panama, Carribean. *Ca. 1940*
- Mother Edith Johnson, United Holiness Church of America, Salala, Liberia, *Ca. 1940–1990*
- Gladys East, NBC, returned to S. Africa. *1944*

Evangelical United Brethren. *1946*

Evangelical Methodist Church. *1946*

- Hakim Scott, Baptist, Mexico, China. *post-1949*
- Dr. Ernest L. Wilson, co-founder of Afro-American Missionary Crusade, fist Black leadership faith mission in the U.S. *1949.* World Christian with ministries in Panama, Central America, Uganda, etc.
- Mother Vera Stephen, United Pentecostal Council of the Assemblies of God (UPC), MA, sent with Child Evangelism Fellowship to Liberia, built a camp, a church, and a boarding school. *Ca. 1950–1994*
- Mother Erma Bailey, NBC, Suen Mission, Liberia. *Ca. 1950–1990*
- Rev. Ruffis Prunty, National Baptist USA, Suhen Mission, Bendue Mission: agriculture and evangelism, teaching grade school, and planting churches. *Ca. 1950–1994*
- Darius Swann, China. *1953–1963*

Coloured Methodist Episcopal Church changed to Christian MEC. *1954*

- Mother Viola Reddish, LCC, Bopolu Bible Mission, Liberia. *Ca. 1954–1955;* Afro-American Missionary Crusade. *1957–Ca. 1970*
- Mother Martha Thompson, Afro-American Missionary Crusade, Bopolu Bible Mission; bush preacher, school principal, assisted orphanage. *Ca. 1955–Ca. 1985*
- Rev. Dennis Leon Foster, independent missionary to Japan, member Nazarine Baptist Church, Philadelphia, PA. *1955–1987*

Free For All Missionary Baptist Church, Inc. *1955*

- Dorothy Webster Exhume, Church of God and Christ, Haiti, West Indies: Bible teacher, preacher, many churches, orphanage, many schools and preachers under her jurisdiction. *1955-1995*
- Mother Maggie Lampkin, Soul Clinic Mission (or Church of the Home Mission), 15 miles outside of Monrovia. *Ca. 1955-1970*

Beginning of African-American Civil Rights Revolution and rapid rise of independent states in Africa. *1956*

Progressive National Baptist Convention, Inc. organized. *1956*

Christian Methodist Episcopal Church. *1956*

- Mother Pearl Grant, Todee, Liberia with her husband; planted a church and mission school, helped rebuild mud brick buildings with concrete blocks. *1956-1963*
- Mother Naomi Lundee, Church of God, Monolu Mission, Liberia, Grabo tribe; pastored church, principal of day school, director of mission and outchurch ministry. *Ca. 1956-1967*
- Andrew Foster (ministered to the deaf), Ghana, Nigeria, Liberia, Ivory Coast, Senegal, Benin, Cameroon, Central African Republic, Zaire, Burkina Faso, Burundi, Gabon, Kenya, Guinea, Sierra Leone, Congo, Ethiopia, Tanzania, Zambia, and Zimbabwe. *1957-1987*

Bible Way Churches of Our Lord Jesus Christ, Worldwide. *1957*

- Elgin and Dorothy Taylor, President, Christians in Action, Okinawa, Japan; UK; Nigeria. *1957-Present*
- Rev. Douglas and Dorothy Oliver, India among Hindus, Muslims, and tribes. *1957-1966*
- Mother Pearl Page, Church of God in Christ, Tubucka Mission, Liberia; church and elementary boarding school. *1958-Ca. 1968.* Philippines. *1959-2002*
- Sister Naomi Doles Mitchell. Carver Foreign Mission, established Monrovia Bible Institute and started a school in King Gray Village (which is now Carver Christian Academy), Monrovia. *1959-Ca. 1970.* Married Luther Mitchell, ministered to Krone and Sappo tribes and then Monrovia under Church of Christ Holiness, Foreign Mission Board. *Ca. 1973-1981*
- Dr. Henrietta Hernon, Carver Foreign Mission, Monrovia, Liberia. Public school Bible teacher, quiz master for Youth for Christ radio broadcast, counselor and mentor for youth, adult literacy facilitator, soccer enthusiast, assisted with church plant at King Gray Village. *1959-1984*
- Verlene B. Farmer Goatey, National Baptist Convention USA, Suhen Industrial Mission. Liberia; third grade teacher, house mother, village evangelist, taught at church. *1959-1966*
- Bob Harrison, Baptist, Philippines, Taiwan, etc.; later established Bob Harrison Ministries. *1960-Ca. 2000*

- Rev. Willie & Mrs. Betty Qumby, Afro-American Missionary Crusade, PA, Bopolu Bible Mission Station; pastored the church, taught grade school, trained preachers in village evangelism, and did mission station orphanage work. *Ca. 1960-1965*
- Daphne Henderson, Afro-American Missionary Crusade, Bopolu Bible Mission; orphanage, teacher at the mission school, preached in the bush. *Ca. 1960-1988*
- Mable McCombs, Carver Bible Institute, Liberia. *1962-1996*
- Mother Cora B. McCleary, Carver Foreign Missions, worked with Mable MCCombs (about 38-42 years) although beginning and ending dates unknown: church planter, field leader, Bible school professor and Christian education, etc.
- Virgil Lee Amos, Mexico, Spain, India, Kenya, Nigeria, N. Africa, etc. *1962-Present*
- Rev. Harold and Sister June Cottman, National Baptist Convention, Krone and Sappo tribes, Murryville, Sinoe County, Liberia; Christian education, church planting, evangelism. *1962-1970*
- Rev. Walter and Vera Gibson, United Pentecostal Council of the Assemblies of God, Cabridge, MA. Bonnika Mission, Cape Palmas, Liberia; church planting, evangelism, Christian education, and preaching. *Ca. 1962-1967*
- Rev. Dr. Joseph C. Jeter, Sr., founded Have Christ Will Travel Ministries with Mrs. Catherine E. Jeter; Uganda, Haiti, West Indies, Liberia, W. Africa, Kenya, E. Africa, S.W. India, and Nova Scotia, Canada. *1963-Present*
- Mother Augusta Tyler, N. Oakland Baptist Church, CA and graduate of Bay Cities Bible Institute. Founded Voice of Africa Mission, Ca. 1963. Went to Liberia to work with Mother Holmes near Town of Clay, Monrovia. Called to Grand Bassa County by Chief Bassa Geah, and there built Voice of Africa Mission for children with Mother Grazelle Settles, to build a mission school, a church, and to start an agricultural project. *1967-Ca. 1995*
- Ruby P. Clarke, United World Mission, Mali, Senegal. *1964-1994*
- Mother Francis Watkins, Kodish Church, Todee, Liberia; Bible teacher, preacher, prayer warrior and administrator. *1964-1985*
- Rev. Barbara Harper, Kodish Church, Todee, Liberia; preacher, teacher, mission administrator, school principal. *Ca. 1964-Ca. 1969*
- Sister Iris Johnson, Church of the Living God Mission, 15 miles past Todee Junction; preacher, school principal, boarding school supervisor, mission field director. *Ca. 1964-1974*
- Mother Maddie Lee Monroe, Founder of Evangelical Negro Industrial Mission, Inc., Oakland, CA, to support Mother Eliza Davis George's work in Liberia. Went to assist preaching and teaching in villages. *Ca. 1965-1970*

Methodist Church merged with Evangelical United Brethren and the Central Jurisdiction was abolished. *1966*

- Rev. Andrew D. and Mrs. Irma Marie Trustee, Afro-American Missionary Crusade, Bopolu Bible Church. *1966-1974*

- Rev. Curtis and Mrs. Maves Holmes, West Indies Mission, Haiti; Church planting, taught Bible by Extention. *Ca. 1966-1975*
- Black Baptists for Church Renewal organized from Methodists. *1968*
- Rev. Donald & Mrs. Charlotte Canty, Carver Foreign Missions, Carver Christian Academy, Liberia. Teachers. *1968-1980*

The Wesleyan Church. *1968*

The United Methodist Church. *1968*

- Benjamin W. Johnson, Sr., Baptist American Sunday School Union, S. Africa, Canada, Losotho, Botswana, Spain, Haiti. *1968-1973*
- Daise Whaley, WEC, International, Ivory Coast, W. Africa. French and Guru languages, Bible teaching, preaching in churches, teaching at women's conventions, counseling, built and ran a girls home. *1969-1998*
- Mother Mary Fossett, Carver Foreign Mission, music teacher and evangelist, Monrovia, Liberia. Worked with Cora McCleary and Mable McCombs. *Ca. 1969-1987*
- Sister Josephine Mentor, National Baptist Convention USA, Suhen Mission, Liberia; Churad Zulu, Malawi, East Africa; nurse, administrator, teacher; Director was Dr. Daniel S. Malekebu. *Ca. 1969-1974*

The American Baptist Churches of the South (predominantly black regional union of the ABC). *1970*

- Elizabeth Proctor, Voice of Africa Mission, Grand Bassa; nurse, teacher and principal at the school, Bible teacher, house mother, village outreach. *1969-Ca. 1974*. Haiti, West Indies. *Ca. 1975-2000*
- Rev. Claude and Althea Austin, Kodish Church of Emmanuel, Pittsburg, PA, sent to Todee mission station in Liberia. *Ca. 1969-1976*. Rev. Austin returned sick to the U.S. with Althea and passed away. Althea Austin returned to Todee. *1970-1985*
- Mother Carrie Ford, Church of the Living God Mission, Todee, Liberia; Bible teacher, principal of grade school. *1969-1989*
- Sister Verna Boman, Kodish Church of Emmanuel, Todee, Liberia; nurse, Bible teacher, preacher, and school principal. *Ca. mid-1970s*

Black Catholic Priests ordained and recognized. *1970*

- Dorris Porter, Christians In Action, Sierra Leone; witnessing, Bible studies. *1971-1982*
- Rev. Kenneth and Mrs. Jean Thorpe, Manna Bible Institute Philadelphia, PA, Afro-American Missionary Crusade, Bopolu Bible Mission, Liberia with Bassa and Keppelli tribes: he was Pastor, Bible teacher of Bopolu Bible Church, field leader of all missionaries, teacher and preacher in the bush villages, and she was teacher at the mission school, record keeper, home school teacher of their children and Bible teacher in the bush villages. *1971-1984*
- Brian Johnson, Carver Foreign Mission, Monrovia, Liberia. Later w/ World Relief. To Benin w/COMINAD. *1973-Present*

- Elaine Joseph, Christians In Action, Sierra Leone. *1974–1986*
- Daisy Russell, Christians In Action, Sierra Leone. *1974–1979*
- Fanney Randolf, Church of God in Christ, Haiti; church planting, orphanage, and children's work. *1974–1981*
- Emma Lee Haywood, Church of God in Christ, Haiti; orphanage work. *1975–1985*
- Bertha Williams-Smith, Christians In Action, Sierra Leone, Monrovia. *1975–1976*
- Jocelyn Buchanan, Christians In Action, Columbia. *1975–1979*
- Diane Jeter (Bryant), Have Christ Will Travel Ministries, Haiti, Western Nova Scotia; group leader, Bible Club, children's camp, evangelism. *1975–1980*

New interest among African Americans for World Mission. *1976*

- Mother Ermma Moreland, Church of the Living God, Todee, Liberia. *1977–1987*
- Julia King, Have Christ Will Travel Ministries, Carver Foreign Missions, Liberia; assisted at mission, nurse, teaching, mission secretary, Christian counseling. *1977; Ca. 1984–1991; 2000–Present*
- Theresa Character, Have Christ Will Travel Ministries, Western Nova Scotia; Bible Club, Bible camp, home visitation, evangelism, ladies Bible classes, assisting churches. *1978–Present*
- Tonya Orozco, CIA, Guatemala, Columbia, Ecuador; Bible studies, church planting. *1978–1990*
- Dr. David Cornelius, Southern Baptist Convention, Director of African-American Church Relations, and Co-director of International Volunteer Fellowships of the International Mission Board of the SBC, USA. Nigeria; water research in West Africa. *1980–1990s*
- James and Gloria Whitaker, Christians In Action, Okinawa. *1981–1996*
- Joy Needles, Christians In Action, Guatemala, UK, Mexico. *1982–Present*
- Dr. Michael and Mrs. Kay Johnson, Zaire, Kenya; hospital administration, surgical care, street children health care, training Kenyan physicians. *1984–Present*
- Jacqueline Huggins, Wycliffe Bible Translators, Philippines, Haiti, Philippine island; scripture translation Kagayanen language. *1981–Present*
- Shirley K. Wright-Masongezi and Wilondia Masongezi, Baptist General Conference, Nigeria, Cameroon. *1983–Present*
- Chester Carney, Christians In Action, Okinawa. *1985–1994*
- Rev. Glenn and Mrs. Kim Mason, Carver Foreign Missions, Liberia. *1990–1991* Director of the Mission. *1999–Present*
- Mary McKelvy, Christians In Action, Sierra Leone. *1990–2006*
- Stephen Craig, Wycliffe Bible Translators, West Africa; tribal translation. *1993–Present*
- Lillian Tanner, Christians In Action, Sierra Leone. *2003–2004*

Bibliography

Adams, C. C., and A. Marshall Halley. *Negro Baptists and Foreign Missions.* Philadelphia, PA: Foreign Board of the National Baptist Convention, 1944.
Andrew, John A., III. "Betsy Stockton: Stranger in a Strange Land." *Journal of Presbyterian History* (52) Summer 1974, 157–166.
Andrews, William I., ed. *Sisters of the Spirit: Three Black Women's Autobiographies of the Nineteenth Century.* Bloomington, IN: Indiana University Press, 1986.
Agbeti, Kofi J. *West African Church History.* Leiden: J. J. Brill, 1986.
Ashley, Willie May Hardy. *Far From Home: A Biography of Emma B. Delaney, Missionary to Africa 1902–1922.* Self published, 1987.
Ayandele, E. A. *The Missionary Impact on Modern Nigeria, 1824–1914: A Political and Social Analysis.* London: Longmans Press, Green and Co., 1966.
Baer, Hans A. *The Black Spiritual Movement.* Knoxville, TN: University of Tennessee Press, 1984.
Banks, William L. *A History of Black Baptists in the United States.* Pennsylvania, PA: Philadelphia, 1987.
Barrett, David B. *World Christian Encyclopedia.* New York: Oxford University Press, 2001.
Barrett, David B., and Todd M. Johnson. *World Christian Trends.* Pasadena, CA: William Carey Library, 2001.
Bedinger, Robert. *Triumphs of the Gospel in the Belgian Congo.* Richmond, VA: Presbyterian Committee of Publication, 1920.
Benedetto, Robert. *Presbyterian Reformers in Central Africa.* Leiden: Brill, 1996.
Bentley, William H. *The Meaning of History for Black Americans.* Chicago, IL: National Black Evangelical Association, 1979.
Bery, Lewellyn L. *A Century of Missions of the AME Church 1840–1940.* New York: Gutenberg Printing Company, 1942.
Bliss, Edwin, ed. *The Encyclopedia of Missions.* New York: Funk & Wagnalls, 1891.
Bradley, David H. *A History of the AME Zion Church.* Vols. 1 and 2. Nashville, TN: The Parthenon Press, 1970.
Brichoux, Felicia S. *Gasper Makil.* North Carolina: Wycliffe Bible Translators, Summer Institute of Linguistics, Wycliffe-JARRS printshop, 1970.
Blyden, Edward. *Christianity, Islam and the Negro Race.* Edinburgh, Scotland: University Press, 1887.
Camphor, Alexander Priestly. *Missionary Story Sketches.* Cincinnati, OH: Jennings and Graham, 1909.
Cauthen, Baker J. et. al. *Advance: A History of Southern Baptist Foreign Missions.* Tennessee: Broadman Press, 1970.
Clendennen, Clarence et. al. *Americans in Africa, 1865–1900.* Stanford, CT: Stanford University Press, 1966.
Coan, Josephus R. "The Expansion of Missions of the African Methodist Episcopal Church in South Africa, 1896–1908." Ph.D. Dissertation, Hartford Seminary, 1961.
Crane, W. Henry. "Presbyterian Work in the Congo." Thesis, Union Theological Seminary, 1960.
Dabney, Mary. *Light in Darkness.* Asheville, NC: Daniels, 1971.
David, Humphreys. *An Historical Account of the Incorporated Society for the Propagation of the Gospel in Foreign Parts.* New York: Arno Press, 1969.
Davis, John W. "George Liele and Andrew Bryan, Pioneer Negro Baptist Preachers." *Journal of Negro History* (3) no. 2, April 1918, 119–127.

Dean, Edith. *Great Women of the Christian Faith*. New Jersey: Westwood Press, 1959.
Dickinson, Richard C. *This I Remember*. St. Louis, MO: Concordia Publishing House, 1995.
———. *Roses and Thorns*. St. Louis, MO: Concordia Publishing House, 1997.
Du Bois, William Edward Burghardt. *The Souls of Black Folk: Essays and Sketches*. Chicago: A.C. McClurg & Co.; [Cambridge]: University Press John Wilson and Son, Cambridge, 1903.
Dvorak, Katharine. *An African-American Exodus: The Segregation of the Southern Churches*. New York: Carlson Publishing, 1991.
Eddy, George Sherwood. *Pathfinders of the World Missionary Crusade*. New York: Abingdon Cokesbury Press, 1945.
Edmiston, Althea. *Maria Fleming*. Atlanta, GA: Committee on Women's Work, 1938.
Executive Committee of Foreign Missions, PCUS. "William H. Sheppard: Pioneer Missionary to the Congo." Nashville, TN: Executive Committee of Foreign Missions, PCUS, 1942.
Fisher, Miles Mark. "Lott Carey: The Colonizing Missionary." *Journal of Negro History* (7), October 1922. 380–418.
Fitts, Leroy. *A History of Black Baptists*. Nashville, TN: Broadman Press, 1985.
———. *Lott Carey: First Black Missionary to Africa*. Valley Forge, PA: Judson Press, 1978.
Foote, Julia A. *A Brand Plucked from the Fire*. Cleveland, OH: Foote, 1879.
Frazier, Franklin, and C. Eric Lincoln. *The Negro Church in America*. New York: Scholken Books, 1974.
George, Carol. *Segregated Sabbaths: Richard Allen and the Emergence of Independent Black Churches, 1760–1840*. New York: Oxford University Press, 1973.
Gregg, Howard D. *History of the African Methodist Episcopal Church*. Nashville, TN: AMEC Publishing House, 1980.
Hagood, Lewis M. *The Colored Man in the Methodist Episcopal Church*. Westport, CT: Negro University Press, 1970. Reprint, 1898.
Harr, Wilbur Christian. "The Negro as an American Protestant Missionary in Africa." Doctoral dissertation, University of Chicago Divinity School, 1945.
Harrison, Bob. *When God Was Black*. Concord, CA: Bob Harrison Ministries International, 1978.
Harrison, William Pope. *The Gospel Among the Slaves: A Short Account of Missionary Operations Among the African Slaves of the Southern States*. Nashville, TN: Publishing House, Methodist Episcopal Church, South, 1893.
Harvey, William J., III. *Sacrifice and Dedication in a Century of Mission*. Philadelphia, PA: The Foreign Mission Board, National Baptist Conventions, 1979.
———. *Bridges of Faith Across the Seas*. Philadelphia, PA: The Foreign Mission Board, National Baptist Convention, 1989.
Hervey, G. Winfred. *The Story of Baptist Missions in Foreign Lands, from the Time of Carey to the Present Date*. St. Louis, MO: Chaney R. Barns, 1886.
Hughley, Clyde E. "An Analysis of Black American Involvement in World Missions." USCWM SE Research Project, Dallas Theological Seminary, 1983.
Jacobs, Sylvia M. "Black Americans and the Missionary Movement in Africa." *Contributions in Afro-American and African Studies* no. 66. Westport, CT: Greenwood Press, 1982.
Jeal, Tim. *Livingstone (Nota Bene)*. New York: Putnam Press, 1973.
Jetter, Joseph C. *The Unknown Soldiers*. Philadelphia, PA: Have Christ Will Travel Ministries, Inc., 2004.
Johnson, Leonidas. God's *Missionary Call to the African-American Church—Wake Up*. Pasadena, CA: William Carey Library, 2006.
Johnson, Thomas Lewis. *African for Christ, or Twenty Eight Years a Slave*. Sixth edition. London: Alexander and Shepherd, 1892.
Johnstone, Patrick J. St. G. *World Handbook for the World Christian*. South Pasadena, CA: World Christian Book Shelf.
Jordan, Artishia W. *The African Methodist Episcopal Church in Africa*. New York: AME Department of Foreign Missions, 1964.

Jordan, Lewis Garnett. *A Brief Record of Negro Baptist Missionaries Who Heard and Obeyed the Command "Go Ye": They Went—Preaching the Word.* N.p, n.d.

———. *Up The Ladder in Foreign Missions.* Nashville, TN: National Baptist Publishing Board, 1901.

Kane, J. Herbert. *Understanding Christian Missions.* Grand Rapids, MI: Baker Book House, 1986.

Kellersberger, Julia. *A Life for the Congo: The Story of Althea Brown Edmiston.* New York: Revell, 1947.

———. *Lucy Gantt Sheppard.* Atlanta, GA: PCUS, Committee on Women's Work, n.d.

King, Willis J. "History of the Methodist Church Mission in Liberia." Typescript in United Methodist Church Commission on Archives and History. Lake Junaluska, NC: Methodist Missions in Africa, 1945.

Lakey, Othal Hawthorne. *The Rise of Colored Methodism.* Dallas, TX: Crescendo, 1972.

———. *The History of the CME Church.* Memphis, TN: CME Publishing House, 1985.

Lincoln, C. Eric and Lawrence H. Mamiya. *The Black Church in the African-American Experience.* Durham, NC: Durham University Press, 1990.

Lapsley, James, ed. *Life and Letters of Samuel Norvell Lapsley.* Richmond, VA: Whittet & Shepperson, 1893.

Lewis, Marilyn. "Independent Study Assignment: The African-American in Christian Missions." Partial fulfillment of Th.M. degree, Dallas Theological Seminary, 1993.

———. "Overcoming Obstacles: The Broad Sweep of the African-American and Missions." *Mission Frontiers* (March–April 2000). http://www.missionfrontiers.org/issue/article/overcoming-obstacles.

Little, John. *The Presbyterian Colored Missions.* Louisville, KY: 1914.

Livingstone, David. *Missionary Travels.* New York: Harper, 1858.

Martin, Sandy D. "Spelman's Emma B. Delaney and the African Mission." *The Journal of Religious Thought,* (41) Spring 1984, 22–37.

———. *Black Baptists and African Missions, 1880–1915.* Macon, GA: Mercer University Press, 1989.

McClain, William. *Black People in the Methodist Church: Whiter Thou Goest?* Cambridge, MA: Schenkman Publishing, Company, 1984.

The Missionary. Richmond, Nashville. 1890–1910.

Mitchell, Joseph. *The Missionary Pioneer, or a Brief Memoir of the Life, Labours, and Death of John Stewart, (a man of colour), Founder, under God, of the Mission Among the Wyandotts at Upper Sandusky, Ohio.* Self published 1827. Reprinted in *The African Preachers.* Harrisburg, VA: Sprinkle Publications, 1988.

Moffett, Eileen F. "Betsey Stockton: Pioneer American Missionary." *International Bulletin of Missionary Research* (19) no. 2, April 1995, 71–76.

Mutshi, Morrisine. *African-Americans in Mission.* Louisville, KY: Worldwide Ministries, Presbyterian Church, 2000.

Myers, John Brown. *The Congo For Christ: The Story of the Congo Mission.* New York: Revell, 1895.

Newton, H. Malcom Trusty. "Missiology From A Black Theological Perspective." Master's thesis, Dallas Theological Seminary, 1984.

Payne, Daniel A. *History of the African Methodist Episcopal Church.* Nashville, TN: AME Church, 1891. Reprint, 1968.

Pelt, Leslie. "Wanted Black Missionaries, But How?" *Evangelical Missions Quarterly* (25) January 1989, 28–37.

Pelt, Owen, and Ralph Lee Smith. *The Story of the National Baptists.* New York: Vantage Press.

Phiri, D. D. *Let Us Die for Africa.* Blantyre, Malawi: Central African Limited, 1999.

Phillips, Charles Henry. *The History of the Colored Methodist Episcopal Church in America.* Jackson, TN: Publishing House of the CME Church, 1898. Reprint 1925.

Pitts, Walter F. *Old Ship of Zion: The Afro-Baptist Ritual in the African Diaspora.* New York: Oxford University Press, 1993.

Plowman, Edward E. "Black Baptists: The Missing Missionaries." *Christianity Today,* October 12, 1973, 56–58.

Poe, William A. "Lott Carey: Man of Purchased Freedom." *Church History* (39) March 1970, 49–61.

Poston, Larry A., and Carl F. Ellis, Jr. *The Changing Face of Islam in America: Understanding and Reaching Your Muslim Neighbor*. Camp Hill, PA: Horizon Books, 2000.

Read, Florence Matilda. *The Story of Spelman College*. Princeton, NJ: Princeton University Press, 1961.

Reapson, James. "Where Are The Black Missionaries, It's Time to Reject the Old Answers." *Evangelical Missions Quarterly* (23) July 1987, 296–297.

Redkey, Edwin S. *Black Exodus: Black Nationalist and Back-to-Africa Movements, 1890–1910*. New Haven, CT: Yale University Press, 1969.

Roth, Daniel F. "Grace Not Race: Southern Negro Church Leaders, Black Identity and Missions to West Africa, 1865–1919." Ph.D. dissertation, University of Texas at Austin, 1975.

Schweitzer, Albert. *On the Edge of the Primeval Forest*. London: Black, 1928.

Seals, Eugene, and John McNeal, Jr., eds. *Waite: A Man Who Could Not Wait*. Carver Foreign Missions, Inc., 1988.

Seraile, William. "Black American Missionaries in Africa, 1821–1925." *Social Studies* (63) October 1972, 198–202.

Shaloff, Stanley. "William Henry Sheppard." In Albert Berrian, ed., *Education for Life in A Multi-Cultural Society*. Hampton, VA: Hampton Institute Press, 1968.

Sheppard, Lucy. *From Talladega College to Africa*. New York: American Missionary Association, n.d.

Sheppard, William H. *Presbyterian Pioneers in Congo*. Richmond: Presbyterian Committee of Publication, 1917.

Shepperson, George, and Thomas Price. *Independent African: John Chilembwe and the Origins, Settings and Significance of the Nyasaland Native Rising of 1915*. Blantryre, Malawi: Christian Literature Association in Malawi (CLAIM). This 2000 edition was made from the 1987 paperback edition.

Sidwell, Mark. *Free Indeed: Heroes of Black Christian History*. Greenville, SC: Bob Jones University Press, 1995.

Slade, Ruth. *English Speaking Missions in the Congo Independent State, 1878–1908*. Brussels: Academic Royale des Sciences d' Outre Mer, 1959.

Smith, Amanda Berry. *An Autobiography. The Story of the Lord's Dealings with Mrs. Amanda Smith the Coloured Evangelist; Containing an Account of Her Life Work of Faith, and Her Travels in America, England, Ireland, Scotland, India, and Africa, as an Independent Missionary*. Chicago: Meyer, 1893.

Smith, Charles Spencer. *A History of the African Methodist Episcopal Church*. Philadelphia, PA: AME Church, 1922.

Synan, Vincent. "The Holiness-Pentecostal Movement in the U.S." Ph.D. dissertation, Eerdmans. Oral Roberts University Library, 2002. www.oru.edu/university/library/holyspirit/pentorg1.html.

Tucker, Ruth A. *From Jerusalem to Irian Jaya: A Biographical History of Christian Missions*. Grand Rapids, MI: Academic Books, Zondervan, 1983.

Tupper, H. A. *The Foreign Missions of the Southern Baptist Convention*. Philadelphia, PA: American Baptist Publication Society, 1880.

Verne, Becker. "A New Era for Black Missionaries." *Christianity Today* (33) October 20, 1989. 38–40.

Walls, William J. *The African Methodist Episcopal Zion Church: Reality of the Black Church*. Charlotte, NC: AMEZ Publishing House, 1974.

———. *Black Americans and the Evangelization of Africa 1877–1900*. WI: University of Wisconsin Press, 1982.

Walston, Vaughn J., and Robert J. Stevens, eds. *African-American Experience in World Mission: A Call Beyond Community*. Pasadena, CA: William Carey Library, 2002 by the Cooperative Mission Network of the African Dispersion (COMINAD).

Walston, Vaughn J. "Ignite the Passion." *Mission Frontiers*. Pasadena, CA: U.S. Center for World Mission, (March–April 2000). http://www.missionfrontiers.org/issue/article/ignite-the-passion.

Williams, Walter L. *Black Americans and the Evangelization of Africa 1877–1900*. Madison, WI: University of WI Press, 1982.

Wills, David W., and Newman, Richard. *Black Apostles: At Home and Abroad.* Boston: G. K. Hall and Company, 1982.

Wilmore, Gayraud S. "Black Americans in Mission: Setting the Record Straight." *International Bulletin of Missionary Research* (10) no. 3, July 1986, 98–102.

Winter, Ralph D., and Steven C. Hawthorne, eds. *Perspectives on the World Christian Movement, A Reader.* Third edition. Pasadena, CA: William Carey Library, 1999.

Wright, Mary Emily. *The Missionary Work of the Southern Baptist Convention.* Philadelphia, PA: American Baptist Publication Society, 1902.

Yates, William L. "The History of the AMEZ Church in West Africa, Liberia and Gold Coast (Ghana), 1880–1900." Master's thesis, Hartford Seminary, 1968.

Young, Rosa. *Light in the Dark Belt, The Story of Rosa Young as Told by Herself.* St. Louis, MO: Concordia Publishing House, 1950.

Index

A
abolishing slavery, 20
Abraham, 92, 240–42
acceptance, 224
achievement, 45, 70, 76, 149, 166, 181
Africa, 10, 20, 22, 25–30, 33, 36–38, 40–45, 47–51, 59–60, 65, 68, 73, 76, 81–83, 86–87, 89–92, 94–101, 105–06, 108–09, 111–17, 119, 126–32, 134–38, 140–50, 153, 155, 158–61, 163–66, 171–75, 177, 179–81, 185–86, 193, 196–99, 203–04, 206, 210–12, 215, 220, 222, 224, 229–30, 234–35, 270–72, 276, 280, 286
African, 3–4, 24–30, 34, 43–45, 49–50, 60–61, 76, 82, 87, 89, 91, 97–101, 106, 109–11, 114, 116–20, 125, 128–31, 134–42, 144, 146–48, 150, 153, 158–66, 171–72, 174–77, 181, 185, 197–200, 203, 206, 211, 232, 234–35, 273, 276, 279–80
    culture, 7, 32, 172
    descent, 10, 199, 265, 275–76
    heritage, 32
African Independent Churches, 141
African Inland Mission, 211
African Methodist Episcopal (AME), 14, 20, 35, 84–87, 89–90
African Missionary Society, 48, 99
Afro-American Missionary Crusade, 179, 187
Aggrey, James K., 26, 28, 30
Ahlstrom, Sidney, 15
Allen, Richard, 19–20, 24
Alphonse, Efrain, 183–84
ambassador
    fellowship, 191, 280
    American
    Revolutionary War, 10, 19, 60
American Baptist Foreign Missionary Union, 59
American Baptist Missionary Union, 99
American Board of Commissioners for Foreign Missions (ABCFM), 63, 66–67, 171
American Colonization Society, 49–50, 127–29
American Negro Academy (ANA), 76
American Protestant Episcopal Church, 19, 59, 81
Amos, Virgil, 191, 280
ancestors, 100, 112, 176, 211, 236, 264
    worship, 38, 176
ancestral
    worship, 112
Angola, 171
Antrom, Virginia, 156
apartheid, 125, 136
Asia, 105, 213–15, 229, 252
Asian, 203, 253
atonement, 14
Azusa Street Mission, 14–15

B
Back to Africa, 159
Baptist Foreign Mission Convention (BFMC), 132
Barbados, 26
Barratt, Thomas Ball, 14
Belgian, 87, 108–09, 114, 116–18, 150, 164, 172
Benin, 197
Bible, 7, 24, 26, 34–35, 41, 44, 47, 49, 54, 62, 64, 70, 82, 92–94, 96–99, 101–03, 111, 113–14, 117, 138, 159, 162, 176, 180, 191, 193–94, 196–98, 201, 203, 213, 219–22, 225, 234, 237–39, 242, 246, 248–51, 253–57, 264, 267–68, 274–75, 278, 283–86, 288
    college, 179, 208, 252
    school, 14, 181, 186, 202, 209–10, 212, 216
    study, 44, 198, 250–51, 258, 260, 274, 278, 285
    teacher, 65, 195
    translation, 184
Bingham, Roland, 70
black missions. *See* missions.
blessing, 12–14, 26, 38, 48, 53, 92, 102–04, 174, 236, 238, 240–42, 259
Boardman, William E., 13
Body of Christ, 150, 208, 216–17, 243–45, 251
Boston University, 30
Bray, Thomas, 7
budget, 274
Burma, 48, 105

C

calling, 3, 19, 53, 129, 135, 152, 175, 186, 256, 262, 265, 273, 277, 281, 285
Cambridge University, 76, 104
Cameroon, 95, 230
Canada, 20, 25, 71, 92, 175, 180, 198, 219, 246
Carey, Lott, 47–51, 59, 127–32, 179
Carey, William, 9, 47, 199
Caribbean, 212, 235
Cartwright, Andrew, 25–27
Carver Foreign Missions, Inc., 180, 224, 231
Carver, George Washington, 224–25
Cheek, Landon, 137, 140, 158–67
chieftaincy, 38
Chilembwe, John, 134–42, 160–67
China, 33, 45, 62, 72, 111, 213, 232, 277–80
Chowan, Reverend Ranford, 7
Christian, 3, 7–11, 13, 20, 24–26, 29, 32, 34, 36, 39, 41–42, 44–45, 50, 52, 55–56, 59–60, 62–70, 72–73, 76, 87, 93, 95–97, 99, 102, 111, 113–14, 118–20, 125, 130–33, 135–36, 138, 141, 144, 150, 152, 155–58, 160, 172–75, 179–80, 192, 195, 198, 200–01, 203, 207–08, 210–11, 213–23, 229–31, 234–37, 239, 241, 243–45, 248, 250–51, 256, 258, 265–66, 268, 278, 280–81, 283–85, 288–89
Christian Methodist Episcopal Church, 23–25, 59, 85–87, 89, 102
Christian Missionary Alliance, 173
Christianity, 3, 8, 19, 21–23, 42, 60, 62, 67, 70, 73, 86, 89, 95, 111, 114, 128, 134–35, 152, 159, 185, 196, 209, 237, 249, 251, 267, 288
Church of England, 3, 7, 26
Church of God in Christ, 14, 82, 179
Church Missionary Society, 59, 134
civil rights, 81, 158, 172, 191, 230, 280
Civil War (U.S.), 14, 25–26, 32, 81–82, 85, 103, 136
civilization, 60, 70, 76, 89, 141, 146, 164, 178
Coker, Daniel, 59
college, 31, 33, 40, 48, 64–65, 82, 95, 113, 141, 143, 159, 179, 186, 192, 196, 198, 204, 207–08, 211, 229–30, 252, 258, 260–62, 267–69, 274, 277–78, 283–84, 286
colonial, 3, 8, 37, 50, 82, 109, 111, 130, 134–35, 138–39, 163–65, 171, 174, 185, 280
colonists, 49–50, 125, 128–30, 171
Colonization Society, 49–50, 127–29
Columbus, Christopher, 10
comfortable, 115, 160, 213, 266–68, 270, 276
COMINAD, 230, 234–35
communication, 130, 148, 163, 235, 287

community, 35, 64–65, 72, 113, 125, 131, 139, 143, 156, 160, 191–92, 194, 199, 205, 211, 215, 229, 254, 256, 281
conflict, 23, 76, 90, 264, 274, 288
Congo, 87–89, 98–99, 107–09, 111–15, 117–20, 132, 150, 164, 197–98, 215
Congregational Church, 35, 59–60, 66, 106, 113–14
Congregationalists, 59–69, 106
Cookman, Alfred, 14
Coptic, 59
Cornelius, David, 243, 260
Cox, Melville Beveridge, 25, 105
Crane, William, 127–28
Crowther, Samuel Ajayi, 95
Crummell, Alexander, 60, 74–77
cultural, 255
  background, 281
  challenges, 230
  differences, 42, 111
  history, 229
  ministry, 283
culture, 7, 32, 37, 45, 60, 76, 85, 100, 112–13, 128, 172, 191, 200, 213–14, 219, 234, 239, 241, 248, 253, 255–57, 275, 281, 288–89
curse, 43, 54, 207, 264

D

Dark continent, 34, 40, 49, 88–89, 136, 160
Davis, Mother May, 156
Day, John, 166
Delaney, Emma, 137, 140–51, 153–57, 160
Demerara, 25
deputation, 287
destiny, 59, 150, 219
dignity, 77, 130–31, 258, 281
discipline, 24–25, 55, 64, 156, 192, 257, 273
discipling, 221, 278
discrimination, 33, 76, 130, 158, 163, 166, 185, 191, 213, 215, 244
disillusionment, 162, 278
doctrine, 14, 34, 53–54, 89, 192, 213
Doe, Samuel, 231–32
Doles, Naomi, 180, 224

E

East, Gladys, 156, 185–87
East, James E., 185–86
East Africa, 144, 146, 148–50, 211
economic development, 234
Edwards, Jonathan, 8
Egypt, 59, 105, 212, 283, 285–89

Egyptian, 285–86, 288–89
Ekong, Jonathan Udo, 37–38, 40–42, 45–46
Elmina Castle, 95, 134
Elon College, 33
Emancipation Proclamation, 93
embassy, 233–34, 263
Embury, Philip, 23
emigrants, 129
equality, 25, 67, 125, 130, 159
equipping, 44, 277
establishment, 20, 23, 44, 66, 89, 99, 139, 171
Ethiopia, 45, 50, 98, 198, 211
Ethiopian, 161–63, 165, 206, 247
ethnic groups, 160, 219, 230–31, 233, 235, 242, 244, 248
Europe, 3, 29, 95, 99, 120, 173, 181, 191, 210, 212, 269, 276, 280
evangelization, 7–8, 44, 59, 87, 89, 109, 111, 114, 132, 171–72, 185, 192, 217
  world, 244
evangelize, 7, 39, 66–67, 69, 83, 111, 165, 219
expatriates, 128, 285, 289
exposure, 158, 203, 230, 285, 289

F

fellowship, 29, 37, 86, 115, 120, 165, 177, 202, 230, 237, 256, 269
financial, 11, 40, 131, 136, 139, 165, 166, 274
  obligations, 165
  support, 25, 137, 159–60, 164, 256, 274, 287
Flower, J. Roswell, 14
foreign missions. *See* missions.
Foster, Andrew, 193–94, 196–98
France, 174, 232, 287
freed slaves, 8, 49, 95
freedmen, 4, 7, 20, 32, 93–94, 98
freedom, 10, 19–21, 23, 25, 47–48, 64, 67, 74, 92–93, 99, 102, 116, 127, 129, 131, 134, 158, 166, 172, 232, 251, 268, 276
Freeman, Thomas Birch, 26
Freetown, 27, 49, 128, 175–78
funds, 25, 35, 40, 48, 50, 75, 81–82, 98–99, 115, 138, 147, 153, 160–61, 163, 173–74, 179, 202, 257

G

Gabon, 197
Galangue station, 171
Garvey, Marcus, 119, 137, 171, 174
George, David, 10
Ghana, 26, 29–30, 45, 193, 196–98, 203–04, 211, 280

ghetto, 209
Gilbert, John Wesley, 86–89
glory, 56, 75, 104, 142, 184, 212, 216, 220, 238–40, 246, 275–76
Gold Coast, 26–30, 129
Gordon, A. J., 14
Gordon, Robert, 125
Great Awakenings, 8, 19, 21
  First, 48
  Second, 48, 59–60, 73
Great Commission, 138, 158, 192, 230, 235, 237, 246
Grenfell, George, 96
Guinea, 22, 99, 176–77, 198, 221
Guyana, 25, 132–33

H

Haiti, 20, 32, 59, 132
Hall, Moses, 12
Harrison, Bob, 206, 208
Harvey, William J., 30, 140, 149, 155
Hayes, James O., 132
heaven, 9, 54, 71, 92, 97, 164, 207, 236–40, 243, 246, 248, 251, 275
heritage, 32, 43, 50, 183, 185, 218, 282
Hillis, Dick, 213–14
Holiness Movement, 13–14, 81–82
Holsey, Lucius, 86
Holy Spirit, 7, 13–14, 55, 87, 103, 138, 173–74, 179, 201–02, 206, 208, 221, 236, 239, 242–44, 246–47, 250–51, 266, 268
Hood Theological Seminary, 30–31
Horton, Ron, 155
hostility, 20, 70, 129, 162, 164, 166, 237
Howard University, 40
Huggins, Jacqueline, 249, 258
hunger, 181, 238

I

identity, 73, 211, 284, 288
India, 33, 47, 50, 105, 132, 191, 280
Indigenous, 15, 44, 118, 136, 161, 230
Indonesia, 215, 285
influence, 24, 26, 37, 40, 54, 70, 73, 86, 95, 110–11, 130, 132, 137–38, 141, 150, 164, 211, 221, 267–68, 281
inner city, 120, 202
Inskip, John, 14, 103
integrated, 81
Iran, 191, 280
Irving, Edward, 13
Islam, 44, 162, 192

INDEX

Islamic
　faith, 277
　fundamentalism, 192
Ivory Coast, 197, 218–21

J
Jackson, Andrew, 194
Jamaica, 9–12, 173–74, 177, 180, 199
Japan, 180, 201
Jerusalem, 49, 241–44, 247
Jesus
　ascension, 206
　death, 195
　lordship, 237, 247
　resurrection, 182, 195, 213, 242
Jim Crow
　laws, 158
　segregation, 276
Johnson, Benjamin, 187
Johnson, Brian, 231–34
Johnson, Michael, 269
Johnson, Thomas, 91, 98–100
Jones, A. L., 60
Jones, Absalom, 19–20
Jones, Howard, 210–11
jungle, 115, 117, 142–43, 147–48, 153, 177, 211, 271

K
Kenya, 198, 210, 268, 270–75, 280
King, Dr. Martin Luther, 266, 276
Korea, 72
Ku Klux Klan, 36

L
Lambuth, Walter Russell, 86–89
Lapsley, Samuel, 108–15, 120
legacy, 139, 153, 275–76
Leopold, King, 109, 117–18, 164
Liberia, 25–29, 45, 49–50, 59–60, 76, 81–82, 94–95, 100–01, 105, 128–30, 132, 140, 145–47, 150–51, 153, 155, 180, 185–87, 203, 211, 222, 224–25, 231–32, 234, 280
Liele, George, 9–12, 199
Livingstone, David, 30, 33, 88
Livingstone College, 25–27, 30–31
local mission. *See* mission.
Lott Carey Foreign Mission Convention, 50, 127–28, 131–32
L'Ouverture, Toussaint, 20, 32
lynching, 276

M
Macaulay, Zachary, 76
machetes, 42
malaria, 109, 113–14, 135, 143, 145, 199, 254
Malawi, 139, 141, 148–50, 158, 166–67
Malaysia, 215, 258
Malekebu, Daniel S., 143, 146–47, 149–50, 154
mandate, 83, 192, 236, 276
Mandingoes, 129, 152
Manna Bible Institute, 218
marriage, 55, 117, 149, 221, 245, 260, 262, 268–69, 273–74, 286–87
McCombs, Mable, 222–24
mediator, 235
Methodist, 8, 13–14, 19, 21–23, 32–36, 52, 60, 71, 103, 106, 183, 200, 210, 223
Mexico, 99, 191, 252, 269, 278–80
Miller, William, 24–25
Ministry, 9, 11–12, 26, 28, 32–34, 37, 44–46, 48, 55–56, 64–65, 88, 105, 108, 113, 120, 128–29, 136, 138–39, 165, 174, 180, 182, 198–99, 201–03, 208–14, 216, 218–25, 230, 232, 234, 242, 244, 251–52, 254–56, 258, 262, 273, 278–81, 285–89
missionary, 9, 26–30, 33, 36–37, 39, 41–42, 45–50, 52, 56, 59–63, 65–67, 69–73, 76, 81–83, 86–89, 96, 98–99, 104–05, 108–09, 113–15, 118–20, 125, 128–32, 134–36, 140–43, 148–50, 153, 155, 157–60, 162–65, 171–81, 183, 185–87, 191–93, 197, 199–204, 210–11, 214–16, 218, 220, 222–25, 229, 231, 240, 252, 255, 257–58, 262, 265, 268, 271–72, 275, 277–78, 281, 283, 285–88
　participation, 191
missions
　agencies, 50
　black mission, 32, 34
　expansion of, 47
　field, 33–34, 37, 41, 45, 48, 60, 81, 87, 113, 119, 130, 140, 160, 179–81, 185, 202–05, 215, 224, 234, 256, 265, 285–86
　foreign, 26, 30, 47–48, 62–63, 89, 114, 125, 127, 131–32, 208, 213, 215, 230, 265
　global, 235, 240, 284
　medical, 132
　movement, 9
　multiethnic, 240
　program, 33, 191
　short-term, 270
　training, 235
　white mission, 162, 280

mob
  violence, 276
mobilize, 235, 246
money, 11, 26, 33–36, 40, 43, 50, 53, 86, 89, 91, 93–94, 103–05, 107, 118, 128, 130, 138–39, 142, 144, 147–48, 152, 155, 158, 163, 174, 176, 194, 202–03, 207, 220, 225, 232, 248, 254, 263, 271, 274, 276, 281, 285, 288
Monrovia Bible Institute, 224, 231
Montgomery, 25
Moody Bible Institute, 211, 280
moral, 25, 30, 34, 67, 159, 164
  character, 75
Moravians, 32, 134
Morehouse College, 82
Morgan, John R. V., 108
mother tongue, 253, 258
motivation, 69, 192, 276
Mozambique, 139
mulatto, 63, 69, 76, 99, 107
multi-ethnic, 244–45
  church, 239, 242, 244
  group, 239
Muslim, 59, 191–92, 220, 222, 277–79, 283, 285–86, 288–89

N
Nairobi, 198, 274–75
National Baptist Convention, 131, 134, 136–42, 147, 149, 153, 156, 159, 165, 186
nations, 14, 44, 54–55, 99, 138, 162, 192, 203, 230, 232, 235–36, 238, 240–41, 246, 248, 265, 276
Native Americans, 59, 273
neighbor, 43, 192, 209, 261, 265, 288
Neighbor, Cal, 283
network, 108, 235, 255, 287
Nigeria, 29, 36–46, 132, 197, 203–04, 230, 262–64, 280–81
North Africa, 276
Nova Scotia, 10
Nubia, 100
Nyasaland, 135–37, 139–44, 147, 149, 158, 160–64

O
obey, 48, 92, 105, 138, 178–79, 246–48, 277
Operation Mobilization, 191, 280
Overseas Crusades, 213–14
Ozman, Agnes, 14

P
pagan, 60, 89, 112, 240, 245
Paine College, 86

Palmer, Phoebe, 14
pan-africanism, 135
paradigm, 289
Parham, Charles Fox, 14–15
partnership, 281, 287
paternalism, 118, 213
paucity, 32
Pentecostal, 13–15, 82
  movement, 13–14, 82
persecution, 11, 44, 84, 213, 247, 278
Philadelphia, 19–20, 24–25, 27, 29, 64, 71–72, 84, 86, 90, 128, 141, 145, 149, 165, 174–75, 180, 186–87, 218, 251, 253–54, 269–70, 272
Philadelphia College of the Bible, 251, 253
Philippines, 213–16, 249, 252–53, 257–58
Pointer, Jonathan, 53
police, 93, 99, 263
political power, 172
politics, 81, 177, 229
polygamy, 42
poor, 9–11, 23, 25, 37, 39, 41, 49, 72, 75, 85, 88, 92–93, 100–02, 105, 109, 111, 117, 119, 139, 141–42, 145, 173, 175, 218, 244–45, 249, 267–68, 285
Portuguese, 139, 150, 171–72
prayer, 7, 12, 34, 37, 43, 48, 52, 64, 82, 87, 90–94, 96, 98, 101, 104–05, 114–16, 146, 155, 173, 175, 178, 181, 195, 202, 210, 213, 216, 220, 222, 244, 255–56, 264, 267, 269, 272, 274, 282, 285
pregnant, 176, 179, 268
prejudice, 62, 67, 76, 161, 163, 206, 208, 244
Presbyterian, 8, 13, 35–36, 59–60, 63–66, 72, 81, 87, 106–08, 111, 113–18, 120, 179, 199, 285
Princeton Seminary, 65
prosperity, 158, 162
Prosser, Gabriel, 20, 32
Protestant, 7, 23, 60, 65, 87, 109, 134, 172
Protestant Episcopal Church, 19, 59, 81

Q
Queen's College, 76

R
racial
  barrier, 45, 194
  discrimination, 158
  identity, 284
  innuendo, 136
  prejudice, 67, 208
  pride, 131
  problems, 213

status, 3
strife, 212
superiority, 208
tension, 72, 163
ties, 60
racism, 20, 48, 76, 104, 191, 230
reconciliation, 231-32, 234-36, 239-40, 245
reconstruction period, 76, 125, 276
recruiting, 125, 281
redemption, 25, 28, 136, 142, 161
relationships, 44, 76, 119, 135, 200, 204, 236-37, 245, 253, 256, 272-74, 281, 284-86, 288
religious zeal, 69
responsibility, 25, 64, 89, 125, 136, 162, 172, 216, 254-55, 264, 281
revolt, 20, 23, 32, 116, 131, 139, 166, 239
Rhodesia, 150, 162
rich, 25, 244, 248
Richmond African Baptist Missionary Society, 48, 130
Ricks Institute, 132
riots, 45, 215
Roman Catholic, 7, 13, 20, 54, 81, 87, 134, 143, 172, 249
Royal Geographic Society, 113, 120
Rush, Christopher, 23-25
Russia, 196, 232
Rwanda, 198

S
sacrifice, 38, 42-43, 49, 76, 112, 158, 167, 194, 208, 218, 220, 241, 266, 281, 289
Samaria, 242-43
Santo Domingo, 20
Satan, 11, 43, 181, 215, 236-37, 239-40, 244, 246, 248, 263
Schmidt, George, 37
Scott, Hakim, 277-79
Scott, June, 24
segregation, 20, 33, 44, 104, 276
self
    assertion, 25
    expression, 23
    governing, 125
    supporting, 82, 114, 146, 159
sending church, 280
Senegal, 191, 197, 234
servant, 7, 10, 27-29, 32, 63-65, 67, 88, 92, 116, 137, 150, 153, 176, 179, 184, 186, 199, 220, 241, 247, 275, 281-82
Seymour, William J., 14-15
Sharpe, Henry, 9-10

Shaw, William, 28
Sheppard, William Henry, 107-20, 164
short-term
    missions trips. *See* missions.
Sierra Leone, 10, 27, 49-50, 60, 95, 109, 128-29, 174-77, 179, 198, 203-04, 211, 232, 234
Simpson, A. B., 14, 174
Singapore, 214-15, 258
skin color, 215
slave, 3-4, 7-12, 19-24, 32-33, 47-49, 63-64, 67, 69-70, 74, 84-85, 91-97, 99-100, 102, 109-10, 113-14, 118-19, 127-28, 131, 137-38, 142, 160, 206, 244, 246
    runaway, 21, 53
    trade, 3, 21-22, 49-50, 100
slavery, 3, 11, 20-24, 32-33, 49, 62, 67, 75, 81, 84, 88, 99-100, 102-03, 107, 131, 136, 150, 152, 211, 270, 273, 276, 280
Small, John Bryan, 26
Smith, Amanda, 102, 104, 106, 175
social
    change, 73
    gospel, 213
    revolution, 8
Society for the Propagation of the Gospel in Foreign Parts, 7
South Africa, 33, 132, 139, 147, 150, 159-60, 164-65, 185-86, 236
Southern Baptists, 210, 263
    Convention, 60, 262, 265
Spain, 280
Spiritual Awakenings, 8
standard of living, 156
statistics, 82
status, 26, 63, 127, 146, 171, 218, 233, 244, 247, 258, 278
stewardship, 4
Stewart, John, 21, 52-56
Stockton, Betsey, 62-67, 69-73
stranger, 22, 43, 53, 62, 69, 88, 112
struggle, 24, 74, 85, 94, 128, 141, 172, 224, 232, 255, 268, 276
Student Volunteer Movement, 125
Sudan Interior Mission, 233
support raising, 175, 179, 224, 253, 274, 279, 285, 287, 289
syncretism, 248

T
Taiwan, 213, 216
Talbot Seminary, 191
Tanganyika, 87

Tanzania, 181
Taylor, Dorothy, 199
Taylor, Elgin, 199–202
Teague, Colin, 59, 128
television, 267, 270
theology, 13–14, 75, 230
Thomas, Samuel, 4
Thorpe, Jean, 311
Thorpe, Kenneth, 311
traditions, 43, 140, 264, 276
tribe, 34, 38, 49–50, 52–53, 74, 87–89, 95, 97, 100, 110–11, 116, 129–30, 135, 138, 143, 150, 152, 159, 162, 166, 175–76, 179–81, 183, 211, 233, 235–41, 243, 245–46
Triennial Convention, 128
Tule, John, 132
Tyler, James, 42–43, 45

U
Uganda, 198, 211
United Brethren in Christ, 175
unrest, 21, 45, 89
Urbana, 56, 252, 258, 285
U.S. Navy, 128

V
Varick, James, 23–24
vernacular
　language, 249, 258
　literacy, 44
Vietnam, 213, 246, 261

W
Waite, Montrose, 172–74, 178–81
Washington, Booker T., 35–36, 82, 107, 118, 137–38
Wesley, John, 13, 22–23, 85, 89
West Indies, 21, 23, 25, 27, 32, 60, 83, 199, 206
Whaley, Daisie, 218
Wheaton College, 211, 216
White, William, 20
white missions. *See* missions.
Whitfield, George, 8
Williams, George, 109
Wilson, Ernest, 37
Woman's Home and Foreign Missionary Society, 25
world evangelization. *See* evangelization.
World War I, 35, 147
World War II, 29, 44, 166, 194, 196, 214, 254
worldview, 65, 270

worship, 15, 20, 38, 44, 54–55, 60, 64, 76, 100, 112, 115, 158–59, 167, 176, 200–01, 237–42, 246–48, 252, 260, 288

Y
Yale University, 15
YMCA, 149, 158
Youth, 9, 29–30, 35, 38, 52–53, 69, 75, 115, 117, 132, 143, 157, 207, 213, 220–21, 251, 258, 281, 285
YWAM, 221

Z
Zaire, 197, 270
Zambia, 139, 198
Zimbabwe, 139, 198
Zion Church, 23–31, 84, 86, 89–90
Zion College, 30
Zulu, 238